Life-Span Developmental Psychology

PERSONALITY AND SOCIALIZATION

CONTRIBUTORS

INGE M. AHAMMER

PAUL B. BALTES

VERN L. BENGTSON

JAMES E. BIRREN

K. DEAN BLACK

NANCY DATAN

WALTER EMMERICH

DWIGHT HARSHBARGER

WILLARD W. HARTUP

ROBERT J. HAVIGHURST

SAMUEL Z. KLAUSNER

NATHAN KOGAN

LAWRENCE KOHLBERG

JACQUES LEMPERS

NORMAN LIVSON

WILLIAM R. LOOFT

ANNE H. NARDI

BERNICE L. NEUGARTEN

K. WARNER SCHAIE

DIANA S. WOODRUFF

LIFE-SPAN DEVELOPMENTAL PSYCHOLOGY

PERSONALITY AND SOCIALIZATION

Edited by

PAUL B. BALTES   and   K. WARNER SCHAIE

College of Human Development
Pennsylvania State University
University Park, Pennsylvania

Department of Psychology
West Virginia University
Morgantown, West Virginia

1973

ACADEMIC PRESS   New York   San Francisco   London
A Subsidiary of Harcourt Brace Jovanovich, Publishers

ACADEMIC PRESS, INC.
111 Fifth Avenue, New York, New York 10003

United Kingdom Edition published by
ACADEMIC PRESS, INC. (LONDON) LTD.
24/28 Oval Road, London NW1

Library of Congress Cataloging in Publication Data

Main entry under title:

Life-span developmental psychology.

    Proceedings of the 3rd of a series of meetings;
proceedings of the 1st are entered under title: Life-
span developmental psychology: research and theory;
proceedings of the 2nd are entered under: Life-Span
Conference, 2nd, West Virginia University, 1971.
    Bibliography: p.
    1.   Developmental psychology–Congresses.
2.   Personality–Congresses.   3.   Socialization–
Congresses.   I.   Baltes, Paul B., ed.   II.   Schaie,
Klaus Warner, Date   ed.
BF712.L54   155   73–797
ISBN 0–12–077150–0

Contents

HISTORY AND THEORY

1. History of Developmental Psychology: Socialization and Personality Development through the Life Span

Robert J. Havighurst

6. Socialization and Sex-Role Development

Walter Emmerich

7. Creativity and Cognitive Style: A Life-Span Perspective

Nathan Kogan

8. Continuities in Childhood and Adult Moral Development Revisited

Lawrence Kohlberg

SOCIAL PROCESSES

9. Intergenerational Relations and Continuities in Socialization

Vern L. Bengtson and K. Dean Black

PROGRAMMATIC INTERVENTION

14. Some Ecological Implications for the Organization of Human Intervention throughout the Life Span

Dwight Harshbarger

Epilogue: On Life-Span Developmental Research Paradigms: Retrospects and Prospects

Paul B. Baltes and K. Warner Schaie

List of Contributors

Numbers in parentheses indicate the pages on which the authors' contributions begin.

INGE M. AHAMMER* (253), Division of Developmental Psychology, Catholic University of Nijmegen, Nijmegen, Netherlands

PAUL B. BALTES (365), College of Human Development, Pennsylvania State University, University Park, Pennsylvania

VERN L. BENGTSON (207), Ethel Percy Andrus Gerontology Center, University of Southern California, Los Angeles, California

JAMES E. BIRREN (305), Ethel Percy Andrus Gerontology Center, University of Southern California, Los Angeles, California

K. DEAN BLACK (207), Ethel Percy Andrus Gerontology Center, University of Southern California, Los Angeles, California

NANCY DATAN† (53), Division of Behavioral Sciences, University of the Negev, Be'er-Sheva, Israel

WALTER EMMERICH (123), Human Development Research Group, Educational Testing Service, Princeton, New Jersey

DWIGHT HARSHBARGER (339), Department of Psychology, West Virginia University, Morgantown, West Virginia

WILLARD W. HARTUP (235), Institute of Child Development, University of Minnesota, Minneapolis, Minnesota

*Present address: School of Behavioural Sciences. Macquarie University, North Ryde, N.S.W., Australia.
†Present address: Department of Psychology, West Virginia University, Morgantown, West Virginia.

ROBERT J. HAVIGHURST (1), Department of Education, The University of Chicago, Chicago, Illinois

SAMUEL Z. KLAUSNER (71), Department of Sociology, University of Pennsylvania, Philadelphia, Pennsylvania

NATHAN KOGAN (145), Department of Psychology, New School for Social Research, New York, New York

LAWRENCE KOHLBERG (179), Graduate School of Education, Harvard University, Cambridge, Massachusetts

JACQUES LEMPERS (235), Institute of Child Development, University of Minnesota, Minneapolis, Minnesota

NORMAN LIVSON (97), Institute of Human Development, University of California, Berkeley, California, and Department of Psychology, California State University, Hayward, California

WILLIAM R. LOOFT (25), College of Human Development, Pennsylvania State University, University Park, Pennsylvania

ANNE H. NARDI (285), Department of Educational Psychology, West Virginia University, Morgantown, West Virginia

BERNICE L. NEUGARTEN (53), Committee on Human Development, The University of Chicago, Chicago, Illinois

K. WARNER SCHAIE* (365), Department of Psychology, West Virginia University, Morgantown, West Virginia

DIANA S. WOODRUFF† (305), Ethel Percy Andrus Gerontology Center, University of Southern California, Los Angeles, California

*Present address: Ethel Percy Gerontology Center, University of Southern California, Los Angeles, California.

†Present address: Department of Psychology, University of California, Los Angeles, California.

Preface

The subject matter of an emerging field, life-span developmental psychology, has been the focus of three West Virginia Conferences which were held in 1969, 1971, and 1972 under the auspices of the Department of Psychology at West Virginia University. Whereas the first two conference volumes dealt with a review of life-span theory, methodology, and basic psychological processes, the current volume addresses the area of socialization and personality. Historically speaking, the selection of this topic as the focus for a third conference may seem out of chronological order, since it is the area of personality and socialization that was largely at the core of initial life-span developmental theorizing and research. Nevertheless, it is gratifying to see, in this volume, a larger contribution by and tribute to those who pioneered a life-span approach to the study of psychological ontogeny. It is testimony to their scientific posture that the present effort yields an impressive array of empirical and theoretical contributions.

It is our hope that this volume will be more than a vehicle for disseminating knowledge. Rather, we trust that it will provide an incentive for the generation of research and the continuous development of more useful theoretical conceptions in the area of human development. At the present moment, in accord with a descriptive life-span view of development, we can only say that time, distance, and death alone will crystallize issues. In the meantime, it is you, the reader, who will judge the success of our efforts by your actions which will lead either to acceleration, deceleration, or modification of the course and the life span of life-span developmental psychology.

In any case, we eagerly anticipate your vigorous response.

Acknowledgments

The editors are grateful to the sponsoring institution, West Virginia University, and especially to Dr. Ray Koppelman, Provost for Research and Graduate Affairs, who so ably carried the burden of administrative risk taking. The assistance of many others associated with West Virginia University and its doctoral program in life-span developmental psychology and the College of Human Development at The Pennsylvania State University, where most of the editorial work was carried out, must also be acknowledged. In a real sense, a host of current and former West Virginia and Pennsylvania State graduate students (William Arnold, Elizabeth M. Barton, Thomas W. Bartsch, William Birkhill, Dana Cable, Wanda Franz, Joseph M. Fitzgerald, Edward Forbes, John Friel, Carol Furry, Frances Hoyer, William Hoyer, Rudolph A. Kafer, Erich W. Labouvie, Gisela Labouvie-Vief, Leighton Stamps, Richard Swanson, and others) were collaborating conference organizers and amiable hosts. They gave their time generously in working with us to make the conference an intellectual and social success. Finally, without the secretarial skills of Mary Kutac and Pamela Evans, and especially the diligent and painstaking work of our able editorial assistant, Elizabeth M. Barton, this volume would not have been completed on schedule and with minimal frustration for the contributors and editors. We gratefully acknowledge our vast indebtedness to all of them.

As to the contributors to this volume, we thank them not only for their scholarly products, but also for their warm, cooperative, and challenging spirit that made it not only enjoyable and edifying to work with them, but also easy to form a number of precious new friendships and to further develop already existing ones. We hold them in high esteem.

HISTORY
AND
THEORY

History of Developmental Psychology: Socialization and Personality Development through the Life Span

ROBERT J. HAVIGHURST

THE UNIVERSITY OF CHICAGO
CHICAGO, ILLINOIS

ABSTRACT

There was no explicit developmental psychology of personality through the life span before the middle of the twentieth century. Prior to 1940, psychologists studying personality generally confined themselves to a limited segment of the life span. The period from 1850 to 1920 saw a good deal of empirical study of child and adolescent development, but almost no attention to adulthood and later maturity. After 1930, a small number of leaders emerged with an interest in life-span development: Charlotte Bühler, Else Frenkel-Brunswik, Erik Erikson, and Hans Thomae. Also, the University of Chicago Committee on Human Development directed its resources into the study of personality development in middle and old age.

Theories of personality which did not prove useful for understanding life-span development were constitutional types, nineteenth century evolutionary theory (G. S. Hall), and psychoanalytic theory. Since 1930, several longitudinal studies of personality development have been producing useful data and theories. Other useful sources are biographies, autobiographies, and systematic case studies. The development of life-span theory probably requires: an organismic theory of personality, which assumes an active organism inter-

acting with the social and physical environment; attention to physical vigor and health as a causal factor; study of career changes and other crises of middle age; and study of the perceptions of aging by the self and the wider community.

I. Introduction

There was no explicit developmental psychology of personality through the life span before the middle of the twentieth century. That is, there was no systematic set of psychological data concerning even half of anyone's life span, and there were no tested theories or models of psychological development covering this much of the human life cycle.

A number of questions about personality development throughout life had been asked and there were some speculative answers to these questions. Some of these basic questions were: (1) Is personality related to the physique—the biological make-up of the individual? (2) Are the principal behavior patterns determined genetically for the individual? (3) To what extent is there a quasi-universal life course for humans that can be described in terms of personality development? (4) To what extent and in what ways can personality be changed after the end of adolescence? (5) How is human personality modified as the individual progresses through the life span?

Though these questions were discussed, from time to time, in a largely speculative way, or in dogmatic terms, they did not get serious, sustained scientific attention prior to the twentieth century.

A. Definition of the Topic of This Paper

This chapter deals with one aspect of human life-span developmental psychology. The broader field has been defined by Baltes and Goulet (1970) as follows: "Human life-span developmental psychology is concerned with the description and explication of ontogenetic (age–related) behavioral changes from birth to death [p.12]."

The aspect of focus here is personality development and the socialization processes that influence personality. Thus, we are not concerned directly with several major areas of psychological development—intelligence, learning, psychomotor development, sensory development, or occupational development.

Within the field of personality and socialization, we are especially concerned with the adult period, since this is a relatively neglected area.[1] Baltes and Goulet

---

[1]This chapter depends heavily on two papers prepared for an earlier symposium and published in the book entitled *Life-Span Developmental Psychology: Research and Theory* edited by Baltes and Goulet. The papers are: "Historical Antecedents of Life-Span Developmental Psychology" by Charles (1970), and "Life-Span Developmental Psychology in Europe" by Groffmann (1970). It is assumed that the reader has access to these papers. The focus of this paper, therefore, has been narrowed from *developmental psychology in general* to the subject of *personality development*.

(1970) point this out when they say that a major objective of life-span developmental psychology is the

> integrative conceptualization of the totality of ontogenetic behavioral changes . . . the bulk of research efforts in developmental psychology has been conducted thus far by researchers whose primary orientation was toward specific age periods such as infancy, etc., without any comprehensive attempts to integrate the findings within the framework of the life span. As a consequence, and with few exceptions, these age-specific research efforts have remained fairly insular and uncoordinated, even though they appear to be intrinsically related through their common goal, the study of age-related behavioral change [p. 13].

B. Trends before 1920

Developmental studies of infancy, childhood, and adolescence originated in the nineteenth century and were flourishing by 1940, when studies of adulthood and aging were just getting started. Some of the people who worked with the earlier stages of development became interested in adulthood and aging, but they did not do serious research at these levels. For example, G. Stanley Hall, who published his influential book on *Adolescence* in 1904, after his formal retirement wrote his book on *Senescence: The Last Half of Life,* published in 1922. In his introduction to the later book, he wrote:

> Our life, bounded by birth and death, has five chief stages, each of which, while it may be divided into substages, also passes into the next so gradually that we cannot date, save roughly and approximately, the transition from one period to that which succeeds it. These more marked nodes in the unity of man's individual existence are: (1) childhood, (2) adolescence from puberty to full nubility, (3) middle life or the prime, when we are at the apex of our aggregate of powers, ranging from twenty-five or thirty to forty or forty-five and comprising thus the fifteen or twenty years now commonly called our best, (4) senescence, which begins in the early forties, or before in woman, and (5) senectitude, the post-climacteric or old age proper. My own life work, such as it is, as a genetic psychologist was devoted for years to the study of infancy and childhood, then to the phenomena of youth, later to adulthood and the stage of sex maturity. To complete a long-cherished program I have now finally tried, aided by the first-hand knowledge that advancing years have brought, to understand better the two last and closing stages of human life [p. vii].

The history of the study of personality development over the life span can be broken into two periods. The period from 1850 to 1920 saw a good deal of empirical study of child and adolescent development, with almost no attention to adulthood and later maturity. Throughout most of this period, it was supposed

---

Parallel to this paper, and written with a systematic basis in general psychological theory, is the chapter by Riegel (1960) on personality theory and aging in Birren's *Handbook of Aging and the Individual*. Riegel analyzes the contribution each of the major theories or schools of thought has made to a systematic theory of personality in the latter half of life. He concludes that "up to the present, no theory exists which takes full account of the aging personality [p. 844]."

that personality was primarily controlled by inheritance—individual and racial. Therefore, research was focused on the description of the unfolding of inborn patterns. Only toward the end of this period did psychologists become aware of the power of the environment in shaping human behavior.

The psychology of personality development hardly moved beyond Shakespeare before 1930. His seven ages of man illustrate the concepts of social role, of stages or periods of life, and of life styles.

> All the world's a stage,
> and all the men and women merely players;
> They have their exits and their entrances,
> And one man in his time plays many parts,
> His acts being seven ages. At first the infant . . .
> Then the whining schoolboy, . .
> creeping like a snail,
>   Unwillingly to school. And then the lover,
> Sighing like a furnace . . .
> Then a soldier,
> Full of strange oaths and bearded like the pard,
> Jealous in honor, sudden and quick in quarrel,
> Seeking the bubble reputation
> Even in the cannon's mouth. And then the justice, . .
> With eyes severe and beard of formal cut,
> Full of wise saws and modern instances; . .
>   The sixth age shifts
> Into the lean and slippered pantaloon,
> With spectacles on nose and pouch on side;
> His youthful hose, well saved, a world too wide
> For his shrunk shank, and his big manly voice,
> Turning again toward childish treble, pipes
> And whistles in his sound. Last scene of all,
> That ends this strange eventful history,
> Is second childishness and mere oblivion,
> Sans teeth, sans eyes, sans taste, sans everything.
>
>   *As You Like It*

II. Emerging Life-Span Views of Personality Development in the Twentieth Century

During the early decades of the twentieth century, psychologists came to see heredity as an interacting force with the social environment in the making of personality. Some of them, the behaviorists, saw the personality as a tabula rasa on which the social environment could stamp almost any pattern of behavior. Others saw the personality as a pattern of behavior that emerged from the interaction of a biological organism with a social environment, in which the organism possessed an active force that made demands upon the social environment and was to some extent shaped by the environment. It was this latter group who became interested in the life-span development of human personality. The period from 1920 to 1960 saw the first attempts by psychologists to put together the concepts needed for a life-span view of personality development.

A. Charlotte Bühler

In the early years of this period, Charlotte Bühler (1933, 1953, 1962a,b), working in Vienna on child development, with her students began to look at the entire human life span, and put her students to collecting life histories from a number of elderly people. She then divided the life span into the following five age periods: (1) childhood—birth to 14; (2) youth—14 to 25; (3) adult I—25 to 45–50; (4) adult II—45–50 to 65–70; (5) aging—65–70——.

She identified two sets of events in life—the biological, and the biographical. These events could be placed on age curves, which rose from a low level in the first two stages, and then differentiated—the biological curve dropping rather sharply after about age 50, while the biographical curve remained on a high plateau from early adulthood to age 55–65, after which it declined also.

Later, Bühler added another useful set of five concepts—those of basic life tendencies, which are acting to some extent at all stages, but have periods of dominance in determining the life-style of the individual. In a paper published in 1962, Bühler combined these two sets of concepts as seen in Table 1. She subdivided the life span further into 10 periods. Her basic life-tendencies are, listed in the order of their first domination of the person's behavior: need-satisfaction; adaptive self-limitation (adjustment); creative expansion; establishment of inner order; self-fulfillment.

B. Else Frenkel–Brunswik

A colleague of Charlotte Bühler in Vienna, Else Frenkel–Brunswik came to Berkeley, California in the 1930s and joined the Institute for Child Development, which was then headed by Harold E. Jones. She became interested in life-span development and under the auspices of the Institute of Industrial Relations at the University of California (Berkeley), she headed a group that studied the social adjustment of men aged 60 and over. This study was carried on during the 1950s and was described in the paper by Reichard, Livson, and Peterson (1962) as the first systematic personality study of men at the age of retirement.

TABLE 1

Bühler's Conception of Phases and Basic Tendencies during the Life Span[a]

Age period	Basic Tendency				
	Need-satisfaction	Adaptive self-limitation	Creative expansion	Establishment of inner order	Self-fulfillment
0–1.5 yr	Trust & love, evolvement & discovery of self-sameness				
1.5–4 yr		Obedience & super-ego ideal versus independence			
4–8 yr			Autonomous, value-setting, ego-ideals aspect of task		
8–12 yr				Attempts to objective self-evaluation in social roles	
12–18 yr	Sex needs & problem of sexual identity			Review & preview of self-development (autobiographical)	Fulfillment of & detachment from childhood
18–25 (30) yr		Tentative self-determination to role in society			
25 (30)–45 (50) yr			Self-realization in occupation, marriage, & own family		
45 (50)–65 (70) yr				Critical self-assessment	
65 (70)–80 (85) yr					Self-fulfillment
80 (85)–death	Regression to predominant need-satisfaction				

[a]Source: Bühler (1962a).

8

C. Erik Erikson

Erik Erikson came from Europe to the United States in the 1930s, and spent much of his first 20 years in this country working at least part–time with one or another of the research projects in child and adolescent development that were going on with financial support from the Child Study Program of the General Education Board (one of the Rockefeller foundations). Erikson worked with Caroline Zachry and others in the Progressive Education Association Study of Adolescents in the middle 1930s. After 1940, he spent some time at the University of California at Berkeley working with Jean Walker MacFarlane on her longitudinal study of children and adolescents who were born about 1930.

In 1950 Erikson published his book *Childhood and Society* which was destined to become, in this writer's opinion, the most influential book of the mid-century on personality development. Erikson set forth a theory of personality development through the life span, with a set of eight *psychosocial tasks,* each of which dominated the development of the individual at a certain stage in his development. Erikson's psychosocial tasks and their age periods are:

Basic trust	Birth to one year
Autonomy	1–6
Initiative	6–10
Industry	10–14
Identity	Adolescence: 14–20
Intimacy	Early adulthood: 20–40
Generativity	Middle adulthood: 40–65
Integrity	Later adulthood: 65——

D. Developmental Tasks

During the 1935–1950 period, a group of people worked interactively first in New York City and then in Chicago under the auspices first of the Progressive Education Association and later of the Child Study Program of the Commission on Teacher Education of the American Council on Education. Both of these research and development programs were financed by the General Education Board (Rockefeller Foundation). The directors of the programs were Caroline Zachry and Daniel Prescott. Associated with them for more than a brief period of time were: Peter Blos, Fritz Redl, Erik Erikson, Caroline Tryon, and Robert J. Havighurst. An important catalyzer and instigator of this activity was Lawrence K. Frank, director of the Child Study Program for the General Education Board. All members of this group shared a dynamic or organismic theory of personality development. In the many staff conferences devoted to discussing and analyzing the complex data on boys and girls whom these people were studying, there emerged repeatedly the need to combine the *drive toward growth* of the individual with the *demands, constraints, and opportunities provided by the social environ-ment*—the family, school, peer group, and community. The research group began to talk about a series of problems or life-adjustment tasks to be achieved by the growing person in relation to his environment. Eventually the phrase *developmental task* came into use, and was employed in the writing of several members of the group during the 1940s.

Havighurst started in 1941 to teach courses in child development and adolescent development at the University of Chicago. The field was new to him (he had been trained in chemistry and physics) and consequently, he was more free than he might have been otherwise to use and develop concepts not in conventional textbooks. He began to organize his courses around the concept of developmental tasks, drawing much material from the seminars, conducted by Daniel Prescott, with experienced teachers on child and adolescent development. Caroline Tryon, a staff member of Prescott's Child Study project, had worked at the Institute of Child Study at the University of California at Berkeley, and found the develop-mental task concept useful in organizing her information on children and adoles-cents from the Berkeley Institute. She took the lead in preparing a monograph on child and adolescent development which was published by the Association for Supervision and Curriculum Development. From his participation with Tryon, Havighurst became very familiar with this material on developmental tasks. There was one difficulty that stood in the way of using this concept for teaching purposes. The research group had defined and analyzed the developmental tasks of boys and girls into large numbers of detailed *task-lets* that tended to obscure a vision of the forest because of the many individual trees. Accordingly, Havighurst deliberately combined the many detailed tasks into a manageable number of broadly defined tasks for any given age level. He set a limit of 10 tasks for a given age, and generally kept below that limit in his own teaching and writing.

In 1948, Havighurst wrote out and had mimeographed much of his lecture material for the use of his graduate students, so that they could read the basics and spend their class time in more intensive discussion. The mimeographed pages were bound and sold at cost through the college book store. Soon there came requests for these materials from outside the university, and eventually Havighurst prepared a published revision (1952). This was a thin paperback booklet that could be sold cheaply and used as a supplement to a college textbook on child or adolescent development. It came into wide use, was reprinted again and again, and, when the demand showed no sign of abating, Havighurst con-cluded that he should update the text in accordance with the development of his knowledge and thinking. A new edition was published in 1972.

Havighurst's age periods are: (1) early childhood—birth to 5 or 6; (2) middle childhood—5–6 to 12–13; (3) adolescence—12–13 to 18; (4) early adulthood—

18–35; (5) middle adulthood—35–60; (6) later maturity—60 and over. He makes use of Erikson's psychosocial tasks as central to his various age periods, but looks also for two principal sources of developmental tasks: the biological changes of the body, which present the individual with new opportunities, needs, and problems of adjustment; and the expectations of the society, which present the individual with a number of changing social roles that change with age and are expected of him by the society and by himself. Thus, Havighurst's theory is one primarily based on biological development and social expectations which change through the life span and give direction, force, and substance to the development of personality.

E. Bernice L. Neugarten

Neugarten became the coordinator of the research team at the University of Chicago that carried on the Kansas City Study of Adult Life from about 1954 to 1964. She was especially interested in the personality studies that emerged as a major factor in the research program. Together with several students she carried on a series of researches with projective techniques, thus exploring the intrapsychic development taking place in men and women from middle age on into old age. She and her students demonstrated a regular progression from an instrumental, outward directed set of attitudes toward *interiority,* a more passive and introversive set of attitudes. Men showed this trend more clearly than women. But the social behavior of the Kansas City adults did not change much with age. Thus, she concluded, "We have evidence from the Kansas City studies that *some* changes in adult personality are to be interpreted as developmental, but others are to be interpreted as the results of situational influences." This statement appears in Neugarten's (1973) contribution to the Report of the Task Force on Aging of the American Psychological Association. There she also provides a useful summary of the pros and cons of disengagement theory, which has an important bearing on life-span developmental personality theory.

This work of Neugarten and her associates was published in the book, *Personality in Middle and Late Life.* The theme of intrapsychic development from middle to old age has been further developed by Gutmann (1969), who was one of the Kansas City team. He made a cross-cultural test of the universality of this phenomenon. Gutmann carried out a set of studies of men ranging from middle to old age in Kansas City, Mexico (Maya), Arizona (Navajo), and Israel (the Galilean Druze). The personality structure of these men changed with age from an active–instrumental set of attitudes to a more introversive, passive, and self-centered complex. These studies were cross-sectional, made at one point in time, but Gutmann has more recently re-examined his Navajo sample after a period of four years, and has found the expected age trend.

F. German Developmental Psychology

Shortly after World War II, Professor Hans Thomae of the University of Erlangen studied children in a quasi-longitudinal way. He became acquainted with American researchers in this area, and when he moved to Bonn as Professor of Psychology in 1959, he had a well-developed interest in life-span psychological research. One of his students and later a colleague was Ursula Lehr, who joined him in an extensive set of developmental studies. Their work included a study of a sample of elderly people from the Rhine region, aged 60–75, who were interviewed and tested several times between 1965 and 1972. The Bonn group studied middle aged and elderly persons between 1960 and 1970, with a substantial output of research reports (e.g., Thomae & Lehr, 1968).

Professor Thomae was the leading figure in the creation of the interdisciplinary International Society for the Study of Behavioral Development, which held its first symposium at Nijmegen, The Netherlands, in 1971, and its second at Ann Arbor, Michigan, 1973 (also see Mönks, Hartup, & DeWit, 1972).

III. Conditions under Which a Life-Span Interest Develops

In presenting these interrelated treatments of the development of personality through the life span, it is useful to note that the persons named are a minority of those working productively and creatively and writing in the field of developmental psychology. The majority, working between 1920 and 1970, focused their work on development in childhood and adolescence, and ignored or paid scant attention to adulthood.

Erikson started with a major interest in development during the first 20 years of life, but found his curiosity and psychological activity carrying him on into the study of adulthood. Erikson's studies of Luther and Gandhi caused him to focus attention on adult development. Bühler's activity as a therapist working with adults in Los Angeles during the 1940s and 1950s initially involved her in thinking about adult development, but her search for antecedents of adult behavior dynamics led her to extend her inquiries into childhood.[2]

Havighurst was Chairman of the Committee on Human Development at the University of Chicago, which after 1945 moved up the age scale from its earlier concentration on child and adolescent development. Havighurst's research from 1940 to 1955 concentrated heavily on childhood and adolescence, but after 1945 he was led by Ernest Burgess, a member of the Committee on Human Development, into a joint project on adjustment in old age. Soon Burgess and

[2]Personal communication, 1972.

Havighurst had a number of graduate students working on problems of aging and had formed a core· of researchers, including Ruth Shonle Cavan, Ethel Shanas, and Bernice L. Neugarten, all with a vigorous interest in adult development and aging. By 1952 these researchers had started the Kansas City Study of Adult Life, with a group of faculty and students including W. Lloyd Warner, William E. Henry, Everett C. Hughes, David Riesman, Eugene Friedmann, Warren Peterson, Martin B. Loeb, Ruth Albrecht, Jean and Joseph Britton, and Sheldon Tobin. Thus, when Havighurst wrote his book on *Human Development and Education* (1953), he was heavily involved in research extending over the life span.

IV. Research Programs and Methods in Relation to Life-Span Study of Personality Development

Among the many people who have worked in the fields of socialization and the development of personality, why did the great majority focus their attention on infancy, childhood, and adolescence, and why did so few concern themselves with life-span facts and theories? It is at once evident that the great practical importance of education and of childrearing would tend to concentrate the work of researchers in these areas. Still, scientific curiosity together with the practical value of adult education and adult psychotherapy should be sufficient to produce a substantial amount of psychological research on adult behavior.

Indeed, there has been a considerable amount of research, and research of good quality, on adult behavior. Much of it has dealt with psychomotor behavior and with intelligence and memory. But this does not have a direct bearing on personality development. In addition, however, during the past 50 years there has been a good deal of study of attitudes, motives, interests, leisure activities, work satisfaction, religious behavior, and political behavior, all of which are relevant to the study of personality and its development.

It is interesting that so much of this study of human behavior during the adult part of the life span has been done as empirical research, without any attempt to produce or to test a theory of development and change during adult life. An example of very good research in substantial quantity is given by the work of Kuhlen. He was one of the most productive researchers on attitudes, interests, and activities of adults. Generally, he treated age as an important variable, but he did not state or use any theory of development through the life span (Kuhlen, 1963).

The work of Eysenck is another example of skillful research applied to adult behavior, but without much attention to development. Eysenck used factor analyses of data to distinguish the cognitive, conative, affective, and somatic or constitutional factors of personality. He paid special attention to *extraversion* and *introversion,* and related those traits to body build. The index to his book on *The Structure of Human Personality* (1970), does not refer either to age or to development. He gives a very useful history of the many attempts to find relationships between body build and personality. It is Eysenck's conviction that human personality is mainly determined by genetic factors, and that the social environment cannot exert any great effect on an individual's personality. At the close of his book, he claims that about 75% of individual differences in personality are caused by heredity. This refers specifically to his two major factors of personality—extraversion–introversion, and neuroticism.

One possible reason for the absence of developmental concepts in the large volume of empirical research on adult personality is that there does not seem to be much change with age during the broad expanse of adulthood, prior to old age. Thus, Havighurst (1968), who was looking for substantial age trends in his study of Kansas City adults aged 40 to 70, found only very low correlations of age with the social role behaviors that were studied.

A. Research Programs with a Developmental Emphasis

Despite the tendency to conduct empirical research on adults without a theory of personality development, a number of research programs after 1930 evolved a life-span interest. That is, programs which started with an interest in child and adolescent development added an interest in adult development, and programs which started with a nondevelopmental interest in middle and old age changed by adding a concern with development.

Programs in the first category seem to have centered in California. The Institute of Human Development at the University of California at Berkeley started a study of adolescents in the Claremont Junior High School of Oakland about 1933. This group was followed through high school with an intensive set of psychological, physiological, and anthropometric studies. Later, Mary Cover Jones and Read Tuddenham interviewed those members of the sample who were still in the San Francisco area. Parallel to this effort was the Guidance Study directed by Jean Walker MacFarlane of the Institute of Human Development. The subjects of this study were every third child born in Berkeley during 1928–29. Parents were enlisted in this study with the promise of counseling and guidance for themselves and their children. The most thorough longitudinal set of psychological studies ever made of infants, children, and adolescents was carried through with the aid of such people as Erik Erikson, who took residence in Berkeley for a period and studied the group in its adolescence. Recurrent studies have been made of the members of this cohort who were available and who are now in their forties (cf. M. C. Jones, 1967).

There was also a study, commenced in 1922 by Lewis Terman of Stanford University, consisting of psychological testing of high IQ children in California schools who were about ten years old. Those in this group who were still available were studied in their thirties and reported by Terman and Oden in *The Gifted Child Grows Up* (1947). The members of this sample, currently in their early 60s, are being interviewed and asked to respond to a questionnaire by Lee Cronbach and Robert Sears. This should be a valuable study, though the lack of measures of childhood and adolescent personality is a handicap.

Programs starting with a sample of adults and developing an interest in recurrent, or longitudinal data collection, are not as well known, but will soon provide much useful information. Among these are the Duke University Study which commenced in 1957 with 260 community residents 60 years of age and older. This study continues, and was supplemented in 1968 with a community sample of men and women over 45 years of age (cf. Maddox, 1968). Another is the longitudinal study of men conducted by Nathan Shock and his colleagues under the auspices of the National Institute of Health at the Baltimore City Hospital. A sample of men from the Baltimore–Philadelphia–Washington area, covering a wide range of ages, come recurrently to Baltimore for intensive biomedical and psychological study.

Finally, there is the Normative Aging Study in Boston under the auspices of the Veteran's Administration, with a sample of 2000 men ranging in age from 24 to 84 in 1971, eight years after the study's initiation (Bell, Rose, & Damon, 1972). The first task of the inter-disciplinary team making this study has been to work out a method of measuring *functional age* as distinguished from chronological age. When they succeed in this, they will have a longitudinal time dimension which will allow them to study developmental change more usefully than the present dimension of calendar years.

B. Life History Research in Psychopathology

Research on deviant behavior has been fruitful in the production of personality theory. It seems to lend itself naturally to longitudinal study, perhaps because the worker in this field is interested in therapy, and hopes for a cure or a remission of the deviant behavior, which can only be ascertained by a follow-up study. In this connection, one should refer to the work of the Society for Life History Research in Psychopathology, which has held several conferences and has collected the papers into two published volumes edited by Roff and others (1970, 1972). Types of pathology treated are schizophrenia, character disorder, delinquency, suicide, drug abuse, and various types of adult maladjustment.

C. Personality Theories That Have Not Given Useful Life-Span Developmental Understanding

Generally speaking, the theories of personality and of personality development which were extant in the nineteenth and earlier centuries have been less than useful to the twentieth century psychologists. Earlier theories have failed to provide the two things that such theories should: They have not differentiated clearly and reliably among various types of personalities; and they have not stated hypotheses of personality change and development through the life span which could be tested by research.

1. Theories of Constitutional Types

The Roman physician, Galen, who lived in the first century, A.D., proposed that adult personality was related to the relative quantities in the body of four juices, or "humours"—blood, phlegm, yellow bile, and black bile. Predominance of one of these four humours made a person sanguine, phlegmatic, choleric, or melancholic. Kant, in his *Anthropologie,* followed the lead of Galen and announced that all men were characterized by one or another of these "four simple temperaments."

Kretschmer, a German physician and psychologist, tried to relate body build to an affinity for one or another form of mental illness. He defined three types of body build as: pyknic (short and fat); asthenic (thin and tall); athletic (stocky and well muscled). The first two types tended toward manic–depressive and schizophrenic forms of mental illness, respectively, if they became ill. Kretschmer's book *Koerperbau und Charakter* was widely read in Europe, and went through 25 editions (perhaps more properly called "printings") between 1921 and 1967. Kretschmer himself was still living and took part in a major revision of the book in 1961 (cf. Kretschmer, 1927, 1967).

Sheldon (1942) developed a theory of the relation of body build to temperament as a basis for a branch of psychology he called "constitutional." He defined three basic types of body build, similar to Kretschmer's, and named them endomorphic, ectomorphic, and mesomorphic. These, he claimed, resulted from a dominance in development of one or another of the three layers of the human embryo. Closely correlated with these body-build dimensions, Sheldon suggested three types of temperament: viscerotonic, cerebrotonic, and somatotonic, respectively. He published reports based on his interviews which showed high correlations between the body build of college students and the personality ratings that he gave them.

There is considerable controversy over the relationships between body build and personality claimed by Kretschmer and Sheldon. In any case, their theories did not contribute to the study of personality change and development through the life span.

While Kretschmer and Sheldon did not have much to say about change of personality with age, Conrad (1963), a German physician, developed a theory of constitutional types which pays some attention to psychophysiological development in childhood and early adulthood. He recognizes two basic constitutional types—the pyknomorphic and leptomorphic—rather similar to Kretschmer's pyknic and asthenic types. He believes that these basic types of body build and personality are genetically determined. But he reports a tendency for the body and the temperament of all people to be pyknic and cyclothymic before adolescence, with a developmental trend which causes the body build to become more leptomorphic after adolescence for the true leptomorphs, while the true pyknics retain their early body build. He writes of "conservative" and "progressive" developmental modalities, the leptomorph showing the more "progressive" development.

2. Human Evolution

Another theory of personality development which had some currency during the nineteenth century was based on the Darwinian theory of evolution of the human species. Since the human body had evolved from a long series of phyla, or animal species, it was deduced that the human mind had evolved from the minds of the preceding species. The German philosopher, Ernst Haeckel, writing on evolution in the middle of the nineteenth century, stated the famous proposition, "ontogeny recapitulates phylogeny." That is, the human body and mind, as they develop, go through stages that are similar to those of prehuman species. This proposition drew some support from the developing science of embryology, which discovered that the human embryo in its early stages was rather similar to the embryos of other animals. Consequently, it was proposed that the human mind and personality must go through stages reminiscent of the evolution of lower organisms and primitive man. Some of this development took place before birth, but much of childhood development consisted of recapitulation of the development of the human race. If this was indeed true, it could be and was argued that children had to repeat the stages of early man. They have to be cave-men, tree-dwellers, nomads, etc. G. S. Hall in his vastly influential book on *Adolescence* (1904) said that during childhood, it was necessary to allow "the fundamental traits of savagery their fling till twelve." But he said that the adolescent personality could and should be influenced by society. Hall's theory was criticized severely by Thorndike (1967). He wrote:

The recapitulatory, or bio-genetic, or bionomic, law that "ontogeny repeats phylogeny" is true in only a very vague and partial way. Only in rough outlines and in the case of a fraction of bodily organs does nature make an individual from the fertilized ovum by the same series of changes by which it made his species from the primitive protozoa.

In intellectual capacities the child of two years has passed all the stages previous to man. It is difficult to find even one instinct in ten that occupies in his ontogeny the same relative position in time that it occupied in his phylogeny. No fact of value about either the ontogeny or phylogeny of behavior has, to my knowledge, been discovered as a result of this theory. Consequently one cannot help thinking that the influence which it has exerted upon students of human nature is due, not to rational claims, but to its rhetorical attractiveness [pp. 241, 244].

James M. Baldwin was a contemporary of Hall and a thoughtful and vigorous researcher. He, too, was a prisoner of recapitulation theory. One fourth of his book (1906) is devoted to this theory, which he called the "biological genesis" of the child's mind. Another half of his book discusses "psychological genesis," reporting results from his empirical research on children's mental and personal development.

These leaders of the "genetic psychology" movement of the late nineteenth and early twentieth centuries were pretty well replaced before 1920 by a new breed of students of child development who created "developmental psychology." But their fixation on the ages of childhood and adolescence gave little stimulus to studies of adult personality. One might say that the students of human personality in 1920 had not advanced beyond Shakespeare in their grasp of personality development through the life span.

3. Freudian Theory and Personality through the Life Span

Psychoanalysts were active in the developmental psychology of the post-1920 period, and they used the three Freudian elements or forces in personality structure as the basis of their theory. The id, ego, and superego, and their interaction accounted for development through infancy, childhood, and adolescence. This group made important contributions to personality theory, but did not produce much of value for the understanding of personality development through the adult years. However, there were some attempts along this line. One was the application of psychoanalytic theory to the personality development of women around the age of the menopause. Deutsch (1944, 1945) proposed that women would show marked personality changes at the time of the menopause, because of the decrease of the hormones involved in menstruation. This proposition, however, did not stand up under the light of a number of empirical studies of the relation of menopause to hypothetical changes in women's personality.

A direct application of Freudian theory to personality change in aging men and women was attempted by Hamilton (1942), one of the early American psychoanalysts, in his chapter written for the second edition of Cowdry's *Problems of Aging*. Hamilton divided the life span into five age periods separated by four transition points, namely: (1) termination of infancy; (2) termination of childhood and beginning of adolescence; (3) transition from adolescence to maturity; and (4) change from a mature to an aging personality.

According to Hamilton, the fourth period—adulthood—is one of great personal stability. The ego, superego, and id are in satisfactory equilibrium. But after the reduction of sex hormones in the blood stream, which occurs at the menopause of women and in a less dramatic way with men in their fifties, the balance of personality forces is upset, and there may be a tendency for *regression* from adult to earlier forms of psychosexual behavior. Hamilton proposed that a kind of *involution* may take place in the period after 60, and psychosexual behavior may reverse its course back through adolescence and childhood. He thought he could observe this in some of his patients and in other older people for whom he had data. However, he was cautious in his claims since the people who would come to his attention were likely to be having unusual personality problems. Hamilton wrote that there is "urgent need for collections of data on psychosexual aging in large samples of the population [p. 815]." His chapter does not appear in the third edition of Cowdry's book, and no other psychoanalyst appears to have felt that the data justify the proposition of a general involution of psychosexual behavior after the age 50 or 60 in women and men.

4. Carl Gustav Jung

Disciples of Jung generally claim that his personality theory was more "developmental" than that of Freud. Some of the titles of his published lectures give that impression—"The Development of Personality"; "The Integration of Personality"; and "Stages of Life." These lectures were given between 1930 and 1940, when Jung was 55 to 65 years old. In those days they may have seemed developmental, but they do not possess much of that quality for a reader who is accustomed to the developmental psychology of the 1950 to 1970 period. In the lecture on "Stages of Life" (1960) Jung said that his task is that of "unfolding a picture of psychic life in its entirety from the cradle to the grave [p. 387]." He divided the life span into four stages: childhood (to about age 12); youth (12 to 40); maturity (40 to 65); and old age (65 and beyond). During the periods of childhood and old age, the individual is said to have no conscious problems because he is completely dependent on his parents or other people for the structure of his life. Puberty brings his first consciousness of problems. Then for the next 30 years, the individual takes more and more responsibility as his life expands in activity, responsibility, and effectiveness. This period, he said, is the "morning of life," which is followed by the "afternoon," when the sun of assurance and initiative is going down. During the period of maturity, from 40 to 65, the person experiences a growing rigidity of personality and a kind of neurosis, with loss of self-confidence. Finally, old age is seen to be a period of complete dependence on others; the individual does not have problems because others take the responsibility.

This and other lectures represented more of a philosophy of life than a theory of life-span development, and they do not offer this researcher much stimulation for planning and conducting research.

V. Textbook Treatments of Personality Development and Socialization

The standard and most widely read textbooks on developmental psychology generally pay very little attention to the adult period. The book by Goodenough entitled *Developmental Psychology* (1934, 1945), with a third edition substantially revised by Goodenough and Tyler (1959), gives relatively little attention to adulthood and old age. The first edition has only ten pages devoted to some descriptive comments on old age, with somewhat more space given to the years between adolescence and old age. The third edition carries a preface by Tyler who says that the structure of the book was effected by her reading of Erikson, Piaget, and Havighurst. Still, out of nearly 550 pages in the book, only 57 are given to three chapters, entitled: "Early Adulthood—The College Years"; "Adulthood—The Twenties and Thirties"; and "The Second Half of Life—The Forties and On."

The book by Pressey and Kuhlen (its second edition entitled *Psychological Development Through the Life Span* [1957]), was a bold attempt when it was first published in 1939 to bring the entire life span to the attention of undergraduate students. The authors announced that they would treat "development in its rapidly changing socioeconomic and cultural environment—not simply as a biological phenomenon." Part three of the book is entitled "Preface to a Life-Span Psychology of the Future," and contains a 13-page chapter entitled "Retrospect and Prospect: Major Concepts and Problems as Seen Integratively in the Life-Span View." This chapter pays special attention to changes in abilities, motivations, and values. It does not use developmental concepts in the structure of the book, and thus tends to be content with empirical data on work life, family life, leisure, and religion, with age as a variable, but without unifying developmental concepts.

Birren published a textbook in 1964 entitled *The Psychology of Aging*. As an introduction, he lists eight phases of the life cycle: 0–2; 2–5; 5–12; 12–17; 17–25; 25–50; 50–75; 75 and over. He then gives data on development with age in special senses, psychomotor skills, learning, intelligence, work and achievement, and personality. This is a useful overview, but it does not treat personality development fully.

The book by the British psychologist Bromley, entitled *The Psychology of Human Aging* (1966), has a strong developmental bent. His chapter on "Personality and Adjustment" reports fully on the five personality types delineated by Reichard, Livson, and Peterson. His appendix on methodological problems deals perceptively with problems of studying development. Bischof's book on *Adult Psychology* (1969) is an eclectic survey of psychological studies over the adult segment of the life span. The overview of the book reports various writers on the stages of life, with special reference to Bühler, Frenkel-Brunswik, and Bromley.

There are some undergraduate textbooks that use development as a framework, though they are not widely used or widely known. The Pikunas text entitled *Human Development: A Science of Growth* (1961, 1969), now in a second edition, has chapters on each of eight age periods, and a treatment of the developmental tasks of each period. Philippe Muller has a text in French, with an English translation in 1969, which is structured around developmental tasks of children and adolescents.

VI. Literary Sources of Life-Span Developmental Information

There are sources in the nonscientific literature that might provide useful data for analysis from the life-span developmental point of view. These are novels, biographies, and autobiographies.

A. Novels

Though the content is fictional, some novels have been written by novelists who have an experience with human nature and human behavior that makes their books interesting and perhaps useful for scientific analysis. These are generally novels that cover family life over two or three generations. Some of them are: *Buddenbrooks,* by Thomas Mann; *The Forsyte Saga,* by Galsworthy; *Jean-Christophe,* by Romain Rolland; *Anna Karenina,* by Tolstoy; *East of Eden,* by Steinbeck.

B. Biographies and Case Studies

The writer of a biography is presumably an expert in life-span study and analysis. His job is to select, arrange, and print a connected account of a human life. Therefore, his work may be a valuable source of data on personality development. The nature and depth of the treatment depends, of course, on the author's perception of what a biography should be, as well as on the quality of the data with which he works, and on his skill as analyst and writer. Especially valuable are biographies written by psychologists who have as subjects people who kept full records of their lives. The great three-volume biography of Sigmund Freud written by Ernest Jones (1953, 1957) is highly useful. The biography of Edward L. Thorndike by Jonçich (1968) is a most interesting work by a sophisticated writer, whose subject did not open his private life readily to inspection. The biography of Eleanor Roosevelt by Lash (1964) will repay study from the point of view of personality development.

Bühler relied heavily on biographies as a source of data in her work in Vienna. Recently she wrote to this author:

> My interest was in the whole of human life, . . . I studied infancy, to get an idea of life's earliest trends. But after some years, I decided that life as a whole could be better understood from its end than from its beginning. Thus my students and I studied *biographies,* which were well enough documented to know them in great detail. We chose biographies, because these lives were closed and one could study their actual end, not only late periods.

Case studies, where the data on the subjects are intensive and extend over a period of time, are valuable, assuming a skillful analysis and a representative sample of cases, in providing a substantial basis for generalization. This procedure has been used with success by several psychologists at Harvard, notably Henry Murray, Robert W. White, and Kenneth Keniston. The set of case studies which forms a main section of the book by Keniston, *The Uncommitted* (1965), gives a convincing picture of this type of personality. White's book, *Lives in Progress* (1952), presents three cases, based on autobiographies and projective tests. The three young persons were seen first when they were of college age, and again when they were in their mid-twenties. Roe's (1953) studies of creative scientists are based upon questionnaires and some interviews. These have the advantage of covering a fairly large segment of the lives of these scientists. Block's book on *Lives Through Time* (1971) follows a California group through adolescence and into adulthood.

C. Autobiographies

The autobiography may be an extraordinarily valuable source of life-span data; or it may have little or no value, depending upon the willingness of the subject to tell the truth about himself, as he sees it, and to select and organize his material so that the true life history is presented. Clifford (1971) says that an autobiography may do any or several of the following: (1) create a work of art; (2) tell a story, based on reminiscence; (3) compile a set of records; (4) convince people of the rightness of some cause or effort which the subject wishes to promote; and (5) apply one's expertise to the understanding of one's own life. In her comments on the brief autobiography that Sidney Pressey wrote, Clifford says that he did fairly well on points 2, 3, and 4, but fell down on the last point. She says also that E. L. Thorndike, like Pressey, wrote his brief autobiography nonintrospectively and with many reservations.

Roger Brown (1969) in a review of volume 5 of the series on the *History of Psychology in Autobiography* (Lindzey & Boring, 1967) writes that in the study of autobiography we hope to acquire "as much as possible of the inner life and private action relevant to our understanding of large events." Since psychologists are trained to understand personality, a psychologist's autobiography "is uniquely suited to the treatment of private lifelong experience as psychological data." He goes on to say that the concepts used in writing an autobiography might be used by any successful man writing his memoirs.

This writer expects that in the future autobiography will become a valuable source of life-span developmental data on personality, but not all autobiography will be equally useful. One has only to read the 80 or more life-stories in the series on *A History of Psychology in Autobiography* to see the great differences, not only among the lives of distinguished psychologists, but also among their ways of writing about themselves and their notions of what is useful or important for people to know about them. Clifford (1971) has commented on the reserved and nonintrospective quality of the self-reports of Thorndike and Pressey. On the other hand, Carl Rogers (1967) has written a highly personal and revealing story.

In the project of the National Society for the Study of Education on the lives of *Leaders in American Education* (Havighurst, 1971), the 11 persons writing brief autobiographies were given a suggestive outline which aimed to cover decisive points and influences in their lives, and to secure data that might be comparable from one to another. Actually, their self-reports were so idiosyncratic that a reader could hardly guess that they had any common outline to to work from.

Some of the more useful autobiographies are those by Bertrand Russell, Anne Morrow Lindbergh, the *Confessions* of Rousseau, and *Sun Chief* (1942), the life story of a Hopi Indian written with help from Leo Simmons, the anthropologist. Less valuable to a psychologist may be *The Education of Henry Adams,* and the life story of Dean Acheson (1965). These deal with the outer world, seen from the point of view of a person who was in a good position to observe "large events," but they do not reveal much of the individual's life. Eleanor Roosevelt's autobiography (1961) on the other hand, gives a remarkable self-portrait of the first 18 years of this woman's life, better, almost, than a psychologist could have done.

VII. Requirements for a Life-Span Theory of Personality Development

In order to have a scientifically fruitful and viable area of study known as *life-span personality development,* it seems that the following conditions should be met:

1. Researchers should work with an organismic theory of personality, assuming the existence of something like a self-actualizing tendency, or the creative expansion of Bühler.

2. The personality theory should assume that the biological organism interacts with the social and physical environment, seeking satisfaction of needs and drives as noted in the preceding paragraph.
3. Researchers should look for evidence of change of personality at all age levels. This change may be judged as desirable, or undesirable.
4. Researchers should concern themselves with *live* problems—including controversial ones. For example, the statement of the theory of disengagement by Cumming and Henry (1961) instigated a good deal of research on the interaction of personality with retirement. Other problem areas that would enrich life-span personality research might include: study of career changes in relation to personality, where the change takes place in middle age; study of the perceptions of aging and of old age by the self, the family, and the wider community; study of personality changes associated with marked change in physical vigor and health; study of the relations between personality and favorite leisure activities of people; study of the attitudes toward death, held by people of various ages and personality types and; study of the correlates of senility.

CHAPTER 2

Socialization and Personality throughout the Life Span: An Examination of Contemporary Psychological Approaches

WILLIAM R. LOOFT

PENNSYLVANIA STATE UNIVERSITY
UNIVERSITY PARK, PENNSYLVANIA

> *The philosophical self is not the human being, not the human body, or the human soul, with which psychology deals, but rather the metaphysical subject, the limit of the world— not a part of it.*

—Wittgenstein

ABSTRACT

Like all people, developmental psychologists possess an organized view of human nature, or a model of man. The model of man held by the psychologist is consistent with the psychological model or paradigm that dominates and guides his scientific activities. Nearly all contemporary psychological approaches to the study of human behavior and development can be characterized as subscribing to one of two general models—the mechanistic model and the organismic model. Five quite diverse approaches to the study of socialization and personality development (Kohlberg's cognitive-developmental approach, social-learning theory, Loevinger's ego-development system, the Chicago approach to adult personality, Cattell's factor-trait approach) are examined. It is found that each can be classified as adhering to the assumptions deriving from either one or the other of the two general models. The claim is made that the changing nature of society and human needs demands the formulation of a new psychological model; this model must emphasize the complex relational, interactional, and dialectic nature of human development within the context of an evolving society.

I. Introduction

Everyone carries around within him a model of man—a personalized conception of the nature of human nature, a common-sense notion about "the way people are." He may not be able to verbalize precisely just what his personal theory about human nature is, but he clearly has one, for it is implicit in what he does to, for, and about other people. The development of his model begins very early in life as he observes and interacts with the persons around him. It probably crystallizes during his late adolescent period and will remain with him throughout his life as a guide or standard for his interpersonal relations. Undoubtedly his personal model undergoes a few minor alterations now and then as he encounters persons and situations that are not readily assimilated into his model structures, but basically it persists as a stable, equilibrated operational schema.

All psychologists, just as all other people, accept, implicitly or explicitly, a model of human nature; it is used as a guide and a rationale for both their theoretical and empirical work. Immediately we are faced with a problem, however, because not all psychologists accept the same model (or "paradigm," to use Kuhn's, 1962, term). Thus, there has resulted, as the outcome of the activities of our multi-modeled psychologists, a confusing array of often contradictory findings about human behavior; one almost wonders if these scientists are even talking about the same creature—that ordinary human being who gets along quite nicely with his own common-sense truths about the way people are.

It is obvious (which some will interpret to mean that there is no evidence for this assertion) that the formal model under which a psychologist chooses to operate is consistent with the psychologist's personal model. His "common-sense" understanding of nature is basic to his choice of scientific problems (Heider, 1958). Baldwin (1967) has stated this premise well: "Science grows imperceptibly from the answers that ordinary laymen find for the questions occurring to them [p. 6]." Later, common-sense and formal theories interact, blend together, and influence the form of each other.[1]

---

[1]There are some intriguing parallels between the theories about "reality" constructed by the developing child and those constructed by scientists in a developing discipline (cf. Piaget, 1933, 1970a). An interesting case example is the understanding of sexual reproduction. Kreitler and

This chapter examines the psychological models found in contemporary research on life-span socialization and personality development. Even more, this investigation should suggest to us something about the psychology of the psychologists conducting the research. Kaplan (1964) has mused that the models extant in any given period of the history of science are reflective of the cognitive style distinctive of scientists at that time. Extending this reasoning, if it could be determined which of the major models is *most* dominant and influential among the current generation of psychologists, we could be tempted to infer the nature of the cognitive style of contemporary society (Looft, 1971b; Riegel, 1972a).

Part II of this chapter presents an overview of psychological models and their corollaries, with emphasis upon the implications these have for the theoretical and empirical activities of scientists operating within them. Part III examines selected approaches[2] to the study of life-span socialization and personality; the premise underlying this discussion is that the assumptions and characteristics of each approach suggest the model within which it operates. The final section presents a strong recommendation for the formulation of a new psychological model to guide our future activities.

II. Dimensions of Psychological Models of Development

In recent years there has appeared a number of cogent presentations on the nature of the models that define the field of psychology in particular and the social sciences in general; the reader is especially referred to the discussions by Kaplan (1964) and by Reese and Overton (1970; Overton & Reese, 1973) in the proceedings of the two previous West Virginia life-span conferences. In view of the excellence and comprehensiveness of these analyses, it is unnecessary to repeat in great detail their arguments; thus, only a cursory overview of the nature of models is provided here.

In essence, the fundamental character of any model is that it is a representation of something—that something being, in the specific case, whatever it is that holds our immediate interest. Accordingly, there can be several levels of models,

---

Kreitler (1966) found that one of the most common theories about pregnancy held by young children is that the baby is actually inside the mother all the time; it just suddenly starts to grow. This belief is nearly identical to that held by physiologists even as late as the eighteenth century. Agreement between children and the preformationists ends here, however, for the latter group could not agree among themselves as to whether the preformed human being was initially inside the mother's body or the father's body.

[2]The term ''approach'' is used in this chapter to designate a systematic theoretical/empirical orientation toward investigating a particular aspect of behavior or development. Thus, an approach means something more than a theory, but it is tied to a general psychological model in the same manner as the theory embedded within it. An approach can usually be identified by the name (or names) of its promulgator (e.g., Cattell, Kohlberg).

arranged along a continuum of concreteness and specificity to abstractness and generality. The primary concern in this paper is the more general models, i.e., the epistemological and metaphysical models that determine the confines of lower-order, more specific theoretical and empirical activities (Reese & Overton, 1970). To use Kuhn's (1962) terminology, models at this level are to be called "paradigms" or "world views."

A model is built around an internally consistent system of assumptions and undefined terms that delimit or signify the basic theoretical derivations that may be drawn from this system. From our psychological perspective, such a metaphysical system, therefore, is an exposition of the nature of "reality," particularly with regard to the essence of human nature. Within a general model there may be developed a family of theories (Reese & Overton, 1970), with each theory somewhat different from the others on specific details, but in agreement with the others on the fundamental nature of man.

Unlike the physical sciences, psychology is beset (perhaps "plagued" is a more appropriate term) with at least two or more general models or paradigms. This situation is problematic in that, as Reese and Overton have so forcefully argued before, differences between paradigmatic assumptions can never be reconciled. These are untestable premises. Controversies among theories within the same model family are potentially resolvable, for these concern only theoretical and empirical issues. However, controversies among theories from *different* model families are futile from the very outset, for these arguments involve metaphysical, epistemological—thus, unbridgeable—assumptions.

There appears to be some disagreement as to the number of paradigms or models that can be found to encompass all of contemporary psychology. Reese and Overton have concerned themselves in their discussions with two models—the mechanistic and the organismic. The former assumes man to be a *reactive* creature, and the latter assumes an *active* organism. Skinnerian theory and Piagetian theory, respectively, are exemplars of each of these categories. Langer (1969) adds a third model to these two (which he has called "the mechanical mirror" and "the organic lamp"): the *psycho-analytic perspective*. Within the psychoanalytic family of theories are found classic Freudian theory and Loevinger's (1966) theory of ego development.

In yet another classification scheme, Riegel (1973) allows for the active and the reactive models of human nature, but he includes a third model, which entails both the active and reactive assumptions of the former models, but with additional assumptions about the complex dialectical nature of the interactions between ontogenetic and historical change. There appear to be almost no entries from American psychology in Riegel's third model cell, although Erikson's (1963) theory of epigenetic development may come closest to meeting its requirements. (Langer, 1969, however, has classified Eriksonian theory into the psychoanalytic camp.) Apparently, Rubinstein's synthesis of Pavlovianism and

Marxist–Leninist dialectical materialism stands as the leading exemplar of this model (see Payne, 1968). As we shall see later in this paper, nearly all contemporary American approaches—including neopsychoanalytic ones—conform to the assumptions of either the mechanistic or the organismic model.

Before discussing specific model issues, it is desirable to re-emphasize that the paradigmatic umbrella under which the psychologist operates defines for him which questions are meaningful to explore. Further, it advocates to him the most appropriate methods for studying these questions, and it suggests the best form for interpreting the data he gathers. Scientific, empirical activities are *second-order* activities; *first-order* activities are model building or model subscription.

Psychological models of behavior and development can be viewed from a number of different perspectives. Each perspective should provide us with a somewhat different understanding of the potential dimensions or issues inherent in the models. In the discussion that follows, a number of dimensions are described in a fairly informal, discursive fashion. In effect, we will scrutinize general psychological models in several slices, with the assumption that our gleanings from these details will ultimately be synthesized to render a more global comprehension of model issues and implications. It should not be assumed that the model slices presented here are the final handiwork of Occam's razor, for no doubt another examining surgeon could slice up our models into a different set of dimensions. It will be seen that most of these dimensions (especially A through H) are highly interdependent: A given model's position on one of these dimensions necessitates, for logical reasons, the model's stand on most of the other dimensions. The major issues (A through H) are presented as bipolarities, but in actuality these should be viewed as continua, for it is possible for a model to fall midway between the extremes of the dimensional boundaries. In addition to the major issues, four additional issues (I through L) that are potentially useful model descriptions are discussed. (As most of these model issues have been described at length elsewhere, the present delineation is mercifully brief.)

A. *External versus Internal Locus of the Developmental Dynamic*

This issue could very well be the most fundamental premise underlying any psychological model, for it pertains to the assumption taken regarding the basic nature of man. In essence, this dimension concerns the question of whether developmental change occurs because of changes *within* the organism or because of changes *external* to it. A model positing the former is typically called the *organismic* model; it assumes man is an active creature—one who changes as a result of his own initiations. In short, the developmental dynamic is *internal* to the organism. On the other hand, the so-called *mechanistic* model assumes the organism changes primarily in response to changes occurring in its environment. The locus of the developmental dynamic is *external* to man.

B. Qualitative versus Quantitative Change

A model assuming qualitative changes insists that the meaning of behaviors and traits changes through the course of ontogenesis. Thus, there are to be found uniquenesses at separate points in one's life: "Reality" is construed or constructed in quite different ways by the toddler and by the teenager. (Van den Daele, 1969, has provided an excellent examination of qualitative-change models.) Change in certain other models is seen to be inherently quantitative: The meanings of behaviors or traits remain invariant over time. The same processes or mechanisms underlie any behavioral change, and therefore development can be quantitatively measured.

The organismic model assumes qualitative change, and the mechanistic model assumes quantitative change.

C. Closed versus Open Model

An issue closely related to the qualitative versus quantitative dimension is that of closed versus open models. Perhaps this latter issue is best viewed as a corollary or refinement of the former. In an open model, development consists in the accumulation of skills, habits, and other behaviors in basically an additive, linear fashion. Human development is viewed as essentially a panorama of more and more, or, perhaps, less and less. The open model is an optimistic one, for implicit to it is the possibility of unlimited growth; there is no necessary end point to development. Most quantitative models can be categorized as open.

Closed models, alternatively, are teleologically flavored, for they posit that capacities are basically fixed or limited, and thus there are end points to development. Specific terms denoting developmental end points (or "maturities") are *Conduites progressives* (Janet), genitality (Freud), ego integrity (Erikson), and formal operational thought (Piaget). Most closed models, however, allow for the possibility of further refinement of skills or knowledge within endpoint stages. Clearly, closed models are most closely related to the organismic paradigm.

D. Continuous versus Discontinuous Change

Initimately related to the qualitative versus quantitative dimension is the issue of whether developmental change is continuous or discontinuous. That is, is growth characterized by steady, quantitative change, or is it a sequence of saltatory, qualitative changes? The latter possibility immediately invokes the question of developmental stages. Developmental psychologists have long labored over the stage concept, but apparently this has not been a labor of love. Disgruntlement with the stage concept has been increasingly voiced by those who work with it. (For recent analyses of the stage issue, consult the following: Flavell, 1971, 1972; Hooper, 1973; Kessen, 1962; Toulmin, 1971; Van den Daele, 1969.) Hooper (1973) aptly captured this sentiment in his conclusion to a review of the use of stage designations in cognitive developmental psychology: " . . . although psychologists are using stages more and more, they appear to be enjoying them less and less [p. 7]."

The mechanistic model assumes continuity of development, and the organismic model assumes discontinuity. Nevertheless, continuity is also inherent to most organismic approaches, in a derivative sense. Essentially, there is a derivative relation between two behaviors such that the two possess common characteristics. The second behavior derives from the first as a consequence of a transformational sequence that is divisible into stages; this is *not*, in effect, a substitution of one behavior for another (Dyer, 1971). The mechanistic model posits that there is no logical necessity for the introduction of the stage notion into theory. If "stage" appears at all in a mechanistically based theory (such as that of Bijou, 1968b), it is used as a convenient descriptive term or as a referent to a naturalistic–empirical phenomenon.

E. Reductionism versus Emergence

The corollary of reductionism, as found in the mechanistic model, accounts for phenomena by events at a "lower" level. It is assumed that any behavioral skill or operation can be reduced down or isolated into simpler, more elementary forms (Gagné, 1968). To avoid the entry of mentalistic entities in their explanations, reductionists seek out *naturalistic* explanations, which generally assume correlated assumptions of quantitative and continuous change mechanisms. Although seldom specifically discussed, certain reductionist positions also imply that explanation is to be at the level of physiology, anatomy, and biochemistry.

Emergence is a philosophical alternative to reductionism: Later forms are not reducible to earlier forms. The emergent position, found in the organismic model, professes that different levels of complexity or analysis can be defined; each level has its own set of governing principles that transcend principles regulating simpler or earlier levels. Change is discontinuous, for the organism undergoes genuine transformations that yield successively different, emergent levels.

F. Elementarism versus Holism

Closely related to the reductionism versus emergence dimension is the part-whole issue. Into the mechanical model is incorporated the corollary principle of elementarism, which, in essence, asserts that the whole (man) can be assembled by piecing together its isolated parts. Stated in another way, the whole can be predicted from its parts. Because responses are assumed to be physical processes, behavior is assessed in terms of its material identity. Thus, physically identical elements have identical "meanings" (Overton & Reese, 1973).

In contrast, the holistic viewpoint insists that the organism possess an organization that disallows a breaking-down-and-piecing-back-together analysis. Behavior is assessed in the context within which it is embedded; included, therefore, must be considerations of the individual at a multitude of levels and perspectives— physical status, goals, self-knowledge, environmental surroundings, and so forth. Two behaviors cannot be assumed to have identical meanings merely because they are physically alike.

G. Structure–Function versus Antecedent–Consequent Analysis

To operate within the confines of the organismic model, one must assume a structure–function perspective. That is, first one must identify or define the functions or objectives of the organism, and then one proceeds to look for the facilitating structures that serve them (Reese & Overton, 1970). A psychological structure is an equilibrated, organized pattern of a particular behavioral realm or system (Piaget, 1970b). The teleological flavor of structure–function analysis is clear: Purpose or form is primary and heavily determinative.

The antecedent–consequent form of analysis is intrinsic to the reactive model of man. No inherent goals or functions are assumed; purpose is a derived category. Any given behavioral phenomenon can be interpreted as the consequence of a set of prior antecedents. Intervening between consequence and antecedents is some form of linking, mediating mechanism; this intervening variable or hypothetical construct provides the explanatory framework for any observed behavior.

H. Structural versus Behavioral Change

Incorporated into both the structure–function and the antecedent–consequent forms of analysis is fundamental concern about just what it is that changes. The mechanistic model focuses attention on specific, observable behaviors or responses; the organismic model is more abstract in this regard, for it directs attention to inferred changes in psychological structures (i.e., the organizational or regulating patterns underlying behavioral realms). The former model assumes changes take place as a result of reactions to external stimuli or reinforcement conditions following a response; the latter model assumes structural changes occur as development proceeds toward an ultimate goal or purpose.

Following are four additional dimensions that can provide even further articulation about the character of a psychological model of development. A given model's status on these dimensions is not as closely dependent upon (i.e., predictable from) the active- versus reactive-organism postulates of the model. Because previous model analyses have not given these issues much attention (compared to issues A through H), considerable discussion will be accorded to them here.

I. The Nature of Individual Differences

How do persons differ, both between and within themselves? A given model's stand on this matter may not be as readily apparent as its stand on most of the dimensions described previously here. This relative ambiguity derives from the tendency for developmental analyses to disregard or minimize individual differences. However, the fundamental fact that individuals do differ and do not respond uniformly to experimental manipulations seems sufficient reason to invest the effort to understand a given theoretical or empirical system's position on the matter.

Emmerich (1968; see also Baltes & Nesselroade, 1973) and Van den Daele (1969) have developed classification schemes that can be applied usefully for our purposes. In Emmerich's system, developmental theories can be classified into one of three general categories. The *classical* view, which assumes an invariant sequence of developmental stages (e.g., Freud, Piaget), generally treats individual differences in relation to age norms of stage or level attainment. Thus, one's *rate* of progression through the sequence is his primary distinguishing characteristic. *Differential* approaches are concerned with how persons get sorted out into various subgroups, differentiated according to status and behavioral attributes, through the course of their development. Factor-analytically derived systems such as those of Cattell, Eysenck, and Guilford are most characteristic of this category. Individual differences are defined in the typical psychometric sense as a person's location on a number of attributes or traits.

The third category is the *ipsative* approach, which examines *intra*individual consistencies and changes in the organization of attributes over time. Accordingly, attention is centered upon changes *within* individuals, not between them. An ipsative approach might examine how the interrelationships among attributes might change with age, the rate of structural change, or perhaps the change in the number of levels in hierarchical organization. Apparently there are few entries in this cell of Emmerich's classification scheme. The idiographic personality theories of Allport and Murray seem to come closest to fitting the ipsative label.

Van den Daele's (1969) scheme seems to apply best to organismic models. Models treat individual differences in one of four ways, according to this two-by-two classification matrix. Development can be viewed as *unitary, multiple,* and *simple,* or *cumulative.* If development is unitary, each person moves along a single developmental track, with interpersonal variation limited only to the rate of movement; if multiple, people can sort themselves out and progress along a variety (divergent, convergent, parallel) of developmental tracks. If a model also views development as simple, a person can occupy only one developmental stage at a time, with intraindividual variability thus being quite limited; if development is perceived as cumulative, there exist simultaneously several developmental structures or levels, and an individual can operate at any one of these levels of complexity.

An example reflecting the assumptions of the simple-multiple model is Erikson's (1963) theory of epigenetic development. His "binary fission" design (Van den Daele, 1969, p. 307) allows for the possibility of several developmental pathways for an individual to follow (thus it is multiple), but a person can be found in only one stage at a time (thus, simple).[3]

With the possible exception of Emmerich's differential category, neither Emmerich's nor Van den Daele's analyses are much applicable to mechanistic approaches. Researchers of this ilk tend to account for differences among subjects on the behavior in question by referring to a number of independent, descriptive status or demographic categories. Thus, people will differ in their performance because of their differential learning experiences with respect to sex, age, socioeconomic status, cohort, ethnic group, personality profile, and so forth. Oftentimes in research the effects of these individual difference variables are minimized or canceled out by the application of experimental or statistical controls.

J. Status of Chronological Age

Although the variable of chronological age has been central to the discipline of developmental psychology, it has received only cursory or limited treatment

---

[3]Extending to the extreme the logic Van den Daele has applied to Erikson's theory, one may conclude that there are a finite number of individual differences with regard to personality "types." According to the branching-tree model implied by this logic, from each of Erikson's eight stages of development, one can proceed onward in only one of two directions, depending on the nature of the resolution of the psychosocial crisis intrinsic to that stage. Within each stage of life, therefore, there exists a limited number of possible forms of ego development. In the first stage (the 2^0 stage), there is only one type, for the individual has not yet resolved the trust vs. mistrust dilemma. In stage two (2^1), the first crisis has been resolved and the person can either be trusting or mistrusting. Thus, at the beginning of any given stage of life, the total possible number of individual differences is 2^n, where n is the stage number minus one. Summing across the entire life span, the tally of all possible developmental locations, including those following the eighth and final crisis resolution, is

$$\sum_{0}^{9} 2^n$$

or 511. (It is probable that Erikson would discourage this sort of interpretation.)

in formal discussions of psychological models. Nevertheless, certain consistent uses of the chronological age variable can be found among the approaches found in different model camps. Many mechanistic approaches are relatively unconcerned about age, for age can be reduced to time, and time itself causes nothing. The same general processes or mechanisms underlie behavioral changes at all ages, and therefore age itself, as a focus of attention, is relegated to minor status. A more extreme version of this viewpoint has been expressed by Bijou and Baer (1961), who claimed that there is really no need to explain age differences at all; the task at hand is to account for behavioral change in terms of the determining mechanisms.

In contrast, organismic theories positing stages of development are characterized by their chronological age boundaries. Probably most members of the organismic school would downgrade the importance of these age norms and might further state that they are provided merely to satisfy the applied worker's curiosity. They would insist that the sequence of emerging stages is primary in importance. Nevertheless, as has been pointed out in recent discussions (Baltes & Goulet, 1971; McCandless & Evans, 1973; Wohlwill, 1970a), age is intrinsic to a sequence of stages. The flurry of attempts to modify or replicate age–normed cognitive developmental functions (such as Piagetian or Kohlbergian stages) attests to the salience of chronological age in the organismic model.

Despite frequent arguments to the contrary, there can be little doubt that chronological age is, and most likely will continue to be, a basic dimension of developmental psychology. There are numerous indicators to substantiate this belief:

1. First of all, developmental journals continue to abound with article titles beginning with the "The Effect of Age upon _____" (the reader is invited to fill in the blank with his favorite dependent variable). Chronological age, as a main independent variable in both descriptive and experimental research, has retained its ubiquitous character.
2. Another indicator is the growing body of data on people's perceptions of time and age. This work initiates from a recognition that these subjective elements possess psychological reality because of people's Kantian, phenomenological perception of age and time (Reichenbach & Mathers, 1959; Riegel, 1972c). In this light, Baltes and Goulet (1971) have recommended the implementation of a research strategy entailing the simulation of age differences in subjective age perceptions (both retrospective and prospective).
3. In an analysis of the meaning of the term *aging,* Birren (1959) concluded that the term is closely tied to chronological-age change but not identical to it. In gerontological research, aging has been used both as an explanation for behavioral change (in the sense of an independent variable) and as something to be explained (in the sense of a dependent variable).

4. The pervasiveness of the age concept is further demonstrated in the editors' introduction to the proceedings of the first West Virginia Conference on Life-Span Developmental Psychology: "Human life-span developmental psychology is concerned with the description and explication of ontogenetic (*age-related*) behavioral change from birth to death [Baltes & Goulet, 1970, p. 12, emphasis added]."

Recently there have appeared two provocative analyses of the status of chronological age in developmental psychology. Baer (1970) has taken the position that the use of the age dimension as a cataloging system to impose order upon the diversity of people has produced, in actuality, an *age psychology*, not a true developmental psychology. Moreover, Baer's position has provocative implications for the nature of our present life-span developmental psychology:

[The age psychologist] studies children only because they represent a condition of the organism in which a great deal of behavior does in fact vary in an orderly way. Typically, as age increases beyond childhood, behavior change becomes less thoroughly ordered by it, and the interest of the age psychologist wanes correspondingly. Late in life, age change may again take on a powerful function in correlating with behavior change; thus a developmental psychology, concerning this time of senescence, again is possible [Baer, 1970, p. 239].

Baer went on to propose the radical notion that the environment is a poor programmer of "normal" behavioral change. Instead of idling about waiting for stages to burst forth, as do Freud and Piaget, Baer suggested that we create experimental environments that are necessary to bring about valuable behaviors much earlier than the laggard natural environment permits. Time and age are simply irrelevant.

In the second analysis, Wohlwill (1970a) has looked upon the age variable considerably more benignly. In response to Baer's age-irrelevant proposal, Wohlwill would probably respond accordingly: Change in response over time is a central characteristic of the diversity of behavior; thus, the age dimension (to the extent that it is not reducible to a set of completely specificable external events that determine the change) is indispensible to descriptive and functional analyses of behavioral change. In actuality, Wohlwill's proposal is more demanding than Baer's. He recommended that age be incorporated into the *dependent* variable in developmental investigations. Thus, the measurements of change would concern the *age at which something happens*, or perhaps the *rate-of-change of something happening*. Wohlwill's methodological suggestions would be restricted to behavioral systems for which the course of development (e.g., form, sequence, direction) remains invariant over a broad range of environmental and hereditary conditions. (These are precisely the assumptions that Baer feels are unnecessary.)

To repeat, the status of age has not been a major concern in most descriptions of psychological developmental models. Nevertheless, it seems worthwhile to examine more closely how various theoretical families treat this variable. A precise, unambiguous classification system for the status of age within different theoretical/empirical approaches is not immediately obvious, but a somewhat looser system, with rather fuzzy boundaries, can be proposed. Psychological models can be viewed as treating age as *intrinsic* or *extrinsic* to development. The intrinsic category would include those approaches that assume age is correlated with invariant, sequential changes; these approaches are likely to hold implicit or explicit assumptions about the importance of biomaturation underlying the change sequence. Also included in this group are those approaches whose focus of study is age-correlated changes in attitudes, statuses, and other phenomenologically-derived entities; these are intrinsic approaches because of the static, solidly entrenched age markers inherent to an age-stratified society (cf. Riley, 1971; Riley, Johnson, & Foner, 1972).

The extrinsic category would include those approaches that relegate age considerations to very minor status. The age dimension may be used as a convenient index variable by some of these approaches, but they do not take the age norms seriously, for age is not inherent to the behaviors observed. Since the same basic processes underlie all behaviors and changes, any given age function could be rendered irrelevant by the introduction of appropriate environmental manipulations.

K. Directionality of Development

The traditional understanding of the concept of development is one of progression, increasing complexity, and expansion. Nagel (1957) provided a good example of this classical viewpoint with his assertion that "changes must be cumulative and irreversible if they are to be labeled *developmental* [p. 16]." Observations of the behavior of organisms, however, suggest that development may not always be progressive and unidirectional. Thus, the possibility of developmental *regression* is raised. The usual psychological definition of regression entails a primitization of behavior, a "going back" to less mature ways of behaving that the individual had previously "outgrown" (Dyer, 1971).

Theorists operating within the organismic model generally deny or ignore regressive phenomena (for recent statements see Flavell, 1970; Piaget, 1972). This position is completely consistent with their model, at its present state of development. An axiom of the organismic model is that observable behavior may or may not reflect a change in psychological structures. Therefore, any behavior that is claimed to be an example of regression can be dismissed by the organicist on the grounds that it does not truly reveal what is happening in the underlying organizational patterns. Behaviors that appear to have changed from relative maturity to relative immaturity only *appear* that way; alternatively, perhaps they were not brought about by the same lower-order structures underpinning similar behaviors in children (Langer, 1969; Looft, 1972; Turiel, 1969). The boldest statement to be advanced by an organismic theorist would be that there is no "true" regression in a developmental sequence, but there could occur some temporary regressions that are indicative of instability of an intermediate point in equilibrium; thus, some individuals find it easier to revert to a surer and more familiar response of an earlier nature than to volunteer a newly achieved and still somewhat uncertain response of a later stage. In short, organicists have left the study of regressive phenomena to the psychoanalysts and the behavior modifiers, for the models inherent to the latter two groups can more readily account for such behaviors.

Despite the organicists' ostrich-like stance on this issue, there exist several indications of developmental regression. Students of personality have long investigated normal and abnormal (i.e., psychopathic) regressions in behavioral patterns. At various periods of crisis throughout the life span, some individuals appear to revert back to the use of earlier or more "primitive" personality forms that may be more immediately functional than the higher structures. Zinberg (1963) has persuasively argued that such "regressions in service of the ego" are especially common in old age. Developmental regressions have been implicated even in many of the phenomena that fall into the domain of study by organismic researchers. Regressions have been noted in the cognitive developmental sequences of children (Almy, Chittenden, & Miller, 1966) and in the moral judgments of college sophomores (Kohlberg & Kramer, 1969). Moreover, although the data are almost exclusively cross-sectional and thus only suggestive of ontogenetic change, there is rapidly accumulating evidence that many older adults evince developmental regression in their understanding of Piagetian conservation and classification tasks (e.g., Ajuiriguerra, Boehme, Richard, Sinclair, & Tissot, 1967; Papalia, 1972; Sanders, Laurendeau, & Bergeron, 1966; Storck, Looft, & Hooper, 1972), their concepts of life (Dennis & Mallinger, 1948; Looft & Bartz, 1969), and in their decentering skills (Looft & Charles, 1971). Current cognitive developmental theory cannot comfortably account for these findings.

Mechanistic and the psychoanalytic systems allow for the possibility of development proceeding other than unidirectionally. The organismic model's insistence upon developmental unidirectionality apparently has been derived from an inadequate understanding of embryology. It places excessive emphasis on a poorly understood process of development at the expense of other equally important aspects and processes of development. Perhaps future examinations of other aspects of the biological model (e.g., considering the organizational patterns within tissues and organs as analogous to "psychological structures") will bring about further articulation of the now incompletely developed organismic model. Such changes might someday permit development to be seen as bi- or even multi-directional, rather than only unidirectional.[4]

L. Universality versus Relativity of Development

Is the course of developmental change common to all human beings, or does each person traverse a unique developmental pathway? Most personologists are apt to answer in the affirmative to both of these questions. This seeming paradox was phrased most eloquently by Kluckhohn and Murray (1949): "Every man is in certain respects (a) like all other men; (b) like some other men; (c) like no other man [p. 35]." That is, all people are alike in some aspects because of the existence of certain personality determinants that are universal to the species (e.g., common biological endowments); some people are like some other people because of their membership in certain units or statuses (e.g., nationality, sex, vocation); and in some ways each person is completely unique (because of his unique genetic composition and his unique experiental encounters).

Each of the predominant psychological models of development also views each human being as a matrix of universals and relativities. However, upon closer examination of a given model, it is usually possible to discern a more fundamental assumption of either universality or relativity of developmental change. The active-man model essentially posits developmental universals: Each individual evolves through an invariant sequence of developmental stages that are common to all biologically intact human beings. Empirical research, to a limited extent, supports these claims of universality. Cross-cultural and cross-social-strata studies have shown that the sensorimotor, preoperational, and concrete operational forms of thought are apparently displayed by children everywhere (cf. Goodnow, 1969; LeVine, 1970); formal operational thought, however, seems to be more relative and dependent upon certain forms of educational and social experiences (Rohwer, 1971; Tomlinson–Keasey, 1972). Further, Kohlberg and others have marshaled evidence that progression through well-articulated stages of moral judgments (Kohlberg, 1969, 1971a) and dream interpretation (Kohlberg, 1969; Lloyd & Light, 1970) is also apparently universal. Obviously, these theorists allow for relativity in the development of thinking,

---

[4]Actually, Heinz Werner long ago pointed to the direction that model builders should take. His position was that psychological differentiation did not necessarily have to occur unidirectionally. In fact, Werner postulated two forms of developmental regression; one form is a "de-differentiation (dissolution) of existing, schematized or automatized behavior patterns," and the other is the "activation of primitive levels of behavior from which undifferentiated (little formulated) phenomena emerge [Werner, 1957, p. 139]." Wernerian development is thus an oscillation via progression and regression around an individual's primary level of maturity. Langer (1969) and Looft (1972a) have also attempted to outline structural accounts for bidirectional developments in adulthood.

moral judgments, and dreams because of the *content* provided by different cultures and subcultures and by the *rate* at which individuals pass through stage sequences, but the underlying structures of these developments are asserted to be universal to people in all human groupings.

Proponents of the reactive model of man, on the other hand, would be likely to assume that development proceeds uniquely for each human being. A person reacts to and is shaped by the forces or stimuli existent in his surroundings; since each person experiences a unique surrounding for a multitude of reasons (sex, birth, order, culture, parental characteristics, etc.), he displays a set of behaviors that are in many ways unlike those of anyone else. The mechanistic model would allow for similarities among people in behavioral development, but these should not be considered universal because the similarities could be dissolved by the application of a unique set of environmental contingencies to each person. It should be acknowledged that the reactive model assumes that uniform processes or mechanisms give rise to all forms of developmental change, but the focuses of the model are the antecedents–consequents of behavioral change.

III. Representative Examples of Contemporary Psychological Approaches

In this section we wish to proceed on a more concrete level and give illustrations of how the 12 model issues discussed previously are actually manifested in contemporary psychological approaches toward the study of socialization and personality development. Five examples were selected for analysis. First of all, however, it would be appropriate to spell out the criteria by which these examples were selected. Basically, the criteria were these:

1. We selected approaches that most psychologists would agree upon as deriving from primarily *psychological* models, as distinct from sociological, anthropological, socio–physical, or other models. Obviously, clear and final distinctions cannot be made among these various sorts of models, but consensus can be reached as to the fundamental nature of each.
2. The approaches selected had to be *developmental* in nature. That is, they must be concerned with behavioral change over time, rather than with static characteristics of, for example, personality traits.
3. Approaches were selected that generate or stimulate considerable empirical, data-gathering activity. (This is perhaps an indication of the author's socialization into the data-bound academic world.) Thus, such systems as that of Erikson were eliminated from further consideration.[5]

[5]It should be noted, however, that Erikson's concepts are being operationalized and tested by an increasing number of researchers (e.g., Baker, 1971; Boyd & Koskela, 1970; Ciaccio, 1971;

4. It was originally intended that the approaches to be examined had to encompass a life-span framework with regard to socialization or personality. However, it quickly became clear that if this criterion were stringently applied (in conjunction with the other criteria), there would have been very little to talk about. There seem to be only two or three psychological approaches that meet all of these criteria. Thus, a compromise was made for the present exposition: Approaches were selected which, taken together, cover the entire life span.

Immediately following is a brief description of each of the examples selected. The purpose of these descriptions is only to give a flavor of each approach and show how it reflects its fundamental model assumptions. (More complete discussions can be found in the representative references that are provided.) It will be seen that each approach conforms rather closely to the model dimensions presented in Section II. A summary statement of the model characteristics of these five systems can be found in Table 1 (see pp. 48–49).

A. Kohlberg's Cognitive–Developmental Approach

Lawrence Kohlberg is most noted for his study of moral development, but additionally he has made important contributions to the study of psychosexual development, dreams, and educational practice. Kohlberg claims that his studies of moral and social processes are guided by what he calls the "cognitive–developmental approach." Similar to the theories of those persons whom he claims were most influential to him (J. M. Baldwin, Piaget, Mead, Dewey), the approach that Kohlberg has developed clearly derives from the organismic model. Thus, development is viewed as involving transformations of cognitive structures that can only be explained by reference to organized wholes and patterns of internal relations. Further, the cognitive–developmental approach incorporates such concepts as action, equilibrium, reciprocity, discontinuity, and emergence; in other words, it contains all the classic characteristics of the organismic model.

With regard to the question of individual differences, Kohlberg's delineation of six stages or levels of moral judgment suggests Emmerich's classical definition; as for Van den Daele's scheme, this approach would clearly be unitary, but there is some question as to the simple–cumulative dimension. Van den Daele (1969) classified Kohlberg's scheme as cumulative, for he felt that an individual is capable of manifesting different levels of moral reasoning at any given time;

Constantinople, 1969; Marcia, 1966; Waterman & Waterman, 1971), mostly on samples of college students. Most typically, however, any mention of Erikson's theory in research reports is to be found in the "Discussion" section; it is used as a sort of after-the-fact framework in which to discuss data already obtained.

however, most likely Kohlberg himself would insist upon the simple designation, for in various places he has indicated that a person basically displays only one stage of reasoning in a given developmental period.

Chronological age is clearly intrinsic to this approach; age norms can (and have been) derived for the appearance of each new stage of development. Thus, age is best viewed as a dependent variable in the sense that Wohlwill has advocated.

As for the directionality question, this approach—like other organismically-derived approaches—assumes *unidirectional* development. However, unlike other organismic proponents, Kohlberg (1969; Kohlberg & Kramer, 1969) has discussed the phenomenon of regression. Apparently, however, moral regressions are not assumed to reflect true structural change.

And finally, Kohlberg claims—quite emphatically (cf. Kohlberg, 1971a; Kohlberg & Gilligan, 1971)—that the sequence of stages of moral (and dream) development is *universal*. Some cross-cultural data to substantiate this position have been gathered.

(For comprehensive reviews of the cognitive–developmental approach to socialization, see Kohlberg, 1963, 1964, 1969, 1971a, and also his chapter in this volume.)

B. The Social-Learning Theory Approach

Contemporary adherents to social-learning theory are many, active, and mostly concerned with infants and children. Moreover, there are a number of variations of the theory. The brief discussion here is an attempt to present a generalized picture of the social-learning approach.

Although social-learning theory has become considerably more complex and sophisticated since its early stimulus-response reformulation of Freudian psychoanalytic theory, the fundamental principle is the mechanistic one—that man came to be what he is in reaction to his environment. Definitionally, "the term 'social learning' simply defines a category of learning that involves stimuli provided by people but that follows the same principles as nonsocial learning [Gewirtz, 1969a, p. 61]."

Inasmuch as it derives from the quantitative model, the social-learning approach does not fit well into either of the individual-difference categorizations of Emmerich and Van den Daele, which basically apply to qualitative models. However, the assumptions of this approach do not seem inconsistent with Emmerich's differential label; the conjunction of the unique learning history of each human being with the common learning histories of persons belonging to identifiable groups (sex, race, etc.) should permit the location of each individual in psychometric space according to learned attributes and traits.

Chronological age is essentially extrinsic to the social-learning approach. Although the acquisition of behavioral systems typically studied by social-learning theorists (e.g., attachment, sex role, delay of reward, etc.) are correlated with age, this correlation is not considered to be fundamentally important, for it is not determined by an internal "maturational" developmental program. Any age trend could be eliminated by appropriate external manipulations.

Social-learning development is *bi-* or *multidirectional* and *relative:* Development proceeds according to the environmental stimuli impinging upon the organism that affect his behavior; although there are commonalities across social environments, the social stimuli that each person encounters are different in many ways from those that other individuals encounter (thus, relativity); and social-learning mechanisms imply no necessary hierarchy or progression to development (thus, multidirectionality).

(For overviews of the social-learning approach, see Bandura & Walters, 1963; Gewirtz, 1969a; and Miller & Dollard, 1941; see also Ahammer's chapter in this volume.)

C. Loevinger's Approach to Ego Development

For the past several years Jane Loevinger has been developing a theoretical base and a system of measurement (using sentence-completion items) for the study of "ego development." As yet a precise definition of "ego development" has not been proffered, but Loevinger has stated that such a definition will ultimately incorporate concepts from other well-studied areas, including moral, psychosexual, intellectual (of the Piagetian variety), role, and self-concept development.

Although this approach is sometimes depicted as representative of the psychoanalytic paradigm (e.g., Langer, 1969), close inspection reveals that it contains nearly all the characteristics of an organismically-based approach. Loevinger asserts that even though differences in ego development can be graded continuously, they are fundamentally qualitative in nature and cannot be reduced to quantitative differences. It is assumed that the newborn possesses the internal structures necessary for ego functioning, and that ontogenetic changes occur as a result of transformational processes.

Loevinger's approach fits Emmerich's classical definition, for the seven stages of ego development can be ordered along an ordinal scale. In Van den Daele's terminology, the invariant sequence of stages calls for the unitary label, and as it is assumed that an individual can occupy only one stage at a time, the approach is also simple.

Although Loevinger emphatically downplays the significance of chronological age in her developmental system, the age variable seems intrinsic to it. As with most other stage approaches, the emergence of new "milestones" in this approach is very likely to be highly correlated with age, especially in an age-stratified society. Thus, age is best viewed as a dependent variable.[6]

The approach assumes unidirectional development. However, Loevinger would probably acknowledge the possibility of regressive phenomena, but as yet her sentence-completion measurement format cannot take this into account. This possibility is apparently some source of concern, for it is admitted that "pathology in a subject is a possible serious source of error [Loevinger & Wessler, 1970, p. 123]."

Nowhere in Loevinger's presentations to date has she explicitly addressed the question of universality versus relativity. It seems appropriate to draw the inference, however, that her hierarchy of ego milestones is assumed to be universal. Perhaps different cultures can be characterized by showing a preponderance of one or the other of these forms of adjustment. In any case, "ego development has been presented not as one interesting personality trait among many, but as the master trait [Loevinger, 1966, p. 205]."

(For elaborated discussions of the ego development approach, consult Loevinger, 1966, 1969; Loevinger & Wessler, 1970; Loevinger, Wessler, & Redmore, 1970.)

D. The Chicago Approach to Adult Personality

For the past several years a group of researchers at the University of Chicago (hereafter called the Chicago group) has conducted a series of cross-sectional investigations of personality and adjustment patterns of adult and aged persons. Although this research program has involved a large number of investigators and many different kinds of investigations, an attempt will be made here to put together a generalized analysis of their approach.

At first glance the Chicago approach defies neat categorization into the organismic/mechanistic scheme used here. This may be due to a number of reasons, including: (a) Their guiding theoretical base remains in a state of evolution and is as yet not well articulated; (b) they tackle more global problems than most researchers operating from other psychological models; and (c) their style of hypothesis-formation and data-gathering varies widely from study to study. The original work from this group appears to have stemmed from hypotheses derived from ego-psychology theory.

Eventually the theory of disengagement was proposed, and later this theory was modified and broadened. Basically the approach appears to be an organismic

---

[6]The limited data collected to date in support of Loevinger's milestone hierarchy strongly indicate its dependence on chronological age. In comparing the relative ego statuses for four different age groups of children and adolescents, there was no overlap between any of the ogive curves (Loevinger & Wessler, 1970, p. 50).

one: Man is assumed to be active and creative of changes upon his environment. However, the organismic designation is clouded by the not infrequent appearance in their work of methodologies and interpretations that are clearly mechanistic in character. For example, in many places we are informed about the underlying "structure" of adult personality and how it undergoes qualitative transformations at certain "stages" of later life; but their empirical approach toward studying these changes, by their own admission, is clearly an antecedent–consequent analysis (e.g., to find the early "predictors" of late-life adjustment).

The continuity/discontinuity issue is another area of inconsistency in this approach. In some places we are informed about the qualitative, structural changes in personality and of the discontinuity of development between age groups because of rigid age roles and expectancies; in other places we are informed that personality changes are above all continuous and due to "accumulations" of past experiences and adaptations to biological and social events (cf. Neugarten, 1969). It appears, however, that the Chicago people approach their empirical work in a manner that is much broader but less rigorous than the social-learning researchers. Overall, the Chicago system more closely approximates the organismic than the mechanistic model.

For these reasons the classifications of the Chicago approach in Table 1 are tentative and, in places, somewhat contradictory. Perhaps these inconsistencies will be resolved in the future as these people continue their work and eliminate some of the lacunae in their theoretical framework.

Individual differences are heavily emphasized in the Chicago approach. Attempts have been made to identify different styles or modes of adaptation to aging and to formulate empirically derived personality types. In this sense the approach conforms to Emmerich's differential description. The approach also seems to fit Van den Daele's multiple/simple qualitative model: Individuals can sort themselves out on a variety of diverging developmental tracks in middle to late life, but persons are primarily seen to operate within one adjustive style (or stage) at a time.

Chronological age is clearly intrinsic to the Chicago approach. In their view, people's phenomenological perspective of time and age is an important determinant of ontogenetic change from birth to death. Society's rigid norms and expectancies bring about and maintain the resulting age-related roles. This view permits age to be incorporated into their researches as a dependent variable.

Later-life development is viewed as fundamentally unidirectional: The process of disengagement inexorably occurs, personality changes from an active- to a passive-mastery style, and personal time perspective changes from time-lived to time-left-to-live. Although the approach allows for relativity in that it maintains that there are multiple patterns of disengagement and adjustment, it would seem that more basically, adult development is viewed as universal: Every society is age-graded, and each person passes through a socially-regulated cycle.

(For more details on the Chicago approach, see Cumming & Henry, 1961; Neugarten, 1964; and several of the articles in the volume edited by Neugarten, 1968a.)

E. Cattell's Factor–Trait Approach to Personality

The Cattellian factor-analytic approach to the study of personality appears to be quite dissimilar to any of the other approaches discussed here. Upon close examination, however, it can be discerned that the uniqueness of Cattell's approach is his methodology; nevertheless, the assumptions upon which the approach is based adhere quite closely to the mechanistic model. It seems warranted to claim that Cattell's system is a highly sophisticated, mathematical interpretation of the reactive model of man. Cattell has been especially important to life-span developmental psychology, for in contrast to other factor-analytically oriented personality theorists (e.g., Eysenck, Guilford), he has made the greatest effort to consider developmental aspects of behavior. Most other researchers in this vein assume a static view of personality, although some of them admit that personality *measurement* is at best only half the question (cf. Nunnally, 1967). Cattell has developed a number of techniques (the well-known *R, P, O, Q, S,* and *T* techniques) designed to illustrate the factorial structure of personality traits over time within and between persons. Moreover, he now has questionnaire factorings covering ages 4 to 70 years.

Cattell begins with a definition of personality as "that which tells what a man will do when placed in a given situation [Cattell, 1965, p. 25]." This definition can be formalized, according to Cattell, to $R = f(S \cdot P)$, where S is the stimulus situation, and P is the nature of the person's personality (i.e., his particular arrangement of "traits"). Traits derive from two sources: learning (conditioning, cultural influence, rewards—even "unconscious" ones) and genetic inheritance. Cattell is quite unambiguous about his position on the origin of personality: "Most debaters are sane enough to recognize that everything is partly environmental and partly hereditary in origin, and the only issue is a quantitative one of *how much* each contributes [Cattell, 1965, p. 32]."

In the present context Cattell's use of the term "structure" can lead to confusion. He defines *trait* as a "mental structure," or "in terms of logical positivism, a 'construct,' and initially an 'empirical construct,' from observations of *behavior* [Cattell, 1950, p. 47]." Moreover, it is assumed that when a structure (trait) is in operation, the resulting behavior has functional unity. Thus, it would appear that, at least superficially, Cattell's approach incorporates the organismic model corollaries of structure–function and structural (as opposed to behavioral) change. However, Cattell's structures do not carry the teleological flavor of purpose or form that inheres in the organismic paradigm.

Of course, given Cattell's psychometric orientation, this approach places great emphasis on individual differences. Indeed, Cattell's system is perhaps the best exemplar of Emmerich's differential category. Although Cattell is concerned with change in personality structure through life, chronological age per se does not play a very important role in his system and is therefore extrinsic. Development is viewed as bidirectional in character. Cattell has dealt with the regression phenomenon quite extensively, and his methodology is ideally suited to be sensitive to regression over time on traits. The approach's stand on the relativity versus universality question is not easily answered. Cattell allows both for "common traits" (which all people possess in some degree) and "unique traits" (which are peculiar to individuals). Data gathered in recent years, however, have led Cattell to speculate that the same basic source traits are evident in all cultures.

(For more complete coverage of the factor–trait approach, consult Cattell, 1946, 1950, 1957, and 1965; see also Baltes & Nesselroade, 1973.)

IV. Recommendations for Future Model Development

The analyses in this chapter have been carried out within the framework established in the two previous life-span conferences by Reese and Overton (1970; Overton & Reese, 1973). They have identified two world views in psychology—the mechanistic and the organismic—and they have quite different truth criteria and are therefore forever irreconcilable. (It is probable that Reese and Overton would admit to the existence of other models, although this admission is not very evident in their papers.)

Although it could be argued that this is an extreme and unnecessary position to take, our own scrutiny here of five quite diverse approaches to the study of socialization and personality has suggested that most all contemporary psychological systems can be rather confidently categorized as derivative of either the mechanistic or the organismic models.

Nevertheless, it would seem that Reese and Overton are too fatalistic. Implicit in their message is that psychologists will forever continue to operate within one or the other of these two unbridgeable paradigms. Their ahistoricity has produced for us a thesis and an antithesis, but no possibility of new alternatives or syntheses has been suggested for the future. It seems entirely possible that the formulation of a new psychological model could simply surpass and transcend the active-man and the reactive-man world views and relegate them to the status of historical curiosities.

Human activity and experience can alter the conceptions people hold about themselves. As people make new discoveries about their world and invent new tools to act upon that world, that very world they inhabit undergoes changes. And as their world changes, people's needs change. Cultural upheavals in recent centuries have brought about revolutions of all kinds—political, industrial, informational, communicational, sexual. Some social scientists have been dimly aware

TABLE 1

A Comparison of the Psychological Model Assumptions of Five Approaches to the Study of Socialization and Personality Development

Model Issues	Five Selected Approaches				
	Kohlberg's Cognitive–Developmental Approach	Social-Learning Theory Approach	Loevinger's Approach to Ego Development	The Chicago Approach to Adult Personality	Cattell's Factor–Trait Approach to Personality
A. External vs. internal locus of the developmental dynamic	internal	external	internal	internal	external
B. Qualitative vs. quantitative change	qualitative	quantitative	qualitative	qualitative	quantitative
C. Closed vs. open model	closed	open	closed	closed	open
D. Continuous vs. discontinuous change	discontinuous	continuous	discontinuous	[continuous?]	continuous
E. Reductionism vs. emergence	emergent	reductionistic	emergent	[emergent?]	reductionistic

F. Elementarism vs. holism	holistic	elementaristic	holistic	[holistic?]	elementaristic
G. Structure function vs. antecedent-consequent analysis	structure–function	antecedent–consequent	structure–function	structure–function	antecedent–consequent
H. Structural vs. behavioral change	structural	behavioral	structural	structural	behavioral
I. Nature of individual differences	classical (Emmerich); unitary–simple (Van den Daele)	(differential? [Emmerich])	classical (Emmerich); unitary–simple (Van den Daele)	(differential? [Emmerich]); multiple–simple (Van den Daele)	differential (Emmerich)
J. Status of chronological age	intrinsic	extrinsic	intrinsic	intrinsic	extrinsic
K. Directionality of development	unidirectional	bidirectional	unidirectional	unidirectional	bidirectional
L. Universality vs. relativity of development	universal	relative	[universal?]	universal	

49

of how these historical alterations have changed the very nature of psychological development within individuals. Freud's model seemed to fit well a traditional, unchanging society: When women always grow up to be wives and childrearers and men always grow up to assume the same vocational niches occupied by their male ancestors before them, it may well have been true that the establishment of a stable sexual orientation was the primary developmental achievement in youth. As the rate of cultural change in the Western world increased, the Freudian model no longer applied as well.

It was the great contribution of Erikson (1963) to elucidate that for youth in modern industrial society, sexuality becomes subordinate to larger questions of identity—role, social, vocational. But now we may be at the threshold of even newer societal transformations that will render Erikson's interpretations inadequate. In a world torn between potentials for tremendous humanitarian improvement and massive destruction of humanity, between incredible affluence and rising unemployment, and between communications media that integrate people together and at the same time create deep cynicism and despair, Freud's sexuality and Erikson's personal identity concerns diminish in importance. Perhaps, as Mead (1970) has so eloquently proposed, the major developmental crisis for future young people will be that of *commitment:* What kind of commitment is one to make to the larger social and historical forces that are in operation?

Furthermore, as the developmental problems of young people have changed during recent historical developments, so have the roles of the elderly in society. In the traditional, nonchanging societies, the aged were the educators and socializers of children and youth; they had lived longest, and thus they were the wisest and knew most about what the future held in store for the new generation. In our contemporary co-figurative society (Mead, 1970), the elderly are left to spend their last years in disengagement, isolation, and reminiscence. The role of the aged in future society can only be speculated.

The examples previously cited hopefully have made a point. The mechanistic and organismic models have been useful and have generated a vast amount of theoretical and empirical activity (and, hopefully, understanding too). Unfortunately, their historicity resides only within the persons who operate within them; they are ahistorical in that they do not take into account the changes that have occurred in the milieus in which human beings develop.

To counter the pessimism that is evoked by the Gordian knot that Reese and Overton (as well as many others) have tied, a more optimistic position can be taken. This alternative stance insists that we can formulate a new psychological model that better accounts for the complexity of change between and within individuals and society. First, it will be necessary to re-emphasize the *prescriptive* nature of model corollaries or assumptions (cf. Watson, 1967, 1971). When our model tells us, for example, that "man is a rational being," we merely assume he is (or, perhaps, we hope he is). These prescriptions—emergence, continuity, holism, rationalism, etc.—orient the psychologist and tell him how to hypothesize, proceed, and interpret. It is entirely possible to adopt a different set of assumptions or prescriptions and formulate a new model.

The alternative model advocated here admits to a new view of reality, one that perceives human social and mental development as the confluence of many interrelated and changing systems and subsystems, including the biological, social, cultural, and historical.[7] The new paradigm may be given a number of different appellations by different proponents, including "rational," "general system theory," "interactional," "dialectic," or "transformational," but all of these titles imply that the model's unifying theme is *relations;* material, elemental, and organismic aspects are of secondary importance. Theorists from the mechanistic and organismic models continue to engage in belabored, useless discussions on causation, nature and nurture, continuity versus discontinuity, and the like.[8] The adoption of the relational model obviates all these debates and propels us to a new level of understanding.

One of the important implications of the relational model of development is that, in effect, psychology diminishes in importance. Indeed, psychology retains its significance only as it fits into the relational network with other developmental sciences, including biology as well as history. Thus, in addition to incorporating developmental biology into our new analytic framework, we must also take into account historical, sociological, and demographic concepts (cf. Ryder, 1965) if we are to formulate a more encompassing understanding of social and mental development. No longer should developmental psychologists focus so exclusively on ontogenetic age functions; each new generation will manifest age trends that are different from those that preceded it, and thus, previous empirical endeavors are reduced to exercises in futility.[9]

[7]By no means, of course, is it to be implied that this is the first plea of this sort. Many persons have advocated similar models in the past. One of the most insistent of the recent proponents for new conceptualizations in developmental psychology is K. Riegel (1972a, b, c).

[8]The following comment is most apropos regarding the troublesome division in psychology:

It would seem that when contemporary psychologists deal with human nature they employ or reject (which is to employ as a counterpoint) a concept developed in another time, in a stage different from our present stage. While psychology is trying to deal with relational (e.g., environmental psychology) problems, it is using a concept of man that is essential: Stage 3 problems treated with a stage 1 concept. It seems very like travelling the interstate highway system on foot [Svoboda, 1972, p. 17].

[9]Most recent discussions calling for revisions in developmental methodology have emphasized the importance of *cohort* change, and appropriately so. However, our new model should not overlook the unique problems encountered by individuals *within* a cohort as they live out their lives in a rapidly changing society that continually demands new kinds of adjustments from its members. Eisenberg (1972) has expressed this concern well:

However wide the range of behaviors man can exhibit—evidenced by the comparison of one society with another [and one generation with another]—the task of developing adaptive attributes is very different when radically changed behaviors are required within an *individual's* lifetime rather than over the history of a people [p. 127].

A probable criticism to the relational model (and one that may very well inhibit its adoption) is that the complexity of its methodological implications can be staggering. (Indeed, it is very likely that one of the reasons the mechanistic and organismic approaches are so well entrenched in our scientific establishment is that they each have highly developed and articulated methodologies; cf. Breger, 1969.) Nevertheless, methodological imperialism should not be allowed to obstruct our desire to look at human development in a new way. Also, it would appear that considerable progress has been made in the formulation of developmental methodology (viz., the work of Schaie, 1965, and Baltes, 1968); further progress in this line is, however, unquestionably needed.

Presentations such as this one too often sound uniformly harsh and condemnatory of our present state of affairs. This is not our intent here. Rather, we should view our discipline as a developing entity in itself and interpretable in the same relational paradigm suggested for the study of the development of the individual human being. Indeed, Foucault (1970) has advanced the argument that the notion of "man" as an object of our investigation and knowledge is a very recent invention, not yet even two centuries old. The impression that our work to date is misguided and woefully inadequate is probably not a healthy one. As Bromley (1970) observed in the first West Virginia life-span conference, it is impossible to say whether a scientific discipline is making satisfactory progress, for there are no developmental norms to be derived from the history of science. The mechanistic and the organismic models of man may have served us well in the past, but our changing human needs demand a new model to guide our future activities.

ACKNOWLEDGMENTS

The author wishes to acknowledge his indebtedness to K. Riegel, C. Svoboda, and R. Eischens. Appreciation is also extended to B. Pickford, A. Higgins-Trenk, F. Hooper, and D. Papalia for their critical reading of various portions and versions of this paper.

The author wishes to acknowledge the insights provided to him by a provocative unpublished paper by Mary Ann Roberton (1972) on the issue of the derivation of an organismic model from embryology as discussed in Part K.

CHAPTER 3

Sociological Perspectives on the Life Cycle

BERNICE L. NEUGARTEN

THE UNIVERSITY OF CHICAGO
CHICAGO, ILLINOIS

NANCY DATAN[1]

UNIVERSITY OF THE NEGEV
BE'ER-SHEVA, ISRAEL

ABSTRACT

Students of the life cycle have given much attention to the biological timetable of human development, but much less attention to the socio-historical context. A few of the major sociological concepts significant for understanding personality are briefly reviewed– namely, social system, social role, and socialization, and each is discussed in relation to a time dimension in looking at the life course. The life cycle is then viewed from each of three dimensions of time: life time (or chronological age); historical time; and social time, or the system of age grading and age expectations which shapes the life cycle. After a brief discussion of age norms as a system of social control, and of age stratification in society, there follows a description of the changing rhythm of the life cycle in American society, illustrating how historical time, social time, and life time are intertwined.

I. Introduction

Students of the life cycle have given much attention to the biological timetable of human development, using such concepts as maturation, age, and stage as

[1]Present address: Department of Psychology, West Virginia University, Morgantown, West Virginia.

major dimensions in mapping significant changes. Much less attention has been given to the socio-historical context and to the development of concepts for mapping changes in the social environment as they affect the way in which an individual's life is lived. Although there have been scattered but significant attempts by psychologists to understand the lives of noted individuals in relation to historical change (such as Freud's [1939] study of Moses and monotheism, and Erikson's [1958, 1969] studies of Luther and Gandhi), for the most part, psychologists have left it to biographers, novelists, and historians to study the personalities of the eminent and to elucidate both the forces that shape the individual and the effect of the individual upon his time.

Developmentally oriented studies have appeared which deal with the impact of single historical events upon the life course of groups of individuals. For example, the effects of World War II have been studied in a variety of ways, as in studies of the long-term effects on British children evacuated from London during the Blitz (Maas, 1963), or the effects of the Depression upon the subsequent social development of children (Elder, 1973), or in a study of middle-aged women 25 years after they had experienced concentration camps (Antonovsky, Maoz, Datan, & Wijsenbeek, 1971).

While there are many such studies of the significance of given historical events, the socio-historical perspective on the life cycle has not as yet received widespread, systematic treatment. On the contrary, studies of development are more often characterized by a search for a universal sequence of personality change comparable to, if not paced by, the maturational timetable, rather than a search for the sequences of personality changes that can be shown to reflect sequences of historical and social events. A major problem lies in the fact that we lack a set of conceptual tools by which to integrate maturational, psychological, sociological, and historical perspectives on the life cycle.

The purpose of this paper is to remind the reader of a few sociological concepts that have been of significance in understanding human personality, and then to turn to the life cycle seen in three dimensions of time: life time, or the individual's chronological age; social time, or the system of age grading and age expectations that shapes the life cycle; and historical time, or the succession of political, economic, and social events that shape the setting into which the individual is born and make up the dynamic, constantly changing background against which his life is lived.

II. Sociological Concepts

From the sociological perspective, personality is generally seen as an emergent of the interaction between the biological organism and the social context, and the task of the sociologist has been to explore this interaction from the standpoint of social organization. Thus, speaking very generally, sociologists often move from a study of the social organization to the consideration of its consequences for personality, viewing personality as the outcome of social learning.

In relating the individual to his social surrounding, the concepts of social system, social role, and socialization have repeatedly been set forth in the sociological and social–psychological literature. (Recent expositions are given, for example, in Brim & Wheeler, 1966; Clausen, 1968; Goslin, 1969; and Riley, Johnson, & Foner, 1972.) Although not each of these concepts was originally intended for this purpose, each can be related to a time dimension in looking at the life course.

A. The Social System and Social Role

Parsons and Shils (1951b) have expressed the distinction between the psychological and sociological levels of analysis in their description of the social system as made up of the actions of individuals. The actions constituting the *social system* are the same actions that make up the personality systems of the individual actors, but these two systems are analytically discrete entities despite the identity of their basic components. The difference lies in the different focuses of organization and each system involves different functional problems in operation. The individual actor is not the unit of study in the social system; rather, for most purposes, it is the *role* that is being examined. A role is a sector of an individual actor's range of action, but it is also a specific set of behaviors having a particular function for a social institution—e.g., fatherhood is a role with specific functions for the family (and thus for the larger society) and at the same time, it is a role with specific functions for the individual. Any role or role constellation has different significance according to whether it is viewed from the individual or the societal perspective; but from both perspectives, the individual learns to think and to behave in ways that are consonant with the roles he plays, so that performance in a succession of roles leads to predictable personality configurations. Indeed, for some sociologists, personality itself is perceived as the sum of the individual's social roles. For purposes of the present discussion, the life cycle can be seen as a succession of roles and changing role constellations, and a certain order and predictability of behavior occurs over time as individuals move through a given succession of roles.

B. Socialization and Social Learning

The process by which the human infant is transformed into a member of a particular society and learns the roles appropriate to his or her sex, social class, and ethnic group, is called socialization. (Social classes have been shown by sociologists to be subcultures with differentiated norms and institutions.) LeVine (1969) has distinguished three different views of the process of socialization which correspond approximately to the disciplinary orientations of cultural anthropology, personality psychology, and sociology. For the anthropologist, socialization involves the transmission of cultural values and traditions from generation to generation. To some psychologists, the major task in socialization is the channeling of instinctual drives into socially useful forms. For the sociologist, socialization is a process of training the child for participation in society, with the emphasis upon positive social prescriptions growing out of the needs of the social structure.

In all three views, however, socialization can be seen as a process of social learning or of training through which individuals acquire the knowledge, skills, attitudes and values, the needs and motivations, and the cognitive, affective and conative patterns that relate them to their socio-cultural setting. The success of the socialization process is measured by the ability of the individual to perform well in the roles he takes on (Inkeles, 1969).

While socialization was once conceived as a process by which the infant was transformed into an adult of his culture, and thus the process was essentially complete at adulthood, more recently, sociologists have come to describe socialization as a lifelong process (Brim & Wheeler, 1966), one that involves new learning in adulthood in response to rapid social change and in response to the succession of life tasks. Although anthropologists such as Benedict (1938) have long pointed to discontinuities in cultural conditioning at various points in the life cycle, the recognition of the need for resocialization in adulthood is relatively new.

In summary then, from the sociological perspective, the life cycle can be described as a succession of social roles, and personality can be described as the product of changing patterns of socialization.

III. Three Dimensions of Time

A. Life Time

From the ancient poets through Shakespeare to Erikson (1950, 1959), people have viewed the life cycle as a series of orderly changes, from infancy through childhood, adolescence, maturity, and old age with the biological timetable governing the sequence of changes in the process of growing up and growing old. Although for the developmental psychologist there are a host of conceptual and methodological issues involved in the use of chronological age or *life time* as an index of change (see, e.g., Baer, 1970; Baltes & Goulet, 1971; Looft, Chapter 2, this volume; Wohlwill, 1970a), chronological age is nevertheless the most frequently used index. It is a truism that chronological age is at best only a rough indicator of an individual's position on any one of numerous physical or psychological dimensions, for from earliest infancy on, individual differences emerge in development. Nor is age a meaningful predictor of many forms of social and psychological behavior, unless there is accompanying knowledge of the particular society as a frame of reference. An obvious example is the fact that in the United States the typical 14-year-old girl is a schoolgirl, while in a rural village in the Near East she may be the mother of two children. The significance of a given chronological age, or a given marker of life time, when viewed from a sociological or anthropological perspective, is a direct function of the social definition of age, or of *social time*.

B. Social Time

Social time refers to the dimension that underlies the age-grade system of a society. Anthropologists were the first to introduce the concept of age grading (see, e.g., Eisenstadt, 1956; Warner, 1958). It is characteristic in a preliterate society to have *rites-de-passage* marking the transition from one age status to the next, such as the passage from youth to maturity and to marriageability (Van Gennep, 1960). Only a rough parallel exists between social time and life time, for although in simple societies a girl may be considered marriageable when she reaches puberty, in a modern society, she is not considered marriageable until long thereafter. In short, social timing is not synchronous with biological timing. There are also different sets of age expectations and age statuses in different societies, further demonstrating that neither chronological age (nor maturational stage) is itself the determinant of age status, but that it merely signifies the biological potentiality upon which a system of age norms and age grading can operate to shape the life cycle.

C. Historical Time

Historical time shapes the social system, and the social system, in turn, creates a changing set of age norms and a changing age-grade system which shapes the individual life cycle. Aries (1962) has traced the social history of family life in Western society, suggesting that not until the seventeenth and eighteenth centuries, with the growth of industrialization, the formation of a middle class, and the appearance of formal educational institutions, did the concept emerge that childhood is a distinct phase of life, a period that has its specific characteristics and needs. The concept of adolescence as a distinctive period in the life cycle appeared in the twentieth century (Demos & Demos, 1969). Keniston (1970) has suggested that in the past few decades, when the speed of social change has been so great, a stage called youth, in which a new form of reconciliation of the self with the changing social order follows upon the earlier task of identity formation, can now be noted. Similarly, the period of middle age is a recently delineated stage in the life cycle resulting from the enormous increase in longevity that has occurred since the beginning of this century, together with the changing rhythm of the work cycle and the family cycle.

Historical time refers not only to long-term processes, such as industrialization and urbanization which create the social-cultural context and changing definitions of the phases of the life cycle. History is also a series of economic, political, and social events that directly influence the life course of the individuals who experience those events. The life cycle of an individual is shaped, then, by the long term historical processes of change that gradually alter social institutions; but the life cycle is also affected by discrete historical events. Some sense of the interplay between historical time and life time emerges if, for example, one considers World War II as it impinged on a young man, a child, or a young mother.

In the first case, a young man who becomes a soldier may achieve some resolution of masculine identity by taking on a highly stereotyped male role. In the second case, the child may go fatherless for the first few years of his life, with the attendant consequences for parental identification and oedipal resolution. In the third case, a mother whose husband has gone to war faces child rearing with reduced economic, physical, and psychological resources as she takes on both father's and mother's roles. This example merely illustrates the obvious point that the same historical event takes on very different psychological meanings depending on the point in the life cycle at which the event occurs.

Behavioral scientists have recognized the importance of the timing of major historical events in the life line of the individual, and *cohort analysis* (cf. Cain, 1967; Schaie, 1968) is a tool originally developed by demographers in an attempt to relate life time to historical time. A *cohort* is a group defined by calendar year of birth (a given year or some prescribed number of years). The characteristics of cohorts are analyzed in an attempt to explore *cohort effects,* that is, the effect of membership in a particular cohort with its unique background and demographic composition (cf. Riley, 1971; Riley *et al.,* 1972). For instance, Cain (1967) has presented sets of data to show that a historical "hinge" or "watershed" developed in America at the end of World War I with regard to levels of education, fertility patterns, sexual mores, reduction of hours in the work week, labor force participation patterns, and so on. This watershed produced a sharp contrast in life styles between the cohort of persons born before the turn of the century (persons who are presently over 70) and the cohort born after 1900 (persons who are now entering old age), with the results indicating that the needs of the new cohort of the aged will be very different from the needs of cohorts that preceded it. Another watershed probably occurred with the Great Depression of the 1930s.

It might be pointed out that cohort, like the dimension age, is in itself without psychological meaning, and that psychologists must eventually be able to specify the events that give meaning to cohort differences. For the present it is not known, except in the most general way, which historical events are more significant than other events in influencing the course of personality development over the life cycle—a problem which must somehow be resolved if cohort analysis is to become a powerful tool in analyzing life histories.

IV. Social Time and the Age Status Structure

The concepts of historical time and life time are well understood, even though they have not often been used in juxtaposition in studies undertaken by developmental psychologists. The concept of social time, on the other hand, probably needs fuller exposition.

Age grade systems are expressions of the fact that all societies rationalize the passage of life time, divide life time into socially relevant units, and thus can be said to transform calendar time (or biological time) into social time. As already noted, the concept of age grading comes from anthropological studies of simple societies where the life cycle may consist of a succession of formally age-graded, ascriptive roles: A male, for example, may pass from infancy to childhood to warrior-apprentice to warrior (and simultaneously to husband and father), and finally to elder, a status terminated by death. Age-strata and age-status systems emerge in all societies; and duties, rights, and rewards are differentially distributed to age groups which themselves have been socially defined. In societies where the division of labor is simple and the rate of social change is slow, a single age-grade system becomes formalized; and family, work, religious, and political roles are allocated and regulated accordingly. A modern complex society, by contrast, is characterized by plural systems of age status that become differentiated in relation to particular social institutions.

American society is characterized by a comparatively fluid and differentiated age-status system; yet despite its fluidity, and despite overlapping systems of age grading, there are some ascriptive age statuses that are systematically tied to chronological age, such as entry into school, age at eligibility to vote, age of legal responsibility, and so on.

The age-grade system institutionalizes cultural values and constitutes a social system that shapes the life cycle. Every society has a system of social expectations regarding age-appropriate behavior, and these expectations are internalized as the individual grows up and grows old, and as he moves from one age stratum to the next. There is a time when he is expected to go to work, to marry, a time to raise children, a time to retire, even a time to grow sick and to die.

As an example of the way in which age expectations are institutionalized, most children in American society must attend school between the ages of

6 and 16; at 18, they acquire the right to vote. This is to say that American society views a lengthy education as a prerequisite for adult responsibility; there are social institutions to provide this education; there is an age-grade and age-norm system that prevents the assumption of adult responsibilities—work, marriage, voting, legal liability—until compulsory education is ended. The total network of age-associated institutions is far more complex than this example can indicate, and the system of age grading is primarily consensual rather than formal, but the example serves to illustrate the close correspondence between age norms and age expectations on the one hand, and social and cultural values on the other.

That these concepts of social time, age grading, age status, and age norms refer to present-day social realities is demonstrated in a series of empirical studies by the first-named author begun over 15 years ago. Many of these studies remain unpublished and some are still in progress, but it will be useful to draw upon them here in elaborating upon the concept of social time.

One of the first in this series of studies explored regularities in age expectations among adults. It was found that middle-aged people perceive adulthood as composed of four different life periods, each with its characteristic pattern of personal and social behavior: young adulthood, maturity, middle age, and old age (Neugarten & Paterson, 1957). Progression from one period to the next was described along one or more of five underlying dimensions of life: career line (e.g., major promotion, retirement), health and physical vigor, the family cycle (e.g., children entering school, children departing the family home), psychological attributes (e.g., "Middle age is when you become mellow."), or social responsibilities ("Old age is when you can take things easy and let others do the worrying.").

From these data it was possible to delineate the first gross outline of an age structure and a system of age expectations that cross-cut various areas of adult life. There appears to be a set of social age definitions that provide a frame of reference by which the experiences of adult life are perceived as orderly and rhythmical. Although perceptions vary somewhat by age and sex, and especially by social class (for example, middle age and old age are seen as beginning earlier by working-class men and women than by middle-class), it was the high degree of consensus that was striking in these data.

Expectations regarding the timing of major life events can also be charted. Interviewees respond easily to questions such as: "What is the best age for a man to marry?"; or "the best age to become a grandmother?" and they readily give chronological ages for phrases such as: "a mature woman"; or "when a man should hold his top job." Moreover, there is widespread consensus on items such as these that deal with the timing of work and family events, attitudes, and psychological characteristics. There also appears to be a prescriptive timetable by which major events are ordered along the individual's life line, and consensual definition of the chronological ages that correspond to phases in the life span. For example, most middle-class men and women agreed that a man is young between 18 and 22, middle-aged between 40 and 50, and old between 65 and 75; and that men have the most responsibilities between 35 and 50. Youth, middle age, and old age were similarly defined for women, but women are seen as moving through major phases of the life line earlier than men (Neugarten, Moore, & Lowe, 1965). There is greater consensus regarding age-appropriate behavior for women than for men; and greater consensus regarding age expectations for the period of young adulthood, as if the normative system bears more heavily on individuals as they enter adulthood than when they move on to successive phases of maturity and old age.

V. Age Norms as a System of Social Control

If the system of age expectations is a normative one, as hypothesized, then it should be more or less compelling for everybody; that is, individuals should feel some degree of social pressure to conform to expectations. One of the ways this issue was pursued was to ask to what extent an individual is consistent in meeting various age norms. The data were examined to identify persons who fell at the extremes of the age distribution on an early life event—for instance, men who had married comparatively early or late—and to see to what extent these persons maintained an early or late position relative to their own social class group on successive life events. Although these data are spotty thus far, and the size of the sample precludes statistical testing, in examining individual cases it was observed that early or late individuals move toward the norm on the next major event in the life line. The implication is, then, that there is a "pull" in the age system, just as there is in other normative systems, so that individuals who are age-deviant on one event tend to move back toward the norm on the next event.

Individuals themselves are aware of age norms and age expectations in relation to their own patterns of timing. In adults of varying ages, it has been found that every person can report immediately whether he was "late," "early," or "on time," on one life event after another (e.g., "I married early," or "I was late getting started, because of the Depression"). This high degree of awareness of timing has been interpreted as further evidence that age expectations form a normative system, that social definitions of age are commonly accepted and meaningful, and that patterns of timing play an important role with respect to self-concept and self-esteem.

Another question relates to the process of socialization by which age norms are learned. Respondents have been asked how their ideas about age norms originated, but people seem to take age-norms so much for granted that they are unable to describe their learning experiences. One conclusion has been that the norms are probably learned in such a wide range of contexts and are so imbedded in experience that it is not feasible to attempt to disentangle the socialization experiences by direct questioning.

It may be reasoned, however, that if a normative system is operating, people are probably aware of the sanctions in the system and are sensitive to social approval and disapproval. Attempts to explore this question through a study of individuals who were "off-time" in major life events convinced the investigators that age deviancy is always of psychological significance to the individual, even though a systematic elucidation has not yet been achieved of the mechanisms involved in the social sanctioning of age deviancy.

Another research approach has permitted some inferences about age norms as a system of social constraints. Such questions as these were asked:

> Would you approve of a woman who decides to have another child at 40? at 35? at 30?

> What about a couple who moved across the country to live near their married children when they are 40? 55? 75?

In analyzing responses to such items, a significant increase with age has been found in the extent to which respondents attach importance to age norms and view age appropriateness as a constraint upon behavior. It can be inferred then, that the middle-aged and the old, who see greater constraints in the age-norm system than do the young, have learned that to be off-time with regard to major life events entails negative consequences, and that, therefore, age and age appropriateness are reasonable criteria by which to evaluate behavior. The young, by contrast, tend to deny that age is a valid criterion by which to judge behavior (Neugarten *et al.*, 1965).

These studies illustrate the point that the age-status structure of a society, age-group identifications, the internalization of age norms, and age norms as a network of social controls are important dimensions of the social and cultural context in which the life course must be viewed. Many of the major punctuation marks of the life cycle are not only orderly and sequential, but many are social rather than biological in nature, and their timing is socially regulated. These concepts point to one way of structuring the passage of time in the life span of the individual; and in delineating a social time clock that can be superimposed upon the biological clock, these concepts are helpful in comprehending the life cycle.

VI. Age Stratification

A complementary perspective on the dimension of age emerges from the literature on age stratification in society. Mannheim (1952b) and more recently, Riley and her associates (Riley, 1971; Riley *et al.*, 1972) have viewed the study of the age structure of society along two dimensions: the life course dimension; and the historical dimension, seen as coordinates for locating the individual in the age structure of society.

The life course dimension is roughly indexed by chronological age which serves as an indicator of the individual's experience, including age-related organic changes affecting physical and mental functioning, and including the probability of certain psychological and social experiences. The historical dimension includes the political, social, and cultural changes in society. In Riley's view, integration of these two dimensions provides a perspective on the life course, and the concept of cohort is a link between the two dimensions.

In Mannheim's concept of a generation, he bridges historical time and life time. Mannheim suggested that the sociological significance of generations is predicated upon, but not defined by, the rhythm of the biological succession of generations. Individuals sharing the same year of birth are endowed with a potentially common location in "the historical dimension of the social process." A common year of birth does not in itself constitute a similarity of location: rather, a generation by its date of birth is limited to a particular range of possible experiences. Similarity of location results from the fact that a particular generation, or what we now call age cohort, experiences the same events at the same points in the life cycle, and thus "these experiences impinge upon a similarly stratified consciousness. [Mannheim, 1952b, p. 310]." The sense of belonging to a generation is only a *potentiality* based upon the biological succession of generations. Furthermore, "whether a new *generation style* emerges every year, every thirty, every hundred years, or whether it emerges rhythmically at all, depends entirely on the trigger action of the social and cultural process [Mannheim, 1952b, p. 310]." Mannheim thus moves from the historical context to the level of individual consciousness by the intervening concepts of "generations" and "generational consciousness."

Riley (1971), using Mannheim's dimensions of historical time and life time, deals with the effect of the process of aging on the social structure of society. After describing a society as a structure composed of age strata, her concern is the sociology of age stratification as the expression of the rhythm of generations. Following Mannheim's conceptualization, each cohort by the fact of its year of birth is limited to a certain range of experience; and the consequence is that when, at a given point in time, individuals of varying age levels are studied, they differ in ways that cannot be accounted for solely on the basis of aging. Instead, each age stratum has its distinctive subculture which is the product of the historical events the individuals experience at a particular period in their lives.

At any point in time, then, society consists of a set of age strata each of which is characterized by its own pattern of labor force participation, consumer behavior, leisure-time activities, marital status, religious behavior, education, nativity, fertility, and childbearing practices. Differences (or similarities) between age strata are to be understood on the two dimensions of life course and historical change.

Both Mannheim and Riley, then, are concerned with only two of the three time dimensions under discussion here, and both of them link historical time to life time by the use of such intermediary concepts as generation and age cohort. The relations between historical time and life time can be better understood, however, if social time is added as a third interrelated dimension and if age statuses and age norms can be seen as forming a social-psychological system that stands parallel to the age-stratification structure.

The conceptual framework put forward here, then, might be restated as follows: The age-stratification structure described by Riley and the age-status structure as described in the present paper can be seen as descriptions of two types of sociological reality. Age norms as a system of social control can be seen as a description of social–psychological reality. All three are based upon age as a dimension of social organization; and all three imply that an individual can be located within an age structure and that his behavior is controlled by the age system of which he is part. Similarly, in turning from concepts of social structure to dimensions of time, historical time and life time need to be complemented by the dimension of social time. In moving from the socio-historical context to the form and content of the life cycle, and in considering the psychological significance of historical events, social time and social age become particularly useful as intermediary concepts. The effects of historical events upon the individual can be said to be "filtered" through the age-status system. For example, the effect of World War II upon an 18-year-old man is different from its effect upon a 25-year-old man not only because the second, having lived longer, is different biologically from the first, but because he is different sociologically from the first. The two individuals have been socially "placed" in different age strata; they have different age statuses, and the age-related expectations of behavior that are binding upon them are different.

Some of these points will emerge again in the following illustration of how historical time, social time, and life time are intertwined in the currently changing rhythm of the life cycle.

VII. The Changing Rhythm of the Life Cycle

As American society has changed from agrarian to industrialized, from small town to metropolis, there have been corresponding changes in the social definitions of age groups, in age norms, and in relations between age groups. Only a few aspects of the changing rhythm of the life cycle will be described here to show how major life events are now differently timed and to indicate that the difference in timing is an accompaniment of underlying biological, social, and economic changes in the society. (Much of this section is taken from Neugarten & Moore, 1968.)

Medical advances are among the many factors that have led to growth and redistribution of the population, with presently high proportions of the young and the old, due in turn to reductions in infant mortality and to a striking increase in longevity. Technological change and urbanization have created alterations in the economic system and the family system which are superimposed upon this changing biological base. One result is a new rhythm of life timing and aging.

Concepts of social age and age status are readily illustrated within the institution of the family. The points along the life line at which the individual moves from "child" to "adolescent" to "adult" are socially defined, although they are timed in relation to biological development. After physical maturity is reached, social age continues to be marked off by relatively clear-cut biological or social events in the family cycle. Thus, marriage marks the beginning of one social age period, as does the appearance of the first child, the departure of children from the home, and the birth of the first grandchild. At each stage, the individual takes on new roles and his prestige is altered in relation to other family members.

As shown by the data for women in Table 1, changes in timing in the family cycle have been dramatic over the past several decades as age at marriage has dropped, as children are born earlier in the marriage and are spaced closer together, and as longevity of both sexes, and consequently the duration of marriage has increased. (The data for men show parallel trends. In 1890, the median

TABLE 1

Changes in the Timing of Life Events[a]

Median age at:	1890	1966
Leaving school	14	18
Marriage	22	20
Birth of first child	24–25	21
Birth of last child	32	26
Death of husband	53	64
Marriage of last child	55	48
Death	68	78

[a] Data are taken from Glick, Heer, and Beresford, 1963. The entries in the table do not, of course, represent the same women, but various groups of women at each of the two calendar years. The timing of future events for, say, women who in 1966 were marrying at average age 20 cannot be directly extrapolated from the table. At the same time, the interpretation of these data may be seen as a quickening family cycle over calendar time. This is but another instance in which developmental psychologists draw longitudinal inferences from cross-sectional data.

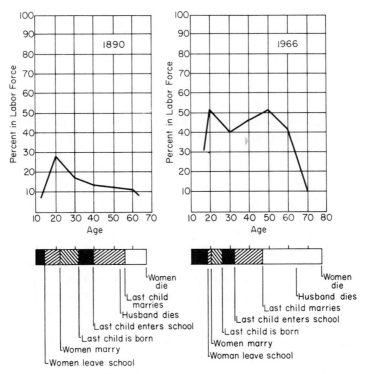

Fig. 1. Work in relation to significant stages in the lives of women. [From Neugarten (Ed.), *Middle age and aging: A reader in social psychology.* Chicago: The University of Chicago Press, 1968. © 1968 by the University of Chicago Press. *Sources:* National Manpower Council, *Womanpower* (New York: Columbia University Press, 1957), p. 307. Right-hand portion of figure has been revised based on labor-force data taken from *1967 Manpower Report*, U.S. Department of Labor, Table A-2, p. 202, and on family cycle data taken from Glick, Heer, and Beresford, 1963, p. 12.]

age at marriage for men was 26; at birth of first child, 36; at marriage of last child, 59; at widowhood, 57. In 1959, the respective median ages were 22, 28, 49, and 66.)

Changes in work patterns have been even more dramatic (see Fig. 1). In 1890 less than 30% of all women at age 20 were in the labor force, and this was the highest percentage for any age group. The proportions dropped by age, so that at age 50 only about 12% were workers. But by 1966, womens' participation in the labor force had increased so dramatically that over 50% of all 20-year-old women were working. The percentage dropped off only a little among 30-year-olds, and then rose again so that over 50% of all 50-year-old women were in the labor force.

Historically, then, the family cycle has quickened as marriage, parenthood, empty nest (and grandparenthood) all occur earlier. The trend is toward a more rapid rhythm of events through most of the family cycle, then an extended interval (now some 16 years) when husband and wife are the remaining members of the household. Widowhood occurs much later, and the life span for women has lengthened enormously.

These general trends are not expected to be reversed, even though today a slight upturn in age of marriage (in 1972, it was 20.8 rather than 20.2 for women), more unmarried families, more communal and other experimental forms of family life may be noted. While the family cycle runs its course a few years later for women at higher-than-average levels of education, the general pattern of historical change just described is the same for both highly-educated and poorly-educated women.

Over the past 80 years, an interesting and important difference has been developing between men and women with respect to the timing of family and work cycles. Marriage no longer signifies that the man is ready to be the bread-winner. With the needs of the American economy for technical and professional workers, the length of time devoted to education has increased for more and more young persons, but there has not been an accompanying delay of marriage. In 1966 of all men attending college or graduate school, nearly one in four was married (for those men aged 25–29, it was nearly three out of four) as was one of every seven women.

The accompanying phenomenon is the young wife who works to support her husband through school. The changing sex-role patterns are reflected in the rising proportion of young married women in the labor force: In 1890, it was only 6% of those aged 14–24; in 1960, it was 31%. While these percentages reflect marriages in which husbands are working as well as those in which husbands are still in school, they show in both instances not only that young wives are increasingly sharing the economic burdens of new households, but also that women are doing so at younger and younger ages. Thus, the age of economic maturity has been deferred for men, but not for women. It has become socially acceptable for men to reverse the traditional sequence of events, and for family maturity to precede rather than to follow economic maturity.

Furthermore, men's work life has been shortened over the past decades as young men are increasingly delayed from entering the labor force (at technical and professional levels, because of increased length of education; at lower occupational levels, because of the diminishing need for unskilled workers) and as older men are increasingly retiring at younger ages (for men over 65, only one of four is now in the labor force). In short, the trend for men is to be older when they start to work, and younger when they retire. Women still spend much less time in the labor force than men, on the average, but the historical trend for women is the opposite—women are younger when they start to work; they work much longer than before, whether or not they are married and whether or not they have children; and they are older when they retire.

The new rhythms of social maturity impinge also upon other aspects of family life. Parent-child relationships are influenced in many subtle ways by the fact that half of all new fathers in the 1960s were under 23 and half of all new mothers under 21. Changes in parental behavior, with fathers reportedly becoming less authoritarian and with both parents sharing more equally in tasks of homemaking and child-rearing, may reflect, in part, this increased youthfulness. It is the relative youth of both parents and grandparents, furthermore, that may be contributing to the complex patterns of help between generations in the family that are now becoming evident, including the widespread financial help that flows from parents downward to their adult children. Similarly, with more grandparents surviving per child, and with an extended family system that encompasses several generations, new patterns of child-rearing are emerging in which child–grandparent relations may be taking on changing significance.

VIII. Toward a Social Psychology of the Life Cycle

Changes in the life cycle, such as those just described, have their effects upon personality, and it is likely that the personalities of successive age cohorts will, therefore, be different in measurable ways, especially if the sociologist's view of personality is adopted. (This is not the occasion to discuss varying conceptions of personality, except to acknowledge their great diversity, and to suggest that from most points of view, including those of psychoanalysis and ego psychology, social change can be expected to have at least some systematic effects upon personality development.) It nevertheless remains for future personality psychologists to turn attention to the interplay between history and personality, as indicated at the outset of this chapter, and to undertake empirical studies that will elucidate, for example, the changes in self-concepts, the sense of efficacy, and even the balance between the rational and the impulsive components of personality as these are affected by the changing social context.

Developmental theorists are lacking, as yet, an overarching theory of development over the life cycle. In part, this is so because we have not fully recognized the complex interplay between maturational sequences and social-cultural forces, and have often tended to view the latter as complications that "obscure" the invariant sequence of developmental change. What is needed is to view maturational change as only one of the major components of development, and to forego the constraining analogy that compels us to search only for corresponding invariant timetables of psychological change. The present authors are not, of course, the first to argue that the specific historical context is as valid a frame of reference for the study of the development of personality as is the maturational timetable, and that both are required. The point can be stated more accurately: namely, the task is to study sequences of change for the purpose of determining *which ones* are primarily developmental (in the sense of being tied to maturational change), and *which ones* are primarily situational —if, indeed, this distinction can be made at all.

For example, how will life-cycle change and social change be related in the life course of present-day youth, a problem that is as current as this morning's headlines and as relevant as any to which the developmental psychologist can address himself? As this chapter is being written, the morning newspaper carries a story about high school radicals and the fact that by the time they reach college they seem to have exhausted their political energies—that is, the "little brother" about whom the campus radical used to warn us only a year or two ago seems already to have burned out and to be leading a more conventional life as a college student than his big brother. What is the relation of *timing* and commitment to social causes, and the relation of both to personality development? What does it mean to become an activist at 15, as compared to 20, or 45?

Shall we re-examine our earlier views that extremism and idealism among the young are an accompaniment of underlying biological change? Why was it the 20-year-old who was the activist in 1968, the 15-year-old in 1970, but neither in 1972? And what difference will it make to the particular individuals by the time they reach middle age?

To take another example, what are the changes in the personalities of women that may be anticipated as the accompaniment of the women's liberation movement? Specifically, what are the effects if the woman is young and is choosing to postpone marriage and childbearing, perhaps to forego them altogether, as compared to the effects if the woman is 40 and engaged in that period of self-evaluation whose outcome will determine the course of her old age?

Obviously the relations of life time, social time, and historical time pose enormously complicated questions, but it is precisely this complexity to which students of the life cycle should be willing to address themselves.

CHAPTER 4

Life-Span Environmental Psychology: Methodological Issues[1]

SAMUEL Z. KLAUSNER

UNIVERSITY OF PENNSYLVANIA
PHILADELPHIA, PENNSYLVANIA

ABSTRACT

Life-span environmental psychology faces the problem of constructing propositions linking a variable in a physical with a variable in a social science frame of reference. Relations among social science variables may be studied while treating variables in the physical system as conditional, holding them constant. Appropriate transformation concepts define the social significance of the physical variable.

When social or psychological facts are circumscribed for study in terms of their orientation to an object, including orientation to age, an entity is posited in the initial existence statement. The concept of development is bound to the idea of such an entity. The criteria establishing the boundary of the entity may not be expressive of the nature of the elements within it . As one consequence, the entity may consist of relatively functionally independent subsystems. Consequently, correlations between elements in distinct subsystems may be low. Development is structural differentiation. New elements emerge with the passage

[1]This study was supported by the program on Society and Its Physical Environment of the Center for Research on the Acts of Man, Philadelphia, and by the National Center for Energy Management and Power, University of Pennsylvania.

71

of time. This may account for some of the low correlations between elements at successive stages of development.

Disciplinary theory, on the other hand, tends to circumscribe relevant facts, within the frame of reference, by establishing empirical associations among them. The result is an object-free theoretical net of general propositions. These propositions may interpret relations among the elements in the orientationally posited entity. The boundaries of such a net are a function of the relations among the elements included. Values of such analytic variables may be said to change, but only entities, orientationally established, may be said to develop. These methodological issues are illustrated through fragmentary life-span environmental psychological analyses of action oriented to space, to noise, and to natural outdoor settings.

I. The Two Problems

Life-span psychology is environmental psychology, at least, in that two methodological problems are common to both. First, both are committed to a rule for selecting facts for study in terms of a focal object of orientation. This is a problem of the *criteria of relevance*. Second, both employ statements expressing associations between physical and human action systems. This is a problem of linking facts defined in disparate *descriptive frames of reference*. (See the excellent discussions of this point in Parsons [1949] and Cassirer [1955, Vol. III].) Since the frame of reference defines the nature of the universe of facts within which the investigation takes place, commitment to a descriptive frame of reference is logically prior to commitment to particular criteria of relevance.

The special sciences are often defined by the frame of reference in which they interpret experience. Social science describes systems of action. These systems are composed of subjective interpretations of events expressed as ideas, feelings, and evaluations. Physical systems are defined in a space-time frame of reference. Physical events are treated as objects, or attributes of objects, located in space.[2] Practical problems always and theoretical problems exceptionally require interdisciplinary explorations. Such explorations may generate propositions connecting facts stated in two frames of references. Life-span psychology, because it links personality to the time and location of a developing body, and environmental psychology, because it links behavior to a situational physical object, both conjoin systems of action and physical systems.

[2]The subjective frame of reference for the study of human action is enunciated in the work of Max Weber (1947). Talcott Parsons and Edward Shils, in "Values, Motives and the Theory of Action," in Parsons and Shils (1951a), develop this orientation as part of the more contemporary role theory. Concepts for stating regularities in human behavior may also be constructed in a space-time frame of reference as, for example, in positivistically oriented psychological theories such as that of Skinner (1938) and in some work in demography and human ecology (Hawley, 1950).

The first major section of this paper comments on the problem of interpretation presented by research in more than one frame of reference, reviewing three common approaches and offering a tentative posture on this issue for the researcher. The second major section begins with some tentative definitions of three criteria of relevance. Examples from history, sociology, and psychology are introduced to clarify these definitions and some implications of the use of each criterion for life-span psychology, with particular reference to the concept of development and the concept of age, follow. The final section takes three environmental areas to illustrate life-span psychological research concepts in the light of each of these methodological problems. This paper does not analyze the subject matter of life-span environmental psychology, but, rather, discusses research methodology in that field.

II. On Propositions Linking Physical and Psychological Variables: A Problem in Explanation

Ontologically speaking, systems of action, biological systems, and physical systems are conjoined. Evolutionary theory bears grand witness to the interdependence of the last two and anthropological studies on culture and habitat, as well as psycho-biological research, continue to document the interdependence of all three systems. However, since our concepts for thinking about these systems are differently constructed, the scientific description of their joint action is difficult. The problem is epistemological. A review of the history of man-environment "theories that failed" (Klausner, 1971) reveals that the key weakness of these earlier attempts to relate geographic and climatic factors to personality and social organization lay in their failure to grasp the epistemological problem. As a result, they directly correlated measures of variables conceptualized in disparate frames of reference arriving at less than meaningful propositions.

Elements of physical and biological systems are conceived as objects located in space and coordinated in time. System boundaries are the loci of exchanges of matter and energy. With some exceptions, social science places behavior in frameworks of meaning. The elements of systems of action are, for instance, norms, values, rules of behavior, motives, and affects, all of which enter into actors' interpretations of their situations—interpretations on which they base choices to act one way or another. A motive rests on the interpreted relation between drives and "cathected" objects. The boundaries of social and psychological systems are social definitional or perceptual. A social group defines its boundaries by rules —criteria of membership.

This epistemological problem of connecting facts in disparate frames of reference is not specific to life-span environmental psychology or to the boundary between physical and social systems. All interdisciplinary research and theory must resolve this issue. Klausner (1967) presents a number of social science examples of interdisciplinary statements. Meaningfulness of such propositions rests on supplying the "missing links" between variables in two frames of reference. These links are *transformation concepts* which function to interpret or explain the relation between the variables. The solution, therefore, rests in a problem of explanation. Three approaches have been proposed for obviating the difficulty: (1) The difficulty only arises because of the recognition of disparate frames of reference; therefore, eliminate theory. (2) Use only one frame of reference for both behavioral and environment events. (3) Treat events in one frame of reference as "control" conditions external to propositions linking events within the other frame of reference.

A. The Denial of Theory

First, that the linking of physical and psychological variables constitutes a problem may be denied by refusing to recognize any theoretical system or abstract frame of reference. Correlations are held to be established between concrete observable events, such as the temperature readings and the suicide rate, and expressed at face value. The expression may take mathematical form. Projections of future behavior may be extrapolated on the basis of such models. However, such correlations are not interpretable—that is, do not become part of a more general statement.

Another "nontheoretical" approach is exemplified by *systems analysis* which places units, attributes, and processes in formal, rather than substantive, categories. Any system may be described in terms of inputs, outputs, feed-backs, and entropy. Thus, in studying man-machine systems, signals become inputs to man and his button-pushing responses outputs. Dial readings, following his responses, may be feedback information controlling future responses. This model, being formal, will accept concrete data, irrespective of how its content is conceptualized. The criterion is not the intrinsic meaning of the datum, but its role or function for the system. While this method is useful in establishing ad hoc procedures, as may be required for developing working policies, the method allows no explanation as to why the various parts play the role they do in the overall system, and, as a consequence, the model is poorly adapted for coping with unforeseen changes in conditions.

B. Reduction to One Theory

Second, the theoretical status of concepts of social behaviors and of environment may be recognized, but, it may be argued, one frame of reference is sufficient for expressing facts of both domains. Sometimes, the frame of reference is an overarching one such as Charles Morris' semiotic (1955). Since symbolism is a language of all science, concepts of the special sciences may all be formulated as rules of symbolism. The rules of symbolism are, in themselves, formal—like the associative and commutative laws of algebra. However, the symbols themselves become meaningful as they express or point to content.

More often, though, the single frame of reference is less extensive than the domains being considered. Both social and physical facts may be conceptualized in a physical frame of reference. This approach is substantively reductionistic. Demographic theory, for instance, may offer a classified enumeration of individuals as spatially located objects, thus providing an intensive and specified description. Only a single frame of reference is used. Behaviors are considered as direct expressions of physiological elements or as predictable from information on physical environmental conditions alone. Parsons (1949) termed such approaches "radical anti-intellectualistic positivism," partly because they admit no mentalistic or volitional constructs to the theory. Greek environmental psychology is an extreme substantive reductionism. Since both personality and the physical world derive from the same primordial elements, the Greeks would understand the developing personality in terms of the physical mixture, say, of heat and water, of which it was composed. Substantive connections between personality and environment are easily asserted, if not established, when but a single frame of reference is permitted.

Genetic psychology has bequeathed a methodological reductionist inheritance to life-span psychology. While a substantive reductionism assumes a single frame of reference, methodological reductionism applies the same model to both mental and physical development. Paralleling biological recapitulation theory, personality is held to develop from its primitive to its civilized stages (Grinder, 1967). The confusing of history and ontogenesis is approached in reverse order in the biological and the mental cases. The race passed through biological evolutionary stages, but ontogenesis does not recapitulate them. Personality evolves ontogenetically from a diffuse undifferentiated process to a stage at which logical thought is possible, but the mental history of the race did not anticipate these stages.

C. Explanatory Transformation Concepts

A third solution retains the separate languages and examines interrelations among variables in one of the systems under some conditions, fixed or sequenced, set by the other system (Klausner, 1972). State of the psychological system may be explored under sequentially changing environmental conditions. A statement about the influence of the state of one system on elements in the other system deals with a point of tangency of the systems. This point, when conceptualized on a concrete level, is shared by both systems. In the analysis, it is interpreted in one frame of reference at a time. The interpretation is a transformation concept through which the link between the frames of reference is established.

The relating of seasonal climate, as measured in physical terms, to the suicide rate, a social event, by Durkheim (1951), is a classic example of this transformation concept. The climatic variable is "replaced" by or transformed into a concept of levels of social interaction. Intensity of social interaction, as it varies by season, is the correlate of suicide. The physical element, climate, becomes relevant for social action, suicide, when it has become the referent for a social term, level of interaction or strength of the norms. Subsequently, the analysis proceeds within the social frame of reference. Studies of the images of cities as a function of the way subjects moved spatially in that city offer another example (e.g., Stea & Downs, 1970). A transportation route, a physical condition, is transformed into a cognitive map. Idiosyncratic personality factors modify the maps of different people traveling the same route. Depending on the actor's values, one person's map might emphasize points of interaction with retailers and another's might be most detailed around church locations.

Some studies, appearing to relate facts in more than one frame of reference, are, on closer examination, reductionistic. For instance, Schachter (1964) found that physiological states induced by norepinephrine affect mood, in part, through the individual's interpretation of those states. This interpretation may depend, in turn, on social climate. If moods are examined for successively higher doses of norepinephrine, with the social situations interpolated for each instance, the statement is interdisciplinary —a part of environmental psychology. If, however, the study analyzes only the relation between affects and social climate, the study is entirely psychological or social psychological. Its propositions are quasi-interdisciplinary.

Some common types of transformation concepts which interpret interdisciplinary social science propositions are catalogued by Klausner (1967). Concepts to bridge the physical science and social science frames of reference are less available. As a result, the best approach, for the moment, seems to be to treat one system as a condition, while studying variations in the other. If the conditional system is physical, the nature of its impact on social action may be pursued by a *verstehende* analysis of the subjective meaning of that physical situation for the actors. The meaning becomes a basis for hypothesizing about possible explanations for the association.

The frame of reference defines a universe of facts for consideration. Interdisciplinary work proceeds in more than one such universe. The location of a particular problem requires the selection of a subset of facts from that universe. These are the facts which, within the elected frame of reference, are considered relevant, worthy of attention, for the description of the problem. The next section discusses criteria for such decisions of relevance.

III. Criteria of Relevance: A Problem in Fact Selection

A. Three Criteria of Relevance

1. Orientations to Physical and Cultural Objects

Criteria of relevance direct the researcher in delimiting facts, within the frame of reference, pertinent to a particular problem. Perhaps, the lion's share of the discussion of this issue in social science has been framed by the sociology of knowledge relating the selection of facts to the researcher's "interests" or "values," the social structure of the research situation, or to his disciplinary culture. The criterion of relevance is a technical matter immanent in the scientific formulation of the problem. This discussion, therefore, is methodological or epistemological.

Three criteria of relevance may be distinguished. The first two may be termed *orientational*. They direct the researcher to include facts which, in some way, cluster around an object. The object may be physical, such as spatial location, and the selected facts might include descriptions of the object and behaviors oriented to or circumscribed by that object. The result is a bounded set of facts around the physical focus which constitute an *entity*. A person, an industrial enterprise, or a territorial state are such posited entities. In much the same way, facts may be selected in view of their orientation to a cultural object, an idea, or a belief. The posited entity might then be a social movement, an institution, or an attitudinal cluster.

With an orientational criterion of relevance, research begins with an "existence statement" referring to the entity. Subsequent empirical work maps the internal structure of the entity and its relation to other entities without seriously questioning the existence of the entity and of the elements which, assumedly, constitute it. Nagel, in his philosophical analysis (in Harris, 1957), making a similar point, places the "notion of a system possessing a definite structure and a definite set of pre-existing capacities," at the core of developmental psychology.

A third criterion of relevance may be termed *analytic*. According to this rule, facts are selected in terms of established connections among them. An existence statement is introduced with respect to the facts, but not a priori, with respect to a system they might constitute. An initial fact is designated in terms of some basic conception of the problem. Additional ones are admitted on the strength of their correlations with the first and, subsequently, with any of the successively admitted facts. The result is a relational net having no "simple location," to use Whitehead's term. Such relational nets are illustrated by the concepts of schizophrenic process and its relata, the process of modernization, or the concept of class conflict and its relata.

Both life-span psychology and environmental psychology take orientation to an object, especially a physical object, as a primary criterion of relevance. Life-span psychology, like some other psychologies, such as clinical, focuses around particular biological organisms. Acts attaching to the developing organism at successive moments become the relevant data. Baer (1970) discriminates between child psychologists, for whom an experimental subject defines the field, and physiological, sensory, or perceptual psychologists who characterize their fields by the processes they study. Bijou (1968a) locates developmental psychology in the ''interaction between a biologically changing organism and sequential changes in environmental events.'' For Baltes and Goulet (1970), ''intra-individual variability,'' the changing values of elements within an entity, is the primary objective of life-span developmental psychology.

Environmental psychology introduces orientation around some extra-personal physical object as an additional basis for data selection. Appleyard's (1970) environmental psychological study of the mental structuring of a city studies acts oriented to a series of territorial locations. The mental structuring, as indicated by a map of the city drawn by the subjects, is treated as a dependent variable. Independent variables include residential location, travel mode, and familiarity with the area. An urban shopping center is the object of orientation for a study by Downs (1970). Decisions of individuals to behave in one or another way with regard to the shopping center are among the facts to be explained. Independent variables include information about the environment, perception of the environment, and environmental conditions as varied as price, pedestrian movement, and traffic.

Environmental life-span psychology is at the intersection of life-span and of environmental psychology. The organism and the external physical object are both objects of orientation. Interest is riveted on acts oriented to the interface of these two objects as they develop over time or, as Baltes and Goulet (1970) say, as they are expressible in an age-related function.

2. The Analytic Criterion

Selecting relevant facts by empirically establishing relations is, perhaps, more common in science than is selection according to an orientational criterion. The selected facts may not be concrete behaviors—say, aggressive acts—but attributes or values of these behaviors—say, degrees of aggressiveness. Systems of such facts may be defined by the pattern of factors with similar loadings or linked in a matrix of intercorrelations by high coefficients. Beginning with a concept such as ''ability to learn'' or ''flicker fusion,'' facts are added as they are established as causes or consequences of the initial ones. Looft (1972), for instance, takes the concept of ''egocentrism'' and, correlating it with social interactional variables, traces the change of this interrelation across the life span.

For sociologists, the classical discussion of criteria of relevance is in Max Weber's study of "Objectivity in the Social Sciences" (Weber, 1949). Weber contrasts the concepts of "historical individual" and "analytic laws," paralleling the distinction here, as selective criteria. Perhaps, taking a hint from Weber, history offers the clearest illustration of these issues. The next few sections of this paper offer some historiographic illustrations, followed by some examples from sociology and psychology in general, and in life-span environmental psychology in particular.

B. Illustrations from History

History, like life-span psychology, is the record of the changing state of some "individual." Historiographic practice reveals some implications of organizing events around a physical or cultural object, or in terms of their intrinsic interrelations. Territorial history selects its facts with respect to a land. The facts of institutional history are oriented to a cultural object, perhaps a body of rules, a social purpose, or a concept of the sacred. Analytic history grows with the empirical establishment of a net of facts.

1. Territorial History

Territorial history relates occurrences within relatively constant territorial boundaries. In this tradition, the Mexican national self is traced to Aztec forebears, and both Aztec and Spanish–Mexican culture become episodes in the history of Mexico. The boundary circumscribing facts relevant to territorial history is not, in general, defined by physical geographic features alone. Rather, an institutional act, such as that of a nation, and, perhaps, tied to the ecological distribution of nationals, delimits the geographic locus. The political institution, a cultural object, thus, joins the land in delimiting the scope of relevant events.

While land is the focus for selecting facts, land, as a physical entity, does not enter directly into the content of historical concepts. Territory is conceptually transmuted into its meanings for social action—that is, in terms of a symbol of national consciousness, or as property law, or as the backdrop for military conflict. The problem of explanations of interdisciplinary propositions was discussed previously.

In territorial history, facts needed for the study of cultural development are not always available within the circumscribed area. Spanish culture cannot be predicted from data about the Aztec civilization. In part, this is a problem of the lack of coextensiveness of physical and socio-cultural systems (Klausner, 1972). A territory circumscribes several social and cultural systems, each following its own developmental trajectory. Change in Aztec language follows a path of development relatively independent of that of transportation arrangements, though the latter may promote conditions for language modification. On the other hand, a socio-cultural system may extend beyond the territory. Mexican architecture would not be comprehensible without introducing Iberian traditions. In general, the physical object of orientation defines an entity in a manner "artificial" with respect to the social or psychological activity. An analogous difficulty arises when life-span psychology attempts to treat personality as coextensive with the organism. In some respects, the same organism may harbor relatively independent dimensions of personality, or an understanding of personality may require data from beyond the boundaries of the organism.

2. Institutional History

Institutional history selects events in virtue of their orientation to a cultural object. A belief system, as in the study of religious institutions, or an empirically implementable "platform," as in the study of political movements, becomes an organizing principle for activities. The researcher, in accepting this focus and the associated activities, is, primarily, following the interpretation of the situation by the actors in that situation. The history of religion, for example, locates and follows Christianity through a cluster of statuses oriented to the "church" and its doctrines. The trajectory may furcate into branches of the church, of dissidents from it, forming around variants of the doctrine. Economic and political climates around the church, while external to the entity, may become part of the equation for explaining events within the church (Troeltsch, 1960; Weber, 1964).

Independence of the data elements—say, lack of demonstrable empirical connection between monasticism in the Eastern church and liturgical reform in the Western church—is irrelevant to the decision to retain them for historical consideration. An historical thread from the Council of Nicea, say, to the Council of Trent joins events within the same developing historical body. Theological concerns of the later council may be explored in the light of their formulation at the earlier council. That the first council occurred on the Mediterranean littoral and the second on the European continent is no obstacle to their joint consideration. The boundaries of an entity developed around a cultural object are established according to cultural rules and, at the same time, elements within those bounds are defined culturally. The boundary would then not be "artificial" with respect to the facts within it, as the case might be when social facts are ordered with respect to a physical object of orientation. The artificiality problem would arise, however, if cultural objects were used to define a boundary for the study of a physical or biological system—as, for instance, in studying plant ecology within political boundaries (Klausner, 1972). The history of a church in a territory, such as "national Catholicism," or a history of the Shrine of Our Lady of Fatima, or of Vatican City, illustrate subjects of investigation that blend territorial and institutional objects.

3. Analytic History

Analytic history borders on sociology in its interest in general propositions that rise about space and time, transcending any particular entity. Studies of "revolutionary potential," economic historical works on modernization or processes of industrialization tend to be informed by a relational criterion of relevance. For instance, chiliastic religious movements are admitted as relevant facts in the study of rapid social change when they are demonstrated, time and again, to be precursors of revolution. The proportion of entrepreneurs in the society, the rate of energy consumption, or the proportion of the population in the labor force are woven empirically into a general model of social and economic development. Such general propositions, developed according to analytic criteria, may be invoked to explain a particular revolutionary development or a particular case of modernization which is circumscribed according to an orientational criterion. The boundaries of an analytically developed system are vague and vary as terms accrete to the theoretical net. Any concept of entity is far in the background—often being no more than a device for deciding upon the locus of measurements.

Toynbee's (1947) conception of the developmental laws of civilizations combines institutional, territorial, and analytic history. Civilizations are vast and flexible over time. The interrelationships of dominant minorities and internal proletariats, for instance, are significant institutional focuses for conceiving of the civilizations as cultural entities. Yet, in the final analysis, Toynbee moves toward analytic history. Comparative studies of civilization are the source of general propositions about development which transcend any particular civilization.

C. Illustrations from Sociology

Each of these criteria of relevance defines a style of sociological research. Like territorial history, sociological study may focus on activities around a physical setting, such as that of a hospital (e.g., Stanton & Schwartz, 1954), an architecturally circumscribed institution. In this locus, the researcher gathers facts about incumbents of nurse, doctor, and patient roles. Sociological research oriented to a wider geographic territorial bound is illustrated by Selznick's (1949) study of the TVA. The posited entity consisted of the various social group activities, communities, lobbies, and labor unions forming around the planned and ultimately built hydroelectric plant are relevant facts. Ogburn's (1950) studies are a classic example of the selection of social and cultural facts around a technological innovation. Cultural rules governing work conditions with respect to the specified technology are at the heart of his analysis.

The work of Troeltsch, mentioned previously, on church and sect, illustrates institutional sociology. Weber's (1947) work on economic and economically oriented behavior is another illustration. Media of exchange, resources, and rational decisions are among the relevant items for observation. This becomes socio-economic analytic theory when the relation between the degree of divisibility of the medium of exchange and the degree of rationality of socio-economic decisions is expressed as a proposition, valid at any time or place and in any economy.

D. Illustrations from Psychology

The growing body as the locus for the initial selection of life-span psychological facts illustrates the orientational criterion of relevance in psychology. The "belongingness" of a behavior to the "individual" is presumed on a priori grounds—as part of the initial existence statement. An individual with attributes such as cognition, perception, and ability to learn is ab initio presumed to constitute an entity. The question as to whether secondary as well as primary qualities "belong" to the entity is recapitulated in the settlement of this existence statement. Behavior in conformity with a cultural norm may reflect an attitude, an internal predisposition, substantively corresponding to that norm and, thus, part of the personality entity. Alternatively, the behavior may simply reflect external conformity and, thus, indicate a fact of culture as such, but not an attribute of the individual. Bleuler's (1951) classic descriptions of hysteria and toxic psychoses begin with a physical symptom and then assemble facts on attributes of personality oriented or empirically related to the physical symptom. A particular bit of technology is the physical focus of research on man-machine systems. Ultimately, the machine display, the physical object, is adjusted in terms of human abilities to discriminate the arrangement of signals. Perceptual processes constitute some of the facts studied (e.g., Chapanis, 1965).

Attitude studies organize personality facts around a cultural object. The subjective apprehension that the disposition to behave is "controlled," in part, by the meanings of the cultural object unifies this entity. The attitude itself, a psychological event, may be the focus around which some associated psychological events are studied. Authoritarian personality research, for instance, accepts personality data expressive of and correlating with the attitude of prejudice into its model (e.g., Adorno, Frenkel–Brunswick, Levinson, & Sanford, 1950). If the retention of each datum depends on its correlation with the attitude, the model moves in the analytic direction. Bruner's work on cognitive growth (e.g., Bruner, Olver, Greenfield, 1966) illustrates how a particular psychological process may be almost reified as an entity focused around a cultural object.

Abstract analytic criteria inform the model-building activities of learning theorists as, for instance, in studies of concept learning (e.g., Klausmeier & Harris,

1966). The prototypical analytic approch is that of Cattell (1950) who admits facts exclusively on the basis of demonstrated factor loadings.[3]

E. The Concept of Development and the Concept of Change

1. Development and Entitivity

The positing of an entity, partly a consequence of selection of facts according to an orientational criterion, is salient to the notion of development. Only an entity may develop. An analytical criterion of relevance, which does not posit an entity, may be concerned with change over time —a broad category of which development is a particular case.

Tracing the average change in scores obtained by members of some group in relation to an age function is not literally developmental psychology. The formal similarity of the measures of change, in general, and of development in particular, underlies some of this confusion between them. Werner (in Harris, 1957) cites Rorschach responses by age. These are developmental measures, if we presume that the same individuals were tested at successive ages. Otherwise, we have cross-sectional quasidevelopmental data. Group means of Rorschach scores of psychotics in various stages of psychiatric intactness measure change in the state of personality and seem, despite the lack of an entity, to parallel the developmental case. On the basis of this parallel pattern of scores, psychoses and early stages in normal development are assumed to be substantively comparable. As the "old saw" in psychology has it, while the behavior of a "regressed" psychotic is child-like, the psychotic is not a child.

A physical anchor for facts offers common-sense assurance that successive measures are assessing the "same" entity. Comparable developmental patterns in numbers of individuals is a basis for developmental laws. By comparing the technical materials in strata in different countries at the same calendar time, archeologists compare stages and rates of development of societies (Childe, 1963). Assuming a relatively fixed developmental sequence of culture, they identify developmental stages by the contents and level of strata. Study of the successive organizations enveloping the industrial processing of a material object involves a similar developmental sequence (Klausner, 1972), not of continuous

---

[3]The culture of science draws its practitioners toward abstract variables and analytic theories. Analyses of social problems, on the other hand, because they are formulated in common sense terms and involve concrete action, tend to cluster facts around an issue, a cultural object, and around a particular time and place, a physical object. Social interest draws facts together with near indifference to verifiable associations. Nationalism promotes interest in territorial history. Developmental psychology arises in those institutional contexts in which social interest is in the individual. These include juridical institutions, which focus on the responsibility and guilt of a particular individual and seek to reform him, the educational system which measures itself by the growth of individuals and the mental health institutions designed to foster individual therapy.

development, but of discrete stages with different actors at each stage. The industrial product, the focus of each organization, binds, sequentially, otherwise disparate organizations.

The association of development with growth of an entity suggests that it is "unidirectional, irreversible and directed toward a certain end state or goal," as Reese and Overton (1970) put it. Werner (in Harris, 1957) expresses this as following an orthogenetic principle that development implies proceeding "from a state of relative globality and lack of differentiation to a state of increasing differentiation." By implication, new attributes of the entity constantly appear. In psychology, these may be new attitudes or new competencies. While processes of increasing differentiation offer a logic of continuity—by specifying the ancestry of dimensions of personality—the emergent nature of new facts may cause actual measurements to be discontinuous.

"Development" is not restricted to progressive change. Regressive phenomena, such as some of those characterizing the end of the life span, are of equal interest. The decline in sensory processes and reduction in the *amount* of environmental information with old age (Lawton & Nahemow, 1973) illustrate regressive processes. A process of differentiation accompanied by or followed by one of dedifferentiation appears manifestly regressive. Aside from senescence, such a regressive process may be a phase of progressive development (Klausner, 1961). The concept of regression in the service of the ego illustrates this.

The belief that development is directed to an "end state" also seems to emerge from the positing of an entity. The "ends," however, are not sharply identifiable. Birth and death, the usually accepted developmental time bounds, are not the sole appropriate limits for study of the life span. Knowledge of fetal growth is relevant to the prediction of postfetal conditions. The development of medical technology in deferring biological death adds to the doubts that death may be pinpointed in time. Social personality may terminate before the body expires, and the social person may continue as a matter of cultural interest after biological death.

The boundaries of the entity are constantly breached during development. Role behaviors are an important class of facts which cannot be understood with reference to the body-encased self alone. For instance, a husband and wife are observed to alternate in periods of illness. The nature of their relationship, requiring a dependent partner, explains the alternation (Opler, 1965). To understand this aspect of self, the criterion of relevance is extended to include facts of personality shaped with respect to the identified body locus, even when they are not of that body. The death or departure of an alter may terminate an aspect of the ego's social "personality."

Change is a broader category than development. Change in the *values* of elements in an entity may occur without development of the entity. Development should be limited to a change in the pattern of relations among the elements, a structural reorganization. This is implicit in Werner's reference to "increasing differentiation." Decreasing differentiation should also be considered a developmental process. Learning qualifies as a developmental process because internalization of a new object implies a change in the general structure of internalized objects.

Change in the values of attributes may be difficult to distinguish from a change in their structure in the light of manifest behavior. To take a social system example, the government, as a collectivity, may become more radical when radical politicians displace conservative ones without any one of them changing his own posture. This is a structural change. On the other hand, the government could become more radical if individuals, while remaining in their posts and maintaining the same positions relative to one another, become more radical in attitude. This is a change in the values of the elements. Attitudinal change might involve individual development without affecting the structure of relations among those individuals. On the collective level, this is cultural change without social change. When rules of assignment to position are not contingent on the content of the attitudes of the occupants of the positions, it is possible to speak of the independence of social development and psychological change.

These are substantive examples of a more general methodological issue. Facts may be selected according to orientational criteria and the reasons for this selection may be independent of the relation among those facts. In other words, the criterion for grouping facts may be external to the nature of those facts. The meaning of the boundary may be extrinsic to the nature of the relations among the included elements. This introduces one of the most difficult issues in environmental psychology. The elements of an entity formed according to an orientational criterion of relevance may well not, in such cases, constitute a single system. When elements are related intrinsically, by an analytic criterion of relevance which admits only correlates, they are, by reason of the criterion, a single system. The boundary of that system is established by the same procedure that establishes the system and is nothing other than another way of viewing the structure of relations among the elements of the system. The magnitude of intercorrelations, an internal criterion, defines this boundary.

Where factor analytic methods present dimensions of personality held to be subsystems of the same personality, rather than simply abstract clusters of traits, the orientational criterion is superimposed on the relational. Without the entity of the personality, these various clusters would fly apart centrifugally. Each part of the more specified concept would receive special study. The entity, as a whole, may not be subject to a process of structural differentiation occurring homogeneously throughout it. Subsystems may undergo their own development. Being part of the same entity, however, these separate developments would not proceed randomly with respect to one another.

Thus, low correlations obtained in studies measuring development at two points in time may be not only because of the emergence of new structural differentiations, but also due to the subsumption of initially differing systems within the bounds. Kagan (1969) points to these low correlations as a general problem of life-span psychology. The poorly correlated behaviors are retained as characterizing the same entity. Kagan (1969) refers to "islands of continuity of process and behavior" to designate the fact that personality data, selected on the basis of orientation to a physical or cultural object, may involve several systems or dimensions. This basis of low correlations at a point in time supplements the argument regarding low correlations between measures in successive developmental stages because of the developmental process of restructuring successive emergent levels.

The differences in relative rates of development of verbal and of performance scores on the Wechsler Adult Intelligence Scale for various subjects illustrates the variant changes in subsystems of the same entity. A person could be at an advanced stage of logical reasoning or of "seriation" (Inhelder & Piaget, 1964) and at an early stage of moral judgment, of respect for rules (Piaget, 1960b). The very discrepancies in these rates of development are personality clues. Such terms as "functional autonomy" (Allport, 1968) or James' (1929) concept of the "divided self," are based on what James calls "a certain discordancy or heterogeneity in the native temperament of the subject [p. 164]."

2. Criteria of Relevance and Methods of Data Analysis

Each criterion of relevance not only directs the selection of facts, but has a particular affinity for a method of analyzing these facts. Baby biographies were, not surprisingly, an early source of insight for child psychology (Charles, 1970). The case study or, specifically, the biography is, in general, the most natural form of study for life-span psychology. The orientational criterion for fact selection assembles those facts into a developing entity which then has a biography. The journey of a changing personality is biographically anchored to a constant, though developing, physical locus. With the search for developmental laws, the qualitative case study gives way to the quantitative study of many cases. Usually, these laws do not encompass the total individual but rather describe change along component dimensions of the individual.

Focus on laws of development of "self-contained systems," as Lohnes (1965) calls them, of an entity, suggests Markov models. In a Markov model, subjects are observed repeatedly over time and the *transition probabilities,* the likelihood of their shifting from one state to the other, are computed. In a hierarchically developing system, a succeeding level may have an emergent character not easily predictable from the attributes of an earlier level, a problem encountered in the previous discussion of fact selection. In general, this is the problem of the differing developmental trajectories of the several subsystems constituting the developing entity. The Markov model partially answers this problem by allowing for differing transition probabilities along each branch. The Markov model is applicable to both continuous and discrete distributions. When continuous variables are available, Livson (see his chapter in this volume) recommends Hotelling's canonical correlation methods which "can display the structure of relationships across domains."

Multivariate statistical models, such as Cattell's (1969) factorial models have been developed for treatment of facts selected according to analytic criteria. Such models in specifying the patterns formed by facts are part of the fact selection process. With specific attention to life-span problems, factorial models have been designed for differentiating *exogenic* (outside the entity) and *epogenic* (through developmental time) factors in life-span curves. The sequential strategy devised by Schaie (1965) offers another option for data treatment within this class of methods. Factorial methods aim to assess the average change in values of attributes of members of a group. That is, the mean scores at T_1 are compared with the mean scores at T_2 and, only then, is the attempt made to separate change over time from variance attributable to the differing initial means of several subgroups. The study of the change in such group averages has heuristic value for deriving explanations for regularities in the development of individuals or other orientationally established entities (Spiker, 1966).

F. Age is like a Physical Object of Orientation

The rate of development of an entity is customarily assessed in terms of its age. In fact, Baltes and Goulet define life-span developmental psychology in terms of a "systematic age-functional relationship" (1970). Technically, age governs the selection of data much as does a physical object. Essentially, it is an orientational focus around which facts may be assembled. Age, like the objects already discussed, is also a factor external to and different in kind from the activities ordered with respect to it. Age is an interval of physical time, a matrix on which events may be located by their successive coordinates. When used in conjunction with the body, as another orientational object, facts must satisfy a double orientational requirement. When age is used in conjunction with relational criteria, it imposes the requirement of contemporaneity, or known sequentiality on the otherwise "free" field of potential correlates.

The role of age as a classificatory factor is sometimes confused with age as a variable. Tables are prepared with age at the top of the column and dependent percentages distributed in the column. The comparative behavior of age "groups" may then be stated on the basis of those data. These are not analytic tables showing the effect of age on the distributed factor. Rather, they are, in reality, comparisons of two sets of marginals —the distribution of a single factor in two populations differing in their age distributions. Similarly, a diagram showing age on the horizontal, and some changing factor on the vertical axis describes, but does not explain, the behavior of that factor over time. Another way of putting this is to say that age is an index variable and not a causal one (see, e.g., Baltes & Goulet, 1970; Reese & Overton, 1970), or, as Wohlwill (1970b,c) says, it is the dimension along which change is studied, a part of the dependent variable. A rate of change or of development is, in a sense, a dependent variable that includes time. Differential rates of development are then studied, dependently, as a function of some independent condition. As Baltes and Goulet (1971) say, the construction of age gradients or age functions is not the final goal of developmental theorizing. What is needed is the "explication" of age-related change in terms of psychological parameters or variables. The research objective consists of eliminating the age dimension by substituting nontemporal conditions.

Another sense in which age imposes a way of ordering facts extrinsic to the character of those facts is in the nature of the scale itself. The temporal ordering by age follows a ratio scale. Yet, none of the developmental processes so scaled may be changing at so regular a rate. Such discrepancies between the scaling of the observed processes and temporal scaling are reflected, for instance, in the distribution of heights associated with each age. The standard deviation of height measures for each corresponding age, especially around puberty, is large enough to cloud the correlation coefficient.

An alternative would be to use temporal scales of development based on "time" sequences intrinsic to the individual. For instance, the ratio of the time in one stage of development to the time in another might be computed for each subsystem. G. S. Hall (1904) seems to have had this in mind in presenting the ratios of the sizes of each organ of the body at various ages to the size of that organ at birth. Erikson's global psychosocial developmental stages might be assessed, not only in terms of the fact that basic trust is developed during the first year and autonomy from one to six years of age, but in the light of the ratio of the time an individual spends resolving the task of autonomy to the time he takes developing basic trust. Individuals might be compared in terms of these ratios. In comparing age cohorts, calendar time is added to the measure of time elapsed from birth. Such calendar time is an external criterion for coordinating a number of individual life histories, standardizing them for common exposure to external events (Riley et al., 1972). The same problem of scaling affects cohort measures.

The discussion of age opened with an assertion that age acts like a physical object with reference to the selection and ordering of facts. That statement may be reversed. What is true of age, is true of physical objects of orientation in general. The physical object, a territorial bound, or a climatic state, may, like age, be a basis for classifying facts, rather than a variable, when social actors take it into account in choosing their acts. The intrinsic character of the physical object is displaced by its significance for the action system. This raises the issue, discussed previously, of coordinating facts conceptualized in disparate frames of reference.

IV. Illustrative Problems for Life-Span Environmental Psychology

The implications of an orientational criterion of relevance for the selection of facts and of the problem of explanation presented by stating propositions in two frames of reference, a physical and a social, will be clearer by illustration. The following sections illustrate social–scientific thinking about environmental problems with reference to the use of space, to noise, and to outdoor recreation. An index of age will be used heuristically to initiate the life-span analysis.

A. The Orientation to Space

The number and scope of physical spatial areas within which an individual interacts in his daily routine seems to change with age. Stea (1970) has used the concept of "home range" to express this fact. Early in life the number of physical settings traversed seems to increase with development. The child's rather uniform and narrowly circumscribed home setting is eventually displaced by the varied settings of adults. Adults may, within a given day, move from the home to the office and to public streets through various kinds of services, such as stores, and, perhaps, entertainment. Late in life, the variety of environments becomes more restricted and the sensory ability to experience environments is more limited. These changes may be traced both to changes in individuals' initiative and to changes in the social rules regarding use of space (Lawton & Nahemow, 1973). How are these changes to be understood?

At the beginning and the end of the series, physical competency plays a direct and primary role. Social controls are imposed in view of the guardian's judgment of the individual's competency. Social rules about space usage, motivational factors, and technological culture seem most significant between childhood and old age. The extent of constraint imposed or facilitation offered by other occupants of the space changes from situation to situation.

The relation of social rules to mobility in space may be examined in the light of the changing complexity of the status set and role set at different ages and the meanings these impose on space. The relevant facts would be the variety of social activities and the physical settings considered appropriate for their enactment. From the physical side, the direct physical map of activities may be analyzed against the physical characteristics of the setting. From the social side, the analysis turns on the social rules and the meanings attributed to the settings. Age is used by society as an index for the allocation of positions in educational, occupational, marital, and other roles. Age and space (grasped in a space-time frame of reference) enter as conditions under which rules, activities, actors (grasped in a social science frame of reference) are examined. Because age is but one of many factors in role allocation, and because there is no fixed correspondence between physical settings and the roles enacted in them, there will be a distribution of environments, at any age, appropriate to given activities. Actors consider and adapt to physical environmental constraints. They also shape environments—often planfully sculpting the setting to match the activity.

Individuals, following social behests, select and structure their settings so as to facilitate role enactment. Patient beds in a hospital are arranged to respond to the conception of patient service—a conception governing staff and patient relations. The structure of the workplace separates managerial and productive functions, as well as the occupants of these statuses. Home arrangements for dining and bedrooms are designed to facilitate appropriate degrees of concentration or dispersion of family members during eating and sleeping.

Changes in role allocation through the life span, without reference to space, define a customary developmental sociological or social-psychological study. Space, as an additional criterion of relevance, and the behavioral data oriented around it followed through the life span defines a problem in life-span environmental psychology.

B. Noise as Part of a Social Event

Noise is an evanescent physical event, but its impact as an environmental despoiler survives it. Literature on the noise environment tends to be couched in the concepts of the acoustician. It is, however, social activities which are despoiled. The psychological literature on noise concentrates, in good measure, on noise and psychological stress (e.g., Kryter, 1970). Some social-psychologically oriented studies report correlations of age and noise tolerance. Children seem able to generate and tolerate a great deal of noise; adolescents seem to enjoy noisy activities, while mature adults and, especially, the aged seem to have a somewhat lower annoyance threshold.

Sound becomes noise when it interferes with some course of action; it is annoying to people not participating in the activity in which it is emitted. Noise reaches beyond the bounds of the activity generating it and captures others for the activity, impressing them into a situation against their will. It is also annoying when it prevents enjoyment of an activity—as when it masks speech. The neighbor's TV bothers the scholar at study and his power mower bothers the night worker trying to sleep late. Annoyance is a function of the extent of disruption of activity as well as of decibel level. Noise, as a physical object, may be taken as a condition under which human relations are examined. At the same time, the meanings of the actors' orientations to it become the basis for analysis. The life-span aspect revolves about the variant social norms and personality characteristics affecting the meaning of noise at successive stages in life.

Noise may become an element in social conflict by precipitating a conflict where there was none, as between airport management and nearby residents. It may also become a weapon in an existing conflict, as a noise of battle. The noise of new neighbors may accelerate the displacement of an earlier population. These are social meanings of noise. Noise evokes a strong response because it taps those levels of the personality which respond to violence by seeming to symbolize or simulate violence. This is a psychological meaning of noise.

Decreasing tolerance for noise among the elderly may express their reluctance for conflict, particularly conflicts with a clash of armor rather than the manipulation of soldiers on a map. Noise may be tolerated by youth who are inclined to be more stress-seeking or stimulus-seeking. The variables to be correlated with annoyance, at each age, are thus not decibel level, but fear of violence and assessment of violence potential—two psychological factors. Successive decibel levels may be taken as conditions under which the social psychological variables are studied. The physical concept of noise is, by symbolic interpretation, incorporated in a psychological frame of reference. Age, as an index for locating periods in the life cycle, joins the physical noise as loci for ordering social and psychological facts.

C. Outdoor Settings for Life Dramas: The Case of Recreation

Outdoor recreational activities are life dramas. Vacations, a special case of outdoor recreation, involve a change in the physical space occupied. Thus, the orientational object is not a single location, but a relation between locations or, more precisely, between the physical attributes of locations. Social units change location and, in the process, change their interrelations.

Social, physical, and psychological dimensions may be used jointly to classify vacations. Socially, vacations may be divided according to whether or not people disperse or congregate at a vacation site. In terms of their natural physical setting, vacations take people to open or to enclosed spaces, or some combination thereof. The data refer to human orientations to these physical characteristics. Psychologically, vacations may be classified according to whether participants are active, working on the social and physical environment, or are passive, primarily served by those environments. Cross-classifying these two dichotomous and one trichotomous dimensions, 12 types of vacations may be identified. A hotel at a beach, for instance, offers an opportunity for people to congregate, be passive, and contemplate the open space of beach and sea. (For further illustrations, see Klausner, 1969.)

The kinds of life drama enacted in each setting give the key to the meaning of that type of vacation and the meaning of the setting. Physical attributes which make one or another setting preferable for one or another life drama become culturally, symbolically, associated with those dramas. The symbolization of some physical attributes, such as up and down, or light and dark, seem to be almost universal symbols of moral good and bad (Cassirer, 1955). Seemingly, in our culture, open spaces are preferable settings for mystic dramas, such as those involving sexuality or religious motifs..The sea has long been associated in myth with motifs of rebirth and the desert has been a site of theophanies. Perhaps the enclosed spaces, like the forest glen, are more appropriate as retreats, points of withdrawal, for a reorganization of the self, rather than for a rebirth of the self.

Age groups may interpret the same sites differently by imposing different social and psychological meanings. Congregating at the sea, actively engaging the setting, seems appropriate for a mating drama. Congregating at the sea, while passively engaging it, seems more of a drama of satiation, as might appeal to the older set. The sea, approached passively and with dispersion of people, the lonely quiet sea, may be a setting for the elderly contemplative mystic.

When the family is the vacationing unit, the relevant age may not be that of the individual, but the stage of the family in its life cycle. Early in the family life cycle, camping is popular. The reason may be in part economic, that is, a function of the way rights to natural resources are distributed in our market economy. In part, it may reflect a penchant for outdoor activities on the part of young parents. Camping, as played out in our culture, challenges the family to meet its routine needs, to obtain a dry place to sleep and cook food, under difficult conditions. To some extent, sex roles shift. The home-residential setting tends to allocate internal home management responsibilities to the woman under the general aegis of male authority. In the camping setting, the man may take the initiative in food preparation or even assume the more ancient role of food gathering and, perhaps, fire-making. His authority is implemented more intimately and immediately. The drama of ancient patriarchalism is enacted. Perhaps, as years go by, family role negotiation settles the case so that the need to negotiate symbolically declines. Then, families are less attracted to camping. In this analysis, behavior is selected for study in virtue of its orientation to the camp site. Analytical propositions about patriarchal authority (such as the implied notion that intensity of control increases with the increased involvement by the authority in details) are drawn upon to clarify the meaning of the activities observed under the territorial criterion.

Vacation sites may become associated with age-homogeneous groupings. This may be explored within a life-span environmental psychology framework. In adult-dominated camps, postadolescents are not subject to general community rules and to little adult supervision. In vacation communities, entire areas may be taken over by youth groups. The history of a vacation site may be traced through this succession of increasingly younger age groups which may dominate it as each older group at the vacation site is succeeded and displaced by a younger one. Here activities over time around a relatively constant physical object are considered relevant. The "developmental" dimension is a regressing series of age cohorts—perhaps offering one of the few opportunities to study life span in reverse.

V. Conclusion and Policy Implications

To recapitulate—life-span environmental psychology faces the problem of constructing propositions linking a variable in a physical with a variable in a social science frame of reference. Relations among social science variables may be studied while treating variables in the physical system as conditional, holding them constant. Appropriate transformation concepts define the social significance of the physical variable.

When social or psychological facts are circumscribed for study in terms of their orientation to an object, including orientation to age, an entity is posited in the initial existence statement. The concept of development is bound to the idea of such an entity. The criteria establishing the boundary of the entity may not be expressive of the nature of the elements within it. As one consequence, the entity may consist of relatively functionally independent subsystems. Consequently, correlations between elements in distinct subsystems may be low. Development is structural differentiation. New elements emerge with the passage of time. This may account for some of the low correlations between elements at successive stages of development.

Disciplinary theory, on the other hand, tends to circumscribe relevant facts, within the frame of reference, by establishing empirical associations among them. The result is an object-free theoretical net of general propositions. These propositions may interpret relations among the elements in the orientationally posited entity. The boundaries of such a net are a function of the relation among the elements included. Values of such analytic variables may be said to change, but only entities, orientationally established, may be said to develop. These methodological issues have been illustrated through fragmentary life-span environmental psychological analyses of action oriented to space, to noise, and to natural outdoor settings.

The methodological problems of life-span environmental psychology clarify similar issues at the boundary of science and social policy. An orientational criterion for the selection of facts constructs an entity in accord with social interests. The resultant grouping may, while being scientifically "unnatural," consist of a pattern of elements occurring in the "real" world. The clustered facts of academic disciplines, perhaps following an immanent law of development, are increasingly selected by analytic criteria of relevance. With respect to events in the "real" world, analytically constructed propositions may express a free-floating science of possibilities. The scientifically "unnatural" entity formed by orientational criteria is closer to the public perception of events and to the focus of social policy. Educational policies, health policies, or environmental policies are all framed in orientationally constructed entities. The orientational entity is a link between applied policy and analytic theory. On the one hand, established analytic propositions may explain the relations found among elements in the orientational entity. On the other hand, the socially determined patterning of facts in that entity suggests new ways in which facts may be linked which, upon test, may extend theoretical propositions.

Science could be pursued as an expressive activity in its own right without attention to the patterns in which social interest clusters facts in the everyday world. Policy, for its part, could proceed on the basis of ad hoc interpretations of the behaviors conjoined in orientational entities without drawing on science to extend the understanding of those associations. Research which is defined by orientational criteria complements and enriches that defined by analytic criteria. Life-span environmental psychology gains depth through its relation to general personality theory.

PERSONALITY VARIABLES

CHAPTER 5

Developmental Dimensions of Personality: A Life-Span Formulation[1]

NORMAN LIVSON[2]

UNIVERSITY OF CALIFORNIA
BERKELEY, CALIFORNIA

ABSTRACT

The notion of developmental dimensions of personality is presented in the context of assumptions and methodologies that appear to follow directly from, and are therefore necessary to a life-span formulation of the proper tasks of a developmental–psychological conceptualization of personality. Certain assumptions are made regarding the nature of personality, its method and level of measurement, and the role of typologies within such a conceptualization. Genotypic continuity—predictability between developmental periods irrespective of the stability of the "same" personality characteristics over time—is regarded as axiomatic for this approach, and the canonical correlation technique is recommended for maximizing continuity, thus defined. Developmental dimensions, obtained in this manner, are regarded as facilitating links with current "dynamic" theories of personality development.

[1]Preparation of this chapter was partially supported by a Grant (HD 03617) from the National Institute of Child Health and Human Development.
[2]Also Department of Psychology, California State University, Hayward, California.

I. Introduction

The general area assigned to be covered by this chapter—personality dimensions—seemed clear enough. It was relatively simple to assume an agreeable definition that went something like this: Personality dimensions refer to an extensive set of general constructs, a consensual language which permits us to describe and spin theories about personality organization and development. A proper set of personality dimensions should provide a decently comprehensive summary description of personality at any given point in development, a point of departure from which we can describe, measure, and theorize about everything we always wanted to know about personality, and weren't afraid to ask.

My mandate, as I saw it initially, was to review various schemes or systems that were currently in use and sometimes in competition, to collate these, and then come up with a reasonably concise and fair-minded distillation of what is available today. My own work over two decades, all in the context of a longitudinal study of personality development, has kept me somewhat aware of the need for a comprehensive inventory of this sort. My current work, in which I have been seeking continuity in personality organization across childhood, adolescent, and adult data (from follow ups both at ages 30 and 40 of subjects in the Berkeley Guidance Study), has made me acutely aware of the need for an extended personality-descriptive schema for the adult years. In part, this is because of the relative inappropriateness of earlier-age dimensional schema for the assessment of adult behavior. However, as will soon become evident, no such succinct schema will be presented. Instead, presented here is an informal, perhaps rambling and overly personal essay, which details some of the issues, problems, and possible solutions that seem inevitably encountered in attempting to work toward such a schema.

II. Some Necessary Tactical Assumptions for the
Life-Span Study of Personality Development

While one is at one's own drawing board working on one's own data, there is little need to reask what is personality, and what are *personality dimensions,* and how are such dimensions best measured. The questions seem naturally answered, at a given moment, by the compass of those data that occupy us in our present research. More crucial, however, is the feeling that life-span personality developmental research must take stands (perhaps "tactical assumptions" is a better term) on a wide range of issues concerning definitions and procedures which make the enterprise viable. I have a hunch that the near-absence of true life-span data in this heavily researched field is because of the relative unpopularity of many of these assumptions and the likelihood that no research program has adopted them all.

One of the first statements encountered in an attempt to evaluate the present status of research in personality development confirmed my initial suspicion; research already in the field did not bode well for life-span work. Adelson in his *Annual Review* chapter on "Personality," presents a gloomy picture indeed. He notes that "at one time we thought of personality as a matter of enduring dispositions, but in recent years this definition has been under sharp attack. Some writers . . . question the generality and consistency of traits and other inner dispositions [and] argue that it is more useful to think in terms of response potentials actuated by situations." Further, "the impulse for synthesis, for finding unities, has for the moment been set aside" and there is currently a "sprawl and diversity in personality [which] can be seen as both a cause and a consequence of the virtual abandonment of large theoretical ambitions." He goes on to deplore "tight designs which limit both stimulus conditions and the range of response" and calls for, as a corrective, "a revival of inductive and naturalistic approaches [1969, pp. 217–218]."

Be not unduly dampened by this shower of quotes; there is hope, or so it will be argued here. The point in this confessed polemic will be—most generally—that the life-span orientation is just what the doctor ordered, that it inherently supplies a "corrective" since it necessarily owes an intense allegiance to "inductive and naturalistic approaches." What is more, from this perspective, one *must* look upon personality "as a matter of enduring dispositions" or, from my reading of what we are about, there is no field of action at all. One may fuss about what is meant by "enduring dispositions," but we most certainly are primarily concerned with searching for and understanding continuities in personality development over the life span. And that, it must be admitted, betrays a large theoretical ambition. To return to tactical assumptions necessary for life-span research, let us go back (in both senses of the term) to a logical first consideration—our conception of personality.

A. Conceptions of Personality

Discussions of personality by Allport and Vernon (1930) and MacKinnon's (1944) essay on the "structure of personality" still provide useful frameworks within which one can classify the numerous contemporary implicit and explicit definitions of personality and define our own proper ground. The "omnibus" or "ragbag" definition of Allport's in which personality is the "sum total" of just about everything a person does, including the influences of innate dispositions and acquired experiences, is still very much with us. Dahlstrom (1970), in his recent overview of the field, found that this remains one of the three main classes of definitions of personality which he labels "personality as the total response repertoire." In this definition "personality" and "behavior" are coextensive, rendering the task of the systematizer within personality an impossible one. Worse, this definition carries the notion of personality as a derivative dependent entity. By defining the behavior of a person as a "response," it appears to leave the field to situational determinants as the prime movers of behavior. It denies an effective role to intrinsic, enduring, predictable (and predictive) traits, motives, character, and other such "inner" constructs as first-order determinants of what people do. Certainly this emphasis on situational determinants is congenial to social-learning theories of personality development, such as those of Mischel (1968), and Bandura and Walters (1963). Such a definition can be taken to imply total malleability of the individual, the familiar *tabula rasa* upon which reinforcement contingencies can inscribe their effects. Clearly Skinner, if he needed a formal theory of personality, would adopt one of this sort.

A second main view of personality, a derivative of the *mask* model, is what Dahlstrom calls "personality as social stimulus value." This is akin to the earlier one and seems to say that personality can only be measured in some kind of dyadic or multiple social interaction. In this view again, enduring features of some "real," continuing person are in the background, and these features to some extent determine the nature and course of specific interplays between the person and other "actors." Whatever regularities may be discerned in personality defined in this way would seem to be social–psychological for the most part, and tell us little of the "inner" structure and functioning of the individual personality. Taken to the extreme, personality can be said not to *exist,* except in the fleeting contexts of momentary social interactions, a position apparently advanced by Carson (1969).

Both of the foregoing views of personality insist upon its evanescence. To exaggerate a bit, they seem to assume that personality reinvents itself with each new stimulus confrontation or in each new social interaction. Quite clearly, by these general definitions, personality lacks "substance"; it is essentially an entity of the moment, perhaps with some accumulated residue from past commerce with stimuli and social stimulus objects.

Integrative definitions (MacKinnon, 1944) represent a quite different conception of personality, and a more tangible one. As MacKinnon describes them, they have typically been adopted by psychologists "who have been willing to conceptualize inner psychological states, processes, and structures and relationships among them in order to make the observed behavior of the individual more meaningful [p. 4]." For Dahlstrom (1970) such conceptualizations represent a "differential approach to personality." In this approach, "the unidimensional, homogeneous psychological trait has come to serve as the core concept in a definition of personality that rests upon salient individual differences [p. 7]." Such *substance* models for conceptualizing personality abound, but none rival Cattell's for complexity, ingenuity, and sheer volume of research investigation. Furthermore, other such systems frequently establish their constructs rationally or, if they do their dimensionalizing empirically, unfortunately begin with an unsystematic and often biased sampling of behaviors from the personality domain. Cattell, in contrast, has sought dimensions, for the most part factor-analytically, within highly comprehensive samplings of behavior from three major domains: life-record (*L*), questionnaire (*Q*), and objective tests (*T*). (Cattell's unabated outpouring of research reports defies adequate citation; for the present purpose, perhaps the most pertinent recent items are Cattell, 1970c, for a succinct introduction, and Cattell, 1970b, for an overview of current thought.)

It is likely that life-span developmental psychologists or, for that matter, anyone with some concern with the structure of personality, is well acquainted with the varieties of Cattell's formulations. Cattell's introduction at this point is largely intended to serve as a shorthand to indicate the general conception of personality required for detecting *developmental dimensions* of personality. This term means nothing more or less than empirically derivable dimensions, which in their very derivation make use of longitudinal information, and which are, therefore, inaccessible to anything but a longitudinal approach. Toward this end, the two features of Cattell's approach to be emulated, and which are irreplaceable for work on personality dimensions within a life-span framework, are his comprehensive and unselective sampling of human charac-teristics (at least in the *L* mode where our effort will be most productive) and his objective–empirical methods for dimensionalizing these characteristics (although different analytic techniques will be suggested for certain points in the process). For the moment, however, Cattell's general conception of per-sonality—a "substance" one that permits, even if it does not require, the assump-tion that personality is a continuous, enduring entity—is adopted to exemplify the *kind* of conception of personality required for a life-span approach to personality development.

B. Modes of Observation

As just noted, the *L,* or life-record type of observation (direct observations, interviews) will tell us most if our aim is to detect developmental dimensions— predictive threads in personality which can be traced throughout the life span. This is really an expression of faith that the most maligned and suspect mode of describing the human personality—ratings —is the method of choice. By comparison, formally constructed personality self-report inventories and ques-tionnaires are currently held to provide a more precise assessment of personality constructs and, though less versatile at the moment, "experimental" procedures are generally preferred over ratings for their ability to define precisely the measure-ment situation. Ratings are generally passé these psychometrically elegant days, so much so that two recent major works on the measurement of personality essentially ignore this approach to the quantification of behavior. The index of Horst's (1968) *Personality: Measurement of Dimensions* has two entries for ratings, while Fiske's (1971) *Measuring the Concepts of Personality* has none. Why this near-total ostracism of a traditional method for describing personality? Admittedly, ratings, whether by self or by others (peers or experts), are subjective, but the fact that personality inventories call for objective written responses hardly insures the validity of personality inferences made from such responses. True, ratings have been shown to be susceptible to "halo effects," "errors of leniency," and the like, but then our professional journals have had to dedicate significant chunks of their page allotments to raging battles over the issues of response sets (e.g., "acquiescence," "social desirability") which generally erode the value of personality inventories.

What has been overlooked in this controversy over the relative merits of these different measurement modes is that ratings have the best potential for yielding useful assessments of the levels of personality traits for those who regard personality as an enduring, pervasive construct. If, as Murphy (1964) estimated, about half of the variance in personality data is associated with situational or context variability, then Q mode and T mode methods of measurement, which by their very nature sample highly limited contexts, should be avoided by those who embrace this conception of personality. At the very least, this conception requires that the person be characterizable as showing a certain stable value on a given trait at a given developmental point in time, even if this value represents an averaging over different observational methods and situations. Of course, averaging in this manner forecloses upon the possibility of detecting method- or situational-related variance. Further, this tactic assumes that the variance that remains (and is carried by the average) is large enough and reliable enough to make the enterprise viable. If it is not, then we would be out of the personality-quantifying business. While admitting to this serious risk, it still seems unarguable that the life-span approach requires just such an orientation to quantification and, for that reason alone, L mode methods—and specifically ratings—should be the measurement method of choice. Furthermore, only ratings seem workable for quantifying naturalistic samplings of behavior over a wide range of situations.

Ratings should also show relative immunity (and, theoretically, could achieve total immunity) from the hazards inherent in any version of the repeated-measurements longitudinal design which is indispensable to the life-span strategy. The chief hazard—the possible nonindependence of measures obtained on different occasions—is one that can easily be eliminated in ratings by insuring that different judges provide the assessments at each point in personality development. What is more, employing a number of raters at each time point not only offers the possibility of sampling a greater range of behavioral situations (promising both greater generality and stability through consensual ratings), but also permits this consensus to be arrived at by *conferencing*. Conferencing—using judges to make independent ratings, compare their ratings with one another and discuss discrepancies, and then obtain a second set of ratings that are then composited—does smack of contamination and other psychometric sins. But the superiority (from a validity standpoint) of conference ratings (and ratings in general when compared with questionnaire and inventory data) for the kinds of personality information needed for life-span study has been demonstrated a long time ago, and the evidence still seems convincing (Murphy, Murphy, & Newcomb, 1937). While embracing such sins it may be argued further that conferencing could and should include raters whose data come not only from observation of the target person but from, for example, interviews with "relevant others." Interview with a spouse, a parent, a child, an intimate friend—all these can and do illuminate facets of a personality which might otherwise have been successfully (and unfortunately) hidden from view. A risky business to be sure, but why deny access to the wealth of first-hand observational data available to these everyday observers and through them transmittable to us. Of course such second-hand data have been filtered through a nonneutral screen, but it is reasonable to trust the ability of sophisticated and well-trained judges to make appropriate corrections.

The fall from grace of ratings as the means for evaluating personality characteristics is attributable to the erosion of the esprit of personologists following recurrent attacks by higher-minded experimentalists. The current vogue of seeking situational determinants of behavior, with an attendant emphasis on Q mode and T mode measurements, has come to dominate the arena of personality research, and this new direction is responsible for much of the "disconcerting sprawl" which Sanford (1968) has seen as characterizing current research in personality. As an evangelical aside, let me call back to the fold of "real" work on understanding a "real" personality those who have been diverted from their proper course and have been diluting their energies by pursuing more precise quantification of less useful phenomena. But for now, let me only restate my conviction that some form of rating is the only viable method for discovering dimensions of personality, given the requirements of a life-span framework.

Permit me to perseverate a bit longer in this atavistic championing of so out-of-favor a method of measurement and to present some informal data which illustrate, if they do not confirm, my preference. As an example, some data will be chosen to describe the degree of reliability and validity achieved in the Berkeley Guidance Study through use of a set of ratings (actually, the California Q set, Block, 1961) which, safely ignoring its ipsative aspect, can be considered a highly comprehensive array of 100 personality-descriptive rating scales. This example seems especially apt since it involved a summary assessment of their "basic" personality for longitudinal subjects of both sexes based on 31 separate sources of data (interviews, tests, inventories, observations, etc.) available from age 21 months to 18 years, and involving the subjects, their families, teachers, peers, etc. (Quantifications in our longitudinal study are, of course, typically age specific, but on this occasion there was need for a developmental overview describing the "enduring core" personality for each subject.)

The data records for each case covered hundreds of pages and required several hours for a single reading; return to certain data sources was frequent and at the option of the rater. This is a horrendous task, calling for the simultaneous, intuitive weighing by the rater of a potpourri of data—data gathered by multiple observers from multiple sources using multiple measuring instruments on roughly 20 developmental occasions over a 16-year developmental span; and one may suspect that reasonably high agreement among raters assigned such a task would be highly improbable. But considering agreement on individual subjects (over 100 items), inter-rater correlations averaged .75, ranging from .44 to .85. (The mean reliability of two-rater composites, therefore, was .86). If conventional validity criteria can be translated into "by individual" from "by variable" terms, discriminant validity is indicated by the ability of this set of descriptive ratings to segregate the subjects into five relatively homogeneous person clusters (and quite different ones) for each sex (Livson, 1962). Convergent validity is suggested by the tendency for other kinds of assessment measures to group together roughly the same persons. Furthermore, between-cluster differentiation was shown for a host of other quantitative and qualitative indices. To take two examples among many, parental occupation reliably discriminated these person clusters, as did their subsequent marital fate (getting married and staying married), and did so in ways that made some theoretical sense. Such findings permit us to infer at least a modicum of construct validity for the rating-based descriptions.

This case history of a difficult rating venture has been presented all too tersely, but it affords at least a glimpse of data to explain my obstinacy in continuing to plump for a personality-descriptive method which, for many today, is regarded as discredited. Arguing to the contrary, not only do ratings generate reasonable, reliable, and valid data but, more importantly, they permit—indeed require—an extraordinary amount of sifting and weighting of evidence which can only be effectively accomplished by experienced human judges. And, to go further, only human judges are equipped to make the additionally necessary and delicate judgments of the *level* of a trait.

C. Levels of Inference

This, once again, is an old issue—but a stubborn one. To be able to identify the threads of predictability that weave through the life span of a personality, our search should focus for primary data at the least manifest level consistent with adequate validity. This suggestion too runs against the current grain since it also encourages human observers to combine and weigh intuitively discrete bits and pieces of interview material, observational reports, test data, etc., in an attempt to estimate the "real" level of a personality trait for a given person at a given time in his development. It might be bolder, but perhaps less politic, to do away with the quotation marks around "real" because, in my view, there is one, real personality structure regnant at each developmental point. Furthermore, a skilled and experienced judge can readily sort out diverse behavioral expressions over various situational settings with varying role demands and social restraints, and somehow arrive at a "true" estimate of a trait value.

In order to measure aggressiveness, for example, do not count the number of times a child strikes another over a number of time-sampled occasions in a standardized free-play nursery school setting. Rather, the judge, armed with his good sense *and* a clear specification of the trait, and the level at which it is to be rated, should range freely throughout the child's natural life space to gather the observational data from which a judgment can be formed. (If Barker and his colleagues can do this, so can we all, even though our ultimate goals may be polar opposites: his, the dominant role of the behavior setting and ours, a setting-free measurement of a pervasive personality characteristic.) Perhaps for certain characteristics or for certain individuals, no single value will prove adequate; then, perhaps, we can begin to learn under what conditions and for what kinds of people a stable, underlying trait cannot be discerned. Better that, than beginning with the assumption that such traits exist nowhere for no one.

Inferences concerning the true values of underlying traits involve what is most often designated as "clinical judgment." For many, this term raises an immediate spectre, as one thinks of the current verdict in the literature concerning the relative merits of "clinical versus statistical" prediction. This verdict—that statistical combining of data more often leads to accurate criterion prediction—is one that is hard to share, and, if space permitted, it would be possible to document that in too many instances the contest has been rigged against the clinical mode. Most often, this is done by an unrepresentative reconstruction of the clinical judgment situation, both in terms of restricting predictor information to what is statistically manageable and, for similar reasons, by selecting a simplified, quantifiable outcome criterion. Baughman (1972), in an excellent overview of the data and issues in this contest, makes much the same point in concluding that a fair, hence valid, verdict is not yet possible.

In the case of the inferential ratings of the type under discussion here, however, it may be suggested that the nature of the criteria—the true, underlying values of traits—and the access in judgment to data from a range of situations, methods, observers, *and* levels, promises an advantage for the clinical decision process. I do not believe, though I cannot provide comparative data, that statistical methods could have yielded as reliable summary personality descriptions, often involving inferential judgments, as those described in the preceding section.

Thus far tactical assumptions have been proposed regarding the nature of personality and its method and level of measurement, assumptions which may be necessary and which appear most congenial for a life-span orientation to the study of personality development. Similar consideration can be given to working assumptions concerning the form that personality dimensions can most usefully take, the prior constraints to be placed upon their organization, and the populational generality of such dimensions.

D. Factors or Functional Unities?

It seems fair (even inevitable) to say that most of what is known regarding the dimensionality of personality has been filtered through the factor-analytic model, applied to empirical data in one of a variety of basically similar forms. At least this is the case for quantitatively-oriented approaches, and especially those that aspire to a comprehensive mapping of the personality domain. Cattell, Eysenck, Guilford—these systematizers come immediately to mind; but even with some effort, it is difficult to cite ambitious searchers of personality dimensions who have not employed a version of this data-reducing tool in formulating their descriptive schema. But to impose this general method—or any method—upon raw observational data in order to perceive its structure is to make certain prior assumptions, and, therefore, to impose certain restrictions concerning the nature of the structure that may be found. In the case of factor analysis, these assumptions are well-known and, in any event, a discourse on them is not appropriate here.

It may be appropriate, however, to point out here an implicit tactical decision sometimes made without full awareness: The earlier the ordering influence of factoring imposed in the course of moving from raw data to final dimensions, the sooner there is a foreclosure of other, later-in-the-game possible and relevant determinants of that final structure. Take Cattell's earliest efforts at dimensionalizing personality, starting from the now-classic list of 17,593 personality-descriptive adjectives (or *trait names*) which Allport and Odbert (1936) had culled from a standard English dictionary. Through a succession of screens—some intuitive, some quantitative, some a bit of both—Cattell succeeded in achieving about a thousandfold reduction in the number of variables necessary to describe personality; his 16 *PF* tests more or less represent the *source trait* essence of this laborious distillation process. The various way-stations along this route are well known, but let me focus on two, or rather on the *space* between them.

One of the way-stations, Cattell's "surface traits," are just that—surface—in the sense that the similarities among the specific trait names that compose each one are readily apparent in their first-order intercorrelations among the raw data. No complex transformation, no process of inference, no reaching for some underlying uniformity is intended at this *clustering* stage. Source traits, on the other hand, do involve just these kinds of transformations as they are effected through factor analysis. There is a discontinuity introduced at this point by the factoring process but, before focusing on it, let us look first at a crucial and sometimes overlooked assumption which has been in effect *up to* this point of discontinuity. The assumption is that the process of sifting and combining from the assortment of dictionary adjectives down through specifying surface traits is inevitable, obvious, and, therefore, theoretically uninteresting. Either manifest redundancy in meaning, or very substantial "going-togetherness" on the surface have been the reducing filters up to this point. This implies an assumption that the final inventory of surface traits is essentially independent of the population from which it was derived. For example, in Cattell's data, the three specific traits "honest versus dishonest," "loyal versus fickle," and "fair-minded versus partial" could be combined into a single surface trait (integrity, altruism versus dishonesty, undependability). The fact that this proved possible in one (or more) samples does not justify what appears to be an implicit assumption that this grouping is a universal phenomenon, one which could be expected to show up in all kinds of people, at any age, and in every time and clime.

Perhaps this is overstating the case, but it should be emphasized that the further along in the reduction process this sort of *a priori,* almost casual collapsing of trait elements is allowed to go, the more we risk a failure to detect—in some group, or at some age, or in some time and clime—a true and theoretically important distinction among traits that are no longer semantic or cultural–behavioral synonyms. Perhaps, generally, a well-educated person in Western society *is* also honest when he is fair-minded, and vice versa, but it is *possible* that a member of a particular subculture can as easily be either, neither, or both. Of course, this is not a quibble on this particular collapsing of traits. The point here is to illustrate that it may be wise to call a halt earlier in such relatively uncritical combining of specific traits, and in that way, to lessen the risk of blurring forever a useful between-trait distinction. Any such distinction, once lost, may continue to plague later attempts to make some theoretical sense of a given set of personality dimensions and their interrelationships.

This precaution holds special importance in the search for life-span dimensions of personality since we must remain able to detect differences in the surface organization of traits throughout the course of development. To heed this precaution is, of course, not parsimonious, either mathematically or fiscally, but it is parsimonious in the crucial sense of not discarding potentially useful information.

There are many possible methodological responses that can be made in response to this precaution and all share the characteristic of assuring extreme "internal homogeneity" for resulting combinations of traits. For now, let me only record my loyalty to Tryon's (1939) notion of *functional unities* (more familiarly clusters, but in his special sense) as the proper level of reduction for handling covariance among traits up to the point when over-time relationships enter the picture. (For the current status of this enormously developed, yet unfortunately neglected approach, see Tryon & Bailey, 1970). Incidentally, Cattell did use a form of clustering in setting up his surface traits; the point here is that such clusters should be very "tight," lest they capture potentially separable, specific traits by casting too wide a net. Departing from Tryon, it is argued here that some variant of the factoring model *does* become appropriate, even necessary, when the reduction process enters the region wherein *underlying uniformity,* by our best guess, is most profitably to be sought and found, if it exists at all. That region, most likely, is the space recurring along the life-span *between* developmental points that developmental dimensions (soon to be defined) are intended to bridge.

E. Where to Factor

Some time back Cattell was left dangling in the factoring-induced discontinuity between his surface and source traits. As just noted, the region within which one chooses to factor is the region where one is placing his bets that truly interesting underlying uniformities are best to be found. To set this region at the interface of surface and source traits is to make, in the usual R factoring of age-specific personality data, two overlapping assumptions: (1) The "truly interesting underlying uniformities" do not require a temporal or developmental source of variance, but can be discovered within a single slice in time, and; (2) When repeated measurements are available, subsequent analyses to explore links among R factors obtained within two or more developmental cross-sections will not be distorted by those prior within-age factorial reductions. In estimating the possible losses risked by these assumptions, it does not at all matter whether or not the "same" factorial structure can be demonstrated for the various age cross-sections to be linked. The point is that whatever power the process of factoring has in defining underlying uniformities—in getting at the infrastructure of personality organization to provide the constructs from which theory building in personality development can proceed—has been invested at the cross-sectional stage.

What this means is that personality structure defined exclusively from data at a given age cannot possibly have been influenced by the relationships of each of the traits at that age with the same traits and *with different* traits measured on the same sample at earlier and at later ages. In short, any developmental continuities that may exist have been precluded from any influence upon the dimensionality of personality at that age. True, correlations of factors among age periods can later be computed. But the resultant network of inter-age correlations may seriously underestimate both the potential strength of the predictive and postdictive relationships among various age periods, and worse, the theoretical sense which can be made of such relationships. Had factoring been applied, instead, to a matrix of interrelationships that *included* between-age correlations, then within-age covariance would have interacted and competed with that demonstrable over ages. Had this been done, the resultant dimensional structure could well have presented a theoretically more heuristic picture. Just this sort of factoring is possible by the technique of canonical correlation (Hotelling, 1935, 1936), of which more later. What is more, employing this method inevitably *maximizes* between-age predictability.

To return to the point of possibly destroying useful developmental information by "premature" factoring within age levels, some time ago (1965), I undertook a search for functional unities at four developmental periods (early and late childhood, early and late adolescence) within sets of personality ratings obtained annually for Guidance Study subjects. Using the BC TRY computer system (Tryon & Bailey, 1966), several obliquely-related clusters were defined for each period. These clusters were substantially different both between sexes and among ages, although identical rating scales had been employed throughout. Parsimony had certainly not been achieved, either in numbers of clusters or in their defining characteristics.

The findings were complex and no attempt will be made to summarize them here. Instead, one example will be given of an interesting developmental sequence which was teased from the network of cluster and individual trait interrelationships. Anxiety was found to be a personality characteristic curiously absent from any clusters in the earlier age periods, although it had been reliably rated and was known to have many substantial first-order correlates with other traits at these earlier ages. What had happened, in early childhood for example, was that anxiety related highly and significantly *and about equally* to all five clusters definable for that age period. Hence, in personality space it bridged all clusters, but joined none of them. Necessarily, it would have achieved a high loading on a factor, and most likely on the first factor, for that age period. Anxiety, as a separate trait continued to drift in personality space in later years, sometimes closer to one cluster, sometimes to another. Finally, in late adolescence, something jelled; anxiety (together with moodiness, social sensitivity, even nightmares) formed its own quite homogeneous, "tight" cluster, one relatively independent of others defined at that same age.

By holding off on factoring, it was discovered that anxiety is a pervasive quality of personality throughout much of early development, and that only at late adolescence does it crystallize into a dimension in its own right. Furthermore, it was noted that this late adolescent dimension had a significant *negative* relation to an early childhood cluster of explosive behavior with which the *contemporary* rating of anxiety had had a significant *positive* correlation. Some sense could be made of this curious transformation through exploring the network of interrelationships in the intervening time span. Certainly this developmental tale could not have been told had we R factored at each age and come up with the three or so factors sufficient to account for the reliable covariance within each developmental period.

The point, after all this, is no doubt obvious: Maintain closely-knit functional unities until you are ready to bridge the developmental chasm. Since such clusters consist of phenotypically highly similar, specific traits, they have the added advantage of being easily nameable. Do not fret over too many dimensions, or lack of orthogonality since premature mathematical elegance may sabotage the developmental enterprise. The message is familiar, possibly banal: Stay close to the data (for as long as you can).

F. The Necessity of Typology

Kluckhohn and Murray (1949), and others very likely, have observed that "every man is in certain respects like all other men, like some other men, and like no other man." Ignoring its now sexist overtones, we can all probably agree with this statement, assert that it speaks directly to the issue of personality structure and, note further, that it commits us to introducing typological considerations into our search for personality dimensions. I hesitate before plunging into this brambly "R versus Q" thicket, but this issue is perhaps *the* most recalcitrant one with which life-span research on personality development must deal.

Permit me a few flat assertions:

1. Personality dimensions derive from interrelationships among personality variables.
2. Persons differ on all useful personality variables.
3. Different groups of persons show different patterns of variable intercorrelation, and therefore, have different personality dimensions. One must detect and work separately with these groups of persons with differing dimensions if there is ever to be a complete and accurate taxonomy of personality, even within a single developmental cross-section.
4. These groups of persons, for want of a less inflammatory term, are called *types*. Somewhere along the way (it is difficult to say where and more difficult to say how), we must break down our population into types.

Having just provoked Nomothesis, the handmaiden of science, some words of justification seem in order. We all well understand the nomothetic approach, but let one spokesman speak, one highly concerned and skilled in the measurement of personality (Fiske, 1971): "The task facing personality today is the identification and delineation of attributes which can be *uniformly* applied to persons, the objects of this science, with the specific applications of each attribute differing *only in quantity, not quality* [emphasis added] [p. 49]." The statement is a recent one, but not the controversy; many of the more cogent comments and attempts at resolution bear less recent publication dates. Selecting a few such samples from a vintage period, both Eysenck (1954) and Cattell (1952) deny any need for the Q factoring approach, their main argument being that it is wholly redundant, that Q results and R results are essentially equivalent, and that one set of results can be derived exactly from the other. (Cattell, curiously, notes that "Q technique has its chief use as a classificatory device for finding the subpopulations in a nonhomogeneous population [p. 520]," which certainly seems agreeable to the present argument.)

Block (1955) specifically questions this full convertibility of Q and R results, asserting that it does not hold true when "the pattern of correlations between variables for one subgroup within the total sample differs reliably from the patterns of correlations derived from other subgroups [p. 356]." He goes on to discuss instances of enormous differences in correlation between the same pairs of personality variables in different groups, in some cases involving major reversals in sign and he claims that this state of affairs is commonly encountered in the personality domain.

If Block is correct on this point and significant variations in patterns of trait intercorrelation do occur within subgroups (his differences were among men from different careers, studied in an assessment setting), what does this imply for the search for a general taxonomy of personality dimensions? Obviously, one cannot ignore these data and proceed as before, assuming homogeneity in trait intercorrelations throughout mankind. Equally obvious, there is no reason to assume that careers optimally segregate persons with similar covariance patterns into homogeneous types. What must be done instead is to devise empirical means for detecting true types, subgroups of persons showing highly similar trait covariance, from within unselected populations.

There are a great number of analytic techniques for doing this and probably a greater number of indexes of profile similarity to generate the inter-person comparison matrices upon which these techniques can operate. There have even been occasional studies reporting empirically-generated types within specific populations. One interesting variant of this approach was conveniently suggested by my wife. Reichard, Livson, and Peterson (1962) sought such "natural" subgroups by means of Q cluster analyses of personality rating profiles of a sample of older men, aged 55 to 84. But rather than applying this method directly to the total sample, they initially partitioned it into two subgroups, one relatively high and one relatively low, on a separate assessment of overall adjustment to aging. Thus, different character types could be reported *within* good and poor "agers," and the personality dynamics of each type could be related to their differential coping with the aging process. Neugarten (1964) used a different type-establishing approach (Q factoring with varimax rotation), although her personality variables, in part, duplicated those from the earlier study. There was no prior partitioning on adjustment to aging. She found quite similar types from separate Q analyses within groups of men and women of approximately the same age range, and these types substantially replicated those found previously by Reichard *et al.* Furthermore, Neugarten was able to demonstrate that these personality types were independent of age, supporting a speculation offered from retrospective data in the earlier study.

This brief digression into aging was made to illustrate an infrequent attempt to compare person types obtained from roughly comparable populations. In this instance, quite drastic differences in typologizing techniques seemed of little importance. That, and the suggestion that the typologies were age independent over a considerable age span might—for those who need it—provide some encouragement concerning the viability of the approach and the relative sturdiness of its results. Whether such optimism would be justified for the typing variant I shall propose may be quite another matter; perhaps one might employ a typologizing technique that takes explicit account of developmental changes. Who gets grouped with whom would, at least in part, be a function of their similarity of personality-development path throughout the life-span; specifically, persons within each type would belong to the *same* person cluster in the Q analyses at each age. Luckily, for the purposes of this chapter, it seems possible to neglect some embarrassing ramifications of this suggestion. For example, an enormous total sample size would be required if reasonable numbers of persons are to populate each type, thus defined.

To return to the issue of nomothetic laws, it should be clear that planning to take into account differing patterns of interrelationship within subgroups is by no means to deny that nomothetic laws are the ultimate goal. Of course, if ever there is to be some "supertheory" of personality development, it must explain all behavior, including that of members of all subgroups (or types), but subgroup membership will by then have entered as a parameter into the explanatory system.

The quarrel, if there indeed still is one—the straw man may have already ridden off into the sunset astride a dead horse, when no one was looking—is not with nomothetic laws, but with nomothetic dimensions. In fact, it can be argued that an insistence upon a single universal set of dimensions defeats the eventual attainment of truly general laws of personality development. To refuse to dimensionalize personality in ways more fitting the data *within* detectable, homogeneous subgroups introduces sheer error. Thus, nomethetic laws of maximum generality would seem to be most probable when personality dimensions and interrelations are determined in a way that least distorts the inherent structure of the data from such subgroups. To opt instead for dimensions describing the "average" structure of the personality domain is to assume no useful and conceptually exploitable heterogeneity among men and women.

It is the rare researcher today who fails to segregate the sexes in analyzing data. If sex is to be an exception to the universal sweep of the nomothetic principle, then why not age, socio-economic status, birth order, occupation, etc. Why not, indeed? Our data can be analyzed comfortably and separately within these subgroups, sometimes finding generality of results across groups, sometimes not. And we often can speculate profitably about why and why not. The latent principle operating in current personality research seems to be that objective distinctions among persons—for example, biological or demographic—are legitimate discriminators, but that psychological ones, which can be made equally objective (even though perhaps confounded with the phenomena being studied), are not.

Dahlstrom (1970) commented critically on the tendency to regard implicitly such objective discriminators as having univocal psychological meaning, regardless of the differing contexts in which they operate. Meehl (1967) has pointed out that socio-psychological parameters of this sort are insufficient for creating meaningful groupings of persons; rather, he suggested setting up such groupings only on the criterion of homogeneity of personality configuration. But these efforts persist. Birth order, an example of such a popular subgroup, cannot possibly be expected to segregate persons in the same way in all populations. One needn't strain to make this point; the psychological meaning of being, say, a first-born male can hardly be expected to be unaffected by variations in whatever still remains of primogeniture in his subculture. Yet, numerous contemporary studies continue to deal with birth order as a major factor in personality development in otherwise unselected populations. Birth order does provide fruitful and interpretable results occasionally when considered within a highly complex nexus of family size, sibling sex and separation, social class, family values, and the like. Take one instance: Smelser and Stewart (1968), looking into the well-known generalization that first borns more often go on to college, found that the sex of later-born siblings was critical. Specifically, in two-child families the "rule" held only when the younger sibling was of the opposite sex.

The fact that, still, so many people working on problems in personality development are lured by the notion of talking about "the psychology of the first born" is itself informative. Other socio-psychological classifications that fare no better, despite their equally "objective" nature, are still attractive. Perhaps their popularity is one good indicator of a sensed need in the field for doing *some* kind of segregating out of the troublesome heterogeneity to be found in personality structure within an unselected population.

Somehow, this issue of what to do with heterogeneity of organisms when seeking universal, nomothetic laws refuses to go away. Perhaps, this is one sign that a research conflict is exposed which at sometime must be dealt with appropriately. Cronbach (1953) recommended essentially that we break down data matrices by applying, alternately, techniques involving correlations between organisms and those involving correlations between characteristics, precisely what we have been talking about here. Since then, McClearn (1967), Melton (1967), and Owens (1968) have stated the need for some reconciliation of what basically are the idiographic and nomothetic approaches; there are probably others.

Owens has, in fact, acted vigorously upon his own suggestions. Working with very large college samples, he has established subgroups with similar profiles on factors derived from biographical data. Several studies are underway to check out the discriminating power of these subgroupings in such diverse areas as perception, cognition, classroom learning styles, academic achievement, and social preferences. This seems to be the only major current effort with the long–range explicit goal of building up to general laws of behavior by seeking first to improve the precision of behavioral prediction within psychologically homogeneous subgroups (Owens, 1971).

Let me finally close off this discussion with a quotation from a recent reconsideration of this same issue. Vale and Vale (1969) concluded that

> individual differences must, necessarily, be the business of *all* of psychology, because there appears to be little opportunity for psychology to become a science of general laws without systematically including individual differences in the search, and *general laws* are the business of all of psychology [p. 1105].

To work within typologies of persons in the search for general laws governing personality development remains an ultimately nomothetic strategy, but one that makes it possible to consider individual differences (in the sense of type differences). As is no doubt clear by now, it is suggested that this strategy is inescapable within a life-span framework.

III. Continuity as Axiomatic for the Life-Span Study of Personality Development

Until now attention has been given only to the conceptual and methodological tactical assumptions that may facilitate a life-span analysis of personality dimensions. Each of the assumptions can be argued, with perhaps lesser fervor and relevance, for approaches to the topic with more limited time span scope, or even with cross-sectional-descriptive goals. But there is an additional assumption so central to the life-span enterprise that it must be considered axiomatic: Personality development *necessarily* is a phenomenon characterized by *continuity*. Put simply, if extremely, we would and should leave the field if, before the fact of our inquiries, we could somehow know that personality can be adequately defined and studied *without* recourse to developmental considerations, and that appropriately extensive data from within any slice in time would be sufficient to the task. The converse of this proposition, perhaps, is that considerations of continuity should take precedence, conceptually and methodologically, in determining what we do study and how we go about it.

A. Dimensional Stability, Phenotypic Persistence, and Genotypic Continuity

A review of the relevant literature for this chapter would exemplify the varieties of meanings that could be assigned to the notion of ''continuity'' in personality development. It may be helpful to categorize these into three main kinds and remark upon each. But only the last of these, as will be seen, is directly related to our main theme.

1. Dimensional Stability.

This term refers to similarities and differences in the structure of personality as they exist in different populations—populations defined by age, sex, subculture, or what have you. (*Factorial invariance* would do as well as a term were it not for its somewhat parochial overtones.) Data on *dimensional stability* can be, and most typically have been, obtained from cross-sectional studies of enormous varieties of samples, using various personality-descriptive schemes and methods, and arrived at by a variety of dimensionalizing techniques.

It is tempting to settle this question once and for all by referring to Eysenck whose claim for his factors of E (extraversion–introversion) and N (neuroticism) sounds definitive: E and N, he states, ''have been replicated with high accuracy in studies carried out on male and female subjects; they appear in different age groups . . . are replicable in different European and non-European countries [and] have appeared in groups of subjects differing widely in education and intelligence [Eysenck & Eysenck, 1969, p. 326].'' However, that temptation must be resisted, being unable to escape the doubt that, occasionally, his efforts and those of his colleagues are as Procrustean as they are Herculean. But he has worked seriously at establishing the dimensional stability of his theoretical scheme. Together with Cattell, he probably tells us the bulk of what we know about the dimensional stability of personality factors under diverse conditions for diverse populations. Their writings are our best source on this issue. A recent sampling of systems for dimensionalizing personality, and some data on their generality is available in Mahrer (1970). And an excellent overview of dimensions found at maturity and old age is provided by Schaie and Marquette (1972). But this body of knowledge need not be of concern here since it can, and usually does, remain silent on whether individuals, in the course of their development, show continuity on various personality dimensions.

2. Phenotypic Persistence

Anyone who has ever done a longitudinal study over whatever time span in which the "same" personality characteristics were assessed for at least two developmental points has had something to say about what may be called *phenotypic persistence*. Not only do data abound on this question but, perhaps for the same reason, so do labels: "isomorphic continuity" (Bell, Weller, & Waldrop, 1971) and "individual stability" (Emmerich, 1964) are recent examples.

It would be madness to attempt a synthesis of the probably hundreds of studies that could qualify for this category. Not only are the sets of personality characteristics measured rarely duplicated, but methods and settings of measurement are equally nonuniform. However, others have made this attempt, though most often confining their overviews of literature on phenotypic persistence to selected portions of the life span. Understandably, the prevalence of reviews for given portions of the life span reflects the relative volume of research activity within each time period. It comes as no surprise, then, that the childhood years and aging years are overrepresented, while the middle years (within themselves or in relation to earlier or later personality) find few summarizers. Risking bias and some exposure of ignorance, only a few will be noted. Yarrow and Yarrow (1964) present a good sketch of what they call "phenotypic consistency" within the earlier years, and several useful summaries for the same period can be found in Iscoe and Stevenson (1960). Stone and Onqué's (1959) abstracts of longitudinal studies of child personality, while less convenient to use, can also be a valuable source. Neugarten (1964) overviews the middle years; her selection of original reports for this time span supplements this source (Neugarten, 1968a). Kuhlen (1964) and, more recently, Chown (1968), provide good reviews of data on later life. Bloom's *Stability and Change in Human Characteristics* (1964) takes a stab at covering infancy to adulthood, but should be read selectively.

If I were to venture a general comment on dominant trends within the phenotypic persistence literature, I would go along with Honzik (1964). In her succinct overview of long-term longitudinal studies, she notes that investigators tend to "invoke intrinsic or constitutional factors to account for their findings [p. 141]." Put in other terms, it does seem that personality characteristics which traditionally are in the sphere of temperament, and for which biological underpinnings are most easily (if not always validly) assumed, are most persistent, possibly throughout the life span. Introversion–extraversion is a prime example.

But this is a very rough impression. By and large, one is not struck by inescapable regularities within the data on phenotypic persistence. And certainly there are no hard data on the persistence of specific personality characteristics throughout development since longitudinal studies of entire lives have not yet been completed. Some current studies, however and happily, may be suspected of that aspiration. The mass of rather chaotic data on this topic leaves the impression that, although little bits and pieces of personality do seem, even replicably, to persist over limited periods of development, no persuasive themes are yet evident. What data there are, almost without exception, refer to the persistence of specific traits, not to general dimensions. Furthermore, it is extraordinarily difficult to tie in those data with any full-blown theories of personality development. This difficulty is inevitable since to be confined to, or even to focus upon, over time persistence of the ''same'' personality characteristics seems a foredoomed enterprise. Even if it were not problematic to assume that the dependency of a two year old is psychologically identical with that of an adolescent, or of a middle-aged adult, it seems at best, a curiously limiting strategy for exploiting longitudinal data. Why not extend to looking at correlations among phenotypically dissimilar traits over time?

The so-called *sleeper effect* (Kagan & Moss, 1962) seems an example of this unnecessary restriction to phenotypically defined channels of development. At least this appears to be the case in one of their two examples of the effect—the greater predictability of ''love-object dependency'' in adult men from phenotypically somewhat similar characteristics (passivity and fear of bodily harm) in the preschool period than from the same characteristics in later childhood and early adolescence. The sleeper effect, in this instance, refers to the relative hiatus in ''continuity'' within the latter period. Kagan and Moss suggest only that ''a covert disposition to passivity may be present during the school years and may find expression in adolescent and adult derivative reactions [p. 278].'' This hypothesis may well be true, but it is hardly an explanation of the phenomenon. One might guess that this gap in phenotypic continuity could have been bridged by looking into what *other* characteristics during this gap period might have been predicted from earlier passivity which, in turn, might have predicted adult dependency.

An illustration of this ''indirect'' approach comes from some work by Livson and Peskin (1967). It was found that adult psychological health (at about age 30) for both men and women in the Berkeley Guidance Study was predictable only from personality characteristics in preadolescence and, furthermore, that none of these predictive characteristics were obviously (and certainly not phenotypically) ''healthy'' traits. Earlier behavior of the child was not predictive, nor, at first glance, was behavior during late adolescence—a kind of sleeper effect, it seemed. Later on, Peskin (1972) was able to show that the chain of causation was indeed unbroken and that, after all, some of the very same late adolescent personality characteristics, when statistically controlled for their early adolescent values, did contribute to the predictability of adult psychological health for both sexes.

The point of this too-abbreviated case history of a research exercise is only to set the stage for another kind of definition of continuity, one which encompasses sleeper effects by focusing on predictability in a manner that gives no priority to instances of phenotypic persistence.

3. Genotypic Continuity

"Continuity" in the sense just mentioned is another axiom for the life-span study of personality development. In this context (although it can be defined more broadly), it refers to the predictability (and postdictability), *in whatever form,* of personality between developmental points all along the life span. Put another way, genotypic continuity subsumes any and all evidence for an unbroken chain of causation, or at least connectedness, linking all occasions at which personality organization is assessed. Phenotypic regularities will provide only a few links in this chain but, insofar as these exist, they will be subsumed within the definition.

It is my unoriginal faith that such genotypic continuity does exist throughout personality development, we should assume its existence, and directly act on this assumption in our research efforts. (Dr. Ahammer's contribution to this volume, Chapter 11, clearly makes, and must make, an opposite assumption.) But this axiom says no more than that "behavior is determined." My impatience with the sleeper effect, incidentally, probably derives from a vague sensing that some have tended to deny this truism, and to use the concept to sound a wondering "gee whiz" over a chasm of ultimate indeterminacy. This "some" no longer includes its originators, if ever it did, since Kagan (1969) drew a clear distinction between "phenotypic continuity" and "genotypic continuity" (his term also).

Since genotypic continuity seems to be a concept as obvious as it is necessary, its formulation should be expected by others also. In addition to Kagan's use of the term, Yarrow and Yarrow's (1964) "dynamic consistency," Emmerich's (1964) "developmental transformation," and Bell, Weller, and Waldrop's (1971) "metamorphic continuity" all refer to a similar, if not identical concept. There no doubt are other conceptual synonyms in the literature that have been missed. The thrust of each of these concepts is to emphasize that developmental continuities are typically complex, rather than phenotypically obvious. Also, Coan's (1966) concept of "factor metamorphosis" appears related; it describes the situation in which "two factors appearing at widely separated age levels could . . . be characterized as qualitatively distinct although they represent a single historical continuity [p. 746]."

Genotypic continuity refers to the sort of developmental regularities most congenial for integration within so-called dynamic theories of personality. And if this particular conception of continuity is in any sense novel, it is because it can be translated into a particular analytic technique which, conveniently, has been waiting in the wings for some time.

B. Maximizing Genotypic Continuity

If, indeed, it is accepted that genotypic continuity is a natural assumption for life-span personality research, techniques for data analysis that permit its assessment are needed. Many such techniques are available, and several have been used. In fact, the only requirement for a technique to be sensitive to genotypic continuity is that it attends, within a matrix of intertrait, interage correlations, to something other than persistence correlations within the "same" trait over time. Cross-trait, cross-age correlations, of course, do just this, as do multiple regression prediction techniques. Then, there is the general approach which may be called *comparative factor analysis* that recognizes genotypic continuity by maximizing the match between factorial solutions of data obtained from the same sample at different ages. Nesselroade, Schaie, and Baltes (1972) have presented a convincing instance of this approach in the realm of adult cognitive behavior based primarily on Meredith's (1964) technique of rotation to achieve factorial invariance.

There is at least one analytic technique that can both *maximize* cross-age relationships between developmental periods and, at the same time, determine within-age personality dimensionality *in accordance with the maximizing criterion*—and that is canonical correlation. This seems precisely what is required if genotypic continuity is to be our primary organizing influence.

1. Predicting the Most Predictable Criterion

Hotelling (1935, 1936), as noted earlier, introduced canonical correlation as a method for analyzing the relationships between two sets of measurements. He regards the method as "predicting the most predictable criterion" in the sense that the canonical correlation is the maximum correlation that can possibly be obtained between linear combinations of variables within each of the two sets. In other words, the result of this procedure is a weighted composite score from each set which, when these two scores (or canonical variates) are intercorrelated, the obtained correlation is the maximum attainable. Each analysis can yield additional canonical correlations, with their accompanying pair of canonical variates, since the procedure can be reapplied to residual covariance matrices. The only restriction is that successive variates are orthogonal to all preceding ones.

What we have here is essentially a form of factoring. In fact, Bartlett (1948) called it "external factor analysis" and spelled out the relationships of canonical correlation to traditional "internal" factor analysis. As Cooley and Lohnes (1971), who provide a succinct summary of the method and a computer program for its implementation, stated: "The canonical correlation model uses the same analytic trick to display the structure of relationships across domains . . . that the factor model uses to display the structure of relationships within a domain [p. 169]."

Finally, then, it is at this point that the factoring process does enter the picture, and does so in a manner that permits *maximum* estimates of *between-age*, or developmental, relationships to play a major role in determining the structure of personality *within* ages. The resultant canonical variates are, in fact, factors. In a certain limited sense then, the variates within any developmental period define the dimensionality of that period. But these factorial "solutions" are by no means unique. There are as many passes at defining the structure for a given period as there are earlier and later periods to which it can be related. Thus, for example, the within-age structure of a set of early adolescent personality measures will almost certainly be importantly different when it is related to late childhood data than to late adolescent data. This multiplicity may not satisfy our parsimonious instincts, but the price may well be worth paying. The payoff should be an optimal solution for the particular time period that most concerns us at the moment. An alternative to this multiplicity is provided by Horst (1961) who has extended canonical correlation to any number of sets of data. Thus, the possibility exists for detecting canonical variates strung through several developmental periods *simultaneously* in a single analysis. Unfortunately, the sample size demands for this technique probably require considerably larger longitudinal samples than have thus far been available. In any event to my knowledge, there is not yet available a means for evaluating the statistical significance of these *m* set canonical correlations.

Canonical variates are not usually regarded as defining the dimensional structures of variables within a given cross-section. Their natural focus, rather, is on the gap between periods, and it is precisely there that our developmental interests properly lie. Because of this, it may be suggested that the canonical solution for personality data between two given developmental periods, or more appropriately, the set of significant canonical variates generated by that solution, be dubbed developmental dimensions of personality.

2. Developmental Dimensions of Personality

As just defined, developmental dimensions are as true as any empirically-derived construct can be to the ideal of genotypic continuity. Such dimensions, necessarily, suggest how to dimensionalize personality in order to exploit the maximum predictability possible between developmental periods, and do so with no preference whatsoever given to phenotypic resemblance. Of course, it may turn out in a given analysis that an assortment of specific traits in early childhood, each weighed about equally and easily subsumable under the label "introversion," yields the maximum possible correlation with a very similar trait assortment in later childhood. Were this to be the case—and this, in fact, was a solution hinted at during a preliminary analysis (Livson, 1965)—then introversion–extraversion would indeed have emerged as a developmental dimension. But typical solutions are far more complex, and a computer printout sprinkled with an array of significant canonical correlations is just a starting point.

Furthermore, to label developmental dimensions is no simple matter. Our language, it seems, is deficient in familiar terms that do justice to the nature of canonical variates as they appear within each developmental period. Perhaps this should be expected, because everyday language intends primarily phenotypic description. It is the task of theory to formulate new constructs that organize the regularities our analytic methods pull out of observational data. It is tempting to invent wholly new terms—and this may well be what must be done if we are to be freed from traditional personality constructs. At the very least, in attempting to "name" canonical variates, one comes to empathize with Cattell's need to turn to neologisms in labeling his source traits. After all, when dealing with underlying uniformities, with the infrastructure of personality development, one perhaps must expect to be confronted with the non-obvious, and to have to invent new constructs. And, in the last analysis, these new constructs will serve as the bases upon which someone, sometime, will be sufficiently ingenious (or genius) to erect an integrative "supertheory" of personality development.

This "naming" task need not be done in the dark. The existing, so-called dynamic theories of personality certainly share our ultimate goal of an all-encompassing integration of personality–developmental data. These theories have admitted defects and lacunae, and many of us may shy away from them, made distrustful by their lack of rigor of inference and of systematic, empirical underpinnings. But it is perhaps to them that we should look for hints as to the nature of the developmental dimensions we uncover. They have, after all, been continually concerned with tracing long-term genotypic continuities within individual development and delight in, rather than balk at, failures of specific personality manifestations to persist in identical form over time. "Developmental-transformations," to return to Emmerich's concept, are just what the Doctor Freud ordered, and psychoanalytic theories accept the challenge of imposing genotypic order upon phenotypically anarchic developmental patterns.

Dynamic theories of personality development all along have been doing *conceptually* what we should have been doing more of. The "we" here refers to those of us addicted to systematic observation, quantification, rigorous rules of proof and inference, and all the proper trappings of an empirical science. But "we," admittedly, haven't been doing too well in our attempts to trace far-ranging genotypic continuities throughout the life span. Worse, many of us have turned to far simpler tasks, with the unhappy consequences for the state of the personality art that Adelson (1969) bemoaned earlier. Perhaps we should join with the dynamic theorist in his ambitious goal, share our quite different though compatible skills and data, and proceed nonetheless according to the canons of our discipline. We both clearly agree on all the tactical assumptions which have been discussed earlier, and continuity is certainly axiomatic for the dynamic approach. While it no doubt is too early to speak of marriage with dynamic personality theory, a long engagement, or at least a mutually stimulating flirtation, may be in order now.

ACKNOWLEDGMENT

Twenty years of work with the subjects and the data of the Berkeley Guidance Study, and with my colleagues on its research staff, must be responsible for whatever good sense is found in this chapter.

CHAPTER 6

Socialization and Sex-Role Development[1]

WALTER EMMERICH

EDUCATIONAL TESTING SERVICE
PRINCETON, NEW JERSEY

ABSTRACT

Recent secular trends have attenuated long-term continuities in sex-role socialization, but sex differences within age periods probably continue to be aspects of one or more ontogenetic series. Knowledge about sex-role development remains fragmentary at all age periods largely because underlying theoretical assumptions have not been satisfactorily incorporated into research designs. It is suggested that each theory of socialization can be translated into a distinct set of predictions for the several parameters of developmental trends in behavior (dependent variables) and for the impact of socializing influences (independent variables) upon these developmental trends. Certain concepts are suggested for sex-role measurement, including the competence-performance distinction. In illustrating these points, particular attention is given to psychodynamic and cognitive theories of sex-role identity, and to internalized normative structures as regulators of sex-role behaviors and development. Implications for a life-span developmental framework are discussed, including the issue of ontogenetic versus secular changes in sex roles, differences between early and later sex-role socialization, and the possibility that sex-role development is subordinated to other ontogenetic sequences during much of the life cycle.

[1]Preparation of this chapter was partially supported by the National Institute of Child Health and Human Development under Research Grant 1 PO1 HDO 1762 to Educational Testing Service. The study on gender constancy in disadvantaged preschool children was supported by Grant H-8256 from the Office of Child Development, United States Department of Health, Education, and Welfare.

123

I. Introduction

Socialization often is characterized as follows: (1) In order to carry out its functions, adult society is differentiated into networks of social structures; (2) socializing institutions and their agents prepare younger members of the society to assume adult statuses and roles; (3) as a result of socialization, the individual acquires (internalizes) psychological attributes needed to enter adult statuses and perform accompanying roles. While this formulation has generated useful research on sex-role development, there are reasons for believing that adult sex roles in modern society have neither the coherence nor permanence required to serve as specific targets of early socialization.

Allocations of complementary activities to different persons increases efficiency and order in social activity. These divisions of labor tend to become crystallized as enduring structures. For example, sex-role differentiation along instrumental-expressive lines is believed to have been a long-standing emphasis in structuring family life and work (D'Andrade, 1966; Holter, 1970; Parsons & Bales, 1955; Zelditch, 1955). In modern society, however, there is little reason to believe that efficiency and order in social life would be disrupted by role allocations in which traditional sex-role lines are gradually discarded. Indeed, a careful analysis of tasks associated with current marital, parental, and occupational roles probably would reveal that successful accomplishment in each is directly proportional to the incumbent's competencies in *both* instrumental and expressive functions (see Chapter 11 in this volume). Certainly the fact that a man or woman may be spouse, parent, and/or worker calls for flexibility rather than primacy with regard to the distribution of instrumental and expressive behaviors in adult life.

Recent secular trends indicate that traditional sex-role differentiations are in fact breaking down, especially in the areas of education and work (Holter, 1970; Neugarten & Moore, 1968; Seward & Williamson, 1970). Critical factors have been rapid technological change and its demands for increasingly high levels of technical mastery and associated interpersonal skills. Social movements such as Women's Liberation can be expected to accelerate societal redefinitions of traditional sex roles. Moreover, recent analyses of socialization during adulthood (Brim, 1966; Neugarten, 1968a; Riley, Foner, Hess, & Toby, 1969) suggest that certain adult statuses and roles form a temporally ordered series. The fact that adult status and role requirements are continually changing throughout adult life implies that earlier socialization cannot be linked directly to a delimited set of enduring structural end points.

Evidence that the long-term goals of early socialization are becoming less clearly differentiated by sex does not deny the existence of sex differences in behavior, nor the need to understand their origins and consequences. Researchers continue to maintain a lively interest in discovering behavioral sex differences and their determinants within all periods of human development.

But it can no longer be assumed that such differences reflect variations on a basic societal theme. Indeed, when resources allow, society seems more likely to foster sex-role equality through socialization practices and institutional arrangements that buffer rather than amplify empirically demonstrated behavioral differences between the sexes.

Of course, secular changes in sex roles are not all of one piece; rather, they selectively influence different aspects of sex-role behavior and do so differentially among subpopulations. Future theory and research in this area undoubtedly will consider gradients of change among sex-role processes, contents, and contexts, different patterns and rates of change among subgroups, how deeply these changes penetrate into earlier and later periods of the life cycle, and the nature of the social and psychological mechanisms used to cope with incongruities arising from differential rates of change in sex-role phenomena.

Secular changes can lead to mismatches between early sex-role socialization and later role requirements. To some extent, the potential for such *developmental discontinuities* has always existed; for example, sex-role norms are known to differ among social strata (Bronfenbrenner, 1967; Carlson, 1971; Hess, 1970; Holter, 1970), and therefore socially mobile individuals presumably have experienced developmental discontinuities in sex-role norms. Developmental mismatches arising from secular change probably are increasing in frequency and severity. For example, a girl's childhood experiences might be consistently and strongly supportive of traditional feminine activities and interpersonal behaviors, whereas her later life circumstances and/or opportunities call for more traditional masculine role behaviors. It would be useful to construct a discontinuity typology for each sex based upon kind of mismatch over time in terms of (1) prescriptions versus proscriptions, applied to (2) traditionally masculine versus feminine behaviors. Each kind of developmental discontinuity generated by this scheme could produce its own set of adjustment problems for each sex. These types could be further refined by including other bases for classifying temporal mismatches in socialization (Brim, 1966).

In this typology, sex-role distinctions are subordinated to the development of a broad range of competencies in both sexes. This shift in emphasis displaces but does not resolve complex problems in connecting early socialization to later role performances. For example, it is generally recognized that attempts to transmit later role requirements to young children can be successful in only the most rudimentary sense. Many competencies of value to adult society appear to be the end points of developmental sequences that cannot be greatly speeded up, and early phases of these sequences may have little direct value to the adult world, as many an exasperated parent can testify. For example, even assuming that society achieves complete sexual equality, adults may still need to respond with amusement rather than alarm when young children express less-than-equalitarian stage-related manifestations of sex typing.

If, as seems likely, sex differences in behavior continue to serve important social functions in the short run, then somewhat different patterns of sex differences would be expected to occur during each period of the life cycle. Within-period appraisals of behavioral sex differences and their determinants can help clarify the nature of these developmental tasks or phases, while between-period comparisons can provide insights on sequences and stages in human development. Since modern theories of socialization deal with these kinds of questions, the discussion now turns to a consideration of these theories.

II. Theories of Socialization

When an individual participates in a social structure, whether in action or fantasy, his behaviors are channeled into social roles. Processes which produce organized role behaviors are collectively known as *socializing influences,* and achievement of a reasonably stable match between a person's behaviors and role expectations is commonly accepted as at least a minimal sign of internalization.

Theories of socialization differ in how they conceptualize the organizing properties of socializing influences. (A comprehensive account of these differences is found in Chapter 2 of this volume.) A major division occurs between theories which attribute structural properties to the personality and those which locate organizing factors in the social environment. It is not yet clear whether this division arises from a fundamental indeterminacy in the subject matter of person–society relationships, or whether a genuine integration of the two approaches eventually will prove possible. What is clear, however, is that recent theories of socialization typically adopt one or the other of these perspectives (Goslin, 1969).

For example, social-learning theories (Bandura, 1969b; Mischel, 1970) emphasize the organizing properties of social contingencies, including patterns of reinforcement, verbal instruction, the behaviors of models, and the publicly observable consequences of the model's behaviors (vicarious learning). These theorists do not deny the existence of personality, but they do characterize persons and individual differences in the language of environmental organizers. Consequently, these theories view socialization as a process in which the individual's behaviors are selectively drawn toward situational (role) definitions through mechanisms of social learning and performance. At the other extreme on this issue are psychodynamic, trait, and cognitive–developmental theories. In cognitive–developmental theory, for example, social interactions are said to be organized by the cognitive processes that they engage (Kohlberg, 1966, 1969). The individual's general cognitive level shapes his social responses, including his definitions of the social situation; e.g., whether he centers on fragmentary aspects of actors' appearances and behaviors or upon their organized behaviors conceived as "roles." The influence of social factors is not denied, but their impact upon behavior is couched in the language of cognitive organizers. This approach views socialization as a process in which selected aspects of the social environment are incorporated into the individual's current mode of thinking and action through assimilation and accommodation.

Theories also differ on the issue of constancy versus change. The question here is whether socializing influences are believed to have essentially the same pattern throughout life or whether development is said to involve basic structural transformations. Theories that emphasize environmental organizers take one of three positions on this issue. Some approaches attend to broad societal forces and values which are believed to have a constant and cumulative impact upon behaviors. These theories assume, for example, that similar sex-role differentiations characterize many socializing contexts during childhood and adolescence, leading to internalizations that are congruent across social settings and developmental periods (Mussen, 1969). A second group of theories asserts that socialization occurs through participation in qualitatively different social structures that are sequentially ordered in development (Parsons & Bales, 1955). According to this view, sex roles become redefined as the individual participates in each socializing structure within the series. A third approach makes fewer assumptions concerning a master plan at the societal level, asserting that socialization produces either constancy or change, depending upon whether specific role requirements call for maintenance of earlier-formed behavior tendencies or for new patterns or behavior (Bandura, 1969b; Mischel, 1970).

Theories which emphasize organizing factors in the personality also differ on this issue of constancy versus change (Emmerich, 1966, 1968). Certain approaches assume that basic personality characteristics are formed relatively early, and that subsequent development consists of accommodations to changing life requirements rather than basic personality reorganizations (Kagan, 1969; LeVine, 1969). In this view, sex-role development after middle childhood involves surface transformations in the expression of deep personality structures. Other theories give greater weight to later formative stages, but even these approaches emphasize that early-formed personality characteristics influence how later stages in life are defined and worked through (Erikson, 1950; Havighurst, Neugarten, & Tobin, 1968; Neugarten, 1968b). Finally, certain theories emphasize sequential, stage-related changes in organizing structures which fundamentally alter the individual's social orientations and behaviors (Kohlberg, 1966, 1969; Loevinger, 1966). While such theories acknowledge that certain attributes are crystallized early in life, they also assert that these attributes are radically transformed in the course of development as they become incorporated into successively more complex hierarchical networks.

III. From Theory to Research

A. *Present Status*

The research literature on sex-role development has been extensively reviewed elsewhere (Biller, 1971; Kagan, 1964; Kohlberg, 1966; Lynn, 1969; Mischel, 1966, 1970; Mussen, 1969). These reviews typically have been position statements for one or another theory of socialization. One might expect, therefore, that a reviewer could provide a reasonably straightforward evaluation of each theorist's claims. For reasons that will be discussed shortly, however, much of the research literature on sex-role development is not well tuned to the task of evaluating the relative merits of theories of socialization.

This problem does not arise primarily from difficulties in operationalizing sex-role phenomena, nor from a paucity of empirical findings. To cite just a sample, research has considered such influences as cross-cultural variations (D'Andrade, 1966; Seward & Williamson, 1970; Whiting, 1963), social structure (Hess, 1970; Holter, 1970), family structure (Biller, 1971; Bronfenbrenner, 1967; Sutton-Smith & Rosenberg, 1970), parent–child relationships (Becker, 1964; Hetherington, 1967; Mischel, 1970; Sears, Rau, & Alpert, 1965), model characteristics (Bandura, 1969b; Mischel, 1970), and cognitive maturity (Kohlberg, 1966; Kohlberg & Zigler, 1967), and has related these and other factors to a variety of sex-role behaviors, including the following: sexual feelings, fantasies, and activities (Simon & Gagnon, 1969); sex-role perceptions, stereotypes, and knowledge (Dubin & Dubin, 1965; Hartley, 1960; Heise & Roberts, 1970; Kagan, 1964; Kohlberg, 1966; Mischel, 1966, 1970); sex typing of social behaviors (Mischel, 1970; Sears, Rau, & Alpert, 1965); preferences (Biller, 1971; Lynn, 1969); achievement standards (Stein, 1971; Stein & Smithells, 1969); social norms (Emmerich, Goldman, & Shore, 1971; Kohlberg, 1966); differential reinforcement by or imitation of male (or masculine) versus female (or feminine) models (Kohlberg, 1966; Mischel, 1970); differential parental imitation or identification (Hetherington, 1967; Heilbrun, 1965a, 1965b; Lynn, 1969; Kohlberg, 1966; Mischel, 1970); sex-typed cognitive abilities and styles (Maccoby, 1966; Witkin, 1969).

Of course, many sex-role phenomena remain to be examined in greater detail, including processes noted earlier in relation to current redefinitions of sex roles. Some relatively unexplored areas considered later in this chapter include sex-role identity, internalized normative belief systems as regulators of sex-role behaviors, and the systematic influence of context upon sex-role norms and behaviors. More critical, however, is the need to incorporate alternative theories of sex-role development into a common research framework. Such translations would not attempt to arrive at a synthesis of extant theories (such an effort seems premature at this time), but rather would sharpen and test differential theoretical predictions within a common body of developmental data. Since theories of socialization make assumptions about the nature of organizing processes extended through time, age comparisons based upon cross-sectional and/or longitudinal data become essential features of such a framework.

The search for organizing processes in sex-role socialization calls for research that relates theoretically derived independent variables to the several parameters of developmental trends in behavior. Specifically, attention needs to be given to all of the following: (1) developmental trends for each aspect of sex-role behavior; (2) developmental relationships among aspects of sex-role behavior, e.g., whether they develop independently, synchronously, or sequentially; (3) analyses of independent-variable influences as *moderators* of the several properties of developmental trends; (4) inclusion within the same study of multiple independent variables derived from *alternative* theories of socialization.

B. Parameters of Developmental Trends

Theories of socialization define their dependent variables in terms of developmental trends and therefore require translations of their assumptions into predictions for one or more properties of developmental trends (Emmerich, 1969b; Wohlwill, 1970a). The implication that properties of developmental trends in behavior reveal organizing factors in socialization does not violate the scientific canon of separating an effect from its cause. Theories of socialization assume that organizing factors can be measured independently of their traces in developmental behavioral trends, but they also make assumptions about how organizing processes "leave their mark" upon the same (or similar) behaviors extended over time.

To illustrate this point, consider the question of whether the boy's sex-role socialization is influenced by the father's absence from the home. Suppose matched samples of father-present and father-absent boys were studied, the latter having experienced no adult male residing in the home throughout early and middle childhood. Suppose further that a variety of sex-role behaviors were assessed at the age of four and expected differences were found between the groups. One might then be tempted to conclude that father-absence is a critical factor in the boy's sex-role development, supporting a theory of early environmental determination. This conclusion would be strengthened, of course, if similar differences occurred at later periods, especially if these differencs increased with age. On the other hand, if differences between the two groups later decreased and eventually disappeared, then one might infer that father-absence merely retards developmental trends which do not depend solely upon early environmental influences, calling for an alternative theoretical explanation.

While this example may appear to carry an obvious message, the fact remains that relatively few studies of sex-role socialization actually have measured the impact of hypothesized influences upon developmental trends in behavior.

Additional parameters of developmental trends are likely to have theoretical import. For example, theories attend to the issue of constancy versus change in the meaning of a behavior, determined by comparing its correlates within a developmental period with those in other developmental periods (Baltes & Nesselroade, 1973; Bronson, 1969; Emmerich, 1968). Other potentially important developmental properties include the behavior's stability correlations across age periods (Emmerich, 1968; Kagan, 1964; Kagan & Moss, 1962) and age changes in individual variability. Any or all of these developmental properties (and perhaps others) provide critical information for evaluating alternative theories of socialization. Indeed, verification of a particular theory for an aspect of sex-role development calls for simultaneous consideration of the theory's predictions for each parameter of the developmental trend. Derivation of each theory's distinct pattern of predictions makes feasible the testing of alternative assumptions within common developmental designs.

The most comprehensive analysis to date on developmental changes in sex-role processes is found in Kohlberg's (1966) discussion, well illustrating how developmental evidence is essential for evaluating the relative merits of theories of socialization. Kohlberg's cognitive–developmental theory postulates a number of age trends, including the following sequence for the boy's sex-role development during childhood: (1) formation of a sex-typed identity (gender identity); (2) expansion of sex-typed interests, attitudes, and values; (3) increased imitation of male figures including the father; (4) increased attachment to male figures including the father. Kohlberg contrasts this sequential order (and supporting evidence) with sequences posited by psychoanalytic and social learning accounts in which achievement of sex-typed identity is the final rather than the initial developmental phase during childhood.

Lynn's (1969) formulation explicitly distinguishes and incorporates each of the following variables into a set of over 30 hypotheses on sex roles: parental preference, sex-role preference, perceived parental similarity, perceived sex-role similarity, parental behavior adoption, sex-role adoption, parental identification, and sex-role identification. With certain exceptions Lynn's hypotheses do not refer explicitly to developmental trends as dependent variables, but his propositions might be amenable to such an analysis. Using similar concepts, Biller (1971) has suggested that sex-role orientation (e.g., gender identity) typically develops prior to sex-role preferences and adoption. Biller's discussion also suggests that a typology based upon the eight high–low combinations of these three attributes may fit an epigenetic model.

In contrasting adult with child socialization, Brim (1966) postulates a number of developmental changes in the personal attributes subject to socialization, including a shift from values to overt behaviors. Brim further distinguishes between knowledge, ability, and motivation as aspects of both values and behaviors, suggesting that the emphasis in socialization shifts developmentally from motivation to ability and knowledge. Implications of these hypotheses for sex-role development appear to be testable through developmental-trend analyses.

C. Nature of Correlational Evidence

It has become common practice to consider correlations among sex-role measures within age periods as evidence bearing on one or another theory of sex-role development (Kohlberg, 1966; Mischel, 1966, 1970; Sears, Rau, & Alpert, 1965). What are the theoretical implications of such correlational evidence in the light of the preceding discussion?

There is considerable evidence that sex-role measures do not intercorrelate to form a unified dimension of masculinity-femininity and that such correlational patterns differ among subpopulations (Hetherington, 1965; Kohlberg, 1966; Mischel, 1966, 1970; Mussen, 1969; Sears, Rau, & Alpert, 1965; Terman & Miles, 1936; Thompson & McCandless, 1970). Also, while measures of masculinity and femininity typically are constructed to yield large mean differences between the sexes, correlations of these scales with other variables raise questions about discriminant validity (Emmerich, 1971; Gray, 1957; Vroegh, 1968, 1971). Moreover, inspection of masculinity-femininity scales often reveals confounding with other processes (Kohlberg, 1966; Lansky & McKay, 1963; Mischel, 1966, 1970), because of such factors as instrument artifacts and response sets, failure to counterbalance for socially valued versus disvalued aspects of traditional sex roles, and difficulties in disentangling sex-role contents from other role contents, including age roles.

This evidence suggests that sex-role measures do not form a unified construct, even when technical shortcomings in measurement are discounted. The question remains, however, whether theories of socialization actually postulate the existence of such a construct. As a first example, consider the hypothesis that the social environment exerts a common influence upon a variety of sex-role behaviors across role settings and developmental periods, thereby producing increased conformity to cultural norms with increasing age. This theory does not predict unidimensionality among sex-role measures within age periods; rather, it is tested by determining whether mean levels for each sex-role measure gradually change and then level off in the course of development, and whether individual variabilities gradually decrease at successive age periods.

It is also questionable whether psychodynamic approaches assume unidimensionality among the behavioral components of sex roles. Psychodynamic theories distinguish between early-formed enduring *genotypes* (deep personality structures) and later age-specific *phenotypes* (surface behavioral characteristics). Socialization of sex roles is said to be a series of adjustments or compromises between external social requirements and internal dispositions, mediated by ego processes or defense mechanisms. Because these mediating processes are believed to be critical, even in young children, this approach assumes that a person's sex-role behaviors in a particular situation or his score on a scale of masculinity–femininity typically is a very weak sign of underlying dispositions, and that inferences from behavioral signs to deeper structures must take account of mediating processes.

With regard to trait formulations, it is true that a trait's existence is called into question when relevant items or scales fail to intercorrelate. However, the typical finding for sex-role measures is not total absence of intercorrelation, but rather correlational patterns indicative of multidimensionality and/or subpopulation differences in dimensionality. Neither of these outcomes is evidence against the utility of a trait approach (Baltes & Nesselroade, 1973; Emmerich, 1968). Indeed, trait theorists continue to disagree among themselves as to the dimensionality of both the cognitive and personality domains. Moreover, multidimensional theorists in the cognitive domain (Guilford, 1967) do not conclude that differentiated cognitive abilities in persons are "unstable" or "situation-specific" simply because they may be numerous. Likewise, evidence for multidimensionality of personality, even within the subdomain of sex-role behaviors, simply implies that sex-role characteristics form a differentiated set of traits.

D. Competence versus Performance

The competence and performance aspects of sex-role development might be fruitfully distinguished in ways analogous to current distinctions in the areas of linguistic and cognitive development (e.g., Flavell & Wohlwill, 1969). For example, Brim draws such a contrast when comparing child and adult socialization: "We can say, therefore, that the content acquired in adult socialization is not so much new material as it is the aggregation and synthesis of elements from a storehouse of already-learned responses, with perhaps the addition of several fragments that are newly learned when necessary to fill out the required social acts [Brim, 1966, p. 28]." In a less universal sense, psychodynamic theories make this kind of contrast when asserting that early-formed individual differences become elaborated in later development without losing their initial meanings.

The distinction between competence and performance also is applicable to the development of behaviors or processes within shorter time spans. For example, cognitive–developmental theory in the Piagetian tradition distinguishes between the presence of a cognitive operation in the individual's repertoire (competence) and its successful performance on a variety of tasks (Flavell & Wohlwill, 1969). Also, social learning theorists distinguish between acquisition (learning) of behavioral tendencies and their manifestations in varied settings (performance) and have applied this distinction both to long and short temporal spans (Ahammer, this volume; Bandura, 1969b; Mischel, 1970).

Thus, despite other important differences among theories of socialization, each, in its own way, seems to incorporate the competence-performance distinction. Explicit recognition of this state-of-affairs could give greater theoretical relevance to research on sex roles, as will be illustrated subsequently in this chapter.

E. Sex-Role Overlap versus Specialization

Current changes in sex roles make it increasingly appropriate for the sexes to behave in similar ways. Sex-role definitions used in the past often emphasized differences rather than similarities and can be seen in retrospect as caricatures of current sex roles. There is continual need to update operational definitions of sex-role phenomena and to validate them against current norms. For example, recent evidence suggests that sex-role overlap is considerable for masculinity-femininity judgments of children; studies have found that the same or similar behaviors indicative of social outgoingness or adjustment tend to be correlated with judgments of *masculinity* in boys and with judgments of *femininity* in girls (Emmerich, 1971; Vroegh, 1968, 1971).

Are there developmental changes in extent of sex-role overlap versus specialization? How do these developmental trends bear on the relative merits of theories of socialization? The evidence to date is unclear on these questions. To cite just a few examples, there is some evidence that sex-role specialization in interpersonal relationships increases with age during childhood (Emmerich, 1971; Vroegh, 1971). Similarly, sex-typed differentiations of certain achievement standards have been found to increase with age (Stein & Smithells, 1969), although there is also evidence that academic skills generally are conceived of as more feminine than masculine during middle childhood with a reversal of this difference during adolescence (Horner, 1969; Kagan, 1964; Maccoby, 1966). A sex difference in analytic style has been found to be maintained over time (Witkin, Goodenough, & Karp, 1967), although this difference may not occur at all periods of the life cycle (see Kogan's chapter in this volume).

Such developmental changes in extent (and direction) of sex-role specialization remain to be investigated in greater detail. It should also be noted that much depends upon how the competence-performance distinction is incorporated into operational definitions of sex roles. Greater overlap between the sexes can be expected for definitions emphasizing competence aspects of sex roles (minimal requirements for adaptive behavior) than for definitions emphasizing performance criteria (behaviors of high frequency, intensity, etc.).

IV. Sex-Role Identity

In order to illustrate more fully some of the issues raised above, two recent formulations of sex-role identity suggested by Kagan (1964) and by Kohlberg (1966) will be discussed. Both of these theories locate fundamental organizing processes in the person, but their differences with regard to other assumptions make these theories especially suitable for the present discussion.

A. Psychodynamic Formulation

Starting with the assumption that the child's understanding of sex-role behaviors in his society is reasonably well developed before adolescence, Kagan hypothesizes that such knowledge serves as a standard against which the individual evaluates himself and that individuals strive to enhance the belief that their own characteristics match this standard. It is further assumed that the degree to which an individual regards himself as meeting sex-role standards defines his sex-role identity. Sex-role identity is believed to be determined by differential identification with models, acquisition of sex-typed skills through social learning, and perceptions that others attribute sex-typed characteristics to the self. The theory also assumes that individual differences in traits associated with traditional sex roles (e.g., dependency, aggression, sex typing) are reasonably well formed by adolescence, but that their phenotypic expressions during later periods of development may change in accordance with their congruence with society's sex-role standards.

One might expect from this formulation that extent of possession of each sex-role attribute would be correlated with sex-role identity judgments, although not necessarily highly, and that these relationships would combine to produce a moderately high multiple correlation. However, there is little systematic evidence on these relationships. Moreover, Kagan emphasizes that integrity of sex-role identity is not directly proportional to extent of possession of sex-role attributes. Thus, the theory may not be testable using *performance* criteria which imply monotonicity between sex-role identity and number (and/or magnitudes) of sex-typed attributes. Perhaps the theory is better translated by assuming that identity judgments are of a more categorical nature and therefore depend upon self-perceptions reaching threshold values. For example, once the number and/or intensity of masculine cues about the self reaches some threshold, additional information that the self is ''masculine'' or ''feminine'' (or neither) may be nonmonotonically related to one's masculine identity.

In addition to fitting Kagan's definition, this translation in terms of competence has a number of other features which appear to be consistent with the theory's broader psychodynamic implications:

1. Two persons having the same sex-role identity could also exhibit very different *profiles* of sex-role behaviors.
2. This translation would be consistent with evidence that individual differences in sex-role identity tend to be stable over time despite qualitative and/or quantitative developmental changes in sex-role performances (Kagan, 1964; Kagan & Moss, 1962).
3. It provides a measurement operation consistent with Kagan's statement that sex-role identity "is but one component of a complex interlocking set of beliefs the individual holds about himself [1964, p. 144]."
4. This measurement operation is clearly distinguished from that signifying the salience of sex-role identity as an organizer in a hierarchical network of interlocking identities, whereas the usual performance measures confound a trait's strength with its salience in such a network (Emmerich, 1968).
5. This translation overcomes the legitimate objection that measures of sex typing, as assessed by performance criteria, are likely to be confounded with other personality variables; e.g., that very high "masculine" scores signify authoritarian attitudes or antisocial tendencies and that very high "feminine" scores signify maladaptive passivity or lack of "ego strength."
6. It also makes explicit the possibility that the same individual has *both* a masculine and a feminine identity (Carlson, 1971, 1972).

B. Cognitive–Developmental Theory

Kagan assumes that sex-role identity derives from sex-role attributes acquired during early and middle childhood through sex-typed identifications, reinforcements, and attributions by others. By contrast, Kohlberg's (1966) cognitive–developmental theory postulates that achievement of a stable cognitive judgment of gender identity provides an early and fundamental organizer upon which later sex-role development builds. In Kohlberg's view, this achievement depends upon the development of aspects of concrete operational thought which give constancy to object categorizations. A firm belief that one is a "boy" or a "girl" is thus distinguished from the child's abilities to identify and verbally label the sexes, abilities which generally are achieved by about the age of three (Kohlberg, 1966). While age-norm data are still fragmentary (De Vries, 1969; Kohlberg, 1966), it is believed that most children become reasonably certain of gender identity constancy by about the age of six or seven. Once firmly established, gender identity is postulated to usher in a new phase of sex-role development in which activities, attitudes, and values become increasingly and consistently sex typed by the child.

Gender identity constancy is assessed using procedures similar to Piagetian techniques for appraising the physical constancies and conservations (De Vries, 1969; Kohlberg, 1966; Shipman et al., 1971). For example, after presenting the child with a picture of a boy and labeling it as such, the examiner verbally and/or pictorially introduces a series of transformations that resemble the opposite sex. Constancy is signified when the child indicates that the standard stimulus remains a "boy" despite the changes suggested by the examiner, and when the child can provide verbal justifications for his choices indicative of gender identity constancy. Since it is known that children's understanding of traditional sex-role differences develops considerably earlier than knowledge of genital differences (Kohlberg, 1966), transformation items are chosen which refer to such attributes as motives (e.g., "If Johnny really wants to be a girl, can he be?"), traditionally sex-typed activities (e.g., "If Johnny played with dolls and did girl things, what would he be?"), and appearance (e.g., "If Johnny puts on girl clothes, what would he be?").

If a child totally lacks gender identity constancy, he probably will fail to give a constancy response, no matter how minor the transformation. And if the child has established a very firm gender identity, he is likely to give a constancy response for all transformations, at least of the type just illustrated. However, gender identity constancy is presumed to develop gradually during early and middle childhood, and so the child would be expected to exhibit a mixed pattern of "passes" and "fails" on gender constancy items throughout these periods. If this is so, then how can we know *when* the child has achieved a firm gender identity in the sense discussed by Kohlberg?

This question is part of the larger problem of detecting transitions from minimal competence to fully functioning performance on Piagetian tasks. A general model formulated by Flavell and Wohlwill (1969) deals with this question, and will serve as a basis for our discussion:

> Let us distinguish at the outset between two determinants of the child's performance in a cognitive task: A, the rules, structures, or "mental operations" embodied in the task, and B, the actual mechanisms required for processing the input and output. . . . We may now specify three parameters that jointly determine a child's performance: P_a, the probability that the operation will be functional in a given child; P_b, a coefficient applying to a given task or problem, and determining whether, given a functional operation, the information will be correctly coded and processed; and k, a parameter expressing the weight to be attached to the P_b factor in a given child. P_a and k are thus parameters characterizing a particular child at a given age level, while P_b characterizes a particular item or task [Flavell & Wohlwill, 1969, p. 98[2]].

In this model, the following equation gives the probability of a child's solving a particular task:

$$P\ (+)\ =\ P_a\ \times\ P_b^{\,1-k}$$

[2]In Elkind and Flavel (Eds.), *Studies in cognitive development: Essays in honor of Jean Piaget.* New York: Oxford University Press.

Flavell and Wohlwill use this formulation to describe four distinct phases in the development of a cognitive structure. In Phase 1, the operation is totally absent from the individual's repertoire; i.e., $P_a = .0$. Phase 2 is a transitional period when it can be said that the child "has" the operation at least to some degree, but cannot perform it consistently because of difficulties in processing related task requirements; i.e., P_a changes from .0 to 1.0 and k remains close to .0. Phase 3 is a period of consolidation when the operation clearly is functional but situational and/or information-processing factors still present obstacles to highly generalized performances; i.e., $P_a = 1.0$ and k changes from .0 to 1.0. The fourth and terminal phase occurs when the child is able to apply the operation successfully despite most situational and/or task-related complexities; i.e., $P_a = 1.0$ and $k = 1.0$.

With regard to correlations among tasks presumed to tap the same operation, Flavell and Wohlwill suggest that such correlations may be more unidimensional in structure (e.g., scalable in the Guttman sense) for a population during the period of consolidation (Phase 3) than during the transitional period (Phase 2). Of course, these intercorrelations will approach zero during Phases 1 and 4 because of the lack of individual-difference variance.

This model may be useful for detecting developmental phases in the formation of gender identity constancy. To illustrate, preliminary findings on a sample of economically disadvantaged children 3½–5 years of age will be reported (Shipman *et al.*, 1971). Each child was individually administered a ten-item task in which items were transformations of the kinds described earlier. There were two sets of five items each. The first set was administered using a girl stimulus as the standard with transformation stimuli depicting traditional "boy" characteristics; the second set used a boy stimulus as the standard with transformation stimuli depicting traditional "girl" characteristics. Responses indicating constancy were scored 1.0, those indicating lack of constancy were scored .0, and ambiguous responses were scored .5. If the child exhibited constancy on a particular item, he also was asked to give reasons for his response; however, the present findings are limited to the choice scores only.

Choice scores were summed for those subjects who gave scorable responses to at least four out of the five items in each set. This score was converted to a proportion based upon the child's total number of scorable responses. This proportion could vary from .0 (no constancy) to 1.0 (perfect constancy).

The results clearly indicated that these children were in an early phase. Proportion scores were highly and positively skewed, with a mean of .225 ($N = 1340$). Ninety percent of the children received a score less than .50, and no child achieved a perfect score.

The Flavell and Wohlwill model suggests that during Phase 2, empirical findings on the relative difficulties of items should correspond generally to independent judgments on relative item difficulties based upon an analysis of task requirements. However, item difficulty levels for the total sample were not clearly ranked as expected, and rankings varied considerably among subgroups for which summed item scores did not differ. Since stable item difficulty ranks could not be assigned, it can be inferred that most children had not yet reached this transitional phase. Moreover, it is during Phase 2 that success on this task should begin to correlate with independent measures of information-processing capacity. This expectation is based upon the assumption that such measures will be indexes of the parameter k in the model. In the present study, subjects were administered an extensive battery of information-processing tasks which were found to define a large general factor (Shipman *et al.*, 1971). However, these measures generally entered into very low correlations with the gender constancy task.

It can be concluded that these children generally were in Phase 1 and had not yet achieved competence on the gender identity task. The possibility remains, of course, that easier items might be developed that would reveal a greater degree of gender constancy in this population during this age period. But at least for the present items applied to this sample at this age, this analysis seems to resolve the question posed initially concerning detection of the kind of competence which Kohlberg postulates is critical for sex-role development.

Before leaving this topic, it should be noted that there was evidence for a clear *multidimensional* item structure. For example, one subscale consisted of four items in which the girl stimulus was the standard for transformations in activities and appearance, and a second subscale consisted of four (similar) items in which the boy stimulus was the standard. These two subscales were internally consistent but uncorrelated with each other. Moreover, these orthogonal measures each had different relationships with such factors as the child's sex, socioeconomic status, and race. For example, with sex and socioeconomic status (partially) controlled, black children had higher constancy scores than white children on the subscale just noted in which the boy stimulus was the standard ($p < .001$), but this race difference did not occur on the same subscale in which the girl stimulus was the standard.

Since most items entered into orthogonal subscales having differential experiential correlates, the findings suggest that fragmentary *pseudo-constancies* are formed during the preoperational period. These pseudo-constancies apparently reflect sex-role beliefs and attitudes formed by *associational* processes in response to environmental influences. For example, black children during this period may be especially resistant to the idea that a boy can become a girl by behaving or appearing like a girl because these children's social experiences have led them to respond negatively to "girlish" behaviors in boys. Of course, if Kohlberg's theorizing is correct, such association-based pseudo-constancies should be replaced by a cognitive reality judgment of gender identity constancy as the child develops concrete operational thinking.

Longitudinal follow-up data on these children at yearly intervals should reveal movement through the phases described by Flavell and Wohlwill. For example, it is expected that items will split off from their pseudo-constancy clusters and be replaced by moderately high correlations between items of similar difficulty and by scalability of items at different levels of difficulty. This shift in item structure would reflect the transition from Phase 1 to Phase 2. Interestingly, this transition may also be characterized by *decreasing* gender constancy on certain items now constituting the pseudo-constancy clusters, since these items were designed to be the most difficult ones for maintaining gender constancy on the basis of a cognitive reality judgment. Subsequently, as these children move well into Phases 2 and 3, scores on the total scale are expected to increase with age and to increasingly correlate with independently measured indexes of information-processing skills.

V. Development of Sex-Role Norms

All theories of socialization give importance to social norms as regulators of social behavior, although, again, theories vary in whether they emphasize normative aspects of social structures (Bandura, 1969b; Brim, 1966; Holter, 1970), motivational-affective factors in the individual which function as internalized controls over behavior (Aronfreed, 1969; Hoffman, 1970), or the child's natural tendencies to evaluate social experiences in moral terms (Kohlberg, 1966, 1969). Even when a distinction is made conceptually between sex-role behaviors (what people do) and sex-role norms (what they ought to do) (Brim, 1957), it is difficult to define the former without having at least implicit notions about the latter. Indeed, fundamental questions for developmental analysis concern when and how the child's descriptive and normative concepts become differentiated from one another. For example, there is evidence that children's conceptions of sex differences in social behavior are similar to their beliefs about what these differences ought to be, with both processes influenced by sex-typed favoring of the same sex (Emmerich, 1959, 1961; Emmerich, Goldman, & Shore, 1971). These findings suggest that the ability to disentangle descriptive and normative aspects of sex-role differences is a relatively late developmental achievement. Moreover, while relationships between the individual's normative concepts and behaviors are not yet clear (Hoffman, 1970), there are grounds for believing that children's responses to situational cues are mediated by normative concepts (Emmerich, Goldman, & Shore, 1971; Kohlberg, 1966, 1969). For this reason, it would be informative if naturalistic and experimental studies of sex-role processes were to include more explicit variations of norms, and were to measure the individual's normative interpretations of situations and of their own responses to these situations. Developmental-trend analyses of these mediating normative processes throughout the life cycle could greatly enhance our understanding of sex-role socialization.

A. Dyadic Sequences

Socialization often occurs within dyadic interaction sequences (Hartup & Lempers, this volume). Since both the child's and adult's "situation" change in meaning from one phase of interaction to the next, each phase may be governed by different motivational, cognitive, and normative processes (Aronfreed, 1969; Emmerich, 1969c; Hoffman, 1970). As an illustration of normative shifts, consider an interaction sequence in which the child persists in disobeying the parent. The child's disobedience first engages (1) a proscriptive norm, perhaps followed by (2) a norm governing parental *tolerance* of this kind of deviance. If and when the parent's tolerance threshold is exceeded, norms regulating applications of (3) discipline and/or more punitive sanctions will be applied. Each phase of a dyadic socialization sequence thus can provide a differentiated normative experience which may differ for the sexes.

With regard to the initial prescriptive–proscriptive phase, there is evidence that parents give priority to *common* (overlapping) behavioral norms relative to those associated with the child's sex status (Emmerich, 1969c; Stolz, 1967). For example, a sample of highly educated parents were found to value obedience, to disvalue aggression, and to take a relatively neutral stance toward interpersonal dependency in their preschool-age children irrespective of the child's (or parent's) sex status (Emmerich, 1969c). On the other hand, there is evidence that socializing agents differentially *tolerate* deviance from general norms depending upon the child's sex and kind of deviant behavior; e.g., interpersonal dependency generally is tolerated more in girls and aggression is tolerated more in boys (Bronfenbrenner, 1961a; Hatfield *et al.*, 1967; Kagan & Moss, 1962; Stolz, 1967). For this reason, there may be an especially close link between social norms regulating tolerated limits in expressing socially undesirable aspects of sex-role behaviors and the formation and maintenance of internal psychological controls. In this regard, it is also of interest that at older age periods individuals relax these controls somewhat and become more tolerant of tendencies in themselves which traditionally are associated with the opposite sex (Neugarten & Gutmann, 1968). This developmental shift appears to be greater in men than in women (Terman & Miles, 1936).

These phases in dyadic interaction differ in other ways that could influence normative concepts. In disciplinary situations, for example, negative affects (e.g., anger, distress) are likely to increase in both parent and child as the sequence moves from less to more highly charged phases, and these emotional changes could have important influences upon the norms associated with each phase (Hoffman, 1970). For example, later phases which arouse especially strong negative affects are likely to be accompanied by increasingly arbitrary, defensive, and face-saving normative justifications differing qualitatively as well as quantitatively from those which precede them. It seems likely, then, that each phase of a dyadic socialization sequence is governed by different norms, and that the norms regulating each phase have different implications for the development of sex differences in social behavior. Perhaps norms associated with each phase initially are assimilated by the child to global judgments of good and bad and only gradually become differentiated from one another in the course of development.

B. Situational Variations

Intraindividual variability in behavior across situations is a well-known fact of social life, and considerable attention has been given to the impact of variations in social structure upon sex-role norms and behaviors (Holter, 1970). Situational variations are clearly multidimensional in nature, based upon intersections of such classifications as sex and age. Within the family, for example, specialized sex-role norms commonly are believed to regulate husband–wife, father–son, father–daughter, mother–son, mother–daughter, and sibling relationships (Ahammer, this volume; Brim, 1957; Parsons & Bales, 1955; Sutton-Smith & Rosenberg, 1970). Contingencies between sex- and age-role classifications have been found at later as well as earlier periods of the life cycle (Neugarten & Gutmann, 1968), and may be especially important for understanding inter-generational relationships (Bengtson & Black, this volume; Riley et al., 1972).

There is evidence that the contingency between sex- and age-role norms shifts developmentally between childhood and adolescence. In a study by Emmerich, Goldman, and Shore (1971), internalized norms governing same-sex versus opposite-sex interpersonal relationships were found to be much more differentiated in relationships with peers than with parents during middle childhood. During this period, boys believe they should act more positively toward other boys than toward girls, and girls believe they should act more positively toward other girls than toward boys, but this sex-typed basis for normative differentiation failed to hold when fathers and mothers were the contrasted social objects. Moreover, during this period children believe they should act more positively toward parents than toward peers irrespective of the child's or parent's sex status. During middle childhood, then, sex-role norms apparently have primacy in governing interpersonal relations between the sexes within the child's generation, whereas age-role norms have primacy in governing relations between the generations irrespective of parent or child sex status. Both of these normative differentiations decrease during adolescence, when sex-typed favoring of same-sex peers decreases markedly (especially in boys) as does the tendency to apply higher standards of conduct in relationships with parents than in relationships with peers.

C. Multiple Reference Figures

If an individual's responses to a situation are at least partially determined by the differentiated normative concepts he brings to it, then his behavior is likely to be influenced by the nature of the match (or mismatch) that exists between his normative concepts and dominant norms in the situation. Certain analyses of identification, internalization, and conscience development have given special attention to processes which produce matches and mismatches between internalized and situational norms (Aronfreed, 1969; Hoffman, 1970; Kohlberg, 1969). Moreover, the individual's "inner voice" probably is differentiated into several perspectives, each arising from social experiences with different significant others or reference groups (Brim, 1965, 1966; Campbell, 1964; Hoffman, 1970; Shibutani, 1962). These different perspectives might draw upon relationships with reference figures from the individual's past, present, or anticipated future, in actual or fantasied relationships, and in kinds of roles that differ from those of the immediate situation.Therefore, the question of match is made even more complex by the possibility that alternative norms for responding to a given situation may be internalized by the individual.

There is evidence that children attribute different sex-role norms to various reference figures, that these attributions differ for the sexes, and that they are subject to developmental changes between childhood and adolescence (Emmerich, Goldman, & Shore, 1971). During middle childhood, boys believe that other boys more than parents (or girls) expect them to establish closer bonds with males than with females. Also, sex-typed norms which boys hold for their own behaviors during middle childhood are most similar to norms attributed to other boys. These differences in attributions decrease with development, however. Thus, there is a developmental change in boys from a highly sex-typed identification with other boys during middle childhood toward more equalitarian sex-role identifications with several reference figures during adolescence.

On the other hand, girls during middle childhood believe that parents and especially other girls (but not boys) expect them to establish closer bonds with females than males. During adolescence, however, there is a shift in the sex-role norms attributed to parents relative to other girls: During this period parents are seen as continuing to expect closer bonds with females than with males while girl peers are seen as decreasing this expectation. Also, the sex-role norms which girls hold for their own behaviors are most similar to those attributed to parents during middle childhood but become more similar to sex-role norms attributed to other girls during adolescence.

These findings reveal the importance of assessing attributions to a variety of reference figures when appraising the individual's sex-role identity and its development. Moreover, several of the developmental changes just cited were found to be moderated by the child's general cognitive level, suggesting that cognitive organizers influence attributions of sex-role norms to reference figures and accompanying developmental shifts in sex-role identity. This study also illustrates several general points emphasized throughout this chapter, including the importance of developmental-trend analyses for evaluating alternative hypotheses, treatment of independent variables as moderators of developmental trends in behavior, and the continued need to update and extend taxonomies of sex-role processes, contents, and contexts.

VI. Implications for a Life-Span Framework

A recurring issue in this and previous volumes of the series concerns the relationship between secular and ontogenetic factors in development (Goulet & Baltes, 1970; Nesselroade & Reese, 1973). This chapter has suggested that recent secular trends attenuate long-term continuities in sex-role socialization, while patterns of sex differences within age periods continue to be aspects of one or more ontogenetic series. The present view is that secular changes in adult sex roles have had only an indirect, and therefore moderate impact upon sex-role socialization at other periods of life. Alternatively, secular changes in norms governing adult sex roles may be diffused to all periods of the life cycle. This viewpoint, which attributes fundamental organizers to the environment, predicts that many ontogenetic changes in sex-role behavior will continue to occur only as long as diffusion of changed sex-role norms to all age-graded environments remains incomplete. Developmental methodologies that disentangle historical from ontogenetic factors should prove useful for evaluating these and other views on the relationship between secular and ontogenetic changes in sex roles (Baltes, 1968; Schaie, 1970; Wohlwill, 1970b).

A related question is whether different assumptions about organizing processes are needed to explain sex-role socialization at different periods, such as childhood versus adulthood. It is reasonably clear that distinct adaptive tasks become salient at different periods of life (Brim, 1966; Erikson, 1950; Neugarten, 1969), and these tasks are likely to have differential implications for the sexes. Nevertheless, other basic questions remain. Are adult responses to developmental tasks essentially different from the child's because adult personality is more crystallized? Are changes in behavior during adulthood less "structural" (Kohlberg, this volume) or "morphogenetic" (Flavell, 1970) than behavioral changes at earlier periods? This chapter has emphasized that such life-span questions can be resolved only by casting theoretical assumptions into differential predictions for the parameters of developmental trends over extended time periods.

Finally, sex roles may not be primary definers of socialization sequences. For example, formation of a firm sex-role identity is an important phenomenon of childhood, and yet this milestone's significance could arise from its placement in an ontogenetic series in which sex-role contents are secondary. A firm sex-role identity may be just one of many manifestations of a general cognitive stage (concrete operations) and/or simply one phase in a lifelong series of identity transformations in which categories other than sex status typically are more salient. A life-span framework thus alerts investigators to the likelihood that sex-role phenomena are subordinated to more fundamental organizing processes in personality development.

ACKNOWLEDGMENT

The author wishes to express his gratitude to Barbara Kirshenblut for her assistance in preparing this chapter.

CHAPTER 7

Creativity and Cognitive Style:
A Life-Span Perspective

NATHAN KOGAN

NEW SCHOOL FOR SOCIAL RESEARCH
NEW YORK, NEW YORK

ABSTRACT

Theory and research on creativity and cognitive styles are surveyed with particular emphasis upon their implications for life-span developmental psychology. Within the creativity domain, particular emphasis is given to the developmental aspects of the creativity-intelligence distinction. Problems of cross-age generality, the influence of the testing context as a function of age, the long-term stability of indexes of creative ability, and age and cohort-relevant aspects of creativity in "real-world" settings are considered. Attention is given to the issue of the usefulness of testing for creativity in adulthood when extrinsic behavioral criteria are generally available. The need for alternative predictive models for creative performance is discussed.

The similarities and differences between cognitive styles, on the one hand, and creativity and intelligence, on the other, are described. A threefold classification of cognitive styles is offered on the basis of distance from traditional ability indexes and inclusion of value judgments in defining alternative poles of the style dimension. Several cognitive styles are reviewed with particular attention to the methodological difficulties in drawing developmental inferences from cross-sectional data. Consideration is given to the developmental relevance of the style-capacity distinction. Finally, the developmental problems associated with the construction of real-world criteria for cognitive styles are discussed.

I. Introduction

The mission of this chapter is to examine from a life-span point of view two topical areas in psychology—creativity and cognitive styles—that have been the target of intensive programs of research over the past 25 years. It would be quite feasible, of course, to devote a separate full-length chapter to each. That I am willing to make an effort to encompass both in a single chapter of modest length necessarily implies that my intention is not that of a thoroughgoing review. Recently published systematic reviews are, in fact, available elsewhere for both areas—e.g., Wallach (1970) for creativity, and Kagan and Kogan (1970) for cognitive styles. My approach, in contrast, will be much less formal, and will offer an amalgam of theoretical speculation, methodological criticism, occasional new data, and extrapolations wherever possible to the enterprise of life-span developmental psychology.

There is no inherent logic to the grouping of creativity and cognitive styles within the confines of a single chapter. Theoretical and empirical linkages have been forged between the two, but the combination offered here simply reflects my closeness to the topical areas under consideration. It is also worth noting that my initial engagement with each of these topics was from the vantage point of cognitive, social, or personality psychology, rather than that of life-span developmental psychology. Almost always, however, the developmental issue would assume great salience. In due course, for example, one is forced to inquire whether phenomena or relationships observed in a sample of subjects of a relatively narrow age range possess stability and continuity across the life span. There are also times, of course, when one anticipates systematic variation in the phenomena of interest as a function of age. Such a developmental perspective brought to bear on the constructs of creativity and cognitive style does not necessarily imply a genuine life-span orientation. As we shall see, such an orientation has characterized but a small portion of the published research in the domains under consideration in the present chapter. There are very few investigations that employ a common set of psychological constructs across a broad age range while employing methods that permit the examination of both ontogenetic and generational change (e.g., Baltes, 1968; Baltes & Nesselroade, 1970; Schaie, 1970).

II. Creativity

A. Definition: Performance, Personality, and Process

It is difficult to imagine a discussion of creativity across the life span that does not start with reference to Lehman's (1953) definitive study of *Age and Achievement*. If one chooses to restrict the creativity construct to the performance of those notable individuals who in the past have made enduring contributions to the arts, humanities, and sciences, Lehman's pioneering work represents the major effort in the field. One may question some of the interpretations offered by Lehman, as Dennis (1956, 1958) has done. Lehman (1960) has effectively responded to these criticisms, however. On balance, it seems highly probable that *Age and Achievement* will continue to stand as the authoritative work on the issue of quantity and quality of publicly recognized creative achievement over the life span.

Lehman's principal finding is that major creative achievements occur relatively early in an individual's productive career—somewhere between the twenties and forties, depending upon field of endeavor. Though incidence of achievement may continue at a relatively high level for many years thereafter before declining in advanced age, these later achievements are generally recognized to be less outstanding and significant than work produced earlier. Where quantity of output alone is at issue, Dennis (1966) has shown that maximal output, in fact, occurs at ages greater than that indicated for highest quality achievement in the research of Lehman. Dennis also reports considerable variation across fields in the degree to which productivity declines with advanced age.

In current parlance, the approach of Lehman and Dennis to the study of creativity can be called product-centered. They have examined the productivity across the life span of the major creative figures in Western civilization over the past few centuries. These investigations demonstrate the value of historical data for genuine life-span developmental research.

We next consider two other orientations to the domain of creativity. One of these is a personality-centered approach in which specific individuals in a particular field of endeavor (e.g., architecture, painting, mathematics) deemed most creative by their peers are subjected to intensive psychological assessments in the interest of uncovering the possible motivational and cognitive bases of the so-called creative personality. Much of this research has been conducted at the Institute of Personality Assessment and Research (located at the University of California, Berkeley) under the general direction of MacKinnon (e.g., 1962) and Barron (e.g., 1963). Developmental concerns have not been the central focus of this research, though it should be noted that retrospective questions about parents and child-rearing experiences have generally been included in the assessment battery.

A third approach to creativity is process-centered. Here, the principal question concerns the kinds of thinking processes presumed essential to current or future generation of creative products. Since a substantial portion of this research has employed children as subjects, the validity issue, i.e., the link between creativity test scores and creative performance in the "real world," often has had to be held in abeyance. The process-centered approach to creativity received its major impetus from Guilford's (e.g., 1967) work on the development of divergent-thinking tests. These constituted a set of cognitive tests that did not demand a single correct answer from the respondent, but rather required that he generate a variety of appropriate alternative answers. The latter in turn can be scored for number (fluency), number of categories (spontaneous flexibility), unusualness or uniqueness of response, and quality (originality) of response. The last of these may well reflect a combination of the unusualness and appropriateness (''good fit'') of the subject's response.

B. Creativity and Intelligence Assessment

As research on divergent-thinking tests progressed during the 1950s and 1960s, attention eventually turned to the issue of whether the proliferation of these new open-ended tests was in fact yielding information of a character different from that produced by the older tests of intelligence. Unless it could be shown that the alleged measures of creative ability clustered together and that each was relatively independent of IQ indexes, there was little point in advancing a new construct of creativity distinct from the older construct of general intellective ability.

Thorndike (1963) and Wallach and Kogan (1965) took a critical look at the published literature available through the early 1960s, and essentially concluded that a genuine statistical separation between creativity and intelligence had not been achieved. Subsequently, Wallach and Kogan, working with fifth-grade children, were able to effect such a statistical separation by operationally defining creativity (at the level of test performance) in strictly associative terms, and by removing the test-like property employed in the typical creativity assessment. The associational definition of creativity was consistent both with prior theoretical statements (Koestler, 1964; Mednick, 1962), and with introspective, autobiographical accounts of the thought processes of recognized creative individuals (Ghiselin, 1955).

The decision to depart from the standard test-like assessment with its emphasis upon time limits, group administrations, and evaluational stress toward a more relaxed, nonevaluative, game-like assessment context stemmed in part from earlier theoretical (Mednick, 1962) and empirical (Christensen, Guilford, & Wilson, 1957) work indicating that uncommon ideas occur later in a sequence of verbal responses (see Ward, 1969, however, for negative evidence). Hence, it seemed reasonable to allow subjects as much time as they wished for responding to an item. It is the author's contention that the two modifications described—tasks of a homogeneous associative character and individual game-like assessment—accomplished the goals of generating a set of open-ended tasks that would cohere as a creativity cluster and remain independent of the domain of general intelligence.

C. Age Generality of the Creativity–Intelligence Distinction

Though the Wallach–Kogan research represented the first definitive demonstration that divergent and convergent thinking abilities were separate entities in empirical fact as well as in theory and measurement operations, that research nevertheless, has spawned a multitude of further issues, some of genuine developmental significance. The most obvious developmental question concerns the degree to which the creativity–intelligence distinction obtained by Wallach and Kogan for 10–11-year-old fifth-grade children (and subsequently replicated by Pankove and Kogan [1968] in children of the same age) can be generalized to younger and older subjects.

Relevant empirical evidence is now available for children of nursery school age (Williams & Fleming, 1969), children of kindergarten age (Ward, 1968), 7- and 8-year-old first and second graders (Ward, 1968), high-school seniors (Wallach & Wing, 1969), and college students (Cropley & Maslany, 1969). Regrettably, there is no published evidence on the creativity–intelligence distinction for individuals beyond the age level of the early twenties. Starting with this age period, however, and descending to 4-year-old nursery-school children, the correlations between the Wallach–Kogan creativity cluster and age-appropriate measures of intelligence have been consistently nonsignificant and have hovered around zero. It should also be noted that the consistency of the relationship across age groups has not been completely confined to middle-class subjects, for the magnitude of the correlation remained neligible in a sample of black, disadvantaged fifth-grade children (Ward, Kogan, & Pankove, 1972). The task for the future, nevertheless, is the examination of the generality of the creativity–intelligence distinction into the period of middle and old age.

Regrettably, virtually all of the test-oriented creativity research on older subjects has been preoccupied with the issue of performance decline. Consider the research reported by Bromley (e.g. 1967), for example. Using the Shaw and Vygotsky tests, Bromley remarks that "rational responses . . . are highly correlated with intelligence and, . . reflect creativity [p. 33]." This is a truly astonishing statement, implying that one can study one kind of thinking process with tasks that also reflect a very different type of thinking process. For Bromley, each test employed could be "regarded as an operational measure of creativity (inventiveness) since each test was 'open-ended' and required the S to produce progressively more ingenious responses [p. 33]." This would imply that any test with a divergent structure is a face-valid measure of creativity. The issue of discriminant validity—the degree to which these tests measure something different from general intelligence—is ignored by Bromley. Further post-hoc justification for the two tests employed—both of which involved the sorting of blocks along such physical dimensions as color, shape, height, and width—is the evidence that the declines with age in uncommon responses on those tests mirror the declines in quality of achievements in Lehman's sample of recognized creative individuals. There is no doubt of a formal similarity here, but such analogical leaps from the test performance of average individuals to the real-world achievements of the major creative figures in the Western cultural heritage certainly can be considered premature in terms of our present state of knowledge.

Though published under the title of "Age and the Rigidities," Chown's (1961) article is quite relevant to the concerns of the present chapter. Included in Chown's battery of measures were several tests of *spontaneous flexibility*. This refers to the number of categories generated to open-ended tests of divergent thinking, a score that tends to correlate quite highly with sheer number of responses *(ideational fluency)*. Whereas the tests of spontaneous flexibility did not load significantly on an age factor (in a sample with an age range of 20 to 82), all of the foregoing tests loaded moderately on a *g* factor, suggesting that a sharp creativity–intelligence distinction was not obtained. Separate factor analyses for young, middle-aged and old subjects paralleled the outcomes reported here for the sample as a whole, though it should be noted that the *g* loadings of the spontaneous-flexibility measures were highest for the young subjects, intermediate for the old subjects, and lowest for the middle-aged group.

In the author's view, it is quite premature to talk about declines in creative ability over the life span when the various tests employed to assess that construct are saturated with *g*. Whatever declines have been observed (and all have involved cross-sectional data) may simply represent a by-product of decline in other intellective functions. Even if age decrements in creative ability were found with intelligence statistically controlled, consideration would have to be given to the possibility that the observed differences reflect cohort or generational effects rather than ontogenetic change. Through the use of combined cross-sectional and longitudinal analyses, Nesselroade, Schaie, and Baltes (1972) have shown how apparent age declines in a dimension possibly relevant to creativity—cognitive flexibility—must rather be interpreted in terms of cohort differences.

D. Testing Context: Developmental Interactions

It will be recalled that the Wallach and Kogan research cited earlier placed much emphasis on the importance of a relaxed, nonevaluative assessment of ideational productivity, if a separation from general intelligence is be achieved. Not surprisingly, a number of investigators have actually tested the Wallach–Kogan hypothesis by administering the identical creativity tasks under evaluative and nonevaluative conditions. Wallach (1971) has reviewed this evidence and concluded that a permissive context is not really necessary to bring about a separation of creativity from intelligence, provided that the former is confined to measures of ideational fluency (e.g., the Wallach–Kogan tasks). The issue does not seem to be closed, however, for correlational differences have been found (e.g., Boersma & O'Bryan, 1968; Kogan & Morgan, 1969; Nicholls, 1971). It is worth noting that evaluative and permissive conditions can be contrasted in terms of several attributes—group versus individual administration; unlimited versus restricted amounts of time; test-like versus game-like (or neutral) description of task; typical institutional versus atypical or home setting for completing tasks; authoritative, demanding versus relaxed, supportive examiner. One or more of these contrasts have been employed in every relevant study, but studies have varied in the number and choice of contrasts employed. No doubt this has contributed to the mixed outcomes reported.

It is in the course of deciding the most appropriate assessment context to employ that one is forced to enter the developmental arena. A permissive context for one age group may be a threatening context for another age group. Correspondingly, a typical evaluational context for one age group may be quite benign for some other age group. To illustrate these points, consider the supportive examiner individually administering a set of educational games without time limits to a ten-year-old child. Such an assessment context is quite credible to a child of that age. The identical assessment context for a 15-year-old adolescent would be greeted with skepticism, and would probably be accompanied by an effort to uncover the "deception" being practiced. In similar fashion, the anxiety-generating power of a test-like context for fifth-grade children would essentially be lost on nursery-school children for whom such evaluations have little meaning in personal experience. The foregoing examples imply that interactions between age and the context of test administration will be the rule rather than the exception.

In the period from nursery school through kindergarten, for example, the contrast between permissive and evaluative contexts should not be especially salient, for the use of tests for evaluative purposes has not yet begun in a serious form. When convergent-thinking (the Peabody Picture Vocabulary Test) and divergent-thinking (the Wallach–Kogan tasks) measures were administered under permissive or evaluative conditions to nursery school children by Williams and Fleming (1969), context proved to be of little importance. The creativity–intelligence separation was obtained in both cases. In sharp contrast to the Williams and Fleming results, Nicholls (1971), working with children 10 to 11 years of age, found substantial differences in correlations between intelligence and divergent thinking when the latter was measured under test-like or game-like conditions. These correlations were negligible and nonsignificant for game-like divergent thinking, and were of moderate magnitude (.32 to .48) and consistently significant for test-like divergent thinking. Comparable correlational differences in 10–11 year olds have been reported by Boersma and O'Bryan (1968). Wallach (1971), on the other hand, has cited other researches that do not report correlational differences as a function of testing context, despite the use of subjects sufficiently advanced in age to comprehend permissive-evaluational difference. None of these studies, however, have employed permissive and evaluational procedures with the same subjects in the fashion of Nicholls, whose work represents the best-designed study in the area to date. It should be noted, finally, that all of the foregoing studies on the effects of testing context owe a considerable debt to the ideas of Campbell and Fiske (1959) concerning multitrait-multimethod matrices.

One of the reasons for the emphasis placed upon context of assessment in the foregoing paragraphs is the growing recognition that such context effects may be especially important where older individuals are under study. Welford (1958), among others, has suggested that elderly subjects react poorly under time pressure, are highly sensitive to the evaluational implications of tests and experimental procedures, and often manifest symptoms of withdrawal from assessment situations. In other words, the elderly often exhibit the characteristics of test-taking anxiety and defensiveness that, in fact, led to Wallach and Kogan's efforts to rid creativity assessment of its evaluational component by turning the tasks into nontimed games.

We presently do not know what the "optimal" context would be for the assessment of divergent thinking in elderly subjects, but conceivably it would be one that involves untimed conditions, the elimination of evaluational pressures, and the examiner adopting a supportive, encouraging manner. Whether such an "optimal" context would in fact yield divergent-thinking scores unrelated to conventional intelligence indexes remains moot in the absence of relevant empirical data on samples of elderly individuals. It is worthy of note, however, that self-pacing and increased time of exposure to stimulus materials in learning experiments (an "optimal" context for the elderly?) did result in improved performance for aged subjects (e.g., Arenberg, 1965; Eisdorfer, 1965.)

No reference has been made thus far to age differences in *level* of ideational productivity and uniqueness. The reason for this omission is that such levels are highly dependent on task and contextual factors. Task factors are apparent in the difference between the verbal and figural procedures in the Wallach–Kogan battery. The verbal tasks seem to yield larger age discrepancies than do tasks of the same associative form using figural stimulus material. For example, the mean productivity difference between the Wallach–Kogan middle-class fifth graders and the Wallach–Wing (1969) college freshmen favored the latter, but the discrepancy was very much larger for verbal than figural items. More critical than the verbal–figural distinction is the indication that ideational productivity is remarkably sensitive to the context of assessment. The most obvious contrast would involve the administration of divergent-thinking tasks under strict time limits, as opposed to administration with unlimited time. The outcome of such a comparison would hardly be in doubt.

More interesting is the evidence that significant differences in ideational productivity and uniqueness emerge as a function of assessment conditions even when the time factor is held constant. Test-like versus game-like conditions yield mean differences in ideational productivity, uniqueness, spontaneous flexibility, and even in response content (Kogan & Morgan, 1969; Nicholls, 1971). There are also strong indications that the level of ideational productivity can be strikingly altered by such simple devices as providing an example item with 10 imaginative responses listed (Hudson, 1968), having subjects role play creative models such as an uninhibited artist (Hudson, 1968; Wild, 1965), by experimenter reinforcement of more original responses (e.g., Levy, 1968; Maltzman, 1960), and by provision of monetary incentives (Ward, Kogan, & Pankove, 1972). Hudson (1968) even reports that the level of ideational fluency in a particular sample reached an unexpected high when he inadvertently acted in a surly, aggressive manner in his role as test administrator.

None of the foregoing outcomes necessarily implies that divergent thinking is completely at the mercy of motivational and situational determinants. Indeed, the research indicates that the mean level of ideational productivity can be systematically raised or lowered by diverse situational manipulations, but the ordering of individuals on that dimension remains constant. An example of this empirical generalization is provided by the outcomes of the Ward, Kogan, and Pankove (1972) study of elementary school children. Note in Figure 1 that the slopes of the regression lines for control and experimental groups are essentially identical, whereas the intercepts diverge. In other words, both

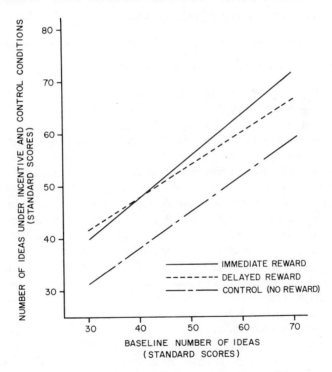

Fig. 1. Regression of incentive performance on baseline creativity.

immediate and delayed monetary rewards for generating responses raised ideational productivity levels to a comparable extent, without in any way disturbing
the rank ordering of the children. In sum, we do seem to be dealing with
individual differences on a capacity dimension.

The implications of the research described for developmental study are quite
discouraging, however. Earlier, we observed that procedurally identical testing
contexts may have quite different meanings across diverse age groups. How
then can one make meaningful age comparisons in mean level of ideational
productivity? Perhaps, it would be necessary to conduct parametric studies in
various age groups to discover the optimal method for enhancing ideational
productivity, subsequent age comparisons then being based on the optimal method
for each age group. Such a proposal for the domain of intellective abilities
has recently been advanced by Furry and Baltes (1973 in press). Those authors
have shown how a fatiguing pretest experience as well as the location of a
particular subtest in a test battery can differentially affect the performance of
children, adults, and elderly individuals. In short, the lack of situational invariance
complicates the interpretation of cross-sectional age comparisons of intelligence.
Furry and Baltes recommend a strategy of "testing the limits" (Schmidt, 1970)
in order to determine what constitutes the optimal assessment context for various
age groups.

E. Long-Term Stability of Associative Creativity

Thus far, the discussion has been confined to developmental trends based
on cross-sectional evidence indicating that the creativity-intelligence separation
remains intact from approximately age 4 to 21. Is there any longitudinal evidence
that can be brought to bear on this issue? Recently, Kogan and Pankove (1972),
working with a sample of children initially tested (individually) in the 5th grade,
were able to retest (either under individual or group administration) the 62.5%
of the original sample who remained in the same school systems 5 years later in
the 10th grade. Regrettably, a simple answer to the question of 5-year stability
was not possible since it depended both on the sex of the subject and the 10th
grade testing context. Marked stability was observed for males under group administration in the case of both ideational productivity and uniqueness. For girls,
in the same testing context, on the other hand, the stability coefficients were
negligible. In the context of individual administration with the examiner and
subject always of the same sex, both boys and girls manifested moderate consistency over the 5-year period.

A speculative interpretation of these results is advanced in Kogan and Pankove
(1972) based on the possible differential impact of impersonal and personal assessment contexts on males and females. At the same time, the need for additional
longitudinal and experimental data on divergent thinking was clearly recognized

as necessary to resolve some of the evident ambiguities and complexities in the Kogan–Pankove pattern of outcomes. Also of interest in the Kogan–Pankove findings is the evidence that creativity and intelligence, which were unrelated for both sexes at fifth-grade level, remained unrelated for girls 5 years later. For boys, on the other hand, the correlations at 10th grade turned positive and significant. The latter outcome represents a striking deviation from cross-sectional results, and no obvious explanation for the discrepancy can be advanced. It is interesting, however, to apply the cross-lagged panel correlational technique (e.g., Rozelle & Campbell, 1969) to the results for males. This suggests that earlier level of IQ is contributing to changes in later level of ideational productivity and uniqueness, rather than the earlier creativity level contributing to shifts in later IQ level.

F. Developmental Changes in Real-World Criteria of Creativity

Developmental change is not confined to the issue of creativity tests and assessment context. The next logical step is to consider similar developmental phenomena in the extrinsic validity (concurrent and predictive) of the creativity dimension. Creativity test scores are essential for purposes of construct validation, but at the same time, we should like to know whether such scores can be used as signs or predictors of important behaviors or accomplishments in the real world. Of particular interest is the question of ontogenetic and cohort-related changes in delineating the concurrent and predictive validity of the creativity dimension. It is quite reasonable to assume that different external criteria of creativity may be appropriate for different age and cohort groups.

Consider first the ontogenetic aspect, starting with children of elementary school age and younger. Although it is possible at this age to ask teachers to rate children for creativity on the basis of classroom behaviors and products, the interjudge reliability of such ratings and their differentiation from conventional intelligence indexes has been thrown into question (e.g., Holland, 1959; Piers, Daniels, & Quackenbush, 1960). More recently, Biggs, Fitzgerald, and Atkinson (1971) have maintained that teachers are capable of differentiating children on the basis of their convergent versus divergent thinking styles. Examination of their data, however, does not yield a single rating characteristic exclusively differentiating children high and low on divergent thinking ability. Wherever such differentiation was observed, a similar differentiation occurred for the children low and high on convergent ability. In short, there is reason to doubt that a creativity criterion can be found at the elementary school level that is more "real" than the performance on divergent-thinking tasks as such.

By junior high school age, the student has had the opportunity to develop a set of leisure-time interests which might conceivably serve as tentative creativity criteria. The student can also be asked to produce literary products that are scorable for imaginativeness of ideas. Vernon (1971) recently examined the correlations of divergent-thinking measures administered under test- and game-like conditions with the foregoing external criteria. The trend in the correlations clearly favored the greater concurrent validity of the divergent-thinking tasks administered under relaxed conditions. Higher correlations were observed for such criteria as "rated creativity of an autobiography," "creativity of a 'draw-a-man procedure'," and "artistic leisure-time interests." In no case was a significantly higher validity coefficient obtained for divergent thinking assessed under test-like conditions.

Beginning in secondary school and proceeding through college, highly meaningful external criteria of creativity become available. At this level, we can discern the development of interests and talents that are not directly connected to classroom learning. The student can engage in a variety of private and organized activities in such diverse domains as science, writing, painting, acting, and composing. He can also assume leadership roles in various groups and can contribute to social service activities. All of the foregoing were examined in a sample of high school seniors (admitted to Duke University) by Wallach and Wing (1969). Rates of participation and accomplishments for the activities listed were significantly discriminated by level of ideational productivity and uniqueness, but not by score on the College Board's Scholastic Aptitude Test. It should be further noted that the significant associations between the divergent-thinking measures, on the one hand, and the activities and accomplishments, on the other, were largely confined to domains in which novel products were required (e.g., art, writing, and science). Associations failed to hold for dramatic and musical activities, which, at the secondary school level, are likely to be more interpretive than creative.

Proceeding beyond college and university training into the period of occupational careers, the most meaningful external criteria of creativity become available. It is at this point that we have come full circle to once again touch base with Lehman (1953, 1960). Of course, Lehman was largely concerned with creativity in the past. By concentrating on individuals no longer living, a complete record of accomplishment—quantitative and qualitative—was guaranteed. Works of high quality must withstand the test of time, and hence, the sheer passage of time contributes to the accuracy of a quality assessment.

If our research is to be contemporary rather than historical, however, assessments of real-life performance will clearly have to be made before a complete biographical record is available. The research carried out at the Institute of Personality Assessment and Research (Barron, MacKinnon, Helson, and others) suggests the presence of a reasonable consensus within current professional groups (e.g., architects, artists, mathematicians) as to those deemed most highly creative. Though such requirements may not stand the test of time in Lehman's sense, they may well be the best we can do if contemporary real-world based creativity research is to proceed.

It is quite a different matter to start with mature individuals deemed creative while working backwards toward possible antecedents than to work forward from a set of creativity test scores to the future incidence of talented activities and accomplishments. The latter poses many more difficulties in regard to the criterion problem. The graduates of our colleges and universities (those for whom we have information on creativity test performance and extracurricular accomplishments) will distribute themselves across a diversity of occupational endeavors. Where the choice of field entails the production of publicly accessible outputs (e.g., scientific or literary articles, art works, patented inventions), we can count the incidence of such products and attempt to evaluate their quality. But what are we to do with those individuals who become practicing lawyers, physicians, accountants, or teachers? Does the mere choice of such an occupation automatically place their incumbents at the zero point of a creativity scale? If these individuals are excluded from consideration in predictive validity studies, for example, the problem of sample attrition would become quite serious. We shall have to deal with the fact that the base rates for genuine real-world creativity are going to be extremely low.

Most of the previous discussion is not directly applicable to the period beyond middle age. In many instances, the onset of old age becomes associated with occupational retirement. What criterion of creativity shall one employ at this time? Conceivably, such a criterion might have more to do with constructive use of leisure time than with persistence in prior occupational activities. If there is any basis to this reasoning, it is the individual with cultivated talents and interests beyond his immediate occupation who can be considered to best fulfill an hypothetical creativity criterion in advanced age. Is it feasible that somewhere in the life span, a switch in emphasis from depth (specialization) to breadth must be made to insure a creative old age? Or does it make more sense to confine the creativity label to the activities and products of young adulthood and middle age, the elderly individual to be considered as still manifesting creativity only to the extent that he continues to engage in such activities and to turn out such products? From this latter perspective, creativity and retirement are truly incompatible. To adopt the alternative view opens the possibility of equating creativity with successful aging, an extension that is so broad and general as to raise questions about the utility of the creativity concept in old age.

Thus far, we have concentrated on likely age-linked effects. A word about cohort or generational differences is now in order. Lehman (1960) makes reference to changing publication practices across generations. A century ago, scientific publication was almost exclusively in the interest of communication of research findings. As incidence of publication has become tied to academic promotion and tenure, however, publication practices have changed quite dramatically for the cohort of scientists completing their graduate training after World War II.

At the present time, we are witnessing a reaction against the publish-or-perish syndrome, with university administrators placing a higher premium on teaching competence. With such a revised reward structure in the academic community, we may well witness another change in the publication practices of that cohort of scientists completing their graduate training within the last 3 years.

Cohort effects may also play a differential role across disciplinary fields. The various sciences have experienced creative and fallow periods. Those cohort groups whose peak productive years coincide with an innovative surge in the field will obviously have a greater opportunity for creative accomplishment. In those fields undergoing frequent rapid change in substance or style, apparent age-based declines in creativity may be nothing more than the periodic regular emergence of different cohorts representing the "new wave."

G. Research Recommendations and Conclusions

The previous discussion has demonstrated how developmental considerations are relevant to the assessment of creative ability and to the evaluation of its extrinsic validity. The nature of the creativity domain virtually appears to demand a life-span perspective. Whether creativity is assessed by means of cognitive tasks or various real-world accomplishments, we must clearly shape our experimental conditions and measurements to the requirements of diverse age and cohort groups.

In addition to issues of assessment, however, a life-span approach forces a consideration of the most appropriate research questions and strategies for generating new knowledge in the creativity domain. For example, talented activities and accomplishments of students in schools, colleges, and universities can be treated as *ultimate* or *intermediate* criteria of creativity. The latter can be defended more readily, since creativity in its purest form is associated with accomplishments in one's chosen occupation or profession. From that point of view, creativity could best be assessed somewhere in the period of middle age. If one adopts this perspective, the activities and accomplishments examined by Wallach and Wing, for example, could be viewed as predictors of subsequent occupational accomplishments in adults. Where the latter constitute the ultimate criterion, one might expect secondary school and college accomplishments to yield better predictions than would a battery of divergent-thinking measures. The latter, after all, are less direct than the intermediate criteria of secondary-school accomplishments. On this basis, one can seriously question the value of administering divergent-thinking tasks beyond the secondary school years. As soon as indexes of talented activities and accomplishments become available, it does make sense to use them as predictors of later creative work. Given the strong commitment of many researchers in developmental psychology to cognitive testing across the life span, however, the consequences of a research strategy questioning the utility of such testing in young adulthood and beyond are very serious indeed.

The problem of prediction is bound to be complicated by the fact that there are likely to be both continuities and discontinuities within a life-span perspective. Consider the depth versus breadth issue, for example. At the level of secondary school and college, students may try their hand at a number of activities, or they may focus intensively on one activity that consumes their interest. Since creativity in adulthood is generally linked to occupational activity, one might expect a single-minded talent in adolescence to form the basis for subsequent occupational choice and performance. Hence, predictability might be best in such a case. A typical example might be the Westinghouse science prize winner in secondary school who chooses a scientific career and eventually contributes to the growth of knowledge in his field. In other areas (the humanities and social sciences, for example), the paths toward adult creativity may be considerably more circuitous with the consequence that the prediction problem becomes quite complex. Along with the assessment of cognitive performances, the inclusion of both motivational and environmental components might well be necessary. Baltes and Nesselroade (1973) have recently discussed the need for both organismic and environmental assessments within a life-span developmental framework.

Some recent research by Kogan and Pankove (1972) is illustrative of one possible approach to the prediction problem just discussed. In that study, the prediction of extracurricular accomplishments in secondary school from assessments of intellective and creative ability in elementary school was found to be quite substantial in a small school system, but negligible in a large school system. The outcomes were consistent with Barker and Gump's (1964) observations of large and small high schools. Within the large school, however, separate analyses for low and high anxious subjects revealed substantial predictability for the former sub-sample and little predictability for the latter. In short, both environmental and motivational contingencies *moderated* the link between cognitive performances in the creativity domain and real-world accomplishments. Elsewhere (Kogan & Wallach, 1961b, 1964), the kinds of analyses described have been discussed under the heading of "moderator variables." The major advantages and disadvantages of the foregoing methodological approach have recently been outlined by Alker (1972) and Bem (1972) in response to Mischel's (1968) criticism of personality trait theories. Of particular importance from the perspective of life-span research in creativity is the indication that simple linear models underlying correlational and regression analysis may not be sufficient to do justice to the complexity of the problem. We must be prepared to expect possible curvilinear effects, and our analytic models will have to do justice to age- and cohort-based organism–environment interactions.

Implicit in much of the foregoing discussion is an essential tension between two disparate orientations or strategies in conducting creativity research. One

is more pragmatic and practical, an orientation that insists upon linking performance on tests and experimental tasks to the ongoing life of the individual.
Thinking processes are of importance only to the extent that they have real-life
consequences. The alternative research strategy is more conceptual and
theoretical. It questions the need to force linkages between fundamental thinking
processes and external behavioral criteria, when the former are not yet thoroughly
understood. The two orientations are not mutually incompatible, of course,
and there is an obvious place for both in a life-span developmental psychology.
The foregoing discussion has tried to encompass both, though it is entirely
possible that the pragmatic side has been emphasized. If so, this bias will undergo
forcible correction in the following section on cognitive styles, an area where
fundamental research has run far ahead of practical application.

III. Cognitive Styles

A. Definition and Conceptual Distinctions
from Creativity and Intelligence

A discussion of the historical origins of the construct of cognitive style would
be no less than a history of cognitive psychology. Obviously, such an effort
is not possible within the confines of the present chapter. Some of the theoretical
antecedents of cognitive styles are discussed in Kagan and Kogan (1970). That
chapter, as well as the chapter by Kogan (1971), treat the various cognitive styles
in considerable detail, but with particular emphasis upon the period of childhood
and possible implications for educational practice. The latter contribution also
offers a definition of cognitive styles, quoted here:

> Cognitive styles can be most directly defined as individual variations in *modes* of perceiving,
> remembering, and thinking, or as distinctive ways of apprehending, storing, transforming,
> and utilizing information. It may be noted that *abilities* also involve the foregoing properties,
> but a difference in emphasis should be noted: Abilities concern level of skill—the more
> and less of performance—whereas cognitive styles give greater weight to the *manner*
> and *form* of cognition [Kogan, 1971, p. 244[1]].

The foregoing definition points to the nature of the distinction between cognitive
styles, on the one hand, and intelligence and creativity, on the other. It is
important to note, however, that these distinctions apply more in principle than
in practice. Where the intellective abilities are concerned, there is no ambiguity
whatsoever. Whether one's preferred theory of intelligence stresses a *g* factor
or orthogonal multiple primary abilities, the measurement dimensions at issue
extend from a high (or accurate) level of performance, at one extreme, to a
low (or inaccurate) level of performance, at the other. In the case of the creative

[1]In Lesser (Ed.), *Psychology and educational practice.* Glenview, Ill.: Scott Foresman. © 1971
by Scott Foresman.

abilities as well, better versus poorer (though not necessarily accurate versus inaccurate) performance can be distinguished. Research in the latter domain received its impetus from Guilford's delineation of the divergent-thinking abilities within a "structure-of-intellect" model. Indeed, Guilford explicitly subsumes the creative abilities within a theory of intelligence. Unlike the latter, however, creativity (as distinguished from the creative abilities) has been endowed with qualities that extend beyond sheer cognitive skill.

Where the cognitive styles are at issue, a threefold classification is possible in terms of their respective distance from the construct of ability as considered previously. First, there are styles whose assessment is, in fact, based on accuracy versus inaccuracy of performance. Indeed, the term *style* employed to designate such performance may be something of a misnomer. Nevertheless, the style label has struck to the construct, possibly because their principal investigators have worked within a developmental- and/or personality-cognition tradition rather than having emerged from a background of psychometric study of abilities. Typical of the foregoing cognitive styles are field dependence–independence (Witkin, Lewis, Hertzman, Machover, Meissner, & Wapner, 1954; Witkin, Dyk, Faterson, Goodenough, & Karp, 1962) and constricted–flexible control (Gardner, Holzman, Klein, Linton, & Spence, 1959; Klein, 1954). Definition and discussion of the foregoing constructs will be offered later in this chapter.

The second type of cognitive style involves assessment procedures whose underlying dimension cannot be characterized in terms of veridicality of performance. Yet, a value distinction is imposed upon the dimension, such that performance at one extreme is considered superior to performance at the other. In the formal respect of this approach, such styles are not fundamentally different from certain of the creative abilities distinguished by Guilford. Ideational fluency, for example, does not concern veridicality, yet the generation of a large number of responses is deemed superior to lower levels of response output. In the cognitive-style domain, Kagan, Moss, and Sigel (1960, 1963) employing grouping and sorting tasks, observed individual variation in the degree of preference for analytic and non-analytic categorizations. Though the former in no sense represents more accurate performance than the latter, the investigators, nevertheless, placed greater value upon an analytic style. More detailed consideration of the foregoing stylistic dimension will be offered later in this chapter.

Finally, there are those cognitive styles where matters of veridicality are irrelevant and where no value judgments are placed upon the kinds of performances derived from the tasks employed to assess the style at issue. These are the cognitive styles that are most purely stylistic. By virtue of that quality, they are most remote from the conventional conceptualizations of the ability domain. Illustrative of such a style is *breadth of categorization* (e.g., Pettigrew, 1958)—the setting of broad or narrow category limits when provided with a measure of central tendency for a category. It should be observed, of course, that the absence of veridicality or other value considerations is *intrinsic* to the initial conceptualization and operationalization of the style at issue. As construct validation proceeds and extrinsic correlates are examined, it is entirely feasible that an initially value-free cognitive style will assimilate value properties which will render it formally indistinguishable from the second type of style just described.

B. General Developmental Considerations

Given the conference emphasis, and given the previously published discussions of cognitive styles in children, it would be preferable to concentrate on the adult period and to introduce the research on children only insofar as it contributes to a genuine life-span perspective. This is not simply accomplished, for the bulk of the developmentally-oriented research on cognitive styles concerns the age period prior to young adulthood. Where elderly subjects are concerned, one draws a virtual blank. One looks in vain for *cognitive styles* in the index to Botwinick's book on *Cognitive Processes in Maturity and Old Age* (1967); nor does one find this listing in the index to the Goulet and Baltes (1970) volume based on the first West Virginia Conference on Life-Span Developmental Psychology. The absence of any mention of the cognitive-style construct in the books mentioned does not mean that relevant research has not been performed. The chapter by Comalli (1970) in the Goulet–Baltes book is very much concerned with cognitive styles, though the term as such is not employed.

With reference to the threefold classification of cognitive styles discussed earlier, one finds great variation in the availability of long-term developmental data. The great bulk of published data on individuals across the life span concerns the first class of cognitive style described—those manifestly closest to the ability domain. There is a very considerable decline in the amount of relevant published data for the second class of cognitive styles discussed—those with inherent value properties that are not focused on veridicality. Finally, genuine developmental data are extremely scarce for cognitive styles of the third class—those without apparent value connotations. It should be observed that the differential availability of life-span data across the three classes of cognitive styles distinguished merely reflects the overall magnitude of the research effort within each of the three.

The large majority of life-span relevant studies in the domain of cognitive styles feature cross-sectional data. As we shall presently observe, the penchant of most investigators in this area of research has entailed the interpretation of age differences in ontogenetic rather than cohort–generational terms. Since the research designs employed do not truly permit such unequivocal interpretation, it will become evident that most of the relevant research is seriously flawed. Though the description of these studies in subsequent pages may seem somewhat critical in tone, the author has attempted as much as possible to avoid a deprecating fault-finding perspective. Rather, in this author's view, relevant prior research can best be conceived of as a necessary preliminary effort toward bringing a life-span perspective to bear on cognitive styles preparatory to more methodologically elegant research in the future.

In subsequent sections, the empirical evidence on cognitive styles will be presented and discussed with particular emphasis on life-span developmental implications. Not all of the cognitive styles have been examined from a life-span perspective, however. Such styles will receive minimal consideration in the chapter. The author's intent is selective rather than exhaustive.

C. Age Comparisons for Selected Cognitive Styles

1. Constricted versus Flexible Control

Klein (1954) coined the term ''constructed versus flexible control'' to describe individual differences in susceptibility to distraction and cognitive interference in tasks containing conflicting cues. Though several procedures have been employed to assess that cognitive style (see Gardner, et al., 1959), the Stroop (1935) Color–Word Interference Test has become the favored standard instrument. Further, it represents the measure of the cognitive style for which life-span data exist (Comalli, Wapner, & Werner, 1962).

The Stroop test has three sections—reading of color words, naming of colors in a series of patches, and naming the colors in which color words are printed (e.g., the word orange printed in green ink). It is the last of these that provides an index of susceptibility to interference. The amount of time required to accomplish the three tasks constitutes the critical variable of interest. Since the present style is concerned with the maintenance of accurate performance under conditions of interference, it clearly belongs to the first type of cognitive style described earlier.

Cross-sectional data presented by Comalli et al., (1962) for the three sections of the Stroop test across the life span clearly show a U-shaped pattern, with children and elderly individuals similar to each other and different from young and middle-aged adults. Further, the slope of the conflicting-cue section of the Stroop is enhanced at the age extremes, indicating that young children and elderly subjects are most susceptible to interference. Though Comalli et al. note that the similarity in achievement of children and elderly subjects does not imply similarity of process, they nevertheless do not offer any interpretation beyond the broad Wernerian categories of progression and regression via differentiation and hierarchic integration, on the one hand, and dedifferentiation and dehierarchization, on the other. Explanation at that level of abstraction does not particularly help in understanding what may actually be going on. Since no controls for cohort differences in education were built into the research design, the strong possibility exists that the observed age differences can be explained on those grounds alone.

Two further studies are less vulnerable to the foregoing criticism. Comalli (1965) compared 65–80 and 80–90-year-old men of approximately equal educational level, and found significantly greater interference in the latter group. Comalli, Krus, and Wapner (1965), in a comparison of institutionalized aged subjects and elderly individuals residing in the community, obtained significantly greater time scores in the former sample on all three sections of the Stroop. This latter set of results rules out any interpretation based on a specific difference in susceptibility to interference.

Objections can also be raised against the Comalli study comparing the 65–80 and 80–90-year-old samples. Though the time scores on the interference section of the Stroop represented the only significant difference between the age groups, the time differences on the other two sections of the test, though falling somewhat short of significance, were clearly in the same direction as the interference scores. The appropriate analytic technique, the one employed by Gardner *et al.* (1959) and others working in the area of cognitive styles, employs regression methods. Since reading speed for color words and/or speed of naming colors are generally correlated with the interference score, one or both should be statistically regressed out of the latter. Such regressed scores represent that portion of the variance attributable solely to interference, and clearly those scores should be used in making life-span comparisons. Comalli and his co-workers have failed to employ these essential regression techniques, and hence the large majority of the age and other differences examined may well represent the operation of the straightforward speed factor, rather than interference as such.

In sum, the foregoing research points to the pessimistic conclusion that life-span data on the Stroop test are not informative in regard to developmental trends in a cognitive style of constricted-flexible control. All of the published work cited can be more readily assimilated to the tradition of research on developmental changes in response speed (see Birren, 1964, Chapter 5).

2. Field Independence–Dependence

Consider next the relevant evidence for the cognitive style of field independence–dependence. The style is most often defined on the basis of the capacity to overcome an embedding context. Three basic measures of the style have been developed. On the Embedded Figures Test (EFT), superior performance requires the rapid location of an element embedded in a geometrically complex figure. The Rod-and-Frame Test (RFT) is an alternative index of the same style, and, in the present case, field independence requires more accurate adjustment of a luminous rod to the true vertical when it is suspended within a tilted frame in a completely dark room. Finally, in the third and least often employed measure of the style—the Body Adjustment Test (BAT)—the subject's task is to adjust his body to the true vertical following rotation of the chamber in which he has been sitting to a non-upright position. In the research of the Witkin group, a composite index based on the three named procedures is often employed. Field indenpendence–dependence fits the first class of cognitive style delineated earlier; field dependence implies poorer performance on all three indexes described.

Extensive cross-sectional data on field independence–dependence across the life span have been reported by Comalli (1965) and Schwartz and Karp (1967). In addition, longitudinal data for two samples, one tested at ages 8 and 13 and the other tested at ages 10, 14, 17, and 24, are described in a study by Witkin et al. (1967). The latter authors also report cross-sectional data for the age periods just cited.

Consider first the results obtained over the period extending from preadolescence to young adulthood. Stability coefficients reported by Witkin et al. for both longitudinal groups were significant and substantial with the coefficients ranging from .48 to .92. Clearly, an individual's relative standing on the Witkin dimension does not change much over the considerable time period under study. Such consistencies are especially impressive in the light of the many developmental tasks that individuals have to master as they pass from preadolescence to early and late adolescence, and into young adulthood (e.g., puberty, reduced dependence on the family, career decisions, and, occasionally, marriage and the birth of children).

It is important to note that the stability just described is interindividual across the age span studied. The subject's standing relative to his age cohort remains highly constant. At the same time, intraindividual change is very much in evidence. Mean levels of field independence rise, reaching a peak at age 17 with little change through age 24. In their cross-sectional data, Witkin et al. obtained a consistent decline across the three independence–dependence indexes (BAT, RFT, and EFT) between ages 17 and 21. As in the case of the intelligence domain (e.g., Baltes, 1968; Schaie, 1965, 1970), cross-sectional data in the area of cognitive styles can evidently be misleading in respect to developmental change. Witkin et al. attribute the discrepancy between the longitudinal and cross-sectional data to special cohort characteristics of their 21-year-old cross-sectional sample.

Given the discrepancies observed for subjects in their early twenties between cross-sectional and longitudinal outcomes, one is somewhat taken aback to find cross-sectional differences over the life span that are directly attributed to developmental processes. Data reported in Comalli (1970) for the various Witkin indexes have a distinct U-shaped form. The performance of children and aged subjects are similar, and both differ from young adults on the various perceptual tasks employed. These curvilinear trends are then interpreted from the perspective of Werner (1948, 1957) as indicative of progressive and regressive age changes over the life span.

It is entirely possible that the life span can be characterized along the lines of the original Werner formulation, but the available published outcomes do not readily permit such interpretation. More parsimonious explanations associated with cohort differences are easily advanced for the declines observed. In the Schwartz and Karp (1967) investigation, for example, the three age groups employed—17, 30–39, and 58–82—differed substantially in educational level, occupation, and country of birth. Examination of mean levels for the three age groups on the BAT, RFT, and EFT indicates a uniform increase in field dependence with increasing age, with the latter inversely related to level of education.

That education rather than age constitutes the major determinant of the observed differences is suggested by the uniformly greater field dependence of the 30–39 relative to the 17-year-old group. The former group, after all, is in the prime of adulthood, and hence their deficit very likely can be attributed to their educational disadvantage. The research of Granick and Friedman (1967) should be mentioned at this juncture. Significant negative correlations between age and performance on an extensive battery of perceptual tests turned nonsignificant in about 30% of the cases with education partialled out. Birren and Morrison (1961) report similar effects on the WAIS.

Less open to criticism are studies by Karp (1967) and Comalli, et al. (1965) in which comparisons were drawn between different types of elderly subjects. In the Karp work, the distinction concerned retired versus employed individuals of the same age. Comalli et al. compared institutionalized elderly subjects with a sample of the same age living in the community. Quite regrettably, the two studies produced inconsistent results. Karp obtained significant differences on the Gottschaldt and EFT Tests. Comalli et al. found no significant differences where perception of verticality was the measure employed. The contradiction between the studies becomes less prominent when we observe that the Comalli et al. contrasting samples were reasonably matched for years of education, whereas the Karp groups were simply matched for age. Hence, the greater field independence of the employed relative to the retired groups in the Karp work may again be reflecting a difference in educational level.

Variables associated with education and other demographic dimensions are not the only ones that require consideration when making developmental comparisons of cognitive styles. Though Witkin and his associates have steadfastly maintained that field independence is related only to those forms of intelligence that are analytic in nature—the Picture Completion, Block Design, and Object Assembly subtests of the WISC, for example—the embarrassing truth of the matter is that various investigators have found significant relations between the Witkin indexes, on the one hand, and measures of verbal, mathematical, and spatial skills, on the other. Kogan (1971) has reviewed this evidence. In the context of cross-sectional age comparisons, it is imperative that these annoying relationships be statistically controlled, so that we can have reasonable confidence that demographically matched subjects are in fact being compared on a cognitive style dimension, and not on a *g* factor of intelligence.

In sum, the published evidence on the field independence–dependence dimension is rather discouraging from the point of view of drawing firm conclusions concerning age versus cohort effects within a life-span perspective. The difficulty in distinguishing between these two kinds of effects is well illustrated in the domain of sex differences. Consider the disappearance of a sex difference in older subjects in the Schwartz and Karp (1967) research. One finds a parallel for the absence of such sex differences in children younger than 8 years of age (Goodenough & Eagle, 1963; Maccoby, Dowley, Hagen, & Degerman, 1965). Sex differences in field independence appear to be maximal between the upper elementary grades and the last year of high school—a period when sex role differentiation may well be maximal. Although it is beyond the scope of this chapter to discuss the diverse interpretations of the causal basis for sex differences in field dependence (see Kagan & Kogan, 1970, for a detailed analysis), it might nevertheless prove instructive to conjecture whether the disappearance of the sex difference in the Schwartz and Karp data represents a cognitive analogue of a trend toward sex role dedifferentiation in advanced age. At first blush, such trends, if proved replicable in future research, would appear to have an ontogenetic basis. Given contemporary cultural pressures toward the reduction of sex-role typing from early childhood through adulthood, however, the age-linked sex differences consistently observed in previous research on field independence–dependence may well prove to be a generational cohort-specific phenomenon.

3. Categorizing and Conceptualizing Styles

These have generally been assessed by means of sorting tests. Most of the life-span oriented research has employed three-dimensional geometric figures varying in such physical attributes as color, form, height, and width. The Weigl, Shaw, and Vygotsky tests are typical specimens. Thaler (1956) used the Weigl Color Form Test as a measure of abstractness–concreteness and concluded that older subjects were more concrete than younger subjects. Bromley (1967) employed the Shaw and Vygotsky tests, from which he inferred that older subjects were less "creative" than younger subjects. Both of the foregoing studies, in short, employed the sorting procedure to make quality distinctions between older and younger persons.

Stimulus materials for sorting tests do not have to consist solely of geometric forms, however. Gardner (1953) employed a sorting procedure consisting of a diverse assortment of everyday objects, the subject being instructed to group them on the basis of the most comfortable number of categories. This score, initially labeled "equivalence range" by Gardner, was subsequently relabeled "conceptual differentiation" (Gardner & Schoen, 1962). The latter provides an excellent illustration of a cognitive style initially conceptualized in strictly value-free terms (the third type of style cited earlier) but subsequently endowed with value properties on the basis of construct validational research. The present dimension would now have to be placed among those styles incorporating value distinctions not based on veridicality (the second type of style described previously).

Generality of this cognitive style across diverse stimulus materials—objects, photos, behavior statements, and attitude statements—has been demonstrated by Gardner and Schoen and by Glixman (1965). Individuals high in conceptual differentiation (i.e., form many groupings with few items per group) are described by Gardner and Moriarty (1968) as having a more constricted, literal, and stereotyped orientation. On the TAT, such subjects do not stray far from the physical properties of the pictures.

Cross-sectional data on children between the ages of 9 and 13 point to decreasing conceptual differentiation over that particular age span (Gardner and Moriarty, 1968). Such findings are consistent with other evidence (e.g., Bruner, et al., 1966; Vygotsky, 1962) indicating a clear progression from childhood to adulthood in the deemphasis of differences and the emphasis on similarity-based synthesis. The recognition of differences can proceed on a strictly perceptual basis; the recognition of similarities generally entails higher-order abstraction and the availability of superordinate terms.

Kogan (1973) administered Gardner's object-sorting test to samples of college students (ages 18–22) and well-educated older people (ages 62–85) residing in the community. Instead of using 50 actual objects, pictures of the objects were employed. Subjects were requested to group the objects into the most comfortable number of categories. As the first row of Table 1 indicates, old–young comparisons for females yielded a highly significant difference, older women manifesting lower levels of conceptual differentiation (i.e., form fewer groupings). The direction of the age difference was the same for males, but was decidedly nonsignificant. Of course, the foregoing research suffers from the liabilities of the cross-sectional design, but the outcomes nevertheless indicate that samples of older individuals of approximately the same educational level as younger samples do not necessarily revert to childlike modes of cognitive functioning. There is no indication in the data that older individuals shift in the direction of a "differences" as opposed to a "similarities" orientation. Indeed, the latter actually appears to be accentuated in the sample of older subjects employed relative to the performance of young adults.

In addition to a count of number of groupings formed, the object-sorting procedure permits the examiner to elicit from the subject the bases on which the various groupings were formed. In contrast to scoring methods (Kennedy & Kates, 1964; Rapaport, Gill, & Shafer, 1945) that emphasize quality distinc-

TABLE 1

Comparisons of Younger and Older Adults on Categorizing and Conceptualizing Styles[a]

	Young males (N = 63)		Old males (N = 76)			Young females (N = 137)		Old females (N = 92)		
	M	SD	M	SD	t	M	SD	M	SD	t
Conceptual differentiation (no. of groups)	9.9	2.9	9.3	3.4	1.19	10.9	2.8	9.4	2.7	3.95**
% Categorical–inferential	81.1	20.2	71.1	25.5	2.57*	80.2	17.3	74.5	24.3	1.96
% Analytic–descriptive	5.3	13.5	3.6	12.4	0.78	5.6	11.8	0.6	2.7	4.76**
% Relational–thematic	13.1	16.6	25.0	24.0	3.44**	12.8	12.5	24.5	23.5	4.37**

[a]Note: Percentages do not total 100 because of a small fraction of unclassifiable responses.
*$p < .02$.
**$p < .001$.

tions in reasons for grouping objects together, Kagan *et al.* (1960) proposed a more value free system—one that appears more compatible with a stylistic as opposed to an ability perspective. A threefold distinction for conceptual classifications is offered. Analytic–descriptive concepts are those in which grouping takes place on the basis of some objective attribute of the stimuli that all share (e.g., all have handles). Categorical–inferential concepts reflect groupings in which objects are treated as whole entities, each object constituting an exemplar of the concept in question (e.g., kitchen utensils). Finally, relational–thematic concepts imply the presence of functional relationships among the objects in a group, with each object thereby deriving its meaning from its link to the other members of that group (e.g., comb, brush, and mirror are grouped because all are implicated in the act of grooming one's hair). As in the case of the previous cognitive style discussed—conceptual differentiation—the initially value-free formulation of Kagan *et al.* (1960) changed into a value position in subsequent publications by those authors (cited in the next paragraph).

Are there developmental trends in the utilization of the three kinds of conceptual classifications described? Kagan and Kogan (1970) have summarized the evidence for the preadolescent period. With a triads procedure in which pictures could be paired on an analytic–descriptive, categorical–inferential, or relational–thematic basis (Kagan *et al.*, 1963), comparisons of children ranging in age from 6 to 11 indicate a progressive increase in the use of the descriptive–analytic classification and a concomitant decline in preference for relational–thematic bases for pairing. Kagan *et al.* (1963) explain these age trends in terms of the greater obviousness of the relational–thematic grouping and the greater subtlety of the analytic–descriptive pairing.

The foregoing explanation suggests that the nature of the stimulus array will be a powerful determinant of age-related preferences for the three kinds of conceptual classifications described. If words rather than pictures are used (Bruner *et al.*, 1966), subjects (6 to 19 years of age) being asked to state the similarity among eight words presented successively, analytic bases for linking the words together decline and superordinate categories increase. The foregoing authors also employed an array of pictures of 42 familiar objects for grouping by categories, and they found that analytic concepts decrease and relational–thematic concepts increase with age in a sample of boys 6 to 12 years old.

The Kagan *et al.* scoring scheme was also applied to the samples of college students and elderly individuals studied by Kogan (1973) and reported in Table 1. Some striking age differences result. (Categorical–inferential groupings predominate (about three-fourths of the total) for both age groups, but are more common for younger males and females relative to older males and females. Analytic–descriptive groupings are infrequent (less than 10% of the total) for all subjects, but are much rarer in old than in young females. The direction of the age difference is the same for males, but falls quite short of significance.

Consistent for both males and females is a striking age difference in the incidence of relational–thematic groupings. They occur about twice as often in the older subjects and the difference is highly significant for both males and females. These various statistical tests are not completely independent, of course, and hence it is the patterning of conceptual classifications across the younger and older subjects that is of primary interest. In the present object-sorting procedure, it is the relational–thematic groupings that are the more subtle. Their generation requires a more freewheeling and imaginative approach to the stimulus materials presented. As we have seen, the older individuals of the present study were more willing to depart from the conventional abstract–conceptual groupings to try their hand at something a bit more adventurous.

How can one explain the striking discrepancy between these findings and the previously discussed outcomes of the Bromley (1967) investigation? Again, the nature of the stimulus materials employed would seem to be crucial. Both of the tests employed by Bromley were comprised exclusively of geometric forms. Successive classifications of such materials must necessarily proceed along abstract–conceptual lines, and, it will be recalled, younger subjects manage to generate a wider diversity of such groupings. Where the stimulus materials are composed of everyday objects, in contrast, there is likely to be a rich associative repertoire linked to each of the objects with the result that the interlacing of these repertoires can produce a diversity of unusual combinations. To the extent that one holds to an associative conceptualization of creativity, the performance of the older subjects on the object-sorting procedure has a distinctively "creative" quality. To the extent, however, that one holds to the view that meaning is a complicating factor in this type of research and hence, prefers to use stimulus materials virtually stripped of meaning, the liabilities of the older individual will assuredly become quite prominent.

4. Reflection–Impulsivity

In a monograph published several years ago by Kagan, Rosman, Day, Albert, and Phillips (1964), a distinction was drawn between a reflective as opposed to an impulsive style of processing stimulus information. In matching-to-sample tasks with response uncertainty, reflective subjects pursued a strategy of carefully scanning all variants before venturing a response; hence, they were both slower and made fewer errors. Impulsive subjects, by contrast, scanned less carefully, and hence, had faster decision times and made more errors. Correlations between response latencies and error scores have ranged from approximately .5 to .7. Reflection–impulsivity belongs to the first type of cognitive style discussed earlier, since accuracy of performance is intrinsic to its assessment.

It should be emphasized that all of the published research on reflection–impulsivity (see Kagan & Kogan, 1970, for a review) is based on preadolescent subjects. Within that age span, there is a clear trend toward increasing reflectiveness with increasing age. Further, reflectiveness appears to be considerably more adaptive than impulsiveness for a wide range of cognitive and school performances. An anxiety-over-error dynamic has been postulated as accounting for individual variation in reflective versus impulsive strategies. Reflective children do not wish to make a mistake and they take their time in order to accomplish that goal. Impulsive children, on the other hand, are considerably more casual about error and hence can afford to respond more quickly.

Relations between response speed and errors have been a favorite preoccupation of experimental psychologists working with elderly subjects (see Birren, 1964; Botwinick, 1967). Very little of this research has focused upon perceptual tasks involving response uncertainty. There is, nevertheless, strong indication that older individuals slow down in order to avoid mistakes. Botwinick (1967) has reviewed a number of studies indicating a tendency for older subjects to prefer errors of omission to errors of commission. Such outcomes indicate a strong tendency on the part of elderly subjects toward cautiousness in venturing responses. Hence, if one were to administer Kagan's Matching Familiar Figures Test to older subjects, we would clearly expect a strongly reflective response—long response latency and few errors.

Reflectiveness is considered to be a highly valued style or strategy in preadolescent children. An analogous style or strategy in older subjects evokes more ambivalent reactions, presumably because it is part of a general pattern of slowdown in both cognitive and psychomotor activities. It may nevertheless be useful to consider the contradictions inherent in the differential value placed upon slowness and accuracy in young and old subjects.

D. Developmental Aspects of a Capacity–Style Distinction

In the threefold classification of cognitive styles drawn earlier, those of the first type appeared to tap capacities, whereas those of the second and third types seemed to involve the assessment of stylistic preferences. From the foregoing distinctions, it can be inferred that field-dependent individuals, for example, must respond in the manner they do on the EFT, RFT, and BAT. The field-independent mode of responding to the three tasks cited is outside of the field-dependent person's repertoire. In striking contrast, an analytic style of responding on a grouping task may well represent a conscious preference. Presumably, other cognitive options are available, but are rejected on grounds of lesser appropriateness or elegance.

The latter example suggests that the stimulus materials employed in research on cognitive styles can have a sizeable influence on the generalizations one can make in regard to developmental change. It is quite likely that a task posing response options for the individual will evoke cognitive preferences offering maximal challenge short of task failure. Given an option perceived to be excessively easy and another option that is more difficult or subtle but still within one's capacity, the latter will probably be chosen. For very young children, the options are likely to be more limited, and hence it is conceivable that the particular cognitive orientation brought to the task is the only one that is in the child's repertoire. With the advent of later childhood, the options are likely to increase, and the one eventually chosen by the subject may seem to be the most subtle, elegant, or "best fitting." These personal definitions are likely to vary with the age of the individual and with the kinds of stimulus materials employed. When the child, by virtue of certain school emphases, has become impressed with the power of abstract–conceptual thought, classifications that incorporate such thought are likely to be preferred. With advancing age, the individual may well become more secure in his abstract–conceptual powers, and hence, become willing to try out other kinds of cognitive orientations. Of course, one can expect that there will be substantial individual differences all along the age spectrum in the degree to which an individual has more than one cognitive option at his disposal as opposed to being "locked into" a single all-pervasive cognitive disposition.

Evidence is now available indicating that the threefold classification of cognitive styles proposed earlier is not invariable across age. Indeed, a stylistic preference in adulthood (i.e., a cognitive style of the second or third type) may well represent a capacity (a cognitive style of the first type) in early childhood. In a study reported in Kagan *et al.* (1963), for example, fourth-grade children were taught to associate nonsense syllables with geometric figures containing figure and ground components. After the associations were learned, the child was shown the figure and ground components separately. Those children classified as analytic–descriptive in their orientation on the Kagan *et al.* (1960) triad procedure were more likely to provide the correct nonsense syllable when the figural component was presented alone. Wachtel (1968) repeated this study with college students using materials appropriately upgraded in difficulty, and failed to replicate the Kagan *et al.* (1963) results. Rather, Wachtel found that Witkin's Embedded Figures Test predicted performance in the figure-ground paired-associates task. This suggests that the choice of analytic concepts in the triads procedure constitutes more of a capacity for ten year olds, and more of a stylistic preference for college students. In order to predict performance in an analytic learning task for adults, it is necessary to switch to an index of analytic capacity (Witkin's EFT).

One may well ask whether cognitive dispositions that were capacities in childhood and stylistic preferences in middle adulthood again become cognitive capacities in old age. Regrettably, there are no data directly relevant to the question. In data based on a sample of well-educated and healthy older individuals (Kogan, 1973), there is more diversity of response than in college students. At the same time, the fifth-graders employed in the Wallach–Kogan research also manifested more diversity than did the college students. The latter group had the strongest penchant for the superordinate categorical–inferential classification. Such age comparisons should be considered highly tentative, of course, in the light of the many methodological problems intrinsic in cross-sectional age comparisons. Nevertheless, these data suggest how identical stimulus arrays can have different psychological meanings at different ages, hence affecting the kinds of developmental inferences one may draw. It is possible to optimize or to minimize a particular style of cognitive functioning at various age levels on the basis of the difficulty or obviousness of the cues linked to that style.

With the kinds of stimulus material currently employed, measures of conceptualizing style in adults will likely reflect stylistic preferences rather than capacities. One can conceive, however, of sorting tasks for adults that might well engage the subjects' capacities. The author is currently engaged in research directed to this issue.

E. Developmental Changes in Real-World Criteria of Cognitive Styles

Unlike the case with creativity, where the inherent nature of the construct demands a real-world referent, research in cognitive styles has proceeded as a more strictly theoretical enterprise. For several cognitive styles, no effort whatever has been made to seek extrinsic behavioral criteria. For others (e.g., reflection–impulsivity), the research has been largely confined to preadolescent subjects, and hence the extrinsic criteria have been limited to school-related behaviors. Given the thorough discussion of the educational implications of cognitive styles in Kogan (1971), and given the life-span focus of the present volume, research concerned with the extrinsic validity of reflection–impulsivity will not be offered here.

Since field independence–dependence represents that cognitive style which has been studied most intensively and extensively for the longest period of time (over 30 years), it is hardly surprising to find several attempts to validate the style against real-world criteria. Except for evidence indicating that extremes of field independence and field dependence may be associated with particular kinds of psychopathology (e.g., Witkin, Lewis, & Weil, 1968), the overall picture regarding relationships between the present cognitive style and real-world behavior criteria is a rather disappointing one.

Where children are concerned, a study by Crandall and Sinkeldam (1964) did not find significant relationships between field dependence and rated dependency behaviors in a free-play situation. More achievement striving was observed in the field independent children, but this finding is explained by the authors in terms of the achievement cues forming part of the testing context for EFT. In support of this explanation, there is little to indicate that field independence enhances performance in school. Indeed, research has appeared (Witkin, Dyk,

Faterson, Goodenough, & Birnbaum, 1966) indicating that boys deemed mentally retarded in school score better (close to the average for their age group) on the Witkin dimension than on more traditional measures of ability. In older samples matched for educational level, Comalli et al. (1965), it will be recalled, found no significant differences in field dependence between those aged subjects residing in the community and those confined to an institution, two groups who might well be expected to vary in actual dependency.

Though frequent lip service is rendered to the view that both field independence and field dependence have their assets and liabilities, the writings of Witkin and his associates reveal a clear value bias favoring the field-independent pole of the dimension. As one examines the cognitive, personality, and motivational correlates of a field-independent mode of functioning as described in the pages of the 1962 Witkin et al. volume, for example, one cannot help but predict a bright future for the field-independent children and a rather dim one for the field-dependents in the sample. Yet, no published evidence based on adult samples could be located that would fulfill the foregoing predictions. Indeed, one can cite evidence of certain strengths in field dependents in the sphere of interpersonal relations. Research by Messick and Damarin (1964) has demonstrated that field dependents are better than field independents at accurately recognizing faces that had been displayed a short time before. Such a skill might be quite advantageous to adults working in a context involving short-term contacts with a large number of people. In another study, Wallach, Kogan, and Burt (1967) observed that homogeneous groups of field-dependent males were able to achieve a unanimous consensus on a series of choice-dilemma problems significantly more quickly than homogeneous groups of field-independent males. Consistent with the foregoing evidence is a study by Linton (1955) indicating that field-independents are better able to resist interpersonal influence. Hence, it appears that field dependence would be a quite desirable quality in conflict situations where a compromise solution is essential for ending a stalemate.

Since the foregoing is a rather pessimistic commentary on the adaptive significance of field independence on the contemporary cultural scene, it is only fair to note that the published longitudinal work on field independence extends only into young adulthood. The future may well yield a number of important behavioral criteria as subjects are followed into and beyond the period of formal higher education. Given the demonstrated fertility of the field-independence–dependence dimension in the personality domain, one should suspend final judgment regarding its eventual utility. After all, the current status of life-span psychology in the domain of the abilities is not much better. After countless years of probing the patterns of stability and decline of the various intellective abilities over middle and late adulthood, we still do not know what impact, if any, such patterns have upon the individual's actual life experience. Thus, one must face up in general to the question of the ultimate value of cognitive test scores during the middle and latter portion of the life span.

F. Research Recommendations and Conclusions

Many of the methodological recommendations advanced for the creativity domain also apply to the area of cognitive styles. At the level of assessment, we have observed that the cognitive processes underlying creative ability and certain cognitive styles are not fundamentally different. That different labels have become attached to the two domains is more of an historical accident than a logical or conceptual development. Empirical linkages between creative-thinking abilities and various cognitive-style indexes have been established (e.g., Messick & Kogan, 1963; Wallach & Kogan, 1965), but such relationships have not been systematically explored within a developmental context. More research is generally needed relating similar constructs that have led separate existences simply because the relevant investigators have emerged from different theoretical traditions.

Within the cognitive-style domain, for example, Gardner et al. (1959) and Santostefano and Paley (1964) discuss a style designated "scanning" or "extensiveness of attention deployment." Psychophysical size-estimation procedures have been employed as the major index of the style, with more accurate size estimation presumed to result from more extensive deployment of attention. Under the creativity rubric, Wallach (1970) on the basis of research by Mendelsohn and Griswold (1964, 1966) and Laughlin (1967) has invoked a construct of "breadth of attention deployment" as a fundamental cognitive process underlying creative ability.

In the foregoing studies, individuals with higher scores on creative ability tests seem able to assimilate information acquired in one context and apply it adaptively in a quite different context. Finally, there is the body of research literature concerned with incidental learning. Botwinick (1970) has reviewed that material from a developmental perspective. Attentional mechanisms must necessarily be involved in the assimilation of information that subjects have not been instructed to learn. There is evident overlap among the three traditions of research cited, yet their interrelationships have not yet been systematically explored. Further, the three vary considerably in the degree to which a life-span perspective has been brought to bear upon them. The domain of incidental learning is most advanced in this respect, though the conflicting empirical findings in the field make generalizations difficult, as Botwinick (1970) has observed. Conceivably, developmentally oriented research on those aspects of cognitive style and creativity relevant to incidental learning might help to clarify the currently murky picture.

While it is important that future research seek significant extrinsic criteria for both creativity and cognitive styles, the problems are somewhat different in the two cases. Looking at the matter from a life-span perspective, it appears as if the adult period provides the most meaningful criteria for creativity, whereas the periods of childhood and adolescence seem to provide the most appropriate criteria for cognitive styles. As stated earlier, the most direct creativity criterion will almost always concern contributions made within one's field, and these will generally emerge during young adulthood and beyond. Criteria advanced prior to that time—during the period of formal schooling—must necessarily have "intermediate" rather than "ultimate" status.

Although there are disagreements about how one evaluates creativity in the real world, there would be almost universal agreement about the most creative geniuses of past and present. Both psychologist and layman have a reasonably accurate conception of what creativity is about. Where cognitive styles are concerned, such obvious guidelines toward constructing relevant and meaningful external criteria for the adult period are essentially absent. As a consequence, most of the research on cognitive styles has moved in three directions—construct validation, developmental comparisons, and relations to school-related performances. The first represents an enterprise in which the relations between various cognitive tests have been examined in order to achieve a better understanding of the structure of the cognitive style domain. Factor analysis has been a favored method in this particular approach, though by no means exclusively so. It is only quite recently that efforts have been made to articulate the foregoing structural approach with genuine developmental concerns (see Kagan & Kogan, 1970). The latter focus, however, has been more in the service of uncovering constitutional and early socialization antecedents of cognitive styles in infancy and early childhood (e.g., Kagan, 1971), rather than exploring continuities and discontinuities into middle and late adulthood. Nevertheless, some research of the latter type has been carried out, as we have seen, though little of it shows much concern with the relevance of the style under study for life experience during adulthood. The real-world referents of cognitive styles outside the context of formal schooling have simply not been spelled out in any systematic fashion.

The foregoing lack does not imply that there has been a detailed articulation between cognitive styles and school-relevant variables. Rather, there has been a growing recognition that learning and thinking in the context of the classroom show wide individual variation. A simple better–poorer achievement dimension does not account for all of this variation; rather, the individual differences seem to be partially stylistic. Accordingly, there has been much discussion about the prospect of matching instructional treatments to subgroups of individuals with distinctive cognitive and motivational characteristics (see Lesser, 1971). We can be sure that the issue of the utility of cognitive styles will be put to a severe test in the course of such an enterprise. As the trend toward additional formal instruction for middle-aged and older persons continues to grow (see the Birren and Woodruff chapter in this volume), the real-world consequences of cognitive styles beyond adolescence may assume greater clarity. Until such a development ensues, cognitive styles will necessarily constitute a theoretically interesting, though esoteric, topic within a life-span developmental psychology.

ACKNOWLEDGMENT

The author would like to acknowledge the invaluable assistance of Augusta Gross for the bibliographic work involved in the preparation of this chapter.

CHAPTER 8

Continuities in Childhood and Adult Moral Development Revisited[1]

LAWRENCE KOHLBERG

HARVARD UNIVERSITY
CAMBRIDGE, MASSACHUSETTS

ABSTRACT

This chapter is addressed to the question of existence of adulthood stages and stage change in moral development. Stage change is defined as directed, sequential, qualitative transformations in psychological structure. The existence of adulthood psychological stage change is theoretically important since such change must be the result of experiential interaction with the environment, rather than being linked to biological maturation.

Evidence of Piagetian cognitive stages indicates continuing development of formal thought past adolescence but no new postadolescent cognitive stage. In contrast, this chapter indicates that there are moral stages that first appear in young adulthood (over 21) in a longitudinal sample. These are the stages of principled moral reasoning (Stage 5, social contract utilitarian orientation and Stage 6, universal principles of justice orientation). An earlier study by Kohlberg and Kramer (1969) reported attainment of principled moral reasoning in high school followed by "retrogression" to a skeptical egocentric relativism. A scoring system which better differentiates structure from content indicates that this skeptical relativism is a transitional state between conventional and principled morality rather than a retrogression. It also indicates that the high school reasoning scored as principled was only an advanced form of conventional reasoning

---

[1]An expanded version of the ideas presented in this chapter will be published as part of a forthcoming book, C. Kohlberg and E. Turiel (Eds.), *Recent research in moral development.*

(Stage 4, member of society orientation). It was suggested that the nature of the experiences leading to adulthood development, e.g., to principled moral thought, were somewhat different than those involved in childhood and adolescent movement to the conventional stages of moral reasoning. Development of moral thought in childhood is an increasingly adequate comprehension of existing social norms and social ideals. Accordingly, it develops through the usual experiences of social symbolic interaction and role taking. In contrast, construction of principles seems to require experiences of personal moral choice and responsibility usually supervening upon a questioning period of "moratorium."

This view of adulthood moral stages linked to experience of personal choice suggests a rapproachement between Erikson's stage theory of adult development and a more cognitive–structural stage theory. This, in turn, invites speculation as to a more ontological or religious seventh stage which might correspond to Erikson's stage of integrity–despair.

I. Introduction

Probably the most important problem for life-span psychology is that of the existence of developmental stages in adulthood. This paper will survey the scanty evidence on the existence of adulthood cognitive and moral stages, and consider the way experience in adulthood could lead to stage change. In this paper, I am going to eat some of the words Kramer and I wrote on this topic 4 years ago (Kohlberg & Kramer, 1969). In the meantime my thinking, as well as that of my longitudinal subjects, has developed.

II. Concepts of Stage in Relation to Adulthood

Before reviewing the evidence, it might be pointed out that the existence of adulthood stages has not yet been the subject of any serious direct systematic study other than my own. In saying this, a rigid and precise notion of the stage concept is used. This notion comes from the structural tradition of Piaget and other cognitive–developmental child psychologists. The notion of stage used in most discussions of adult change is not structural; it is, rather, the notion of socio-cultural or social role-defined *developmental tasks*. In this conception, a culture (responding, in part, to maturational events) outlines a rough sequence of roles or tasks from birth to death, and adaptation to this task sequence leads to age-typical personality changes. Such *stages* are defined primarily by new socio-cultural environments or roles as they impact upon already established maturational capacities and acquired response patterns. To research such adult stages involves all the complexities of sampling and design elaborated by Schaie (1973b). The relation of the stage to age must be defined independent of cohort, and it must be defined across a representative sample for the culture or subcultures for which the stage is postulated.

Often opposed to such socio-environmentally defined stages are biological-maturational stages. In the psychological realm, an example would be the stages of classical psychoanalytic theory, psychosexual stages, defined by the biological activation of a new organ. This may be called the embryological stage model. Oral, anal, and phallic psychosexual stages correspond to the neurological sensitization or libidinalization of new organs. Such a direct biological model of stages is unlikely to postulate adult stages. After early adulthood, biological notions of development are notions of either stabilization or decrement in biological functioning, rather than of new biological activation of a structure or qualitative biological change in a structure.

The cognitive–developmental or structural model of stages involves both different theoretical postulates and a different research strategy than do socio-cultural and maturational concepts of stages. The cognitive–structural model starts with the distinction between quality and quantity in age-related change. Most age-related changes are changes in quantitative rather than qualitative (structural–organizational) aspects of responses. A related distinction to quantity–quality is competence–performance. Structural theories treat most quantitative changes as changes in performance rather than changes in structural competence. As an example, there are decrements in speed and efficiency of immediate memory and information processing with age, but such changes do not imply a regression in the logical structure of the aging individual's reasoning process. In general, structural theory does not treat any change as a change in structural competence unless the change is evident in a qualitatively new pattern of response. Qualitative novelty involves the distinction between form and content. A really new kind of experience, a really new mode of response, is one that is different in its form or organization, not simply in the element or the information it contains.

In summary, the kinds of age change relevant to a stage model are restricted to those implied by the distinctions between quality and quantity, competence and performance, and form and content. In addition to focusing upon quality, competence, and form, a cognitive–developmental stage concept has the following additional general characteristics (Piaget, 1960a):

1. Stages imply distinct or qualitative differences in structures (modes of thinking) which still serve the same basic function (e.g., intelligence) at various points in development.
2. These different structures form an invariant sequence, order, or succession in individual development. While cultural factors may speed up, slow down, or stop development, they do not change its sequence.
3. Each of these different and sequential modes of thought forms a structured whole. A given stage-response on a task does not just represent a specific response determined by knowledge and familiarity with that task or tasks similar to it; rather, it represents an underlying thought-organization. The implication is that various aspects of stage structures should appear as a consistent cluster of responses in development.

4. Stages are hierarchical integrations. As noted, stages form an order of increasingly differentiated and integrated *structures* to fulfill a common function. Accordingly, higher stages displace (or, rather, reintegrate) the structures found at lower stages.

There is, then, a hierarchical preference within the individual, that is, a disposition to prefer a solution of a problem at the highest level available to him.

The characteristics of stages just mentioned, while defined by structural theory, are amenable to research examination. It is possible to ask whether there are qualitative changes in adulthood forming an invariant sequence in any sociocultural environment, which form a generalized structured whole, and which hierarchically relate to earlier qualitative developmental change. The research strategies used to answer these questions are very different from those usually entailed in the study of aging. The questions entail little in the way of establishing age norms for different populations, or disentangling age from cohort, from time, from testing effects. Rather, they require the careful analysis of a small number of longitudinal cases. The number of cases required is not large. Piaget's three infants defined an invariant sequence of sensorimotor intellectual stages which has since been shown to hold for the development of large numbers of infants in very different environments. Stages are not established by longitudinal analysis of one's own children, but they are established by fairly small numbers of cases testing the limits of a universal sequence by longitudinal study of a variety of types of people in a variety of environmental settings. A single case of longitudinal inversion of sequence disproves the stage theory if it is not a manifest case of measurement error.

Accordingly, those ideological enemies, the Skinnerians and the structuralists, agree on the careful use of small numbers of cases to demonstrate universalities in behavior change. A law of learning disobeyed by a single rat is no law; a stage sequence disregarded by a single child is no sequence. Verification of conclusions reached in this chapter then rests in the reader's agreement with the classification of cases presented in various papers by myself and colleagues as reflecting sequential qualitative change, rather than in the statistical significance of means.

In addition to the formal characteristics of stages and the kind of data relevant to their verification, there is need to note briefly the theory of the role of experience in development which lies behind structural stages. Stages are viewed neither as the direct reflection of maturation, nor as the direct reflection of learning in the sense of specific environmental stimulus exposures, reinforcements, etc. Stages represent, rather, the equilibrated pattern of interaction between the organism and the environment. If the child's responses indicate a different structure or organization than the adult's, rather than a less complex one, and if this structure is similar in all children, it is extremely difficult to view the child's mental structure as a direct learning of the external structure. If stages cannot be accounted for by direct learning of the structure of the outer world, neither can they be explained as the result of innate patterning. If children have their own logic, adult logic or mental structure cannot be derived from innate neurological patterning because such patterning should hold also in childhood. It is hardly plausible to view a whole succession of logics as an evolutionary and functional program of innate wiring, particularly in light of the fact that the most mature logical structures are reached only by some adults.

What has been said about the interactional theory of stage development suggests the possibility of the existence of adult stages and the importance of studying adult stage development. Some theories, like Gesell's, treat stages as direct products of maturation. Other socio-cultural theories of developmental tasks treat them as fairly direct products of social learning or social experience. It is highly unlikely that there are maturational stages in adulthood. It is also highly unlikely that direct social learning or experience could produce structural stages in adulthood. The existence of adult structural stages could best be explained by an interactional or equilibration theory of the effects of experience on development, as will be attempted later on.

The importance of adult stages in this regard springs from the fact that childhood *interactional* or *structural* stages cannot be completely distinguished from maturational stages. As an example, while Piaget asserts that his cognitive stages are "interactional" and not maturational, they are closely tied to the maturation of the nervous system. If one combines a knowledge of the child's chronological age with a knowledge of his long-term IQ, with its hereditary component, one can predict quite well a child's Piagetian stage (Kohlberg & Mayer, 1973). Presumably, chronological age and the hereditary component of IQ generate an index of maturation with which Piaget stages are correlated. Until maturation is completed, presumably in adolescence, then, it is impossible to disentangle roles of maturation and experience in generating stages or stage change.

Accordingly, it falls upon the student of adult development to determine whether there are structural stages that arise through experience. Furthermore, it is primarily the student of adult development who may be able to distinguish the roles of personal experience and of generalized-symbolic experience in development, a distinction centrally dividing "emotional" and "cognitive" theories of personality development.

III. Cognitive Stage Development in Adulthood

In raising the issue of adult cognitive stages, it is necessary to discriminate between the existence of adult stages and the existence of continuing stage development in adulthood. Piaget, himself, does not postulate adult cognitive stages, but he does postulate continuing cognitive development through early adulthood (Piaget, 1972). Piaget's highest stage, formal operations, is defined by him as appearing in the era of early adolescence, ages 12 to 15. While Piaget views the onset of the highest stage as occurring in adolescence under typical or favorable conditions, he sees continuing development of formal operational thought as occurring in early adulthood.

This continuing development is of the following sort:

1. Adolescents who have been slow in cognitive development because of biological and cultural conditions and who are still concrete–operational at 15 may develop formal operational thought in early adulthood.
2. There is continuing *horizontal decalage* of formal–operational thought in early adulthood so that it is applied to more spheres or activities.
3. Related to this decalage, there may be *stabilization* of formal thought, i.e., increased subordination of, or rejection of, lower forms of thought for formal–operational thought in adulthood.

The available evidence is of exactly this sort. Age trends in the development of formal operational thinking in two tasks, the pendulum and correlation problems, in 265 California subjects between the ages of 10 and 50 were studied by Kuhn, Langer, Kohlberg, and Haan (1974). The results are presented in Figure 1. As Figure 1 indicates, the correlation problem was a more difficult

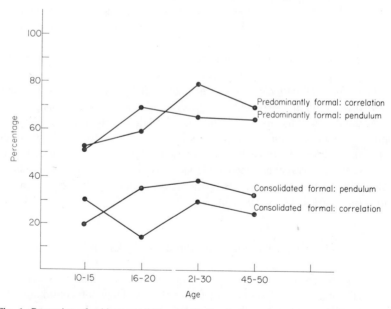

Fig. 1. Proportion of subjects exhibiting predominantly formal operations (III, II, and above) and consolidated formal operations (IIIA/B or IIIB), by age group.

problem to solve at the formal-operational level than was the pendulum problem; it represents a form of *horizontal decalage* in formal thought. On this task there was continuing development to formal-operational thought after ages 16–20, but on the pendulum problem there was not. In addition to horizontal decalage of formal thought, there was also development in this period in the form of *stabilization* in the pendulum task. This is indicated in Figure 2. The mixture of concrete and formal operational thought present in 10–15% of adolescents, disappears in the 20–30 age group.

Three types of cognitive development in adulthood have been discussed: (1) continued development among the "slow;" (2) developers' horizontal decalage; and (3) stabilization. The critical question, however, is whether any new cognitive stage may be found in adulthood. The three forms of continuing development discussed could all exist without the existence of any new cognitive stage in adulthood. If these forms of development exist without a new adult stage, it would follow that formation of a stage demands experience as well as neurological maturation, i.e., that neurological maturation in early adolescence is a structural condition necessary for a new cognitive stage. The actual appearance of the cognitive stage may lag way behind the maturational change, or may never occur because of experiential factors. However, in that case, the maturational change is still a necessary, if not sufficient, condition for the existence of the stage. This conclusion is consistent with Piaget's view. Piaget does not rule out the possibility of a stage beyond formal operations, citing Godel's proof

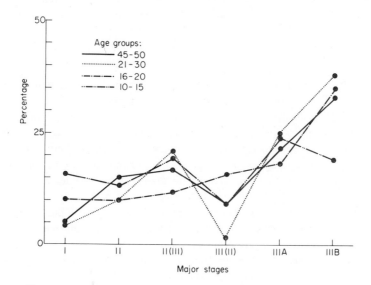

Fig. 2. Pendulum problem: percentages of each age group at major stage.

that the impossibility of another form of logic cannot be proved by formal-operational logic. However, he does seem inclined to believe that there is no later cognitive stage.

Now, if there is some new adulthood stage, it is not likely to appear in logical-cognitive tasks as such. This may be concluded for two reasons: First, as noted, Piagetian cognitive growth is correlated to both the hereditary and the age-maturational factors found in general intelligence. Secondly, logical stages are by definition relatively experience-free. If anything, experience appears to represent something of a hindrance to pure formal-logical thought as evidenced by the fact that the greatest work in mathematical and pure physical theory has been commenced in late adolescence.

IV. The Existence of Adulthood Moral Stages—Background Considerations

The question arises, however, whether there may not be adulthood stages that are not *logical* but still have a cognitive–structural component. This possibility is raised by moral stages; that adult moral stages might exist is suggested by the fact that moral change is clearly a focal point for adult life in a way cognitive change is not. Erikson's studies of Martin Luther and Mahatma Gandhi are not needed to know that the crises and turning points of adult identity are often moral. From Saint Paul to Tolstoy, the classic autobiographies describe the dramas of maturity as the transformations of the moral ideologies of men.

While dramatic moral changes occur in adulthood, the question is whether such change is structural stage change. It is known that there are structural moral stages in childhood and adolescence. These moral stages are defined in the right-hand column of Table 1. The stages have been demonstrated to meet the requirements of structural stages in the following ways:

1. They are qualitatively different modes of thought rather than increased knowledge of, or internalization of, adult moral beliefs and standards.
2. They form an invariant order or sequence of development. Fifteen-year-longitudinal data on 50 American males in the age periods 10–15 to 25–30 demonstrate movement is always forward and always step-by-step. (These data are discussed later in this chapter.) More limited 6-year longitudinal data on Turkish boys also indicate invariant sequence as do cross-sectional age data in many cultures (Kohlberg & Turiel, 1973).
3. The stages form a clustered whole. There is a general factor of moral stage cross-cutting all dilemmas, verbal or behavioral, with which an individual is confronted (Kohlberg & Turiel, 1973).
4. The stages are hierarchical integrations. Subjects comprehend all stages below their own and not more than one above their own. They prefer the highest stage they comprehend (Rest, 1973; Kohlberg & Turiel, 1973).

TABLE 1

Relations between Piaget Logical Stages and Kohlberg Moral Stages

Logical Stage	Moral Stage
Symbolic, intuitive thought	Stage 0: The good is what I want and like.
Concrete operations, Substage 1 categorical classification	Stage 1: punishment-obedience orientation
Concrete operations, Substage 2 reversible concrete thought	Stage 2: instrumental hedonism and concrete reciprocity
Formal operations, Substage 1 relations involving the inverse of the reciprocal	Stage 3: orientation to inter-personal relations of mutuality
Formal operations, Substage 2	Stage 4: maintenance of social order, fixed rules and authority
Formal operations, Substage 3	Stage 5A: social contract, utilitarian law-making perspective Stage 5B: higher law and conscience orientation Stage 6: universal ethical principle orientation

Before asking questions about adult moral development, it is necessary to clarify the relation of moral stages to Piagetian logical-cognitive stages. First, if moral stages are cognitive–structural, they must have some relationship to Piagetian logical stages. The relationships found are presented in Table 1, which indicates that for every moral stage there is a parallel logical stage or substage. These relationships have been empirically confirmed (Kuhn, *et al.*, 1972; Colby, 1973; Fritz, 1973). These relationships raise a problem as to adult moral stages. If moral stages parallel logical stages, are they not simply a horizontal decalage of logical stages to a moral content area? In that case, there could be no adult moral stages but only more of the adult horizontal decalage of logical stages, which has been discussed. In fact, this is not the case (Kohlberg, 1973). The empirical relations found are that a given logical stage *is a necessary but not sufficient* condition for the parallel moral stage. As an example, all principled (Stage 5 and 6) subjects are formal operational, but many formal operational subjects are not principled. These formal operational nonprincipled subjects may display elements of formal reasoning in responding to moral dilemmas and still display no use of moral principle in the dilemmas.

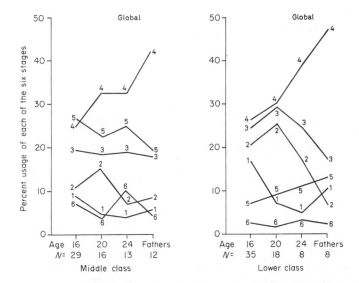

Fig. 3. Moral judgment profiles (percentage usage of each stage by global rating method) for middle- and lower-class males at four ages. [From Richard Kramer, "Changes in Moral Judgment Response Pattern During Late Adolescence and Young Adulthood," Ph.D. Dissertation, University of Chicago, 1968; reprinted in Kohlberg & Kramer, 1969.]

Our theory holds that moral and logical stages are structurally parallel, but different. Moral stages involve social role taking and the equilibration of role taking in the form of reversible justice structures, structures of reciprocity and equality (Kohlberg, 1971a). Principles of justice involve a reciprocity-operation with a parallel in logic, but the use of principles of justice is not merely the application of logical reciprocity to moral situations.

With regard to adult moral stages, then, biography and common experience indicate dramatic or qualitative changes in adulthood in moral ideology; our theory of moral stages would be consistent with the notion that such changes represent moral-stage change.

V. The Existence of Adult Moral Stages—
The Kohlberg and Kramer Conclusions

While the existence of adult moral stages seems plausible, the conclusions drawn 4 years ago were that the facts on moral development in adulthood were similar to those just summarized on logical development in adulthood (Kohlberg & Kramer, 1969). In that paper, it was reported that no new structural

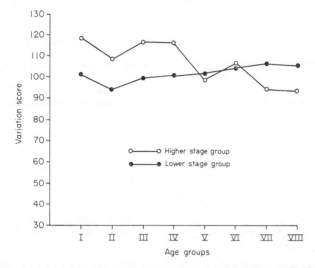

Fig. 4. Mean variation scores for higher-stage and lower-stage subjects in the Kramer group at the following eight age ranges: 14.0–15.11 (I); 18.0–18.11 (II); 17.0–17.11 (III); 16.0–18.11 (IV); 19.0–20.11 (V); 21.0–22.11 (VI); 23.0–23.11 (VII); and 24.0–26.11 (VIII). [From Kohlberg & Kramer, 1969.]

moral stage could be found in adulthood. Instead, forms of development which have just been summarized with regard to logical stages were reported. It was found that some subjects at lower stages of moral judgment (Stages 1–3) continued to develop toward Stage 4 from age 16 to 24. This result parallels the tendency for subjects not yet formal-operational to become formal-operational in the period 16 to 25–30. These trends from Kohlberg and Kramer (1969) are presented in Figure 3.

Other findings suggested stabilization among the higher-stage subjects with age. Higher-stage subjects (Stages 4, 5, and 6) increasingly dropped out lower-stage thinking with age and became more consistently high-stage. This stabilization of moral thought is not only reflected in the trends of stage usage for the group as a whole, but it is also reflected in the trends of variability of stage usage within individuals.

Figure 4 presents the trends in decreased variability with age found by Kohlberg and Kramer (1969). Although the major moral change past high school was noted to be stabilization of higher stages rather than the formation of a new stage, it was reported that this stabilization was often a dramatic developmental process. Prior to stabilization at a higher or principled stage, *retrogression* was found on an increased usage of preconventional Stage 2 thinking. Under ordinary conditions, individuals are capable of using all stages below their own, but prefer to use the highest stage they understand and are capable of using (Rest,

1973). However, at around the college sophomore age, individuals often did not seem to use the highest moral stages of which they were capable, but instead made use of preconventional thought previously abandoned.

The findings on retrogression and return to the social contract were interpreted in terms of Erikson's concepts of moratorium, identity crisis, and renewed commitment. It was suggested that after an individual had formed the capacity for morally principled thought, he still had to commit himself to do so. This commitment often was part of the resolution of an identity crisis or moratorium in which the individual displayed retrogression in moral thought.

An interpretation of retrogression and return in terms of Eriksonian ego development may be juxtaposed with the interpretation of the same phenomena as structural stabilization. Thus, a Piaget–Kohlberg structural stage theory could interpret the phenomena only as stabilization, not as adulthood structural stage change. What could be seen by structural theory only as stabilization could be seen from another theoretical perspective, the Eriksonian, as adult development. Accordingly, it was suggested that if there were adult stages and development in adulthood, such stages would have to be defined in terms of Erikson's *functional* stages, rather than in terms of structural stages or of qualitatively new patterns of thought and judgment.

For a variety of reasons, the conclusions of Kramer and Kohlberg just summarized, need revision. These revisions arise from:

1. a more careful analysis of the sense in which moral stage theory can tolerate regression, provided by Turiel (1973a);
2. a thorough revision of the stage-scoring system to reflect more directly the structure rather than the content of moral thought;
3. a further wave of longitudinal interviews on the subjects.

Once these revisions are made, a new conclusion arises; the conclusion is that there are indeed adult stages. Fully-principled or Stage 5 and especially Stage 6 thinking is an adult development, typically not reached until the late twenties or later. Structural development and stabilization are not two different things. The fact that the apparently Stage 5 thinking of high school students was vulnerable to retrogression or was not yet stabilized was, in fact, evidence for the fact that such thinking was not really principled.

Each of the three points that lead to this revision will now be considered. With regard to the first point, the theoretical status of regression, the apparent resurgence of Stage 2 reasoning in college sophomores had been interpreted as a *structural retrogression,* i.e., a return to a lower structural stage, but a *functional advance.* It was a functional advance in flowing from a questioning of previous commitments and standards necessary before these standards could be stabilized as "one's own identity." This question, in turn, reflected a new awareness of the relativity of value and choice which was a developmental advance, though the response to it appeared to be a regression to Stage 2 instrumental egoism.

It was suggested, then, that one could regress in the service of development. In the breakup of one stage and the movement to a higher stage, one could recycle to an earlier position. This view, of course, is held by Gesell, Werner, and other developmental theorists. Turiel holds that the apparent regression involved in stage development is a disequilibrium of transition very different than the disorganization or dedifferentiation involved in regression. According to Turiel, relativistic regressions to Stage 2 are in a disequilibrated transitional stage in which the breakup of conventional morality is easy to confuse with the resurgence of preconventional morality.

This issue leads directly to the next: the distinction between content and structure in moral thought and the development of a new stage-scoring system which more adequately represents the distinction. It is the current opinion of this author that the older stage-scoring procedures confused the *structure* of moral thought with the *content* of moral thought.

This confusion led some subjects to be scored too high and others too low in their thought. Take, first, the retrogressors. According to the old scoring system, at the end of high school they were Stage 5 with some Stage 4. As college sophomores, they retrogressed to a mixture of Stage 2 and Stage 4 thought. Post-college, they returned to Stage 5. It was claimed earlier (Kohlberg & Kramer, 1969) that their Stage 2 usage in college was a response to a new awareness, the awareness of relativism, and was to that extent, a functional advance in development. Nevertheless, their thinking was viewed as still structurally Stage 2. Thus, it was functionally an advance, but structurally a regression.

A more careful analysis of these college-sophomore responses indicated that it was incorrect to label them as structurally Stage 2 and that they should, instead, be labeled Stage 4½. The apparent Stage 2 thinking of the longitudinal subjects was not actually a return to an earlier pattern of Stage 2 thought used when they were younger, but was actually a pattern of thought used in the *transition from* conventional to principled reasoning. The thinking of the transitional relativists in our sample could best be characterized as Stage 4½, i.e., as a way of thinking that equated morality with Stage 4 thought and then questioned the validity of morality conceived in Stage 4 terms.

Within the old scoring system, Stage 4½ subjects would appear not as a distinctive type but as a mixture of Stage 2 and Stage 4. In fact, however, there are characteristics of Stage 4½ thinking which clearly distinguish it from either Stage 2 or Stage 4. There were two related salient characteristics of these retrogressed interviews that were scored as Stage 2. The first was ethical skepticism or extreme ethical relativism—the assertion that the "morally right" or "moral duty" *were relative* to the actor's wishes or needs and had no further validity. The second related assertion was ethical egoism or ethical individualism —the assertion that a "good" moral reason, rule, or principle was one which appealed to the actor's self-interest or to his point of view, where the actor's individual point of view is "natural," "outside society," "amoral" or independent of acceptance of the rules and expectations of others. Subjects who responded with this latter assertion were classified as Stage 2 because they stated that a choice based on the individual's own egoistic interests was as legitimate as any other choice since all choices are relative. This use of a more or less egoistic choice is, however, more a similarity of content between Stage 2 and the Stage 4½ sophomores, than a similarity of the structure of their moral thought.

The notions of relativism and egoism held by Stage 4½ subjects are quite different from those of "naive" or "true" Stage 2 subjects. In particular, the Stage 4½ subjects respond at a much more "abstract" or "philosophical" level than do either the preconventional (Stage 2) or conventional (Stage 4) subjects. In order to deal with this difference, *levels of abstraction, levels of discourse,* or *levels of reflectivity* in moral judgment have been defined. In brief, these levels are:

Level I   Justifying moral judgment to an individual selfish actor.
Level II   Judging a general practice (institution), or justifying a
             practice from the point of view of other institutions, or
             from the standpoint of a generalized member society.
Level III   Defining a *moral theory* and justifying basic moral terms
             or principles from a standpoint outside that of a member
             of a constituted society.

The reanalysis of moral judgments in late adolescence and early adulthood has led to a different view of the existence of adult moral stage change. When a clear distinction between Stage 4-B and true Stage 5 thought was made, none of the longitudinal subjects under the age of 23 displayed true Stage 5 thought.

In summary, longitudinal data now suggest that Stage 5 is a stage reached in adulthood, not in adolescence. With regard to Stage 6, something similar is to be said. Thinking which had been labeled Stage 6 in high school was misclassified. No longitudinal subject in high school had been predominantly Stage 6, nor has any become predominantly Stage 6 by the age of 30 (although we will not predict that none will reach Stage 6). Essentially, the material that was scored as Stage 6 was another form of sophisticated Stage 4 thought, one which appealed to "conscience" and "moral law" instead of to "the will of the majority" and "the welfare of the greatest number."

VI. Adult Experiences Involved in Moral Stage Development

If new moral stages do form as a result of adult experience, it would be well to understand how this happens. In particular, Piaget's cognitive–structural model of experience leading to development needs to be integrated with a model of adult personal experience. The bulk of moral stage development occurs in childhood and adolescence and does not require the extensive personal experience of moral choice and responsibility found in adult life. Elsewhere an account has been presented of the role of experience in leading to moral development that does not stress personal experience of moral choice and responsibility. Instead, following Piaget, it stresses the role of cognitive conflict between and within contradictory judgmental structures as leading to development (Turiel, 1973a). Following this theory, a one-stage-up movement has been induced for the moral judgment of a majority of preadolescents and adolescents with the logical capacity for reasoning at the next stage (Blatt, 1973; Hickey, 1973).

These findings support the notion that the experience necessary for moral stage development in childhood and adolescence is largely cognitive and symbolic and does not require large amounts of personal experience. In using the term "cognitive," as opposed to "personal," it is not intended to oppose cognition to the emotional, the social, or the behavioral. The moral structures of judgment studied as stages can be hotly emotional, are manifestly social, and determine choice and action. But in calling moral stages cognitive, it should be implied that they are centrally forms of *thinking;* they are *generalized* and *symbolic.* Accordingly, the experiences which generate stage movement have a strong general and symbolic component; they are experiences involving thinking.

It has been noted that the experiences involving thinking leading to moral development are not simply logical experiences. Moral stage development is not merely the horizontal decalage of logical thought to social situations. In order for a formal operational adolescent to attain morally principled reasoning, he must undergo social and moral experiences that cannot be conceptualized as experiences that aid him in transferring logical principles to social situations. They are experiences, rather, that lead him to transform his modes of judgment of the morally right and the fair. Often, the experiences that promote such change have a fairly strong emotional component. As emotion enters into experiences leading to change, it is, however, the emotion that triggers and accompanies rethinking.

The most successful format for a moral discussion group is not impersonal in the sense that didactic cognitive teaching is impersonal; the best discussions, themselves, are often personal, often emotional. Genuine personal interchange and challenge appear to be an educational precondition for thinking or rethinking and for believing that one's thinking makes a difference. But, obviously, the role of emotion in stimulating development in a group moral discussion program is only that of a trigger to general thinking. It is a different matter than the role of emotion in a concrete moral choice, the consequences of which one lives with and emotionally experiences long afterward. Furthermore, the recognition and "choice" of the next stage up is general and "cognitive"; it is not a personal choice in the moral sense of the term.

A new stage is a new general solution to moral problems and its greater adequacy is evident on cognitive grounds. If the higher stage solution is "seen," it is then preferred to the lower stage solution, whatever the particular experiences with either stage solution. This is because part of seeing the higher stage is seeing why it is better than the lower stage solution. One of the most striking findings of the Rest (1973) study was that adolescents preferred reasoning at the next stage up to reasoning at their own stage; they were not "personally committed" to their own stage of reasoning.

The Turiel (1973b) experiments and the Kohlberg–Kramer moral discussion groups are extreme examples of the possibility of vicarious symbolic experience for promoting moral stage development. The more general formulation of this experience has been called *role taking* and the occasions stimulating development were called *role-taking opportunities*. Each stage is both a cause and a result of a wider and more adequate process of taking the perspectives of others, personal and societal, upon social conflicts. Such widening role taking can go on without extensive personal experiences of responsibility and choice. A formulation of the experience leading to moral stage movement as vicarious, cognitive, symbolic, and general fits the naturalistic findings on moral development in childhood and adolescence quite well.

Because structural moral stages represent general forms of thinking, both the capacity for higher stages and the preference for higher stages can develop relatively speedily in a cognitively and socially rich environment. A great deal of experience of personal moral decision and choice is not necessary for movement from one stage to the next in childhood and adolescence. The tentative finding, however, that principled thinking does not appear until adulthood suggests that perhaps a different kind of experience is required for attainment of principled moral judgment than is required for attainment of the prior stages. While our cognitive developmental theory stresses that the child constructs each new stage "for himself," the sense in which the individual constructs the stage of principled moral reasoning for himself is somewhat different than the sense in which he constructs earlier stages for himself. Through Stage 4, each new stage represents a wider and more adequate process of role taking, of perception of the social system. Principled thinking, however, is not a more adequate perception of what the social system *is;* rather, it is a postulation of principles to which the society and the self *ought to be committed*. To be principled in moral judgment is not just to cognitively "see" principles. It is: (1) to see their ideal adequacy in spite of the fact that they are not a social reality to conform to; (2) to see a basis for commitment to these ideals; and (3) at the same time, to see a commitment to a real society in which one acts consistently with these ideals. This seems to require more than the vicarious experiences of role taking sufficient for movement through the stages to Stage 4, which represents a fairly adequate cognition of the social system.

While the evidence is limited, there appear to be two different sorts of "personal" as opposed to vicarious-symbolic experiences important in movement to principled thought. Both share common features and both occur, at least typically, only after high school. The first experience is the experience of leaving home and entering a college community with conflicting values in the context of moratorium, identity questioning, and the need for commitment. As indicated earlier, this experience precipitates the relativistic crisis of Stage 4½. In the earlier interpretation (Kohlberg & Kramer, 1969), it was thought that the sophomore "identity-crisis" questioning of moral values was a retrogression from Stage 5 principled thinking, and that the mid-twenties commitment to moral values through a social contract was a stabilization of moral thought. With the revised definition of the stages, it may now be said that the sophomore questioning and the young-adult commitment to the social contract are part of the process of movement to Stage 5, rather than a process of questioning of and commitment to morality, separable from moral stage development itself.

The importance of the college moratorium experience is suggested by the following findings:

1. None of the longitudinal subjects who did not attend college, but went directly into the army and/or to adult occupations developed principled thinking.
2. As noted, none of the high school longitudinal subjects showed principled thinking.
3. Working with classroom moral discussion, Blatt succeeded in moving high school Stage 3 students to Stage 4 (and Stage 2 students to Stage 3). But he failed to move any Stage 4's to Stage 5 (Blatt, 1973).
4. In contrast, a moral discussion program led 40% of the Stage 4 freshmen and sophomore participants in the program to move to a Stage 5 orientation (Boyd, 1973).

These findings suggest an interaction between cognitive experience components of moral development and experience in a particular life phase. One study even suggests that high school cognitive experience has a sleeper effect, manifest only after the college moratorium–independence experience. Beck, Sullivan, and Porter (1972) found that a high school moral discussion class showed no upward moral change on posttest in high school, compared to controls. On college follow-up, however, the class showed considerably more Stage 5 thought compared to the control group.

In stressing an interaction between cognitive stimulation and moratorium experience components of college experience, it should be emphasized that questioning one's identity and resolving it by commitment is far from sufficient to lead to principled moral thought. As discussed in the next section, a study by Podd (1969) suggests that college students can go through the questioning and commitment process with regard to identity without moving to principled moral thought. When identity questioning, however, is combined with explicit cognitive-moral stimulation as in the Boyd (1973) college moral discussion programs, movement to principled thought is more likely.

In addition to the moral-stimulation component often missing in the college period of identity-questioning and commitment, there are personal experience components also frequently lacking in a student-moratorium period. This moratorium period is one of new responsibility only for the self; it is primarily an experience of attained freedom to make one's own choices for oneself. Until college, the adolescent usually lives within a world he did not make and in which the choices he must make are circumscribed. Insofar as there is movement to principled thought in the college period, it is in relation to anticipated commitment. Now free, the student seeks the moral terms or contract which he should accept in terms of future commitments. Only later, however, does the student typically have the experience of *sustained responsibility for the welfare of others* and the experience of irreversible moral choice which are the marks of adult personal moral experience, and which Erikson makes central to the development of the ethical sense in the state of generativity.

It is obvious that, in themselves, experiences of responsibility do not lead to movement to a stage of moral principle. Most adults have such experiences; most never become principled. For some young adults, however, experiences of moral responsibility are the sources of moral reflection leading to principles, just as for some young adults, experiences of freedom or moratorium are the sources of reflection leading to principles. This occurs particularly when responsibility, accepted on a conventional basis, leads to some conflict with the universally human. For example, in war, as opposed to American young men in vociferous moratorium, one thinks of Israeli young men in full commitment to a group code. When these men encountered, in the six-day war, a real crisis of moral choice born out of responsibility, many seemed to engage in the kind of reflection leading to principle.

In summary, personal experiences of choice involving questioning and commitment, in some sort of integration with stimulation to cognitive-moral reflection, seem required for movement from conventional to principled (Stage 5) thought. It is probably for this reason that principled thought is not attained in adolescence. The conditions for movement to fully-principled or Stage-6 thought are probably even more of this order, though no real data exist on movement to this highest moral stage.

VII. Relations between Cognitive–Structural Moral Stages and Erikson's Ego Stages

The earlier summary of the Kohlberg and Kramer (1969) paper noted that its conclusion was to juxtapose structural moral stage theory and Eriksonian functional ego stage theory. What, from the point of view of structural theory, was only stabilization, from the point of view of functional ego theory, was stage development. The Kohlberg and Kramer conclusions as to the "facts" of moral postadolescent development were in essential agreement with Erikson's (1964) perception of the "facts." These conclusions supported Erikson's belief that the adolescent is capable of awareness of universal ethical principles, though only the adult can consistently *be ethical*.

While Erikson believes that cognitive awareness of ethical principles arises in adolescence, this adolescent awareness of principles is not itself *ethical;* it is *ideological*. From the point of view of ego development, cognitive and moral–cognitive structures are capacities uncertain in their uses, and the ego must make a series of decisions or commitments as to how to use these structures. From this point of view, an awareness of moral principles can cognitively arise in adolescence, but a *commitment* to their use requires testing and choice; it requires their embodiment in an ideology to which one can test one's fidelity and the fidelity of others, and which is part of a commitment to an identity.

This post identity crisis commitment, in turn, entails a social contract which is a somewhat "conservative" commitment to "my society," "my relationships" from the point of view of universal principles, a contract which is Stage 5 rather than Stage 6 in Kohlberg–Kramer terms.

According to Erikson, the ethical sense or power of the adult depends not only upon resolving his identity, but upon establishing relations of care or generativity toward others. In Erikson's view, when this generativity combines with a more inclusive identity with the human species, there may result a lived ethic which is universal or Stage 6 in Kohlberg–Kramer terms. Typically, such a truly ethical stage does not develop until full adulthood, or even middle age, as in the case of Gandhi.

The Kohlberg and Kramer report, then, agreed with Erikson that while the cognitive awareness of principles develops in adolescence, commitment to their ethical use develops only in adulthood. The retrogression of the subjects and their adult return to principled-conventional thought was seen to be an indication that adolescent awareness of ethical principles was not genuine ethical use of principles. Agreeing with Erikson on "the facts" of ethical development, from the point of view of structural theory, these facts represented development as stabilization, rather than as structural stage change. For Erikson, the outstanding characteristic of the adolescent ideological as opposed to the adult ethical stage is the imbalance and inconsistency of the ideological stage.

The Kohlberg and Kramer paper found the adolescent to be an inconsistent mixture of verbal idealistic moral principle (with occasional accompanying sacrificial action) and egocentric hedonistic response. The retrogressed or transitional subjects were seen as extremes of such a contradiction; they were individuals who had begun to try to act on their high school verbal moral principles and became aware of the contradictions between these ideals and the reality of society and of their own impulses without resolving these contradictions. The retrogressors were seen as having made a step forward toward stabilization over their high school position because they were attempting to cope with contradictions, rather than blandly verbalizing conventional or principled moral reasoning while often acting in self-centered ways. The young adult subjects had partially resolved this conflict and, hence, had stabilized, having come to a greater consistency and equilibrium between moral ideals and reality and between moral thought and action.

In summary, then the Eriksonian adult moral development was seen as increased stabilization, as an equilibration between adolescent moral ideals or norms and perceptions of reality.

In the current revised conclusions, however, what had been interpreted as stabilization related to Eriksonian notions of ego development was viewed as moral stage change. There were not two kinds of moral development, but only one, and a theory of adult moral development could not be a theory of stabilization or ego development, as opposed to being a theory of moral-structural change. Accordingly, in the previous section it was suggested that an adequate account of experience leading to principled thought must integrate Piagetian cognitive–structural accounts of experience with "personal experience of choice," accounts of experience central to Erikson's theory into a single whole. While this cannot be done now, there is increased clarity about the relations of structural moral stages to functional ego stages. Erikson's formulation suggests that for all individuals there should be an adult movement from an ideological to an ethical orientation, as there is ego progression through the phases of identity crises and commitment. Similarly, our account of stabilization suggests that adulthood should lead to increase in stabilization for all individuals. In contrast, a "single" view of development implies that the experiences of youth and adulthood lead to a stabilized or ethical use of moral judgment only in the relatively few adults who also move to a principled stage in this period. It would be expected that some, but not all youths, go through a recognizable phase of identity crisis and its resolution, and that still fewer youths move from conventional to principled morality. All those moving to principled morality would be expected to go through this identity progression. The movement from conventional to principled morality is one which must be considered as a matter of personal choice and as a choice of a self in a sense not true of earlier moral stages. Accordingly, it might be hypothesized that an Eriksonian identity-crisis and its resolution might be a necessary part of such movement. It may also be said, however, that movement from conventional to principled morality requires cognitive–moral stimulation and conditions not contained in the Eriksonian stage descriptions. While necessary, Eriksonian stage progression would be far from sufficient to produce principled morality. In summary, a loose fit between the following stages is implied.

Ego Stages	Moral Stages
Ascribed identities accepted	Conventional morality
Identity crisis or moratorium	Traditional or retrogressed relativism
Identity achievement	Principled morality

It has also been implied, however, that the ego progression could occur without the moral progression, with the adolescent starting as principled and returning to principle or starting as conventional and returning to convention. In addition, both the ego progression and the moral progression could be absent in persons permanently conventional and nonquestioning of identity (Kohlberg & Gilligan, 1971).

A broader basis of integration between the Kohlberg–Kramer structural theory and Erikson's theory of ego stages in adulthood may now be suggested, but before so doing it may be profitable to review briefly the differences between the two approaches, as summarized in Table 2.

The first central distinction between the models is the fact that the structural model starts with relatively rigid distinctions which the functional model slides over. These are the distinctions between structure and content, between competence and performance (behavioral use) and between quality and quantity in development. Related to the rigidity of these distinctions is the fact that the structural model insists that: (1) The nature of each new stage has a definitely definable structure, a structure defined by a logical system; and (2) Each higher stage is logically, cognitively, or philosophically more adequate than the preceding stage and logically includes it. Insisting on initial abstraction of structure from content in description, structural theory is able to empirically find culturally universal invariant sequence in its stages. The price it pays, however, is abstraction from life history. Structural stages do not tell us what is on the individual's mind. The individual, more or less, knows he is in the phase of identity crisis; he does not know he is moving from moral Stage 4 to Stage 5. In contrast,

TABLE 2

Erikson Functional and Piaget–Kohlberg Structural Stages

Piaget	Erikson
Nature of Stages	
Stages are different structures for a single function, e.g., moral judgment, logical reasoning. Accordingly, later stages replace earlier stages. Experience leading to development is cognitive experience, especially experiences of cognitive conflict and match.	Stages are choices or uses of new *functions* by an ego—earlier functions or choices remain on background to the new stage. Experience leading to development is personal experience, especially experiences and choice of personal conflict.
Focus of Stages	
The developmental change is primarily a changed perception in the physical, social, and moral world. The outcome of movement is perceptual change. The stability of the new stage is not the result of choice.	The developmental change involved is primarily a self-chosen, self-perception identification with goals. The outcome of a movement is relatively permanent and results in a choice or a commitment.
Later stages are more cognitively adequate than earlier stages: (1) including the earlier stage pattern, (2) resolving the same problems better, and (3) in being more universally applicable or justifiable, i.e., in the universality and inclusiveness of their ordering of experience.	Later stages are more adequate than earlier stages, not in cognitive inclusiveness, but in virtue or ego strength, i.e., in their ability to order personal experience in a form that is stable, positive, and purposive. Attainment of a stage and adequacy of stage use are distinct, however.

Eriksonian stages, empirically unverified as universal sequences, are used to write biographies or life histories.

Structural theory purchases its abstraction from life history by its empirical verifiability as historically and culturally universal. It gains another gift with this abstraction; a clear logical or moral-philosophical justification as to the sense in which each later stage is better or more adequate than its predecessor (Kohlberg, 1971a). In contrast, Eriksonian theory relies on psychological rather than on logical or moral-philosophical accounts of the way in which each stage brings new "strength" or "wisdom" to the individual. As a result, in its moral and other aspects, Erikson's account is more culturally relative (though not "relativistic") than the structural account.

The second basic distinction between the stage models, then, is that in moving away from pure structuralism in defining stages, a psychological rather than a logical account is obtained of the sense in which a later stage is more adequate than its predecessor.

This distinction between logical and psychological adequacy is, in turn, related to the third basic distinction; the focus of ego stages upon the ego or the self as that which changes and becomes more adequate with development. Both structural and functional stage theory hold that there is a parallelism between development of the self and orientations to the world, but cognitive and moral stages stress the world-pole, and functional stages stress the self-pole.

Piaget's cognitive stages and Kohlberg's moral stages represent a series of increasingly adequate cognitions of a relatively constant physical and social world. The objective moral world the child lives in is grossly or basically the same throughout his development from the point of view of structural theory. The basic changes in the child's moral world come from the developmental changes in his perception of it. In contrast, the focus of the Erikson model is upon changing self. While the socio-moral world is more or less constant, the child's self, his competence, and his position in that world is constantly changing. Erikson attempts to characterize these changes around an invariant sequence of challenges to, and accretions of self, either as a sense of the self's competence, which defines an order of increased adequacy in the sense of an increase of ego strength, ego integration, or as solidity of a sense of self-worth.

The self-focus of ego stages, in turn, implies another basic contrast between Piaget's and Erikson's stages: that of Erikson's focus upon choice. Stages of perception of the world cannot be defined directly as choice. In contrast, stages in the perception of and movement of the self are stages in a self's choice. Moral decisions and moral development may be viewed as either a choice (or change) in the moral self or as a change in perceived moral principles. The former is the central perspective of Erikson's stages, the latter of the Kohlberg moral stages.

In summary, both the function upon self and the focus upon choice coincide with the notion of stages of an ego, of an executor or chooser who uses cognitive and other structures. In contrast, the focus of the Kohlberg moral stages is upon the form and content of "objective" moral principles, rather than upon the process of their choice, use, or application to the self. An integrated theory of social and moral stages would attempt to combine the two perspectives.

VIII. Notes toward a Seventh Stage

Erikson's ideal man passes through his seventh stage of generativity and becomes an ethical man, an ideal corresponding to the Kohlberg Stage 6. There remains for Erikson's man a task that is partly ethical, but more basically religious (in the broadest sense of the term religious), a task defining an eighth stage whose outcomes are a sense of integrity versus a sense of despair. The problem of integrity is not the problem of moral integrity, but the problem of the integration and integrity of meaning of the individual's life and its negative side, despair, which hovers around the awareness of death. This problem is also psychological. The concept of the self's integrity is psychological, but the concept of the integrity of the meaning of the self's life is philosophical or religious. As Santayana (1954) says:

> This struggling and changing force of religion seems to make for an ultimate harmony within the soul and for an ultimate harmony between the soul and all that the soul depends upon. So that Religion, in its intent, is a more conscious and direct pursuit of the Life of Reason than is society, science or art. For these approach the ideal life tentatively and piecemeal, hardly regarding the goal or caring for the ultimate justification of their instinctive aims. Religion also has an instinctive and blind side, but it soon feels its way toward the heart of things and veers in the direction of the ultimate [p. 181].[2]

A discussion of a Stage 7 in our own series, a discussion purely hypothetical and based on no data, is primarily an effort to make Erikson's concept more explicitly philosophical. It is related to Fowler's (1972) efforts to define religious stages which parallel both this author's moral stages and Erikson's ego stages. A first basic notion is that there is a postconventional religious orientation, as there is a postconventional ethical orientation. A second basic notion of a Stage 7 is that an adequate postconventional religious orientation is both dependent upon, and demanded by a Stage 6 orientation to universal human ethical principles.

After attainment of a clear awareness of universal ethical principles valid against the usual skeptical doubts, there remains the loudest skeptical doubt of all: the doubt of "Why be moral?" "Why be just, in a universe that is largely unjust?" This is, of course, one of the problems thought to be unanswerable at the stage of transitional relativism and skepticism. The Stage 5 answer, the social contract, is essentially a compromise answer, the answer that one's own happiness is pursued socially or with due regard to the rights and welfare of others. While Stage 6 ethical principles offer a more complete solution to the problem of relativity of values than Stage 5, it has an even less complete solution for the problem "Why be moral?" There is a sharper contrast between ethical principle and egoistic or hedonistic concerns than there is between the social contract and hedonism.

The answer to the question "Why be moral?" at this level entails the question "Why live?" (and the parallel question, "How face death?") so that ultimate moral maturity requires a mature solution to the question of the meaning of life. This, in turn, is hardly a moral question per se; it is an ontological or a religious one. Not only is the question not a moral one but it is not a question resolvable on purely logical or rational grounds as moral questions are. Neverthe-

[2]Reprinted by permission of Charles Scribner's Sons.

less, a purely metaphorical notion of a Stage 7 may be used as pointing to some meaningful solutions to this question which are compatible with rational science and rational ethics (Kohlberg, 1971b). The characteristics of all these Stage 7 solutions are that they involve contemplative experience of nonegoistic or nondualistic variety. The logic of such experience is sometimes expressed in theistic terms, but it need not be. Its essential is the sense of being a part of the whole of life and the adoption of a cosmic, as opposed to a universal humanistic (Stage 6) perspective.

The concept of such a Stage 7 is familiar, of course, both in religious writing and in the classical metaphysical tradition from Plato to Spinoza. In most accounts the movement starts with despair. Such despair involves the beginning of a cosmic perspective. It is when we begin to see our lives as finite from some more infinite perspective that we feel despair. The meaninglessness of our lives in the face of death is the meaninglessness of the finite from the perspective of the infinite. The resolution of the despair which we call Stage 7 represents a continuation of the process of taking a more cosmic perspective whose first phase is despair. It represents, in a sense, a shift from figure to ground. In despair we are the self seen from the distance of the cosmic or infinite. In the state of mind metaphorically termed Stage 7, we identify ourselves with the cosmic or infinite perspective, itself, and value life from its standpoint.

Spinoza, a believer in principled ethics and in a science of natural laws, could still achieve this state of mind, which he termed "the union of the mind with the whole of nature." Even most persons who are not "religious" temporarily achieve this state of mind when on a mountaintop or before the ocean. At such a time, what is ordinarily background becomes foreground, and the self is no longer figure to the ground. The unity of the whole and the self as part of that unity are sensed. This experience of unity, often treated as a mere rush of mystic feeling, is also associated with a structure of conviction. The reversal of figure and ground felt in the contemplative moment has its analogy in the development of belief. This development, in turn, has some parallels to the movement of moral thought. The adolescent crisis of relativism, Stage 4½, can occur only because there is a dim apprehension of some more universal ethical standard in terms of which the cultural code is relative and arbitrary. To thoroughly and consistently explore the crisis of relativism is to decenter from the self, reverse figure and ground, and to see as figure the vague standpoint of principle, which is the background of the sense of relativity. Similarly, one may argue that the later crisis of despair, when thoroughly and courageously explored, leads to a figure–ground shift that reveals the positive validity of the cosmic perspective implicit in the felt despair.

Because the logical structure of Stage 7 is vague and its philosophic adequacy hard to justify, our concept of it must rest more on the psychological testimony of lives than upon structural analysis. In this testimony, it appears that the men from Socrates to Martin Luther King, who are most easily pointed to as having lived and died for their ethical principles, have had something like a strong Stage 7 orientation in addition to a commitment to rational principles of justice.

Turning from world history to our longitudinal study it is found that the concerns and ideas necessary for anything like a Stage 7 seem absent in all our longitudinal subjects in their twenties, even those at the highest moral stage in the sample, Stage 5.

Of the longitudinal subjects, even those who have reached postconventional Stage 5 morality, none has gone far toward development of a postconventional religious orientation. This appears to be at least negative evidence for Stage 7, indicating an area in which later adult morally-relevant development may occur. Although this area will probably not be amenable to a structural approach, with its philosophic notion of adequacy, the chief value of studying this area is philosophical, and requires a philosophic approach. One of the major aims of a life-span psychology may be to aid in communicating from generation to generation such wisdom as humans accumulate. Our experimental ,studies demonstrate that higher structural stages are not understood by lower stages, and that stage psychology is an aid to such understanding.

As an example, one of the chief values of the study of moral stages is the tentative isolation of a Stage 6 trend of moral thought. The number of adults who reach Stage 6 makes the study of this advanced moral stage meaningless for the description and explanation of most lives. It helps very much, however, for making understandable and viable a more adequate and difficult mode of moral thought. Our experimental college course suggests that the isolation and formulation of this stage helps Stage 5 students to transform the academic study of moral philosophers into a reformulation of their own thoughts to a more adequate level. In suggesting a more diffuse, but still philosophically articulated stage in the development of the sense of the meaning of life corresponding loosely to Erikson's seventh stage, it may be suggested that the study of lives may someday aid in the comprehension and communication of more adequate life meanings.

In conclusion, then, the questions to be asked in the study of lives are not simply those brought from psychology or sociology as disciplines. In the end, lives are studied so humans will learn how to live better. To ask questions of life-span psychology from this point of view is to engage in philosophy.

SOCIAL PROCESSES

CHAPTER 9

Intergenerational Relations and Continuities in Socialization

VERN L. BENGTSON
K. DEAN BLACK

UNIVERSITY OF SOUTHERN CALIFORNIA
LOS ANGELES, CALIFORNIA

ABSTRACT

The concept of "generations" is important in analyses of socialization, representing a crucial link between individual development and the broader social and historical context. Intergenerational relations are characterized in this chapter in terms of macro- and micro-perspectives on time, social structure, and socialization. The concept "generation" is defined in two ways: generation as cohort and as lineage, corresponding to these two levels of analysis. Relations between generations are seen as a continuous bilateral negotiation in which the young and the old exchange information and influence from their respective positions in developmental and historical time. There are inevitable intergenerational differences, stemming from contrasting types of contact with cultural institutions, differences in orientation toward future time, age differentials in social position, and within-cohort solidarity. There are also inevitable intergenerational similarities, resulting from inter-dependence, explicit attempts at transmission, and mutual effect-informational dependence. These factors which lead to difference and similarity between generations can be seen as one element in broader socio-cultural change, as generational units are involved in the production, testing, and selection of cultural alternatives in a feedback process.

207

I. Introduction

Socialization may be defined in its broadest sense as *the attempt to ensure continuity of a social system through time*. One of the classic dilemmas of human society has been the maintenance of a functioning social order despite successive invasions of neophytes: a younger generation lacking the skills and values to perform the intricate social roles of adulthood. The problem of generations, from this perspective, is to successfully transmit information that enables the young to function effectively in the increasingly complex social positions they encounter in adult life.

Such is the structural–functional approach which characterizes much that has been written on the phenomena of intergenerational relations. This perspective may be termed macro-analytic; it characterizes generations as age-based social aggregates whose interaction in the process of socialization has historical and cultural implications. Such a perspective is useful because much of socialization cannot be understood without reference to the broader schema of social structure and function of which they are a part.

However, the structural–functional approach omits several important considerations regarding socialization and relations between generations. For one thing, though issues of socialization have societal and cultural implications, their negotiation generally involves a personal confrontation between individuals (for example, within the family). For another, that negotiation of roles and standards of behavior usually results in a greater level of intrafamily similarity than is necessary to meet the requirements of social structure or function alone. A functional political order, for example, may be structured in many ways; but from conservative parents usually come conservative children with a regularity that transcends any structural requirement for continuity. In addition, socialization is a bilateral process: The old learn from the young, just as the young learn from the old. And in a constantly-changing society, the young and the old learn together as changes created by technological innovations, demographic shifts, and contact with other cultural groups alter the framework of the social system.

The purpose of this chapter is to examine issues of intergenerational relations as they affect both individual socialization and continuity of culture. The perspective taken allows consideration of both structural–functional and interpersonal–interactional aspects of generational analysis. Consistent with the focus of this volume, the chapter will deal primarily with those aspects of intergenerational relations that relate to socialization. For this reason, most attention will be given to the relationship between youth, entering adulthood, and the parenting generation. During these transition years, socialization issues most clearly influence the nature of the generational bond—as is highlighted in contemporary concern over the generation gap. Relations between other intergenerational units, however, will be examined as well. For the contrasts between elderly parents and middle-aged children allow examination of transmission effects lasting far into maturity, as well as exploration of cohort-historical and ontogenetic parameters of individual development.

The central argument of this chapter is that socialization and intergenerational relationships should be viewed from two perspectives of time and social structure: a macro-level, involving analysis of generations as large age-based aggregates and examining cultural continuity or change within the context of historical time; and a micro-level, in which generations are represented by lineage members and examining interpersonal interaction within the context of individual developmental time. There are six substantive points which will be made in support of this argument.

First, consideration of the *larger social structure is necessary* to a comprehensive view of socialization and interpersonal generational relations. The nature of the relationship between representatives of different generations within the family is, to a significant extent, determined by events experienced and attributes acquired by each generation as a result of membership in a particular set of age peers. Consequently, the relationship of family members to larger social and cultural elements within a historical time frame—the macroperspective—forms an important context for the generational relationship.

Second, *attributes linked to individual development* also form a significant context for the generational relationship. Each of the interacting parties—the old as well as the young—is a developing individual; each brings to the relationship a set of issues and concerns that are largely the result of his personal developmental experiences.

Third, the *generational relationship should itself be viewed as a developmental phenomenon* (that is, subject to systematic change over time). Both cultural change and individual developmental change may take place within the life span of a generational relationship, and so the relationship itself must also be seen as a continuously developing entity.

Fourth, the socialization relationship should be characterized as a continuous *bilateral negotiation*. Socialization is not a unidirectional process, with transmission inevitably proceeding from the older generations to the younger. Each member approaches the relationship as an agent of his own developmental interests; and so each influences and is influenced by the socialization process and its outcomes.

Fifth, the elements involved in the four themes just listed lead to the existence of two sets of factors that characterize the intergenerational relationship: those leading to intergenerational similarity and solidarity, and those leading to intergenerational difference. *The socialization process may be viewed as an interactional confrontation between developing individuals in which those factors leading to continuity and those leading toward difference are negotiated.*

Finally, *socio-cultural change* may be seen as the macro-level *result of the confrontation of similarity and change between generations.* This social-psychological perspective, implicit in many discussions in the sociology of social change, can be seen more clearly utilizing the concept of "feedback."

The discussion of these six themes begins with an overview of several dimensions of generational analysis. In the second section, the focus shifts to specific factors that lead to intergenerational differences or similarities. A concluding section makes some speculative comments on generations and social change.

II. Dimensions of Generational Analysis: Time, Social Structure, and Socialization

What *is* a *generation?* The term is increasingly used, both in life-cycle analyses and in the sociology of social change; nevertheless, there is little clear-cut agreement concerning its definition. For example, Troll (1970) has identified five distinct ways in which the concept of generation has been employed by social scientists. Part of the reason for this confusion is the failure to recognize that generations represent two distinct dimensions of social structure and function, as well as two kinds of temporal context; they characterize relationships at the societal level (as in the "youth vote"—a macro-dimension), and at the individual level (as in the family—the micro-dimension).

In this chapter, therefore, a distinction is made between two types of generational units: cohort and lineage. The *cohort* type of generational unit is composed of individuals of different ages who form social aggregates which have common characteristics. For example, members of the same cohort are at a similar stage of life-cycle development; they probably have experienced together the impact of historical events in their lifetime; and they may share substantially similar locations in age-related social positions (such as the family). This definition of generation emphasizes that age is a defining characteristic in social organization, with political and ideological implications for the broader society. In this sense, different generations are linked together at the macro-level of social relations much as social class is a parameter of social organization (Riley, 1971).

The *lineage* type of generational unit—seen at the micro-level—involves individuals of different ages who are linked in an explicit interpersonal relationship, defined socially or biologically. A crucial aspect of their interaction is the exchange of information: values, norms, and behaviors are transmitted across age-grades. Generation in this sense is a defining characteristic in interpersonal interaction. It implies not only that participants are of different ages, but also that socialization is a primary purpose of their interchange. The most obvious example of generation as lineage is seen within the family, but any socialization relationship may be characterized by the lineage type of generation.

TABLE 1

Dimensions of Social Structure, Time, and Socialization Related to Intergenerational Analysis

| Analytical level | Social structure | | Temporal context | Socialization issues |
	Generational unit	Dimensions of generational relationship		
Macro	Cohort: age-based social aggregate	Intercohort solidarity: 1. attitudes toward each other (sentiment) 2. interactions and confrontations in institutional contexts 3. difference (or similarity) in attitudes and behavior	Historical time	Continuity of social institutions: cohort replacement and succession
Micro	Family members of different generations	Lineage solidarity: 1. affect 2. association 3. consensus	Individual developmental time	Preparation of individual for maturity; transmission of attitudes and behaviors

In this section the distinction between these two types of generational units—cohort and lineage—is used to build a typology of generations in terms of social structure, time, and socialization. The typology, based on the contrast between macro and micro levels of analysis, is schematically summarized in Table 1.

First, in terms of the *unit* in the social structure, the generational component at the macro-level is the cohort—a social aggregate based on age (or year of birth). At the micro-level, the generational unit is the individual lineage member of a family differentiated by ranked descent. Second, the dimension of generational *relationship* corresponding to the macro-level is intercohort solidarity (these terms will be defined later); at the micro-level, it is lineage solidarity. Third, the temporal context of generations at the macro-level is historical time; at the micro-level it is individual developmental time. Finally, the dimension of *socialization* corresponding to the macro-level focuses on cultural continuity: cohort succession in the social institutions of the culture—politics and the economy, for example. At the micro-level, the issue is the development of motives and behaviors.

These dimensions, though represented for simplicity in Table 1 as independent, are in fact interrelated—as will be seen throughout the discussion to follow. For example, lineage solidarity is affected by the context of historical time as well as the individual developmental location of each member. Similarly, family socialization involves training for positions in the social structure as well as the teaching of moral attitudes and behavior.

A. Generations as Age-Based Social Aggregates: The Macro-Level

1. Generations and Social Organization

In the late nineteenth century, continental social historians—for the most part followers of Hegel—began systematically to explore generations as a dimension of social organization and political change. As summarized by Heberle (1951), Mannheim (1952a), and Marias (1968), they attempted to document the thesis that the rhythm of changes in ideas and political institutions is associated with the emergence of new biological generations. Their perspective implied that age-group differences are an important dimension of social organization and that age groups, and the interaction between them, are parameters of social differentiation as well as change over time. These ideas, first suggested by pre-Socratic social historians, have led to a resurgence of interest recently within sociology as may be seen in the work of Eisenstadt (1956), Goertzel (1972), Musgrove (1964), Parsons (1967), and Riley, Johnson, and Foner (1972).

As Mannheim describes it, the goal of the early continental sociologists was to define some unit of social time to account for change in the nature of the social fabric from period to period. There were two types of explanations corresponding to positivist and romantic–metaphysical definitions of generations—a distinction which is still useful when applied to current perspectives on generations. The early *positivist* school tied the movement of history to the fact that persons growing up in an identifiable span of time experience basically the same set of social events—wars, economic conditions, political movements—as they come of age. A new generation, arising with predictable regularity every 25 to 30 years, produces an identifiable historical era and represents a distinct link in the chain of progress. By contrast, the *romanticists* defined generations, not in terms of time span, but in terms of common sharing of experiences of a purely qualitative sort. A generation is defined by the shared *Zeitgeist* of an era which colors all its products and is in a sense, independent of chronological time. Thus, the classical period in art lasted for three calendar generations, while the expressionism of the late nineteenth century lasted only one. From this viewpoint, then, a generation lasts as long as a single art form or mode of expression prevails.

Mannheim proposes that the concept of generation be used as a kind of identifier of location in time, embracing related age groups who are embedded in a historical–social process. There is a trigger action of social and historical events which determines whether a new generation emerges every year, or every thirty or one hundred years, or whether it emerges at all. Thus, during some periods, generations do not appear as social change agents because there has not been a catalyst to produce their consciousness and cohesiveness as a generational unit.

The classical sociological perspective of generations just summarized has been employed most often to explain the rise of political movements. Feuer (1969), Flacks (1971), Goertzel (1972), Heberle (1951), and Mentre (1920) have applied the concept to the rise of national parties, to political movements, or to shifts in international policy. For example, Heberle has suggested the concept of "decisive politically relevant experiences" to interpret the institutions of society in different ways. He emphasizes that the entire generation will not have identical objective experiences, and a generation will include many subdivisions (social classes, for example) that create differences within them. Still, he suggests, intragenerational divisions are less pronounced than differences between generations. Such contrasts between generations will be greater in periods of rapid social change. The longer a generation stays in power politically (a "gerontocracy"), the sharper will be the clash with the youngest generation. Feuer (1969, p. 12) adds an ideological dimension to such intercohort confrontation: the "moral deauthorization of the older generation" has been a principal component of revolutionary change based on generational distinctions.

2. Generations and Continuity of Culture

Some more recent analyses, while not minimizing the importance of social change, have paid more explicit attention to social system continuity, looking at the processes that lead to a uniform cultural product, the persistence of cultural institutions over time, and even the maintenance of a "national identity" (Inkeles, 1968). The mechanisms involved in such processes are seen to reside in the *social system:* those efforts, formal and implicit, that prepare the individual for the new role he is assuming. Each culture preserves its own set of maxims, fairy tales, and moral stories. Games and national sports are developed and maintained that demand certain personal features which become highly valued.

Each society is also characterized by certain structural features that preserve within broad limits a particular cultural pattern. Consider, for example, the extent to which the configuration of the political and economic systems must influence certain personal attributes of the members of that society. Living in a capitalist economy has implications for personal behavior (McCelland, Atkinson, Clark, & Lowell, 1953). Societies can be seen to structure their socialization settings so as to produce relevant motives as well as behaviors in the young, as Bronfenbrenner (1970) and Inkeles (1966) have noted in comparisons between Soviet and American socialization settings.

3. Cohorts and Age Stratification

Whether the emphasis is on cultural change or social system continuity, it is apparent that, in this functionalist perspective, the outcomes of the socialization processes transcend the lives of single individuals. In this application, the focus of socialization is on the shaping of large-scale aggregates who are the carriers of culture. Although the immediate and intended outcome is the shaping of an age cohort, the same processes are ones through which cultures are changed and history is registered.

Interest in such considerations has received a major impetus with the emergence of a new subfield within sociology—the study of age stratification (Riley, 1971; Riley *et al.,* 1972). The major element in the age structure of society, and therefore the major analytic unit in the study of age stratification, is the *cohort*. The term cohort most often refers to those people who were born in the same period of history and thus are of approximately the same chronological age. However, a cohort may be defined by a common experiencing of any significant social event (Ryder, 1965). Indeed, it is often the case that membership in a cohort defined by some event other than birth may be more important behaviorally than membership in an age cohort. For example, a 40-year-old who returns to graduate school may have more in common behaviorally and attitudinally with his 25-year-old fellow students than with those of his own age who are involved in full-time employment. For purposes of simplicity, however, throughout this chapter, a cohort is defined as a group of people who share a common time of birth. The important implication is that they thus share many important, but often unrecognized, characteristics that mark them as a social aggregate:

experiencing events of history—war, economic depression, fashion, political upheavals—at the same point in ontogenetic development.

Four issues have emerged from the study of age stratification that are of interest to students of the intergenerational relationship (Riley, 1971). First, the observation that an individual's location in the changing age structure of society channels the way he feels and acts has led to the study of *cohort differences in attitudes and behaviors*. This line of inquiry has received major impetus from the contemporary concern about the generation gap. As has been pointed out elsewhere (Bengtson, 1970), three perspectives on the gap have emerged from scholarly analysis. For example, some feel that there is indeed a great gap between cohorts today that may lead to revolutionary change in the current social fabric (Friedenberg, 1969a,b; Mead, 1970; Reich, 1970; Richman, 1968; Slater, 1970). Others contend that the "gap is an illusion," having been over-played in recent years in a kind of mass-media overkill; this position is to some extent supported by growing evidence that the intercohort relationship is charac-terized by continuities in a variety of behavioral domains (Gamson, Goodman, & Gurin, 1967; Thomas, 1971a; Troll, 1970; Westby & Braungart, 1968). A third perspective ("selective continuities and differences") attempts to incor-porate the contradictory evidence concerning differences in attitudes and behavioral types between cohorts by positing a continuity in core goals and life orientations ("values"), but differences in such peripheral arenas of behavior as political opinions and sexual attitudes (Keniston, 1968; Thomas, 1971b).

A second dimension of the intercohort relationship, suggested by Riley (1971), involves their *attitudes toward and interactions with each other*—their age-based behavioral and attitudinal stances. This issue has generally been conceptualized under the general heading of age-grading. To what extent do people of the same age share a common orientation toward self and others that is based on age differences? Several gerontologists (Palmore & Whittington, 1971; Riley, 1971; Rose, 1964; Streib, 1965) and sociologists interested in youth (Berger, 1971; Flacks, 1971; Goertzel, 1972; Laufer, 1972; Wood, 1972) have speculated about the development of age-group consciousness, or a social cohesion based primarily on the underlying dimension of chronological age ("intracohort sol-idarity").

The third dimension involves the *mobility of cohorts through the social institutions*. Riley (1971) has couched this in terms of individual development, a perspective which the study of "careers" (Becker & Strauss 1968; McCall & Simmons, 1966; Spence & Lonner, 1971) has developed. However, we wish to turn attention beyond the individual toward the broader social implications of cohort flow. As Ryder (1965) has demonstrated, problems may be created when the adjacent cohorts differ greatly along the critical demographic dimen-sions. Cohorts may be differentiated in terms of size, age and sex distribution, and racial, language and socio-economic dimensions. Social institutions—for example, the number of jobs available, or positions at a university—are shaped along the dimensions of the preceding cohort. Thus, the succession of a younger cohort is often accompanied by problems that are a function of the differences in the extent of heterogeneity of the preceding and succeeding cohorts. In this sense, cohort differences may tear at the fabric of the existing social institutions.

The movement of cohorts through time and social institutions is very much related to the fourth dimension of interest in the study of intercohort relationships: *social change. Cohort succession is one basis for change in structure and composition of the population,* as well as the fundamental process in the introduction of novelty into the cultural pool. But the relationship between cohorts and social change is one of feedback and reciprocal interaction in that cohorts are shaped by their experience of historical change, and may in turn forge out the cultural future within that same confrontation. We will return to this theme in the last section.

The importance of age cohorts is not limited to their function as structural dimensions of large social systems. For example, within developmental psychology, an individual's membership in an age cohort is recognized as a significant determinant of the nature of developmental change. Many important methodological advances in recent years have come from efforts to determine the relative contribution of ontogenetic and cohort–historical factors (Baltes, 1968; Cattell, 1970a; Schaie, 1965; Wohlwill, 1970b). And because of the relationship between cohort membership and individual development, characteristics of age cohorts and their relationship within the large social structure are important social-psychologically as significant contextual elements in any interaction in which the participants differ in age. Certainly this is true of the interpersonal generational relationships within the family. It is to this interpersonal context that we turn next.

B. Generations in an Interpersonal Context: The Micro-Level

1. Lineage Effects and Socialization

The interpersonal generational relationship defines the generational tie as one denoting a lineage relationship. Generation as lineage refers to the vertical structural relationship in which the linkages are based either in blood ties (as in the family) or in the social designation of an explicit socializing relationship between neophyte and incumbent (as in the school). Although the focus of this chapter is on lineage within the family context, it should be emphasized that the concept proposed here has much broader application in socialization. Indeed, a lineal effect can be observed whenever there is an explicit attempt at information exchange between an incumbent and a neophyte regarding the latter's learning of a new social position.

Two alternative perspectives may be noted in the study of generations on a micro-analytic level. The first involves a focus on the *individual* and on the *product and process of socialization:* how he learns behaviors, skills, and motives appropriate to the social position he will eventually occupy. Analyzing the process of socialization involves investigating the methods by which learning of new roles or standards takes place; examination of the product of socialization focuses on the content of such learning. Various mechanisms have been proposed to characterize this learning: internalization (Aronfreed, 1969); role learning (Brim, 1966; Spence & Lonner, 1971); social comparison (Aronson, 1969); or transformation of identity (Strauss, 1969). The last term, originating from the interactionist perspective in sociology, has particular appeal in terms of its global characterization of continuity and discontinuity over time. It connotes the fact that the individual who has been successfully socialized to the new position carries with him a new outlook, a new set of skills, which spill over into other social positions; in a sense, the social system has changed his identity. From this perspective, one can clearly see that the issue of continuity in a social system over time may be a profitable starting point in the study of socialization (see Baldwin, 1969; Child, 1954; Inkeles, 1968; Maccoby, 1968; Strauss, 1969).

The second perspective focuses more directly on the intergenerational relationship itself, usually emphasizing cohesiveness or conflict. The main thrust of this perspective derives from the acknowledgement that, while the emphasis on the outcomes of socialization for the individual is important and enlightening, socialization is in fact a process of *bilateral negotiation* between the agent and inductee. Thus, it draws attention to what McCall and Simmons (1966, p. 202) call the "career of a relationship." Each participant approaches the arena of negotiation with his own set of developmental challenges. His approach to the socialization relationship, and the issues he brings to the intergenerational "negotiating table," are a product of those personal developmental challenges.

This focus on the relationship between generations is represented in the classical sociological perspective by Kingsley Davis (1940) in his discussion of the sociology of parent–youth conflict. His position can best be seen in contrast to the macro-perspective reviewed at the beginning of Section I. Whereas Mannheim, Pinder, and Heberle focus principally on historical and structural conditions producing differences between generations, Davis focuses more on interpersonal and developmental issues. Whereas Mannheim considers conflict between age groups frequent but not inevitable, Davis suggests that it is unavoidable.

For Davis, conflict between generations is the result of three universals in human development, modified by four variables having to do with the particular societal context of socialization. The three universal factors leading to parent–child conflict are: (1) the basic birth cycle difference between parent and child; (2) the decreasing rate of socialization with the coming of maturity; and (3) the resulting intrinsic differences between parents and children in the physiological, sociological and psycho-social planes of behavior. These constants in ontogenetic development, according to Davis, lead to interpersonal conflict; but the degree of that conflict in any given social system depends on several variables: (1) the rate of social change; (2) the complexity of the social structure; (3) the degree of integration of the culture; and (4) the velocity of movement within the culture; that is, social mobility.

Both of these perspectives—the analysis of socialization processes and products, and the analysis of intergenerational conflict—illuminate many important issues, but deal with somewhat limited aspects of the generational relationship. First, many intergenerational concerns do not deal with issues of socialization: helping patterns, ritual deference, affection, and effects of differential mobility on interaction, for example. Certainly the emphasis on socializaiton in intergenerational relations decreases as the younger generation becomes more independent. Second, to focus only on conflict ignores many other important dimensions of the interpersonal relationship between generations. The concept of *lineage solidarity*, discussed next, allows a more general characterization of the intergenerational relationship.

2. Lineage and Interpersonal Solidarity

It is apparent that discussion of some aspects of the generational relationship, as well as comparisons between the generational relationship and other interpersonal relationships, would be facilitated by taking a broader perspective than has heretofore characterized investigations of lineage relations. The dimensions of such a perspective would feature those characteristics that are common to interpersonal social relationships in general.

Homans (1950) has posited three basic social processes which characterize any human group: similarity, sentiment, and interaction. Similarity refers to those elements of behavior which interacting persons do in similar ways; in terms of opinions or values, the pair may be said to have reached a consensus. Sentiment has to do with the expression of affect regarding the relationship—how much one likes another. Interaction refers, of course, to associative behaviors: what they do together, and how often. At the macro-level, these processes were implicitly discussed earlier (see Table 1 and Part 3 of Section I) in terms of intercohort solidarity and contrasts: (1) differences between cohorts in attitudes and behavior; (2) attitudes (sentiments) of one cohort toward another; (3) interactions and confrontations between cohorts within the broad context of social institutions. The application of these solidarity processes are, however, more immediately apparent at the micro-level focusing on interaction between individuals (as in the family).

The idea that "consensus," "affect," and "association" represent basic ways in which individuals relate to one another has been borne out in the work of several other social scientists (see the review by Haddad, 1971). For example, Thibaut and Kelly (1967) found that the more cohesive the group, the more the group members will agree on group norms (i.e., consensus). Deutsch and Krauss (1965) found that the greater the group cohesiveness, the more they tend to work together (associate), and to place a high value upon one another (affection).

The family is a special type of small group. It follows, therefore, that if consensus, affect, and association are indexes of solidarity in groups generally, then they should perform a similar index function with regard to the lineage relationship within the family. Such a three-dimensional index of intergenerational solidarity has been developed in an ongoing study of family relations in three generations (see Bengtson, Olander, & Haddad, 1971; Haddad, 1971).

While the generational relationship shares common characteristics with other interpersonal relationships, there are also some important differences. For example, lineage ties—representing ascribed roles with strong if informal sanctions—are more permanent than many interpersonal social relationships. This suggests that if there is to be any real degree of solidarity, the relationship must change over time as the members themselves change.

The introduction of time into generational analysis at the micro-level opens up a new set of interesting developmental questions. How do intergenerational patterns of affect, association, and consensus change as family members move through the set of biological, psychological, and social experiences associated with growth and development? The next section deals with the temporal context of the generational relationship as a developing entity.

C. Time and the Generational Relationship

It is, of course, misleading to refer to *the* generational relationship as though its nature were static and unchanging. Rather, it exhibits change through time on two levels. First, with the passage of *historical* time, the lineage relationship as a social institution changes in nature just as any social organization alters its organization and structure through the years. Second, any individual lineage relationship changes within the shorter time framework of *individual development;* as each member moves through his own life course, the relationship changes. The purpose of this section is to examine the temporal context on these two levels and its implications for the generational relationship as a developing entity.

1. Generations and Historical Time

Concepts of time and age are not uncommon in the sociology of social institutions. As Nisbet (1969) has noted, the metaphor of growth and development applied to societies is one of the oldest sociological ideas of Western man.

Organizations (such as Veterans of Foreign Wars) can be said to grow old; and institutions (such as societal religious patterns or the military) are quite different in structure and function at different points of historical time within the same culture. However, the analysis of time and change is not as highly developed in sociology as it is within developmental psychology. The chapter by Neugarten and Datan in this volume elegantly summarizes issues of historical time as related to social time and life time. (See also Riley *et al.*, 1972.)

Any time scheme is basically a means of marking off the passage of events (Riegel, 1969). The time frame underlying the development of social institutions is based on events which signal an important change in the nature of the social fabric. Such events, noted Riegel, may be seen either as causative triggers or merely as symptoms of historical change. The time of their occurrence represents a time of transition to a new cultural condition. It is difficult to chart such events because they bear little systematic relationship to chronological time; their rate of occurrence is not fixed. At times, events such as wars or political crises may follow one another in rapid succession; at other times, there are periods of substantial cultural stability. Riegel (1969) has suggested that social change often depends on the interaction between historical figures and interest groups within the population. The rate of such change may increase continually over time as the number of such figures and groups increases. However, it is likely that such regularity is confounded by transient historical factors which, in interaction with more constant features of generational succession and social structure, generate historical epochs of continually varying lengths.

The variability in the rate of historical time is an important contextual element in the development of the intergenerational relationship. In times of rapid cultural change, a given generational relationship may witness (within the relatively brief limits of its life span) a number of significant events that influence the family members' relationship to one another. In fact, the rate of flow of historical time may be an important variable in its own right, regardless of the nature of the changes involved (Toffler, 1970). At any rate, it should be apparent that explanations of the development of an intergenerational relationship must take into account its location in historical time.

Some changes in the cultural condition bear directly on the generational relationship. Other cultural changes affect the intergenerational relationship more indirectly through their influence on the development of attitudes and behaviors of family members. Historical factors, transmitted to the individual through membership in an age cohort, have come to be recognized within developmental psychology as significant determinants of the nature of individual developmental change.

Important methodological advances in recent years have come from efforts to determine the relative contributions of ontogenetic, cohort, and historical factors in individual development (Baltes, 1968; Cattell, 1970a; Schaie, 1965;

Wohlwill, 1970b). The search for new strategies was precipitated by the observation that data on age-related phenomena will differ depending on the strategy used in data collection. The differences are due to the confounding of three sources of time-related variation: maturation, cohort membership, and historical factors present at the time of measurement. Several analytic techniques have been developed to sort out the various sources of influence and have generated some debate among proponents (described in Schaie, 1970). Discussion of those techniques is beyond the scope of this chapter. The important point is that, recently, researchers using such techniques have discovered that factors whose variations are based on historical time are significant sources of change in individual attributes and behaviors (see, for example, Baltes & Nesselroade, 1972). Such studies lend empirical support to the assertion that cohort-historical factors are important contextual modifiers of those interpersonal relationships— such as the generational relationship—that derive much of their nature from the characteristics of the persons involved (Clausen, 1972; Riley *et al.*, 1972).

2. Lineage Relationships and Developmental Time

Although historical factors do have developmental implications, most developmental events are meaningful only within the shorter time framework of the individual life span. When dealing with phenomena of individual development, the most commonly used time dimension is, of course, chronological time, with its associated concept of chronological age. Although age per se has often been used as an explanatory variable, it should be recognized that its value comes only because it is to some extent systematically related to the occurrence of events that have significant developmental importance. (The function of age in development studies is thoroughly discussed in Baltes & Goulet, 1971; and Wohlwill, 1970b). Such *developmental events* are important because: (1) They are experienced by most individuals during the course of life; and (2) they have some systematic influence in the ordering of human behavior.

Developmental events may be biological, psychological, or sociological in nature. Biological events include the attainment and loss of reproductive capacity, and the experiencing of growth and decline. Psychological events include the development of cognitive capacities, and changes in the experiencing of expansion and contraction of life, with consequent changes in orientation toward future events or life goals. Sociological events include the entrance into and exit from the major arenas of social interaction, along with succession to positions of greater or lesser responsibility and power within social positions.

It was stated earlier that time is basically a way of marking off the passage of events. It would seem reasonable, therefore, to posit a *developmental time* that marks off the passage of the developmental events just mentioned. However, such a time scheme introduces a complexity not found when dealing with chronological age. Chronological age is an unidimensional time scale: People are compared by age as points along a single time line. Such comparisons are very difficult when considering developmental time, especially when dealing with social events that are not structured by a fixed sequential ordering. A 20-year-old who is economically independent and holding a full-time job may perhaps be considered developmentally ''older'' than an age-mate who is being supported through college by his parents. However, if the college student is married, and the full-time worker is not, the matter of defining which is developmentally the ''oldest'' depends on the context of the social institution.

This example points out that developmental time is best considered a multidimensional time space, with each developmental event being represented by a separate dimension. An individual's developmental age would be represented by a set of numbers, each representing the number of years since the occurrence of a particular developmental event. Such data have been found to be significantly related to personal and interpersonal attributes (Rahe, McKean, & Arthur, 1967). Black (1972) asked 341 married couples to indicate how long it had been since they had experienced several events of developmental importance to the marriage relationship. Recency of occurrence of such events as experiencing a major illness, birth of the first child, achieving a major personal success, and having troubles with the boss were found to be associated with variation in such variables as the experiencing of negative feelings in marital interaction, and the self-esteem of the marriage partners.

Parents and children have experienced different sets of developmental events. An obvious consequence is the existence of accompanying differences between generations in attitudes and behaviors. Insofar as those differences influence the relationship that is developed, their identification becomes a fundamental issue in any discussion of the generational relationship.

III. The Negotiation of Difference and Similarity

The discussion to this point has presented the generational relationship in terms of general dimensions of time and social structure. The focus now shifts to a discussion of specific factors that influence a particular intergenerational relationship: forces that lead to differences, and forces that lead to similarity, between the individuals involved.

The prototype of the generational relationship is that within the family exists a personal, diffuse, vertical social relationship between people who are linked by genetic endowment and by an explicit socialization relationship. This relationship will be characterized as *lineage solidarity*. The discussion to follow will be couched in terms of this prototype, but the elements presented can be applied equally to generational relations at the macro-level (as between age-based aggregates in the society) or, indeed, between nonrelated individuals of different ages involved in a socializing relationship (as between teacher and pupil). Such relations may be termed *intercohort solidarity*. (For a slightly different formulation see Riley *et al.*, 1972, pp. 434–438.)

It has been suggested that the generational relationship should be viewed as one of bilateral negotiation in which the issues negotiated are based in several important contextual elements. First, each lineage member belongs to an age cohort, a membership that has implications for behavior, both as independent individuals and with respect to one another. Second, the relationship exists within a context of variable historical time, such that the issues negotiated on a personal level may also have cultural and historical consequences. Third, each lineage member is a developing individual; within the relationship, each represents a unique set of concerns in working out those problems that face him as a result of his own personal developmental experiences.

At the most general level, the outcome of the process of intergenerational negotiation at any point in time may be characterized in terms of the degree of solidarity between the lineage members. As was previously discussed, interpersonal solidarity is conceptualized as having three components: affect, association, and consensus. However, to consider the development of all three dimensions of solidarity would introduce a degree of complexity in the discussion to follow that would prove unwieldy. As a consequence, the term lineage solidarity will be used from this point to refer to a global characterization of the strength of the relationship, recognizing that some precision is lost through this expediency.

The purpose of this section is to describe the development of lineage solidarity as a result of the interaction of the three contextual modifiers of the generational relationship as summarized. The discussion will proceed in two parts. The first part focuses on those elements of the relationship that generate intergenerational differences and the dissolution of lineage solidarity. The second part deals with those elements which favor the development of lineage solidarity and the production of intergenerational similarity or continuity.

A. *Intergenerational Differences and Strains on Lineage Solidarity*

It should be noted at the outset that differences between generations do not necessarily result in the dissolution of lineage solidarity or in disruptive intergenerational conflict. There can be marked differences in political views, for example, within a highly cohesive family marked by high affection, a great deal of interaction, and consensus regarding moral philosophy. Nevertheless, from the definitional interrelationship among the three elements of interpersonal solidarity proposed by Homans (1950), any differences between members represent a potential strain on the cohesion of the relationship. In this section some inevitable differences are discussed which arise from the temporal context of generational relations.

It was noted earlier that members of different generations face each other from contrasting points in developmental time. The following are four ways in which the differential location of lineage members in developmental time creates conditions that tend to produce intergenerational differences and, consequently, the prospect of a reduction of lineage solidarity and continuity. These factors can be seen not only in parent–youth relationship, but also in terms of differences between the elderly and the middle-aged. They apply not only within the micro-structure of the family, but also within the macro-structure of the society.

1. The Phenomenon of "Fresh Contact"

As an individual moves through his life, he achieves a continually greater exposure to the political, educational, economic, and religious institutions of society. His adaptation within those institutions depends on his capacity to understand their nature and identify his relationship with them. These are, of course, social settings in which members of older generations have already achieved some level of adaptation. Consequently, part of the adaptive process involves learning to some extent what he is told by the incumbents. However, the things he is taught are subject to verification by actual experience. He must immerse himself personally in the social setting. In so doing, he is able to come to an empirical understanding of its operation. Preconceptions usually succumb to the weight of experience, so his adaptations are largely of his own making, notwithstanding the admonitions of his elders.

Mannheim (1952a) refers to this process of individual adaptation as the phenomenon of "fresh contact." Fresh contact, he says, is the result of the biological fact that:

> Cultural creation and cultural accumulation are not accomplished by the same individuals— instead we have the continuous emergence of new age groups.
> This means, in the first place, that our culture is developed by individuals who come into contact anew with the accumulated heritage. *In the nature of our physical make-up,* a fresh contact (meeting something anew) always means a changed relationship of distance from the object and *a novel approach in assimilating, using, and developing the preferred material* [1952, p. 294; emphasis added].

Since learning is a process of ordering new experiences, those things that do not make sense will stand out with disturbing clarity. The inconsistent and the undesirable will claim the major attention of the young as they try to understand the adult world. In other words, the "fresh contact" generally has the result of revealing the inconsistencies in the cultural fiber, inconsistencies that are most easily seen when entering from the outside.

Because of this capacity of the young for identifying the cultural inconsistencies, their fresh contact with the cultural heritage has usually resulted in the adoption by the young of utopian ideals—ideals that demand consistency and condemn hypocrisy (Davis, 1940; Erikson, 1950, 1965; Feuer, 1969; Keniston, 1968; Mannheim, 1952a; Musgrove, 1964). Such internally represented ideal states are important in that they inform the behavior selection process: that behavior is selected which is seen as most likely to lead to the attainment of the internally represented ideal. Consequently, along with ideals, the young adopt novel forms of behavior that may be incomprehensible—even obscene—to their parents, who do not share their perceptions of social reality. There is a conflict in definition of what is "sacred" and what is "profane" (Durkheim, 1927). In the presence of such unshared perceptions, mutual understanding is problematical, and change is very difficult, since to each it involves a denial of reality.

2. Future Time and the Developmental Stake

The preceding discussion suggested that some interage differences are the result of different perceptions of the *same* external reality. However, it is apparent that the old and the young do not, in fact, share the same perception of external reality (see Ahammer & Baltes, 1972; Andersson & Ekholm, 1971; Bengtson & Kuypers, 1971). One significant difference in the real worlds perceived by the different generations is their relative positions with respect to the biological facts of growth and decline and a finite life span. The young are experiencing growth and expansion and a relationship to time that includes a seemingly limitless future. On the other hand, their parents are approaching a time of decline and contraction, and the finite limits of their future are becoming increasingly apparent.

One result of this difference in location within life span is a difference in orientation toward future time (Bortner & Hultsch, 1972). Kingsley Davis speaks of this difference in orientation to future time, and its impact on the generational relationship:

> On the one hand, the young person, in the stage of maximum socialization, is, so to speak, moving into the social organization. His social personality is expanding, i.e., acquiring an increased amount of the cultural heritage, filling more powerful and numerous positions. His future is before him, in what the older person is leaving behind. The latter, on the other hand, has a future before him only in the sense that the offspring represents it. Therefore, there is a disparity of interest, the young person placing his thoughts upon a future which, once the first stages of dependence are passed, does not include the parent, the old person placing his hope vicariously upon the young [1940, p. 383].

The suggestion here is that the difference in orientation to the future contributes to another important generational difference: discrepancies in the way different generations view their relationship to one another. One recent study (Bengtson & Kuypers, 1971) found that parents and youth do indeed differ in the way they characterize their mutual relationship. Parents tended to minimize the distance between the generations, emphasizing intergenerational similarity, while the young tended to maximize differences. The authors suggested that the contrast in perception was because of differences in the extent to which each member is committed to that relationship as a means of attainment of personal goals. The older generation appears to have a developmental stake in the young in that they are concerned with the creation of social heirs. This explains why an older generation might tend to minimize the differences perceived between themselves and their children.

The developmental stake of the young is quite different. They have a strong investment in establishing their personal life styles, in forming their attitudes toward major issues and institutions which are, of course, often changing as the result of technical innovations or demographic changes. The young have a greater investment in the *creation,* as opposed to the *validation,* of values and strategies. Such issues imply the need for freedom to experience and develop.

It is likely that this difference in the developmental stake of parents and children has an important influence in the relative power of each to determine the course of the relationship. This suggestion is based in the *principle of least interest* as proposed by Willard Waller (1938), who suggested it as an explanation of exploitation in the courtship process. The principle of least interest asserts that the person who is *least* committed to the maintenance of the relationship is in the best position to bargain for influence, for he has the least to lose if the relationship is broken. On the other hand, the person with the greatest commitment must often make concessions to the will of the other person in order to avoid an implied threat of break-up. This principle has interesting implications for the generational relationship. The parent has an explicit, socially defined authority over the child. However, the principle of least interest suggests that the child has a de facto power over the parent which operates contrary to social definition. Under such conditions, exercise of parental authority carries with it an implied threat to the stability of the relationship, and so parents may tend to minimize differences.

3. Differences in Social Position

The difference in socially defined power just described suggests a general proposition regarding age and social structure: Status within a social institution tends to increase with age. This fact gives the older person both greater rewards in the institution or social position and a greater stake in the status quo—at least until the occurrence of the withdrawal from social positions that often accompanies old age. This can be seen at the micro-level in the family (Schaefer, 1959), or at the macro-level, in terms of political powerlessness of youth (Martin, Bengtson, & Acock, 1972). In short, one aspect of generational differences involves contrasts in social status in which the young and the old are usually disadvantaged by comparison to the middle aged.

There is a second implication of generational differences in social position that may be perhaps best understood by focusing on the concept of the *developmental task*. Robert Havighurst has been primarily responsible for the development of this concept (see chapter by Havighurst, this volume). In an earlier paper (1956)[1], he defined it as "a task which arises at or about a certain period in the life of an individual, successful achievement of which leads to his happiness and to success with later tasks, while failure leads to unhappiness in the individual, disapproval by the society, and the difficulty with later tasks [p. 215]." Later he emphasized that "a developmental task is a *social role* which is expected of most people in a society and which most people come to expect and desire for themselves [pp. 215–216; emphasis added]."

Developmental tasks are anchored in the social structure; they are therefore particular to the individual's social situation. Since the lineage members occupy different positions in the social structure, it is apparent that their respective developmental tasks will orient them toward different activities. A portion of the developmental tasks of each will reside in their relationship to one another. Each generation, and particularly the younger generation, also has a set of developmental tasks in social arenas that are not shared by the adjacent generation. This implies that, although parents share to some extent the child's concern with his adaptation to his changing social world, differences in their respective developmental tasks will undoubtedly cause them to have different approaches to the adaptive process.

McArthur (1962) employed the developmental task concept to understand parent–youth conflict. For example, the parental task of assisting the adolescent to become a responsible adult may conflict with the young person's task of achieving emotional independence from parents. Similarly, if parents have difficulty with the reestablishment of their marital relationship in the "empty nest" period, they may cling to their child and hamper his efforts to achieve new and more mature relations with age mates of the opposite sex.

There is also evidence that changes in developmental tasks have an impact on the relationship between elderly parents and their children. Streib (1965) found that following retirement an elderly parent is likely to place less importance on his children's occupational success than he did before. As an explanation for this finding, Streib suggests that the social changes taking place at retirement cause a lowered awareness of achievement and an increased orientation toward family ties that achievement may be seen to threaten. Retirement also confronts an older person with an increase in leisure time. Although there is evidence that the freedom of the geographical ties of work leads some retired parents to migrate to be near their children (Troll, 1971), little is known about the extent to which associations with children and grandchildren are used by retired people to meet the challenges of increased leisure.

[1]Research on developmental task concept. *School Review*, **64**, 215–233. Published by University of Chicago Press. © 1956 by University of Chicago Press.

4. The Development of Within-Cohort Solidarity

Another important social determinant of an individual's relationship with family members of different generations is his membership in an age cohort. The previous sections documented that cohort membership is an important determinant of human behavior. However, the impact of cohort membership is augmented with other cohort members (Riley *et al.*, 1972, pp. 434–439). Cohort consciousness seems to result when an age group feels that it shares a common condition that is not experienced by other cohorts. This seems most often to characterize the young, and is most manifest during periods of great social change. Mannheim (1952a) speaks of youth's sense of participation in a common destiny. Feuer (1969) describes the alienation felt by the young in their relationship with a "morally de-authorized" adult generation.

The common condition of the young is in part a function of their relationship to historical time. Mead (1970) likens parents in our rapidly changing society to pioneers in time, living in a new era, but linked in memory to another time. Their children cannot share and comprehend their memory. Being unhampered by the memories, the children are better able to comprehend the new era. As the parents try to meet new problems with old solutions, their children observe their failure and know that something must be done, but not how to do it. Their search for solutions, what Mannheim has called their "collective strivings," generates the sense of common destiny and alienation from the adult generation that many have seen as the basis of cohort consciousness.

The common condition of the young is a function not only of their relationship to historical time, but also of their common location with respect to developmental phenomena (see Chapter 3, this volume). In fact, it is probably the fact of their common location in developmental time that gives cohort consciousness its accompanying emphasis on chronological age as an organizer of human experience. As was pointed out earlier, developmental time is multidimensional, with chronological age only one of the dimensions. However, it is readily apparent that, in contrast with later life, the years of development prior to adulthood are characterized by a movement along all dimensions of developmental time that is strongly determined by an individual's chronological age.

This fact is particularly evident when considering the sociological components of the developmental time space. As one moves through the early years of life, entrance into new social engagements is very closely linked to chronological age, sometimes by law. Consequently, age grading forms the primary time-based behavioral constraint since movement in the various social arenas takes place somewhat in "lock-step" fashion; the result is that members of the same chronological age cohort are treated as an undifferentiated group, when in fact they may be heterogeneous in character. Age grading enhances cohort solidarity.

However, one might ask if those same conditions do not characterize the old. They are in a period of life when chronological age once again is an important determinant of participation in social positions—heterogeneous in ability to carry on in a job, they are nonetheless undifferentiated by rules that require retirement at age 65. There is evidence that the old are similar to the young in their feeling of alienation (Martin, Bengtson, & Acock, 1972). Kalish (1969) even argues that the young and the old share so many common characteristics that they are generation gap allies; and although they do not appear to perceive themselves as having substantial similarities (Bengtson, 1971), it is not unreasonable to suggest that the same conditions that generate cohort consciousness among the young do the same for the old. Such considerations have generated debate as to whether the old are beginning to form a distinct subculture, complete with class consciousness (Palmore & Whittington, 1971; Rose, 1964; Streib, 1965). If such age consciousness among the old exists, it might be asked to what extent that allegiance to age peers comes at the expense of the lineage bond with younger family members. One would suspect that the developmental stake of the old in the young would work strongly in favor of family as opposed to age peer allegiances if they were in conflict.

B. Intergenerational Similarity and Lineage Solidarity

The discussion in the preceding section would lead one to conclude that differences and discontinuity characterize the generational relationship more often than not. However, the components that generate intergenerational difference do so in the presence of other, perhaps even more potent, forces which engender generational continuity. Such forces derive from the inescapable interdependence of adjacent cohorts, at the macro-level, and even more directly from the explicit transfer of information between generations at the micro-level of analysis.

1. Interdependence and Generational Continuity

Adjacent cohorts, though differing in age, share a common location in historical time; they also share a common culture. For this reason, contrasting cohorts are interdependent—the characteristics of one in many ways determine configurations of the second.

Several examples can be given which highlight the interdependence of cohorts. First, consider ideologies. As discussed earlier, analyses of youth movements stress the importance of the ideologies that develop and give them shape and substance (Feuer, 1969; Flacks, 1971; Goertzel, 1972). But such ideologies arise in response to, and have meaning in relation to the ideas dominant in the current social structure. In addition, those ideologies emerge in response to the problems the cohort faces during critical developmental years. Since the focus of the problems facing an emerging cohort is almost always the incumbent generation, the attempt to solve those problems will shape the younger cohort in a way that is a function of the ideologies of the parent cohort. In short, the value base of cohort solidarity is often a reaction to the previous generation—often positive, as in a reaffirmation of those values, occasionally negative, resulting in revolution. The coexistence of adjacent cohorts in the face of such developmental problems is accomplished through a process of negotiation of a "social contract" (Elkind, 1970). The bilateral nature of such contracts implies the interdependence of the characteristics of each cohort.

A second example is the "structural fit" between an emerging cohort and the positions or institutions they are moving into. The fact of generational succession means that the younger cohort must eventually occupy most of the institutions currently occupied by the parent generation. Since those institutions take on structural features that are to a great extent determined by the demographic characteristics of the incumbent cohort, social institutions become a sort of procrustean bed for the incoming generations (Ryder, 1965, 1972). When the demographic composition of the younger cohort differs markedly from that of the parent cohort (characterized by greater numbers, or better education, etc.), problems will arise. Furthermore, characteristic cohort features will develop as a result of the requirement that the neophyte generation take on some structural features that are at least minimally compatible with the current institution's structure.

2. Similarity and Effect-Information Dependence between Generations

There are other features of intergenerational interdependence, seen best at the micro-level, which lead even more directly to the maintenance of continuity from one generation to the next. This is the usual connotation of the term *transmission;* it is the focus of research on the product of socialization. In what ways can this more direct manifestation of generational interdependence be seen? Although a complete discussion of this issue is beyond the scope of this chapter (see Clausen, 1968; Goslin, 1969; Riley *et al.* 1972, for reviews), some aspects can be briefly suggested.

First, although the emphasis in preceding sections was on the idea that the old and the young experience social reality from different viewpoints, the old and young share an immense foundation of common experience. Even in times of social change, most of the cultural features remain fairly constant and are similarly perceived by both young and old. Each individual experiences only a small portion of the total social reality. The segments of reality experienced by different persons overlap to some extent, and it is probably in the family that the overlap is greatest, though this becomes less so as the child grows older. It is not surprising, therefore, that many behaviors and predispositions—for example, standards of morality, political involvement, and religious participation—evidence substantial similarity from one generation within the family to the next (Thomas, 1971a; Troll, Neugarten, & Kraines, 1969).

Second, there is the more direct issue of the dependence of children on their parents. Jones and Gerard (1967) have developed an innovative conceptualization concerning two kinds of dependence manifest throughout life. Effect dependence refers to the reliance on another for the direct gratification of needs. Information dependence refers to the reliance on another for the explanation and interpretation of external events. Both information and effect dependence of a child on his parents decrease as the child develops. However, even though the parental monopoly over the regulation of childhood experiences ceases, it is reasonable to suspect that the effects of that monopoly—including a perceptual framework within which experiences are interpreted—persist well beyond the period of actual dependency. To the degree that this is true, the "fresh contact" described by Mannheim (1952a) is not entirely "fresh," but a reinterpretation within some broad limits of perception imposed by the early regulation of experience and explanation. The generational overlap of perceptual approaches is one of the factors which leads to intergenerational similarity.

A third issue involves application of the concept of information dependence to role modeling. The intrafamily continuity described is likely to become most apparent as the younger lineage member moves into full adult status and encounters critical life-cycle transition points already experienced by older family members (Strauss, 1969). These include not only the transitions into the new adult social institutions such as marriage, parenthood, and occupation, but later-life transitions such as child-launching and retirement as well. Because age peers tend to move in somewhat similar schedules through life, they are not always able to function as role models for one another to ease the life-cycle transitions. Parents are often the most likely role models for life's transitions. The result is a degree of intergenerational behavioral similarity that may exist even in the face of ideological differences grounded in peer relationships (Hill & Aldous, 1969).

IV. Conclusion: Generational Relations and Cultural Change

The preceding sections have described a developmental process in which the young person's approach to the adult world leads to an awareness of community with other young people, the development of an utopian ideal with respect to adult functioning, and his eventual integration into the adult social structure with a consequent loss of cohort cohesiveness and utopian ideals. However, this description has included only in passing the broader outcome of these socialization considerations: cultural change. Through what process do the innovations of youth become the established social order?

This chapter concludes with a speculative answer to that question, applying the concept of *feedback* to the macro-level of generational relations. Feedback as a principle of human behavior has been developed within the general theoretical approach that has come to be known as systems theory. Feedback involves the following: (1) an internally represented goal or ideal state; (2) a process that allows the production of behaviors that may lead to the goal; (3) a means of selecting the behavior to be used that involves (a) trying out or testing the various alternatives, and (b) observing the consequences.

Here it is suggested that cultural change may occur through just such an interpersonal feedback process: the cycle of generations allows man to (1) produce an idea about an ideal state; (2) generate alternative cultural patterns intended to reach that state; (3) test or try out the alternatives in order to see which does indeed lead to the attainment of the ideal state; and (4) select and maintain one or more of the alternative cultural patterns that then become the new social order.

A. The Production of Cultural Alternatives

In Section II-A, it was emphasized that the utopian ideals which young people share because of their similar location in developmental time are a major integrating force in the development of cohort cohesiveness. However, the ideals have another important function: they are a continual source of alternatives to the cultural status quo. The current debate about the status of conventional marriage provides an interesting case in point. As the young approach the culturally recommended age for marriage they observe that at least half of the marriages of the current adult generation end in either divorce or separation, or are characterized by tension, hate, and failure. An understandable reluctance to become involved in that kind of social situation has led to an increasing experimentation with viable alternatives: living together; trial marriage; childless unions; and compound or communal unions.

The mechanisms for the perpetuation and propagation of these cultural alternatives can be seen in the attention given them by the communications media, and in the social prophets who predict which of the cultural alternatives will survive (Toffler, 1970; Rozak, 1969).

B. The Testing of Cultural Alternatives

Predictions get tested; the alternatives get tried out and their consequences observed. There is one interesting feature of this experimental process in the arena of cultural change: The young are not only the theory builders, but are their own experimental group. They develop many of their ideals as outsiders—as nonmembers of the very world they want to change; then they must test their own ideals as they become participants in the adult social institutions.

It is inevitable, however, that most of the cultural alternatives will not survive. In any operation of feedback principles, behavior selection is accomplished through a successive narrowing of a once large set of alternatives. It appears that contemporary American society is characterized by an unusually large number of cultural alternatives. It will be comforting to some to know that, through the operation of feedback principles, most of the new life styles will die out. However, it should also be comforting to others, who, distressed by the inequalities and rigidity of the present social order, hope for a more tolerant and humane society in the future. For such a large array of cultural alternatives increases the probability of finding those behavior patterns which are closest to cultural ideals.

C. The Selection of Cultural Alternatives

There are two aspects to the interdependency of the young and the current adult generation which influence the selection process. The first has to do with the fact that testing is risky and it takes time. When the young become functioning members of the adult society there are pressures to be up and about the business of being an adult. Such pressures may not be easily ignored, and since the testing process takes time and may not be productive, it may often be foregone in favor of some "safer" behavior pattern.

This suggests that if something were to relieve some of the pressure to move quickly into functional adult roles, the cultural selection process would be more successful. For example, added time in the socially "irresponsible" youth role should mean that more alternatives may be generated and perhaps tested, and more extensively as well. To the extent that that is true, the extended adolescence described by Berger (1971) may be functional from the point of view of society, though perhaps creating some difficulties on the level of individual development.

The second aspect of generational interdependency is related to the first. However, it refers not to pressures toward conventional adult behavior, but to the proscriptions against the more deviant cultural alternatives. In the process through which the generations negotiate their relationship, the adult generation must tolerate some deviations from the accepted standards of adult performance. If it is true that the young cannot test all of the alternatives before pressures toward functional adulthood force selection, it is likely that the new forms that are tested will be those that fall close enough to the range of tolerance that they may be allowed to occur without disturbing some minimal level of social stability. If more deviant alternatives are to be tested, youth must sever the interdependent relationship, hence the development of communes and other youth communities. It is often these most deviant forms that are given the greatest attention in the media so that, even though in practice they are carried out in relative isolation from the adult social world, they are observed by adults and are symbolically available to the young as they order their social experiences.

There is another point that must not be ignored in this discussion. It has so far been assumed that the ideals of youth remain constant, that what is tested and selected are the alternative pathways to those ideal states. However, one result of the attainment of functional adulthood may be a restructuring of ideals. Experience may teach the young that what they once condemned has some redeeming features when viewed from the inside; or they may discover that their ideal states, when attained, reveal some undesirable and unanticipated features.

From this perspective, cultural change has its origins in the relationship between generations. It is a process which generates a superficial appearance of a massive overhaul of the current conditions; but it also includes feedback mechanisms that insure a more gradual transformation of society.

CHAPTER 10

A Problem in Life-Span Development:
The Interactional Analysis of Family Attachments[1]

WILLARD W. HARTUP
JACQUES LEMPERS

UNIVERSITY OF MINNESOTA
MINNEAPOLIS, MINNESOTA

ABSTRACT

Family attachments are traditionally analyzed with reference to the individual personalities of family members, and attachment development is commonly thought to begin with the infant–mother relationship. Such personological models are questioned, and interactional alternatives are proposed for conceptualizing the infant–mother relationship as well as other family attachments.

I. Attachment and the Personological Perspective

. . . we pictured the relation of ego–libido to object–libido in a way which I can make plain to you by an analogy from zoology. Think of those simplest of living organisms (the amoebas) which consist of a little-differentiated globule of protoplasmic substance. They put out protrusions, known as pseudopodia, into which they cause the substance of their body to flow over. They are able, however, to withdraw the protrusions once more and form themselves again into a globule. We compare the putting out of these

[1]Preparation of this paper was supported by Grant No. HD05027-02, National Institute of Child Health and Human Development.

protrusions, then, to the emission of libido on to objects while the main mass of libido can remain in the ego; and we suppose that in normal circumstances ego–libido can be transformed unhindered into object–libido and that this can once more be taken back into the ego [Freud, 1916, p. 416 (see Freud, 1963)].

Freud (1957) first used the pseudopod as an analogue to attachment in his essay "On Narcissism: An Introduction" in 1914. It was used later in the 1916 "Introductory Lectures" (Freud, 1963) and elsewhere, and it remains the most vivid simile to be found in the psychoanalytic literature on object relations. In this formulation, social attachments were conceived as outcomes of invisible projections of the child's libidinal protoplasm. They are sent forth into the social world, clapped onto pleasure-giving objects such as the maternal breast, and function thenceforth as bonds that hold the child in proximity with the social object.

According to Freud, the first signs of attachment activity appear in infancy; the activity is erotic. Other writers (e.g., Bowlby, 1969) have pointed to a broader significance of these early object relationships in that they promote survival by protecting the infant from predators. Whatever the initial function, attachment necessities do not cease when the child is better able to fend for himself. Attachments represent the foundations of socialization throughout the life span and have important implications in the ontogeny of social institutions and in cultural evolution.

Within psychoanalytic theory, all social relationships are thought to begin with a tie to the primary caretaker based on feeding and the provision of other gratifications. Attachments to persons other than the caretaker—fathers, siblings, peers, teachers, lovers, spouses, and offspring—represent complex extensions of the initial attachment to the caretaker, and are thought to be similar to it in many ways. Social learning theorists have also highlighted the primacy of attachment to the mother and have assumed that this social bond plays a role in the later development of attachment to peers and other nonfamily members. Persistent bids for attention—be they from a child, an adolescent, or an old person—are thought to be partly generalized aspects of the early behavior repertoire vis à vis the mother. Thus, quite diverse theorizing suggests that affiliation begins with the development of pseudopodical bonds to the mother and that these, in turn, influence attachments formed to other persons.

The life-span significance of such conceptions of attachment (i.e., attachments defined as characteristic of persons) revolves around the following problems: (1) determining the time at which first specific attachments emerge; (2) the emergence of specific attachments to individuals other than the original object; (3) the morphology of the attachment repertoire (i.e., the repertoire that promotes proximity with specific objects); (4) changes in the attachment pattern that are correlated with chronological age; and (5) changes in the regularity with which specific situations elicit attachment behavior.

Nearly all life-span analyses of attachment are based on models of childhood development. That is, the processes governing attachment formation in adulthood, relinquishment of attachments in old age, and reaction by adults to separation and loss are most often conceptualized as modifications of the prototypic social relations of childhood (Riley, Foner, Hess, & Toby, 1969). By and large, such analyses have proved superficial and lacking in power, partly because the circumstances of attachment realignment in adulthood are not the same as the circumstances of attachment formation in early childhood. For example, social withdrawal is expected of aging persons, but such withdrawal is neither sought nor sanctioned for the young child. Erikson (1950) recognized this failure to achieve goodness of theoretical fit between models of childhood socialization and the circumstances of the aged person, but his impact on the empirical life-span literature has been minimal.

The pervasive importance of first attachments has also been questioned by students of comparative psychology (e.g., Harlow). It is proposed, alternatively, that early proximity-seeking in primates develops as at least two separate behavioral systems: an adult affectional system, and a peer affectional system. The hypothesis that these systems are independent of each other is supported by findings showing that: (1) Young primates use different behaviors to express affection to adults and to peers; (2) A given condition will elicit attachment behavior differentially, depending on whether the available object is an adult or peer; and (3) Adults engage in certain activities with their offspring, such as play, much less frequently than peers do (Maccoby & Masters, 1970). Thus, there is genuine doubt that attachment is a single, endlessly differentiating system. On the contrary, there may be multiple classes of attachment activity which are differentiated from one another mainly by type of social object. Although only attachment to parents and to peers has been mentioned, such theorizing would imply that attachment bonds, as manifested by parents for their offspring, by lovers for each other, and by numerous other dyads are ontogenetically independent response classes.

Without arguing this point further, the following feature of contemporary theorizing should be underscored: Attachment is nearly always conceptualized as a tie or bond having *its locus in the individual*. It is conceived as a characteristic of infants, of children, of spouses, of parents—i.e., it is a characteristic of the individual's. Even though the attachment is focused on some particular object, the attachment is conceived as an attribute of the individual himself.

Most contemporary empirical studies follow in the personological tradition. Some assessments of individual differences in infant or child attachment have involved maternal interviews (e.g., Schaffer & Emerson, 1964) while others have involved observation of mother–child interaction. One common strategy in studying the mother–infant relationship has been to observe sequences of motor behavior during periods when the mother and infant can interact under quasi-natural, relatively unconstrained conditions. (Studies of this general sort have been conducted by Ainsworth & Bell, 1970; Bishop; 1951; Coates, Anderson, & Hartup, 1972a; Hatfield, Ferguson, & Alpert, 1967; Lewis, 1972; Maccoby & Feldman, 1972; and Smith, 1958.) Frequencies, latencies, or response durations may be observed that refer to glances made by the infant to his mother, the number of times he locomotes toward her, the times he touches her, instances of clinging or grasping, the frequency of his vocalizations to her, and his replication of portions of her motor repertoire (mimicry). Parallel data may be obtained showing maternal glances at the infant, approaches to him, talking, touching, grasping, and mimicking of the infant, and, by means of sequential analysis, we can construct a picture of mother–infant interaction made up of short response chains. In this way, Gewirtz and Gewirtz (1969) found that infant smiles elicit adult smiles, and others have provided normative data concerning the elicitation of infant smiles by adult smiles (e.g., Washburn, 1929); also, vocalization has been found to stimulate vocalization (Lewis, 1972). Seldom does the response chain get longer in sequential analysis than three units (that is, A's Response $\rightarrow$ B's Response $\rightarrow A$'s Response) although Markovian models may be extended to longer chains (Freedle & Lewis, 1971).

Ordinarily, the interactional potential of such observations is ignored; instead, the data are used to describe but one individual—the infant. Thus, Ainsworth and Bell (1970) studied the behavior of one-year-old infants in a strange situation; and others (Coates, Anderson, & Hartup, 1972a,b; Lewis & Ban, 1971) studied interrelations and stability of various approach behaviors directed at the mother as well as the occurrence of separation-induced crying. In all of these cases, an interactional phenomenon has been reduced to a set of individual differences and attachment characterized as an appendage of the organism rather than as a dimension of the social intercourse in which the organism is engaged.

II. Toward Dyadic Conceptions of Attachment

There are several limitations to the personological tradition described above. Most significantly, it deals with only a portion of the phenomenon which is to be understood. Attachment always involves at least two persons and, thus, it is easy to suppose that the infant's attachment to the mother cannot be fully understood without knowing something about the mother's attachment to the infant. Bowlby (1969), Ainsworth (1969), Blurton Jones and Leach (1972), and others have taken great pains to recognize the mutual nature of human attachments, and they go so far as to suggest that the mother's response to her baby may have innate mechanisms underlying it just as such mechanisms may underlie the infant's responses to the mother.

At one point in his book, Bowlby describes the mother and the older infant as showing "dynamic equilibrium." This term denotes the *balance* of instigating forces in mother–child interaction; it is not synonymous with attachment. To understand why the mother takes the initiative on some occasions and the child in others, however, it is necessary to consider four behavioral systems: (1) the child's attachment behavior; (2) the child's behavior that is antithetic to attachment (e.g., exploratory activity and play); (3) the mother's caretaking (attachment?) behavior; and (4) behaviors of the mother that are antithetic to caretaking. The outcome—equilibrium—is thus a kind of criterion variable in a multiple regression equation in which behavioral references to the individual participants become the predictors. It should be noted that dynamic equilibrium is also an independent variable: The occurrence of smooth interaction has different implications for the development of children's attachment than does interaction involving persistent conflict and rejection.

Bowlby (1969) refers to some fascinating equilibrations that occur in mother–infant interaction as a function of changes in the two individual actors. Some of these are found in all primates, of which one is the change—over time—in responsibility for instigating physical proximity. In early infancy, owing to limitations in the offspring's motor repertoire, proximity maintenance is achieved mainly as a function of the mother's activity. In many subtle ways (through changes in visual orienting, vocalizing, and reaching) the infant acquires greater and greater interactional control (Lusk & Lewis, 1972), and a major shift occurs at about six months. After this, the baby plays a larger and larger role in determining proximity, even though he does not execute proximity-maintenance very well. The mother remains dominant in instigating physical contact (in the sense that she finally determines whether contact between herself and the infant occurs), but the child's locomotor competencies give him increased capacity to effect physical union with her. Later, the locus of control shifts still further and, during childhood, proximity may be maintained as much by the child as by the mother. Through adolescence, mothers increasingly assign primary responsibility for the instigation of proximity to their children. Even so, this responsibility is never completely turned over to the child. Offspring have maximal control over proximity maintenance during early adulthood, but partial control is often re-exerted by parents when they themselves reach retirement and old age. Generational and subcultural differences in these patterns of change are, of course, enormous.

These phases, or shifts, in individual responsibility for proximity maintenance represent fascinating problems for descriptive, developmental study. Is there greater universality in the shifts that occur during infancy than in those that occur during adolescence or adulthood? The literature of life-span developmental psychology contains only the sketchiest evidence relating to these changes (e.g., Chapple & Arsenberg, 1940; Lusk & Lewis, 1972). To study them would provide important data about children's social development and would also correct the long-standing tradition in both theoretical and practical child psychology which stresses environmental effects on child behavior rather than the effects of child behavior on the environment.

The literature on social development is slowly beginning to incorporate bits and pieces of descriptive fact showing the many specific ways that infants and children influence the behavior of their parents rather than vice versa. Gewirtz and Gewirtz (1969) reported, for example, that there were probabilities ranging from .52 to .82 for one six-month old that the infant's vocalizations would be followed by adult talking. Other research shows that these probabilities are highest for upper- and middle-class mothers and infants while being lowest for pairs from lower-class groups. The middle-class mother, however, proves not to be more responsive overall to her infant than the lower-class mother. On the contrary, she less frequently touches the baby when the latter vocalizes and less frequently vocalizes when the infant cries or frets. "Vocalize–vocalize," then, is merely the particular pattern that characterizes the middle-class infant–mother dyad (Lewis & Wilson, 1972). From other observational studies conducted by Lewis and his colleagues have come communication matrices showing the full range of maternal behaviors elicited by infant vocalizations (Lewis & Freedle, 1972).[2]

Bell (1971) has reported a study by Harper of one three-hour segment of mother–infant interaction in which 29 instances of mother-looking-at-infant were observed. Of these, 15 were preceded by the crying of the infant. It was also found that 9 of 13 observed instances of cuddling were preceded by crying or fussing. Finally, it was reported that both maternal orienting and maternal cuddling were precipitated by wakefulness: American mothers, unlike mothers in certain other cultures, do not wake their children in order to stimulate them.

This study also shows how the infant may precipitate a large, predictable, sequentially-ordered repertoire of maternal behavior that "runs-off" regularly in some instances but not in others. One mother was observed, for example, to respond to the crying of her offspring as follows: She talked to him first; then stressed his musculature and tried to burp him; then jiggled, rubbed, and patted him. As he quieted, she resumed talking to him. Repeated crying by the infant reactivated the entire maternal sequence. All of the evidence, however, suggests that these orderings are subject to both intramother differences in patterning and consistency and intermother differences (Lewis & Freedle, 1972).

In still another recent paper, Harper (1971) documented both facilitating and inhibiting effects of infants upon their mothers. The former class of behaviors is divisible into triggering, sensitizing, and orienting stimulation of the infant, and the latter can be discussed in terms of checking, desensitizing, and disorienting stimulation. Facilitating types of parent behavior, as elicited by child actions, have been documented in a fairly substantial way in studies of both human

---

[2]These matrices are based on two-unit sequences occurring within ten-second intervals during unstructured observations.

and nonhuman infant–mother pairs. For example, Moss (1967) found that increased smiling and vocalization by babies is accompanied by an increase in affectionate behavior by parents during the third month of life. Lusk and Lewis (1972) reported that proximal caretaker behaviors (e.g., touching) dominate when the baby is very young, while more distal caretaking actions (e.g., smiling and vocalizing) dominate later.

There is little more than anecdotal evidence concerning the elicitation by children of inhibiting behavior by their parents. For example, it is commonly believed that parental aggression directed toward children is elicited with great consistency by direct, personal attacks on the parent by the child. This sanctioning behavior on the part of parents apparently exists in all societies. Nevertheless, documentation of this occurrence is sketchy. In *Patterns of Child Rearing,* Sears, Maccoby, and Levin (1957) reported that 89% of the study parents punished their children from moderate to severe levels when child aggression was directed toward the parents themselves. But it is not known when parents begin to respond this way or how the motor patterns used in punishing children for this type of aggression may change over the course of the parents' and children's lives with each other. Such questions—questions of life-span developmental proportions—have received no systematic study as far as is known.

It is one thing to document the fact that mother–child interaction involves bidirectional effects; it is quite another to account for them psychologically. In 1951, Sears proposed a theoretical model for the study of social interaction and emergent social relationships, and it remains as nearly the only attempt to grapple with problems of theory construction in this field.[3] Unfortunately, the analysis composed by Sears has had comparatively little impact on socialization research even though it has been disseminated widely.

This paper showed how social learning theory could be used to analyze parent–child interaction. In most any social instance, it was argued, the behavior of the child serves stimulus functions for the parent by either triggering, motivating, or rewarding parental action, and even brief sequences of interaction are composed of a tightly-woven double strand of psychological events involving the behavior of both individuals. An important supplemental hypothesis was intended to account for continuity in social relationships. It was hypothesized that the "glue" underlying stable, as opposed to unstable, human relationships consists of each individual's *expectancies* about the behavior of the other. In other words, partnership features (Bowlby, 1969) and mutual regulation (Erikson, 1950) in parent–child interaction were explained in terms of anticipatory tendencies.

The thrust of a growing number of recent papers on parent–child interaction (e.g., Bell, 1968; Gewirtz, 1969b; Harper, 1971) seems to be in the direction

---

[3]A recent analysis by Gewirtz (1969b) is similar to that proposed by Sears (1951) although certain constructs are not utilized by both writers.

of the problem to which Sears addressed himself. There is some agreement, then, that advances in the study of attachment and the study of numerous aspects of family interaction could be improved if we ceased to depict the infant as an eternal receiver of stimulation and instead began to view him as a giver of such stimulation.

III. Toward Interactional Conceptions of Attachment

To recognize that the infant exerts an influence on the mother is not necessarily to generate an interactional analysis of attachment. To show that three-month-old talk precipitates maternal talk, that infant smiles produce a larger cluster of simultaneous maternal responses than any other infant action, and that infant fretting is more likely than infant vocalizing to precipitate maternal touching (Lewis, 1972) is only to provide interesting sequential detail about mother–infant interaction. Such detail increases the thoroughness of any topographic representation of the interaction, but the sequential information references individual differences in persons as much as in interactive processes.

What does sequential analysis do? It shows the proportion of variance in the behavior of one individual that can be accounted for by the particular activities of another individual. Thus, the behavior of each member of the dyad is predicted within the context of interaction, but the criterion variable remains some aspect of individual behavior (e.g., the mother's behavior or the child's behavior) and does not consist of some parameter of the interaction itself.

We would like to propose that attachment be regarded as characteristic of neither the mother nor the infant, but as a structural property of mother–child interaction. We believe that contemporary theorizing about attachment requires a kind of conceptualizing that does not localize the phenomenon with respect to individuals. Such theorizing would be complementary to personological conceptions (in which reference is made to the infant or to the mother as individuals) and would not supplant them. In order to understand the mother–child pair as a social system, it is necessary to enlarge the focus of analysis beyond the child's approaches to mother (and how these change over time), beyond the mother's approaches to the child (and how they change over time), and beyond simple sequential (talk–talk) statements.

There are limitations to any analysis of human social development that is always conducted in personological or quasi-dyadic terms. Important features of the ontogeny of interaction between mother and child may escape notice simply because of the time-honored insistence that variance in human social activity must be explained in terms that reflect back to individual actors rather than back to their interaction. In this instance, then, a viewpoint is presented here that may be more in the spirit of Bales (1950) than in the spirit of Sears (1951).

Why might this approach be fruitful? Bales (1950) put the problem thus:

> Suppose we were to take a total profile for one of our groups . . . and make a breakdown to show the profile of each individual member. Suppose these profiles turned out to be very different from each other and yet fitted together to make a total group profile just like the other total group profiles. If the profiles for these individual members differed from each other more than the total profiles for the series of groups differed from each other, we would have some justification for saying that there is a system-influence which is distributed between members, so that one discovers *the pattern of the system* only by looking at the total activity of all members put together over the total time or, in other terminology, by looking at the social system and not simply at the individual roles [p. 58; emphasis added].

Viewed in these terms, most existing analyses of family attachments do not represent the mother–child dyad as a social system, do not consider individual action as a component of such a system, and do not assume that individual action may be better understood by systemic analysis. Sociological analysis of attachment is virtually nonexistent.

A. Construction of Group Profiles

One interactional approach to the attachment problem consists of fitting together individual behavioral profiles (the mother's, on the one hand, and the infant's, on the other) to form a *group profile*. Thus, one could count total units of approach behavior without reference to the identity of the initiator or, alternatively, one could average the approach frequencies displayed by the two members of the dyad. Then, one could examine the total profile of vocal exchanges, physical contact, and visual orientation in comparison to the distribution of instances of such activities within the dyad. Indeed, the full impact of developmental shifts in the distribution of these actions across the two members of the dyad may be appreciated only when compared to the developmental shifts in the group profile. Thus, the morphology of attachment, and its developmental course, may be meaningfully revealed only in terms of the group profile, even though that morphology may change over time as distributional changes occur (see Bowlby, 1969), or as changes occur in the absolute frequencies of component activities.

For example, when locomotion emerges in the repertoire of the infant, this event is likely to produce a distributional shift in the locus of proximity-instigation; the infant instigates relatively more instances than previously. This developmental change is accompanied by other changes, however, so that the whole modus operandi of attachment becomes very different (e.g., Lusk & Lewis, 1972). With changes in the infant's locomotion, come changes in dyadic eye-to-eye contact, changes in the deployment of vocalizations, changes in pursuit of a "departing other," and so forth. As the child evidences increased competence at locomotion, the mother may decrease her locomotor approaches to him (a distributional change). Simultaneously, the mother may increase vocalizing from a distance while the infant's vocalizing also increases (a nondistributional change). Thus, individual rate changes may have maximal significance only in relation to a profile established by fitting the two individual profiles together and comparing this profile to others obtained from other dyads.

B. *Selection of Dyadic Measures*

A second conception of attachment in terms of social interaction is based on the use of response measures that reference the dyad rather than the individual. Lewis has distinguished four "levels" of interactive analysis, each of which is characterized by a different type of measurement (Lewis, 1972; Lewis & Freedle, 1972; Lewis & Wilson, 1972). The simplest of these consists of frequencies—the total count of such behaviors as vocalizations, smiling, glances, and physical approach as exhibited by the infant, and the total count of such behaviors as exhibited by the mother. Various features of infant–mother interaction can be elucidated by the use of these measures (e.g., through correlations between child frequencies and maternal frequencies). Nevertheless, such measures are not really dyadic in nature; their referent is the individual and not the dyad.

Another relatively low level of interactional analysis consists of the frequency of temporal units (e.g., 10-second intervals) during which both the mother and the infant do something vis à vis each other. This measure does not reference either the nature of the interaction or the initiator of it and, in a sense, it represents the *social activity level* of the dyad. There is little information attesting to the usefulness of such a measure in the study of early attachment processes, but there can be no question that it is a parameter of interaction rather than a parameter of individual behavior. An intermediate level of interactive analysis consists of the number of short temporal units (e.g., 10 seconds of elapsed time) in which pairs of specified actions by the mother and the infant occur. Determination of the initiator of the sequence is not made at this level, but the nature of the interaction is specified. Thus, one counts temporal units in which both mother and infant vocalize, in which one moves and the other smiles, in which both engage in similar motor activity (i.e., mimicry), and so forth.

The highest level of interactive analysis, according to Lewis, is specification of directionality in behavior sequences. This consists of counting the number of instances per unit time in which specified infant actions are responses to maternal actions or initiators of them. Most of the available information about such sequences consists of probability statements showing the proportion of observed instances in which a particular act is followed by a particular activity in the other member of the dyad. As indicated previously, the proportions themselves refer to individual differences as much as to interaction. However, the frequencies with which specified sequences occur—either those which occur within short interactive time intervals or those which occur in longer intervals—may prove to be valuable measurements. Other promising sequential parameters include sequential latencies, sequential length, and sequential densities.

The four levels of analysis specified by Lewis do not represent points on an information continuum. Ordinarily, the term *levels of analysis* refers to the ordering of concepts in terms of *levels of abstraction* and thus, one speaks of the range from micro-levels of physiological analysis to macro-levels of sociological analysis. The continuum proposed by Lewis is clearly not of this type. In fact, there appears to be little justification for ordering these interactive measures in hierarchical fashion since none is more basic or utilitarian than the others (although this seems to be implied). True, the "higher" levels, as ordered by Lewis (1972), are focused somewhat more squarely on functional properties of interaction and the "lower" levels somewhat more on descriptive properties. It should be remembered, however, that no particular level of analysis (whatever the basis for ordering) is better or more fundamental than any other (Gewirtz, 1969b).

1. Distance

Spatial distance between mother and offspring has been widely used in research on infant social development (e.g., Rheingold, 1969), although invariably in a monadic sense: The basic datum is the maximal distance the child will move from the mother's side or, alternatively, how much time he remains standing or sitting next to her chair. Most investigators have brought mothers and their infants to the experimental quarters and programmed the mother in a manner such that she must be minimally responsive to the infant. (This partially removes the confounding influence of her actions upon his *re*actions.) Then, the distance the child will move away from the mother is measured (Ainsworth & Bell, 1970; Coates *et al.,* 1972a,b; Maccoby & Feldman, 1972; Rheingold, 1969; Rheingold & Eckerman, 1969).

Such procedures are entirely appropriate for testing individual differences in the propensity of babies to move to and from their mothers. But in nearly every natural situation, mothers and their locomoting infants move in a mutually regulated fashion. One will move toward or away from the other; at other times, movement will be simultaneously toward contact or toward separation; at still other times, movement by the members of the pair will be antagonistic. Thus, distance, with or without information concerning how changes in distances are effected, is a dyadic datum of vast potential.

Hall (1963) has demonstrated the usefulness of spatial distance ("proxemics") in studying group behavior in relation to varied situational constraints. He distinguishes *intimate distance, casual-personal distance, social-consultative distance,* and *public distance,* categories which probably do not apply well to the analysis of mother–infant attachment but may be more relevant to other family attachments. The general model, however, is germane to any attachment situation involving any two family members at any point in the life span. Distance, without reference to who precipitates contact or separation, can serve as a dependent variable (e.g., to reflect the impact of danger or stress on mother–child interaction) or as an independent variable (e.g., to study the effects of distance in eliciting distress in the individual members of a dyad).

Proximity-maintenance can also be studied using any one of several parameters: maximum separation-distance tolerated before reunion is effected; the proportion of observed time in which members of the dyad remain side-by-side; latency of reunion movement; frequency and latency of following. By selecting the appropriate parameter, it should be possible to secure a dyadic index of proximity-maintenance in any open field situation, including proximity-effectance following separation or exposure to fear-producing stimuli.

2. Dyadic Gazing

Dyadic measures are available for nearly every portion of the behavioral repertoire thought to mediate attachment. Another of these, mutual visual regard, has been the basis for a group of studies by Moss and his associates (Moss & Robson, 1967, 1968a; Robson, 1967; Robson, Pedersen, & Moss, 1969). The basic procedure employed in these studies requires naturalistic conditions (the home) and a time sampling schedule whereby simultaneous eye-to-eye contacts between mother and infant can be counted. The logic for selecting vis à vis as a social variable is described by Robson (1967), who points out that it is both an early and a continuing channel of communication within the mother–child dyad. Moreover, it is a component of such other communication exchanges as smiling, talking, and mimicry.

The published work by Moss and Robson reveals the following facts about vis à vis: (1) It predicts infant gazing at static faces but not at other objects; (2) it increases from one to three months, and occurs with equivalent frequency for both sexes; (3) it is relatively stable across this early period; (4) it is correlated with maternal attitudes during pregnancy (for both sexes at one month; for females at three months); and (5) measured at one and three months, it is positively correlated with gazing at strangers and social approaches to them at nine months, primarily for males. These and a few other bits of information comprise the total findings—not a rich lode of data. Moreover, Moss and Robson have not explicitly related their interest in dyadic gazing to the phenomenon of attachment, so there is less information in these reports than one would like concerning the relation between dyadic gazing, separation-induced distress, proximity-maintaining behaviors, and the like.

With Eric Iverson, the authors have begun an observational study of dyadic behavior using video tape records of mother–infant interactions in relatively unconstrained situations. One infant provides interesting data about dyadic gazing. At 6 months of age—when she could not crawl—she was observed for 20 minutes in nonstructured interaction with her mother. During this time 19 instances of dyadic gazing were found. Twelve of these instances of mutual visual regard were accompanied by at least one other mode of dyadic contact: Four accompanied physical proximity, 6 involved touching, and 7 accompanied some form of imitative interaction (usually with prompting by the mother). Put another way, the observation showed that of 6 instances of proximity, 4 involved dyadic gazing; of 9 instances of touchings, 6 involved gazing; and of 8 instances of imitation, all involved gazing.

When this infant was 10 months of age, the role of dyadic gazing in mother–infant interaction shifted considerably. Again, there were 19 instances of dyadic gazing during a 20-minute period of interaction, indicating no appreciable change in this aspect of the group profile. The conditions of interaction were quite similar to the earlier session, except that a couple of new toys had been added, and a table was present which had not been there before. The child could walk by grasping the table or the mother. At this point only 7 gazes were accompanied by other modes of dyadic contact. Six involved physical proximity or touching and 5 involved imitative interaction. Reversing the description, of 7 instances of contact or touching, 7 were now accompanied by gazing, and of 10 instances of imitation, 5 involved gazing.

Of the several shifts reflected in this protocol, three are worthy of comment. First, there seems to be no decline from 6 to 10 months in total amount of dyadic gazing, but there is a decline in the proportion of gazes that are accompanied by other forms of contact. Second, approximately two-thirds of the touching episodes at 6 months were accompanied by gazing, but all such episodes were accompanied by gazing at 10 months. (To interpolate, the mother was the primary agent of touching contacts at 6 months, whereas the infant took this role exclusively at 10 months). Finally, all of the imitative episodes at 6 months were accompanied by dyadic gazing, but only half of such episodes were so accompanied at 10 months. Here, there were two correlated shifts: Most of the imitation sequences were ''partial'' or ''incomplete'' at 6 months and involved much prompting by the mother; a greater number were fully imitative at 10 months even though 70% were clearly initiated (i.e., deliberately modeled) by the mother. But in addition there was a shift from physical imitation to verbal imitation at the same time as the shift occurred from quasi-imitation to full imitation.

An hypothesis has thus emerged, based on the assumption that dyadic gazing functions to maintain proximity of mother and child and thus, mediates attachment during later infancy: As the cognitive and motor apparatus of the child changes, the proportion of gazes in conjunction with other modes of contact decreases.

At the same time, when instances of physical contact occur, they are accompanied by an increased proportion of simultaneous dyadic gazing. In this manner, the factor structure of attachment seems to change.

3. Dyadic Mimicry

Studies of dyadic mimicry may also profitably proceed within the context of attachment. The interplay between object-choice and imitation (identification) has been a primary feature of psychoanalytic theory for as long as the pseudopodia. This theory suggests that object-choice forms a background for identification, although it does not imply that there should be a direct correlation between the infant's *ability* to replicate a given motor pattern and the extent to which he and his mother seek proximity with each other. On the contrary, the theory suggests that introjection and mimicry are *mechanisms* used by the infant to ensure the continuity of his cathexes. In both fantasy and reality, imitative activity is thought to be a device or a channel for maintaining or mediating the attachment relation. In ethological terms, imitation serves to bind mother and child together, thereby protecting the child. It may serve other functions as the child grows older, including the facilitation of language and cognitive development, but it can be posited that imitation functions in infancy mainly as an attachment mediator.[4]

Recent attempts at charting the course of imitation in the first two years of life have been based on the assumption that the occurrence of successively more difficult forms of imitation—either immediate or deferred (Piaget, 1951)—reflect changes in the child's cognitive capacities or abilities. Consequently, imitative skill has been tested by standard psychometric procedures and the limits of the infant's imitative abilities have been established by performance on items ranging from simple mimicry to deferred imitation (cf., Uzgiris, 1972). It is difficult, however, to know how to use data of this sort in studying the functional role of imitation in the early development of object relations since there is no reason to posit a correlation between imitative skill and attachment within specific age groups.

Our own observation is that mothers "prompt" imitation in great amounts long before the imitative repertoire of the child gains enough proficiency to mediate attachment. The mother of the 6-month old infant described previously engaged in the following behaviors: She rolled a ball to the infant and urged her to roll it back, with no success; she said "pat-a-cake," then went through the motor pattern, and then clapped the infant's hands together even though the infant moved her hands up and down; the mother then attempted "peek-a-boo" on a mutual basis, but without success. Then, when the infant let out a gasping sound, the mother emitted a similar, drawn-out "oh, my." Next, the infant

---

[4]The linguistic literature sometimes seems to suggest that the sole function of imitative interaction between mother and child is to foster the child's language development. This is probably a mistaken emphasis.

emitted the sound, "uhhh," and moved her torso back and forth, after which the mother did the same things. Finally, the infant gave an "ahahahah" and hit her hands against her lap; the mother repeated this with a "huhuhuhu" sound and replicated the infant's motor movements.

This mother played an active role in both prompting mimicry by her baby and spontaneously, herself, mimicking the infant. These are interesting phenomena in themselves since we know very little about the effects of early parental imitation on the behavioral development of children. Some writers (e.g., Hartup & Coates, 1970) have speculated that such mimicking plays an important role in the ontogenesis of generalized imitation but data on this point are lacking. Here, it should be pointed out that, when left to themselves for 20 minutes, this mother and 6-month-old infant interacted in imitative or quasi-imitative ways on 8 different occasions. All of these interactions involved dyadic gazing (as has been reported), and half involved touching or close physical proximity.

A month later, 10 instances of imitation were observed during the 20-minute sequence (most were elicited with less prompting than formerly). Nine instances of imitation still involved dyadic gazing, 7 involved close physical proximity, and 3 involved touching. All included maternal talking, although only one produced a sequence that might be labeled dyadic speech. Note, however, the functional role of these imitative sequences: They all resulted in proximity-maintenance.

At 9 months of age, there were eight instances of imitation (not differentiated according to who modeled whom). Six of these produced gazing, and all eight produced either touching or close physical contact (including one instance in which the mother mimicked the infant's cries after the latter fell and hit her head). At 10 months, there were ten imitative interactions, only five of which involved gazing, and four of which involved touching or close proximity. At this point, dyadic imitation became increasingly verbal and, as reported earlier, dyadic gazing itself was no longer accompanied regularly by the other attachment mediators. It thus appears that changes in deploying the distance receptors clearly change the patterning of the interaction. Imitation remains no less frequent, and much of it consists of maternal mimicking of the child, but it is interwoven with the other attachment mediators in a different manner.

4. Other Dyadic Measures

Several additional possibilities exist for extraction of dyadic measures from observations in natural or quasi-natural situations. Vocalizing, like imitation, often occurs in closely-spaced sequences, and there may be a special significance in those vocal sequences that occur within several seconds of one another. The literature already shows the regularity with which maternal speech follows infant vocalizing (Gewirtz & Gewirtz, 1969; Lewis, 1972) but the frequencies of such sequences are not ordinarily regarded as attachment mediators. Coates et al., (1972a) found nonsignificant correlations between vocalizations to the mother and measures of visual regard and proximity-maintenance at 10, 14, and 18 months of age. Note, however, that their measure of vocalizing was monadic and that it referred to the child's behavior in the presence of a minimally reactive mother (she was instructed to respond to overtures of the infant, but only "in kind"). There is no assurance that a dyadic measure of vocal interchange would interrelate differently with measures of dyadic gazing and proximity-maintenance, although the authors' new records indicate that when the mother is free to interact with her infant, this may be the case.

Touching is another act which may be defined dyadically, and which may have implications as an attachment mediator.[5] As mentioned, it appears to be more regularly accompanied by dyadic gazing in older infants (when they can instigate the touching) than in younger infants (who engage in touching mostly when instigated by the mother). Here again is an instance in which a particular dyadic component may play a different functional role in attachment mediation at different ages.

Finally, it is possible to measure responses to separation in a dyadic fashion. Mothers have frequently been reported to be highly sensitive to the crying of their young, and Schaffer and Emerson (1964) have shown that infant crying upon separation from the mother is common beginning in the third quarter of the first year. Blurton Jones and Leach (1972) report that mothers of criers (when left at nursery school) touch their children more at reunion than mothers of noncriers, so it may be that the dyadic pattern should be examined much more closely under conditions of separation than has been done heretofore.

IV. Final Comment

In considering the infant as a socializing force with respect to its parents, Rheingold (1969) has said:

> In pondering these matters, it has become increasingly clear to me that our usual methods of studying mother–infant interactions are open to question. Although we can talk about who socializes whom, neither the infant's contribution nor the parent's can be separated when the dyad is studied in real life situations. The child's behavior modifies the parent's behavior, even as his behavior is being modified by theirs. As variables for analysis, they are completely confounded. . . . The problem in parent–child interactions can be solved only by the experimental manipulation of the behavior of one or the other of the partners to the interaction.[6]

---

[5]Mutual clinging (a rare occurrence) should also be studied since such a measure has assumed a great importance from several theoretical viewpoints (Ainsworth, 1969).

[6]From Harriet L. Rheingold, "The Social and Socializing Infant," in David A. Goslin (Ed.), *Handbook of Socialization Theory and Research*, © 1969 by Rand McNally and Company, Chicago, p. 789.

It is important to solve the confounding problem, of course; predicting the behavior of the individual actors in family dyads remains a critical issue. But major advance in the study of family attachments requires a more "social" approach than has been taken in the past.

Much can be learned about the course and functional significance of attachment from research in which the natural confounding of parent and infant influences is allowed to remain confounded. This does not preclude experimental analysis of certain important attachment phenomena because manipulations can be applied in quasi-natural situations to both members of the dyad and effects on the profile of the interaction noted.

The interactional strategy proposed in this chapter can be extended to family attachments at many points in the life cycle. Such a strategy would help to elucidate developmental transitions in attachment occurring at pubesence, at departure from the nuclear household, in courting, during various phases of the marital relationship, and at parental retirement. Certain other attachments (e.g., between siblings in adulthood) should be studied interactionally simply because their functional significance in adult socialization is presently unknown. In most cases, however, interactional analysis would supplement existing demographic or descriptive data.

The literature of family sociology contains survey information on several parameters of family interaction which in adulthood are analogous to the measures proposed in our analysis of mother–infant interaction: (1) residential propinquity (measured both functionally and in terms of absolute distance); (2) frequency of face-to-face visiting and other forms of interpersonal contact; (3) type of interaction; (4) patterns of mutual aid; (5) affective qualities of the family bond as reported by the subjects themselves; (6) shared values, rituals, and norms; and (7) indicators of family solidarity (Troll, 1971). Residential propinquity is a truly dyadic proximity measure although its functional significance in adult development is mostly unknown. Proximity is positively correlated with amount of parent–child interaction, and developmental changes have been identified. In the United States, the preferred pattern after marriage is for parents and children to maintain separate households and this preference continues into the old age of the parents. Such is the case even though increased propinquity occurs as a function of aging: 84% of persons over 65 live less than an hour away from one of their children and over 30% actually live in the same household (Shanas, Townsend, Wedderburn, Frus, Mehhaj, & Stehouwer, 1968). Face-to-face visiting has also been studied, kinds of interaction tabulated, and contact comparisons made between rural and urban samples, social class groups, and particular family members (e.g., mothers and daughters, mothers and sons, grandfathers and granddaughters, etc.).

This survey information may prove to be a valuable base for devising new interactional strategies for studying attachment. For example, Shanas *et al.* (1968)

found that the flow of contributions, help, and support between aging parents and their offspring is not one-way but two-directional. If, within a parent–child dyad, help is given at all, the proportion of older persons who help their offspring exceeds the proportion who obtain help from their children. Patterns of economic interdependence have, of course, no analogue in mother–infant interaction except helpseeking. Their functional value as indicators of adult affectional development is unknown. Nevertheless, it has intriguing potential—certainly enough to extend study of mutual aid from the demographic to the functional psychological level.

At the moment, there is no way to draw clear isomorphic lines between the measures used in studies of mother–infant attachment and measures which might be used to study mother–child attachment at other points in the life cycle. There is nothing but speculation to suggest that examination of residential propinquity, shared norms, and mutual aid may assist in research on problems of family attachments including separation and loss, phenomena such as "the empty nest," and the psychological concomitants of retirement and death of a spouse. But the kind of conceptualizing presented in this chapter is inherently applicable to a wide variety of psychosocial dimensions in family development, most of which have previously been conceptualized in narrow, personological terms.

ACKNOWLEDGMENTS

The authors are deeply grateful to Eric Iverson for his contributions and also acknowledge a debt to all the previous work in family sociology which has stressed the nature of the family as a social system (e.g., Parsons & Bales, 1955).

CHAPTER 11

Social-Learning Theory as a Framework for the Study of Adult Personality Development

INGE M. AHAMMER[1]

CATHOLIC UNIVERSITY OF NIJMEGEN
NIJMEGEN, THE NETHERLANDS

ABSTRACT

An attempt was made to analyze behavioral changes in the adult years as a function of major life events (marriage, parenthood) in terms of social-learning principles. Social-learning theory seems particularly suited for this analysis since, in contrast to most personality theories, it is very sensitive to detecting behavior changes as a function of changing environments. People were assumed to move into new environments and come into contact with new people throughout the entire life span and were, therefore, assumed to continue changing throughout life. Marriage and parenthood were analyzed as new situations causing behavioral change in all participants as a function of interaction of spouses and parents and children respectively which result in mutual behavioral change, and as a function of role expectations and prescriptions, which define the reinforcing consequences of the new role behaviors.

I. Introduction: Why Social-Learning Theory?

Adult development, when studied at all, has typically been investigated from a sociological point of view in which adult personality changes are examined

---

[1]Present address: School of Behavioural Sciences, Macquarie University, North Ryde, New South Wales, Australia.

either in terms of changing roles (Brim & Wheeler, 1966), in terms of developmental tasks (Havighurst, 1952), developmental conflicts (Erikson, 1950), or major life events (Neugarten, 1966). These approaches, by definition, deal with molar variables or sociological summary indexes (on both the independent and dependent variable side) and are not primarily concerned with detailed analyses of the mechanisms of behavior change.

In the present chapter, a molecular process-oriented analysis of adult personality development is attempted emphasizing functional relationships between the social environment (stimuli) and the individual's behavior (responses). For this purpose, principles from learning theory (to describe the mechanisms of change) and from the "life-outcome oriented approach" (Neugarten, 1966) (to describe change-producing events in adulthood) are borrowed in the attempt to analyze the molar life events into stimulus–response functions and thus to examine the process of adult behavior change as a function of these life events.

Adult development has typically been neglected by developmental psychologists (1) because of the psychoanalytic domination in the field of child psychology with the notion that basic personality traits are established in the first few years of life, and only modifications thereof occur in the adult years, and (2) because of the domination of the biological growth–maturity–decline model in the field of life-span psychology with the assumption that adulthood is a period of stability or maturity without systematic behavior change (see models by Bühler, 1933; Kuhlen, 1959). Developmental stage models, such as those of Piaget and Kohlberg, similarly preclude the study of adult development since they are tied to a maturational concept of development and since "it is not immediately obvious . . . that there is a biological process indigenous to the adult portion of the life span that could impose such definite and strong constraints on [behavior] change [as there is in childhood] [Flavell, 1970, p. 249]." These theories, by definition, conceive of adult behavior change as the stabilization of earlier achieved behavioral change, rather than as development to new, qualitatively higher stages (Kohlberg, 1969; Kohlberg & Kramer, 1969) (see chapter by Emmerich, this volume).

While we do not doubt that behavior can be and is partially stabilized early in life (see Kagan & Moss, 1962) and that behavior change becomes more difficult as the organism ages, it is assumed that systematic age-related behavior changes do occur in the adult years as a function of programmed or unprogrammed experiences (see Flavell, 1970), and that the study of these changes has been neglected because of unduly restricted conceptual frameworks.

Social-learning theory seems particularly suitable for the study of adult changes, first, because the theory implies no a priori concept of development and thus, considers all systematic age-related changes as subject matter for investigation, regardless of the shape of the developmental curve (Baltes & Goulet, 1970; Reese & Overton, 1970). Secondly, the theory postulates no new mechanisms of behavior change for organisms of different ages and thus, insures continuity of explanatory principles over the life span (Gewirtz, 1969a). This feature of the theory seems to approximate a major objective of life-span developmental psychology as stated by Baltes and Goulet, *namely "the integrative conceptualization of the totality of ontogenetic behavior changes* [1970, p. 13]." A third advantage of social-learning theory relates to its emphasis on experimental methodology and on parametric studies of the variables relating to behavior change (Hartup & Coates, 1970) resulting in an approximation of "exact" laws of behavior change.

Finally, although social-learning theory is not a developmental theory (see Bijou, 1968a; Hartup & Coates, 1970), it seems uniquely suited for the study of developmental processes because of its emphasis on molecular antecedent–consequent relationships, that is, on stimulus–response functional relationships that are particularly sensitive to detecting behavior change. Where molar analyses reveal few changes, molecular analyses might reflect minute shifts in response probabilities (see Patterson & Cobb, 1971). Considering response-maintaining or change-producing stimuli on the one hand and behavior on the other hand, social-learning theory appears equally suitable for the investigation of both behavioral stability and change. This characteristic of learning theories can best be expressed in Mischel's words: "When the eliciting and evoking conditions that maintain behavior change, . . then behavior surely will change also. When response consequences and valences change so do actions; but when maintaining conditions remain stable so does behavior [1969, p. 1016]." This is a particularly important characteristic of social-learning theory since theories which one-sidedly capitalize on stabilities rather than change, for example, trait or differential theories (see Emmerich, 1968, 1969a), would be less apt to find evidence for adult development.

In choosing social-learning theory as the framework for studying adult development, a *mechanistic* model of development is chosen (Reese & Overton, 1970) in which sources of behavior change are looked for in the external environment rather than in self-propelled organismic changes. Age is considered in this formulation of development only insofar as it describes the organismic capabilities (i.e., defines which responses an organism is capable of emitting) and provides a rough index of the history of an individual's past experiences with stimuli provided by the environment (Baer, 1970; Gewirtz, 1969a). When examining adult personality development from a social-learning viewpoint, changes in observable social behavior will be considered as a function of a particular combination and sequence of experiences in the adult years which are assumed to interact with the age of the organism. By social behavior is meant the behavior of two or more people in interaction with one another, or with respect to a common social environment (Bijou, 1970; Skinner, 1953).

The task of the present chapter consists of the delineation of those experiences that are typical for the adult years and of the observation of corresponding behavior change. The rationale for seeking the prime source of adult behavior change in experience is best expressed in Flavell's words:

> If one could discount the nature of the organisms involved (for instance, that young children might be regarded as intrinsically more environmentally malleable than adults), one could argue that adulthood is the nearest thing we have to a pure experiment-in-nature for assessing the change-making power of experience alone, that is, relatively unconfounded by significant and directional biological changes [1970, p. 250].

Some of these powerful, almost-universal experiences in adulthood are marriage, parenthood (child rearing), occupation, post-parenthood (launching of children), retirement, grandparenthood, widowhood, and others (Neugarten, 1966). Some of these events seem to occur in universal or almost-universal sequence (such as marriage, which typically occurs before parenthood and which always occurs before widowhood) thus ensuring relative uniformity of development. The ordered sequence of adult experience, as dictated by societal age-grading systems that prescribe the age to marry, the age to raise children, (see Neugarten & Moore, 1968, and chapter by Neugarten & Datan, this volume) does not imply, however, that individuals respond identically to these events since the responses to new change-producing events are determined to a great extent by past experience (see Maccoby, 1968). In the present chapter, two of these experiences, marriage and parenthood, will be chosen and an attempt will be made to demonstrate how social-learning principles aid in analyzing the processes of behavior change as a function of these experiences.

As mentioned before:

> There may be no fundamental difference between the laws characterizing behavior changes early in life and those characterizing behavior change during other, later, time spans. All involve the determination of sequential, functional relations between stimulus input and behavioral output in the individual's experience [Gewirtz, 1969a, p. 106].

Even though the same laws governing response strengthening and response weakening may hold across widely differing age spans, parameters describing the stimulus–response functional relations may vary with the age of the organism. Surely, certain stimuli will have different reinforcing efficacy for a child than for an adult, whereas other reinforcers may remain effective through the whole life span. However, developmental information concerning the role of incentives is sadly lacking with respect to children's observational learning (Hartup & Coates, 1970) and with other forms of children's learning (Stevenson, 1968). Even less information is available concerning developmental changes in incentive functions over the adult years. It is conceivable that other variables such as response categories, stimulus attributes, task characteristics, etc. also interact with the age of the organism. Again, few such developmental studies have been performed with children as subjects (Hartup & Coates [1970], found only eight developmental studies measuring children's imitation), and even fewer have been conducted with adults.

Thompson (1968) further suggests an interaction between predominant forms of learning (habituation, classical conditioning, instrumental learning) and the age of the organism which seems determined by the biophysical differentiation of perceptual and response systems in childhood. Again, empirical data are still missing to specify which variables determine what form of learning in the adult years. Until such developmental data are forthcoming, an analysis of adult behavior change in the social-learning framework will have to remain speculative. The analysis in the present chapter will be based on the working assumption that the same laws characterizing learning hold for all age groups, an assumption which, upon accumulation of appropriate developmental data, may well have to be modified and refined. In this sense, the purpose of the present chapter is not to formulate a well-rounded theoretical analysis, with specification of the relevant parameters, but to present a framework that points to many areas of research that have been neglected by developmental psychologists, but seem worthy of investigation.

II. Principles of Social-Learning Theory as Related to Life-Span Development

Social-learning theory, based on Skinner's operant conditioning principles and the classical conditioning paradigms, describes behavior change as a function of stimuli provided by the social environment. The key assumption of social-learning theory is that all behavior potentially is learned and can be changed (Bandura, 1969a). The theory is primarily concerned with the study of social behavior which is conceived of as following the same laws as nonsocial behavior (Gewirtz, 1969a).

Behavior change occurs when discriminative conditions and response contingencies change (Mischel, 1968). These are expected to change whenever an individual interacts with people he has not interacted with before, or whenever he comes into a new environmental setting. Since people are assumed to interact with new people throughout the life span (such as spouse, children, friends, colleagues, neighbors, etc.), and/or come into new environmental settings (such as different jobs, countries, neighborhoods, dwellings, etc.), they are expected to show behavior change throughout the entire life span.

In the following section, two major principles of behavior control will be reviewed with particular emphasis on the conditions producing behavior change,

namely, (1) *stimulus* or *cue control,* and (2) *outcome control.* Bandura (1969a)
postulates symbolic regulation (such as thoughts, verbal mediators, and images)
as a third form of behavior control which will be discussed only briefly.

A. Stimulus or Cue Control

"Behavior comes to be regulated by antecedent stimulus events that convey
information about probable consequences of certain actions in given situations
[Bandura, 1969a, p. 19]." A stimulus that signals that a response, if emitted,
is likely to be reinforced or not reinforced is called a *discriminative stimulus*
(see Gewirtz, 1969a). Much of our behavior, in particular, interpersonal behavior,
comes under discriminative stimulus control. A person exerting stimulus control
over another specifies the responses that are relevant for the interaction by
providing the conditioned stimulus which was previously associated with reinforcement (Jones & Gerard, 1967). Stimulus control is important in any interaction
between two or more people where the response of one person serves as discriminative stimulus for the subsequent behavior of the other person.

B. Stimulus Control and Behavior Change

When people enter into new situations (new social environments, new social
relationships), they bring with them behavior systems that have been maintained
by particular stimuli in previous relationships. Since it is unlikely that the behavior
of two interaction partners has been maintained by the same discriminative
stimuli, *relearning* or *new learning* has to take place whenever two previously
unacquainted people interact. That is, each partner probably will present stimuli
to the other signifying information about appropriate responses which may differ
from previously learned information with respect to this stimulus.

When social environment changes, the nature of the initial responses will
depend on the similarity of the stimuli provided by the new social environment
to the stimuli that controlled the behavior previously. The nature of each partner's
adjustment to the new social environment (when the latter consists of an interaction with a "new" person) will depend on (see Gewirtz, 1969a): (1) whether
or not both partners recognize the relevant discriminative stimuli for each other
and provide them appropriately; (2) whether or not both partners, through learning
occasions with each other, acquire the responses appropriate to the new social
environment, that is, an acceptable behavioral repertoire for the new situation;
and (3) whether or not stimuli in this setting acquire discriminative (and reinforcing) value for each other. If these conditions are not fulfilled, or if the environmental shifts are extreme and sudden, it is conceivable that many behaviors of
the partners may be weakened and cease (since the previously controlling stimuli
are no longer available) and that no appropriate substitute behaviors will be
formed (if the discriminations made in the new setting are inappropriate).

It appears that the more similar the discriminative stimuli provided in the new social environment relative to the previous setting, the less behavior change will result, and conversely, the more dissimilar the discriminative stimuli or the higher the proportion of previous discriminative stimuli no longer available, the more behavior change will be expected. This behavior change may take the form of relearning of previously established behavioral repertoires, or of new learning of previously nonexistent behavior systems.

C. Outcome Control

Much social and nonsocial behavior is regulated by its immediate consequences (response contingencies) which are called reinforcing stimuli. Response consequences (reinforcements) can be either externally administered (by the social environment), vicariously experienced through observation of response consequences to others, or self-administered (Bandura, 1969a). The following discussion will focus on externally administered reinforcements. It should be noted, however, that vicarious reinforcement seems to be governed by variables (such as schedules of reinforcement) in essentially the same manner as when the reinforcements are applied directly to the observing subject. Self-reinforcing responses which seem to be learned through differential reinforcement by socialization agents and through modeling processes, may be the mechanism whereby behavior is maintained under conditions in which there is minimal external support (Bandura, 1969a).

Externally administered reinforcements are vital in interpersonal relations in which one person exerts control over another person. Any social interchange results in mutual behavior change of all interaction partners through the provision of reinforcing stimuli for one another (Patterson, 1971). In interaction sequences, the response of one partner simultaneously serves as reinforcing stimulus for the preceding response of the other partner. While learning formulations often imply that an individual's behavior is controlled by a more or less fixed environment to which his behavior eventually adapts, in the present chapter the reciprocal nature of this change process will be stressed. Whereas socialization is often seen as a unidirectional process in which the socializee's behavior (e.g., the child's behavior) is shaped by a socialization agent (e.g., parents, teachers) in a rather passive manner, it will be emphasized here that "psychological functioning, in fact, involves a continuous reciprocal interaction between behavior and its controlling conditions [Bandura, 1969a, p. 46]." (See also Bell, 1968, 1971; Hartup, this volume; Sears, 1951.)

D. Outcome Control and Behavior Change

When people enter new social relationships, they bring behavior repertoires into the situation which have been maintained through response consequences in previous relationships. As previously mentioned, it is unlikely that two people will have the same behavior repertoires and thus, it is likely that they will demand behavior change in one another, especially when the behaviors of the "other" person are experienced as aversive. The necessity for mutual behavior change will arise particularly in extended interactions in which two or more people live closely together, such as marriage partners, parents and children (see Patterson & Hops, 1971). The nature and the amount of behavior change will depend partly on the similarity of the responses reinforced in the new setting to those strengthened or weakened previously.

Whether or not behavior change is achieved in a new social relationship depends on the effectiveness of the other person as reinforcing agent. "It should be noted that both partners in a dyadic interaction interchangeably serve as reinforcement agent and reinforcement receiver, in other words, that both reinforce each other [Gewirtz, 1969a]." One person has reinforcing control over another when the stimuli he provides have reinforcing efficacy, that is, when they are desired by the other (see Jones & Gerard, 1967). Whether or not a given stimulus serves as a reinforcer for a given response will depend on a number of factors (Gewirtz, 1969a; Patterson, 1967).

1. Reinforcement History with the Stimulus

Stimuli which were consistently presented preceding or concomitant with primary reinforcement subsequently serve as social reinforcers (Gewirtz, 1969a). Since different individuals probably had different experimental histories with different stimuli, different social stimuli will serve as reinforcers for different people,(see also Bandura, 1969a).

2. Experimental History with Reinforcing Agent

Whether the reinforcing agent has been primarily a source of positive reinforcement, or primarily of negative reinforcement, or of both to an equal extent will qualify the efficacy of the reinforcing stimuli provided by this agent. A linear relationship seems to exist between the proportion of positive reinforcements associated with the reinforcing person and the attraction to (or liking of) that person (Byrne, 1969; Sapolsky, 1960). That is, stimuli provided by people associated primarily with positive reinforcements appear to be more effective rewards.

3. Relationship between Reinforcing Agent and Reinforcement Receiver

Two dimensions describing interpersonal behavior, which seem to characterize most social interchanges (Foa, 1961; Leary, 1957; Metz, 1962; Schaefer, 1959; Straus, 1964; Triandis & Lambert, 1961), may be useful to describe both the *amount* of influence interaction partners exert over one another and the *kind* of control they use, namely, the dimensions of *social power* (social status, control versus persmissiveness, authority etc.), and positive versus negative control (warmth, love versus hostility etc.). *Social power* may be defined in terms of an individual's capacity to elicit behavior change in others (Hartup, 1970), and dependence as the inverse of power, may be defined in terms of the extent to which an individual's behavior is modified as a function of exposure to social models or as a result of social reinforcers. *Positive* versus *negative control* can be operationalized in terms of the proportion of positive versus negative reinforcements, as well as in terms of additional parameters such as timing of reinforcement, schedules of reinforcement, etc. Social interactions with respect to the power dimension seem to be characterized by complementarity (such that, if one person shows frequent dominant behavior, the other's dominance decreases, and vice versa; if one person is less assertive, the other's dominance behavior seems to increase; see Gellert, 1962; Gewirtz, 1972; Raush, Dittman, & Taylor, 1959; Raush, Farbman, & Llwelleyn, 1960). The positive versus negative control dimension, on the other hand, seems to be characterized by reciprocity in the sense that high positive correlations were found between the frequency of positive reinforcements given and received (Charlesworth & Hartup, 1967), and between the frequency of negative reinforcements given and received (Patterson & Reid, 1969).

Outcome control seems to account for a large proportion of behavior change over the life span. Since it seems reasonable to assume that people at any point in the life span come into contact with new people who will bring different response repertoires, as well as different reinforcement contigencies and expectations (as to which behaviors they are likely to reinforce) into the relationship, behavior change is expected to occur at every stage of life. It is furthermore conceivable that behavior change occurs not only as a function of encountering new people (or new settings), but also in interaction with the same partner over time (such as marriage partners, friends). Long-time partners are expected to keep changing one another as long as at least one of the interaction partners (e.g., husband, children) stands under outcome control of agents outside of the relationship (e.g., work colleagues, peers), or as long as the partners encounter new situations to which each reacts in an idiosyncratic way (depending on his reinforcement history). On the other hand, it might also be conceivable that people, after long periods of living together, would get "locked" into a fixed interaction sequence with one another in which behavior change resulting from outside sources exerts minimal influence on the interaction if the partners do not acknowledge the change in the other (Patterson & Hops, 1971).

E. S–R Chains

Social interactions can best be conceptualized as S–R chains such that the smallest chain would consist of a discriminative stimulus, a response, and a reinforcing stimulus (Gewirtz, 1969a). "Stimuli in S–R chains appear generally to function both as conditioned reinforcers for responses preceding them and as discriminative stimuli for responses following them [Gewirtz, 1969a, p. 71]."

Conceptualizing social interactions as S–R chains has a definite advantage in that the process of interaction is emphasized and the systematic changes in behavior can be analyzed at successive points in time (see Gewirtz, 1969a), even though research only rarely examines the sequential nature of social interactions. Conceptualizing social interchanges as S–R chains further emphasizes the reciprocal nature of social interaction in which each actor changes the social environment at the same time as he is influenced by it.

F. Symbolic Regulation

Symbolic processes, such as hypotheses about appropriate responses, verbal or imaginal mediators, etc., can control behavior as much as overt events. They are conceived of as discriminative stimuli for directing instrumental behavior in essentially the same way as external stimuli direct behavior (see Bandura, 1969a). Since accurate hypotheses about appropriate behavior in a given setting tend to be followed by correct responses and inaccurate hypotheses tend to be followed by incorrect responses, "symbolic events are selectively strengthened, maintained or extinguished by the differential reinforcements to the more distally occurring overt behavior [Bandura, 1969a, p. 566]."

G. Symbolic Regulation and Behavior Change

Social role theorists see in the adoption of new roles and new role behaviors one major source for behavior change over the life span (see Brim, 1968; Brim & Wheeler, 1966). Prescriptions for new role behaviors will very likely be experienced as rules and regulations which "represent social facilitators or constraints on behavior systems [Gewirtz, 1969a, p. 90]," that is, which indicate the reinforcing consequences of the respective behavior. Symbolic processes, in the form of role prescriptions (and role expectations), will exert a particularly powerful influence on behavior change when an individual moves into a social situation (role) that is distinctly different from previous situations and when the behaviors appropriate for the new situation differ from previously appropriate behaviors and are clearly specified (such as marriage, parenthood, etc.).

III. Marriage

In the following two sections, we will attempt to account for (or predict) possible behavior changes resulting from the new social situations of marriage and parenthood in terms of social-learning principles. Marriage and parenthood are not discrete events, since marriage is preceded by dating and courtship (see Broderick, 1971), and both marriage and parenthood describe social situations which are constantly changing as a result of the aging of the spouses as well as the growing up of the children.

> As one looks at families interacting, either in the laboratory or under natural conditions, it is clear that change constantly occurs. Roles are switched, and family members learn new strategies and techniques for interacting with each other. Furthermore, these changes are not random ones but, instead, seem to be related to other variables such as the imposition of a new task on the family, the maturation of the child, or the loss of a member [Waxler & Mishler, 1970, p. 284].

Since investigators of family processes have been little concerned with the study of these changes, the present analysis will emphasize the impact of marriage and parenthood as static events (which are new to the individual) and just occasionally, yet whenever possible, point to the changing nature of these events.

The following discussion about marriage as a change-producing event is centered around two topics: (1) interaction of spouses, and (2) social role prescriptions and role expectatons, as sources of behavior change.

A. Interaction of Spouses

In the previous section, it was discussed how people, through coming into contact with previously unacquainted persons or through entering new social relationships, exert influence over one another which results in mutual behavior change. The mechanisms in terms of which the behavior change was accounted for were stimulus and outcome control. Some factors which were discussed as essential in determining both the effectiveness and the amount of behavior change in both partners were: similarity of reinforcement history, similarity of history with discriminative stimuli, experiential history with the partner, social power of each partner in relation to the other, and kind of behavior control employed.

In this section, behavior change in spouses resulting from interaction with one another will be discussed. It should be noted again that the mechanisms of mutual behavior change are assumed to be no different for married partners than for any other interaction dyad. A variable which may, however, differentially influence the interaction between strangers and married partners is length of acquaintance but since it has not been sufficiently researched, it will be largely neglected in the following discussion.

1. Similarity of Spouses

Although one major argument of the present chapter is that systematic and significant behavior changes do occur in the adult years, a tendency seems to exist among adults to seek environments which support previously learned behavior. In this sense, people tend to choose marriage partners who are similar to themselves in a number of respects (e.g., regarding educational level, age, race, religion, ethnic origin, social class, values, interests, and personality variables) (Barry, 1970; Laws, 1971). Although the complementarity hypothesis is revived from time to time, the overwhelming part of evidence supports *homogamy* as a basic norm in mate selection (reviews by Barry, 1970; Laws, 1971; Tharp, 1963).

A number of explanations can be forwarded to account for people's preference for similar rather than dissimilar others. Griffitt (1969), for example, advanced the hypothesis that attraction to a stranger as a function of attitude similarity is mediated by anticipated positiveness of the interaction with the stranger. An explanation for the positiveness of the interaction between people who are similar to one another could be found in the fact that they tend to be under control of similar discriminative stimuli. Thus, similar social cues will signal similar social behaviors, as appropriate for a given situation.

As discussed at length before, the more similar the stimuli controlling the behavior of two people, the less relearning will be necessary. And relearning seems to be very costly to the person doing the relearning. First, it does not immediately ensure a maximum of rewards (until the new behaviors are learned). Secondly, relearning or behavior change in ordinary social interactions seems to be rather unpleasant or aversive since people seem to have a tendency toward aversive rather than positive control when attempting to change each other's behavior (Bandura, 1969a; Patterson & Hops, 1971; Stolz, 1967). If relearning implies an increased proportion of negative reinforcements relative to the situation in which no new learning has taken place, the generalized reinforcing power of the "teacher" will diminish and so will the attraction to him. If it were true that people with similar backgrounds demand less behavior change from one another (because behavior is controlled by similar stimuli), this would imply that they would have to rely less on aversive control and would present a higher proportion of positive reinforcements for each other's desired behaviors, which would in turn increase the mutual attraction (Byrne, 1969).

A second reason for the preference of similar others may be found in the fact that overlapping behavior systems between people seem to represent a major source of reinforcement for the people (see Patterson & Reid, 1969). Social psychological studies, for example, found a positive relationship between similarities in behavior and the duration of social interactions (or friendships) (Newcomb, 1961; Precker, 1952). Other studies reported a relationship between similarities in behavior repertoires (as measured by the sex of the interaction partners) and the frequency of mutual reinforcement (Charlesworth & Hartup, 1967; Fagot, 1967; Patterson & Reid, 1969). Similarly, a study of married couples revealed more cooperation between the spouses in a Prisoner's Dilemma

Game when the partners were similar to one another (on the personality dimensions of achievement and inclusion) and when they perceived themselves as similar than when they were or perceived themselves as dissimilar (Bean & Kerckhoff, 1971).

Since people with similar backgrounds tend to have a larger proportion of overlapping behaviors than people with dissimilar backgrounds, and since these similar behaviors tend to be a source of reinforcement, and furthermore since they probably will demand less behavior change from one another thereby relying less on aversive control, the proportion of positive reinforcements over all reinforcements given tends to be higher the more similar the partners. As mentioned before, the latter tends to increase the mutual attraction (see Byrne, 1969).

Last but not least, people with similar backgrounds and reinforcement histories will have associated similar stimuli with reinforcing consequences. Therefore, the stimuli they provide for each other will more likely have reinforcing value for the other, and conversely, they will be more responsive to the reinforcing stimuli provided by the other (which again would tend to increase the attraction to each other).

Since similarity in behavior repertoires between people tends to be reinforcing and tends to be reinforced frequently, Patterson and Reid (1969) speculate that

> . . . it seems likely that . . . persons would "shape" each other to be *increasingly similar*. The behaviors of [person] A which are most likely to elicit reinforcement from [person] B are those behaviors which are already in the repertoire of B . . . confirmation of the present hypothesis . . . would require that couples become increasingly similar as time progresses [in addition to the selection of a spouse based on similarities] [p. 17].

Some confirmation of this hypothesis is provided in a study by Newcomb (1961) in which students who lived together in dormitories and formed friendships tended to converge in attitudes and values. Similar results were obtained by Uhr (1957) who reanalyzed Kelly's (1955) data of an 18-year follow-up study of engaged couples. He found that the couples who were reported to be happy in their marrige had become more similar to one another whereas couples who perceived their marriage as unhappy became more dissimilar to one another with respect to personality dimensions. These findings, then, seem to support Patterson and Reid's (1969) hypothesis that couples do become more similar over time if the interaction is reinforcing (if the marriage is perceived as happy).

In postulating that adults have a tendency to choose environments similar to previous environments and people similar to themselves, the theoretical question arises as to whether or not this tendency is a developmental phenomenon. That is, if children had the choice to freely seek interaction partners and social environments, rather than moving through programmed environments, would they also choose environments that sustain previously learned behaviors and people who are similar to themselves? Do children change relatively more than adults only because the environments for them as well as the environmental shifts are programmed (e.g., from nuclear family, to preschool peer group, to school environment, to work environment, etc.) whereas less of these events are programmed for adults?

2. Social Power of Spouses

The previous section detailed the way in which similarity in the behavior repertoires of spouses leads to a satisfactory relationship partially because a minimum of behavior change is demanded from one another and also because existing behavior systems tend to be reinforced. Even though a tendency exists to choose a spouse who is similar to oneself, there undoubtedly will occur occasions in which the partners will demand behavior change from the other. According to Patterson (1971), requests for behavior change are a normal part of living together. Much mutual behavior change, however, also seems to occur without explicit requests for such change, and many times without the awareness of the partners. People may even shape behaviors they dislike in one another, through unplanned and unsystematic distribution of rewards and punishments, for example.

Whether the behavior change is planned or unplanned, the effectiveness of the spouses in shaping each other's behavior is, in part, a function of their social status (social power) in the eyes of the other. Social status has to be distinguished from role status, the former referring to the effectiveness of a person in influencing the other, the latter implying the totality of prescribed, expected, and typical behaviors of the spouses (see Waxler & Mishler, 1970). Parsons and Bales (1955) postulated a positive relationship between role status and social status, that is, the person with the high power role is assumed to be more influential than the person with the low power role.

In traditional marriages, the high power role is ascribed to the man, and power is defined in terms of availability of material and educational resources (see Blood & Wolfe, 1960), in terms of external control, relative involvement, and availability of attractive alternatives (see Broderick, 1971; Heer, 1963). The partner with the fewest alternative opportunities tends to be more dependent on and committed to the marriage relationship, and is less powerful than the other (Blau, 1964; see Laws, 1971). In traditional marriages in which the wife is bound to the house and is dependent on the husband for material and also for social rewards, and in which the nonworking wife has few alternatives to the relationship, the power differential clearly tends to favor the husband.

Studies reviewed by Laws (1971) indicate that early in marriage, especially when the wife is working, the power status is less differentiated, that is, a more equalitarian pattern of power distribution seems to prevail (Blood & Wolfe,

1960; Geiken, 1964). However, with the advent of children a more traditional husband-dominated pattern seems to replace the earlier symmetrical relationship. The power differential between husband and wife seems to be greater the younger the wife at marriage, the shorter the time before the birth of the first child, and the closer the spacing of children (Campbell, 1967; Laws, 1971), that is, the less alternative options the wife has to the marriage relationship.

Some indirect evidence exists for the hypothesized relationship between the power role and effectiveness as a change agent (social status). Barry (1970), in a recent review article in *Psychological Bulletin,* came to the conclusion that marital adjustment and marital happiness is primarily determined by husbands' and *not* wives' personality factors (such as emotional stability, masculine identity, self-confidence) and by husbands' not wives' background factors (such as age at marriage, educational level, close attachment to his father). Similarly, the analysis by Uhr (1957) which was described previously, revealed that the behavior changes in happy marriages, in which the spouses became more similar to one another over an 18-year period, were because of the wives becoming more similar to their husbands rather than vice versa. In the unhappily married groups, it was the husbands' behavior change which resulted in increased dissimilarities between the spouses. Further studies indicate that the wives' perceptions of their husbands as emotionally mature (Dean, 1966), as dominant (Kotlar, 1965), as congruent with the sterotyped conception of a "good" husband (Corsini, 1956 in Barry, 1970) predicted marital happiness, while husbands' perceptions of their wives were not related to marital adjustment. These studies seem to indicate, then, that more behavior changes are made by the wife, and husbands seem to be more influential than wives in determining the relationship.

Since none of these studies measured observable behavior but were based on self-reports of happiness or on scores on personality tests, and since none of them examined cause–effect relationships, that is, the interaction sequence between spouses, tentative conclusions at best can be made from these data. Studies coming closest to examining interaction sequences between spouses are the systematic observations of family interactions at home carried out by Patterson and collaborators. Unfortunately, however, these authors did not analyze their data in terms of stimulus–response sequences, but summarized stimulus–response categories over the observation intervals.

Because of these methodological problems, the studies cited just do not provide conclusive support for the hypothesized relationship between role status and social status. Furthermore, it should be noted, that the majority of studies indicating more behavior change in the wife than in the husband are based on one particular, if not most common pattern of marriage, that is, the traditional, orthodox, or institutional marriage pattern. In this marriage form, complementary roles are ascribed to husbands and wives; the instrumental role to the husband and the expressive role to the wife, with the assumption that these roles cannot be played by the same individual (Blood & Wolfe, 1960; Parsons & Bales, 1955). The instrumental role refers to the orientation to and solution of tasks (e.g., providing material resources, establishing social status; see Laws, 1971), while the expressive role refers to the emotional aspect of the relationship in which the wife is responsible for the quality of the interaction and the cohesion of the family (see Waxler & Mishler, 1970).

While this model of marrige has guided most research and has unquestioningly been accepted by most investigators (see Laws, 1971 for a review), the theory of marital role differentiation has received very little empirical support (see Laws, 1971; Waxler & Mishler, 1970). Several studies indicate rather that both partners share in both expressive and instrumental roles (see Kotlar, 1965) and that similar roles for husbands and wives enhance satisfactory marital relationships (Chilman & Meyer, 1966; Gurin et al., 1960; see Laws, 1971; Levinger, 1964; Navran, 1967). Studies by Leik (1963) and Kenkel (1957) indicate that both parents were high on task activity, and that the mothers at the same time had a high rate of emotional activity (as did their daughters). These studies indicate, then, that the traditional marriage pattern represents but one special case of role distribution in marriage.

The relationship between power role and power status postulated by Parsons and Bales (1955) may be restricted to the traditional marriage forms. The relationship between these two variables rather seems to be much more complicated, as suggested by several studies (Kenkel, 1957, 1961; Leik, 1963). Kenkel (1957) found that highly expressive women are more influential in decision making than instrumental women and more influential than their husbands. The more expressive the women, the more influential they appeared to be. Expressive men, on the other hand, were found to be less influential than instrumental men and less influential than expressive wives. Considering that stimuli are effective reinforcers only when they are desired by the receiver, and conversely, that one person has power over another only when he has "resources" which are desired by the other, then these findings become intelligible. Thus, highly expressive behavior by the wife may have acquired high reinforcement value for the husband, while on the other hand, the husband's high expressiveness may be less valued by the wife.

It is conceivable that both husbands and wives have at their disposal a whole array of responses which may have reinforcing value for the partner and by means of which they exert influence over the partner, but which have not typically been assessed by the traditional role measures. Whether one partner is more influential than the other probably will depend on a number of factors in addition to the relative rewardingness of their available response systems. It seems important, for example, to consider which behavior the spouses attempt to change in one another. Whether the particular behavior is being changed easily will depend on such factors as which stimuli sustain it and whether those are removable, on its learning history, its resistance to extinction, availability of alternative response systems, etc. Safilios-Rothschild (1970) in the review of the family power structure literature speculates that "the relative degree to which the one spouse loves and needs the other may be the most crucial variable in explaining total power structure [p. 548]."

None of these variables have been investigated and therefore little is known about who influences whom, by what means, with respect to which behavior, and on what occasions. To systematically analyze the intricacies of the mutual influence process between spouses over their married life, multivariate sequential analyses would have to be performed, taking into account a variety of responses by both partners, situational determinants, the sequence of the interchanges, rewardingness of the spouses' behavior repertoires, etc.

3. Positive versus Aversive Control by Spouses

Although many studies in the family literature have been concerned with the assessment of the family power structure (however varied and molar the concept is typically defined), surprisingly few studies have investigated how power is exerted. Hallenbeck (1966) has suggested a distinction between reward power and coercive power referring to the exertion of control through administering rewards or punishments similar to the previously mentioned concepts of positive versus negative control.

Using the molecular operational definitions of positive control in terms of providing stimuli that result in an increase of response probabilities and negative control in terms of providing stimuli that result in a decrease in response probabilities, only Patterson and coworkers examined this process in families. Based on observations of family interactions, Patterson reported "an equity in the giving and receiving of positive and aversive consequences [Patterson & Reid, 1969, p. 11]" between spouses (see also Patterson & Cobb, 1971).

Most studies on spousal interaction, however, measure the "exchange" of more broadly defined reinforcers, such as money, interest, services, social approval, and others, rather than merely of positive and aversive consequences. Some studies on marital interaction in game situations and contrived conflict situations bear indirectly on this issue of positive versus negative control, when cooperation can be said to reflect positive control and retaliation to reflect aversive control. Rapaport and Chammah (1965), for example, found men in general to be more cooperative than women in the Prisoner's Dilemma Game. Women playing against women were most uncooperative and tended to retaliate most while men playing against men tended to be most cooperative (see Barry, 1970).

A study by Swain (1970) reported similar results in experimentally arranged conflict situations between husbands and wives. Husbands in general were found to be more conciliatory, less rejecting, less coercive, and to use more appeal than their wives. The interaction style between husbands and wives tended to interact with stages of marriage. That is, wives become more conciliatory and cooperative in later stages of marriage (pregnancy, after childbirth). Bean and Kerckhoff (1971) likewise found husbands to be more cooperative in the Prisoner's Dilemma Game than wives. In their study, cooperation and coercion was found to interact with actual and perceived similarity between spouses.

If the reciprocity hypothesis is correct, and if husbands generally are more conciliatory and cooperative (using positive control) than their wives, "one would expect that the first move (or the greater number of moves) toward cooperation and trust would have to come from the men [Barry, 1970, p. 52]." Barry (1970) and Swain (1970) explain their findings in terms of the greater power (and inner security) of the men. But studies describing dimensions of interpersonal behavior point to orthogonality of the dimensions "power" and "warmth" rather than to relatedness (Foa, 1961; Leary, 1957; Metz, 1962; Schaefer, 1959; Triandis & Lambert, 1961). That is, whether a person uses positive (cooperation) or negative (coercion) control seems to be independent of his power. Furthermore, as discussed at length, power may be a situation-, task- and partner-specific rather than a general characteristic of husbands.

Patterson and Hops (1971) see the main determinants for the use of coercion in the situational variable of living closely with another person in which situation people "quickly" reach the point where it is necessary to alter some behavior of the other person [p. 3]," but have not been trained to use positive control (see also Bandura, 1969a; Stolz, 1967). According to these authors, one determinant for the use of positive or aversive control may be found in the learning history of the partners. It is open to question though why women who have been found to be less cooperative should have been less well trained in the use of positive control than men.

A second antecedent may be found in the learning history with the partner. Thus, according to principles of stimulus generalization, stimuli presented by a partner who is typically associated with positive reinforcement will more likely serve as rewards, whereas stimuli presented by a partner who is typically associated with negative reinforcements will more likely function as punishments. In support of these propositions, Patterson (1971) observed that after sufficient exposure to aversive stimuli presented by a partner, the mere presence of the partner may serve as aversive stimulus. And aversive stimuli frequently call for coercive responses (Patterson & Reid, 1969) which then, as already discussed, tend to be reciprocated. These aversive interchanges are assumed to intensify and "may escalate with commensurate increases in the bitterness of the attack unless one person gives in or leaves the situation [Patterson & Hops, 1971, p. 3]," and are furthermore assumed to reduce the ability of either partner to change the behavior of the other.

An escalation of the interaction chain may be predicted in the positive direction as well, although there exist no direct observational data to test this proposition.

Previously cited data which indicate increasing similarity between the spouses as a function of age of marriage may provide indirect evidence for the increasing positiveness of interaction between the spouses.

Whether spouses use positive or negative control in a given instance may depend on number of variables such as situational variables, responses being "shaped," learning history of the spouses, relation of the spouses, similarity of the spouses, age of marriage, and complex interactions thereof. But presently, little seems known about the exact parameters determing the nature of interaction strategies. Except for the Patterson observations, no learning analysis of spousal interaction has been produced.

B. Social Role Prescriptions and Role Expectations

In the sociological literature of life-span development, marriage is frequently conceived of as an event of which the time of occurrence and the occurrence itself is programmed by society (see Brim & Wheeler, 1966; Neugarten & Moore, 1968). Prescriptions concerning the appropriate (social) behavior of husband and wife as well as the spouses' expectations concerning their "right" behavior are assumed to exert a powerful influence on behavior change (through mechanisms of symbolic regulation). In the process of socialization, to some extent, children of both sexes are socialized in an anticipatory manner into the later roles of husband and wife, father and mother, etc., with their prescribed role behaviors. Some of these behaviors will only be performed, however, when the age and social status at which the behavior is appropriate is reached. The process of anticipatory socialization, that is, of learning behavior systems which are not performed until many years later, is explained by social-learning theorists through the mechanisms of covert rehearsal (Bandura, 1969a; Maccoby, 1959) and symbolic coding (Bandura, 1969a; Bandura, Grusec, & Menlove, 1966).

In addition to anticipatory socialization, children are directly socialized into male and female roles (as defined by society) through observational learning and through differential reinforcement by the socialization agents. These sex-typed behaviors (see Mischel, 1970), to an extent may insure continuity from childhood behavior repertoires into adulthood, insofar as they continue to be supported by environmental contingencies beyond childhood (for discussion of this topic, see Emmerich's chapter, this volume). Further learning of appropriate role behaviors may occur in the years before marriage or even after marriage through observation of peers, mass media, etc.

In discussing behavior change as a function of role prescriptions and expectations, a distinction must be made between the performance of previously learned behavior patterns which were never performed before (such as sharing in household duties) on the one hand, and the acquisition of new behavior patterns (which were not previously learned) on the other hand.

For learned behavior to be performed, reinforcement either vicarious, self, or externally administered, is essential. That is, if the behavior systems which were previously learned and which are to be activated in marriage are to be performed, they must be reinforced either by the spouse (or significant others) or by the individual himself (vicarious reinforcement seems less likely in this situation). It would be possible, for example, for a woman to exhibit new behavior in the marriage situation, such as extreme cleanliness, in the absence of reinforcement from her husband or even in face of sanctions from the spouse. Her behavior pattern would be sustained by self-administered reinforcements, the standards for which might have been learned earlier through observation of her mother's criteria for self-reinforcement of appropriate housewife behavior. Nonadherence to the high standards of behavior might result in self-produced negative reinforcements (or guilt feelings) (Bandura, 1969a).

When the behavior to be performed, however, differs widely from previously performed behaviors, it is likely that the new behavior must also be sustained by external reinforcements. Thus, some evidence indicates that, if external contingencies are discrepant from self-created contingencies, behavior eventually tends to come under control of external reinforcements (Ayllon & Azrin, 1964; see Bandura, 1969a).

In summary, an individual brings into the marriage situation behavior repertoires, some of which are learned but never previously performed and others which are learned and performed (in the process of sex typing) that more or less prepare him for the new situation. The extent to which an individual will have to learn new behaviors or modify existing behavior systems will depend on the similarity of the behaviors required (expected) in the new situation relative to the behavior systems he has learned in the more or less distant past.

Some research from the marriage literature that points to behavior changes because of the new role status will be reviewed now and an attempt will be made to account for these changes in terms of the principles just discussed.

Most marriage research, psychological and sociological, seems to indicate that the woman must make a greater adjustment in marriage than the man and therefore, that more behavior change is required of her (Barry, 1970; Bernard, 1964; Burgess & Cottrell, 1939). Barry, in a recent review article, comes to the following conclusion:

> It is likely . . . that the first years of marriage are particularly more stressful for women. In the first place, the newlywed stage seems to be much more of a transition period for wives than for husbands. Wives, generally, move from a career orientation of some sort to a new orientation of housewife and mother with all the anxieties any drastic change can induce [1970, p. 50].

Since the change of situation for the newlywed wife in a traditional marriage (as just described) seems to be great and stressful, that is, since there seems to exist little overlap between behaviors performed previously and behaviors performed after marriage, we could predict that the new behavior cannot be maintained solely on the basis of self-produced contingencies (if conflicts are to be avoided). We would predict, then, that the wife's new role behavior has to be maintained by external reinforcements provided by the husband (or parents, peers, etc.). If these reinforcements are not forthcoming, but the new behavior is required either by husband or the wife herself (through autonomous standards of performance), conflicts will ensue which may result in unhappiness and maladjustment.

Studies reviewed by Barry (1970) do, in fact, indicate the best role adjustment for those women (measured in terms of marital satisfaction of happiness) whose husbands are conciliatory and supportive (Barry, 1968), which may indicate that they provide positive reinforcements for the wife's new role behavior. A further study seems to indicate that in marriage patterns in which the husband–wife communication style is nonaffectionate, wives tend to be closely involved with their parents (Goodrich, Ryder, & Raush, 1968). These couples are further characterized as closely involved with friends and child-centered (in an anticipatory manner since no children were present), whereas couples who score high on affectionate expression tend to have cut themselves off from their families and tend to be less interested in the prospects of child care. These findings may indicate that in marriages in which partners do not receive appropriate reinforcements from the spouse for the new role behavior, they tend to seek reinforcements from sources outside of marriage.

It will be noted that the studies indicating a more difficult adjustment for the wife than for the husband are based on the traditional marriage pattern and thus, might not generalize to other forms of marriage. In making predictions about behavior change as a function of role expectations and prescriptions in marriage, three factors need to be considered: (1) the extent of instrumental and/or expressive behavior a child has learned (and performed) in the course of sex typing (where instrumental and expressive behavior are each assumed to represent a continuum from high to low expressiveness and high to low instrumentality); (2) the extent to which a child has learned (but never performed) instrumental and expressive role behaviors that are not performed until marriage; and (3) the extent to which the spouses experience the prescription for husband–wife role separation (in terms of social pressures, expectations of the spouse or self-imposed). The amount of behavior change, meaning change in expressive and instrumental behaviors respectively (implying also "new" behaviors, such as task distribution in household, child care, etc.), will depend on the degree of similarity between the factors. Factors (1) and (2) may be related to one another but need not be; thus, parents may reinforce one kind of behavior in their child, while representing a model for differential parental and marital role behaviors (e.g., a father may reinforce instrumental behavior in his son but may be a model of high expressiveness in relation to his wife or son).

The following example may demonstrate the interplay of these three factors in determining the amount of behavior change with the advent of marriage. A child, for example, who has been trained to be highly expressive and little instrumental (typically, the behavior pattern of girls in traditional sex typing), but who at the same time has learned through observation of the same-sex parent both instrumental and expressive role behaviors for marriage, and who marries a partner who expects a highly instrumental role (as would typically be the case, if this individual were a man) and if social pressure supported the instrumental role prescripton, we would predict that the expressive behaviors would be weakened and eventually cease. At the same time, the instrumental behaviors, which have been learned through anticipatory socialization, would be strengthened, and new instrumental behaviors (which have not been reinforced in childhood) would have to be learned (see Chapter 6, this volume for a similar analysis).

IV. Parenthood

While family sociologists have long recognized the continuity of changes in family members over the *family life cycle* (Broderick, 1971), psychologists have largely ignored this topic as subject matter of investigation. From the sociological viewpoint, several family developmental models have been suggested in which years of marriage or stages in the life cycle are used not as independent variables but "crucial turning points" (Bolton, 1961; Kirkpatrick, 1967; Magrabi & Marshall, 1965) or developmental tasks (see Broderick, 1971; Hill & Rodgers, 1964). While those models have produced little research as yet, numerous life-cycle studies have been performed of typical behavior change as a function of years married (or as a function of structural variables, such as advent of children, age of children, etc.) using marital adjustment or satisfaction as the typical behavior being assessed.

Most of these family life-cycle studies did not analyze the *process* of behavior change or stimulus–response functional relationships, nor did they assess observable behavior; typically they were based on self-report data. Therefore these studies—which predominate in the family literature—are of limited usefulness for the present discussion.

It is surprising that despite the popularity of the family life-cycle approach in sociology, this emphasis has barely begun to catch on in psychology. Only recently have child psychologists begun to direct their interest to children as change agents for parental behavior (Bell, 1968, 1971; Gewirtz, 1969b; Osofsky, 1970, 1971; Yarrow, Waxler, & Scott, 1971).

But these studies have not been performed in the framework of family life-cycle theory since children are not conceived of as one stimulus complex in a continuously changing series of stimulus complexes in adult life. Child psychologists are interested rather in children's effects on parental behavior from the vantage point of reciprocal relationships between parent and children, who both exert influence over one another. That is, in a critique of unidirectional socialization theory, these investigators (Berberich, 1971; Osofsky, 1970, 1971; Yarrow, Waxler, & Scott, 1971) attempted to show that children control parental behavior as much as parents control children's behavior. These studies, since they are experimental and use observable behavior as dependent variables, will constitute the core of evidence for the following discussion.

The next section analyzes parenthood as an event producing behavior change in adults and will be organized around the same two topics as the marriage section: (1) interaction between children and parents; and (2) role prescriptions and role expectations concerning the parental role causing behavior change in parents.

A. Interaction between Children and Parents

Even though in recent years increasingly more emphasis has been placed on the reciprocal nature of parent–child relationships, it has been surprisingly little researched. Some observational studies (Bell, 1971; Gewirtz, 1969b; Moss, 1967) have allowed the extrapolation of children's effects on maternal behavior in addition to maternal influence on the child. Furthermore, a few experimental studies examined the unilateral effect of child behavior on adults (Berberich, 1971; Osofsky, 1970, 1971).

The mutual shaping of mother and child seems to begin early in a baby's life. Thus, Moss and Robson (1968a) and David and Appell (1961) observed that infants' crying successfully controlled caretaker behavior. David and Appell (1961), for example, observed that nurses spent 15 times more time with the infants when they were crying than when they were not. The infants' ceasing to cry when receiving attention may have reinforced the nurses' attention-giving behavior. Gewirtz (1961) similarly observed that childrens' smiling, "eating well," and cessation of crying are potent reinforcers for adult behavior. (For a review of these studies, see Chapter 10, this volume).

Based on observations of mother–infant interactions in the first three months of life, Moss hypothesized that the very young infant exerts more control over his mother's behavior than the older infant. Since Moss' hypothesis is one of very few developmental hypotheses concerning children's influence on parental behavior, it is cited here at more length.

> In summary, we propose that maternal behavior initially tends to be under the control of the stimulus and reinforcing conditions provided by the young infant. As the infant gets older, the mother, if she behaved consistently toward his signals, gradually acquires reinforcement value which in turn increases her efficacy in regulating infant behaviors. Concurrently, the

earlier control exerted by the infant becomes less functional and diminishes. . . . Thus, at first the mother is shaped by the infant and this later facilitates her shaping the behavior of the infant [1967, p. 29–30].

Since Moss' (1967) study did not include infants beyond three months of age, it may be safe to conclude that his hypothesis does not extend beyond that age range. Nevertheless, it would seem interesting to speculate about developmental trends in the balance of control between mother and child (see chapter by Hartup, this volume), or, in the earlier used terminology, in the changing power status of mothers vis-à-vis their children.

1. Social Power of Children versus Parents

Richer (1968), in a theoretical essay on parent–child relationships based on social exchange theory, presents such an analysis. Richer (1968) contends that rational social exchange occurs in families as in other social groups and he makes two basic assumptions for his analysis. First, it is assumed that the "the primary goal of parents is to maximize compliance from their children [p. 462]," and secondly that "people able to provide valued resources can rise to power in a group. This rise is accelerated if two conditions hold: 1. The recipients of the resource have no alternative sources of supply, and 2. they do not possess a resource of equivalent value with which to reciprocate [p. 462]."

Based on these assumptions, Richer (1968) hypothesizes that a child in the first few months of life is unilaterally dependent on his parents who are the sole providers of social and material rewards. If Moss' (1967) previously cited hypothesis is correct, the infant's unilateral dependence on his parents could not occur until his mother has acquired reinforcement value. With increasing age, as the child comes to realize that he also has a valued resource, namely, his compliance (age 3–4), the first parent–child exchange is hypothesized to occur. At first, compliance may still be obtained for small costs, such as a smile, praise, etc., but as the child reaches school age, he becomes increasingly aware that his compliance has high "market value." At the same time, the school-aged child acquires alternative suppliers of (mostly social) rewards in his teachers and classmates. With each additional source of reinforcement (e.g., siblings, extended family, relatives, peers), the child becomes more powerful, that is, less dependent on his parents for reward. Richer (1968) hypothesizes that with increasing power, the child will comply less and become more defiant, and that "he will raise the price for his compliance [p. 464]." With the advent of adolescence, the child is assumed to reach a point where he is to a great extent independent of his parents for social and to some extent of material rewards. In the extreme case, parents might have become unilaterally dependent on their children if they cannot "pay the price" and still desire their children's compliance. Based on this general analysis, Richer (1968) advances a number of specific hypotheses concerning the exchange process between parents and children as a function of the child's integration in the peer group, the number of children in the family, the availability of other adults (e.g., relatives) as sources for reinforcement, none of which have been experimentally tested.

Although Richer's (1968) analysis may not be correct in its present form, it represents an interesting approach to parent–child relationships, in fact, the only approach known to us (in addition to Moss' short-term hypothesis). It may not be justifiable, as Richer proposes, to assume any single goal of socialization since different parents probably will each have a multitude of socialization goals (which may differ from individual to individual parent, or be social class specific). Thus, Richer's model might have to be extended into a multivariate one. On grounds of experimental data, it is further questionable whether the *resource theory* of power (Blood & Wolfe, 1960; Heer, 1963) is tenable. Safilios–Rothschild (1970),for example, has cited a number of studies (regarding married couples) that refute the hypothesis that the person with the higher resources (material, educational, number of alternatives) has more power (Komarovsky, 1967; Safilios–Rothschild, 1969). A number of further studies show that the power of the child relative to his parents depends on his social class (Liu, 1966) and membership in cultural groups (Strodtbeck, 1951, 1958). These studies, as well as others on power distribution between married couples, suggest that the resource theory of power operates only in those cultures (and social classes) in which power is not assigned by traditional norms, but is allowed to be distributed dynamically.

When extending resource theory to social (affectionate) rewards in addition to material rewards, as Richer (1968) suggests, the linear relationship he postulates between the availability of alternative resources and influencing power may not hold up. Dependence on one source of social rewards (e.g., parents) may run parallel and remain uninfluenced by the availability of additional sources of social reward (e.g., peer group). A child, for example, in experiencing the rewardingness of peer contacts may become no less dependent on his parents as a consequence. On the other hand, Richer's prediction about increased parental dependence on their children as these grow older, may also prove to be incorrect when the extended resource theory, that is, social and material resources, is accepted as model. Parents with a high emotional investment in their young child and a lesser involvement with their older child, for example, will tend to be more controlled and manipulated by the younger child. Thus, age of the child, rather than showing a curvilinear relationship with parental dependence, as predicted by Richer (1968), will probably interact with parental investment in the child and with variables that determine the latter (e.g., personality of child, number of children in the home, birth order).

In order to extend Richer's (1968) analysis into a multivariate model accounting for the shifting balance of parent–child influence, the following variables may be considered: (1) A matrix of behaviors for each parent and child, which they wish to "teach" the other. For parents, these are typically called socialization goals, while for children they may be called desired parental behaviors; (2) A matrix of reinforcers employed by each parent and child to "teach" the desired behavior. While the desired behavior, when exhibited by the other, tends to have reinforcing value (Berberich, 1971), there may be additional responses which merely serve as reinforcers but are not explicit socialization goals.

An examination of developmental trends, examining parent and child response systems simultaneously, may reveal complex interactions between these various response systems. Thus, it is conceivable that children of increasing age exert influence on increasingly more and increasingly varied parental behaviors, while parents may control neither more nor less the behaviors of their children. A young child, for example, may only control parental behaviors that are restricted to the parent–child interaction (e.g., care-taking activities) while the older child or adolescent may successfully attempt to change parental behavior outside of their interaction (such as grooming, dress style, political involvement). This may be a result of children of increasing ages becoming competent sources of additional information through education, for example. At the same time, children of higher ages may be in a better position to control parental behavior by having a better knowledge about parental reinforcement histories, that is, by knowing better which child behaviors are desired as reinforcers for their parents.

2. Positive versus Aversive Control

The dimension of warmth–hostility, in addition to control, has emerged as major dimension characterizing parent–child relationships (Becker, 1964; Schaefer, 1959). Most studies examined the effect of warmth, as a more or less pervasive dimension characterizing parental child raising behavior, on children's behavior. "Warmth" of child behavior has never been measured, although it is conceivable that it similarly exerts a powerful influence on parental behavior.

As discussed earlier, warmth can be operationalized in terms of the proportion of positive reinforcements over all reinforcements given, in terms of timing of reinforcement, schedules, etc. A number of observational studies seem to support the notion that children's positive or negative reinforcements influence parental behavior in much the same way that parental reinforcements influence child behavior, and that these tend to be reciprocated. Thus, Robson and Moss (1969) report the infants' smiling and looking at the mother served as potent reinforcers for the mothers. In extended inverviews, mothers did not report strong personal affective bonds until the infant appeared to "look at" and "smile at" the mother. Moss (1967) similarly reports increase in maternal affectionate behavior when the infant was three months of age at which time his rate of looking at the mother, smiling, and vocalization had increased.

Negativistic behavior (negative reinforcements) in infants and young children seems to be reciprocated in much the same way as positive reinforcements. Thus, Provence and Lipton (1962), investigating foster home adjustment of 1- and 2-year-olds, reported that foster home parents appeared to reduce their emotional investment (e.g., rate of positively reinforcing child behavior) when children entered a stage of aggressive, provocative, and negativistic behavior (see Harper, 1971).

In a series of studies, Raush and coworkers (Raush, Dittmann, & Taylor, 1959; Raush, Farbman, & Llewellyn, 1960), based on Leary's (1957) system, directly tested the reciprocity hypothesis. Ten-year-old hyperaggressive boys were observed in interaction with peers and adults over a period of a year and a half and compared to 8–10-year-old control boys. "It was clear that among the children aggression begot aggression: the averages of 'sent' hostile actions were paralleled by the averages of 'received' hostile actions [Raush *et al.*, 1960, p. 321]." This finding was true for both interaction with peers and with adults. Thus, the group most hostile toward adults received the most hostility and the group least hostile received the least. A trend over the one-and-a-half-year period indicated a decrease in boys' aggressiveness as a function of receiving relatively less aggression (25%) from adults than sending (45%).

Further studies demonstrate that children's reinforcement can shape adult behavior. Berberich (1971), for example, showed that children's correctness in a learning task controlled adults' teaching strategies. This study is the only experimental study that investigated the effects of children as reinforcement agents for adults. Since the child was a "dummy" (simulated) child, the study did not examine the simultaneous behavior change in the child as a function of adult behavior. Yarrow, Waxler, and Scott (1971), in an observational study of kindergarten children, also found children to be effective reinforcement agents for adult behavior. They report that children's positive responsiveness to adult-initiated approach responses resulted in an increase of these adult responses. Children's positive responses seemed to have brought adult behavior to some degree under control.

In discussing the efficacy of children as reinforcing agents for adults and for their parents much more evidence will be needed to determine the parameters modifying the reinforcement process. While it is typically the case that older, high status subjects are more effective reinforcers, we would not want to make a prediction concerning child reinforcers. The young infant might be just as effective a reinforcer as the older child or the spouse. Most certainly, there will exist some intricate interactions between the response systems being reinforced, some personality characteristics of the child and parent, the relationship between parent and child, and the effectiveness of the reinforcements.

3. Child Characteristics

Similar to parent characteristics and response tendencies which in the socialization literature typically are found to influence child behavior, child characteristics and response tendencies also seem to influence parental behavior. A large number of studies have demonstrated differential parental treatment as a function of sex of child, response tendencies such as dependence–independence, nurturance, and others.

a. Sex of Child. Parents seem to behave significantly different if their infant is a boy or a girl, even though the overt behavior of the infants may be identical. Moss (1967), for example, observed that mothers of 1–3-month-old girls repeated vocalizations significantly more often than mothers of 1–3-month-old boys, even though girl and boy babies did not differ in amount of vocalization. Meyer and Sobieszek (1972) found that adults rated an infant differently if they were told it was a boy or a girl.

Hampson (1965) notes that the external morphology of an infant can elicit a complex of attitudes that can persist through the entire child-raising process. Thus, O'Rourke (1963) observed that whether a parent chooses the expressive or instrumental role depends on the sex of the parent and the sex of the child. Bronfenbrenner (1961b) likewise reported different child-raising techniques as a function of the child's sex. The behavior of parents toward the child, in part, seems determined by their expectations about appropriate sex-typed behavior (symbolic regulation). That is, parents will reinforce different behaviors in boys than in girls and in turn will be influenced by the degree to which their children exhibit appropriate sex-typed behaviors. This tendency to treat boys and girls differently seems to be so dominant that, even when adults are trained to behave uniformly in an either nurturant or nonnurturant way, they deviate from the trained role behavior, depending on which sex child they interact with. Thus, adults who were trained to exhibit only nurturant responses did initiate negative contacts to boys (when they behaved dependently) but not to girls (Yarrow *et al., 1971*).

b. Dependence–Independence. Yarrow *et al.* (1971) observed fluctuations in adults' nurturance and nonnurturance respectively as a function of children's bids for attentions (operationally defined as bids for help, bids for approval, and clowning bids). The adults, for example, who were trained to behave nurturantly, increased their amount of positive contacts with children when those asked for help while the adults who were trained to remain nonnurturant, increased their amount of negative contacts after bids for help.

Osofsky (1970, 1971), in the only experimental study assessing children's effects on parental behavior, assessed maternal behavior in interaction with 10–12-year-old girls (not their own) who were role playing independent, dependent, and stubborn behavior. Behavior ratings of mothers' behavior were obtained on the dimensions of warmth, teaching method, and providing reinforcements. Mothers were consistently warm across the different child behaviors but differentially reinforced child behavior. Thus, when the children acted independent, mothers tended to reinforce independent behavior; when they acted stubborn, mothers tended to reinforce dependent behavior; and when the children acted dependent, mothers reinforced neither dependent nor independent behavior.

These studies, taken together, seem to support Bell's (1968) contention that socialization studies should be reinterpreted in light of the notion that child behaviors seem to determine parental socialization techniques as much as parents' child-raising practices influence child behavior.

B. Social Role Prescriptions and Role Expectations

Just as in marriage, society prescribes appropriate role behavior for parenthood. Again, as was the case with marital role behavior, most of the parental role behaviors may be acquired long before parenthood. Maccoby (1959), for example, in an explanation of the identification process, emphasizes that in mutually dependent interactions of parent and child both participants learn, anticipate, and covertly rehearse (Bandura, 1969a) each other's customary responses. The child in interactions with his parents thus learns parental role behaviors, as well as his own role behaviors (see also Parsons & Bales, 1955). Parental role behavior can also be learned in the years immediately preceding parenthood (through observation of parental peers, for example) or through direct reinforcement and coaching at the beginning of parenthood. No matter how parental role behaviors are learned, it is assumed that they exert a powerful influence effecting behavior changes in both parents.

A number of recent sociological review papers devoted considerable attention to the difficulties of transition to the roles of father and mother which eventually came to be called *parenthood as crisis* (Hobbs, 1965, 1968; Jacoby, 1969; Meyerowitz, 1970; Rossi, 1968). In the parenthood as crisis studies, crisis was more or less specifically defined in terms of "feeling bothered by" the arrival of the first child (Hobbs, 1965, 1968), reporting difficulties (Meyerowitz, 1970), experiencing discontinuities in old behavior patterns (LeMasters, 1957), and was inferred from interview data, rating scales, and check lists.

Studies of intact marriages describe moderate to severe crises in both husbands and wives in adjusting to the first child. The crisis was more profound for women who were professionally trained and had working experience (LeMasters, 1957). Meyerowitz (1970) noted husband ambivalence toward the imminent parenthood and Gavron (1966) stated that the married couple may have been reluctant to surrender their recently found mutuality to their child. The crisis was less severe when good marital adjustment was reported among the couples and was also less severe among those couples who had been married three years or longer (Dyer, 1963; Hobbs, 1965, 1968; see Arasteh, 1971 for a review). The crisis and adjustment to the first child was greater when the child was unplanned or unwanted (Rossi, 1968).

From these studies it appears that the advent of the first child may be an event causing powerful behavior changes in parents. It should be noted, however, that the studies did not specify with which behaviors the parents experienced the greatest discontinuities with the advent of the first born. Nor did they examine whether these "new" or changed activities (e.g., caretaking activities) only have aversive quality, as is implied by the concept of crisis, or whether they are not balanced out by other child-related activities which may be positively reinforcing. Although no studies seem to test these propositions, it may be safe to assume that with the advent of children, a number of behaviors have to be performed which may have been previously learned (e.g., through observation of models) but not previously performed and that some existing responses have to be modified.

These behavior changes, which to a great extent will be a function of role prescriptions and role expectations in the sense that they define their reinforcing consequences, will be considerably greater if the parents accept the traditional notion that the child needs continuous care by its biological mother and that the woman should give up other sources of satisfaction for the sake of the child (Laws, 1971). This traditional parental role expectation seems widely accepted, although there is no empirical evidence to support, for example, the notion that working mothers have damaging effects on their children (Ferguson, 1970).

The relative amount of behavior change (e.g., in expressive and instrumental behavior) with the advent of parenthood may depend on the similarity of role expectations of parenthood to the role expectations of marriage. Women, for example, who perceive expressiveness as appropriate marital role behavior probably will show less behavior change as a function of parenthood than those who perceive it appropriate for parental role behavior only. Laws (1971) interpreted the family literature as indicating that the advent of children in most instances is responsible for a shift in power-role from egalitarian to husband-dominated, and that parenthood, rather than marriage, results in a shift from instrumental to expressive wife behavior. Since parenthood is also conceived of as decreasing the number of alternatives to the marriage relationship, especially for the wife (Campbell, 1967; Laws, 1971), it may be assumed that it results in relatively more pronounced behavior change than marriage, especially in the wife.

V. Retrospect

While marriage and parenthood were used as examples to demonstrate the usefulness of the social-learning approach for an analysis of adult behavior changes, it should be clear that the present analysis could likewise have been extended to other marker events earlier or later in an individual's course of life. Thus, starting school, beginning to work, post-parenthood, retirement, widowhood, etc., may be viewed in terms of the same principles with a corresponding degree of parsimony. It should also be clear that less spectacular events, such as changing the place of work, moving into another neighborhood, or relocating the elderly may result in behavior changes which, like more molar life events, may be analyzed in terms of social-learning principles.

While some of the phenomena discussed in the present chapter may just as plausibly have been described in terms of alternative theoretical models (for example, social role expectations by means of cognitive theories), one major strength of the present approach is its heuristic value, as it suggests areas of research which typically have been neglected by the majority of existing research emphases. Furthermore, such a social-learning approach focuses on the analysis of organism–environment interchanges and the examination of age-related changes in environmental fields (see also Baltes & Nesselroade, 1973). Accordingly, detailed analyses of a person's changing social environment at any age would be a consequence of the present approach.

In the interest of conciseness, the working assumption in the foregoing was that the same principles account for behavior changes over the whole life span. However, it is now in order to make some concessions to this assumption. First, it should be noted that there may be a difference in *speed* of behavior change among younger and older people. With a focus on environmental contingencies and on an interactionistic view of organism–environment interchanges, two explanations emerge.

On the one hand, as discussed earlier in this chapter, people seem to have a tendency to seek environments that support their previously learned behaviors. That is, they seek environments and interaction partners similar to previously experienced environments and to themselves, when given the choice. Therefore, age groups having the greatest freedom of choosing their environments (mostly, the adult age group), should show relatively less behavior changes than the age groups for whom environmental changes are largely programmed from the outside (children and a large percentage of older people).

On the other hand, behavior of adults may change less quickly than the behavior of children because it is maintained by very different and sometimes discrepant sources of reinforcement (Patterson, 1971). The husband, for example, who might try to retrain his wife to be less "busy" might not succeed since his wife might be reinforced by people outside of the family for exactly these behaviors (e.g., neighbors, mother-in-law admiring the perfectly clean household). This intermittent reinforcement may result in stabilization of the behavior that one intends to change. It would appear likely that the more different and conflicting sources of reinforcement (interaction partners) there are in a person's life, the less behavior change would result from any particular source of reinforcement. Controlled environments, therefore, such as institutional settings (schools for children, homes for the aged) with a consistent program may produce the greatest amount of behavior change.

A second concession to the assumption that the same principles explain behavior change at all ages relates to the fact that the *parameters* describing the learning process may differentially interact with the age of the organism. Before an analysis like the foregoing can be refined, detailed developmental studies examining the relationship among characteristics of the reinforcing event, incentive values, reinforcement history, etc., must be performed. Obviously, social-learning oriented research will have to deal with similar issues as the last decade has witnessed in the area of, say, developmental research in verbal learning (e.g., Goulet in Nesselroade & Reese, 1973).

These restrictions notwithstanding, it is concluded that the present application of social-learning principles to adult development has resulted in a rich field of theoretical and interventive perspectives. In addition to offering a powerful model for conceptualizing behavior change, the application of social-learning principles to adult development implies a persuasive argument for the notion that adult behavior is not largely stable, but part of a dynamically changing organism, especially in the context of a changing social matrix. This dynamic, developmental view of the adult personality, which is somewhat contrary to the lack of empirical research in the area, seems however in good agreement with a life-span view of human development.

CHAPTER 12

Person-Perception Research and the Perception of Life-Span Development

ANNE H. NARDI

WEST VIRGINIA UNIVERSITY
MORGANTOWN, WEST VIRGINIA

ABSTRACT

Developmental psychologists have addressed themselves to the issue of a phenomenologically oriented approach to augment existing experimentally derived theories. Within a life-span frame of reference such an approach can be utilized to focus upon perceived changes and differences in life-span processes. Consideration is given to the perceptual process involved in person perception in order to underscore the relevant variables which interact with both the developmental process itself as well as the perception of this process. Within this framework, attention is directed to the consideration of perceived or subjective differences in age-functional behavior.

Research focusing upon perceived age stereotypes is discussed as a historical antecedent to the current consideration of perceived age differences and age changes in life-span research. Major findings related to the perception of age-functional behavior are discussed and implications for methodological considerations are stressed. Emphasis is placed upon the role of perceived developmental change as crucial in effecting subsequent objective change in personality systems. The relevance of a phenomenological approach to investigate the role of perceived age-functional behavior is considered in relation to the impact such perceptions possess for life-span socialization processes.

I. Introduction

Within the context of personal and social variables relevant to the process of development, several authors have suggested the importance of investigating perceived age differences in additon to actual age differences (Ahammer, 1970;

Baltes & Goulet, 1971; Bengtson & Kuypers, 1970; Labouvie & Baltes, in press; Nardi, 1971; Riegel, 1972c; Thomae, 1970). To place this emphasis within the context of life-span developmental research, the role of perceived age-functional behavior may possess crucial implications for the perception of the developmental process. It is Thomae's contention (1970) that perceived change in contrast to objectively occurring environmental change is frequently the antecedent to change in behavior. Bühler (1961), for example, observed that the perception of age change was more important for old age adjustment than was actual change in function. In addition, the influence of subjective (perceived) age differences has been noted by Ahammer (1970; Ahammer & Baltes, 1972) to be significant in determining interage and intergenerational interactions.

In this framework, the importance accorded to perceived age changes and age differences mirrors several important research perspectives. Return to a phenomenological approach has been suggested by Riegel (1972c) as a means of supplementing existing theoretical and experimental approaches. Within this context, the perception of age change merits consideration in its own right, presumably to provide the basis for the development of a phenomenologically oriented developmental theory. Furthermore, perceived age changes and the perception of age differences possess significance for uncovering the developmental antecedents of the patterns and directions of ontogenetic change (Baltes & Goulet, 1971; Thomae, 1970). Both Bengtson and Black (see their chapter, this volume) and Riley (1971; Riley, Johnson, & Foner, 1972) have made substantial contributions to the latter area in their work in intergenerational perceptions. The use of age stratification (Riley et al., 1972) to emphasize the distinct roles of chronological age and cohort membership is most germane to the present topic for its focus upon the impact of societal age structure on the patterning of ontogenetic change.

The structure of the present chapter includes a consideration of the process of person perception and the factors involved therein, followed by a selected review of the literature related to perceived age-related characteristics and lastly, discussion of potential avenues for research on the perception of the developmental process across the life span.

II. The Process of Person Perception

Person perception is the term referring to the sum total of the processes involved in knowing the external and internal states of other people (Tagiuri & Petrullo, 1958; Warr & Knapper, 1968). Tagiuri and Petrullo (1958) used the term to imply that the perceiver regards the perceived "as having the potential of representation and intentionality [p. x]." Furthermore, he distinguished three major elements of the perceptual process: (1) the *situation*, (2) the *person* perceived apart from situational context and (3) the *perceiver* himself as an index of perceptual selectivity. These elements are useful in terms of specifying important components that relate to the subsequent perception and have, in addition, been substantiated by other investigators in terms of their impact upon person perception (Bruner & Tagiuri, 1954; Secord & Backman, 1964; Shrauger & Altrocchi, 1964; Tagiuri, 1969; Tagiuri & Petrullo, 1958; Warr & Knapper, 1968).

The model proposed by Warr and Knapper (1968) represents a parsimonious schematization of the various elements that interact in the perceptual process (see Figure 1). They have hypothesized the operation of an input selector mechanism that governs the information processed in the perception; this subsumes the joint influence of present stimuli as well as stored information about the perceived. Present stimuli include both social and behavioral aspects of the situation, while the stored content component refers to accessible information which the perceiver may employ in forming conceptual judgments. Other factors affecting the perceptual process refer to the perceiver's characteristics and are further differentiated in terms of (1) stable characteristics, and (2) current state. The component of stable characteristics includes the following variables: age, social class, attitudes, cognitive style, and personality traits. In contrast, the current state of the perceiver defined in terms of *Einstellung* or perceptual readiness may influence cue selection at a given point in time.

Warr and Knapper have further distinguished three components directly related to response output. Their involvement in the process is subsequent to the action of the processing center, which is defined as the perceiver's set of "decision rules" concerning stimulus input. These components involve first of all, the attribution of covert and overt characteristics to the perceived, secondly, the generalization of a set of expectancies related to the attributive responses, and lastly, affective responses centered in the perceiver's evaluations of the attributive responses and expectancies.

Warr and Knapper describe the perceptual process as a dynamic series of interactions among the various components; obviously, these interactions are complex and are reflected in the hypothesized feedback loops between input and output components. Within this system, the expectancy component is accorded a role of central importance. When an individual perceiver makes attributional judgments about a stimulus person, he assumes a set of expectancies related to the perceived (Kelly, 1955; Warr & Knapper, 1968). These in turn affect the selection of input information processed in later perceptions. In addition, expectancy as a factor may affect both input and output tendencies in the form of a feedback loop to the stored information component.

Several of the components specified by Warr and Knapper are relevant to the consideration of perceived age-functional behavior. A modification of the Warr and Knapper model of the perceptual process is depicted in Figure 1.

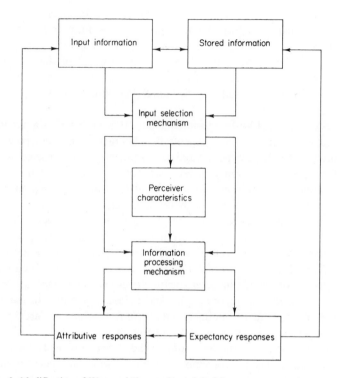

Fig. 1. Modification of Warr and Knapper's model of the person-perception process.

As may be observed in Figure 1, the relevant variables in inter-age perceptions are classified as follows:

1. *Salient characteristics of the perceived.* These incorporate the components of present input information as well as stored information about the stimulus or target person.
2. *Perceiver characteristics.* The variables of chronological age, cohort membership, years of education, and other variables assumed to possess functional relevance to age would be considered under this area.
3. *Attributive and expectancy responses.* Combined, these constitute the perception per se, thus accounting for their central role in the present discussion. Furthermore, the expectancy component is presumed to influence subsequent perceptions through a feedback loop to the stored information component.

According to the proposed model of the perceptual process, attention initially is focused upon the characteristics of the perceived. Secondly, this is differentiated into present stimulus input (target person and contextual setting) and stored information which are selectively coded into the selection mechanism. The majority of age-perception research has capitalized on the component of stored information by minimizing the amount of detail in present stimulus input available. For example, Tuckman and Lorge (1953) instructed college students to describe the perceptual target "older people" in terms of given stereotypes. Such use of minimal stimulus information in an experimental setting is assumed to emphasize stored information and prior perceptions of the target person or group. This approach is prototypical of the research strategies employed in age-perception investigations (Golde & Kogan, 1959; Laurence, 1964; Neugarten, Moore & Lowe, 1965).

The influence of perceiver characteristics has long been acknowledged to be central to the perceptual process within the person-perception literature (Bruner & Tagiuri, 1954; Shrauger & Altrocchi, 1964; Tagiuri & Petrullo, 1958; Warr & Knapper, 1968). However, this concern has not been reflected in age-perception research prior to the present decade. More recent investigations (Ahammer & Baltes, 1972; Higgins–Trenk, 1972; Labouvie & Baltes, in press; Nardi, 1971) have examined the effects of systematically varying perceiver characteristics (defined in terms of chronological age) upon perceptions of age-functional behavior. These investigations, to be discussed in detail in a subsequent section, indicate differential effects of perceiver characteristics for certain personality and attitudinal variables pointing to the crucial influence exerted by this component on the perception of age-related characteristics.

The interaction of perceived and perceiver characteristics is reflected in the perception of the complex of attributive and expectancy responses. Research on the perceptions of aging has for the most part centered upon attributive responses (Eisdorfer & Altrocchi, 1961; Kastenbaum & Durkee, 1964a,b; Kogan & Shelton, 1962a,b; Tuckman & Lorge, 1953, 1958a). While Neugarten et al. (1965) have incorporated the expectancy component in an investigation of age-appropriate behavior in adults and older people, the influence of expectancies on age-related behavior is a recent research emphasis (Ahammer & Baltes, 1972; Labouvie & Baltes, in press; Nardi, 1971).

III. Perception of Age: Stereotypes

The majority of research on age-related perceptions centers upon the dimension of stored stimulus information, since the principal focus has been upon stereotypes of particular age levels. Stereotype, in this case, is taken to refer to a social stereotype that reflects consensual beliefs (Brigham, 1971; Gardner, Rodensky, & Kirby, 1970) about the target or perceived group. As has been noted by other reviewers (Ahammer & Baltes, 1972; McTavish, 1971), research has been concentrated upon perceptions of old age; unfortunately, there is a lack of similar research with other age levels as perceptual targets.

The investigations of Tuckman and Lorge (1952c, 1953) are historically relevant for focusing attention on attitudes toward old people. Their scale of stereotypes pertaining to the perceptual target of "older people" has been used with groups of college students (Tuckman & Lorge, 1953), older people in institutional and community settings (Tuckman & Lorge, 1952a, 1952b, 1958b), college students and their parents (Tuckman, Lorge, & Spooner, 1953), and people with varied amounts of experience with the aged (Tuckman & Lorge, 1958a). In general, the perceptions of old age are essentially negative in all of the studies mentioned, irrespective of the type of subjects involved. Old age is perceived as a period characterized by isolation and social withdrawal, by passivity, and an orientation toward the past in contrast to the future. In addition, it is perceived as a period beset with physical as well as psychological problems and dependency.

While Kogan and his associates have examined age-related perceptions with various procedures (Kogan, 1961; Kogan & Wallach, 1961a), the investigations employing a sentence completion test to assess attitudes toward old people (Golde & Kogan, 1959; Kogan & Shelton, 1962a, 1962b) are especially pertinent to the present discussion. In the first place, such a task permits the construction of a matched set of control items to assess the hypothesis that perceptions of older people are qualitatively different than those held for people in general. Secondly, such an approach eliminates the problem of response set found with the Tuckman and Lorge scale.

The first investigation (Golde & Kogan, 1959) utilizing college undergraduates indicated that the perceptual target of old people is perceived to be qualitatively distinct from the referent people in general. In addition, the perceptions of old people were not always cast in an entirely negative framework. These findings were subsequently substantiated (Kogan & Shelton, 1962a) with older subjects who also perceived the two perceptual targets as distinct. The concluding investigation by Kogan and Shelton (1962b) involving both college undergraduates and older subjects reported age differences that are suggestive of intergenerational conflict as well as misperceptions between generations. Their data indicate that young subjects misperceive old people (when the criterion is the response of older subjects) as being preoccupied with death, more often in need of assistance, more interested in their families, and resentful of young people.

IV. Perceptions of Aging: Diversity of Variables

In addition to the use of *likert-type* scales of attitude held toward the older generation employed by Tuckman and Lorge as well as by Kogan and his associates, other investigators have employed a variety of approaches. Within the body of research on perceptions of the aged, use has been made of the *semantic differential* (Eisdorfer & Altrocchi, 1961; Kogan & Wallach, 1961a; Rosencranz & McNevin, 1969); approaches using *content analysis* (Golde & Kogan, 1959; Hickey, Hickey, & Kalish, 1968; McTavish, 1971; Neugarten & Gutmann, 1958); *age appropriate attitudes* (Kastenbaum & Durkee, 1964a, 1964b); an *age constraint scale* (Neugarten et al, 1965; Troll & Schlossberg, 1970); and *generation rating scales* (Cameron, 1971).

The assessment of age constraint scores (Neugarten *et al.*, 1965) reflects an intriguing approach to investigate the degree to which individuals ascribe increasing importance to societally governed expectancies for age-appropriate behavior. The instrument utilized measures the extent to which subjects agree to age restrictions for certain adult behaviors in areas of dress, social behavior, marriage, etc. Their data indicate the presence of age constraints for certain behavioral areas and furthermore present evidence indicating that with increased age, subjects tend to report that their own behavior is more in accord with the reported constraints (see also Neugarten & Datan, this volume).

For the most part the examination of perceived age differences has been psychogerontological in emphasis. Studies which have employed subjects of various age levels (Axelrod & Eisdorfer, 1961; Laurence, 1964) have varied the age levels of the perceivers primarily to validate the perceptions of older people by subjects of various ages. Typically there has been no examination of the effects of the perceiver characteristics. Interestingly enough, when comparisons have been made between the responses of old and young subjects (Aaronson, 1966; Eisdorfer & Altrocchi, 1961; Hickey *et al.*, 1968; Hickey & Kalish, 1968; Kogan & Shelton, 1962b; Kogan & Wallach, 1961a), the age groups appear to possess distinct perceptions regarding old age, with the views of the older respondents being uniformly less negative.

To relate the findings from aging research to the Warr and Knapper model, it is apparent from reviewing the available literature that most investigators have utilized the stored information component which provides a minimal amount of present contextual information in the experimental setting. There are exceptions to this in the age-judgment research (Britton & Britton, 1969; Kogan, Stephens, & Shelton, 1961; Looft, 1971a; Looft, Rayman, & Rayman, 1972) whereby age discriminability is assessed in young children; the emphasis is generally to examine the development of age perceptions with pictures as stimuli. While increased perceptual accuracy with increased age has been noted (Looft, 1971a; Looft *et al.*, 1972), the data related to preschool subjects are somewhat conflicting with Britton and Britton (1969) reporting extreme inaccuracies in discriminations in contrast to Kogan *et al.* (1961) who report clear age discriminability at age four.

While the role of the expectancy component is felt to be crucial in age perceptions, it is interesting to note that of all of the literature just reviewed, only the Neugarten *et al.* (1965) investigation was directed primarily toward examining age-related expectancies by means of the age constraint score. While no direct assessment of expectancies has been cited within the body of aging literature, given the hypothesized interactive status of this component in the Warr and Knapper model, one must assume that it is functioning in conjunction with the stored information component central to the research.

The literature on age-related perceptions does offer limited information on the effects of stable perceiver characteristics, albeit this factor was not central to the design of the majority of these investigations. Undoubtedly, one of the foremost variables to consider in this context is the chronological age of the perceiver. As already noted, distinctions between perceivers on the basis of age indicated the existence of differential perceptions of the aged across age groups (Aaronson, 1966; Hickey & Kalish, 1968, Kogan & Shelton, 1962b; Kogan & Wallach, 1961a). Furthermore, such differences are typically in the direction of more positive perceptions reported by the older subjects.

Social class of the perceiving group is an additional variable that has demonstrated a certain degree of relationship to reported perceptions. According to Hickey *et al.* (1968) and Rosencranz and McNevin (1969), a negative relationship exists between social class and agreement with negative stereotypes of aging. In contrast, McTavish (1971) reports no relationship between the two variables in his own research. In view of the complex interaction presumed to occur in the perceptual process, it is not surprising that a unidimensional approach resting solely on social class would yield conflicting results.

Similar discrepancies have been observed in regard to a variable relating experience with aged individuals to reported perceptions. Drake (1957) reported no relationship between experience with older people (in the form of daily contacts) and reported perceptions. Subsequently, Tuckman and Lorge (1958a) observed no lessening of stereotypical perceptions in subjects with experience in dealing with older people and, in fact, reported higher degrees of agreement on certain items. More recent data reported by Bengtson (1970) indicate a differentiation in a perceived generation gap when the context of the perception is restricted to primary group members in contrast to perception of the older generation in a broad societal context. The refinement of situational variables suggested by Bengtson offers a promising means of operationalizing the multidimensional status of age-related perceptions.

In summary, the literature on perceptions of the aged at present possesses limited applicability for life-span perception. The foremost methodological difficulties reside in the instrumentation. Lack of technical precision, as well as the sheer diversity of instruments utilized, contribute to the complexity of reported findings. The presence of an evaluative factor (Eisdorfer & Altrocchi, 1961; Kogan & Wallach, 1961a; Rosencranz & McNevin, 1969) has been reported in factor analytic procedures. Given the structure of the majority of instruments used in this field, the influence of such a factor may be an additional source of confounding. Undoubtably, the restrictions of most investigations to unidimensional approaches with little consideration given to the influence of perceiver characteristics has resulted in the variety of observations noted.

V. Perception of Age-Functional Behavior

According to the hypothesized interactions discussed previously, examination of the perception of the developmental process should focus upon systematic investigation of the following variables: stored information, perceiver characteristics, and the expectancy component (Ahammer & Baltes, 1972; Nardi, 1971; Shrauger & Altrocchi, 1964; Warr & Knapper, 1968). Since it is difficult to disentangle interactions between stored information and expectancies, consideration of age-related expectancies implies the influence of previous experience as coded in the stored information component.

Expectancies for age-appropriate behavior are incorporated into a system of explicit and implicit norms for behavior within all cultures (Eisenstadt, 1956; Parsons, 1942). Riley et al. (1972) in their treatment of age in a sociological context stress the societal aspects of age as reflected in the age structure of a society. Thus, age stratification within a society reflects the influence of two separate yet interrelated processes: aging and cohort flow (see also Bengtson & Black, this volume). Aging consists of the movement across age levels or strata from infancy to old age. In contrast, cohort flow is reflected in the aggregates of individuals born at the same point in history who successively enter a society. Distinguishing between these two aspects of societal age structure points to the interaction between an individual's life course and his location within a given historical period.

Concomitant with the model proposed by Riley and associates (1972) is a division of its elements into population-related dimensions of *age strata* (persons of given ages) and *age-related acts* (or capacities) and a role-related dimension of the *age structure of roles* and *age-related expectations and sanctions*. The recognition that age functions as a normative criterion in regard to the latter dimension for both role entry and exit, as well as for age-appropriate behavior, makes explicit the central role of age in life-span socialization.

It is Neugarten's contention (Neugarten et al., 1965) that these expectancies function as "prods and brakes" upon behavior within the sphere of social events. Neugarten et al. (1965) examined the interaction between perceived societal age norms and the extent to which these norms were perceived to have personal validity. Their data indicate increasing convergence with age between the two sets of perceptions (see Figure 2).

As may be observed in Figure 2, age trends within each set of perceptions are opposite in direction. For personal opinions, there is a highly significant increase in scores with age; however, for perceived societal norms ("most people's opinions"), there is a significant decline in score values with age. The investigators interpreted these data in conjunction with a theory of adult socialization, that is, with increased age, individuals become more aware of the norms for age-appropriate behavior which coincides with an increase in beliefs in the personal relevance and validity of the norms. The lack of correspondence between personal opinions and those attributed to a generalized other (except for the oldest subjects) is frequently observed with other types of norms as well (Neugarten et al.,1965). For older people, the high degree of congruence between personal beliefs and those of the generalized other may represent internalization of age norms through the process of adult socialization. Neugarten and her associates have noted that the age norms reported are perceptions of "ideal norms" which in this instance may very well be age norms held by older individuals.

The very existence of age-grading systems and age-homogeneous groups (Bengtson, 1969, 1971; Campbell, 1969; Neugarten et al., 1965) implies that not only are age groups perceived distinctly, but that they also are accorded differential sets of expectancies (Riley et al., 1972). It is not surprising that research on intergenerational perceptions reflects contemporary concern with intergenerational conflicts. Interestingly enough, several recent investigations of personality and attitudinal variables have indicated that perceived age differ-

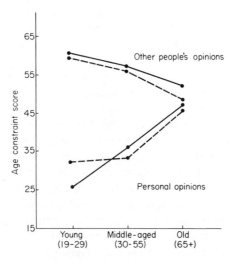

Fig. 2. Perception of age constraints in adulthood, by age and sex. Dotted line—women; solid line—men. [From Neugarten, Moore, and Lowe, Age norms, age constraints, and adult socialization. *American Journal of Sociology,* 1965, **70,** p. 714. © 1965 by The University of Chicago Press.]

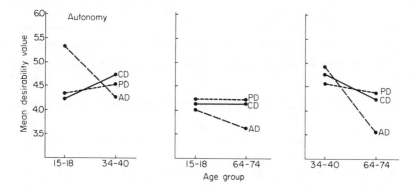

Fig. 3. Personal Desirability (PD), Cohort Desirability (CD), and Age Desirability (AD) of autonomy. Each segment of the graph shows the relationships between two age groups. [From Ahammer and Baltes, 1972, p. 49. Reprinted by permission of the Gerontological Society.]

ences frequently fail to reflect actual age differences between generations (Ahammer & Baltes, 1972; Bengtson, 1969, 1971; Kalish, 1970; Nardi, 1971).

Ahammer and Baltes (1972) concluded that some of the generation differences for a limited number of personality variables are subjective in nature rather than reflections of objectively occurring age or cohort differences. Their intent was to compare perceived and actual age differences for adolescents, adults, and older people on the desirability values of certain personality traits. Objective age differences were defined in terms of the personal desirability of the trait, whereas perceived age differences were assessed by means of an age desirability condition; a third condition, cohort desirability, was included as a method control. For the traits of both autonomy and nurturance, perceived or subjective age differences were reported in the absence of objective age differences, while for affiliation and achievement, perceived and objective age differences did not differ significantly.

The age by instruction interaction for the trait of autonomy may be noted in Figure 3. Adults perceived adolescents to place a higher value on autonomy than they actually did. In addition, both younger groups perceived older people to value autonomy as significantly less desirable than the oldest group described themselves or their own age group.

Ahammer and Baltes (1972) underscored an interesting aspect of their results related to the middle-aged group. The adult age group was never misperceived, in that the results of all instruction conditions coincided for the adult target age. Yet the same group could be frequently described as misperceiving since in all cases of misperceptions (observance of subjective age differences in the absence of actual age differences), the adult group was one that misperceived. In contrast, the older age group was one that was always misperceived on the dimensions where misperceptions occurred (autonomy and nurturance). Similarly, Riley *et al.* (1972) stated that the discrepancy between societal expectations and behavior is most pronounced for adolescence and old age.

Ahammer and Baltes (1972) interpreted these findings in light of the role assumed to be exerted by adults in the socialization process. It is their hypothesis that the adult group functions as the primary agent of socialization. Within this framework, their perceptions of adolescents and older people may reflect age norms and socialization goals set for the other two age groups. Similar ideas have been proposed by Bengtson and Kuypers (1970) in the concept of the *developmental stake,* representing the vested interests of the adult group in the process of life-span socialization (see also the chapter by Bengtson & Black, this volume).

Ahammer (1971) examined the effects of retrospective and prospective perceptions of personality dimensions. Her intent was to determine if perceived differences in behavior were ontogenetic or generational in nature. She assessed these differences using 10 scales of the Jackson Personality Research Form with young adults (CA 18–23) and older people (CA 64–84). Under prospective instructions, young subjects reported self-perceptions of change on only three dimensions: defensiveness, achievement, and impulsivity. The older subjects reported extremely stable self-perceptions under retrospection with the exception of the trait of dependence. Ahammer interpreted the overall conclusions as indicating perceived personality differences to be generational in nature reflecting cohort differences.

Perhaps the most comprehensive work conducted to date is a life-span approach to the investigation of perceived age differences in personality by Nardi (1971). She systematically varied the perceiver characteristic of age to examine the effects on age-related perceptions in adolescents, adults, and older people using the Jackson Personality Research Form. A major finding of her investigation was that all subjects (whose actual ages corresponded to the target age groups studied) shared similar perceptions of each target age (15, 40, and 65 years) investigated. In other words, the targets representing adolescence, adulthood, and old age were differentially perceived, yet this distinction did not reflect actual age effects.

Differential effects of perceiver age were noted for only two personality dimensions: aggression and play. In both instances, adolescents perceived all target ages as being higher on the traits than did older subjects. This finding can be interpreted in terms of adolescents attributing a higher degree of saliency to aggression and play for all stages of ontogeny than adults and older people. This is somewhat supported by the finding that adolescents were perceived under heteroperception as possessing greater degrees of both traits.

In addition to examining differential perception of three marker ages, Nardi also included a variable termed *perception level* which referred to whether the subject was instructed to describe himself at a given target age (autoperception)

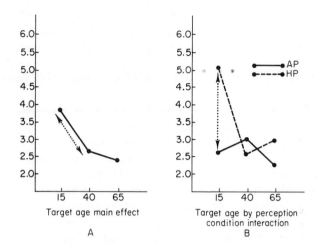

Fig. 4. Mean scores for aggression. (AP=Autoperception; HP=Heteroperception.)[From Nardi, 1971.]

or the "average person" of that age (heteroperception). It is in respect to this variable that an interesting interaction was noted in the data.

Nardi's results indicate that adolescence is perceived to be quite distinct from both of the upper two age levels. However, this interpretation must be qualified by the presence of target age by perception level interactions centered primarily at the adolescent target age. Therefore, much of this differentiation of perceptions of adolescence is attributable to differential perceptions of the average adolescent in contrast to self-perceptions.

An example of the target age by perception level interaction may be observed in Figure 4. The graphs in this figure contrast differential target-age perceptions (Figure 4A) and the interaction of target age with perception level (Figure 4B) for the dimension of aggression. The contrast between self-perceptions as an adolescent (which include retrospective reports as well as concurrent measures) and the heteroperceptions indicate the general tendency in the data whereby self-perceptions for the target of adolescence are quite similar to perceptions of the upper two target ages. The primary distinction in perceptions of adolescence is centered in the heteroperceptions (which again include concurrent as well as retrospective reports).

The data from the Nardi investigation suggest that for the most part all three age groups share fairly similar conceptions of personality patterns characteristic of the three target ages. The absence of marked differentiation between perceptions of adulthood and old age may reflect differential saliency of the personality dimensions investigated as well as a change in the conceptual judgment of what constitutes old age.

The major findings from this study emphasize that the perception of distinct age-related behavior patterns may reflect shared socialization expectancies for age-appropriate behavior as also noted by Neugarten *et al.* (1965) and Riley *et al.* (1972). The absence of major age differences in the perception of the three marker age periods suggests that these perceptions have strong stability across age. Lastly, the clear distinction between autoperceptions and heteroperceptions of the adolescent period strongly hints at the perception of personal stability in personality across age in contrast to marked generation differences for a generalized other. The latter observation is paralleled by Bengtson's data (1971) on perceived generation gaps. Labouvie and Baltes (in press) using age simulation instructions (Baltes & Goulet, 1971) within the adolescent period report similar distinctions between self and peer perceptions on personality dimensions. Their data also indicate that autoperceptions reflect better personal adjustment than do peer perceptions during the adolescent period.

One further investigation of perceived age-functional behavior in adolescence is that of Higgins–Trenk (1972). Higgins–Trenk's data indicate that adolescents' self and peer perceptions reflect stereotypes of adolescence except for the perception of young males (CA 12) by older females (CA 18) and vice versa. Furthermore, her results indicate that females' perceptions are more in accord with cultural stereotypes than are males'. The Higgins–Trenk data attest to the reality of a cohort gap since the reported perceptions are distinct from those frequently reported by adults about adolescence. However, the overall interpretation of her data on the basis of the two cohorts investigated confirms the ontogenetic nature of perceived personality development observed by Nardi (1971), in contrast to the generational impact noted by Ahammer (1971).

The existence of differential age expectancies has been verified both in regard to age-appropriate social behavior as well as in perceived personality dimensions. In addition, age expectancies appear to interact strongly with the self versus generalized-other perception instructions (Labouvie & Baltes, in press; Nardi, 1971; Neugarten *et al.*,1965). This observation merits examination in light of the age-related patterns noted thus far in the research. The discrepancy has been noted thus far with both adolescence (Labouvie & Baltes, in press; Nardi, 1971) and old age (Neugarten *et al.*, 1965), yet is strikingly absent in perceptions of adulthood (Ahammer & Baltes, 1972). Since the adult age group represents a scarcely researched age level, the Ahammer & Baltes (1972) observation of "never misperceived, frequently misperceiving" bears further consideration.

VI. Perception of Change: Implications for Developmental Research

One of the major implications of age-perception research for developmental psychology is stated by Thomae (1970). It is his contention that in the case of personality systems, perceived change, rather than external stimulation, is the critical factor in behavioral change. That perceptions may exert a deterministic influence upon objective behavior has been frequently observed in research on conforming behavior. In those studies, conformity was effected by creating discrepancies between an individual's behavior and that of the total group (Jones & Thibaut, 1958; Thibaut & Strickland, 1956). Subsequent behavioral change in the direction of closer correspondence with the norm of the group behavior is attributed to the perception of an existing discrepancy (Tajfel, 1969). An analogous argument serves as the basis for Thomae's postulates concerning the perceptions of change in age-related behavior.

Similar inferences may be drawn from data presented by Neugarten et al. (1965). Their data substantiate the existence of normative expectancies for age-appropriate behavior in areas such as dress, marriage, and social behavior. In addition, the investigators reported a heightened awareness of these expectancies in older subjects. The suggestion of a deterministic influence which increases with age may be extrapolated from the close correspondence between expectancies and self-reports at upper age levels not observed for younger subjects.

If one accepts Thomae's postulates, then perceptions of age-related behavior may determine age-functional behavior in much the same normative manner through which other socialization standards operate (LeVine, 1969). The existence of such perceptual determinants can be inferred from the roles which are age-related in the existing social structure (Inkeles, 1969; Riley et al., 1972). In addition, the continued existence of age status and age-grading systems within the Western social structure underscores the importance implicitly attributed to age in socialization processes (Neugarten & Moore, 1968; Riley et al., 1972; Williams, 1960). Although both are loosely defined concepts, they are reflected in the cultural expectancies concomitant with biological maturation and aging in all societies (Eisenstadt, 1956; Linton, 1942; Neugarten & Moore, 1968; Parsons, 1942; Riley et al., 1972).

The verification of distinct age-related perceptions for widely separated target or perceived age levels is felt to be sufficient to warrant further examination of this behavioral dimension. Furthermore, the hypothesis that an implicit theory of age-related change may operate as a behavioral determinant remains plausible (Ahammer, 1969; Ahammer & Baltes, 1972; Higgins–Trenk, 1972; Labouvie & Baltes, in press; Nardi, 1971; Thomae, 1970). Evaluation of the parameters suggested by current life-span investigations of age-related perceptions may prove profitable in designing future research strategies.

The interaction between perceived and objective behavior across generations has been cited as a clear instance of intergroup perceptions which are age-defined (Ahammer & Baltes, 1972; Bengtson, 1970; Higgins–Trenk, 1972; Nardi, 1971). Bengtson (1971) has examined additional parameters of such interactions in terms of the *relationship* between perceiver and perceived, further specified in terms of the *context* of the perceiver–perceived relationship (primary group versus generalized collectivity). His data indicate that while considerable cohort gaps are acknowledged within a broad societal context, smaller lineage gaps are perceived within the primary group.

Further specification of contextual variables in the manner suggested by Bengtson yields rich information related to the age-perception process. It is felt that such an approach, utilized with systematic variation of perceiver and perceived characteristics, will augment existing attempts to attribute causality to perceptual and behavioral variations. Cryns and Monk (1972) have employed these specification instructions in the examinations of older adults' perceptions of the young. Using three targets to represent young, Cryns and Monk report decreasing positive attitudes toward the targets in the following order: "our boys in Vietnam," "today's young people," and "college students." Secondly, the investigations examined the perceiver characteristics of life satisfaction and quality of filial relationship with their own offspring. Cryns and Monk report the existence of a direct relationship between these two perceiver characteristics and positive perceptions of the young.

The data of Grifitt, Nelson, and Littlepage (1972) are of interest to consider in terms of an attempt to investigate perceived age differences by further specifying the perceptual setting. They report that young and old groups of subjects in their sample did not rely on age stereotypes to evaluate nonpeers in an experimental setting using a "between groups" design. Additional comparisons of specification procedures would appear mandatory in view of the findings reported in these three investigations.

A major point under consideration relates to the role of implicit theories of change. Within this context, the utilization of longitudinal sequences becomes mandatory since the cross-sectional designs employed in current research investigations restrict observations to perceived age differences and further confound age and cohort differences (Baltes, 1968; Schaie, 1965). Longitudinal research available on personality change (Kelly, 1955; Woodruff & Birren, 1972) indicates that objective change in personality is slight for the time span from late adolescence to adulthood in contrast to perceived adolescent personality as assessed under a retrospective condition.

The data of Higgins–Trenk (1972) related to the perception of adolescent stereotypes indicate that across a relatively short time period (6 years to be precise), differential perceptions, in the form of age by sex interactions, are reported by adolescents of adolescence. Such a time span is certainly amenable for short-term longitudinal strategies which in turn are mandatory for the evaluation of the hypothesized implicit theory of ontogenetic change.

A promising research strategy which is easily accomplished within conventional cross-sectional designs involves the use of retrospective and prospective instructions (Ahammer, 1971; Baltes & Goulet, 1971; Nardi, 1971). With this procedure, the investigator has at his disposal a means to examine age-related perceptions from a specified time perspective in addition to perceiver and perceived characteristics. The use of manipulative or simulation strategies with age perceptions represents a central point in combining experimental strategies within a phenomenological approach to life-span developmental psychology (see Ahammer's chapter, this volume; Baltes & Goulet, 1971).

VII. Conclusion

Research on the perception of age-functional behavior and perceived age differences has moved from the status of preliminary investigations into the perception of aging to sophisticated methodological efforts to assess perceived age differences along a diversity of dimensions. Peterson's (1971) assessment of priorities in age perception research rightfully stresses the importance of conducting such investigations within a life-span framework.

The broad implications that research in age-related perceptions possesses for life-span developmental psychology are reflected in the rapid increase in this body of literature within the past decade. It is felt, perhaps optimistically, that the discrepancies and even glaring gaps in the currently available data will provide stimulating issues for future research in life-span socialization.

PROGRAMMATIC INTERVENTION

CHAPTER 13

Human Development over the Life Span through Education

JAMES E. BIRREN
DIANA S. WOODRUFF[1]

UNIVERSITY OF SOUTHERN CALIFORNIA
LOS ANGELES, CALIFORNIA

ABSTRACT

This chapter focuses on the potential usefulness of the life-span developmental perspective in education and on strategies for enhancing human development over the life span through educational intervention. Means and prospects for implementation of life-span education are also considered. In the first part of this chapter is a review of contemporary criticisms of education, and evidence is presented which demonstrates that a number of social, historical, economic and scientific realities preclude the effectiveness of youth oriented educational practices. From these issues a rationale for life-span education is developed. After this emphasis on the need for education over the life span, attention is directed to implications for education action. Pointing out flaws in educational systems is not sufficient if developmental psychologists are to assist in the planning of educational programs. Specific recommendations in language and aims which are familiar to educators must be developed. Failure of previous early childhood intervention programs can be partially attributed to an overly pragmatic approach and to the absence of theoretical guidelines. To ensure the success of life-span intervention programs, strategies which incorporate developmental concepts and theories must be designed. The intervention strategies proposed in this chapter represent an attempt to apply concepts from life-span developmental psychology to educational practice. These proposals are presented with the hope that they will serve as stimuli for educators and psychologists who will be involved in the planning and design of programs to enhance development over the life span.

[1]Present address: Department of Psychology, University of California, Los Angeles, California.

I. Introduction

To cope with the demands of accelerating social change in the twentieth century, the orientation of educational institutions must be altered from one of exclusive concern with the first two decades of life to involvement with education over the entire human life span. Sixteen years ago Pressey and Kuhlen (1957) asserted that as a consequence of the lengthening of life expectancy and the acceleration of change in society, this country needed educational programming throughout life. In spite of this early recommendation, the prospect of human development over the life span through education has not, until quite recently, received serious consideration for implementation. Perspectives of educators appear to be changing, however, and new attitudes on the part of society appear to be leading to alterations in the nature of educational institutions as well as in the educational process itself.

In 1971 the Carnegie Commission on Higher Education gave emphasis to some of these issues in its publication, *Less Time, More Options*. The report was of the opinion that length of time spent in undergraduate college education could be reduced by one fourth without any reduction in quality. Furthermore, a deemphasis on the value of college education per se in lieu of professional work experience was suggested. Recommendations of direct relevance to this chapter were: "More educational, and thus career, opportunities should be available to all those who wish to study part-time, or return to study later in life, particularly women and older persons. [Carnegie Commission on Higher Education, p. 2]." Social gain was also stressed in the recommendation that,

> Society would gain if work and study were mixed throughout a life-time, thus reducing the sense of sharply compartmentalized roles of isolated students. The sense of isolation would be reduced if more students were also workers and if more workers could also be students; if the ages mixed on the job and in the classroom in a more normally structured type of community; if all members of the community value both study and work and had a better chance to understand the flow of life from youth to age. Society would be more integrated across the lines than now separate students and workers, youth and age [Carnegie Commission on Higher Education, p. 2].

Clearly this is a call for the subject matter of a life-span developmental psychology.

One aim of this chapter will be to document the usefulness of the life-span approach for educators who are attempting to meet new demands arising from social, historical, and economic changes and from generational differences. In addition to providing a rationale for life-span education, we will consider some implications for educational action. Whenever possible, we will discuss the feasibility of implementing our plans for action in terms of the more general issues of education and social planning.

It is relevant to point out that psychology has presumed to have some knowledge of the nature of man or, if you will, the way his behavior is organized. Psychology as an empirical science was antithetical to the theological origins of most institutions of higher learning. Before the advent of psychology, educators might have assumed that mankind was either fundamentally evil, or stupid, or both, and consequently students had to be disciplined along the straight and narrow. Alternatively, man could have been viewed as essentially a virtuous being. From this perspective, if students were protected from excessive temptation and allowed to choose their own way, they would fall into the arms of truth. Psychologists have a fundamental contribution to make regarding self-concepts. In this manner psychologists can provide important information about what should constitute an optimum educational environment. Within psychology, the concepts of personality development, cognitive development, and development and maintenance of social roles and skills are part of the information the educational planner can examine for ideas about how to organize educational institutions.

To make significant contributions to education, however, psychologists must be willing to go beyond merely providing ideas. Psychologists must be willing to translate psychological theory and research into educational terms, and they must be willing to take a more active role in development than that of mere observers. Formal education does not involve objective description; rather, it is interventionist in nature (Bruner, 1966; Rohwer, 1970). Hence, by working with educators, developmental psychologists may find themselves intervening to alter or accelerate the course of ontogeny in addition to measuring and recording developmental sequences.

The potential usefulness of interdisciplinary cross fertilization between developmental psychology and education has been clearly indicated (e.g., Baltes & Labouvie, 1973; Eklund, 1969; Rohwer, 1970). It has also been pointed out that educators and developmental psychologists use different models and perspectives, and such differences may cause difficulty in communication between disciplines. Since we are writing this chapter for educators as well as psychologists, it is important to clarify the meaning of certain key terms. We are defining education in the formal sense to mean the activities of schools and related institutions of our society that are organized to develop the individual's abilities, knowledge, skills and character through systematic teaching, study, training, and guided experience.

One of the key words in the definition of education was *development*. The term development is a difficult one to define, especially development over the life span (Harris, 1957). For the purposes of this chapter, development is defined as the processes whereby the individual goes from a less differentiated to a more differentiated state, from a less complex to a more complex organism, from a lower or early stage to a higher or later stage of an ability, skill, or trait. This assumes that the psychologist can measure where the individual is along some dimension from low to high development. Kohlberg (this volume) illustrates this point of view for moral development in that he describes a progression from lower to higher stages of moral development. In the present context, it is not assumed that development or differentiation ceases at some point in the life span, such as the attainment of physical maturity, but that differentiation proceeds throughout the life span (e.g., see chapters by Emmerich, Neugarten & Datan, this volume). Education is one of the most important ways a society can intervene to optimize development not only of social roles, but development of all aspects of cognitive and affective behavior throughout the life span.

II. Rationale for Life-Span Education

A. Contemporary Reservations about Education

Educational institutions are always subject to criticism. Hopefully people will continue to regard their educational institutions as inadequate and the educational processes they promote, less than perfect. One of the things that characterizes an institution of higher learning is the fact that it continually cultivates a spirit of academic reform. The goals of institutions of higher learning must be continually examined not only with respect to the students who are in the system, but also with respect to society at large which supports the institution. Many groups in society in addition to the students themselves have begun to question the relevance of what goes on in institutions of higher learning to problems and issues of society. There has been, in fact, some evidence that state legislatures are not supporting their institutions of higher learning with characteristic enthusiasm because elected legislators are not convinced the voting public is highly supportive of educational institutions.

Perhaps one of the widest spread criticisms of American higher education is that it has not prepared teachers to serve the needs of the community and of youth of minority group backgrounds. Although ethnic studies courses are being incorportaed into the undergraduate curricula of universities and community colleges, educators and psychologists have only begun to consider the usefulness of constructing and incorporating alternative views of development into curricula. Is it necessary to construct a Black developmental psychology, an Indian developmental psychology, or a non-Western developmental psychology? Such options are possible, and Riegel (1973) has suggested a means of developing these alternative views. The most powerful developmental psychology, of course, would be that which transcended the particulars of any one culture or subgroup in a society. Whether or not specific training on the development of ethnic group members was available, elementary and high school teachers would undoubtedly respond better to the needs of particular groups of students and to the community if they had some background in life-span developmental psychology.

Since cognitive development in minority group members does not appear to be fostered in American elementary and high school education, limited numbers of students from the ranks of minority groups have been admitted to institutions of higher learning. Consequently, a lack of persons of minority group backgrounds is also seen in faculty and administrative positions. Riegel (1973) attributes current admission policies of the so-called institutions of higher learning to nineteenth-century elitism. He argues that supportive fellowships are provided to outstanding students "to make the best better (or at least more arrogrant) [Riegel, 1973, p. 20]." Disadvantaged students who never had the opportunity of working under such ideal conditions might actually show greater improvements than the "outstanding" students as they have more gains to make. It is also suggested by Riegel (1973) that programs that segregate students by ability level alienate the more rapidly developing students instead of directing their attention to individuals who could benefit from extra attention from these more advanced students. In this manner, social responsibility is discouraged rather than rewarded. Clearly a balance is called for in maximizing learning at all levels of ability such that no groups, such as the slow learners or the accelerated learners, are neglected.

Other criticisms of our educational system have included the fact that it stresses an overachievement orientation or competing for grades without an orientation toward the subject matter and the ultimate goals of the educational process. Some schools have adopted a pass–no-pass system coupled with a qualitative evaluation of students. Other schools are now returning to a grade point system under the pressures of the very students who earlier had wanted a pass–no-pass system. The grading of students needs a very thorough examination, hopefully from a developmental perspective, e.g., that which sustains motivation for further development and learning over the life span.

The apparent lack of social responsibility on the part of outstanding faculty members has been another criticism leveled at universities. It has been noted that faculty members sometimes have become empire builders of their own research while neglecting the development of their students and the needs of contemporary society. Thus, less and less confidence has been expressed in the value of research per se for the well-being of society.

The criticism could be directed at professional educators and schools of education for the fact that there has been such an exclusive emphasis on educational research on the childhood years. A 1969 survey of educational research and development in the United States (U.S.D.H.E.W., 1969) showed almost no recognition of the fact that research on education should also be concerned with evaluating the lifelong outcomes of education as well as with immediate outcomes. The report concluded with policy implications that stressed early learning, and this meant early childhood and individual differences. Recognition was given to the fact that elementary schools will be less full as the birthrate drops. No question was raised, however, about whether the school space should go unused or whether it should be used for educatonal programs for adults.

In brief, the professional educational system in administration, research, and teacher training seems to have concentrated inordinantly upon the young child. Very little attention has been given to the goals of a life-span orientation to education. This would seem to be important, particularly in a society where jobs will be of shorter duration, multiple careers will be increasingly frequent, and grey-haired students will be as common as youth on our campuses. Perhaps at no time has there been a greater need to present a life-span developmental perspective to teachers and to schools of education. Education through the life span should become the theme of professional education and its technology should be deeply rooted in an understanding of the biological, psychological, and social differences and capabilities of individuals. Educational institutions have a responsibility to serve all of society, and only one of their functions is to educate young persons to fill the roles of serving society.

B. Social and Historical Changes

1. Changing Age Structure of Society

We are examining the issue of human development over the life span in a period when the balance of power in states has shifted away from legislatures that would enthusiastically endorse educational programs, in a period of time when the economy is quite constricted, and also in a time when the demographic picture of the country has changed. There have been some dramatic demographic changes in the age structure of our society, and the trends appear to be going to continue for the foreseeable future. Figure 1 illustrates the changing age structure of the population in the United States. Since about 1920, the older population of the United States has grown at a more rapid rate than the population as a whole. The current birthrate is low and it is likely to remain low in view of the wide-spread public sympathy for restricting the number of children in order to obtain a zero population growth. What is not so widely recognized is the fact that a low birthrate to achieve a zero population growth will result in a much older average age of the population. In addition to the falling birthrate, the low level of immigration also has reduced the number of young persons in the population. Furthermore, reductions in the death rate has also led to shifting age structure such that the United States is no longer a young country. An adjustment of attitudes should take place including those on the part of educational institutions. How do they best serve a society with an old age structure?

Together with the rise in the proportion of older persons in the population there has also been a downward trend in the age of retirement. Not only does a contemporary individual spend more time in school before he enters the labor force, because of the requisite knowledge required in a technical society, he also tends to leave the labor force earlier because his skills are antiquated or

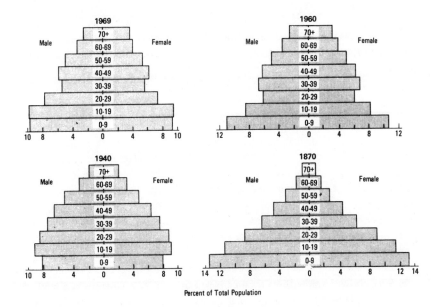

Fig. 1. Distribution of the population by age and sex: 1870–1969. [*Source:* U.S. Bureau of the Census, *Current Population Reports,* P-25, 441 (Washington, D.C.: U.S. Government Printing Office, 1970).]

no longer required. Soon will be the time when the average member of society will spend more than half of his or her life outside of the labor force. In the face of these social changes, the goal of education should not be exclusively that of educating for productive skills, but also that of providing continuing opportunity for relearning or learning new skills and providing a broader basis for an orientation toward the psychological, social, and cultural aspects of the individual's life.

Most persons in institutions of higher learning feel that this is a bleak period in which to contemplate any new educational program, a time when old programs are fighting hard for their survival in the budget battles of academia. At a higher educational level, there is even a widespread belief that we have over educated and have produced too many Ph.D.s, and that we should restrict graduate education. It has been pointed out by Cartter (1971) that the smaller number of entering undergraduates in the future will require fewer Ph.D.s as teachers and, therefore we should constrict the number of present graduate students. Little (1972) presented data indicating that undergraduate enrollment will increase until 1982 when it will decline as a consequence of the present low birth rate. The population under ten years old today is less than it was ten years ago. About 1981 there will be fewer youth of age 18 than those aged 19 (U.S.

Bureau of the Census, 1968). While the overall future job market for Ph.D.s in psychology and educational psychology may seem to be bleak (Little, 1972; Wolfle & Kid, 1971), this general picture is not adjusted to the fact that whole new areas of academic teaching and research and applied jobs await development in serving the middle-aged and older adult (Birren, Gribbin, & Woodruff, 1971).

2. Declining Enrollment of Undergraduates

The popularity of institutions of higher learning with youth seems to have decreased notably. Youth has been expected to go to college as a way of attaining adult membership in a culture that has emphasized education. For many, going to college has been a social and economic escalator to a higher standard of living. Recently, however, youth seems to have lost some zeal for higher learning and college enrollments and applications for admission have dropped. The question in the minds of youth apparently is not where one is going to college, but whether one is going to college.

Future of enrollment decline will also be because of the fact that the cohort of youth of college age will be smaller (see Little, 1972). Current applications, however, are showing a reduction that cannot be attributed to reduction in the size of the age group. In April, 1972, freshmen applications to the University of California system were 4% lower than in 1971. An even larger drop, 8%, was reported by the Independent Association of California Colleges and Universities. This association has 52 members so the reported drop in applications reflects a trend, rather than what is happening at one institution (Los Angeles Times, April 30, 1972).

Along with lower interest of youth in going to college, there may be a rising interest on the part of middle-aged and older adults in higher education. The Institute of Lifetime Learning sponsored by the American Association of Retired Persons (AARP) and the National Retired Teachers Association (NRTA) report a wide range of courses for older adults and impressive enrollments that would not generally be included in national educational statistics. Since its conception in 1964, the Institute has offered courses on more than 90 topics at 12 locations across the country. Thousands of elderly students have enrolled in these courses and in correspondence courses, and additional hundreds of thousands have been reached through courses broadcast over the radio.

3. Education of the Elderly

To argue against the practicality of education over the life span, it might be noted that the contemporary cohort of the aged has taken little advantage of what educational opportunities are open to them (Donahue, 1956; Webber, 1963). Of the total number (479,912) of students enrolled in adult basic educaton programs in 1969, only 13,210 (2.7%) were 65 and over (National Center for Education Statistics, 1970). However, Pressey (1956) pointed out that there have been few occasions when educational opportunities were directed to the needs and goals of the elderly. On a national level, large retirement organizations are taking important steps in assuring that educational opportunities are available for older individuals. The means for continued progress in the education of the aged has been discussed by McClusky (1971) in the source paper on education for the 1971 White House Conference on Aging, and continuing efforts in the form of resolutions, recommendations, and legislative proposals are being made by national and regional committees to upgrade education for the elderly (e.g., U.S. White House Conference on Aging, 1971). Such efforts are useless, however, if older individuals are basically not interested in education.

There is clear evidence indicating that subsequent cohorts of aged individuals will be increasingly interested in education. Johnstone and Rivera (1965) found that the higher an individual's education, the more likely he would be stimulated by education and want to be involved in it. Subsequent cohorts of aged will be better educated. According to the 1970 census figures, only 29.3% of the individuals now over 65 were educated through high school or beyond (U.S. Bureau of the Census, 1971). The census bureau projected that by 1985, 61% of those 65 and older will have at least a high school education (U.S. Bureau of the Census, 1965). Of the cohort aged 30–39, 57% stated that they had taken at least one adult education course in contrast with 30% of the cohort over 60, even though the older people had lived longer and thus had a longer opportunity in which to take the course (Johnstone & Rivera, 1965). Hence, it is highly probable that a greater proportion of future cohorts of elderly will turn to education as a source of activity in their retirement. Educational opportunities over the life span will be increasingly in demand.

At present, it can be said that we are increasingly sensitized to the fact that what may appear to be age differences arise less because of ontogenetic changes than because of historical reasons and culture change in the population. The point is illustrated in the trend toward diminishing illiteracy in the population. An estimate of the trend in illiteracy from 1900 to the present (U.S.D.H.E.W., 1969) shows that in the year 1900, 11.3% of the population was estimated to be unable to read and write a simple message in either English or any other language. By 1910, it had dropped slightly to 8.3% and in 1960, it was estimated to be 2.4%. Similarly, in 1940, 13.5% of adults 25 years and over had not completed 5 or more years of elementary school. The number of such persons in the upper age group who have not spent sufficient years within educational institutions to attain a high level of literacy is going to continue to decline. Also, the educational institutions many adults attended were not particularly oriented to develop an attitude of life-long learning in the individual. Therefore, one may expect in the future more adults attending educational institutions because participating in education is going to be a part of pattern of life in our society.

4. The Impact of Accelerating Change

The educational notion that an individual completes his education by receiving the baccalaureate or higher degree and then lives his life on the basis of what he has learned is simply inadequate. Perhaps in the last century it was appropriate to use the innoculation model of education in which an individual received a sufficient dose of education early in his life which would immunize him from the need for additional formal learning. Snow (1959) suggested that until this century, social change was slow enough so that during an individual's life span there was no noticeable change. In contemporary society, however, the rate of change has accelerated dramatically by almost every conceivable index, from urbanization to economic growth to scientific advances. The phenomenal acceleration of change has been clearly documented by Toffler (1970). Hence, we are coming to a point in time when continuing education over the life span is not only desirable—it is a necessity.

5. Changing Career Patterns

Changing career patterns in society have occurred in relation to technological change. With expansion of productive capacity through automation, there is little need to retain a skilled man in industry as long as he is able to perform. Not only do our buildings and our appliances become antiquated quickly and have to be replaced, but jobs and job skills themselves are shorter lived than in the past. Thus, along with discarding the notion that one's college education will last a life time, we must also discard the view that one's occupational skills will necessarily last a life time. In industry, the trend has been such as to eliminate the less skilled jobs and place a higher premium on education and abstract knowledge. Industries have commonly moved toward a pattern of computer control and continuous flow of production with the range of skills from supervision to the maintenance of equipment requiring a high level of education. Each time an industry upgrades its method of production, it usually upgrades requirements on staff such that fewer people of higher levels of education are employed to the disadvantage of large numbers of persons with low skills and low salaries. With the disappearance of their jobs, workers may be faced with the choice of undertaking training for a new job, or dropping out of the labor force at many points in the work life span.

6. Multiple Careers

Multiple careers are increasingly being seen in our society in which the individual elects, after a period of employment, to retire from his position and accept a new one. One of the common sources of such personnel seeking new positions is the military retirement system of the Navy, Marine Corps, Army, and Air Force, which provide for retirement after 20 years of continuous service.

Since men in the military services (with the exception of physicians and other professionals) tend to enter service early, they become available for second careers at a young age, even at age 42 if they entered with a bachelor's degree. Accommodation of such persons into the work force represents a psychological and social adjustment for the individual.

Garber (1971) made a study of the adjustment of military retirees and found there is a problem in the fact that the retired military man changes his work environment from one in which there is a clearly defined ethos to one in which there may be a high degree of individuality or permissiveness. Also, when the military man moves from station to station, there is a common identity with the organization, with friends and contacts. In a move in private industry from company to company, the families have a much more stressful period of adaptation since there are fewer people in the community with whom they are identified.

There has been a consistent downward trend in the average age of retirement, such as the Federal Civil Service, where one has some option about the time one chooses to retire after meeting some minimum amount of obligation. It is being found that employees may not choose to continue work until the upper limit or mandatory age is reached. That is, given adequate income many or possibly most individuals would prefer some new styles of life to work that may be characterized as hedonistic or self-actualizing, depending upon one's values.

7. Changing Roles of Women

Among the more striking contemporary issues is the desire on the part of many women for a change in social roles. If major shifts in womens' roles occur (see chapter by Neugarten & Datan, this volume), they will have decided implications for educational institutions and for concepts of life-span development that are now held by the educator and public alike.

Within educational institutions, particularly those of higher learning, women are making their voices heard with regard to an equal distribution of positions and salaries, a distribution that now favors men. Court actions have been taken on behalf of women for equal opportunities in universities. Not only are changes in the family organization affecting our institutions, but also technological, economic, political, and cultural changes are altering the succession of roles of women through the life span. In this regard, the university could function to develop objective information about the changing roles of women and to open the issues for discussion in the productive climate of a progressive, academic atmosphere.

Clearly, if university employment practices are altered with regard to women, there will be the consequence that fewer men will be hired. Thus, in discussing the culture changes affecting women in a period when differential employment practices may be changed in favor of women, we are simultaneously or implicitly discussing culture changes on male roles as well. Contemporary discourse tends to be focussed on the needs and roles of women and less on the concomitant social forces that will alter roles of men. Changing roles of both men and women should be part of the subject matter of a life-span developmental psychology.

Since highly educated women are beginning to participate equally with males in the labor force, and since they are likely to be married to educated high-income producing husbands, their families will have a much greater economic potential than would, for example, Spanish-speaking Americans who have not participated extensively in the educational system of the country. Thus, along with considerations of equal opportunities for individuals, equal opportunities for family units must also be considered so that the lowest educated family units will not further fall behind in economic opportunities of society.

Emphasis on a life-span approach to education, with the assumed consequence of lessening the prejudice against middle-aged and older students, might be of special benefit to women. Women graduate students will frequently marry during their education and drop out of formal education for a period to raise children. More than men, they will then seek to return to the university in their thirties and forties to pursue their education beyond the Master's degree. If there were more opportunities for returning students, more women would be able to return to school and develop a subsequent career after launching their children.

Another impact of the changing roles of women may be felt in educational institutions at the primary and secondary level. Elementary and high school teachers in the United States have typically been women, and education and educational institutions may thus carry connotations of nonmasculinity. Improving the status of women may, in turn, improve the status of education. Contemporary cohorts of middle-aged and aged men may not be inclined to participate in or support educational institutions, because they may view education as effeminate. If future generations have greater respect for women's abilities, the members of future cohorts may support and participate in education in greater numbers.

C. Generational Differences

By the very nature of the existence of social change, consequences of unique experiences accumulate to result in individual and generational difference in values, attitudes, and behavior. Educators for that matter are probably not adequately aware of the extent of changes that have occurred in physical maturation let alone attitudinal changes. Concurrent with the trend toward earlier physical maturity, adolescents, for example, have become increasingly responsive to peer group influences. The lessening of family controls in favor of peer group controls has been underway for some time in American society. For black and Spanish-speaking groups, peer group control further enlarges the communicaton gap between generations. Young members of militant minority groups may actively reject their older family members as being too accommodating or passive in their struggles for economic independence. Again, however, if one takes a life-span approach to such issues in the materials introduced in the elementary and high school levels, younger persons entering society would at least have some information about the processes and perhaps skill and sensitivity to reduce the generational tensions.

Understanding between cohorts will be enhanced by exposing elementary and high school students to facts about biological, psychological, and social transformations over the life span. Current negative attitudes held by older persons toward educational institutions and toward youth will likely be reduced as more middle-aged and older adults enroll on campuses to retread their skills and to participate in general educaton. Also, as educational institutions begin to serve the older population, it would seem that there will be less hostility in the older voters and more favorable legislative action may be expected to be taken on budgets. Not only will rejecting attitudes of the older adult toward the young student diminish, but it is expected that some of the attitudes of the young toward the old will also become more positive in mixed aged classes. In addition to classroom activities, there is always an informal information exchange associated with educational activities that can contribute to the setting aside of a stereotypic picture of another age group than one's own. The often quoted phrase, "Never trust anyone over 30," had obviously arisen in a brain factory for the young, one relatively isolated from the interests, talents, and aspirations of those over 30. Perhaps psychologists, more than any other professional or scientific group, should be given the greatest blame for the narrow view of the life span that most educators and university faculty have.

Educational institutions are, of course, not unresponsive to social change. High school and junior high school students today are often asked to write essays on contemporary social problems. Their reading lists contain the titles of books about a wide range of current issues such as the changing roles of women. Writings of contemporary black political leaders are read and discussed, as are materials on the problems of ecology, environmental pollution, and the use of drugs. Young students may thus be expected to have more information and less sensitivity about discussing many current social issues than would their parents or grandparents. In bridging a generation gap, there is the dual problem of the extent to which people have relevant information and whether or not topics are desensitized so they can be discussed openly and constructively.

III. Implications for Educational Action

There is clearly a significant rationale for life-span education. Indeed, factors such as the extension of human life expectancy, the increasing availability of leisure time, and the acceleration of rapid technological and social change preclude the continuation of contemporary youth-oriented educational practices. To meet the needs of individuals in the last decades of the twentieth century, immediate action must be undertaken. Carefully planned strategies to alleviate existing deprivation as well as strategies to enrich and prevent deprivation will have to be developed on a large scale if educational institutions are to progressively serve society.

A. Educational Intervention at All Age Levels

Intervention to enrich lives and to relieve and prevent the effects of deprivation is increasingly being discussed by developmental psychologists. While developmental researchers in previous decades concerned themselves primarily with the description of relationships between behavior and age, contemporary developmentalists have become fascinated with the prospects of intervention which they might define as the introduction of planned programming, deliberately timed to accelerate, decelerate, or otherwise alter anticipated age functions. It is not difficult to understand why intervention strategies have become popular. In addition to insights about development which can be gained from manipulating age functions, intervention provides prospects for improving the quality of life. Intervention can be used as a means of expanding scientific knowledge about development and as a means of enhancing development. Given these prospects, the current preoccupation with intervention strategies has become so pervasive in developmental psychology that interventionism is said to have attained the status of a fad (Looft, 1973).

While most intervention activity has been focused on the early stages of the life cycle, large-scale intervention programs need not be reserved for the young. Strategies for interventionism have been proposed and tested in other phases of the life cycle (e.g., Baltes, 1973; Baltes & Goulet, 1971; Hoyer, 1973; Lindsley, 1964; Schaie, 1973a; Woodruff, 1971). For example, techniques to reverse the observed age changes in performance on cognitive tasks are in the experimental stage (Hoyer, Labouvie, & Baltes, 1971; Woodruff, 1972). Consideration has also been given to the fact that interventionism may have the greatest implications for society if it is directed to cohorts in middle age, as the locus of power in society is concentrated in this group (Schaie, 1973a).

The educational institutions in modern society, public and private schools at all levels, are a likely setting in which intervention strategies can be carried out. More than any other institution, education has the necessary resources for intervention. Facilities, equipment, and trained personnel are already available, and with relatively little modification and retraining, educational settings could be geared to enhancing development at all levels. While the thrust of educational institutions is primarily aimed at individuals in the first two decades of their lives, it has been predicted in an earlier section of this chapter that educational institutions will also be increasingly open to mature and aged adults. Hence, educational intervention as a means for development throughout the life span is a feasible as well as a necessary undertaking.

In spite of the impetus for immediate educational action, interventionists must look at the failures of early childhood intervention programs before future programming is undertaken. Sigel (1971) suggested that a major flaw in the pioneer programs was that the programs were not designed in terms of developmental theory. Instead of a broad theoretical approach, a number of eclectic programs were designed which Sigel (1971) described as "fraught with a series of logical and psychological problems [p. 1]." Given that there are few clearly articulated life-span developmental theories available, it may be necessary to halt program development until theories are better researched (Labouvie, 1973). A more expedient alternative would be to design programs using the available developmental concepts and continue research in the program itself (Charles, 1973a). The continued research and development of theories of life-span ontogeny, as well as the implementation of available concepts of behavioral ontogeny in educational programs, would undoubtedly improve the quality of contemporary education.

1. Goals of Intervention

Provided with the prospect of educational intervention over the life span, one might ask, intervention for what. What are the goals of interventionism? The goal of intervention can be viewed from numerous perspectives, and Baltes (1973) pointed out that interventionists' perspectives are sometimes narrow. The complaint Baltes (1973) had was that interventionists are too often merely concerned with immediate alleviation of deficient behavior rather than with enrichment and with prevention of deficiencies. Intervention over the life span must be applied immediately for short-term alleviation of educational deprivation, but long-term attempts at enrichment and prevention also merit implementation if educational intervention is to have impact beyond that of a postdictive remedial strategy.

a. Alleviation. The alleviation of educational deprivation is the most typical aim of intervention programs, and the life-span perspective, which includes comparisons of educational attainment between cohorts, provides a clear example of the need for immediate alleviation of educational deprivation. Like the poor and the members of ethnic and other minority groups, the aged suffer from educational deprivation (Baltes & Labouvie, 1973; Birren & Hess, 1968; Charles, 1971; Eklund, 1969; Granick & Friedman, 1970). Educational deprivation in the aged is absolute inasmuch as roughly 67% of individuals over 65 have had no more than an eighth-grade education, and it is relative as this education was obtained in the early 1900s. In 1960, only 17% of the individuals aged 25–29 had merely an eighth-grade education (U.S. Bureau of the Census, 1960), and even these individuals had a more current education than the aged cohorts. These statistics led Eklund (1969) to state that, except for reading, writing, and arithmetic, the great majority of the aged are scholastically handicapped. Such a circumstance requires immediate alleviation through educational intervention. Such intervention would be remedial inasmuch as it would involve bringing the cohorts of aged individuals to an educational level at least comparable to the level attained by middle-aged individuals.

Education over the life span could facilitate understanding between cohorts by assuring maximum development of abilities at all age levels. For example, Granick and Friedman (1970) suggested that education may play a role in enabling the aged to maintain their intellectual effectiveness. A number of years ago, investigators called attention to the fact that the relatively lower educational status of older cohorts could account for the apparent decline in intellectual functioning with age (e.g., Birren & Morrison, 1961; Granick & Friedman, 1967; Lorge, 1955). Coupled with the longitudinal data on well-educated adults who showed little or no intellectual decline (e.g., Bayley & Oden, 1955; Owens, 1953, 1966), it became apparent that the reported decline with age in intelligence was largely an artifact. There is clear evidence that the elderly can perform well on intellectual measures (see Baltes & Labouvie, 1973; Jarvik, Eisdorfer, & Blum, 1972), and they have considerable potential to benefit from education. Hence, by providing the elderly with educational opportunities equal to that of younger cohorts, harmful stereotypes about intellectual deterioration with age could be shattered.

A proposal for remedial education for the elderly would require relatively little retraining on the part of teachers who would need to be oriented to interests and abilities of their elderly students. Since the subject matter would be that which is currently taught in secondary schools, few new materials would be required. Thus, the resources necessary to provide a "catch-up" education for the aged would not be staggering.

Serious consideration is already being given in some states to the prospect of extensive programs of education for the aged. Recently, the president of the University of Hawaii, Harlan Cleveland, took an innovative position. He expressed the opinion to the state legislature of Hawaii that a senior citizen's bill of educational rights should be passed. His basic thought was that an individual who has completed his period of employed work life, and thereby made his contribution to society through his products and his taxes, should be entitled to an earned period of time in educational institutions to further his development. This is a philosophy similar to that of the post World War II GI Bill of Rights in which the returning soldier was entitled, after his service, to a period of free education in a program of his choice. Why not, by analogy, several years of free education to individuals who have completed their service to society through their work life and careers?

The University of Hawaii is also responsible for the Senior Center in Honolulu as well as the community colleges. Most universities and colleges would be quite surprised if they were asked to take responsibility for administering a senior citizens center, though many of them are responsible for nursery schools and laboratory schools for young children and adolescents. Why shouldn't universities have an educational responsibility across the life span, including the organization of senior centers for the conduct of a wide range of activities of an educational, research, recreational, and counseling nature? One reason universities might be embarrassed to take on such responsibilities is that few of them have any faculty or administrative staff that know anything about the older adult, his social, psychological, and biological nature, and the needs of the retired population.

b. Enrichment. By contemporary standards, remedial education for the elderly could be an example of enrichment as well as of alleviation as it has been used in the previous section of this chapter. It is unfortunate that such an inequity has arisen in society, but contemporary social inequities must not set the standard by which enrichment is gauged. Eklund (1969) correctly stated that enrichment involves more than remedial education. Thus, one example of an intervention goal in terms of educational enrichment might be to stimulate interest in learning as a process. From when they first enter school to when they are near death, individuals should be involved with education (Eklund, 1969). Rather than teaching content, educators should concern themselves with *meta learning*—conceptual model building, information use, problem solving skills. Eklund proposed that students be oriented to continuing education so that after graduation from high school or college, the student would enter into a period of largely self-directed, postgraduate continuing education. Thus, educational enrichment in this sense would involve creation of a new norm of continuing education, rather than the current emphasis on fixed units of education. "The duration of education needs to be seen in biological terms, ceasing only when the human organism stops functioning. Perhaps, and not altogether facetiously, the only meaningful terminal degree will be granted by the mortician [Eklund, 1969, p. 327]."

To realize enrichment such as the development of life-time learning, habits would require vast change on the part of educational institutions which are only beginning to consider the initiation of remedial education for older cohorts.

Nevertheless, life-time learning is a goal to which thousands of aged invididuals have indicated a commitment. As an example, the AARP-NRTA Institute of Life-time Learning is dedicated to the continuing education of older adults, and the Institute is continually surveying the learning capacity and interests of its constituency to develop innovative programs and educational strategies (e.g., Hixson, 1969). University extension programs and public school system adult education courses are additional examples of attempts to provide life-time learning opportunities. Hence, while educational enrichment through the development of skills and motivation for life-time learning is a goal that educational institutions are far from reaching, there is evidence in middle-aged and aged cohorts of a desire and a willingness to participate in life-time learning experiences. The existence of such motivation in individuals, who as children and adolescents received little training in life-time learning skills, provides a strong case for the potential success of enrichment through life-time learning.

c. Prevention. Consideration of life-span development might lead educators to reflect upon the late life consequences of early educational experience. In this manner, some of the difficulties in adjustment in middle and old age might be avoided. For example, retiring individuals who derived their identity from their occupation face a difficult adjustment when their self image as a productive member of society is lost. Such life crises are at least partially implicated in the high incidence of suicide in older white males (Farberow, 1968; Rachlis, 1970; Shneidman & Farberow, 1957). In spite of these late life consequences, typical classrooms in most American elementary schools and high schools are structured and oriented to developing extrinsically rather than intrinsically motivated individuals. Students are taught that grades and scores on standardized tests are the measures of achievement and the keys to entrance in colleges and universities. Classrooms in which children pursue their individual interests and compete with themselves at their own pace are rare, and since children in such classrooms may not be trained in a manner that will make them highly skilled on the tasks measured on standardized tests, they may not be as successful as traditionally educated children on such tasks. Hence, students who are trained to pursue their own interests may not be as successful on college entrance exams, and might be less likely to be accepted into colleges and universities. There are means available for producing individuals who are self-directed and noncompetative, but such individuals may fail in the contemporary educational system which is geared to competition for grades and to productivity measured by the system rather than by the individual.

What is the merit of developing individuals who are not oriented to extrinsic measures of productivity and achievement? While observable productivity and achievement have been the hallmarks of successful living in American society, the continued emphasis on what is popularly known as the "work ethic" may not be conducive to personal adjustment in a society in which individuals will spend over half of their lives out of the work force. The extension of available leisure time is a hallmark of the future. It is already apparent in cohorts of retirement age that individuals who have derived their status and identity solely through their career may have difficulty in adjusting to the loss of that role. The cohorts currently of retirement age have been imbued with the notion that success is measured in terms of productivity and economic gain. Ideally, intervention for adjustment to retirement should begin long before individuals leave the work force, but it may also be possible to preclude the need for such desensitizing in retirement preparation if individuals learned early in life that both leisure and employment can be productive.

Intervention to modify the current orientation toward productivity and achievement could not be realized if intervention strategies were devised only at one educational level. The standards and criteria of evaluation of the educational system would of necessity have to be revised to provide for the integration of students who were not trained to produce and achieve. The cost to society of such a revision would be small if such preventive intervention would lower suicide rates and preclude in future generations of aged some of the tragic loss of self-esteem which currently incapacitates countless retired or jobless individuals.

2. Foci of Intervention

There are a number of options available to interventionists as to the components and mechanisms at which they aim their strategies. Baltes (1973) simplified a model of some levels of intervention activity discussed by Jacobs (1972), also Harshbarger (this volume). The usefulness of this model rests with its emphasis on the diversity of intervention parameters which are categorized into (1) goals, (2) target behaviors, (3) settings, and (4) techniques. Table 1 presents the Jacobs–Baltes model with examples of educational intervention strategies devised from the perspective of life-span developmental psychology. Baltes (1973) pointed out that this model does not include an exhaustive list of intervention parameters, and the examples of intervention presented here are not necessarily the only or even the best strategies available. We do want to point out, however, that a variety of useful programs could be devised. Since we have already discussed the goals of intervention, this section will be devoted to target behaviors, settings, and techniques.

a. Target Behaviors. In children, cognition has been the target behavior for almost all of the intervention programs which have been implemented. In this manner, the intervention programs undertaken on a large scale in this country have reflected the value contemporary Western society places on youth and on cognitive and intellectual ability. The two best-known programs for intervention are the Federal program, Project Headstart, and the commercial television venture, "Sesame Street." Both programs are aimed primarily at children of

TABLE 1

Selected Parameters of Psychological Intervention Strategies
with Examples for Application in Life-Span Education[a]

Parameter			
Goals	Means	Target behavior	Target group
Alleviation	*Training*	*Attitudes*	*Children*
Educational deprivation of middle-aged and aged (IIIA1a)[b]	Of teachers and researchers (IIIA3)	Intergenerational perceptions (IIIA2a)	Preparation for life-span roles (IIIB2)
Negative stereotype of aged (IIIA2a)	About the life span (IIIB2)	*Affect*	*Adolescents*
Enrichment	For life-time learning (IIIA1b)	Life-span development of (IIIA2a)	Changing attitudes to higher education (IIB2)
Learning as process over life span (IIIA1b)	*Communication*	*Cognition*	*Adults*
Prevention	Between psychologists and educators (I)	In young and old (IIIA)	Changing Careers (IIB5, IIB6)
Loss of self-esteem with age (IIIA1c)	*Political Action*[c]	*Intelligence*	Middle-aged returning to college (IIIB1)
Suicide increase with age (IIIA1c)	*Health Delivery*[c]	Maximizing in aged (IIIA1a)	*Aged*
Behavior decrements with age (IIIA2a)	*Economic Support*[c]	*Motivation*	Alleviate educational deprivation in (IIIA1a)
		For life-time learning (IIIA1b)	Attitudes to (IIIA2a)
		As topic in life-span education (IIIB2)	Potential of operant conditioning and group therapy for (IIIA2c)
			Women
			Impact of changing roles (IIB6)
			Men
			Adjustment to changing roles of women (IIB6)

TABLE 1 (*continued*)

Parameter			
Target level	Setting	Mediator	Technique
Individual Operant conditioning (IIIA2c)	*Educational institutions* (IIIA2b) University College High school Elementary School	*Communications media* Television To reach very young, old and handicapped (IIIA2b) Radio Programming for aged (IIIA2b)	*Operant conditioning* At all age levels (IIIA2c)
Small group Group therapy (IIIA2c) "Parlor" groups (IIIA2b)			*Group interaction* For aged (IIIA2c)
Community[c]	*Public buildings* (IIIA2b) Church Recreation center Union hall	*Printed media*[c] Newspapers Magazines	*Sensitivity training*[c]
Cohort Understanding between cohorts (IIC) The aged (IIIA1a)	*Home* (IIIA2b) Communications media Correspondence courses "Parlor" groups	*Mail* Correspondence courses for aged (IIIA2b)	
Society Productivity orientation (IIIA1c)			

[a] Adapted from Baltes (1973) and Jacobs (1972).
[b] Numbers and letters denote section in present chapter where the issue is discussed.
[c] Potential strategy is not discussed in this chapter.

preschool age, and both represent an attempt to enhance the development of language and cognitive skills. While the goal of improving and accelerating language and intellectual development in children jibes well in a youth-oriented culture dominated by the Protestant ethic, it does not reflect the broad perspective of goals that might be achieved through interventionism. Cognition is only one of a variety of behaviors that might serve as a target for intervention, and it may not be the most pragmatic behavior in which to accelerate development. For example, Looft (1973) suggested that the most useful strategies might focus on affective rather than on cognitive traits. Enhancement of target behaviors such as cooperation, compassion, and contentment might better fulfill the needs of individuals in contemporary society. Indeed, in terms of the ultimate survival of the human species, such an emphasis could have important significance. The current popularity of yoga, transcendental meditation, and alpha conditioning, which emphasize affective rather than cognitive experience, provides suggestive evidence of a readiness on the part of many individuals to develop affective as well as cognitive dimensions of their personality.

Another significant target behavior for intervention are attitudes toward the aged. There is evidence that suggests that perceived age differences are greater than real age differences (e.g., Ahammer & Baltes, 1972; Woodruff & Birren, 1972), and it has been suggested that perceived rather than real age differences are of the greatest significance in determining interage and intergenerational behavior (Ahammer, 1970; Bengtson & Kuypers, 1971; Thomae, 1970). Contemporary attitudes and orientations to aging and the aged involve misperceptions and negative stereotypes accepted by young and old alike (see also Chapter 12, this volume; Peterson & Peters, 1971; Riley, Johnson, & Foner, 1972 for reviews). Schaie (1973a) argues that most negative stereotypes of the elderly are not valid, as the deficient behavior attributed to the aged either does not occur in great frequency or it is the result of social expectations rather than an outcome of natural development. Hence, individuals act on perceived rather than real age differences and perceive that the aged are deficient. The aged, too, accept the perception that they are deficient and they behave according to the expectation. In this manner, the perception of decline in the elderly becomes a self-fulfilling prophecy. Clearly, intervention strategies to change attitudes toward the elderly would be useful in the short term to improve the status of the aged, and in the long term to prevent expectation of decrement in future cohorts of elderly.

b. Settings. One of the least problematic aspects of educational intervention is the educational setting. Education can and has taken place almost anywhere, and the only limitation educational planners will have in devising settings for life-span education is their own lack of creativity. The most logical setting for life-span education is in the educational institutions themselves. Facilities of local elementary and secondary schools are often available in the evenings, and careful scheduling might also provide space in colleges and universities. In such settings, however, middle-aged individuals may feel intimidated by lack of familiarity, so it is also important to consider union halls, community recreation centers, and churches. Transportation is difficult or impossible for very young, elderly, and handicapped individuals. For this reason, education in the home through communications media and correspondence courses has vast potential for life-span education.

Since the mid-1950s with Himmelweit's (1958) study of English children as a television audience, attention and concern have been directed toward the young as a viewing audience (e.g., Schramm, 1961; Witty, 1966, 1967). The impact of these studies which culminated in sweeping changes in programming and the establishment of new policies for children's programming has also drawn attention to the potential of this media for life-span education (Anderson, 1962). Davis (1971) commented: "A 'Sesame Street' may give 4-year-old viewers some valuable tools for living. Where is 'Sunset Street' to give similar tools to a 74-year-old? [p. 159]." Aged individuals spend a median of three hours a day watching television—more time than they devote to any other single activity (Gelwicks, Feldman, & Newcomer, 1971; Nielsen, 1970; Riley & Foner, 1968; Schramm, 1969). Research indicates that while there are few educational programs directed to the elderly audience (Davis, 1972; Marshall, 1970), the aged use television for entertainment, information, and companionship "to keep up with things" (Davis, 1971; Gelwicks, Feldman, & Newcomer, 1971; Schalinsie, 1968). More than any other mass media, television reaches a representative cross-national sample, including individuals of little education, the culturally disadvantaged, and the elderly (Roper, 1971). As a source for life-span education in the home setting, television is ideal.

While television provides a significant source for educational intervention in the home, public service broadcasting time is limited and broadcasters are not willing to donate time they can sell at a profit. One means to increase life-span educational programming would be to attract sponsors to educational programs and convince them that the programs reach a consumer audience. Other less expensive means of reaching home audiences are radio programming and correspondence courses. The NRTA-AARP Institute of Life-time Learning has adapted eight of the most popular Institute courses for standard radio format. Each course is a sequence of thirteen half-hour programs. A recent survey indicated that over 900 stations have used these programs, and at a given time the programs are simultaneously broadcast on 110 stations across the country (L. E. Hixson, Dean of the Institute of Life-time Learning, personal communication, 1972). Home correspondence courses were also initiated by the Institute of Life-time Learning which have involved 1900 elderly participants from every state and from four foreign countries.

c. Techniques. One of the important contributions psychology can make to education is in the form of techniques for teaching. Psychologists in areas such as learning and clinical have been interested in modification as well as description and explanation of behavior, and they have often succeeded in their attempts to alter behavior. Learning psychologists use operant conditioning to change behavior while clinical psychologists have found that group therapy is a useful technique. The implications of these techniques for development over the life span are significant.

Operant conditioning involves increasing the incidence of a desired response by rewarding the response. The technique can also be used to maintain or eliminate behaviors. It was pointed out by Hoyer (1973) that operant techniques have been used successfully as intervention strategies in the early portion of the life span (Bijou, 1968b, 1971; Bijou & Baer, 1961; Gewirtz, 1969a), but they have not been applied in the later years. Lindsley (1964) argued that operant techniques would be particularly useful in late life, as they are effective quickly and place emphasis on immediate behavioral change, and they can be individualized if necessary to suit each member of the highly differentiated older population. Research evidence suggests that operant techniques are useful in increasing social interaction and self-improvement (Mishara, 1971) and physical exercise (Libb & Clements, 1969) in aged institutionalized patients, in modifying rigidity in young adults (Bry & Nawas, 1969), and in improving intelligence test performance in elderly community residents (Hoyer, Labouvie, & Baltes, 1971). The availability of the powerful technique of operant conditioning with its demonstrated potential for behavior modification led Charles (1973a) and Hoyer (1973) to recommend its immediate use as an intervention strategy.

Group therapy appears to be a technique which works especially well with aged individuals (Allen, 1962; Apake & Sanger, 1962; Liederman, Green, & Liederman, 1967; Linden, 1953, 1954; Pomeroy, 1972; Turner & Goldfarb, 1953; Wolff, 1957). Group interaction counters isolation and loneliness in the elderly, and it provides them with a peer group from which they can learn self-acceptance and adjustment to new roles (Lowy, 1962). Organizations such as the NRTA-AARP are using such insights from clinical psychology in the design of educational programs. Currently being developed is a "Parlor Institute" of home study courses involving groups of five or more in which individuals would invite friends and neighbors to join them in a multi-media program of study. This technique might also be successful with small groups of young and middle-aged individuals, such as housewives who could gather in neighborhood groups.

3. Training for Intervention

If today Congress set aside millions of dollars to be used immediately for life-span education, it would be impossible to undertake educational action for several years as the manpower required for such a task is simply not available. Teachers who are currently employed in educational institutions as well as teachers who are presently being trained are not prepared to teach middle-aged and aged adults; they are not trained to teach the meta learning concepts discussed previously which would prepare children and adolescents for life-time learning, and they are not provided with information on the biological, psychological, and sociological aspects of life-span development which should be taught at all age levels. These are some of the deficiencies in contemporary teacher training programs which preclude the introduction of life-span education. Space in this chapter does not permit an in-depth treatment of this significant issue, but we have discussed the demands, prospects, and means for training in development and aging in other publications (Birren, Gribbin, & Woodruff, 1971; Birren & Woodruff, 1973; Birren, Woodruff, & Bergman, 1972; Woodruff & Birren, 1973).

For the goal of alleviating educational deprivation in aged cohorts, we proposed remedial education for the aged. To meet such a need, teachers must be trained to teach older adults. Such training need not be extensive, as older individuals can and do learn in environments designed for young learners. If, for example, teachers of adult education would be made aware of sensory deficits and greater difficulty with speeded tasks in the elderly, they could teach the aged more effectively. Also, adult educators must be concerned with the attitudes and motivation differences in contemporary aged cohorts. Since the elderly might be over-anxious in learning situations and hence perform more poorly, adult education must reinforce and reassure older learners of their abilities. Such examples serve to demonstrate that teachers could be more effective with older learners if they had some training in adult development.

In a subsequent section, we will suggest the importance of training in life-span development early in life to prepare individuals for roles they will fill as they mature. To teach life-span development to children and adolescents, teachers would need rather extensive exposure (at least one undergraduate level course) to the content of life-span development. Few departments of psychology, let alone departments of education, offer courses in life-span developmental psychology. On the undergraduate level, only 71 courses which included some content in adult development and aging were offered in the entire United States in 1968 (U.S.D.H.E.W., 1968). Hence, to provide teachers for the elementary and high school teachers, personnel at the Ph.D. and Masters level must be trained.

B. Life-Span Models, Research, and Intervention

It has been suggested that the early childhood intervention programs were overly pragmatic and largely service oriented. These programs might have been more successful had they been designed with a greater input from developmental theory (Labouvie, 1973; Siegel, 1971). Again one should stress a life-span perspective even with regard to consequences of early environmental enrichment to favor cognitive development and creativity (Kogan, this volume). In order to avoid some of the limitations of those pioneer programs, it is essential to carefully develop programs in accordance with the information provided by life-span developmental research. Sigel (1971) also suggested that intervention programs should be designed in terms of a sophisticated job analysis where steps are taken to find the necessary and sufficient conditions for success (e.g., academic success) by operationally defining the criteria for success (e.g., skills, attitudes, motivation) and then training the target individuals for such achievement. The role of developmental psychologists in such endeavors would be to identify the crucial variables operating in educational settings and to develop measuring techniques to monitor the relevant environment as well as the target behavior(s). From this perspective extensive pilot research is required before programs are initiated.

Scientists are often accused of over-caution and ineffectiveness in translating information in a manner useful to society, and they frequently appear disinterested in social and political issues (Birren, Woodruff, & Bergman, 1972). By rigidly taking the stance that more research is necessary before any new programs can be initiated, developmental psychologists might find that programs will be designed without their input. While we firmly believe that research and theory construction in life-span developmental psychology has scarcely begun, we are convinced that some of the models and concepts that have been researched will provide useful guidelines for educational planners. The following concepts and implications serve as examples of the usefulness of life-span developmental models for education.

1. Separation of Ontogenetic and Generational Change Components

An important contribution to developmental psychology was made by Schaie (1965) and Baltes (1968) who clearly distinguished between generational and ontogenetic change and presented research designs to separate these change components. When generational and ontogenetic components have been compared, cohort differences have been much greater than age changes (e.g., Nesselroade, Schaie, & Baltes, 1972; Schaie & Strother, 1968; Woodruff & Birren, 1972). Hence, it appears valid to assume that large behavioral differences exist and will continue to exist between subsequent generations of individuals. Such a concept implies that educational planners must continually monitor target cohort groups and re-evaluate intervention programs for succeeding cohorts (Labouvie, 1973; Birren, Woodruff, & Bergman, 1972). For example, programs suitable for cohorts over age 65 in 1972 may not meet the needs of aged cohorts in 1982. Specific intervention programs must not be institutionalized.

Since large cohort differences exist, educational planners (who are typically members of middle-aged cohorts) must consider the values and attitudes of the target cohort and avoid imposing their own values on that target cohort. Effective education for the elderly might best be planned with elderly individuals serving as consultants. Children and adolescents would undoubtedly provide novel, useful suggestions for educators planning programs for those respective cohorts.

Another consideration involves the reorientation of individuals who are returning to educatonal institutions for retraining. If someone educated 20 or more years ago in an American institution of higher learning had been out of touch with his school and only recently returned for a visit, there would be many things that would surprise him. The old grad would be surprised at the number of groups on campus asserting their rights and prerogatives. The presence of politically active blacks, the assertiveness of women, the gay liberation groups claiming legal status would cause wonderment. In addition the presence of active recruitment on campus of cults like the Hare Krishnas, and the evangelical Christian cults might give rise to the feeling that schools and educated persons were abandoning natural science traditions. Aware that social change is reflected in colleges and universities, many middle-aged and aged individuals might be unwilling to return and face such "culture shock." Such is the consequence of the age grading in society which exists in the United States. Schaie (1973a) proposed age integration to solve this problem with educational and recreational facilities planned for individuals with similar interests rather than similar ages.

Educators are conditioned by their own early educational experience in which age grading was the way of arranging groups of students to be educated. It is therefore quite likely that educators would conceive of community college and undergraduate students as being homogeneously grouped by age. The picture of an undergraduate class ranging in age from 18 to 60 or more and a graduate class from age 22 to 50 would be bothersome to many. For one thing, it seems to imply a softening of the educative process with the assumption that the older members are least likely to be able to participate fully. Such need not be the case, however. What we know about changes in intellectual capacities of individuals in adult life suggests that there is little in the way of important differences between young, middle-aged, and aged adults. On the other hand, there may be considerable advantages in having heterogeneous age grouping by providing for a greater mixture of experience in interpreting existing information. Our thoughts about age grading will be tested as more and more older adults come into the campus of institutions of higher learning. The question will be whether to mix them with the previous "regular' student body of young adults or to retain them in special classes for homogeneous grouping. The criterion for optimal grouping should take into account not only the direct learning that results from classroom activity but also the incidental learning.

It is not yet apparent whether the needs of middle-aged adults returning to institutions of higher learning are different than the young person. Perhaps more importantly than the needs of older students is the readjustment of attitudes on the part of those who are concerned with selection for admission and subsequently for job placement. Admission committees are usually concerned with likely duration and quality of the services the person will render in return for the education received. For this reason, women are frequently discriminated against on the grounds that they are not as likely to continue in a career as long as men in the same type of activity. A suspicion about the middle-aged person is that the reason they are changing careers is that their previous career was unsuccessful and being relatively unsuccessful they are regarded as poor risks in an alternate career. This of course would reject the possibility of ontogenetic change. Interests and motivations can change over the life span. That is, an engineer might become increasingly interested in issues of human behavior and a lawyer might be increasingly concerned with the social and psychological basis of deviant behavior he faced in legal practice.

At this time when the number of applicants for graduate school is being restricted, there will be a tendency to concentrate more and more on the model candidate by background to the exclusion of the middle-aged person who is recycling through the educational system. While the middle-aged person who is recycling may offer unusual potentials and possibilities, the basis for evaluating these is not clearly obvious. Conceivably faculty members will become expert in assessing the motivation and background of an older adult and predict the likelihood that they offer some unusual potentials for a new career, justifying therefore the position of a regular graduate student in a higher education institution.

2. Developmental Tasks

One of the forces that gives direction to the development of the individual are the developmental tasks facing the individual at characteristic times during the life span. The term *developmental task* came into use in the early 1940s to describe the demands, constraints, and opportunities provided by the social environment (see Chapter 1, this volume). In this conception, there are broadly defined tasks each age level must face in our society. Successful coping with the tasks at one age level results in the development of competence and differentiation of skills and personality so that more complex tasks at the next age level can be met.

While the early developmental psychologists who used the concept of developmental tasks had primarily the development of children in mind, the concept is also useful in describing the continually changing events during the adult life span; events that give direction to experience and seem to divide the human life span into phases with typical concerns. Developmental tasks often change with biological changes in the organism and with the expectations of society for developing social roles approporate for an age level. Clearly these two sources interact, for when a child is expected to learn to walk, talk, and start to school he is conditioned by what the culture believes to be a biological readiness. Late in life, health changes provide complex challenges for the individual to cope with. This approach is "primarily a theory based on biological development and social expectations which change through the life span and give direction, force, and substance to the development of personality [Havighurst, this volume]." The changing developmental tasks facing the individual result in shifts in preoccupations, that is, there are changes in the dominant concerns of individuals over the life span (Smoller, 1971). Such changes in the focus of life concerns have prompted Havighurst (1953), Bühler (1951), and Erikson (1959) to formulate life-span theories of personality to explain age differences in interests, activities, and emotions.

In large part, the purpose of education for older adults is to aid the individual in meeting the developmental tasks for his age level. For example, Smoller (1971) points out that the middle-aged person (45–64) is characterized by the tendency to uphold internal order. At the same time, the individual is responding to other demands in life resulting in reassessment of past goals and his present circumstances with the result there are often at this age level changes in vocational roles and marriage partners. These issues suggest that the individual must react to a range of facts and feelings not unlike in character, if different in content, to those facing the adolescent who is establishing heterosexual relationships and vocational goals, assessing his abilities and interests, while acquiring wide range of school-taught skills and knowledge.

Knowledge in depth of the developmental tasks facing adults at various age levels would appear to provide a focus and a degree of relevancy to adult education that is often lacking since it is easier to serve "rewarmed" material already organized for adolescents or young adults. This would suggest problem-centered courses for the older adult, similar in intent to the courses on "adjustment" for high school students. Such courses are often not particularly well thought of from the point of view of subject matter, and often the students dislike such courses for being so "watered down" as to not be relevant to the real concerns of the age level. Nevertheless, the issue remains—how to assist the individual to handle developmental tasks of any age level through educational intervention. Perhaps what is often lacking is a balance between three components of education: cognition, affect, and motivation. Usually instructors are not able to deal effectively with all three, and it may be necessary to consider educational intervention with separate techniques for dealing with the informational, emotional, and motivational aspects of adult developmental tasks.

Preparing the young through education in a society that has a changing age structure and job life span requires a new orientation. The point has been made that less emphasis should be placed upon the skills of the young adult productive stage than upon the development of a view of the life span as consisting of many transformations of individual function and role. Along with the present thrust for environmental planning and ecological balance, man's own life cycle should receive more attention at the elementary school level. Only small beginnings have been made in introducing elementary school children to concepts and information about the human life cycle. A life-span approach to biological and social function is still a rare inclusion in elementary school and high school curricula. Institutions of higher learning do not prepare teachers by way of exposing them to information about the biology, psychology, and sociology of the life span. In teacher training institutions, developmental psychology for the most part has meant child psychology. Departments of psychology have characteristically included a program on child psychology, but rarely one on the developmental psychology of the adult and old age. Recent estimates of the amount of publication and training document how limited are academic activities on the adult portion of the life span (Birren, Gribbin, & Woodruff, 1971; Birren & Woodruff, 1973; U.S.D.H.E.W., 1968). A change seems to be coming and it seems quite likely that by the end of this century every department of psychology in a university or college will have at least one faculty member who is prepared to teach on the psychology of adult life and aging and to carry out research. This will provide the information base for giving a background to persons in teacher training, who will in turn provide the young with a perspective on the life span appropriate to the culture in which they live.

IV. Summary and Conclusions

The purpose of this chapter has been to discuss the need and means for enhancing human development over the life span through education. The possible strategies and prospects for implementation of life-span education proposals were considered (the reader is referred to Harshbarger's chapter in this volume for a more extensive survey of the prospects for large-scale intervention at the community and national level). In the following paragraphs, presented in summary form are the major ideas discussed in this chapter. The first set of facts and ideas provide a rationale for life-span education, and the second body of information and suggestions represents implications for educational action.

A. Rationale

1. The concept that development ends with biological maturity is fallacious. Differentiation continues until death, and education should have an important

role in helping individuals to meet the challenge of developmental tasks throughout the life span.

2. Educational institutions are being criticized as they are not meeting the needs of society. Attending to life-span needs of individuals through education is a relevant goal, and if a greater proportion of the population were recycled through educational institutions, they would be less likely to criticize them.

3. Educational institutions and educators are rigid and narrow in their objectives. They aim primarily at youth rather than at individuals of all ages. They emphasize technological rather than social issues. They focus on extrinsic rather than intrinsic rewards, hence producing individuals dependent on external reinforcers who despair when those reinforcers are taken away. They develop cognitive abilities and ignore development of affect and motivation.

4. Advances in medicine, health delivery, and economic standards of living have extended life expectancy by almost 30 years since 1900. This fact, coupled with a declining birth rate and a decreasing rate of immigration, have changed the age structure of American society so that a greater proportion of the population is old. Educational institutions must meet the needs of this expanding age group.

5. If the birth rate continues to decline, the demand on educational institutions by youth will be less, and the additional facilities and personnel needed to teach the large cohorts of youth from 1950–1970 could be used to teach adults.

6. As succeeding cohorts reach higher educational levels, the demand for education in the adult years will increase as with higher levels of educational attainment comes greater participation in adult education.

7. The rate of social and technological progress continues to accelerate, and an individual can no longer be programmed for his entire life by education in the first 20 years of his life span.

8. An increasing number of individuals are forced out of careers as their techniques become obsolete, and others simply choose to pursue multiple careers. Educational opportunities for retraining should be available to these people.

9. Leisure time and time out of the work force is increasing as individuals enter the work force later and retire earlier than in previous decades. Education is a useful activity for leisure time.

10. With the availability of educational opportunities at all age levels, more women could have careers as more could return after rearing a family.

11. With the improvement of the status of women may come the improvement of the status of education. Most elementary and high school teachers have been female and hence of low status. This may explain why adult men have been particularly resistant to adult education. As women's roles change, early education may also be less dominated by women.

12. Educational deprivation exists in the poor, in minority group members, and in the aged, and this situation is intolerable. The intellectual decline attributed

to the aged is largely a consequence of educational deprivation. Generational differences are accentuated by differences in educational opportunity.

B. Implications

1. Intervention which involves planned programming deliberately timed to alter ontogenetic age functions could enhance development over the life span. Intervention programs have been undertaken to alter early development, and from these programs, life-span interventionists can learn that programs must be guided by developmental theory.

2. The goals of intervention must not be short-sighted but must involve long-term as well as short-term consequences. An immediate goal should be to alleviate educational deprivation in the aged through remedial education at the elementary and high school level. The goal of educational enrichment could be met by teaching meta-learning concepts rather than teaching information and simple skills and by training individuals to be motivated for learning throughout their life time. Consideration of the detrimental late life outcomes of early emphasis on external (e.g., grades) rather than internal (e.g., happiness) rewards might prevent despair and difficulties in adjustment to retirement in the elderly.

3. Educators should focus on the development of affective experience and motivation rather than being concerned exclusively with cognitive skills. Hence, course content should be changed and methods such as small group discussions of personal experiences and attitudes should be attempted. To successfully achieve such a shift in emphasis, teachers must be trained in life-span developmental psychology.

4. Strategies aimed at altering negative stereotypes toward aging and the aged should be developed. These might include some age integration of classes at all levels and training in the content of life-span development at the elementary, high school, and undergraduate levels.

5. A variety of settings, including the educational institutions themselves can be used for life-span education. To reach more people, public buildings such as union halls, recreation centers, and churches could be used. Attempts should also be made to reach individuals confined to their homes. This might include the very young, the aged, and the handicapped.

6. Communications media, such as television and radio, have great potential for reaching aged individuals in particular. Since "Sesame Street" has been so successful with the young, a "Sunset Street" designed with equal care and insight might enjoy success with the elderly.

7. The potential of correspondence courses for the elderly is also receiving little exploration and should be tried on a larger scale. Multi-media courses for use by small neighborhood groups in the home could also be developed and might be particularly successful for the elderly. Group interaction should be stressed for the aged.

8. Operant conditioning techniques must be incorporated into educational programs as operant conditioning has proved successful in altering behavior at all ages. Teaching machines and programmed texts should be adapted for learners of all ages.

9. Teachers who are knowledgeable in life-span development are scarce. Short term training programs for practicing teachers as well as training programs and courses at the undergraduate and graduate level must be developed if life-span developmental psychology is to have an impact on education.

10. Since cohort differences in behavior are sometimes large, care must be taken to design flexible intervention programs which will meet the needs of subsequent cohorts. Programs must be monitored to ensure continued effectiveness with each cohort. For example, strategies aimed at adolescents in 1972 may be ineffective with adolescents in 1977.

11. Awareness of cohort differences should also lead planners to use members of the target group for consultants. The elderly should be consulted in the planning of old age programs just as children should advise in the planning of child intervention programs.

12. Courses should be designed around interest groups rather than around age groups.

13. If recycling in education is to become a reality, methods to assess middle-aged and aged returning students must be developed. These methods must not simply involve imposing the standards for young students on the middle-aged and aged.

14. Consideration should be given to the design of courses directed at specific developmental tasks to help individuals who are undertaking these tasks to cope with the task more successfully. Such courses should involve affective and motivational aspects of developmental tasks as well as providing information useful in undertaking the task. Examples of topics for such a course are: career selection, marriage, child bearing, child rearing, retirement.

Documentation has been presented for the fact that a life-span developmental psychology should be cultivated by educational institutions and encouraged within psychology. For many reasons our educational institutions of the future will be serving the needs of a much wider span of ages than has been true in the past. This requires long-range educational planning. There are important contributions to education to be made by life-span developmental psychologists if they wish to meet the challenge of influencing human development rather than just describing it.

CHAPTER 14

Some Ecological Implications for the Organization of Human Intervention throughout the Life Span

DWIGHT HARSHBARGER

WEST VIRGINIA UNIVERSITY
MORGANTOWN, WEST VIRGINIA

ABSTRACT

The purpose of this chapter is to examine organizational and ecological dimensions of human intervention, and through the use of a life-span approach, to develop some possibilities for intervention alternatives that might more positively alter patterns of community life. Human services are examined as complex organizations and as active agents of bio-social intervention. Organizational characteristics which make the human service organization relatively unique and problematical are examined, as are some of the consequences of intervention efforts in the U.S.

It is suggested that in planning and developing human service intervention efforts consideration should be given to ecological dimensions of community life, such as the degree of environmental control and sequential environmental linkages. Certain aspects of the language of biology and system theory is suggested as useful for the integration of human services, as well as organizations which have been historically characterized by a high degree of professional and linguistic specialization. A life-span model for the assessment of patterns of community problems and intervention efforts is proposed, and its uses in the planning of intervention strategies are discussed.

Finally, professionalism and its impact in human service organizations is discussed, and some suggestions are made regarding changes in professional training programs.

I. Introduction

In the darkest days of the economic depression of the 1930s, Americans glimpsed the potential reality of an unworkable society, one that might no longer survive. It was a frightening vision then, and remains a haunting one today. It was during that turbulent period that major political policy decisions created irrevocable commitments by federal and state governments to large-scale social intervention through the use of public sector funds. These commitments have expanded over the years to include a vast network of agencies and programs which have come to be organized within the areas of health, education, and social welfare. They comprise what is referred to as the human services.

In terms of the organizational development of these agencies, the human services have, like Topsy, "just growed" into a large, and intricate human service complex. The organizational evolution of health, education, and welfare related agencies has often resembled what Braybooke and Lindbloom (1963) have referred to as "disjointed incrementalism." There has been incremental organizational growth lacking in coherent direction, hence growth which is organizationally disjointed. Little in the way of planning or rational development has characterized the growth of this industry. Our approaches to bio-social problem solving have typically involved a categorical organization of intervention resources following the identification of a categorical problem and the development of a categorical source of funds. This disjointed, but incremental approach has typified the growth of the human services, with larger numbers of organizations being developed to meet an ever increasing number of problems. Today the human services complex might be accurately described as the human services maze.[1]

For better or worse, this situation represents our best efforts to organize public sector strategies of intervention and change in American society. And, while the human services may be organizationally less than desirable, they represent large, powerful, and vast resources in the American economy. For example, in 1971 about 30% of the gross national product came from both public and private sector human services. Almost 70 billion dollars were spent on health alone. In 1972–1973, the budget of the Department of Health, Education, and Welfare may very nearly equal, and possibly surpass that of the Department of Defense. (It would appear quite possible that government support of the economy during the 1950s and 1960s, through a large defense establishment, will, in the 1970s and 1980s, be carried out through expanded human service organizations.)

And yet, the problems do not seem to diminish. Depending upon where the criteria are set, up to 30% of all elementary school children are in need

[1]It is less than surprising that every Secretary of Health, Education, and Welfare has pointed to the immense size and labyrinthine qualities of HEW as one of his major, continuing problems.

of specialized intervention. In both concentrated inner city environments, as well as in dispersed areas such as parts of Appalachia, it is not uncommon to find one-third of the families on some form of public assistance, and drug addiction and alcoholism continue to devastate untold numbers of lives. Although mental hospital populations are decreasing, the number of persons entering both mental hospitals and mental health centers continues to increase and effective preventive public health programs that go beyond infectious disease control remain problematical and marginally effective.

Further, it seems unfortunate, but true, that human problems do not oganize themselves in the same ways that the human services have been organized. Categorical organization of intervention strategies, reflecting ineffective political compromise and inadequate planning, has been highly incongruent with the noncategorical ways in which problems organize themselves. Learning disabilities, juvenile delinquency, substandard housing, and physical and mental health problems tend to occur simultaneously. The multi-problem family and neighborhood is the rule, not the exception. Unfortunately, the human service organization with multiple intervention strategies is the exception, not the rule.

Nature seems to relate its problems logically, with the patterns of these problems reflecting significant transitional zones in the life span. Unfortunately the realities of the life span are only occasionally reflected in the organization of intervention efforts.

II. Organized Intervention: Has It Made Any Difference?

Although it is difficult to assess the consequences of organized intervention in any clear-cut manner, some perspective can be gained on this problem through the examination of various descriptive statistics. For convenience, these statistics have been grouped as indicators of social disorganization and as indicators of health.

A. Indicators of Social Disorganization

1. Family Related

Table 1 describes four types of problems that are likely to have major impact on families. All have increased over the past 30 years.

2. Crime

Table 2 compares the frequency of occurrence and rate of increase of two major categories of crimes in 1960 and 1970. Both have increased over 100% in 10 years.

The economic loss to the public because of crimes committed in 1970 was $20 billion, while the total cost of local, state, and federal law enforcement

TABLE 1
Family Related Indicators of Social Disorganization[a]

	1940	1970
Divorces[b]	2.0	3.5

	1940	1968
Illegitimate[c] live births	7.1	24.1

	1950	1969
Suicide[d]	11.4	10.9
Homocide[d]	5.3	7.2

[a] The data for Tables 1–11 are based on *The American Almanac: The U.S. Book of Statistics and Information,* U.S. Department of Commerce (New York: Grosset and Dunlap, 1972).
[b] Rate per 1000 population.
[c] Rate per 1000 unmarried women.
[d] Rate per 100,000 population.

TABLE 2
Crime Related Indicators of Social Disorganization[a]

	1960	1970	Rate of increase
Crimes of violence	285,000	731,000	144%
Property crime	1,700,000	4,800,000	147%

[a] Data from U.S. Department of Commerce, 1972.

TABLE 3
Juvenile Delinquency as Indicator of Social Disorganization[a]

	1960	1969
Delinquency cases per 1000 persons 10–17 years old[b]	20.1	30.9
Total number cases	510,000	989,000

[a] Data from U.S. Department of Commerce, 1972.
[b] Excluding traffic offenses.

was $7.3 billion. Thus, the total measurable cost of crime to the public of the United States totaled over $27 billion in 1970.

Table 3 gives some indication of the scope of juvenile delinquency problems as seen in 1960 and 1969. The size of the problem has almost doubled.

3. Mental Health and Mental Retardation

Tables 4, 5, and 6 indicate the frequency of mental health problems which come to the attention of public or private institutions.

It is interesting to note that while the institutional population has decreased, the number of persons involved in mental health treatment has increased markedly. Table 7 contains data indicating relevant dimensions of mental retardation treatment problems in institutional settings.

B. Some Indicators of Health

1. Mortality Rates

Tables 8 and 9 describe changes in the mortality rates, across races and age groups for the years 1919 and 1967. Among persons aged 65, only the white female has a mortality rate in 1967 which differs appreciably from that of 1919. White and black males continue to experience mortality rates which

TABLE 4
Patients in Mental Hospitals[a]

	Public	Private	Total
1955	618,150[b]	15,850[b]	634,000
1965	490,899	12.874	503,773
1968	399,152	10,454	409,606

[a]Data from U.S. Department of Commerce, 1972; average daily hospital census.
[b]Estimated.

TABLE 5
Admissions to Mental Hospitals[a]

	Public	Private	Total
1965	314,027	70,921	384,948
1968	365,455	89,138	454,593

[a]Data from U.S. Department of Commerce, 1972.

TABLE 6
Number Persons Receiving
Outpatient Mental Health Care[a]

	Total
1960	211,000
1965	436,000
1968	796,683

[a]Data from U.S. Department of Commerce, 1972.

TABLE 7
Institutional Data on Mental Retardation[a]

	1950	1969
Number public retar-dation facilities	96	180
Number residential patients	103,377	192,848
Rate of admission[b]	6.9	7.4
Deaths in institutions	1,971	3,692

[a]Data from U.S. Department of Commerce, 1972.
[b]Rate per 100,000 population.

TABLE 8
Annual Rate of Mortality at Age 65[a] [b]

	White		Black	
	1919	1967	1919	1967
Male	34.99	33.61	38.93	46.85
Female	31.68	16.17	43.36	34.69

[a]Data from U.S. Department of Commerce, 1972.
[b]Per 100,000 population aged 65.

TABLE 9
Annual Rate of Mortality at Birth[a] [b]

	White		Black	
	1919	1967	1919	1967
Male	80.25	22.82	105.01	39.20
Female	63.92	16.82	87.49	32.39

[a]Data from U.S. Department of Commerce, 1972.
[b]Per 100,000 births.

are nearly as bad, and in some cases worse, in 1967 than in 1919. Although the mortality rate for black females has decreased rather substantially, it remains significantly higher than that of white females.

2. Death Rates from Selected Causes

Table 10 indicates rates of death from causes selected on the basis of there having been intervention programs aimed at the reduction of these rates. Overall, with the exception of infectious diseases, these problems have worsened.

3. The Cost of Intervention

Table 11 describes the total costs of intervention programs in health, education, and social welfare. It also indicates the percent of the United States gross national product that has been based on each of these areas of intervention.

At the present time, the costs of organized intervention in the human services make up about 30% of the GNP, or $280–300 billion. As one examines the increases in problems indicated in the given tables, such as mental health, mortality, etc., it is difficult to avoid asking some searching questions regarding the apparently increasing cost and decreasing effectiveness of these constantly expanding intervention systems. It is equally difficult to avoid the conclusions that through organized bio-social intervention, we have changed the human conditions very little, seen some things get considerably worse, and in a few areas we have barely held our own.

However, our culture has not been static. In the recent past, we have experienced what Hauser (1968) has termed the "social morphological revolution." There have been major changes in the size, density, and heterogeneity of the population of the United States. These changes have occurred with increasing rapidity, and have been characterized by what Hauser refers to as population implosion, or increasing concentrations of people in smaller areas.

For example, it required over 300 years for the population of the U.S. to reach 100 million, and only 50 years to add the next 100 million people to

TABLE 10
Rates of Death from Selected Causes[a] [b]

	1950	1969
Tuberculosis	22.5	2.6
Syphillis	5.0	.3
Cardio-vascular disease	494.4	499.7
Cirrhosis of liver	9.2	15.0
Malignancies	139.8	160.1
Pneumonia	26.9	31.4

[a]Data from U.S. Department of Commerce, 1972.
[b]Per 100,000 population.

TABLE 11
*Total Federal, State, and Local Expenditures[a] in Areas of
Health, Education, and Welfare and Expenditures Percentage of
the Gross National Product (GNP)[b]*

	1935	1950	1970
Health			
total	—	12,130	67,240
% GNP	—	4.6	7.0
Education			
total	3,234 (est.)	8,796	70,600
% GNP	3.1	3.4	7.6
Social welfare			
total	6,548	23,508	143,046
% GNP	9.5	8.9	15.0

[a]Data from U.S. Department of Commerce, 1972.
[b]In millions of dollars.

the census. And, while the population density of the U.S. was one person per square mile, in 1600, it had risen to 29.9 by 1920, and to 57.5 persons per square mile by 1970. All this, while the rural population decreased from 49% of the total census in 1920 to 27% in 1970.

To complicate things a bit further, our life styles have undergone considerable change. Bennis and Slater (1968) have suggested that we are becoming a "temporary society," one characterized by high rates of mobility and short-term social relationships. These life-style patterns, Bennis and Slater suggested, are incongruent with our historical values and modes of developing, maintaining, and breaking social relationships, leading to considerable social strain. We may be moving toward what Slater (1970) has described as *The Pursuit of Loneliness: American Culture at the Breaking Point.*

The major shifts in pattern of living are serious, and are likely to have had, and will continue to have, far reaching implications on the ease with which family and community bio-social adaptation can occur. While there have been strong currents of social and population changes which have, in and of themselves, created serious problems in human adaptation in the U.S., certain organizational dimensions of human service organizations make it exceedingly difficult for this type of organization to be responsive to the immediacies of environmental demands. Further, the models through which human service organizations view their constituencies and their problems need overhauling if responsiveness is to be developed.

III. The Human Service Organization

To understand more fully the relative effectiveness or ineffectiveness of human service organizations as agents of human intervention, it might be helpful to examine some of the characteristics of this form of social organization. In doing so, it should be noted that there are certain characteristics and constellations of characteristics that are unique to human service organizations, when compared to, say, private sector production organizations. These characteristics render the human service organization a unique form of organization, one that produces organizational behavior that cannot be understood by simple extrapolation from research on most product-oriented organizations, even though the latter form of organization is one that has consumed a disproportionate share of the organizational research efforts.

In an earlier paper (Harshbarger, 1971a), a number of dimensions which might distinguish the public sector human service organization from the private sector production organization have been suggested. These dimensions, while not wholly unique to either form of organization, were singled out because, collectively, they give rise to an awareness of the real and substantive differences between these forms of organizations; they are indicated in Table 12.

Moreover, these dimensions of organizational structure and function have important consequences for our understanding of the design and delivery of human services. They represent the parameters that surround organizational behavior in human service organizations.

One dimension of organizational ecology is particularly worthy of individual attention—that of the reticence of human service organization members to enter the political arena. Because this behavior defines the interface of the organization and its environment, it is of major importance in defining strategies of resource

TABLE 12
Contrasting Organizational Dimensions of Production and Service Organizations

Organizational dimensions

Private sector, technical production organizations	Public sector, human service organizations

Resource base

1. Resources obtained from private, individual or corporate, sources.	1. Resources obtained from public, tax or bond based resources, or private monies donated to the public sector.
2. Resource stability is directly affected by economic market fluctuations.	2. Resources stability is affected only by relatively long term economic fluctuations.
3. The potential for risk and loss is relatively high.	3. The potential for risk and loss is relatively low.

Organizational structure and process

1. The organization is structured and organized in accordance with production cycles-systems.	1. The organization is structured and organized in accordance with professional values and membership subgroupings.
2. Type of power is primarily utilitarian.	2. Type of power is primarily normative.
3. Organizationally defined tasks provide the primary bases of social segregation and interaction.	3. Professional membership groups provide the primary bases of social segregation and interaction. Task definition is usually developed by these groups.
4. Social hierarchies and social power are based in the formal organizational distribution of power.	4. Social hierarchies and social power are based in professional hierarchies, and their relative possession of power.
5. Intraorganizational norms and behaviors are largely based in production standards of desired efficiency (in both formal and informal organizational subsystems).	5. Intraorganizational norms and behaviors are largely based in the values of professional and organizational membership groups.
6. The individual member's involvement is primarily calculative.	6. The individual member's involvement is primarily moral.
7. The first allegiance of an individual is to his organizational membership group.	7. The first allegiance of an individual is to his professional membership group.
8. The allegiance of the individual to the organization is assumed, and is not an area of major conflict.	8. The allegiance of the individual to the organization is problematical, and may be an area of major conflict.
9. No (or very limited) use of job tenure.	9. Widespread use of job tenure.
10. Organizational and role performance of the individual is assessed by a profit criterion.	10. Organizational performance of the individual is assessed by criteria based in professional-social values.
11. Personnel are hired and retained largely in terms of their effectiveness in organizational production.	11. Personnel are hired and retained largely in terms of professional value judgments.
12. The consumption of materials is product oriented.	12. The consumption of materials is means, or process oriented.

348

TABLE 12 *(continued)*

Organizational dimensions

Private sector, technical production organizations	Public sector, human service organizations

Output

1. Relatively clear definition of end product.
2. Cost-effectiveness indexes are relatively easily developed.

3. There is an end-product orientation; the end product is given high organizational salience.
4. The overall mission or purpose of the organization is established by a small group (e.g., board of directors) which' acts in the best interests of the organization and its ownership.
5. The primary criterion for the development of new purposes for the organization is that of organizational survival.

1. Relatively unclear definition of the end product.
2. Cost-effectiveness indexes are difficult to impossible to develop; the major problem is the measurement of effectiveness.
3. There is a quasi-end product orientation; the salience of means is often higher than the salience of ends.
4. The overall mission or purpose of the organization is estabished by a relatively large group (e.g., legislators) which acts in the best interests of the public.
5. The primary criterion for the development of new purposes for the organization is the public interest. It is assumed that meeting public needs will give certainty to organizational survival.

Beneficiaries

1. Primary beneficiaries are owners.

2. Secondary beneficiaries are staff and clients or consumers.

1. Primary beneficiaries are usually clients, but sometimes staff.
2. Secondary beneficiaries are usually staff and the general public; sometimes they are the clients.

Organizational ecology

1. Economic indicators (profit-loss) are indexes of effectiveness of an organization's adaptive strategies.

2. Involvement in political decision-making in surrounding environment is legitimate and seen in the interest of the organization.
3. The nature of political involvement will be structured by organizational norms.

1. Degree of judged adherence to professional and social values, through derived behavioral and ideological criteria, are indicators of effectiveness of organization's adaptive strategies.
2. Involvement in political decision-making in the surrounding environment is seen as questionable and probably not in the interests of the organization.
3. The lack of political involvement will be maintained by organizational norms.

acquisition, interorganizational relationships, and other relationships that have long-term consequences for the organization.

Schaefer (1962), in a study of public health officers' views of their political involvement as professionals, found that this group denied legitimacy to their own political involvement. But, at the same time, they were very concerned about local political pressure or domination. When compared to politicians, Schaefer's public health officers saw their personal motives as "right and pure," and their professional roles unfettered by political influence. Since the "motivations of those with whom he (the public health officer) is dealing were regarded as venal or base, effective negotiation and adjustment may have been impossible [Schaefer, 1962, p. 326]."

Such a perspective on the realities of organizational life in the human services is incredibly naive. Although there may have been some changes in this perspective in the ten years since the Schaefer study was completed, those changes, if they have occurred at all, have tended to be relatively small, geographically localized, and limited in scope.

Similarly, Latz (1965), in his examination of the impact of professionally generated research findings on public policy, has concluded that if there has been any impact, it has been restricted to very narrow spheres of public policy. Demone and Harshbarger have noted that "what seems so missing, and so necessary, is a view of instrumental political behaviors as both essential and legitimate in the roles of those persons administering or delivering services in human service organizations. Professional ideologies, with their clear and present views of the past must undergo change [1973, in press]."

In summarizing this organizational analysis of human service organizations, it might be said that these organizations are laden with professional value judgments which usually form the basis for organizational decision making. Such a stance is particularly true to the extent that information feedback regarding organizational effectiveness in the community environment is ambiguous, a situation which holds true most of the time. The combination of organizational ideologies and relative stability of funding have been major supports for the creation of organizational insularity, both with respect to relationships with other human service organizations and the community served by these organizations.

IV. Some Ecological Considerations for Intervention at the Community Level

The following section of this chapter will deal primarily with intervention considerations; however, for convenience, it will focus on the theme of mental health, defined in a rather broad sense. Hopefully, some of the principles of ecological intervention which are developed in a mental health framework might generalize to other areas of human intervention.

Two primary concerns have guided the recent efforts to develop some ecological considerations for mental health intervention. The first of these is a felt need for the development of some concepts that might provide a language and some programmatic guidelines for viewing human behavior in its fullest ecological complexity. The second is a concern about what is done with our knowledge. To know about the complexity of relationships in human communities is not enough. What is needed are strategies of intervention that might improve the human conditions represented by the rather bleak statistical picture alluded to earlier.

Too often the conceptual models that guide research efforts do not approach a representation of the real world; hence the conversion of the respective findings into strategies of action is likely to lead to intervention efforts that are ineffective and faultily conceptualized. Similarly, intervention efforts which are rich with resources but are channeled through conceptually deficient intervention strategies, are likely to produce minimal results.

As a point of departure, some very basic questions need to be asked about how mental health problems at the community level are viewed, for many community and clinical psychologists continue to commit the error that experimental psychologists became aware of in their laboratory research some time ago. That is, we have become so accustomed to viewing problem behaviors in artificial environments, such as treatment settings, that we have almost totally neglected the environmental contingencies supporting or producing these behaviors in the person's natural environment, a problem dealt with by Willems (1973) at the 1971 Life-Span Conference.

In the field of mental health, many of the most cherished historical and contemporary views of treatment have harbored highly individualistic, relatively nonecological points of view. Troubled persons are noticed typically only when they cross the boundary into some organized treatment environment, through breaking a law or violating community norms. Despite the occasionally voiced concern that community mental health problems should be dealt with in communities, not in institutions, most states continue to spend over 90% of their mental health budgets on institutional costs. And, because that is where resources are, these institutions are used for the training of researchers and practitioners, who in later life plan careers in institutional programs, etc.

However, some programmatic changes do occur. The implementation of the 1963 Community Mental Health Centers Act has led to the development of approximately 300 Comprehensive Community Mental Health Centers throughout the nation, and has given structure to what has been labeled as the third revolution in mental health treatment. This catch phrase may grossly overstate the impact of this shift in intervention priorities, but it does reflect a new direction; one which may work more fully in the public interest.

At the community level, two general types of ecological intervention in mental health problems have emerged, both relating to the degree of control exerted over the immediate environment. They might be loosely conceptualized as intervention in relatively controlled and relatively uncontrolled environments.

A. Intervention in Controlled Environments

Controlled environments refer to behavior settings (Barker, 1968) in which the parameters of the immediate environment are subject to a relatively high degree of control. This would include such behavior settings as a classroom, a mental or physical hospital ward, offices, living rooms, community activity centers, and many others.

In controlled environments, decisions can be made regarding the creation of environmental conditions that are likely to lead to desirable behavior patterns among users of that environment. This might include such decisions as a movement from a rather traditional form of classroom organization to something resembling the open classroom, or a restructuring of furniture in a mental hospital ward. Or, these decisions might involve changes in the structure of the social environment, such as providing scheduling options for the students in a secondary school, ward government in a mental hospital, and group activities in a geriatrics center.

Representative of the work in this area are such investigations as Osmond and Izumi's (Osmond, 1957) examination of sociofugal and sociopetal space in mental hospital wards: Sommer's (1966) treatment of the ecology of privacy in libraries; Barker's (1968) ecological examinations of behavior settings; Simon and Lawton's (1967) study of the formation of friendship patterns among high-rise buildings for the elderly; and James Kelly's (1969) inquiry into the ecology of adaptation in high school social environments that differ in terms of environmental fluidity and constancy.

The theme which characterizes much of the research in this area is that of the effects of congruence or incongruence between interpersonal and environmental characteristics on individual and small group behavior and interpersonal adjustment. The findings would suggest that, to the extent that relevant environmental variables can be brought under social control, more ecologically adaptive behavior can be induced. This is most likely to occur if environmental conditions can be made relatively congruent with the characteristics of the individuals who inhabit that environment. To the extent that there is incongruence between characteristics of persons and their surrounding environment, the more likely it is that maladaptive behavior will occur.

As a basis for ecological intervention in communities, this kind of research presents as many problems as it contains promises. First of all, research on environmental determinants of behavior tends to focus on discrete micro-environments. That is, it tends to deal with relatively small, definable environmental units, such as a school, office, library, or hospital ward. Typically, this research does not attempt to examine the sequential linking of functionally related but different environments and the corresponding behavioral ecology. In this sense, it deals only with one part of the real world. In community intervention, the sequences of behavior settings that are utilized in the normal traffic of life cannot be ignored, and, in and of themselves, are an important intervention consideration.

A second major problem arises when individuals concerned with community intervention become involved in the internal dynamics of organizations over which they have no authority or control. The redesign of classroom or hospital ward environments is a highly political process, involving delicate negotiations with the staff of organizations who have worked out their own behavioral ecology in organizational behavior settings. To propose environmental change, however viable that change might appear based on research findings, is to place often delicate nets of interpersonal and person–environment relationships in potential jeopardy.

To suggest caution in the politics of intervention in controlled micro-environments is not enough. What is demanded is that the intervenor project the ecological consequences of the proposed intervention for all persons ecologically related to behavior settings in the micro-environment that will be affected by the intervention. Not to do so is to risk failure through the occurence of unanticipated consequences, consequences that might be predictably anticipated were the intervenor's map of ecological relationships more fully developed.

B. Intervention in Uncontrolled Environments

In contrast with controlled environments, uncontrolled environments refer to a much more global or macroscopic view of community life, and include environments in which there is a pluralism of agents, each possibly controlling certain segmented parts of those environments, and some environments in which there are no stable controls. For example, a community or a neighborhood would be a relatively uncontrolled environment, even though it would contain within it a number of smaller controlled environments, such as schools, hospitals, etc.

It is at this level of analysis that human service specialists, as intervenors, must begin to fully develop ecological guidelines to structure organizational behavior. James Kelly (1966, 1968) has articulated a number of principles which have been of help to those who have attempted to make some bio-social sense out of the tangled web of community relationships. He suggested that (1) the interdependency of social units, (2) the cycling of resources, (3) the effects of environment on styles of adaptation, and (4) the evolution of natural communities ought to be major considerations in beginning to understand community ecology.

Representative research in this area includes such work as Faris and Dunham's (1939) examination of mental disorders in urban areas; Hollingshead and Redlich's *Social Class and Mental Illness* (1958); the ongoing work of the Leightons in Nova Scotia (1959, 1963); Gans' (1962) analysis of the ecology of urban social life; the recent work of the Dohrnwends (1969) on social status and mobility and mental disorder; Levy and Rowitz' (1971) examination of ecological attributes of neighborhoods with high and low rates of mental hospital utilization; as well as Harshbarger's (1971b) research which has attempted to integrate various health, housing, and social relationship data into a coherent ecological picture of Appalachian neighborhood life.

In giving structure to the conceptualization of intervention efforts in community environments, it might be helpful to look closely at those parameters that structure behavior within community subsystems, and in the process borrow from the language of biology and system theory.

C. The Concept of Habitat and Niche

For some time, biologists have effectively used the concepts of habitat and niche to define place and role relationships, with habitat defining the place where an organism lives, and niche referring to an organism's role in the ecosystem (Odum, 1963). Different habitats and niches accommodate themselves to one another in ways that, collectively, define a larger ecosystem. Those concerned with intervention in human relationships in their natural environment might do well to consider the application of these concepts to their efforts in communities.

Certain problems do arise when these biological concepts are applied to relatively psycho-social problems. For example, a rabbit may live out his life in a relatively small geographic area, and engage in rather straight-forward sexual and social relationships. However, humans tend to roam the landscape and the skies and indulge in relationships that might be characterized as anything but straightforward. But, these activities do not occur randomly; human behavior tends to have systematic patterns that link work, recreational, and residential lives, and communities reflect these patterns in terms of characteristics of neighborhood habitats.

The following habitat–niche characteristics are suggested as dimensions that might enable effective comparisons and contrasts across neighborhood environments:

1. Line features. Gibbs (1961) has pointed to the use of line features such as railroad tracks, streets, etc., in establishing the boundaries of a neighborhood.

Within those boundaries, certain characteristic social relationships are likely to occur.

2. Homogeneity–heterogeneity. Ethnic, educational, and occupational characteristics of a neighborhood are likely to consist of relative degrees of heterogeneity or homogeneity. In stable neighborhoods, homogeneity is likely to be most probable, and in unstable neighborhoods heterogeneity will increase. A reliable indicator of these conditions seems to be the style and condition of the neighborhood's housing; to the extent that it might be characterized as diverse and heterogeneous, it is probable that the neighborhood also has similar characteristics.

3. Population density. How many persons are there per unit of living space, and how many living units are there per unit of neighborhood space?

4. Age characteristics. What is the distribution of the population over the life span? Are there habitat-specific patterns?

5. Rate of change. The rate at which out and in migration occurs should be noted. Certain neighborhoods might be described as highly temporary, others as highly stable in residential patterns.

6. Availability of resources. A neighborhood can be described as relatively high to low in the availability of resources that affect life support systems and human development. The most prominent of these resources is economic income, and this is closely linked to the availability of or access to other resources such as schools, medical services, etc. Other social resources, such as the presence of extended families, should be considered.

7. Stress level. If the preceding dimensions are conceptually combined, it is then possible to begin to think of neighborhood environments that differ in their overall levels of stress, and relative ratios of stress to resources. This dimension should prove increasingly valuable as it is related to the incidence of neighborhood–community problems in an ecological framework. In the Appalachian Human Ecology Project it serves as one of the fundamental bases for contrasting ways of life at neighborhood and community levels of analysis.

Other researchers, such as Michaux, Gansereit, McCabe, and Kurland (1967), Dohrwend (1961), Freudenberg, Jenkins, and Robertson (1956), Hinkle (1965), Langner (1960), drawing in part on Selye's (1956) stress theory, and in part on ecological models, have begun to specify the nature of the relationships between environmental stress and behavioral and emotional pathologies.

Overall, it is within the framework of the community habitat contingencies, created by different levels of the preceding dimensions, that human development occurs. It is here that one might begin to put together bio-social outcome predictions regarding such diverse problems as early childhood nutrition, identity development, bio-social pathologies, and many others, and frame predictions within specifiable habitats with known dimensional characteristics.

D. Community Systems and Dynamics

In dealing with the problems of human ecology and human intervention it is unlikely that the language of biology will be entirely adequate to deal with the complexities of human behavior, although it serves as a productive point of departure. Systems of human relationships, while having biological roots and intricate bio-social linkages, do contain properties that transcend the commonly shared language of biology. These relationships are also likely to go beyond the languages of psychology, economics, psychiatry, and sociology. It might augur well to consider the fuller use of a different language for the required concepts, one that might facilitate the sharing of information and the generation of multifaceted interdisciplinary community research.

It might be profitable to take a long and serious look at the application of general system theory as a potentially productive way of dealing with the problems of designing community intervention. Over the past 20 years, the principles and language of system theory have grown and evolved to the point that it is no longer in the domain of engineers and computer technologists. System theory is rapidly becoming a part of the academic language, and in terms of the present *Zeitgeist*, is "in." Unfortunately, skilled use of system concepts is still "out." There has been a tendency not to apply these concepts to the understanding of community dynamics and their pressures on community life-span problems. Bertalanffy (1951), Boulding (1956), Ashby (1958), and more recently Buckley (1967, 1968) have attempted to provide overviews of this approach. It has been referred to as "the skeleton of a science" and "a new discipline."

In the human services, such work as Baker's (1970) treatment of systems theory, research, and medical care; Lee and McLaughlin's (1970) examination of public health services as a system; Baker and Schulberg's (1970) conceptualization of community health care-giving systems: and Howland's (1970) suggested community health system model have given substance and direction to a different view of human service planning intervention.

With respect to the application of system theory language to the understanding of community dynamics and community problems, the following dimensions are suggested as starting points for the development of a systems model of community problems:

1. Serially chained environments. It should be possible to identify, by user group, habitats that are serially chained in terms of their use patterns by different community groups. This would include work, recreation, and living environments.

2. Patterns of pathologies and growth in serially linked environments. Certain serially linked environments are likely to be associated with the occurrence of relatively high and low rates of varying kinds of bio-social pathologies and

adaptive growth. The key to understanding functional and dysfunctional ecological adaptation may lie as much in the accurate linking of chained environments as it does in understanding any one environment or the characteristics of environment users.

3. Life-span related crises. Within separate habitats, as well as in the total community, consideration should be given to the rate of occurrence of life-span related crises. This would include sharp increases in the incidence of problems at certain critical transition points in the life span, such as socialization into occupational career roles, childbearing, leave-taking of one's children, career resocialization, retirement, etc. It is likely that these will differ for community groups and/or habitats, depending upon the constellation of dimensional characteristics mentioned earlier in the discussion of habitat and niche.

4. Resource exchanges. In different neighborhood environments, there should be an examination of the resource exchange patterns within those environments, as well as between the internal and external neighborhood environments. More specifically, the interdependencies between human service organizations and specific client groups in terms of their resource exchanges with those groups should be carefully examined.

5. Costs of habitat maintenance. The dollar costs for the physical maintenance of habitats should be calcualted. Such cost should also be translated into the proportion that must come from the public sector and that proportion which comes from the private sector. When assessed against the relative health–pathological nature of the environment, it should be possible to estimate cost-benefit ratios of habitat maintenance.

6. The texture of the human service organization–community interface. It should be possible to define, both quantitatively and qualitatively, the use patterns that have emerged for certain human service organizations in given habitats. These patterns will differ both in terms of their client demands and problems (e.g., the type and rate of mental health problem) as well as in terms of the inclusion–extrusion characteristics of the service giving organizations in that environment. Ryan's classic *Distress in the City* (1969) pointed to many of the problems that people experience once they cross the boundary into a help giving organization, not the least of which is that organizations are often programmed to extrude many of those who would make demands upon its resources.

All of these dimensions, collectively, begin to define the active system properties of community environments and their relationships to intervention organizations. By accurately assessing these dimensions, intervention organizations can begin to map the system properties of the client–environment–intervention terrain, and begin to plan strategies of intervention that are likely to maximize productive human adaptation to environmental stresses. While such a task is conceptually complex, present computer technologies render it a manageable one.

V. The Ecological Assessment of Community Intervention:
A Life-Span Model

Unfortunately, because of the categorical nature of funding for community intervention organizations, there is rarely any focus on the overall patterns of resources deployment in communities by the organizations involved in those comrmunities. However, if effective intervention strategies are to be designed, it is imperative that some means be developed for the assessment of the deployment of intervention resources at the community level. The following model is suggested as a vehicle for moving toward this goal.

The model in Figure 1 incorporates the three major dimensions of (1) type of intervention, (2) life-span age groupings, and (3) relative stress-resource relationship, into a view of community intervention resource deployment.

With respect to the types of preventive intervention referred to in the model, the following definitions apply.

Primary prevention	intervention strategies designed to reduce the frequency of occurrence of specified problems
Secondary prevention	intervention strategies designed to reduce the duration of problems when they occur
Tertiary prevention	intervention strategies designed to reduce the amount of time taken for a person to return to a relatively productive life style

Life-span age groups refer to statistical groupings of persons around the variables of age and stage of development in a community definition of life-span development. For functional purposes, these life-span groupings might best be developed around age-related periods of time which are characterized as role transitional or role stable. That is, they represent life-span pattern characteristics of a community's culture that give rise to relatively stable or relatively transitional personal and community definitions of roles and positions (e.g., beginning, continuance, and termination of schooling; marriage–divorce; entering, continuing, leaving an occupation; entering widowhood, etc.).

The relative levels of stress to resources indicated in Figure 1 refer to bio-social environmental stresses, as discussed earlier in this chapter, in relation to the immediate resources possessed by persons in given life-span groups. Thus, a given habitat is characterized by both its relative stress level and the life-span characteristics of its occupants.

The internal cells in the model should contain two kinds of data. First, as indicated, the statistical frequency of persons in the community who fit a certain life-span description, and are living under certain estimated conditions of environmental stress, should be entered. Second, there should be entered in each of

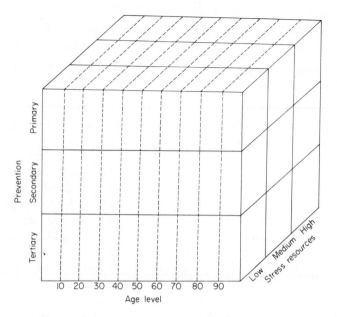

Fig. 1. A life-span model for assessing intervention resources.

the cells containing life-span data, the estimated (dollar value?) intervention resources that might currently affect those problems projected on the basis of habitat-stress and life-span factors.

Completing such a task will be neither simple nor easy. It will require a comprehensive knowledge of existing intervention systems, information about the distribution of life-span groups across habitats, bio-social indicators that will permit reliable estimates of ratios of habitat stress to resources, and social–psychological data on community dynamics that affect age-graded relationships in that community.

Ultimately, what should emerge is a comprehensive picture of the relative congruence or incongruence between the distribution of community intervention resources and the occurrence of community problems in a life-span and habitat-stress framework. Such a statistical representation might indicate, not surprisingly, that persons of all ages living in relatively high stress environments are likely to receive less than their proportional share of intervention resources. Further, it is probable that this will be particularly true for the very young and the very old.

A community focused statistical representation such as this should also indicate where there is a disproportionately rich deployment of intervention resources. Again, it is unlikely that the results will be surprising. However, a data-based representation of community needs and intervention resources is likely to transcend prejudices or historical patterns of resource allocation, and should operate as a more rational basis for change in a community's human service system. It might also serve as a basis for beginning to examine potential cost-benefit ratios of intervention across community habitats and age groups.

VI. Designing Intervention: The Future as Reminiscence or Rebirth?

It is likely that within the short time span of a few years, we will be spending over $300 billion per year on health, education, and social welfare intervention in the United States. To continue our present patterns of organizational efficiency and effectiveness is to court the kind of biological and sociological disaster that will allow historians to place upon us the epitaph: the pathological society.

The organizational resources committed to the maintenance and growth of present patterns of intervention are, indeed, formidable. Vast federal, state, and local bureaucracies have codified and routinized their interorganizational ecology to the point that significant organizational changes of any kind are difficult, vexing, and usually doomed to failure. The future of human intervention as an experience reminiscent of times past, is highly probable.

However, it has been said that things remain the same until change becomes less painful than the status quo. In the unlikely event that that condition might occur, and the perhaps even more unlikely probability that we would have sufficient time to effect change should that condition occur, the following section suggests guidelines for strategies of change in systems of human intervention.

VII. Strategies for Organizational Change in the Human Services

Given our poor track record at successfully generating organizational change in the human services, combined with our penchant for designing new delivery systems that are only marginally effective, the prospects for the future are not particularly bright. But, for those who understand, and perhaps even enjoy, the loneliness of the long distance runner, the following strategies of change are suggested.

A. Affecting the Infrastructure of Service Delivery

First, the allocation of new public funds should be increasingly contingent upon the development of collaborative service delivery strategies at the community level among related, but historically independent, human service organizations. The integration of services is essential to avoid the unnecessary and expensive duplication of those services, and to deal realistically with the intricate complexities of human problems in communities.

What is meant by the integration of services or interagency collaboration should be specified by funding agencies in terms of behavioral indicators, such as the number of manhours and activities spent in joint service delivery programs.

Secondly, there should be an increasing use of cost-benefit models in the analysis of agency programs and the expenditures of agency resources, such as staff time. It is possible to compute, for example, the direct and indirect costs of teaching a retarded adult certain job skills, or the maintenance of a community crisis-intervention program, or the operation of a senior citizens program. Based on the programmatic outcomes of intervention strategies such as these, it should be possible to estimate benefits to the specific people involved and to the community as a whole (e.g., keeping a person in his job via outpatient care, as opposed to the costs of inpatient treatment).

The development of cost-benefit analysis methodology in the human services is still in its infancy and the sophistication with which such analysis can be performed is quite limited. However, this is a critical area of development if we are to increase our own and the public's capabilities for making decisions that maximally serve the public interest.

In addition, there should be an increasing use of target-contracting methods between human service organizations and their funding agencies, focusing on specific habitat environments and their unique life-span related problems. A simple example of this is the geographic catchment area developed by public health agencies, and adopted in the legislation affecting the operation of comprehensive community mental health centers. This strategy should increase the possibilities that agency and interagency responsibilities can be specified. In turn, this should lead to increased accountability among community agencies regarding community problems.

An important by-product of such a strategy is the probability that as agencies become more accountable for certain community groups and problems, there is a tendency for those agencies to become advocates for those same groups and their problems. Furthermore, the probability decreases that any community agency can successfully engage in the extrusive practices that prevent clients from receiving needed services.

B. Affecting the Human Service Overlay

The problems of segmented, conceptually limited service delivery systems go far beyond the delivery systems themselves. Very often, it is likely that delivery system problems are manifestations of the structure of interorganizational relationships that overlay the human services. Hence, if lasting changes in delivery systems are to be accomplished, for example, through affecting the service delivery infrastructure, it is essential that the structural overlay of these organizations be dealt with. One suggestion might include the structural integration in the executive office. At the state level of human service organization, the heads of most major departments in the human services are appointed by state governors. These consist of such offices as Commissioners of Health, Alcoholism, Education, Aging, Drug Abuse, Mental Health, Welfare, etc. In most states they report directly to the governor's office, and submit independent budgets to that office. It is a budgeting, reporting, planning, and decision-making process that is normally characterized by administrative and organizational segmentation, a problem that is reduced only to the extent that the governor's office is large, diverse, and unharried enough to deal with the problems of the human services.

The creation of a structure for the organization of the human services which places an administrative overlay on these historically independent subsystems would seem to be the kind of organizational development that would maximize the probability of our successfully achieving and maintaining changes in the service delivery infrastructure.

One recent example of an attempt to accomplish this end is the creation of a governor's cabinet position of Commissioner of Human Services in the state of Massachusetts. Under this program of reorganization in state government, those departments which in the past comprised what were loosely referred to as the human services, and reported directly to the governor, now are administratively grouped under the office of the Commissioner of Human Services. Their programs and budget requests are subject to approval by the commissioner's office, a process which, it is hoped, will facilitate a more effective integration of services and program planning.

It is unrealistic to ask for the development of ecologically oriented, and organizationally integrated patterns of service delivery under organizational parameters that structurally support and sanction independent agency efforts; the overlay must be integratively altered.

VIII. Concluding Comments

This chapter began by examining both some of the outcomes and organizational dimensions that characterize efforts at human intervention. It will conclude by asking again that consideration be given to the social–psychological dimensions of human service organizations.

If one performs an implicit factor analysis of the number of variables necessary to account for the numerous dimensions of organizational life mentioned earlier regarding human service organizations, it takes little time to realize that "professionalism" is a variable of major importance. Given the legal codes and civil service requirements which have grown profusely around human service organizations, it is very probable that this will remain true for the foreseeable future. The allocation of resources in human service organizations will continue to be politically and behaviorally dominated by persons who label themselves professionals of various stripes and hues.

It might be well to consider some of the implications for professional training required to move toward more ecological, life-span oriented community programs in the human services. Some suggestions are made in the following paragraphs.

First, many hours are spent training students to develop methodological rigor in the production of research. But the consumption of research, or the translation of research findings into strategies of intervention is dealt with only as a by-product of our efforts—one that is usually low in the status hierarchy of training priorities.

The logic of this process is that students cannot be expected to be effective consumers of research unless they understand how to produce research, a premise that is not without merit. However, we then go on to devote the vast majority of our training resources to the latter. If universities are to maintain visibility and relevance as training organizations, even fuller and much more systematic treatment must be given to the consumption and implementation of research findings in graduate training programs.

Second, while many graduate training programs place students in a variety of field settings, the opportunity for students to abstract and systematically examine those experiences around the theme of organized systems of intervention, and intervention effectiveness, is too often lacking. What typically happens is that the student becomes involved in a small number of research or clinical experiences that become the locus and focus of his activities, and he is usually provided neither the opportunity nor positive sanctions for examining, say, the system properties of the community-organization interface. In the process, he is socialized into a mode of perception that ignores some important variables in the intervention process.

Finally, there continues to be talk of interdisciplinary approaches to problems, but little is done to translate such talk into reality. Few academic departments with graduate training programs employ anyone without a credential in that respective discipline. Further, little is done to encourage academic or social contacts of students outside their particular disciplines, a sanctioning process which more often than not reflects preferred academic and sometimes nonacademic life styles. Somehow the belief is maintained that persons can be trained to be the intervention agents of the twenty-first century by training them in organizational structures that reflect, at best, the latter nineteenth or early twentieth centuries.

The human services represent major resources for the development of a viable society. They are perhaps the best hope for the rational development of social change strategies that operate in the public interest. However, if this is to be accomplished, important and far reaching changes in the organizations themselves must occur—changes that will personally affect all those who wear the label "professional."

It is difficult to be optimistic about the probability of rapidly and successfully generating these changes. To quote a recent ecology poster

> We have met the enemy
> And they are us.

On Life-Span Developmental Research Paradigms: Retrospects and Prospects

PAUL B. BALTES

PENNSYLVANIA STATE UNIVERSITY
UNIVERSITY PARK, PENNSYLVANIA

K. WARNER SCHAIE[1]

WEST VIRGINIA UNIVERSITY
MORGANTOWN, WEST VIRGINIA

ABSTRACT

Some model characteristics of a life-span approach to the study of psychological develop-ment are reviewed and discussed. Focusing on a selected set of model attributes related to the tasks of describing, explaining, and modifying intraindividual and interindividual patterns of development (continuity versus discontinuity of antecedent–consequent relation-ships, concurrent versus historical paradigms, time-lag relationships, treatment by history interactions, etc.), it is maintained that the usefulness of a life-span view of development has been demonstrated with regard to the task of description, with developmental change in most behavior classes occurring throughout the human life course. As to explanation and modification objectives, the power of a life-span perspective is primarily dependent upon

[1]Present address: Ethel Percy Andrus Gerontology Center, University of Southern California, Los Angeles, California.

365

the significance of long-term historical (time-lag) relationships as they interact with immediate antecedents and the joint significance of an ontogenetic discontinuity–continuity model. It is asserted, however, that a life-span developmental orientation is mandatory and immediately useful if the task is one of optimization of human development in a changing societal context.

The various contributions to this volume are reviewed in light of the paradigm framework outlined. It is shown how a life-span approach to the study of development modifies the substance and methodology of age-specific developmental models and contributes to a reorientation of existing developmental research. Although the general conclusion of this review is that life-span paradigms are not yet shown to be of great empirical precision and scope, particularly when explanation is at stake, it is also argued that a life-span view of development explicates, in its extreme form, some of the general pitfalls inherent in any developmental approach. In fact, it is contended that such theoretical and methodological constraints may easily be overlooked if an age-specific rather than a life-span view is applied to the study of development.

I. Introduction

The editors of the previous two life-span developmental psychology volumes which were generated by the West Virginia Conference Series (Goulet & Baltes, 1970; Nesselroade & Reese, 1973) elected to say their piece by means of a preface or a brief introductory chapter. Although the present editors are obviously not fully aware of all of the previous editors' intentions, it appears that the primary reason for this choice was to rationalize the very attempt, by showing why the diverse offerings presented in a piece-meal fashion belonged together, and/or the insight that a comprehensive synopsis of life-span developmental issues was premature and probably subject to conceptual failure or sterility.

The present epilogue does not depart significantly from this somewhat fatalistic approach, since we believe that life-span developmental theory, despite major efforts, has not yet reached a level of maturity that permits succinct enunciation of its conceptual and empirical network. Thus, while a growing body of research is clearly evident, we believe that the optimism surrounding the increasing acceptance of a life-span view may easily outrun its scientific utility, if not properly channeled and regulated on a conceptual and methodological level.

In this spirit of conceptual and methodological search, therefore, it is the intention of this epilogue to carry the mission one step further by beginning to delineate the major paradigms that may guide life-span developmental research. It is hoped that such a focus will (1) assist in explicating the unique aspects of a developmental approach in general, and a life-span approach in specific, (2) pinpoint some of the theoretical and methodological features and hazards that characterize life-span research, and (3) suggest research activities that may test the usefulness of life-span developmental models in greater clarity than has been true thus far. In this vein, the present epilogue is a logical extension of the ideas presented in the introductory chapter (Baltes & Goulet, 1970) to the first volume (Goulet & Baltes, 1970) of the West Virginia Conference Series.

In line with the primary intention of increasing the level of theoretical and methodological awareness of a life-span developmental analysis, the following epilogue is organized into three parts. First, an attempt is made to specify the basic nature of paradigms and questions that are prototypical of life-span developmental research. Second, in the paradigm framework outlined, the various chapters to this volume and other research contributions will be examined with particular regard to assessing the degree of empirical usefulness and deployability of life-span paradigms. Finally, suggestions will be made for future research with a focus on sharpening and refining the type of scholarly activities that may be of particular significance in clarifying the survival value of life-span developmental models.

A. Life-Span View of Development

It seems fair to conclude that the rising interest in a life-span view of developmental psychology and other areas of human development witnessed over the last years brings to fruition what some prominent scholars began some decades ago, though in a largely isolated manner (e.g., Bayley, 1963; Bühler, 1933; Bühler & Massarik, 1968; Havighurst, 1948; Hofstatter, 1938; Neugarten, 1968, 1969; Pressey & Kuhlen, 1957, etc.).

Despite the fact, however, that the life-span approach seems to have acquired a certain faddish character, the theoretical and empirical rationale for a life-span developmental view is still vague, and, perhaps even misunderstood. Thus far, the battle to establish firmly a life-span perspective seems to have centered on winning one primary objective: that development occurs at *all* ages (infancy, childhood, adolescence, adulthood, old age) and that, from a theory-construction perspective, it is not only shortsighted, but sometimes even useless and damaging to construct age-specific developmental models that ignore interage networks and other aspects of long-term ontogenetic linkages.

For the most part, this aspect of the battle has been waged and most developmental researchers do accept the notion that developmental change is not restricted to any specific stage of the life span and that, depending upon the psychological function and the environmental context, behavior change can be pervasive and rapid at all ages. The various chapters in Goulet and Baltes (1970) and the present volume are ample testimony to this aspect of a life-span posture. In fact, one finds the statement (e.g., Bayley, 1963) that it seems reasonable to assume that, generally speaking, the rate of change is greatest in infancy and old age. The area of intellectual development (see Baltes & Labouvie,

1973; Horn, 1970; Schaie, 1970, for reviews) offers an empirical example for this hypothetical relationship. Rate of change in intellectual functioning declines systematically during the early part of the life span (e.g., Bloom, 1964) reaching a fairly low rate of change during adulthood (e.g., Nesselroade, Schaie, & Baltes, 1972; Owens, 1966), with adults exhibiting a high degree of trait-like stability over extended periods of time. The years preceding death, however, are again characterized by a significantly accelerated rate of change often labelled as terminal change (e.g., Riegel & Riegel, 1972).

Another case in point is the developmental-task model discussed in this volume primarily in the opening chapter by Havighurst. This model is based on the notion that different types of tasks highlight various periods of the human life span (e.g., Havighurst, 1948, 1972, Chapter 1, this volume). Related to the notion of an "active learner interacting with an active social environment [1972, p. vi]," Havighurst postulated that the individual is engaged in mastering a variety of tasks throughout his life. Thus, the overall rate of change exhibited by a given person throughout the life cycle can be thought of as representing some kind of composite effect of changes on a multitude of behavior subclasses. Obviously, it will bepend upon the scalability of response measures and other assumptions about the additivity of measures to what degree such a model can be translated into the empirical world. However, the developmental-task model illustrates a life-span view of development and exemplifies how a task-specific view of development can bias and sterilize a given researcher in the direction of viewing a specific age period (such as childhood) as being the critical one relative to the impact of developmental processes. Emmerich's chapter on sex-role development presents another very persuasive argument on this point when focusing on the dynamic model attributes necessary when viewing sex-role genesis in a life-span framework.

What is less clear to many developmentalists is whether the nature of life-span changes is such that they are inclined to label them as "developmental change" throughout all phases of the human life span. This issue, though significant in light of the history and variety of world views associated with the concept of development (e.g., Harris, 1957; Looft, Chapter 2, this volume; Overton & Reese, 1973, Reese & Overton, 1970) is less important in the present context. In line with earlier positions (Baltes & Goulet, 1970, 1971), it is asserted here that the distinction between developmental change and aging change is largely a metatheoretical issue, discussion of which generates more heat than light, since it does not lend itself easily to empirical investigation, and assigns on an a priori basis behavior "increments" and "decrements" to distinct age periods. This position, delegating a lesser role to the distinction between development and aging, however, should not be taken as negating the possible significance of decrement models. It is implied only that assigning development to childhood and youth, and aging to the adult and elderly population is resulting in preconceived models of ontogeny that may be of little validity when confronted with empirical data.

B. Explication of Life-Span Changes

Starting then from the conclusion that marked behavioral change does occur at all age levels, i.e., that life-span change does indeed exist on the level of description, the central theme of scholarly efforts is to explicate the phenomenon of life-span change in terms of antecedent conditions and their associated mechanisms. Obviously, this process of explicating change is a tedious one. In general, the authors are inclined to concur with Riegel's (1966, p. 99) position that developmental psychology has not yet provided us with the type of theories that are apt to account for the "why" of development, though most researchers would maintain that impressive advancements have been made. This is particularly true for the ontogenetic change characteristics of the older person, i.e., aging,[2] where most psychogerontologists still seem to rely on "counting and classifying the wrinkles of aged behavior [Kastenbaum, 1968, p. 280]," and on expecting time per se to carry the onus of explanation.

Attempts at explicating behavior change sequences are manifold, yet they are all based on the postulate that time per se is not a causative factor (see Baltes & Goulet, 1971; Riegel, 1972; Wohlwill, 1970a, also Neugarten & Datan, Chapter 3, this volume, Bengtson & Black, Chapter 9, this volume). Time, like chronological age, is a nonpsychological variable whose theoretical meaning must always be deduced from further research aimed at the systematic explication of behavior changes in terms of the antecedents and processes that occur over time. Such a strategy reduces the time dimension to an enumeration of ordered events or event combinations. Baltes and Goulet (1971) have discussed some basic research paradigms that allow for such an analytic explication of developmental change phenomena, as have other researchers such as Wohlwill (1970a), Baer (1970), and Sutton-Smith (1970). In the context of aging, it was Birren (1959, 1970) who presented this issue in great clarity when he said that "aging may be used to refer to relationships involving chronological age with the implicit assumption that such relationships are inevitably in transition to being explained by other variables without recourse to the use of the term 'age' [Birren, 1959, p. 8]."

The quest for an explication of ontogenetic change in terms of antecedents or time-correlated processes leads to a specification of the paradigms that are

---

[2]It may be important to observe that the writers do not see aging as being synonymous with decrement. The type of behavior change observable in old age can take many forms, in terms of structural quality and directionality, depending upon the context and behavior class under consideration.

unique to a developmental view of analytic behavioral research. Obviously, such a task is embedded in one's world view relative to methodology and theory construction in the behavioral sciences (see Reese & Overton, 1970; Looft, Chapter 2, this volume; Klausner, Chapter 4, this volume). However, a summarizing discussion, though metatheoretically biased, seems useful if it clarifies and exemplifies the framework from which it is possible to deduce a theoretical rationale for a life-span view of development. In the following, an attempt is made to outline the type of framework that the present editors have developed over the years when exposing graduate students to a developmental approach to the study of behavior. For the most part, this discourse is not intended to represent a theoretical posture, but to illustrate what we may call the *"developmental orientation"* in the behavioral sciences.

II. Developmental Research Paradigms

A life-span view of development suggests that the behavior of an individual and interindividual differences in behavior are the product of ontogenetic history, that the past is a prologue to the present, and that the present is a prologue to the future. What does such a proposition imply in terms of research paradigms and theoretical corollaries?

A. Basic Paradigms

Previously, it was stated that delineation of research paradigms is always done within a metamodel, and that such a task cannot be geared toward truth criteria. The acceptance of such a relativistic world view is important for the considerations to follow, since the research model used to illustrate the nature of a life-span view of development is not necessarily the one other researchers may embrace. However, the intention is not to propagate a specific research metamodel, but to systematize the generic properties of a developmental orientation.

Within a deterministic and mechanistic metamodel, for example, it has been proposed that research paradigms in the behavioral sciences be organized around the elements described in the upper part of Fig. 1: response variables *(R)*, stimulus variables *(S)*, and organismic variables *(O)*. Other classifications are possible (see Kerlinger, 1964; Spence, 1963 for discussions), and it is recognized that for some researchers the separation in the three types of variable systems proposed is unsavory to begin with (see focus on "true" interactionism à la Piaget or on general systems theory).

First, the metamodel contained in Fig. 1 postulates that behavioral responses

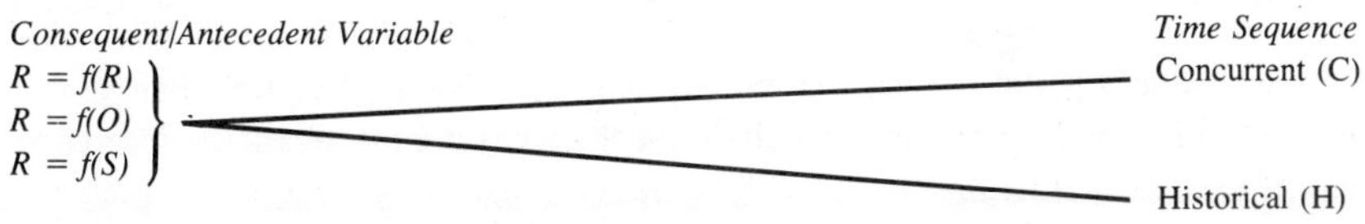

Consequent/Antecedent Variable   *Time Sequence*

$R = f(R)$ Concurrent (C)

$R = f(O)$

$R = f(S)$

Historical (H)

Multivariate Expansion

$R(1, 2, \ldots, r) = f\big[(R1, 2, \ldots, r), (O1, 2, \ldots, o), (S1, 2, \ldots, s)\big]_{\text{C, H}}$

Developmental Formulation

$R(1, 2, \ldots, r)_{T_t} = f(R, O, S)_{T_t}, \; g(R, O, S)_{T_{t-1}}, \; h(R, O, S)_{T_{t-2}}, \; i(R, O, S)_{T_{t-t}}$

Fig. 1. Illustration of possible variable relationships characterizing psychological research (historical or time-extended paradigms are seen as prototypical of developmental research; nature of developmental "cumulation" or "linkage" is goal of explication). Developmental research is aimed at explicating intraindividual change and interindividual differences in intraindividual change.

(R) constitute the dependent variable *(explicandum)* of psychological research. Second, it postulates that the explanation and prediction of behavior by reference to antecedent variables proceeds by relating the target, dependent variable (behavior, R), to either other *response variables* $\big[R = f(R)\big]$, *organismic variables* $\big[R = f(O)\big]$, or *stimulus variables* $\big[R = f(S)\big]$. Substantive examples for these three paradigms are, for instance, the attempts to explain and predict a given dependent variable, say, 'anxiety'' in terms of other response categories (e.g., agression, guilt), organismic variables (e.g., blood pressure, heart rate), or stimulus variables (e.g., darkness, isolation).

Thirdly, the metamodel contained in Fig. 1 states that variable relationships can be *concurrent* (C) or *historical* (H). In other words, the attempt to account for a given target variable or consequent behavior can be based on antecedent variables that are concurrent to, or at least in antecedent proximity to, the target variable; or the account can be based on antecedents that occurred earlier in the time sequence. The latter historical relationships, involving significant time differentials between the consequent and antecedent conditions, are sometimes called "distal" relationships. Obviously, the dichotomy between concurrent and historical relationships is somewhat arbitrary and needs interpretation in a given context. From a pragmatic vantage point, however, it is useful. Consider, for example, the following situation dealing with the explanatory interpretation of the anxiety concept. A concurrent relationship involves the attempt to predict "anxiety" by reference to exposure to a concurrent anxiety-provoking stimulus situation (e.g., threatening father), while the attempt to predict anxiety by an anxiety-provoking stimulus situation that occurred at an earlier period, such as the experience of a threatening father in early childhood, is an example for a historical antecedent-consequent relationship.

Finally, the developmental formulation shown in Fig. 1 states that the major task of developmental research is the explication of intraindividual change and interindividual differences in intraindividual change (the consequent) by reference to time-related interactions between response, organismic, and stimulus variables. It is the product of such long-term interactions that defines the behavior of an individual and interindividual differences at a given point in time (T). Note in this context that T_t and T_{t-1} shown in Fig. 1 parallel concurrent and historical relationships respectively; further, that the use of multiple indices (f, g, h, i) is intended to allow for differential functions at different points in time (see later discussion of continuity versus discontinuity issue). Note further that the developmental paradigm described focuses on a contextual analysis (S, O, R) of the change process in that it does not assume a fixed organism–environment system but explicitly advertises consideration of time-related changes in environmental (S) patterns as well. This dynamic view of man–environment systems, though not typical for American behaviorism (Baltes & Nesselroade, 1973; Klausner, Chapter 4, this volume), is of prime significance in understanding the gist of life-span research.

Obviously, this view of research paradigms is incomplete. On the one hand, it is apparent that for any given response category, there may be a multitude of concurrent and historical antecedents in operation which are not necessarily based on a fixed set of elements as is expressed in the multivariate format paradigm contained in Fig. 1. On the other hand, we need to clarify precisely how historical conditions (the nature of f and g, etc.) are translated or transmitted into the present context. However, it is indeed this notion of a changing system of antecedent-consequent relationships, operating over time to produce a given behavior product and a series of such products (Riegel, 1972), that is at the core of developmental theory construction.

Therefore, in the following, an attempt is made to pinpoint which aspects of the described paradigms are fertile for developmental considerations and, at the same time, which aspects of these paradigms suffer from the weakness inherent in the developmental formulation itself. Whenever possible, this will be done in the framework of the present volume and the area of intellectual ontogeny which is one of the research areas common to both authors.

B. General Objectives of Developmental Research

Thus far, it has been stated that a developmental, life-span view of psychological ontogeny, if translated into empirical operations, must employ historical paradigms. Conversely, it may be said that if concurrent, contemporaneous paradigms are sufficient to account for ontogenetic phenomena, a life-span view is not particularly exciting. Moreover, it is maintained that a life-span view must focus on a cumulative process analysis of response–organismic–stimulus (man–environment) systems. Thus, another corollary can be deduced from this analysis. It is concluded that a life-span view of development is not conceptually distinct from any other developmental approach to the study of behavior such as the attempt to account for the emergence of Piagetian conservation behavior in children. The only difference is one of length and number of the historical relationships involved. This conclusion, though theoretically obvious, is an important one to arrive at, since life-span developmental research is often seen as being conceptually distinct from, say, conventional child development research to name one age-specific counterpart.

In order to examine the usefulness of such a historical, cumulative view of psychological ontogeny, the following discussion proceeds in two steps. First, some general objectives of developmental theory building will be described in terms of the research paradigms presented. Second, a set of questions prototypical of life-span research will be derived and briefly examined in light of the findings presented in this volume.

The frame of reference for the prototypical questions to be discussed is that, ideally, the scope, precision, and deployment of theories should allow one to *describe, explain,* and *modify* a given phenomenon as described in Baltes and Goulet (1970). Moreover, it was asserted in that paper that, in terms of components of variance, developmental research is aimed at describing and predicting both *intraindividual change and interindividual differences in intraindividual change.* How can these objectives of developmental research be explicated by reference to the research paradigms described above? Note again that the following is intended to have primarily didactic and not metatheoretical or metamethodological value.

1. Description of Developmental Change

In this context, description is seen as involving the empirical, systematic report of developmental changes (with respect to both intraindividual and interindividual aspects) as they occur during the life span of an individual. This aspect of the task of theory building involves the left part of the paradigms in Fig. 1 and those components of the right part which deal with response systems. In other words, the question of description is one of (a) identifying the response categories (R 1, 2, . . ., r) constituting the behavior system, and (b) of quantifying time-related changes (T 1, 2, 3, . . ., t) in those response categories in terms of both quantitative and structural attributes and intra- versus interindividual difference parameters (e.g., Baltes & Nesselroade, 1973; Van den Daele, 1969). Often, the initial attempt at description focuses on age-functional relationships. In principle, however, it is the ordered, time-related sequence of behavior events that lies at the core of developmental description (e.g., Baer, 1970; Riegel, 1972; Wohlwill, 1970a).

As long as the time-related behavior sequences described are of the R–R type, even though they involve historical relationships, one may argue that such statements are primarily oriented towards predictive rather than explanatory description. However, this distinction is a matter of taste rather than logical necessity.

2. Explanation and Prediction of Developmental Change

Explanation of developmental phenomena, in this chapter, refers to the explication or clarification of behavior products and changes in interindividual differences by showing their relationships to their concurrent and/or historical contexts. The central question is which antecedent conditions (S, O, other R) or processes (learning, maturation, etc.) are sufficient and/or necessary to account for the occurrence of a developmental event. While in description the primary focus is on unbiased observation, the emphasis in explanatory or analytic analysis is on the evaluation of the explanatory value of variable relationships in accounting for intraindividual change and interindividual differences in such change sequences. In this context, it does not seem worthwhile to dwell on the relative merits of other aspects of explanatory analysis such as whether the strategy chosen is "constructive" or "reductive." Important, however, is the recognition that explanatory attempts are not at all restricted to R–R relationships.

As indicated earlier, the task of explanation centers about assigning the right-hand side of the paradigm depictured in Fig. 1 the status of antecedent conditions, irrespective of whether this relationship is concurrent or historical. The task of explanation becomes predictive when a given variable relationship is used to project into the future as opposed to explicating the past in an ex post facto manner. The approach towards explanation (and prediction) is developmental, if the nature of the variable relationships is such that distal (historical) events or processes are linked to each other in the attempt to account for intraindividual change and individual differences that exist at a given point in time. It is apparent in this context that knowledge about time-related changes or lack of changes in S–O–R conditions, that is, "developmental" information, becomes mandatory if prediction is at stake. In other words, prediction of future behavior becomes less and less accurate, the less is known about the S–O–R context that "develops" over the time period involved in the prediction task. For some researchers particularly of the "strong" developmental type (see Harris, 1957; Reese & Overton, 1970; Kohlberg, Chapter 8, this volume, for discussions), such a developmental approach at explanation and prediction has particularly high explanatory power, if the antecedents invoked involve so-called "basic" processes (e.g., Piaget's processes of assimilation and accommodation) and if they account for universal, directional, and irreversible change sequences (e.g., stage models) in psychological structure. Such directional change sequences may also imply that certain subsequent behaviors have a specific set of antecedent behaviors as historical prerequisites.

The multivariate expansion of the developmental paradigm contained in Fig. 1 points to a complicating feature of a developmental analysis. The multivariate paradigm not only states that the number and structure of variable elements may change during ontogeny, but also that a given developmental phenomenon may result from a variety of antecedent combinations involving not only different sets and amounts but also differential, time-related delivery schedules. Note that such a perspective expands on the conventional definition of a continuity–discontinuity dichotomy.[3] Generally, this dichotomy is restricted to measurement aspects of the dependent variable continuum.

The present view, in line with Kagan's (1969) position, implies that a developmental analysis of the continuity–discontinuity issue should include a focus on the degree of homology involved in the sequential linkage of antecedent-consequent relationships of the $S–O–R$ matrix. Baltes and Nesselroade (1973) have discussed this aspect and pointed out that the degree of interindividual and intraindividual homogeneity in the activation or delivery of developmental matrices may indeed be much smaller than generally assumed by nomothetic models of ontogenetic development. The pervasive effects of historical time or cohort effects (Neugarten & Datan, Chapter 2, this volume; Bengtson & Black, Chapter 9, this volume; Kogan, Chapter 7, this volume), for example, are indeed apt to demonstrate wide differences in the degree of homogeneity in developmental antecedent patterns.

3. Modification and Prevention (Optimization) of Developmental Change[4]

In terms of the research paradigms developed in Fig. 1, the final major task of developmental theory building concentrates on the generation of a know-

[3]The terms "continuity" and "discontinuity" are used in the present manuscript to convey multiple meanings relative to descriptive, explanatory, preventive, and interventive discontinuity versus continuity. In each case, the central theme is that the phenomena are not easily accountable by application of simple additive models but that consideration of interactive, non-nomothetic, and nonhomologous relationships is useful. It is conceded that this diverse use of the continuity–discontinuity distinction does not convey a precise, theoretical concept but only a theoretical orientation.

[4]Readers whose personal terminology comes primarily from the literature on operant psychology, which has so impressively contributed to a better understanding of the modification rationale, may prefer different terms when discussing modification objectives. The authors in this case propose the usage of corrective versus preventive versus optimizing modification of developmental change.

ledge base that would not only allow for explanation, but also for a priori (prevention) or a posteriori (alleviation) alteration or modification of developmental phenomena both on the level of intra- and interindividual differences dimensions. Obviously such attempts at modification assume a knowledge base about the description and explanation of developmental change, although modification attempts are not restricted to such "developmental" information.

In principle, *modification* attempts can involve knowledge about concurrent and historical relationships relative to stimulus, response, and organismic variables and their interaction. However, knowledge of the "naturalistic" antecedent conditions (whether concurrent or historical) may not be sufficient nor efficient when engaging in successful intervention. For instance, some of the antecedents (e.g., heredity, physical trauma), though powerful, may not be easily manipulable. Further, the developmental product, particularly if it is the result of a long-term process and if the organism is beyond critical periods of sensitivity, may be irreversible and chronic. Moreover, it may be useful to apply treatment variables (e.g., drugs) that were not directly involved in the "developmental" generation of the matrix of developmental differences.

Generally it is maintained that a developmental approach to modification of development phenomena makes maximum usage of its potential, if it is oriented towards *prevention* (e.g., Urban & Looft, in press; Birren & Woodruff, Chapter 13, this volume; Harshbarger, Chapter 14, this volume) and *optimization* (Brandstadter & Schneewind, in press) rather than alleviation. This posture implies that—at least with regard to the level of individual analysis—the most effective way to alter the course of development is to alter the man–environment context *(S, O, R)* that typically produces it and, in a preventive fashion, to plan developmental contexts that are apt to enhance psychological ontogeny using optimization principles. Obviously, such a perspective is appealing since, at least theoretically, it attacks developmental dysfunctions at their ontogenetic roots rather than contributes to their continuous perpetuation by improving the sophistication of "nondevelopmental" modification strategies.

The research paradigms, then, illustrate that modification attempts, in principle, can incorporate developmental (historical) considerations, they can be based on concurrent (nonhistorical) variable relationships; and they may bear no similarity to the developmental history that produced the behavior outcome observed. Further, modification attempts can try to maximize their effectiveness by focusing on prevention and optimization rather than alleviation. The latter strategy requires full knowledge of the entire developmental matrix *(S, O, R)* in a prospective orientation.

To illustrate this view on modification, prevention, and optimization of developmental patterns by concrete examples, let us consider an older person who shows decrements in auditory sensitivity (McFarland, 1968, for review). First, in line with a nondevelopmental modification strategy and without much consideration for the history of the auditory loss, one may decide to provide the elderly person with hearing aids (a concurrent, behavioral prosthetic à la Lindsley, 1964) to compensate for the deficiency. Second, with a focus on prevention, one may counsel the person to avoid further exposure to high noise levels which presumably, in their cumulative operation, were among the major ingredients in the developmental production of the auditory sensitivity loss. Finally, with a focus on optimization of the ontogeny of future cohorts, one may decide to control exposure to noise throughout the life span of individuals, to design noise-protective devices, and/or to develop educational programs (for example, through differential reinforcement) that raise the sensitivity of aging individuals to those frequencies that normally show marked sensitivity losses in advanced age, etc.

III. Prototypical Questions of Life-Span Research on Development

With a focus on the tasks of describing, explaining, and modifying human development, the following questions are seen as being critical for the usefulness of a life-span approach to the study of psychological development. For the most part, illustrating examples are taken from the domain of life-span research on intelligence. Specific references are typically not given in the text. However, the reader may consult the following items (Baltes & Labouvie, 1973; Baltes & Nesselroade, 1973; Bayley, 1970; Cattell, 1971; Charles, in press; Horn, 1970; Jarvik & Cohen, 1973; Schaie, 1970) for overviews on this topic. A subsequent section will apply the same paradigms when selectively summarizing the chapters contained in the present volume.

A. Concurrent versus Historical Models of Description

To what extent is the developmental phenomenon under consideration (e.g., intelligence, personality variables, social processes) more comprehensively and/or differentially describable, if related to earlier parts of the life span?

Consider intellectual functioning as an example. There are prototheoretical models that exemplify both a concurrent and a historical approach to description. On the one hand, there is Guilford's structure of intellect model which, at least with regard to its structural properties, is basically nondevelopmental since it postulates an ontogenetically invariant system of abilities. On the other hand, there is Piaget's theory of cognitive development which explicates a historical view by specifying a distinct set of cognitive stages following each other in a fixed developmental sequence with minimum allowance for variation. Finally, there is the Cattell–Horn model (Horn, 1970) with its focus on hierarchical ability structures and the fluid-crystallized distinction which, in principle, permits both structural and quantitative ontogenetic change sequences, though being less wed to a fixed sequence than is true of Piaget's model.

Obviously, the task of description is modified by the extent to which models of development allow both for quantitative and structural change during ontogeny. However, there is nothing sacred about either a historical or a concurrent approach if they cannot be tied to relative degrees of usefulness. At first glance, for example, one might argue that a historical approach is more useful, since it permits the task of description to occur in a *system* of time-related changes with each phenomenon being linked to antecedent (past) and consequent (future) phenomena in the sense of a continuity model. At the same time, however, such a life-span continuity view of intellectual development embeds the phenomenon in a larger context that modifies the nature of the description; it not only provides for continuity of the descriptive task, but possibly also for misrepresentation of, or insensitivity to, the unique aspects of a phenomenon.

Indeed, in the area of intelligence one may conclude that the life-span view has occasionally misguided the descriptive task, since the emphasis has been too much on the use of instruments and procedures that have been developed for younger populations. Accordingly, since the notion of a continuity life-span model prevailed (largely in the interest of *R–R* type prediction), the domain of gerontological intelligence may not have been properly mapped. Conversely, the lack of an adult-centered model of intelligence (the area of creativity provides for a good example, see Chapter 7 by Kogan, this volume) when conceptualizing models of cognitive development in children may have resulted in child development research that, for the most part, is child-centric and does not orient itself toward adult outcomes.

Another example for the questionable usefulness of a life-span, continuity view of behavior change is the widespread use of a "decremental" regression model for aging populations which tends to categorize gerontological changes in terms of dimensions and criteria that are developed within the context of younger age segments. Neugarten (1969) phrased a conceptual "discontinuity" position most persuasively when she said: "We shall not understand . . . adulthood by projecting forward the issues that are salient in childhood [p. 121]," and, "what is most striking is the lack of predictability from childhood to adulthood with regard to life outcomes [p. 128]." All these examples are given to counteract the widespread belief that continuity models are necessarily superior to discontinuity models (see also Woodruff, in press). On the contrary, a life-span perspective becomes especially attractive if both continuity and discontinuity can exist conjointly, though for different time periods and behavior classes.

B. Concurrent versus Historical Models of Explanation

To what extent is the developmental phenomenon determined or accountable by reference to concurrent versus historical antecedents (cumulative and time-lag variable relationships)?

Consider again intellectual performance in the elderly as a substantive example. Setting aside the dilemma that the accumulation of history must be transmitted to the present organismic state of the organism in order to be effective, the question is whether intellectual decline in the aged is due to concurrent or historical systems of antecedents *(S, O, R)*. As Butler (1968) stated in another context: "Evidence . . . supports the conclusion that the immediate . . . situation influences the adaptation of the aged [p. 234]," and "The . . . adaptation of people at any age depends . . . upon the immediate situation and past history [p. 247]." Obviously, similar conclusions can be found in the literature on intellectual ontogeny in childhood.

An empirical case for a *concurrent* model of explanation, for example, relates intellectual decrements and interindividual differences in such decrements in the elderly to aging-correlated changes in the psychophysiological state of the aged's organisms, to the deprived educational context in which the elderly live, or to their high degree of test anxiety or cautiousness when responding to intelligence tests.

In contrast, explanatory attempts that are *historical* in nature focus, for example, on the performance-inhibitory processes that result from long-term cumulative learning as is implicit in various types of interference conceptions. Similarly, the prevalent, cumulative effect of life history associated differences in educational and social contexts on intellectual performance in the elderly (see Charles, in press; Schoenfeldt, unpublished) can be used to account for the aged's difficulties in coping with cognitive tasks and in explaining interindividual differences in cognitive functioning. Further, the perspective that a given intellectual response is necessarily subsequent to a specific antecedent response (as implied in cognitive stage models) is the most simple case of a historical explanation of intellectual ontogeny, most simple since it is cast in the framework of *R–R* relationships alone.

The prototypical questions that push the quest for historical paradigms to its extreme involve lengthy *time-lag* explanation as contained, for example, in the notions of critical periods (Kessen, 1968) and sleeper effects (Kagen & Moss, 1962). Consider again the domain of intelligence. Examples of remarkable time-lag relationships are implicit in data on heredity contributions to late adult functioning, data on the relationships between childhood socialization conditions and adult intelligence, and findings on the relationship between adult professional status and intellectual performance during old age. Similar arguments are made in the context of senile dementia. Kral (1972), for example, summarizes the gist of a literature review by stating that (when contrasted with the effects of physiological, cerebral aging) a genetic disposition (to senility) and stress endured in the remote or recent past may be of greater etiological importance.

On a more general theoretical level, the notion of a *sleeper effect* (Kagan & Moss, 1962) is a concept that has been developed to account for time-lag relationships as has the concept of *anticipatory socialization,* especially when utilized in conjunction with a competence–performance distinction. Both concepts assume that certain conditions, operating at an earlier time, do not manifest themselves behaviorally until the proper performance context arises. The distinction between acquired competence and performance is a clear-cut illustration of this view. Acquisition of grandparental behavior, for example, may occur in early life by such a mechanism as observational learning. Most performance aspects of grandparental behavior, however, will not be shown until late adulthood and old age. Other examples for extended time-lag relationships can be found in the biophysiological literature on development, where impressive data on the effect of early nutritional and hormonal deficiencies on later ontogeny are quite common (e.g., Finch, in press).

C. History by Treatment (Intervention) Interactions in Modification Attempts

To what extent is the developmental phenomenon more effectively manipulable if the strategy of intervention considers interactive effects involving the developmental history of the individual?

As discussed in an earlier section, this prototypical question has at least two aspects to it. One concerns the a posteriori treatment of developmental dysfunctions; the other the *prospective* prevention of dysfunctions and/or the optimization (enrichment) of the course of development. It was also stated above that it is the prospective stance which requires the fullest knowledge of the life-span matrix of developmental phenomena.

In general, it seems fair to conclude that, due to the multiplicity and dynamics of developmental antecedents that might produce the same behavior outcome and the interactive nature of man–environment systems, it is questionable whether behavioral scientists will ever be able to demonstrate the type of treatment and prevention effects that characterize much of the classical biological and medical sciences (e.g., preventive pediatrics and family medicine; Pattishall, in press). In any case, however, the complexity of the problem of human development intervention is apt to require massive, multivariate treatment patterns as expressed in perspectives generated by systems theory (Urban & Looft, in press), education (Birren & Woodruff, Chapter 13, this volume) and ecological programs involving large components of the man–environment system (Harshbarger, Chapter 14, this volume). This appears particularly important if long-term effect patterns are at stake, as is clearly true for life-span optimization attempts.

Consider again the domain of intelligence. With a focus on a posteriori treatment, are there data, for example, to suggest that persons respond differentially to a given set of treatments (organismic, environmental, etc.) depending upon the organism's developmental history? Unfortunately, data are scarce in this respect. However, there is some tentative evidence to suggest the hypothesis that older cohorts benefit more from a retest experience if they have had an average or below average educational history rather than one that is superior in terms of length and quality. Similarly, there are suggestions and hypotheses to the effect that older subjects respond less well to various biological treatments aimed at increasing cognitive performance if they have had a medical history of biophysiological traumata. Furthermore, in line with a cognitive, phenomenological view of personality in late adulthood (e.g., Thomae, 1970), it could be suggested that a given educational intervention is differentially effective depending upon a given individual's prospective, cognitive expectancy about the phenomenon of aging itself; an expectancy which is for most people in Western cultures one of intellectual decrement (see Chapter 12 by Nardi, this volume). Aging subjects, however, differ in the degree of intensity of such expectations and, accordingly, one would predict subject-related history by intervention interactions. Similar arguments could be put forward on the basis of strong cohort differences in intellectual aging (Nesselroade *et al.*, 1972). If the childhood educational system for today's elderly generation is significantly less satisfactory than that for coming generations of aged individuals, one is tempted to predict that a given intervention strategy may be effective with today's aged population but not with the aged of the future, etc.

Such history by intervention interactions is also especially explicit, if a "strong" developmental theory is accepted which implies that developmental theory and intervention must be carefully matched (e.g., Kohlberg, 1968; Rohwer, 1970; Sigel, 1971). Assume for the moment that a given intellectual theory involves four structural and sequential stages (e.g., Piaget). Obviously, if subgroups of the aged had been functioning during adulthood at either the third or fourth level, a fourth-stage intervention package would have differential effects depending upon a given aged person's previous level of attainment. Again, from a design perspective, the outcome would be a history by treatment interaction.

In sum, the proposition of this third prototypical paradigm and question is that the effects of a given treatment are not nomothetic, but that effectiveness is "moderated" by subject-related historical variables; the farther such subject-related variables go back into the ontogenetic history of an individual, the stronger is the case for the usefulness of life-span developmental paradigms.

The question of prevention and optimization translates the treatment by history interaction model (Baltes & Goulet, 1971) into practice. In addition, the search for optimization is aimed not only at a better understanding of the naturalistic course of development itself from a retrospective view; on the contrary, the focus is on examining the effectiveness of intervention in a prospective (preventive) fashion and on redesigning the man–environment context in which development occurs.

Predicting with satisfactory precision the nature, timing, and delivery schedule of developmental antecedents for specified outcomes, of course, is the dream of any scientist including the developmental psychologist, since this task interlocks—conceptually and empirically—the generation of a knowledge base with its application. One might take the posture that such hopes are premature in life-span developmental psychology. At the same time, however, the two chapters in this volume devoted to programmatic intervention (Birren & Woodruff, Chapter 13; Harshbarger, Chapter 14) contain a number of innovative suggestions that are apt to redirect the form and structure of current developmental intervention attempts.

Attention is drawn in these chapters to environmental (ecological) and community, rather than primarily person-centered, intervention programs; to the redistribution of educational efforts through the entire life course of individuals; to the need for considering, in a prospective manner, adult and gerontological educational goals in childhood education; to continuing, adult, and second-career education; and to consideration of the detrimental impact of pervasive and rapid cultural change on the long-term effectiveness of educational programs that are "massed" into the first third of the human life span. The effect pattern of an early life-massed educational effort, for example, is particularly obvious in the area of cognitive functioning, where there is growing and compelling evidence (Baltes & Labouvie, 1973 for review) that intellectual deficits observed in advanced adulthood and old age are largely due not only to cohort effects, but also to reinforcement and practice deficiencies (Labouvie, Hoyer, Baltes, & Baltes, 1973) that characterize the educational ecology of this age population.

It is in the context of preventive human development intervention, then, that a life-span view of development shows immediate power by illustrating the tremendous narrowness and superficiality of current modification attempts. In short, conventional educational and other intervention efforts seem gloriously outdated, though firmly established, by being geared largely towards a stable society, childhood and adolescence, and the cognitive behavior domain. The life-span paradigm, on the other hand, points to intervention for cultural change rather than stability, life-long education, and a host of noncognitive developmental objectives. Concerted examination of the prototypical question posed at the beginning of this section will help us in the design of such life-span intervention programs.

IV. Personality Variables

We shall now raise the previously formulated questions regarding the utility of life-span models and approaches within the context of the substantive contributions of this volume in the area of personality development and social processes.

This strategy will allow us to combine the task of summarizing the thrust of this book with our aim to delineate a conceptual framework for life-span developmental research. In some instances, however, since the contributors did not prepare their manuscripts under the same conceptual auspices, this analysis may place slightly different accentuations on the various chapters than was intended by the authors.

Livson (Chapter 5, this volume) takes the dogmatic stance that there must, by empirical credo, be continuity in personality dimensions between earlier and later life stages. He repeatedly emphasizes that, all evidence to the contrary, investigators are preoccupied with phenotypic data, particularly of a self-report nature. It is his argument that a complete description of personality should be a genotypic one which searches out the different ways in which genotypes can be expressed at different life stages. Such a comprehensive search for inter-age linkages is, of course, feasible only if one follows evidence in the same individuals, over much of the life course. In Livson's perspective, then, descriptive continuity exists at the level of genotypic analysis which he considers axiomatic for life-span study.

On the issue of the importance of concurrent as against historical antecedents and the modifiability of behavior, Livson's chapter, due to its focus on R–R type trait models, does not offer rich evidence. It is hinted, however, that we have confused substantive and methodological issues. That is, any cross-sectional analysis of personality structure must of necessity deal with concurrent data and cannot therefore provide us with any true developmental clues as to the emergence of personality structures at any given level of development. Much of the important work of authors like Guilford, Cattell, or Eysenck may therefore be quite irrelevant to the developmentalist, because it implicitly assumes the concurrent nature of personality structure without incorporating designs which could allow alternate data and conceptions to emerge. Only longitudinal data or some type of sequential approach, which has the possibility of linking structures emerging at different developmental stages, and models that allow for both quantitative and structural ontogenetic change, can be expected to provide data which would truly bear on the issue of historical antecedents to current personality structure (see also Baltes & Nesselroade, 1973; Schaie & Marquette, 1972).

With regard to time-lag variable relationships, Livson argues that sleeper effects have in the past been unnecessarily restricted to phenotypically defined channels of development (Kagen & Moss, 1962). He may be quite right that this is a major dilemma, since there is no obvious reason (except perhaps for major environmental change) why a given behavior at one level of development should necessarily disappear and reappear in identical form at a different stage. Livson cites a study by Peskin (1972) which illustrates unbroken chains of causation in the transformation of attitudes, and recent work by Meili and Meili (1972) presents similar data in the area of temperament traits. These studies show that general reorganizations of behavior as a function of developmental transformation make it likely that behavioral expressions of genotypes do become reorganized, and may not be at all recognizable in any form during extended periods of such reorganizations. Clearly, models that specify explicit connections between phenotypic- and genotypic-type concepts are desirable when accounting for sleeper effects.

A rather different stance is taken by Emmerich (Chapter 6, this volume) in his discussion of sex-role differentiation and socialization. It is easy to interpret his contribution as suggesting that there may be obvious responses to the prototypical questions we have raised, but that they will depend to a large extent upon the theoretical position of the respondent rather than the nature of their data. With regard to the descriptive task, Emmerich emphasizes the need for a conjoint analysis of person- and environment-centered attributes as he focuses on the impact of secular trends in shaping the relative degree of sex-role continuity. Emmerich's chapter is also rich in illustrations for structural changes and structural transformations, possibly of the discontinuity type, in sex-role development, particularly as they evolve from cognitive–developmental conceptions. Moreover, attention is drawn to a careful analysis of the nature of the sequence and relationships among multiple aspects of sex-role behavior, since properties of developmental trends reveal organizing developmental factors of sex-role ontogeny.

When one examines the evidence for the relative importance of concurrent versus historical antecedents in sex-role development, the theoretical evidence for formation of sex-role behavior in early childhood through dyadic parent–child interactions is strong, especially during childhood and adolescence. However, the impact of concurrent situational and the subordination of sex-role phenomena to more fundamental, concurrent organizing processes in personality development cannot be denied. The evidence for time-lag relationships involving adult sex-role phenomena is much more scarce, leaving us, for the most part, with conjecture. On the one hand, there is the possibility of increased situational dependency and increased dominance by multiple reference figures. On the other hand, there is the helping hand provided by the competence–performance distinction (Brim, 1966). That is, the observed discontinuities may be in the area of performance (as being inhibited or transformed by social change), even though the individual's behavior repertoire would permit role functions acquired early in life. Obviously, in this respect the performance–competence distinction bears great similarity to the genotype–phenotype model as alluded to also by Emmerich himself.

While it is not clear then whether we can make direct predictions from early ontogenetic events in the development of sexual identification and sex-role norms, there is nevertheless both evidence and opinion that argues for the reemergence of such everly events at later life stages, albeit in different transformations (e.g., Erikson, 1950; Neugarten, 1969; Parson & Bales, 1955). Sleeper effects in this area tend to have the form of elaboration of sex differences at the adult level, using forms and basic identifications which occurred at earlier developmental stages. Again, the usefulness of such life-span continuities will in the long run hinge on the possibility of constructing models that elevate genotypic (competence) and phenotypic (performance) relationships from the level of theoretical conjecture and interpretation to one of empirically testable assertions.

In examining the life-span developmental implications of Kogan's chapter (Chapter 7, this volume), it is necessary to recognize that he is, in fact, covering separately the topics of creativity and cognitive style. With regard to creativity, Kogan distinguishes between approaches which are either product-, person-, or process-centered. On the level of description, the product-centered approach [for which Lehman's work (1953) clearly represents the most noteworthy exemplar] has generated persuasive evidence for the usefulness of a life-span paradigm, although issues associated with the relative impact of cohort effects on cross-sectional age differences and with concerns about age- and cohort-related validity differentials in creativity assessment make the evidence on the descriptive ontogeny of creativity less than unequivocal. One aspect of Kogan's presentation makes a particularly good case for a life-span approach. Kogan maintains that in future creativity research it will be particularly important to search for "real-life" referents for creative behavior. To this end he argues that it is during the period of adulthood and advanced age that such real-life assessment is possible, whereas during childhood and the period of formal schooling creativity assessment "must necessarily have 'intermediate' rather than 'ultimate' status." Obviously, this view of prospective time lags in the emergence and assessment of cognitive products leads to a sine qua non of life-span research.

Kogan's chapter contains little information on the historical antecedents of creativity and the degree to which its developmental course can be modified. Longitudinal data seem to suggest, however, that creativity-type tests exhibit fairly high long-term stability in the sense of trait patterns. It appears, therefore, that historical events (whether environmental or genetic) are of substantial importance, even though, as in other ability areas, long-term stability of creativity seems more clearly substantiated in male than in female subjects. Whether or not differential correlations by sex between IQ level and later measures of creativity are indicative of possible time-lag effects is open to further inquiry.

What about the evidence with respect to cognitive style as summarized in Kogan's chapter? Here again somewhat different conclusions may be drawn depending upon what stylistic aspects one is concerned with. Kogan deals with a threefold classification. The great bulk of published data appears to relate to the assessment of accuracy versus inaccuracy of performance with respect to measures such as field dependence–independence and constricted versus flexible controls. The second class of variables does not involve veridicality as such, but still implies assigning value to one end of the given dimension as in the case of Guilford's ideational fluency. Finally, and here life-span data are almost completely lacking, there is a class of styles where veridicality is not at issue as in the case of breadth of categorization.

First of all, on the descriptive level, all evidence points to age-related changes throughout all periods of the life span relative to cognitive styles as well. Here, as in other cognitive tasks, substantial differences are found between outcomes of cross-sectional and longitudinal studies pointing again to the need of considering both ontogenetic and culture–historical components when studying long-term developmental trends. As to explanatory evidence, there do not seem to be any data which would bear on the issue of time-lag relationships, but certainly significant interactions between historical and concurrent events are likely. For example, there is at least indicative evidence (Schwartz & Karp, 1967) that age differences in field dependence might be accountable as a function of educational level covarying with the age continuum, as well as studies showing expected differences between retired and employed individuals at the same age.

The utility of examining behavior over time is even more apparent for categorization and conceptualizing styles, since development seems to depend upon the maturation of cognitive structures as well as the environmental context to which these structures are then applied. Of particular interest here is Kogan's account of the departure of older subjects from abstract–conceptual groupings to relational–thematic groupings. Are we again in the presence of genotypic transformatons, or do we find here truly emergent behavior? It may well be that it is in the area of complex cognitive styles that we will encounter the so often talked about wisdom of the old, rather than performance decrement on trivial tasks represented by our conventional test-like measures of convergent thought. In any case, Kogan seems to conclude that the establishment of cognitive styles is probably rooted in early life, while the demonstration of creative behavior (at least as expressed in indicators of social consequence) must be deferred to young and middle adulthood. His review of the literature, however, appears to indicate the presence of interactions between early development and current life experiences for both the creativity and cognitive style construct.

It is most interesting to note that Kohlberg (Chapter 8, this volume) in his essay on moral development has dramatically shifted from his earlier contention (Kohlberg & Kramer, 1969) that moral development ended with adolescence. Very much in accord with the findings on shift in peak attainment in the cognitive domain (see Schaie, 1970), Kohlberg now concludes that full development of his stage 6 is not reached until early adulthood. But this is not all. Interestingly enough, Kohlberg finds it necessary now to introduce a hypothetical stage 7, which involves a transformation which Kohlberg finds difficult to describe in the Piagetian system which he had so successfully applied to the domain of child development. Stage 7 behavior appears to be a transcendental development which is restricted to the unusual person who can go from the merely moral principle to the universal or cosmic stance.[5]

On the descriptive level, Kohlberg's chapter, far more than any other thus far discussed, illustrates the importance of relating earlier to later aspects of the life span—as one would expect from a cognitive–developmental world view. Particularly significant, however, is the fact that Kohlberg, contrary to Flavell's contribution to the first life-span volume (Goulet & Baltes, 1970), assigns major structural transformations to the adult period. In line with a cognitive–developmental view, the new stages proposed are indeed different transformations, but they can only be understood if they are perceived as emerging from the earlier formulations. Once the extension is made, however, Kohlberg finds a rapproachment with Erikson's theory and, with a more satisfactory data base, may well be on the way toward a genuine descriptive life-span theory of moral development.

Kohlberg's chapter also contains statements about interactions between concurrent events and developmental histories, particularly in regard to his attempt at explanation. Attention is drawn to a true "explanatory discontinuity" by the speculative assertion that adulthood psychological stages may be the result of experiential interactions with the environment (e.g., frequent experiences of personal moral choices), whereas moral development during childhood and adolescence is assumed to be largely linked to biological maturation. Obviously, though Kohlberg does not draw this conclusion himself, such an explanatory discontinuity perspective—contrary to classical Piagetian thinking—is apt to suggest the utilization of experiential training programs in modifying or optimizing moral development throughout adulthood. This view of a cognitive–developmentalist of the Piegetian tradition, derived from a life-span approach, would indeed seem to be a major theoretical innovation.

---

[5]Once we consider the possibility of such growth for the select few, to a level which may not be unrelated to Nietzschean concepts, we may be postulating that the stage 7 person is really beyond good or evil! If this is indeed the case one might propose a further transformation which would introduce a little humility into a possibly new rationalization of man as the super-being. In a dinner conversation at the conference which led to this volume one of us (Schaie) therefore seriously proposed to Kohlberg that one should at least entertain the existence of a stage 8, bearing the formulation: "If there has to be a God, it might as well be me." That is, the transformation from stage 7 to 8 occurs when the great man at the cosmic level accepts the fact that his thinking has become the point of reference for moral behavior, rather than morality residing in some abstract, consensual, and societally determined set of precepts. And it might be argued further that not a few of us who have some responsibility over other peoples' lives may tend to develop such stage 8 behavior. Whether or not this seems suspiciously close to what Kohlberg describes as stages 2 and 3 is at issue only if we believe in a regressive model of adult behavior, otherwise it clearly deserves its own described stage.

V. Social Processes

We have somewhat arbitrarily distinguished for organizational purposes between those contributions which seemed to relate primarily to individual differences in intrapersonal processes and those chapters which specifically addressed themselves to interpersonal processes involving at least dyadic interaction. As for the chapters on personality variables, we will again raise in each case the question of the status of life-span description as well as the nature of the explanation and modification in terms of the relative contributions of historical and concurrent events and their interaction.

Bengtson and Black in their chapter (Chapter 9, this volume) on intergenerational relations and continuities make the central argument that socialization and intergenerational relationships must be viewed at the macro-level in terms of cultural continuity or change within the context of historical time, and at the micro-level in terms of the interpersonal interaction of lineage members within the context of individual developmental time. In line with a historical–sociological vantage point, Bengtson and Black attack the question of developmental change with the full understanding that ontogeny does not occur in an ecological vacuum or a stable environmental context, but in a continuously changing societal frame of reference. Accordingly, on the descriptive level, the existence of life-span change is obvious; if anything is conceptually difficult to derive in this framework, it is a high degree of age-related continuity and stability, which so easily structures the world for most developmental psychologists. Indeed, this immediate recognition of change on an a priori basis is refreshing and provocative in light of the prevalent "nondevelopmental" mood among developmental psychologists (for a similar position see also Neugarten & Datan, Chapter 3, this volume).

Bengtson and Black, however, struggle with aligning developmental concepts formulated on different levels of analysis. Their dealing with history by ontogeny interactions when attempting to explain developmental change is interesting in that they do consider such interactions to involve not only individual but also cohort histories. Thus, we must trace the behavioral patterns of successive generations in order to study cultural continuities and discontinuities at the macro-level, as well as on the micro-level, the specifics of individual ontogeny when attempting to understand the unique outcomes of interage and intergenerational negotiations. Bengtson and Black call attention to four salient issues in delineating the process and outcomes of intergenerational transactions. These are cohort differences in attitudes and behaviors, attitudes towards interaction between successive cohorts, the mobility of cohorts through the social institutions, and cohort succession as a basis for change in the structure and composition of the population. In all these four cases, historical information is not only essential but, due to the prevalence of curvilinear historical trends, it is likely that cohort (history) by age interaction is rather common. Parenthetically, it may be mentioned that recent application of sequential–longitudinal designs to the study of adolescent and adult personality development (Baltes & Nesselroade, 1972; Nesselroade *et al.*, 1972) point to rather dramatic, empirical support for such history by ontogeny interactions.

Of particular interest for the present analysis are apparent time-lag or sleeper effects that emerge in cohort analysis as presented by Bengtson and Black. What is referred to here is, for instance, the tendency toward intensive conflict between adjacent generations arising out of differences in interest, but common, intergenerationally shared phenomena (be they felt isolation from social institution, feelings of powerlessness, or the like) occurring for generations separated more widely in time. It is argued then that the old and the young may share rather common characteristics which do not appear in midlife (Kalish, 1969; Schaie, 1973a) or which tend to reappear due to cyclical phenomena in socio-cultural progression.

On the matter of cohort by ontogenetic change interaction, or in Bengtson and Black's terminology, differential macro- and micro-level relationships, it should be noted that cohort membership can be defined in terms of developmental stage as well as chronological stage. That is the socio-cultural circumstances of a given cohort at a specific age may be more characteristic of a different developmental stage for another cohort. In a life-span context, this phenomenon giving rise to interactions would be particularly noticable when retirement ages are changed, when adolescent dependency is prolonged or shortened, or when socially recommended ages of marriage, or acceptable range of ages between marital partners alter during historical time.

In many ways, Bengtson and Black's final comments on intergenerational con-flicts and cultural change implicitly deal with natural, selective modification at-tempts. They argue that interage and intergenerational systems are likely to per-mit a great deal of experimentation by successive cohorts and age groups and that such natural experimentation will result in the production, testing, and selection of cultural alternatives. From an optimization and prevention perspective, Bengtson and Black's model is an intriguing one, since it introduces a Darwinian variation model into modification considerations. History by ontogeny relationships is clearly part of an exciting area apt to revitalize the classical phylogeny–ontog-eny issue, though this time with a focus on developmental concepts as formulated in the social rather than biological sciences. A life-span perspective makes this reorientation quite natural.

Hartup and Lempers' discussion (Chapter 10, this volume) of family attach-ments, on the level of ontogenetic description, addresses an area that has a definite place in life-span conceptions. In many ways it is surprising that develop-mental psychologists have restricted their attention primarily to the early phases of the family life cycle, since the changing system of family relationships (in-cluding premarital and postmarital interactions) is not only a fascinating subject matter, but also has stimulated a series of developmental conceptions in other psychological circles (e.g., Broderick, 1970 for review; Ahammer, Chapter 11, this volume). Thus, Hartup and Lempers' chapter, while emphasizing work with infants, fits well within the life-span framework emphasizing the need for an interactional analysis of the attachment process at all stages of the life span. Again, on a descriptive level, the regarding of attachment not as a characteristic of the mother or the infant, but as a structural property of the mother–child system, makes this approach fertile for application of developmental considerations including structural transformations such as age-related changes in the number and relationships of the person elements involved. Unfortunately, there appears to be a paucity of relevant data; however, Hartup and Lempers provide some provocative hints on how their concerns and methodological proposals might be extended to adult behaviors and relationships.

Although the analysis of attachment behavior emphasizes concurrent or rather proximal events, and in that sense is ahistorical, it illustrates in a time-compressed manner the importance of previous history and the sequence of organism–environment interchanges in the production of attachment. Time-lag effects tend to appear in the study of attachment in at least two distinct ways. First, we note that early attachment behavior (dyadic gazing) seems not to have direct sequellae, but is necessary, although not sufficient, to induce the mother–child proximity which will later lead to the utilization of vocalization and social activity as a means of interactional behavior. Second, we may note that proximity between parent and offspring is universal in early life, is diminished, and more often than not ceases throughout midlife, but that in old age again becomes close to the norm (Shanas et al., 1968). In this context, Hartup and Lempers point to the fact that attachment may represent several distinct behavioral systems (e.g., adult affectional versus peer affectional system) with divergent or at least separate ontogenetic histories. Obviously, such interpretation invites a life-span perspective and a search for history by experience interactions.

It is hinted that there are enormous generational and subcultural differences in patterns of parent–child proximity as well as the initiation of proximity at various life stages (that is whether parent or child initiates contact). But little is known about such differences at this time, and consequently it is difficult to assess whether and in what way early patterns of attachment establishment may interact with socio-cultural change. This seems to be a particularly fruitful area of inquiry, however, particularly in the presence of an increasing number of alternate child rearing patterns and alternate life styles within our own society. We tend to conclude that it is a life-span focus which facilitates the generation of innovative thinking about this area of research. In fact, we believe that earlier recognition of life-span changes in the field of parent–child research would have prevented child developmentalists from taking for such a long time a sterile, unidirectional, personological approach. The most clear-cut evidence for this conclusion is that a similar paradigm sterility never developed in the area of family relations (see Ahammer, Chapter 11, this volume). In the same vein, one might continue and argue that the dearth of effective modification attempts in the field of parent–child attachments may also be partially due to the long tradition of viewing the parent–child relationship in the framework of unidirectional effect patterns with the parent being the center of action.

While Hartup and Lempers emphasize early childhood as the prototypic life episode for the examination of models of social interaction, Ahammer (Chapter 11, this volume) chooses to examine the utility of social-learning theory in understanding development of interactional behavior in adults. It is argued quite convincingly that social-learning theory is particularly appropriate because it does not contain an a priori concept of development and can therefore consider any age-related phenomenon regardless of the nature of the developmental trend. Also, even more important, no new mechanisms or explanatory principles are required to explain behavior changes of organisms at different ages, thus ensuring at least conceptual continuity over the life span. Obviously, social-learning theory shares this initial persuasiveness with the operant model.

On the level of life-span description, Ahammer presents a persuasive case for the fact that behavioral change in regard to intimate interactional systems (parenthood, marriage) is a pervasive phenomenon; moreover, similar to Hartup and Lempers' view, she emphasizes more discontinuity than continuity aspects, although it is true that people entering into new situations will bring with them experiences from previous relationships, and in that sense knowledge of the organism's previous history is of interest. But Ahammer points out that it is unlikely that partners involved in the solving of new developmental tasks (marriage, post-parenthood, retirement, widowhood, etc.) maintain the same discriminate stimulus patterns and, consequently, new learning has inevitably to occur whenever there is an interaction between previously unacquainted individuals. Historical continuity seems much more important for outcome control. That is, within the interaction process each partner will attempt to shape or control the outcome of the behavior of the other as a function of his previous experience, and also as a function of his effectiveness as a reinforcing agent.

Ahammer's chapter also contains a wealth of information relative to historical explanatory attempts and fragmented pieces that suggest that it is important to consider the nature of reinforcement histories in explanatory attempts since they interact with concurrent learning conditions. This conclusion, incidentally, is similar to a number of trends in operant learning, where the interactive effect of reinforcement histories is increasingly recognized (e.g., Bijou, 1968). For example, Ahammer points out the overwhelming finding that successful (read lasting) marriages are a consequence of similarity in the background and personality traits of the marriage partners, and that behavior change is typically obtained by the more powerful partner in the relationship. Consequently, in traditional marriage patterns the behavior characteristics and power position of the husband will be most highly predictive of marital stability. Likewise, parenthood appears to be most reinforcing to the parent who exerts significant control over his or her offspring, with the price of parenthood becoming increasingly greater as children develop independence. Furthermore, Ahammer points to the important contribution that a developmentally and individual-differences indexed analysis of social reinforcers may have for the modification or maintenance of behaviors.

Social-learning theory also has some contributions to make to the understanding of time lag in behavioral development in conjunction with the often espoused notion of a competence–performance distinction. Ahammer cites the acquisition of instrumental behaviors in childhood via modeling, e.g., learning household skills, values regarding marital interaction, etc., which do not become fully activated until they receive external reinforcement at a later stage. It may be questioned, however, whether sequential–longitudinal studies might not show such time lags to be partially in the nature of cohort by age interactions. In general, though, Ahammer's chapter, both on a conceptual and an empirical level, presents extensive evidence and suggestions for the usefulness of life-span developmental paradigms relative to description, explanation, and modification of social interactions during adulthood.

The final contribution in the section on social processes by Nardi (Chapter 12, this volume) is concerned with a phenomenological, person- and perception-oriented approach to the study of life-span development. Much of the literature reviewed by Nardi has been accumulated in the past few years, and this literature certainly supports the contention that individuals attribute change patterns to all stages of the life span, both under prospective and retrospective instructions. Moreover, it is quite clear that when age-homogeneous and age-heterogeneous perceptions are suitably varied, information is found about stereotypes regarding different age groups which do not at all conform to so-called common sense notions nor to age differences as they are typically observed with objective measures and self-report data. As to the issue of descriptive continuity versus discontinuity, it is interesting to note that continuity and stability (i.e., lack of marked age differences) seem to result when individuals are asked to "perceive" (prospect or retrospect) their own life courses, whereas discontinuity prevails when the task involves the attribution of developmental change to other persons (heteroperception).

Little work has been done to relate historical data to such attribution of developmental change other than the predictive use of demographic variables which may be seen as a sort of historical antecedent. Of course, the recency of this line of research has as yet precluded following changes in perception over time within cohorts with experimental conditions superimposed, the kind of data which would be required to elicit the developmental histories that might lead to an understanding of the development of age–function stereotypes. Similarly, beyond speculative assertions (e.g., Thomae, 1970), little is known about the degree to which age stereotypes and age expectations determine the nature of future change or interact as historical antecedents with concurrent socialization influences. Some interesting interactions, however, between the developmental status of perceivers and perceived emerge from the literature. For example, members of that developmental stage which is in societal control (the middle-aged) are rarely misperceived, while adolescents and the elderly are more often than not described by other age cohorts in terms not shown in self-attribution. Yet what little longitudinal evidence on self-reported personality change is available argues toward stability from adolescence into late adulthood. It will also be enlightening to examine whether knowledge of historical antecedents will facilitate the design of intervention programs which thus far are close to being nonexistent in this rapidly growing area of research.

VI. Conclusions

The primary objectives of this epilogue were to further clarify the rationale of life-span developmental theory by delineating a basic frame of reference for life-span research in developmental psychology, and to relate the various contributions in this volume to such a framework. We can summarize the position emerging from this review as being that in many ways the attempt to formulate a conceptual framework and to examine the evidence that can be marshalled results in more questions than answers. Life-span developmental research is still in its infancy. However, a consoling perspective may be that one of the criteria for judging the usefulness of new theoretical orientations is indeed their potential heuristic fertility and ability to clarify and expand on paradigm questions.

Let us summarize the gist of this epilogue by formulating two sets of conclusions. The first deals with the usefulness of the life-span developmental approach itself; the second with its implications for current development research in general.

A. Rationale for Life-Span Developmental Paradigms

1. A life-span view of development, with regard to the descriptive task, is based on the fact that behavioral change, which can properly be labelled developmental change, is observable at all stages of the life span. The rate, directionality, and sequentiality of such changes depend not upon the age of the organism, but upon the relative degree of stability in the man–environment context relevant to a specific behavior class over a given period of time. A life-span perspective also suggests attention to a joint description of the individual and the environment as changing systems.

2. A life-span view, with regard to developmental explanation, illustrates any developmental approach in its extreme form. Its usefulness is dependent upon the joint action of continuous and discontinuous antecedent-consequent models. In terms of paradigms, the focus is on change rather than stability, on historical (potentially time-lag) relationships, nonhomologous or nonnomothetic principles, history by treatment interactions, and the conjoint analysis of man–environment systems. The deployment of such paradigms will often require

more refined methodology than is currently available such as the utilization of experimental, multivariate strategies, systems analysis, models to intertwine genotypic and phenotypic analysis, and designs that center about the explication of the dynamic interplay between ontogenetic and historical change conditions.

3. In regard to corrective, preventive, and optimizing modification, the life-span view of development draws attention to dramatic modifiability of development at all periods of the life span. In terms of substantive proposals, a life-span view suggests a redistribution of interventive efforts throughout the life span, a much stronger emphasis on massive, molar environmental (and genetic) modification than is currently practiced, and a focus on the consideration of developmental history variables (both in a retrospective and prospective fashion) when designing intervention programs. Finally, a life-span view is apt to stimulate scholarship aimed at prevention and optimization rather than alleviation, particularly with regard to adulthood, advanced age, and noncognitive classes of behavior.

B. Implications for Developmental Psychology

1. The life-span view seems to illustrate the conceptual sterility that age-specific developmental psychology (particularly of the child development type) has imposed on developmental scholarship. There is the widespread focus on the following: personological models both of the organismic and mechanistic type, unidirectional cause–effect patterns, developmental stability rather than change, cognitive classes of behavior, and lack of concern with the assessment of prospective and retrospective behavior outcomes.

2. The life-span view, with an emphasis on methodology, suggests increasing use of alternate methods of data collection. Attention is drawn to the potential fertility of revitalizing phenomenological avenues in order to encapsulate people's conceptions of change; employing not only concurrent but also retrospective and prospective methods of data collection; considering much more carefully issues of measurement equivalence (age-invariance of reliability and validity criteria) and scalability; using sequential rather than simple cross-sectional or longitudinal designs when the measurement of ontogenetic change is at stake; and, finally, to the dramatic need for the development of age-sensitive environmental or man–environment measures.

3. A life-span perspective, with an emphasis on developmental theory construction, suggests formulation of theories and models that are dynamic and nonpersonological. The explicit focus is on models of man–environment relationships that extend far beyond $S-R$ positions which are static rather than dynamic, on models which incorporate notions about individual–society interactions and cultural–biological change parameters, and permit for descriptive and explanatory discontinuities. Recent essays on the usefulness of dialectic models, the developmental emergence and transformation of trait–state phenomena, the separation

of ontogenetic from historical change components, the application of systems theory and cybernetic concepts, and on aligning psychological with sociological conceptions of development are but a few examples for the type of metatheoretical reorientation that life-span developmentalists find challenging and desirable.

C. Prospects

In the thirties, Charlotte Bühler and Sidney W. Pressey and their colleagues more than any others began to explore and chart the course of a "life-span revolution" in developmental psychology. The various contributions to the three volumes generated by the West Virginia Conference Series on Life-Span Developmental Psychology (Goulet & Baltes, 1970; Nesselroade & Reese, 1973; and the present volume) attest to the fact that it appears easier to start a revolution than it is to carry it to impressive heights or even victory. Nevertheless, it is hoped that the progress witnessed is substantial enough to prevent most of the actors and audience from returning to the pre-life-span period; and further, that the spectrum of data, theories, and conclusions presented offers enough in terms of persuasion and fertility to attract more researchers to the laborious, but potentially enlightening process of conducting the type of long-term and dynamic work that is basic to a life-span developmental approach.

In any case, however, the intent of this epilogue is not only to convey vigorous optimism about the unique advantages of a life-span developmental view, but also to alert us to the need for methodological reflection so that the growing spirit surrounding life-span developmental scholarship does not outrun its scientific value. Further discussion and clarification of the paradigms underlying life-span developmental research cannot help but contribute to advances in the field.

ACKNOWLEDGMENTS

The authors would like to thank Margret M. Baltes, Elizabeth M. Barton, Donald H. Ford, William R. Looft, and John R. Nesselroade for their critical reading of a draft version of this manuscript. Their insightful comments, though not always in full agreement with the stance taken, were very helpful in improving the quality of this chapter.

References

Aaronson, B. Personality stereotypes of aging. *Journal of Gerontology,* 1966, **21**, 458–462.

Aaronson, E. Some antecedents of interpersonal attraction. In D. Levine (Ed.), *Nebraska symposium on motivation,* Lincoln: University of Nebraska Press, 1969.

Acheson, D. *Morning and noon.* Boston: Houghton-Mifflin, 1965.

Adelson, J. Personality. *Annual Review of Psychology,* 1969, **20**, 217–252.

Adorno, T. W., Frenkel-Brunswik, E., Levinson, D. J., & Sanford, R.N. *The authoritarian personality.* New York: Harper & Row, 1950.

Ahammer, I. M. Desirability judgments as a function of item content, instructional set, and sex: A life-span developmental study. Unpublished doctoral dissertation, West Virginia University, 1969.

Ahammer, I. M. Alternative strategies for the investigation of age differences. Paper presented at the Regional Meeting of the Southeastern Conference of the Society for Research in Child Development, Athens, Georgia, 1970.

Ahammer, I. M. Desirability judgments as a function of item content, instructional set, and sex. A life-span developmental study. *Human Development,* 1971, **14**, 195–207.

Ahammer, I. M., & Baltes, P. B. Objective versus perceived age differences in personality: How do adolescents, adults, and older people view themselves and each other? *Journal of Gerontology,* 1972, **27**, 46–51.

Ainsworth, M. D. S. Object relations, dependency, and attachment: A theoretical review of the infant-mother relationship. *Child Development,* 1969, **40**, 969–1025.

Ainsworth, M. D. S., & Bell, S. M. Attachment, exploration, and separation: Illustrated by the behavior of one-year-olds in a strange situation. *Child Development,* 1970, **41**, 49–67.

Ajuriaguerra, J. de, Boehme, M., Richard, J., Sinclair, H., & Tissot, R. Désintégration des notions de temps dans les démences dégénératives du grand âge. *Encephale,* 1967, **5**, 385–438.

Alker, H. A. Is personality situationally specific or intrapsychically consistent? *Journal of Personality,* 1972, **40**, 1–16.

Allen, R. E. A study of subjects discussed by elderly patients in group counseling. *Social Casework,* 1962, **43**, 360–366.

Allport, G. W. *Values and our youth. The person in psychology.* Boston: Beacon Press, 1968.

Allport, G. W., & Odbert, H. S. Trait names: A psycho-lexical study. *Psychological Monographs,* 1936, **47**, Whole No. 1.

Allport, G. W., & Vernon, P. E. The field of personality. *Psychological Bulletin,* 1930, **27**, 677–730.

Almy, M., Chittenden, E., & Miller, P. *Young children's thinking*. New York: Teachers College Press, 1966.

Anderson, J. E., Jr. Aging and educational television: A preliminary survey. *Journal of Gerontology*, 1962, **17**, 447–449.

Andersson, B. E., & Ekholm, M. Actual and perceived attitudes among adolescents and adults towards each other: A study of Swedish teenagers and their parents. STUG—Project Report #3, Pedagogiska Institutionen, University of Goteborg, 1971.

Antonovsky, A., Maoz, B., Datan, N., & Wijsenbeek, H. Twenty-five years later: A limited study of sequelae of the concentration camp experience. *Social Psychiatry*, 1971, **6**, 186–193.

Apake, T. K., & Sanger, K. B. The group approach in a general hospital. *Social Work*, 1962, **7**, 59–65.

Appleyard, D. Styles and methods of structuring a city. *Environment and Behavior*, 1970, **2**, 100–117.

Arasteh, J. D. Parenthood: Some antecedents and consequences: A review of the mental health literature. *Journal of Genetic Psychology*, 1971, **118**, 179–202.

Arenberg, D. Anticipation interval and age differences in verbal learning. *Journal of Abnormal Psychology*, 1965, **70**, 419–425.

Aries, P. *Centuries of childhood*. New York: Random House, 1962.

Aronfreed, J. The concept of internalization. In D. A. Goslin (Ed.), *Handbook of socialization theory and research*. Chicago: Rand McNally, 1969.

Ashby, W. R. General systems theory as a new discipline. *General Systems*, 1958, **3**, 1–6.

Axelrod, S., & Eisdorfer, C. Attitudes toward old people: An empirical analysis of the stimulus group validity of the Tuckman-Lorge questionnaire. *Journal of Gerontology*, 1961, **16**, 75–80.

Ayllon, T., & Azrin, N. H. Reinforcement and instructions with mental patients. *Journal of the Experimental Analysis of Behavior*, 1964, **7**, 327–331.

Baer, D. M. An age-irrelevant concept of development. *Merrill-Palmer Quarterly*, 1970, **16**, 230–245.

Baker, F. General systems theory, research, and medical care. In A. Sheldon, F. Baker, & C. P. McLaughlin (Eds.), *Systems and medical care*. Cambridge: MIT Press, 1970.

Baker, F. Measures of ego identity: A multitrait-multimethod validation. *Educational and Psychological Measurement*, 1971, **31**, 165–174.

Baker, F., & Schulberg, C. Community health care-giving systems. In A. Sheldon, F. Baker, & C. P. McLaughlin (Eds.), *Systems and medical care*. Cambridge: MIT Press, 1970.

Baldwin, A. L. *Theories of child development*. New York: Wiley, 1967.

Baldwin, A. L. A cognitive theory of socialization. In D. A. Goslin (Ed.), *Handbook of socialization theory and research*. Chicago: Rand McNally, 1969.

Baldwin, J. M. *Mental development in the child and the race*. New York: MacMillan, 1906.

Bales, R. F. *Interaction process analysis: A method for the study of small groups*. Cambridge: Addison-Wesley Press, 1950.

Baltes, P. B. Longitudinal and cross-sectional sequences in the study of age and generation effects. *Human Development*, 1968, **11**, 145–171.

Baltes, P. B. (Ed.) Strategies for psychological intervention in old age: A symposium. *Gerontologist*, 1973, **13**, 4–36.

Baltes, P. B. (Ed.) Life-span models of psychological intervention in old age: A symposium. *Gerontologist*, in press.

Baltes, P. B., & Goulet, L. R. Status and issues of a life-span developmental psychology. In L. R. Goulet & P. B. Baltes (Eds.), *Life-span developmental psychology: Research and theory*. New York: Academic Press, 1970.

Baltes, P. B., & Goulet, L. R. Exploration of developmental variables by manipulation and simulation of age differences in behavior. *Human Development*, 1971, **14**, 149–170.

Baltes, P. B., & Labouvie, G. V. Adult development of intellectual performance: Description, explanation, modification. In C. Eisdorfer & M. P. Lawton (Eds.), *The psychology of adult development and aging*. Washington, D.C.: American Psychological Association, 1973.

Baltes, P. B., & Nesselroade, J. R. Multivariate longitudinal and cross-sectional sequences for analyzing ontogenetic and generational change: A methodological note. *Developmental Psychology*, 1970, **2**, 163–168.

Baltes, P. B., & Nesselroade, J. R. Cultural change and adolescent personality development. *Developmental Psychology*, 1972, **7**, 244–256.

Baltes, P. B., & Nesselroade, J. R. The developmental analysis of individual differences on multiple measures. In J. R. Nesselroade & H. W. Reese (Eds.), *Life-span developmental psychology: Methodological issues*. New York: Academic Press, 1973.

Bandura, A. *Principles of behavior modification*. New York: Holt, Rinehart & Winston, 1969. (a)

Bandura, A. Social-learning theory of identificatory processes. In D. A. Goslin (Ed.), *Handbook of socialization theory and research*. Chicago: Rand McNally, 1969. (b)

Bandura, A., Grusec, J. E., & Menlove, F. L. Observational learning as a function of symbolization and incentive set. *Child Development*, 1966, **37**, 499–506.

Bandura, A., & Walters, R. W. *Social learning and personality development*. New York: Holt, Rinehart & Winston, 1963.

Barker, R. C. *Ecological psychology: Concepts and methods for studying the environment of human behavior*. Stanford: Stanford University Press, 1968.

Barker, R. G., & Gump, P. V. *Big school, small school*. Stanford: Stanford University Press, 1964.

Barron, F. *Creativity and psychological health*. Princeton: Van Nostrand, 1963.

Barry, W. A. Conflict and marriage: A study of the interactions of newlywed couples in experimentally induced conflicts. Unpublished doctoral dissertation, University of Michigan, 1968.

Barry, W. A. Marriage research and conflict. An integrative view. *Psychological Bulletin*, 1970, **73**, 41–54.

Bartlett, M. S. Internal and external factor analysis. *British Journal of Psychology (Statistical Section)*, 1948, **1**, 73–81.

Baughman, E. E. *Personality: The study of the individual*. Englewood Cliffs: Prentice-Hall, 1972.

Bayley, N. The life-span as a frame of reference in psychological research. *Vita Humana*, 1963, **6**, 125–139.

Bayley, N. Development of mental abilities. In P. H. Mussen (Ed.), *Carmichael's manual of child psychology*. New York: Wiley, 1970.

Bayley, N., & Oden, M. H. The maintenance of intellectual ability in gifted adults. *Journal of Gerontology*, 1955, **10**, 91–107.

Bean, F., & Kerckhoff, A. C. Personality and perception in husband-wife conflicts. *Journal of Marriage and the Family*, 1971, **33**, 351–359.

Beck, C., Sullivan, E., & Porter, N. Effects of a moral discussion program on moral judgment. Unpublished manuscript, Ontario Institute for Study of Education, Toronto, Canada, 1972.

Becker, H. S., & Strauss, A. L. Careers, personality, and adult socialization. In B. L. Neugarten (Ed.), *Middle age and aging: A reader in social psychology*. Chicago: University of Chicago Press, 1968.

Becker, W. C. Consequences of different kinds of parental discipline. In M. L. Hoffman & L. W. Hoffman (Eds.), *Review of child development*. Vol. 1. New York: Russell Sage Foundation, 1964.

Bell, B., Rose, C. L., & Damon, A. The normative aging study: An interdisciplinary and longitudinal study of health and aging. *Aging and Human Development*, 1972, **3**, 5–18.

Bell, R. Q. A reinterpretation of the direction of effects in studies of socialization. *Psychological Review*, 1968, **75**, 81–95.

Bell, R. Q. Stimulus control of parent or caretaker behavior by offspring. *Developmental Psychology*, 1971, **4**, 63–72.

Bell, R. Q., Weller, G. M., & Waldrop, M. F. Newborn and preschooler: Organization of behavior and relation between periods. *Monographs of the Society for Research in Child Development*, 1971, **36**, No. 142.

Bem, D. J. Constructing cross-sectional consistencies in behavior: Some thoughts on Alker's critique of Mischel. *Journal of Personality*, 1972, **40**, 17–26.

Benedict, R. Continuities and discontinuities on cultural conditioning. *Psychiatry*, 1938, **1**, 161–167.

Bengtson, V. L. The generation gap: A review and typology of social-psychological perspectives. *Youth and Society*, 1970, **2**, 7–32.

Bengtson, V. L. The "generation gap": Differences by generation and by sex in perception of parent-child relations. Paper presented at the meeting of the Pacific Psychological Association, Seattle, 1969.

Bengtson, V. L. Inter-age perceptions and the generation gap. *Gerontologist*, 1971, **11**, 85–89.

Bengtson, V. L., & Kuypers, J. A. The drama of generational difference: Perception, reality, and the developmental stake. Paper presented at the Meeting of the American Psychological Association, Miami, 1970.

Bengtson, V. L., & Kuypers, J. A. Generational differences and the developmental stake. *Aging and Human Development*, 1971, **2**, 249–259.

Bengtson, V. L., Olander, E. B., & Haddad, A. E. The generation gap and aging family members. Unpublished manuscript, Andrus Gerontology Center, University of California, 1971.

Bennis, W. G., & Slater, P. E. *The temporary society*. New York: Harper & Row, 1968.

Berberich, J. P. Do the child's responses shape the teaching behavior of adults? *Journal of Experimental Research in Personality*, 1971, **5**, 92–97.

Berger, B. *Looking for America*. Englewood Cliffs: Prentice-Hall, 1971.

Bernard, J. The adjustment of married mates. In H. T. Christensen (Ed.), *Handbook of marriage and the family*. Chicago: Rand McNally, 1964.

Bertalanffy, L. General system theory: A new approach to unity of science. *Human Biology*, 1951, **23**, 303–331.

Biggs, J. B., Fitzgerald, D., & Atkinson, S. M. Convergent and divergent abilities in children and teachers' ratings of competence and certain classroom behaviors. *British Journal of Educational Psychology*, 1971, **41**, 277–286.

Bijou, S. W. Ages, stages, and the naturalization of human development. *American Psychologist*, 1968, **23**, 419–427. (a)

Bijou, S. W. Child behavior and development: A behavioral analysis. *International Journal of Psychology*, 1968, **3**, 221–238. (b)

Bijou, S. W. Reinforcement history and socialization. In R. Hoppe, G. A. Milton & E. C. Simmel (Eds.), *Early experiences and the process of socialization*. New York: Academic Press, 1970.

Bijou, S. W. The critical need for methodological consistency in field and laboratory studies. Paper presented at the First Symposium of the International Society for the Study of Behavior Development, Nijmegen, July, 1971.

Bijou, S. W., & Baer, D. M. *Child Development: A systematic and empirical theory*. Vol. 1. New York: Appleton-Century-Crofts, 1961.

Biller, H. B. *Father, child and sex role*. Lexington, Massachusetts: D. C. Heath, 1971.

Birren, J. E. Principles of research on aging. In J. E. Birren (Ed.), *Handbook of aging and the individual: Psychological and biological aspects*. Chicago: University of Chicago Press, 1959.

Birren, J. E. *The psychology of aging*. Englewood Cliffs: Prentice-Hall, 1964.

Birren, J. E. Toward an experimental psychology of aging. *American Psychologist*, 1970, **25**, 124–135.

Birren, J. E., Gribbin, K. J., & Woodruff, D. S. *Training: Background*. Washington, D. C.: White House Conference on Aging, 1971.

Birren, J. E., & Hess, R. D. (Eds.) Influences of biological, psychological, and social deprivations upon learning and performance. In *Perspectives on Human Deprivation*. Washington, D. C.: USDHEW, Government Printing Office, 1968.

Birren, J. E., & Morrison, D. F. Analysis of the WAIS subtests in relation to age and education. *Journal of Gerontology*, 1961, **16**, 363–369.

Birren, J. E., & Woodruff, D. S. Academic and professional training in the psychology of aging. In C. Eisdorfer and M. P. Lawton (Eds.), *The psychology of adult development and aging*. Washington, D.C.: American Psychological Association, 1973.

Birren, J. E., Woodruff, D. S., & Bergman, S. (Eds.) Research, demonstration, and training: Issues and methodology in social gerontology. *Gerontologist*, 1972, **12**, 49–83.

Bischof, J. *Adult psychology*. New York: Harper & Row, 1969.

Bishop, B. M. Mother-child interaction and the social behavior of children. *Psychological Monographs*, 1951, **65** (11, Whole No. 238).

Black, K. D. Systems theory and the development of the marital relation. Paper presented at the Annual Meeting of the American Sociological Association, New Orleans, Louisiana, August, 1972.

Blatt, M. Change in moral judgment through the classroom discussion process. In L. Kohlberg & E. Turiel (Eds.), *Recent research in moral development*. New York: Holt, Rinehart & Winston, 1973, in press.

Blau, P. M. *Exchange and power in social life*. New York: Wiley, 1964.

Bleuler, E. P. *Textbook of psychiatry*. New York: Dover Publications, 1951.

Block, J. The difference between Q and R. *Psychological Review*, 1955, **62**, 356–358.

Block, J. *The Q-sort method in personality assessment and psychiatric research*. Springfield, Illinois: Thomas, 1961.

Block, J. *Lives through time*. Berkeley: Bancroft Books, 1971.

Blood, R. O., & Wolfe, D. M. *Husbands and wives: The dynamics of married living*. Glencoe, Illinois: Free Press, 1960.

Bloom, M. Life-span analysis: A theoretical framework for behavioral science research. *Human Relations*, 1964, **12**, 538, 554.

Bloom, B. S. *Stability and change in human characteristics*. New York: Wiley, 1964.

Blurton Jones, N. G., & Leach, G. M. Behavior of children and their mothers at separation and greeting. In N. G. Blurton Jones (Ed.), *Ethological studies of child behavior*. London and New York: Basic Books, 1972.

Boersma, F. J., & O'Bryan, K. An investigation of the relationship between creativity and intelligence under two conditions of testing. *Journal of Personality*, 1968, **36**, 341–348.

Bolton, C. Mate selection as a development of a relationship. *Journal of Marriage and the Family*, 1961, **23**, 234–240.

Bortner, R. W., & Hultsch, D. F. Personal time perspective in adulthood. *Developmental Psychology*, 1972, **7**, 98–104.

Botwinick, J. *Cognitive processes in maturity and old age*. New York: Springer, 1967.

Botwinick, J. Learning in children and in older adults. In L. R. Goulet & P. B. Baltes (Eds.), *Life-span developmental psychology: Research and theory*. New York: Academic Press, 1970.

Boulding, K. General systems theory—the skeleton of science. *Management Science*, 1956, **2**, 187–208.

Bowlby, J. *Attachment and loss*. Vol. 1. *Attachment*. New York: Basic Books, 1969.

Boyd, D. A developmental approach to undergraduate ethics. Unpublished doctoral dissertation, Graduate School of Education, Harvard University, 1973.

Boyd, R. D., & Koskela, R. N. A test of Erikson's theory of ego-stage development by means of a self-report instrument. *Journal of Experimental Education*, 1970, **38**, 1–14.

Brandtstadter, J., & Schneewind, K. A. Optimal human development: Psychological aspects. In H. B. Urban & W. R. Looft, (Eds.), *Human development intervention*, in preparation.

Braybrooke, D., & Lindbloom, C. *A strategy of decision*. New York: Free Press, 1963.

Breger, L. The ideology of behaviorism, In L. Breger (Ed.), *Clinical-cognitive psychology: Models and integrations*. Englewood Cliffs: Prentice-Hall, 1969.

Brigham, J. Ethnic stereotypes. *Psychological Bulletin*, 1971, **76**, 15–38.

Brim, O. G. The parent-child relation as a social system: Parent and child roles. *Child Development*, 1957, **28**, 343–364.

Brim, O. G. Adolescent personality as self-other systems. *Journal of Marriage and the Family*, 1965, **27**, 156–162.

Brim, O. G. Socialization through the life cycle. In O. G. Brim & S. Wheeler (Eds.), *Socialization after childhood: Two essays*. New York: Wiley, 1966.

Brim, O. G. Adult socialization. In J. A. Clausen (Ed.), *Socialization and society*. Boston: Little, Brown, & Co., 1968.

Brim, O. G., & Wheeler, S. *Socialization after childhood: Two essays*. New York: Wiley, 1966.

Britton, J. O., & Britton, J. H. Discrimination of age by preschool children. *Journal of Gerontology*, 1969, **24**, 457–460.

Broderick, C. B. Beyond the five conceptual frameworks: A decade of development in family theory. *Journal of Marriage and the Family*, 1971, **33**, 139–159.

Bromley, D. B. *The psychology of human aging*. Baltimore: Penguin, 1966.

Bromley, D. B. Age and sex differences in the serial production of creative conceptual responses. *Journal of Gerontology*, 1967, **22**, 32–42.

Bromley, D. B. An approach to theory construction in the psychology of development and aging. In L. R. Goulet & P. B. Baltes (Eds.), *Life-span developmental psychology: Research and theory*. New York: Academic Press, 1970.

Bronfenbrenner, U. Some familial antecedents of responsibility and leadership in adolescents. In L. Petrullo & B. M. Bass (Eds.), *Leadership and interpersonal behavior*. New York: Holt, Rinehart & Winston, 1961. (a)

Bronfenbrenner, U. Toward a theoretical model for the analysis of parent-child relationships in a social context. In J. C. Glidewell (Ed.), *Parental attitudes and child behavior*. Springfield, Illinois: Thomas, 1961. (b)

Bronfenbrenner, U. The psychological costs of quality and equality in education. *Child Development*, 1967, **38**, 909–926.

Bronfenbrenner, U. *Two worlds of childhood: Child rearing in the U.S.S.R. and in the U.S.A.* New York: Basic Books, 1970.

Bronson, W. C. Stable patterns of behavior: The significance of enduring orientations for personality development. In J. P. Hill (Ed.), *Minnesota symposia on child psychology*. Vol. 2. Minneapolis: University of Minnesota Press, 1969.

Brown, R. The secret drawer: Review of a history of psychology in autobiography. Vol. 5. *Contemporary Psychology*, 1969, **14**, 51–53.

Bruner, J. S., *Toward a theory of instruction*. Cambridge: Harvard University Press, 1966.

Bruner, J. S., Olver, R. R., & Greenfield, P. M. *Studies in cognitive growth*. New York: Wiley, 1966.

Bruner, J. S., & Taguiri, R. The perception of people. In G. Lindzey (Ed.), *Handbook of social psychology*. Vol. 2. Reading, Massachusetts: Addison-Wesley, 1954.

Bry, P. M., & Nawas, M. M. Rigidity: A function of reinforcement history. *Perceptual and Motor Skills*, 1969, **29**, 118.

Buckley, W. *Sociology and modern systems theory*. Englewood Cliffs: Prentice-Hall, 1967.

Buckley, W. (Ed.) *Modern systems research for the behavioral scientist*. Chicago: Aldine, 1968.

Bühler, C. Maturation and motivation. *Personality*, 1951, **1**, 184–211.

Bühler, C. The curve of life as studies in biographies. *Journal of Applied Psychology*, 1953, **19**, 405–409.

Bühler, C. *Der menschliche Lebenslauf als psychologisches Problem.* (1st ed.) Leipzig: Hirzel, 1933. (2nd ed.) Goettingen: Verlag fuer Psychologie, 1959.

Bühler, C. Meaningful living in the mature years. In R. W. Kleemeier (Ed.), *Aging and leisure.* New York: Oxford University Press, 1961.

Bühler, C. Genetic aspects of the self. *Annals of the New York Academy of Sciences,* 1962, **96,** 730–764. (a)

Bühler, C. *Psychologie im Leben unserer Zeit.* Munich: Droemer-Knaur, 1962. (b)

Bühler, C., & Massarik, F. (Eds.) *The course of human life.* New York: Springer, 1968.

Burgess, E. W., & Cottrell, L. S. *Predicting success and failure in marriage.* Englewood Cliff, N. J.: Prentice-Hall, 1939.

Butler, R. N. Toward a psychiatry of the life-cycle: Implications of socio-psychological studies of the aging process for the psychotherapeutic situation. *Psychiatric Research Report,* 1968, **23,** 233–248.

Byrne, D. Attitudes and attraction. In L. Berkowitz (Ed.), *Advances in experimental social psychology.* Vol. 4. New York: Academic Press, 1969.

Cain, L. D., Jr. Age status and generational phenomena: The new old people in contemporary America. *Gerontologist,* 1967, **7,** 83–92.

Cameron, P. The generation gap: Beliefs about adult stability of life. *Journal of Gerontology,* 1971, **26,** 81.

Campbell, D. T., & Fiske, D. W. Convergent and discriminant validation by the multitrait-multimethod matrix. *Psychological Bulletin,* 1959, **56,** 81–105.

Campbell, E. Adolescent socialization. In D. A. Goslin (Ed.), *Handbook of socialization theory and research.* Chicago: Rand McNally, 1969.

Campbell, E. Q. The internalization of moral norms. *Sociometry,* 1964, **27,** 391–412.

Campbell, F. L. Demographic factors in family organizations. Unpublished doctoral dissertation, University of Michigan, 1967.

Carlson, R. Sex differences in ego functioning: Exploratory studies of agency and communion. *Journal of Consulting and Clinical Psychology,* 1971, **37,** 267–277.

Carlson, R. Understanding women: Implications for personality theory and research. *Journal of Social Issues,* 1972, **28,** 17–32.

Carnegie Commission on Higher Education. *Less time, more options.* New York: McGraw-Hill, 1971.

Carson, R. C. *Interaction concepts of personality.* Chicago: Aldine, 1969.

Cartter, A. M. Scientific manpower for 1970-1985. *Science,* 1971, **172,** 132–140.

Cassirer, E. *The philosophy of symbolic forms.* Vol. 3. New Haven: Yale University Press, 1955.

Cattell, R. B. *The description and measurement of personality.* New York: World Book, 1946.

Cattell, R. B. *Personality: A systematic theoretical and factual study.* New York: McGraw-Hill, 1950.

Cattell, R. B. The three basic factor-analytic research designs—their interrelations and derivatives. *Psychological Bulletin,* 1952, **49,** 499–520.

Cattell, R. B. *Personality and motivation structure and measurement.* New York: World Book, 1957.

Cattell, R. B. *The scientific analysis of personality.* London: Penguin, 1965.

Cattell, R. B. Comparing factor trait and state scores across ages and cultures. *Journal of Gerontology,* 1969, **24,** 348–360.

Cattell, R. B. Separating endogenous, exogenous, and ecogenic component curves in developmental data. *Developmental Psychology,* 1970, **3,** 151–162 (a).

Cattell, R. B. (Ed.) *Handbook of modern personality theory.* Chicago: Aldine, 1970 (b).

Cattell, R. B. The integration of functional and psychometric requirements in a quantitative and computerized diagnostic system. In A. R. Mahrer (Ed.), *New approaches to personality classification.* New York: Columbia University Press, 1970 (c).

Cattell, R. B. *Abilities; Their structure, growth and action*. Boston: Houghton-Mifflin, 1971.

Chapanis, A. *Man-machine engineering*. Belmont: Wadsworth, 1965.

Chapple, E. D., & Arsenberg, C. M. Measuring human relations: An introduction to the study of the interaction of individuals. *Genetic Psychology Monographs*, 1940, **22**, 3–147.

Charles, D. C. Historical antecedents of life-span developmental psychology. In L. R. Goulet & P. B. Baltes, (Eds.), *Life-span developmental psychology: Research and theory*. New York: Academic Press, 1970.

Charles, D. C. The older learner. *Educational Forum*, 1971, **35**, 227–233.

Charles, D. C. Comments on papers by Labouvie, Hoyer, and Gottesman. *Gerontologist*, 1973, **13**, 36–38. (a)

Charles, D. C. Explaining intelligence in adulthood: The role of life history. In P. B. Baltes (Ed.), Life-span models of psychological aging: A symposium. *Gerontologist*, 1973, in press. (b)

Charlesworth, R., & Hartup, W. W. Positive social reinforcement in the nursery school peer group. *Child Development*, 1967, **38**, 993–1002.

Child, I. L. Socialization. In G. Lindzey (Ed.), *The handbook of social psychology*. Cambridge: Addison-Wesley, 1954.

Childe, G. *Social evolution*. London: Collins, 1963.

Chilman, C., & Meyer, D. L. Single and married undergraduates measured personality needs and self-rated happiness. *Journal of Marriage and the Family*, 1966, **28**, 67–76.

Chown, S. M. Age and the rigidities. *Journal of Gerontology*, 1961, **16**, 353–362.

Chown, S. M. Personality and aging. In K. W. Schaie (Ed.), *Theory and methods of research on aging*. Morgantown, West Virginia: West Virginia University Library, 1968.

Christensen, P. R., Guilford, J. P., & Wilson, R. C. Relations of creative responses to working time and instructions. *Journal of Experimental Psychology*, 1957, **53**, 82–88.

Ciaccio, N. V. A test of Erikson's theory of ego epigenesis. *Developmental Psychology*, 1971, **4**, 306–311.

Clausen, J. A. (Ed.) *Socialization and society*. Boston: Little, Brown & Company, 1968.

Clausen, J. A. The life-course of individuals. In M. W. Riley, *et al.*, (Eds.), *A sociology of age stratification*. New York: Russell Sage Foundation, 1972.

Clifford, G. J. Essay on the autobiography of Sidney L. Pressey. In R. J. Havighurst (Ed.), *Leaders in American education*. Chicago: University of Chicago Press, 1971.

Coan, R. W. Child personality and developmental psychology. In R. B. Cattell (Ed.), *Handbook of multivariate experimental psychology*. Chicago: Rand McNally, 1966.

Coates, B., Anderson, E. P., & Hartup, W. W. Interrelations in the attachment behavior of human infants. *Developmental Psychology*, 1972, **6**, 218–230. (a)

Coates, B., Anderson, E. P., & Hartup, W. W. The stability of attachment behavior in the human infant. *Developmental Psychology*, 1972, **6**, 231–237. (b)

Colby, A. Relations between logical and moral development. In L. Kohlberg & E. Turiel (Eds.), *Recent research in moral development*. New York: Holt, Rinehart & Winston, 1973, in press.

Comalli, P. E., Jr. Cognitive functioning in a group of 80–90 year old men. *Journal of Gerontology*, 1965, **20**, 14–17.

Comalli, P. E., Jr. Life-span changes in visual perception. In L. R. Goulet & P. B. Baltes (Eds.), *Life-span developmental psychology: Research and theory*. New York: Academic Press, 1970.

Comalli, P. E., Jr., Krus, D. M., & Wapner, S. Cognitive functioning in two groups of aged: One institutionalized, the other living in the community. *Journal of Gerontology*, 1965, **20**, 9–13.

Comalli, P. E., Jr., Wapner, S., & Werner, H. Interference effects of Stroop color-word test in childhood, adulthood, and aging. *Journal of Genetic Psychology*, 1962, **100**, 47–53.

Conrad, K. *Der Konstitutionstypus*. Berlin: Springer, 1963.

Constantinople, A. An Eriksonian measure of personality development in college students. *Developmental Psychology*, 1969, **1**, 357–372.

Cooley, W. W., & Lohnes, P. R. *Multivariate data analysis.* New York: Wiley, 1971.

Corsini, R. J. Multiple predictors of marital happiness. *Marriage and Family Living,* 1956, **18**, 240–242.

Cowdry, E. V. *Problems of aging.* Baltimore: Williams & Wilkins, 1942.

Crandall, V. J., & Sinkeldam, C. Children's dependent and achievement behaviors in social situations and their perceptual field dependence. *Journal of Personality,* 1964, **32**, 1–22.

Cronbach, L. J. Correlation between persons as a research tool. In O. H. Mowrer (Ed.), *Psychotherapy: Theory and research.* New York: Ronald Press, 1953.

Cropley, A. J., & Maslany, G. W. Reliability and factorial validity of the Wallach-Kogan creativity tests. *British Journal of Psychology,* 1969, **60**, 395–398.

Cryns, A., & Monk, A. Attitudes of the aged toward the young: A multivariate study in intergenerational perception. *Journal of Gerontology,* 1972, **27**, 107–112.

Cumming, E., & Henry, W. E. *Growing old: The process of disengagement.* New York: Basic Books, 1961.

Dahlstrom, W. G. Personality. *Annual Review of Psychology,* 1970, **21**, 1–48.

D'Andrade, R. G. Sex differences and cultural institutions. In E. Maccoby (Ed.), *The development of sex differences.* Stanford: Stanford University Press, 1966.

David, M., & Appell, G. A. A study of nursing care and nurse-infant interaction. In B. M. Foss (Ed.), *Determinants of infant behavior.* London: Methuen, 1961.

Davis, K. The sociology of parent-youth conflict. *American Sociological Review,* 1940, **5**, 523–535.

Davis, R. H. Television and the older adult. *Journal of Broadcasting,* 1971, **15**, 153–160.

Davis, R. H. A descriptive study of television in the lives of an elderly population. Unpublished doctoral dissertation, University of Southern California, 1972.

Dean, D. G. Emotional maturity and marital adjustment. *Journal of Marriage and the Family,* 1966, **28**, 454–457.

Demone, H., & Harshbarger, D. *The planning and administration of human services.* New York: Behavioral Publications, 1973, in press.

Demos, J., & Demos, V. Adolescence in historical perspective. *Journal of Marriage and the Family,* 1969, **31**, 632–638.

Dennis, W. Age and achievement: A critique. *Journal of Gerontology,* 1956, **11**, 331–333.

Dennis, W. The age decrement in outstanding scientific contributions: Fact or artifact? *American Psychologist,* 1958, **13**, 457–460.

Dennis, W. Creative productivity between the ages of 20 and 80 years. *Journal of Gerontology,* 1966, **21**, 1–8.

Dennis, W., & Mallinger, B. Animism and related tendencies in senescence. *Journal of Gerontology,* 1948, **4**, 218–221.

Deutsch, H. *The psychology of women.* Vol. 1. *Girlhood.* New York: Grune & Stratton, 1944.

Deutsch, H. *The psychology of women.* Vol. 2. *Motherhood.* New York: Grune & Stratton, 1945.

Deutsch, N., & Krauss, R. M. *Theories in social psychology.* New York: Basic Books, 1965.

De Vries, R. Constancy of generic identity in the years three to six. *Monographs of the Society for Research in Child Development,* 1969, **34**, (Whole No. 3, Serial No. 127).

Dohrnwend, B. P. The social psychological nature of stress: A framework for causal inquiry. *Journal of Abnormal and Social Psychology,* 1961, **62**, 294–302.

Dohrnwend, B. P., & Dohrnwend, B. S. *Social status and psychological disorder: A causal inquiry.* New York: Wily, 1969.

Donahue, W. T. Learning, motivation, and education of the aging. In J. E. Anderson (Ed.), *Psychological aspects of aging.* Washington, D. C.: American Psychological Association, 1956.

Downs, R. M. The cognitive structure of an urban shopping center. *Environment and Behavior,* 1970, **2**, 13–39.

Drake, J. T. Some factors influencing students' attitudes toward older people. *Social Forces,* 1957,

35, 266–271.

Dubin, R., & Dubin, E. R. Children's social perceptions: A review of research. *Child Development,* 1965, **36**, 809–838.

Durkheim, E. *Les règles de la méthode sociologigue.* Paris: Alcan, 1927.

Durkheim, E. *Suicide.* Translated by J. A. Spaulding & G. Simpson. Glencoe, Ill.: Free Press, 1951.

Dyer, E. Parenthood as crisis: A restudy. *Marriage and Family Living,* 1963, **25**, 196–201.

Dyer, G. B. Continuity and discontinuity of development in the equilibrium model. *Journal of General Psychology,* 1971, **84**, 201–211.

Eisdorfer, C. Verbal learning response time in the aged. *Journal of Genetic Psychology,* 1965, **107**, 15–22.

Eisdorfer, C., & Altrocchi, J. A comparison of attitudes toward old age and mental illness. *Journal of Gerontology,* 1961, **16**, 340–343.

Eisenberg, L. The *human* nature of human nature. *Science,* 1972, **176**, 123–128.

Eisenstadt, S. N. *From generation to generation: Age groups and social structure.* Glencoe, Illinois: Free Press, 1956.

Eklund, L. Aging and the field of education. In M. W. Riley, J. W. Riley, Jr., M. E. Johnson, A. Foner, & B. Hess (Eds.), *Aging and society:* Vol. 2. *Aging and the professions.* New York: Russell Sage Foundation, 1969.

Elder, G. H., Jr. *Children of the great depression.* New York: Markham Press, 1973, in press.

Elkind, D. Exploitation and the generational conflict. *Mental Hygiene,* 1970, **54**, 490–497.

Emmerich, W. Young children's discriminations of parent and child roles. *Child Development,* 1959, **30**, 403–419.

Emmerich, W. Family role concepts of children ages six to ten. *Child Development,* 1961, **32**, 609–624.

Emmerich, W. Continuity and stability in early social development. *Child Development,* 1964, **35**, 311–332.

Emmerich, W. Stability and change in early personality development. *Young Children,* 1966, **21**, 233–243.

Emmerich, W. Personality development and concepts of structure. *Child Development,* 1968, **39**, 671–690.

Emmerich, W. Models of continuity and change in development. Paper presented at the Biennial Meeting of the Society for Research in Child Development, Santa Monica, California, March, 1969. (a)

Emmerich, W. Models of continuity and change in development. *Disadvantaged children and their first school experiences: From theory to operations.* Princeton: Educational Testing Service, 1969. PR-69-12. (b)

Emmerich, W. The parental role: A functional-cognitive approach. *Monographs of the Society for Research in Child Development,* 1969, **34**, (Whole No. 8, Serial No. 132). (c)

Emmerich, W. *Disadvantaged children and their first school experiences: Structure and development of personal-social behaviors in preschool settings.* Princeton: Educational Testing Service, 1971. PR-71-20.

Emmerich, W., Goldman, K. S., & Shore, R. E. Differentiation and development of social norms. *Journal of Personality and Social Psychology,* 1971, **18**, 323–353.

Erikson, E. H. *Childhood and society.* New York: Norton, 1950, 1963.

Erikson, E. H. *The young man Luther.* New York: Norton, 1958.

Erikson, E. H. Identity and the life cycle. *Psychological Issues,* 1959, **1**, Whole No. 1.

Erikson, E. H. *Insight and responsibility.* New York: Norton, 1964.

Erikson, E. H. *The challenge of youth.* Garden City, New York: Doubleday, 1965.

Erikson, E. H. *Gandhi's truth on the origins of militant nonviolence.* New York: Norton, 1969.

Eysenck, H. J. The science of personality: Nomethetic? *Psychological Review,* 1954, **61**, 339–342.

Eysenck, H. J. *The structure of human personality.* London: Methuen, 1970.

Eysenck, H. J., & Eysenck, S. B. G. *Personality structure and measurement.* San Diego: Knapp, 1969.

Fagot, B. The effect of sex of child upon social interaction and sex role behavior in a nursery school setting. Unpublished doctoral dissertation, University of Oregon, 1967.

Farberow, N. L. *Suicide: Psychological aspects.* New York: Crowell, Collier & Macmillan, 1968.

Faris, R. E., & Dunham, H. W. *Mental disorders in urban areas: An ecological study of schizophrenia and other psychoses.* Chicago: Chicago University Press, 1939.

Ferguson, L. R. *Personality development.* Belmont, California: Brooks Cole, 1970.

Feuer, L. *The conflict of generations: The character and significance of student movements.* New York: Basic Books, 1969.

Finch, C. Modifying biological system functioning and development. In H. B. Urban & W. R. Looft (Eds.), *Human development intervention,* in preparation.

Fiske, D. W. *Measuring the concepts of personality.* Chicago: Aldine, 1971.

Flacks, R. *Youth and social change.* Chicago: Markham, 1971.

Flavell, J. H. Cognitive changes in adulthood. In L. R. Goulet & P. B. Baltes (Eds.), *Life-span developmental psychology: Research and theory.* New York: Academic Press, 1970.

Flavell, J. H. Stage-related properties of cognitive development. *Cognitive Psychology,* 1971, **2,** 421–453.

Flavell, J. H. An analysis of cognitive-developmental sequences. *Genetic Psychology Monographs,* 1972, in press.

Flavell, J. H., & Wohlwill, J. F. Formal and functional aspects of cognitive development. In D. Elkind & J. H. Flavell (Eds.), *Studies in cognitive development: Essays in honor of Jean Piaget.* New York: Oxford University Press, 1969.

Foa, U. G. Convergences in the analysis of the structure of interpersonal behaviors. *Psychological Review,* 1961, **68,** 341–353.

Foucault, M. *The order of things: An archaeology of the human sciences.* New York: Random House, 1970.

Fowler, J. Toward a developmental perspective on religious faith. Unpublished manuscript, Harvard University Divinity School, 1972.

Freedle, R., & Lewis, M. Application of Markov processes to the concept of state. Unpublished Research Bulletin No. RB-71-34, Educational Testing Service, Princeton, 1971.

Freud, S. *Moses and monotheism.* Translated by K. Jones. New York: Knopf, 1939.

Freud, S. *On narcissism: An introduction.* London: Hogarth Press, 1957.

Freud, S. *Introductory lectures on psychoanalysis.* London: Hogarth Press, 1963. (Also published under the title *A general introduction to psychoanalysis* by Liveright Publishing Corporation, New York.)

Freudenberg, R. K., Jenkins, V. M., & Robertson, J. P. S. Personal stress in relation to psychiatric diagnosis and treatment. *Archives of General Psychiatry,* 1956, **76,** 215–219.

Friedenberg, E. Z. Current patterns of generational conflict. *Journal of Social Issues,* 1969, **25,** 21–38. (a)

Friedenberg, E. Z. The generation gap. *Annals of the American Academy of Political and Social Science,* 1969, **382,** 32–42. (b)

Fritz, B. Relations between formal-operational thought and moral judgment development. In L. Kohlberg & E. Turiel (Eds.), *Recent research in moral development.* New York: Holt, Rinehart & Winston, 1973.

Furry, C. A., & Baltes, P. B. The effect of age differences in ability-extraneous performance variables on the assessment of intelligence in children, adults, and the elderly. *Journal of Gerontology,* 1973, **28,** 73–80.

Gagné, R. M. Contributions of learning to human development. *Psychological Review,* 1968, **75,** 177–191.

Galton, F. *Inquiries into human faculty and its development.* London: MacMillan, 1883.

Gamson, Z. F., Goodman, J., & Gurin, G. Radicals, moderates, and bystanders during a university protest. Paper presented at the Meeting of the American Sociological Association, San Francisco, August, 1967.

Gans, H. J. *The urban villagers*. New York: Free Press, 1962.

Garber, D. L. Retired soldiers in second careers: Self-assessed change, reference group salience, and psychological well-being. Unpublished doctoral dissertation, University of Southern California, 1971.

Gardner, R., Rodensky, R., & Kirby, D. Ethnic stereotypes: A critical review. Department of Psychology Research Bulletin No. 157, University of Western Ontario, July, 1970.

Gardner, R. W. Cognitive styles in categorizing behavior. *Journal of Personality*, 1953, **22**, 214–233.

Gardner, R. W., Holzman, P. S., Klein, G. S., Linton, H. B., & Spence, D. P. Cognitive control: A study of individual consistencies in cognitive behavior. *Psychological Issues*, 1959, **1**, (Monograph 4).

Gardner, R. W., & Moriarty, A. E. *Personality development at preadolescence*. Seattle: University of Washington Press, 1968.

Gardner, R. W., & Schoen, R. A. Differentiation and abstraction in concept formation. *Psychological Monographs*, 1962, **76**, (41, Whole No. 560).

Gavron, H. *The captive wife*. London: Routledge & Kegen Paul, 1966.

Geiken, K. F. Expectations concerning husband-wife responsibilities in the home. *Journal of Marriage and the Family*, 1964, **26**, 349–352.

Gellert, E. The effect of changes in group composition on the dominant behavior of young children. *British Journal of Social and Clinical Psychology*, 1962, **1**, 168–181.

Gelwicks, L. E., Feldman, A. G., & Newcomer, R. J. Report on older population needs, resources, and services: Los Angeles County model neighborhood. Los Angeles: Andrus Gerontology Center, University of Southern California, 1971.

Gewirtz, J. L. A learning analysis of the effects of normal stimulation, privation and deprivation on the acquisition of social motivation and attachment. In B. M. Foss (Ed.), *Determinants of infant behavior*. London: Methuen, 1961.

Gewirtz, J. L. Mechanisms of social learning: Some roles of stimulation and behavior in early human development. In D. A. Goslin (Ed.), *Handbook of socialization theory and research*. Chicago: Rand McNally, 1969. (a)

Gewirtz, J. L. Levels of conceptual analysis in environment-infant interaction research. *Merrill-Palmer Quarterly*, 1969, **15**, 7–41. (b)

Gewirtz, J. L. Some contextual determinants of stimulus potency. In R. D. Parke (Ed.), *Recent trends in social learning theory*. New York: Academic Press, 1972.

Gewirtz, J. L., & Gewirtz, H. B. Caretaking settings, background events and behavior differences in four Israeli child-rearing environments: Some preliminary trends. In B. M. Foss (Ed.), *Determinants of infant behavior*. Vol. 4. London: Methuen, 1969.

Ghiselin, B. (Ed.) *The creative process*. New York: Mentor, 1955.

Gibbs, J. P. Some demographic characteristics of urbanization. In J. P. Gibbs (Ed.), *Urban research methods*. New York: Van Nostrand, 1961.

Glick, P. C., Heer, D. M., & Beresford, J. C. Family formation and family composition: Trends and prospects. In M. B. Sussman (Ed.), *Sourcebook in marriage and the family*. New York: Houghton-Mifflin, 1963.

Glixman, A. F. Categorizing behavior as a function of meaning domain. *Journal of Personality and Social Psychology*, 1965, **2**, 370–377.

Goertzel, T. Generational conflict and social change. *Youth and Society*, 1972, **3**, 327–352.

Golde, P., & Kogan, N. A sentence completion procedure for assessing attitudes toward old people. *Journal of Gerontology*, 1959, **14**, 355–363.

Goodenough, D. R., & Eagle, C. J. A modification of the embedded-figures test for use with young children. *Journal of Genetic Psychology*, 1963, **103**, 67–74.

Goodenough, F., & Tyler, L. E. *Developmental psychology*. New York: Appleton-Century-Crofts,

1959.

Goodnow, J. J. Problems in research on culture and thought. In D. Elkind & J. H. Flavell (Eds.), *Studies in cognitive development: Essays in honor of Jean Piaget*. New York: Oxford University Press, 1969.

Goodrich, W., Ryder, R. G., & Rausch, H. L. Patterns of newlywed marriage. *Journal of Marriage and the Family*, 1968, **30**, 385–390.

Goslin, D. A. (Ed.) *Handbook of socialization theory and research*. Chicago: Rand McNally, 1969.

Goulet, L. R. The interfaces of acquisition: Models and methods for studying the active, developing organism. In J. R. Nesselroade & H. W. Reese (Eds.), *Life-span developmental psychology: Methodological issues*. New York: Academic Press, 1973.

Goulet, L. R., & Baltes, P. B. (Eds.) *Life-span developmental psychology: Research and theory*. New York: Academic Press, 1970.

Granick, S., & Friedman, A. S. The effect of education on the decline of psychometric test performance with age. *Journal of Gerontology*, 1967, **22**, 191–195.

Granick, S., & Friedman, A. S. The influence of education on the maintenance of intellectual functioning in the aged. Paper presented at the 78th Annual Meeting of the American Psychological Association, September, 1970.

Gray, S. W. Masculinity-femininity in relation to anxiety and social acceptance. *Child Development*, 1957, **28**, 203–214.

Griffitt, W. Attitude-invoked anticipatory responses and attraction. *Psychonomic Science*, 1969, **14**, 153–155.

Griffitt, W., Nelson, J., & Littlepage, G. Old age and response to agreement-disagreement. *Journal of Gerontology*, 1972, **27**, 269–274.

Grinder, R. E. *A history of genetic psychology*. New York: Wiley, 1967.

Groffmann, K. J. Life-span developmental psychology in Europe: Past and present. In L. R. Goulet & P. B. Baltes (Eds.), *Life-span developmental psychology: Research and theory*. New York: Academic Press, 1970.

Guilford, J. P. *The nature of human intelligence*. New York: McGraw-Hill, 1967.

Gurin, G., Veroff, J., & Feld, S. *Americans view their mental health*. New York: Basic Books, 1960.

Gutmann, D. The country of old men: Cross-cultural studies in the psychology of later life. Occasional Papers in Gerontology, No. 5, University of Michigan—Wayne State Institute of Gerontology, 1969.

Haddad, A. A. Family vertical solidarity and mental health in Lebanon. Unpublished doctoral dissertation, University of Southern California, 1971.

Hall, E. T. Proxemics: The study of man's spatial relations. In I. Galdston (Ed.), *Man's image in medicine and anthropology*. New York: International University Press, 1963.

Hall, G. S. *Adolescence*. New York: Appleton-Century-Crofts, 1904. 2 vols.

Hall, G. S. *Senescence: The last half of life*. New York: Appleton-Century-Crofts, 1922.

Hallenbeck, P. N. An analysis of power dynamics in marriage. *Journal of Marriage and the Family*, 1966, **28**, 200–203.

Hamilton, G. V. Changes in personality and psychosexual pehnomena with age. In E. V. Cowdry (Ed.), *Problems of aging*. Baltimore: Williams & Wilkins, 1942.

Hampson, J. L. Determinants of psychosexual orientation. In F. A. Beach (Ed.), *Sex and behavior*. New York: Wiley, 1965.

Harper, L. V. The young as a source of stimuli controlling caretaker behavior. *Developmental Psychology*, 1971, **4**, 73–88.

Harris, D. B. Problems in formulating a scientific concept of development. In D. B. Harris (Ed.), *The concept of development*. Minneapolis: University of Minnesota Press, 1957.

Harshbarger, D. Environmental turbulance and limited resources in Human Service Organizations:

The basis for a predictive model of communication patterns. Paper presented at the Symposium on Systems Approaches to Community Problems, Annual Meeting of the American Psychological Association, Washington, D. C., September, 1971. (a)

Harshbarger, D. Toward ecological intervention. *Journal of Environmental Health,* 1971, **34,** 311–315. (b)

Hartley, R. E. Children's concepts of male and female roles. *Merrill-Palmer Quarterly,* 1960, **6,** 83–91.

Hartup, W. W. Peer interaction and social organization. In P. H. Mussen (Ed.), *Carmichael's manual of child psychology.* Vol. 2. New York: Wiley, 1970.

Hartup, W. W., & Coates, B. The role of imitation in childhood socialization. In R. A. Hoppe, E. C. Simmel, & G. A. Milton (Eds.), *Early experiences and the processes of socialization.* New York: Academic Press, 1970.

Hatfield, J. S., Ferguson, L. R., & Alpert, R. Mother-child interaction and the socialization process. *Child Development,* 1967, **38,** 365–414.

Hauser, P. M. The chaotic society: Product of the social, morphological revolution. Presidential Address, 63rd Annual Meeting of the American Sociological Association, Boston, August, 1968.

Havighurst, R. J. *Developmental tasks and education.* New York: David McKay, 1948, 1952, 1972.

Havighurst, R. J. *Human development and education.* New York: David McKay, 1953.

Havighurst, R. J. Research on developmental task concept. *School Review,* 1956, **64,** 215–223.

Havighurst, R. J. Personality and patterns of aging. *Gerontologist,* 1968, **8,** 20–23.

Havighurst, R. J. (Ed.) *Leaders in American education.* Chicago: University of Chicago Press, 1971.

Havighurst, R. J., Neugarten, B. L., & Tobin, S. S. Disengagement and patterns of aging. In B. L. Neugarten (Ed.), *Middle age and aging: A reader in social psychology.* Chicago: University of Chicago Press, 1968.

Hawley, A. *Human ecology.* New York: Ronald Press, 1950.

Heberle, R. The problem of political generations. In R. Heberle (Ed.), *Social movements: An introduction to political sociology.* New York: Appleton-Century-Crofts, 1951.

Heer, D. M. The measurement and bases of family power. *Marriage and Family Living,* 1963, **25,** 133–139.

Heider, F. *The psychology of interpersonal relations.* New York: Wiley, 1958.

Heilbrun, A. B. The measurement of identification. *Child Development,* 1965, **36,** 111–127. (a)

Heilbrun, A. B. An empirical test of the modeling theory of sex-role learning. *Child Development,* 1965, **36,** 789–799. (b)

Heise, D., & Roberts, E. The development of role knowledge. *Genetic Psychology Monographs,* 1970, **82,** 83–115.

Hess, R. D. Social class and ethnic influences on socialization. In P. H. Mussen (Ed.), *Carmichael's manual of child psychology.* Vol. 2. New York: Wiley, 1970.

Hetherington, E. M. A developmental study of the effects of sex of the dominant parent on sex-role preference, identification, and imitation in children. *Journal of Personality and Social Psychology,* 1965, **2,** 188–194.

Hetherington, E. M. The effects of familial variables on sex typing, on parent-child similarity, and on imitation in children. In J. P. Hill (Ed.), *Minnesota symposia on child psychology.* Minneapolis: Lund Press, 1967.

Hickey, J. Changes in moral judgment through a prison intervention. In L. Kohlberg & E. Turiel (Eds.), *Recent research in moral development.* New York: Holt, Rinehart & Winston, 1973, in press.

Hickey, T., Hickey, L. A., & Kalish, R. A. Children's perceptions of the elderly. *Journal of Genetic Psychology,* 1968, **112,** 227–235.

Hickey, T., & Kalish, R. A. Perceptions of adults. *Journal of Gerontology,* 1968, **23,** 215–220.

Higgins–Trenk, A. An adolescent is an adolescent is an adolescent: Stereotype or reality? Unpublished master's thesis, University of Wisconsin, 1972.

Hill, R., & Aldous, J. Socialization for marriage and parenthood. In D. A. Goslin (Ed.), *Handbook of socialization theory and research.* Chicago: Rand McNally, 1969.

Hill, R., & Rodgers, R. H. The developmental approach. In H. T. Christensen (Ed.), *Handbook of marriage and the family.* Chicago: Rand McNally, 1964.

Himmelweit, H. T. *Television and the child.* London: Oxford University Press, 1958.

Hinkle, L. E., Jr. Studies of human ecology in relation to health and behavior. *Bioscience,* 1965, **15**, 517–522.

Hixson, I. E. Nonthreatening education for older adults. *Adult Leadership Magazine,* 1969, **18**, 84–85.

Hobbs, D. F. Parenthood as crisis: A third study. *Journal of Marriage and the Family,* 1965, **27**, 367–372.

Hobbs, D. F. Transition to parenthood: A replication and an extension. *Journal of Marriage and the Family,* 1968, **30**, 413–417.

Hoffman, M. L. Moral development. In P. H. Mussen (Ed.), *Carmichael's manual of child psychology.* Vol. 2. New York: Wiley, 1970.

Hofstatter, P. R. Tatsachen und Probleme einer Psychologie des Lebenslaufs. *Zeitschrift fur Angewandte Psychologie und Charakterkunde,* 1938, **53**, 274–333.

Holland, J. L. Some limitations of teacher ratings as predictors of creativity. *Journal of Educational Psychology,* 1959, **50**, 219–223.

Hollingshead, A. B., & Redlich, F. C. *Social class and mental illness.* New York: Wiley, 1958.

Holter, H. *Sex roles and social structure.* Oslo, Norway: Universitets-forlaget, 1970.

Homans, G. C. *The human group.* New York: Harcourt, Brace & World, 1950.

Honzik, M. P. Personality consistency and change: Some comments on papers by Bayley, Macfarlane, Moss and Kagan, and Murphy. *Vita Humana,* 1964, **7**, 139–142.

Hooper, F. H. Cognitive assessment across the life-span: Methodological implications of the organismic approach. In J. R. Nesselroade & H. W. Reese (Eds.), *Life-span developmental psychology: Methodological issues.* New York: Academic Press, 1973.

Horn, J. L. Personality and ability theory. In R. B. Cattell (Ed.), *Handbook of modern personality theory.* New York: Aldine, 1970.

Horner, M. Fail: Bright woman. *Psychology Today,* 1969, **3**, 36–38, 62.

Horst, P. Relations among *m* sets of measures. *Psychometrika,* 1961, **26**, 129–149.

Horst, P. *Personality: Measurement of dimensions.* San Francisco: Jossey-Bass, 1968.

Hotelling, H. The most predictable criterion. *Journal of Educational Psychology,* 1935, **26**, 139–142.

Hotelling, H. Relations between two sets of variates. *Biometrika,* 1936, **28**, 321–377.

Howland, D. Toward a community health system model. In A. Sheldon, F. Baker, & C. P. McLaughlin (Eds.), *Systems and medical care.* Cambridge, Massachusetts: MIT Press, 1970.

Hoyer, W. J. Application of operant techniques to the modification of elderly behavior. In P. B. Baltes (Ed.), Strategies for psychological intervention in old age. *Gerontologist,* 1973, **13**, 18–23.

Hoyer, W. J., Labouvie, G. V., & Baltes, P. B. Operant modification of age decrements in intellectual performance. Paper presented at the 79th Annual Meeting of the American Psychological Association, Washington, D. C., September, 1971.

Hudson, L. *Frames of mind: Ability, perception and self perception in the arts and sciences.* London: Methuen, 1968.

Inhelder, B., & Piaget, J. *The early growth of logic in the child.* Translated by E. A. Lunzer & D. Piaget. New York: Harper & Row, 1964.

Inkeles, A. Social structure and the socialization of competence. *Harvard Educational Review,* 1966, **36**, 265–283.

Inkeles, A. Society, social structure, and childhood socialization. In J. A. Clausen (Ed.), *Socialization and society.* Boston: Little Brown, 1968.

Inkeles, A. Social structure and socialization. In D. A. Goslin (Ed.), *Handbook of socialization theory and research.* Chicago: Rand McNally, 1969.

Iscoe, I., & Stevenson, H. W. (Eds.), *Personality development in children.* Austin: University of Texas Press, 1960.

Jacobs, A. Strategies of social intervention: Past and future. In A. Jacobs & W. Spradlin (Eds.), *The group as agent of change.* Chicago: Aldine, 1972.

Jacoby, A. P. Transition to parenthood: A reassessment. *Journal of Marriage and the Family,* 1969, **31**, 720–727.

James, W. *The varieties of religious experience.* New York: Modern Library, 1929.

Jarvik, L. F., & Cohen, D. A. biobehavioral approach to intellectual changes with aging. In C. Eisdorfer & M. P. Lawton (Eds.), *The psychology of adult development and aging.* Washington, D.C.: American Psychology Association, 1973.

Jarvik, L. F., Eisdorfer, C., & Blum, J. E. (Eds.) *Intellectual functioning in adults: Psychological and biological influences.* New York: Springer, 1972.

Johnstone, J. W. C., & Rivera, R. J. *Volunteers for learning.* Chicago: Aldine, 1965.

Jonçich, G. *The sane positivist: A biography of E. L. Thorndike.* Middletown, Conn.: Wesleyan University Press, 1968.

Jones, E. *The life and work of Sigmund Freud.* 3 vols. New York: Basic Book, 1953, 1957.

Jones, E. E., & Gerard, H. B. *Foundations of social psychology.* New York: Wiley, 1967.

Jones, E., & Thibaut, J. Interaction goals as basis of inference. In R. Taguiri & L. Petrullo (Eds.), *Person perception and interpersonal behavior.* Stanford: Stanford University Press, 1958.

Jones, M. C. A report on three growth studies at the University of California. *Gerontologist,* 1967, **7**, 49–54.

Jung, C. G. The stages of life. *The collected works: Structure and dynamics of the psyche.* Vol. 8. Translated by R. F. C. Hill. New York: Panthean, 1960.

Kagan, J. Acquisition and significance of sex typing and sex role identity. In L. Hoffman & M. Hoffman (Eds.), *Review of child development.* Vol. 1. New York: Russell Sage, 1964.

Kagan, J. The three faces of continuity in human development. In D. A. Goslin (Ed.), *Handbook of socialization theory and research.* Chicago: Rand McNally, 1969.

Kagan, J. *Change and continuity in infancy.* New York: Wiley, 1971.

Kagan, J., & Kogan, N. Individual variation in cognitive process. In P. H. Mussen (Ed.), *Carmichael's manual of child psychology,* Vol. 1. New York: Wiley, 1970.

Kagan, J., & Moss, H. A. *Birth to maturity: A study in psychological development.* New York: Wiley, 1962.

Kagan, J., Moss, H. A., & Sigel, I. E. Conceptual style and the use of affect labels. *Merrill-Palmer Quarterly,* 1960, **6**, 261–278.

Kagan, J., Moss, H. A., & Sigel, I. E. Psychological significance of styles of conceptualization. In J. C. Wright & J. Kagan (Eds.), Basic cognitive processes in children. *Monographs of the Society for Research in Child Development,* 1963, **28**, Whole No. 2 (Serial No. 86).

Kagan, J., Rosman, B. L., Day, D., Albert, J., & Phillips, W. Information processing in the child: Significance of analytic and reflective attitudes. *Psychological Monographs,* 1964, **78**, (1, Whole No. 578).

Kalish, R. A. The old and the young as generation gap allies. *Gerontologist,* 1969, **9**, 83–89.

Kalish, R. A. The generation gap: Real or contrived? Symposium presented at the Meeting of the American Psychological Association, Miami, 1970.

Kaplan, A. *The conduct of inquiry: Methodology for behavioral science.* San Francisco: Chandler, 1964.

Karp, S. A. Field dependence and occupational activity in the aged. *Perceptual and Motor Skills,* 1967, **24**, 603–609.

Kastenbaum, R. Perspectives on the development and modification of behavior in the aged: A developmental perspective. *Gerontologist,* 1968, **8**, 280–283.

Kastenbaum, R., & Durkee, N. Elderly people view old age. In R. Kastenbaum (Ed.), *New thoughts on old age.* New York: Springer, 1964. (a)

Kastenbaum, R., & Durkee, N. Young people view old age. In R. Kastenbaum (Ed.), *New thoughts on old age.* New York: Springer, 1964. (b)

Kelly, E. Consistency of the adult personality. *American Psychologist,* 1955, **10**, 659–681.

Kelly, J. G. Ecological constraints on mental health services. *American Psychologist,* 1966, **21**, 535–539.

Kelly, J. G. Towards an ecological conception of preventive interventions. In J. W. Carter, Jr. (Ed.), *Research contributions from psychology to community mental health.* New York: Behavioral Publications, 1968.

Kelly, J. G. Naturalistic observations in constrasting social environments. In E. P. Willems & H. L. Rausch (Eds.), *Naturalistic viewpoints in psychological research.* New York: Holt, Rinehart & Winston, 1969.

Keniston, K. *The uncommitted: Alienated youth in American society.* New York: Harcourt, Brace & World, 1965.

Keniston, K. *Young radicals.* New York: Harcourt, Brace & World, 1968.

Keniston, K. Youth as a stage of life. *The American Scholar,* 1970, **39**, 631–654.

Kenkel, W. F. Influence differentiation in decision making. *Sociology and Social Research,* 1957, **42**, 18–25.

Kenkel, W. F. Dominance, persistence, self-confidence, and spousal roles in decision-making. *Journal of Social Psychology,* 1961, **54**, 349–358.

Kennedy, K., & Kates, S. L. Conceptual sorting and personality adjustment in children. *Journal of Abnormal and Social Psychology,* 1964, **68**, 211–214.

Kerlinger, F. N. *Foundations of behavioral research.* New York: Holt, Rinehart & Winston, 1964.

Kessen, W. "Stage" and "structure" in the study of children. *Monographs of the Society for Research in Child Development,* 1962, **27**, (Serial No. 83), 65–82.

Kessen, W. Comparative personality development. In E. F. Borgatta & W. W. Lambert (Eds.), *Handbook of personality and research.* Chicago: McNally, 1968.

Kirkpatrick, C. Familial development, selective needs, and predictive theory. *Journal of Marriage and the Family,* 1967, **29**, 229–236.

Klausmeier, H. J., & Harris, C. W. *Analyses of concept learning.* New York: Academic Press, 1966.

Klausner, S. Z. The social psychology of courage. *Review of Religious Research,* 1961, **3**, 63–72.

Klausner, S. Z. Links and missing links between the sciences of man. In S. Z. Klausner (Ed.), *The study of total societies.* New York: Doubleday-Anchor, 1967.

Klausner, S. Z. Recreation as social action. In, *Program for outdoor recreation research.* Appendix A. Washington, D.C.: National Academy of Sciences, 1969.

Klausner, S. Z. *On man in his environment.* San Francisco: Jossey-Bass, 1971.

Klausner, S. Z. Some problems in the logic of current man-environment studies. In W. R. Burch, Jr., N. H. Cheek, Jr., & L. Taylor (Eds.), *Social behavior, natural resources, and the environment.* New York: Harper & Row, 1972.

Klein, G. S. Need and regulation. In M. R. Jones (Ed.), *Nebraska symposium on motivation.* Lincoln: University of Nebraska Press, 1954.

Kluckhohn, C., & Murray, H. A. (Eds.) *Personality in nature, society and culture.* New York: Knopf, 1949.

Kluckhohn, C., & Murray, H. A. Personality formation: The determinants. In C. Kluckhohn & H. A. Murray (Eds.), *Personality in nature, society and culture.* New York: Knopf, 1949.

Koestler, A. *The act of creation.* New York: MacMillan, 1964.

Kogan, N. Attitudes toward old people: The development of a scale and an examination of correlates. *Journal of Abnormal and Social Psychology,* 1961, **62**, 44–54.

Kogan, N. Educational implications of cognitive styles. In G. S. Lesser (Ed.), *Psychology and educational practice*. Glenview, Illinois: Scott & Foresman, 1971.

Kogan, N. Categorizing and conceptualizing styles in younger and older adults. Unpublished manuscript, Department of Psychology, New School for Social Research, 1973.

Kogan, N., & Morgan, F. T. Task and motivational influences on the assessment of creative and intellective ability in children. *Genetic Psychology Monographs*, 1969, **80**, 91–127.

Kogan, N., & Pankove, E. Creative ability over a five-year span. *Child Development*, 1972, **43**, 427–442.

Kogan, N., & Shelton, F. Images of "old people" and "people in general" in an older sample. *Journal of Genetic Psychology*, 1962, **100**, 3–21. (a)

Kogan, N., & Shelton, F. Beliefs about "old people": A comparative study of older and younger samples. *Journal of Genetic Psychology*, 1962, **100**, 93–111. (b)

Kogan, N., Stephens, J., & Sheldon, F. Age differences: A developmental study of discriminability and affective response. *Journal of Abnormal and Social Psychology*, 1961, **62**, 221–230.

Kogan, N., & Wallach, M. A. Age changes in values and attitudes. *Journal of Gerontology*, 1961, **16**, 272-280. (a)

Kogan, N., & Wallach, M. A. The effect of anxiety on relations between subjective age and caution in an older sample. In P. H. Hoch & J. Zubin (Eds.), *Psychopathology of aging*. New York: Grune & Stratton, 1961. (b)

Kogan, N., & Wallach, M. A. *Risk taking: A study in cognition and personality*. New York: Holt, Rinehart & Winston, 1964.

Kohlberg, L. Moral development and identification. In H. W. Stevenson (Ed.), *Child Psychology: The 62nd yearbook of the National Society for the Study of Education*. Chicago: National Society for the Study of Education, 1963.

Kohlberg, L. Development of moral character and moral ideology. In M. L. Hoffman & L. W. Hoffman (Eds.), *Review of child development research*. Vol. 1. New York: Russell Sage, 1964.

Kohlberg, L. A cognitive-developmental analysis of children's sex-role concepts and attitudes. In E. E. Maccoby (Ed.), *The development of sex differences*. Stanford: Stanford University Press, 1966.

Kohlberg, L. Early education: A cognitive-developmental view. *Child Development*, 1968, **39**, 1014–1062.

Kohlberg, L. Stage and sequence: The cognitive-developmental approach to socialization: In D. A. Goslin (Ed.), *Handbook of socialization theory and research*. Chicago: Rand McNally, 1969.

Kohlberg, L. From is to ought: How to commit the naturalistic fallacy and get away with it in the study of moral development. In T. Mischel (Ed.), *Cognitive development and epistemology*. New York: Academic Press, 1971. (a)

Kohlberg, L. The ethical life, the contemplative life and ultimate religion—notes toward Stage 7. Unpublished manuscript, Harvard University, 1971. (b)

Kohlberg, L. Continuities and discontinuities in childhood and adult moral development revisited. In L. Kohlberg & E. Turiel (Eds.), *Recent research in moral development*. New York: Holt, Rinehart & Winston, 1973, in press.

Kohlberg, L., & Gilligan, C. The adolescent as a philosopher: The discovery of the self in a postconventional world. *Daedalus*, 1971, **100**, 1051–1086.

Kohlberg, L., & Kramer, R. Continuities and discontinuities in childhood and adult moral development. *Human Development*, 1969, **12**, 93–120.

Kohlberg, L., & Mayer, R. Early education: A cognitive developmental view. II. The developmental-philosophic strategy for defining educational aims. In L. Kohlberg & E. Turiel (Eds.), *Recent research in moral development*. New York: Holt, Rinehart & Winston, 1973, in press.

Kohlberg, L., & Turiel, E. Overview—Cultural universals in morality. In L. Kohlberg & E. Turiel (Eds.), *Recent research in moral development*. New York: Holt, Rinehart & Winston, 1973, in press.

Kohlberg, L., & Zigler, E. The impact of cognitive maturity on the development of sex role attitudes in the years four to eight. *Genetic Psychology Monographs*, 1967, **75**, 89–165.

Komarovsky, M. *Blue collar marriage*. New York: Vintage Books, 1967.

Kotlar, S. L. Middle class marital role perceptions and marital adjustment. *Sociological Social Research*, 1965, **49**, 283–293.

Kral, V. A. Senile dementia and normal aging. *Canadian Psychiatric Association Journal*, 1972, **7**, 25–30.

Kreitler, H., & Kreitler, S. Children's concepts of sexuality and birth. *Child Development*, 1966, **37**, 363–378.

Kretschmer, E. *Koerperbau und Charakter* (1st and 25th Edition). Berlin: Springer, 1927, 1967.

Kryter, K. D. *The effects of noise on man*. New York: Academic Press, 1970.

Kuhlen, R. G. Aging and life-adjustment. In J. E. Birren (Ed.), *Handbook of aging and the individual*. Chicago: University of Chicago Press, 1959.

Kuhlen, R. G. Age and intelligence: The significance of cultural change in longitudinal versus cross-sectional findings. *Vita Humana*, 1963, **6**, 113–124.

Kuhlen, R. G. Personality change with age. In P. Worchel & D. Byrne (Eds.), *Personality change*. New York: Wiley, 1964.

Kuhn, D., Langer, J., Kohlberg, L., & Haan, N. The development of formal operations in logical and moral judgment. *Genetic Psychology Monographs*, 1974, in press.

Kuhn, T. S. *The structure of scientific revolutions*. Chicago: University of Chicago Press, 1962.

Labouvie, G. V. Implications of geropsychological theories for intervention: The challenge for the seventies. *Gerontologist*, 1973, **13**, 10–15.

Labouvie, G. V., & Baltes, P. B. Adolescents' perceptions of adolescent change in personality and intelligence. *Journal of Genetic Psychology*, in press.

Labouvie, G. V., Hoyer, W. J., Baltes, M. M., & Baltes, P. B. Operant analysis of intellectual behavior in old age. *Human Development*, in press.

Langer, J. *Theories of development*. New York: Holt, Rinehart & Winston, 1969.

Langner, T. S. Environment stress, degree of psychiatric impairment and type of mental disturbance. *Psychoanalytic Review*, 1960, **47**, 3–16.

Lansky, L. M., & McKay, G. Sex-role preferences of kindergarten boys and girls: Some contradictory results. *Psychological Reports*, 1963, **13**, 415–421.

Lash, J. P. *Eleanor Roosevelt: A friend's memoirs*. Garden City: Doubleday, 1964.

Latz, M. T. *Priority study–Study of decision-making on Public Welfare programs for the aged*. Harrisburg: Department of Public Welfare, Office for the Aging, 1965.

Laufer, R. S. Sources of governmental consciousness and conflict. In P. B. Altback, & R. S. Laufer (Eds.), *The new pilgrims: Youth protest in transition*. New York: David McKay, 1972.

Laughlin, P. R. Incidental concept formation as a function of creativity and intelligence. *Journal of Personality and Social Psychology*, 1967, **5**, 115–119.

Laurence, M. Sex differences in the perception of men and women at four different ages. *Journal of Gerontology*, 1964, **19**, 343–348.

Laws, J. L. A feminist review of marital adjustment. The rape of the locke. *Journal of Marriage and the Family*, 1971, **33**, 97–137.

Lawton, M. P., & Nahemow, L. Ecology and the aging process. In C. Eisdorfer & M. P. Lawton (Eds.), *The psychology of adult development and aging*. Washington, D.C.: American Psychological Association, 1973.

Leary, T. *Interpersonal diagnosis of personality*. New York: Ronald Press, 1957.

Lee, S. S., & McLaughlin, C. P. Changing views of public health service as a system. In A. Sheldon, F. Baker, & C. P. McLaughlin (Eds.), *Systems and medical care*. Cambridge: MIT Press, 1970.

Lehman, H. C. *Age and achievement*. Princeton: Princeton University Press, 1953.

Lehman, H. C. The age decrement in outstanding scientific creativity. *American Psychologist,* 1960, **15**, 128–134.

Leighton, A. H. *My name is legion.* New York: Basic Books, 1959.

Leighton, D. C., Harding, J. S., Macklin, D. B., Macmillan, A. M., & Leighton, A. H. *The character of danger.* New York: Basic Books, 1963.

Leik, R. K. Instrumentality and emotionality in family interaction. *Sociometry,* 1963, **26**, 131–145.

LeMasters, E. E. Parenthood as crisis. *Marriage and Family Living,* 1957, **19**, 352–355.

Lesser, G. S. Matching instruction to student characteristics. In G. S. Lesser (Ed.), *Psychology and educational practice.* Glenview, Illinois: Scott, Foresman, 1971.

LeVine, R. A. Culture, personality, and socialization: An evolutionary view. In D. A. Goslin (Ed.), *Handbook of socialization theory and research.* Chicago: Rand McNally, 1969.

LeVine, R. A. Cross-cultural study in child psychology. In P. H. Mussen (Ed.), *Carmichael's manual of child psychology.* Vol. 2. New York: Wiley, 1970.

Levinger, G. Task and social behavior in marriage. *Sociometry,* 1964, **24**, 433–448.

Levy, L. H. Originality as role defined behavior. *Journal of Personality and Social Psychology,* 1968, **9**, 72–78.

Levy, L., & Rowitz, L. Ecological attributes of high and low rate mental hospital utilization areas in Chicago. *Social Psychiatry,* 1971, **6**, 20–28.

Lewis, M. State as an infant-environment interaction: An analysis of mother-infant behavior as a function of sex. *Merrill-Palmer Quarterly,* 1972, **18**, 95–121.

Lewis, M., & Ban, P. Stability of attachment behavior: A transformational analysis. Paper presented at meetings of the Society for Research in Child Development, Minneapolis, 1971.

Lewis, M., & Freedle, R. Mother-infant dyad: The cradle of meaning. Paper presented at a symposium on "Language and thought: Communication and affect." Erindale College, University of Toronto, 1972.

Lewis, M., & Wilson, C. D. Infant development in lower-class American families. *Human Development,* 1972, **15**, 112–127.

Libb, J. W., & Clements, C. B. Token reinforcement in an exercise program for hospitalized geriatric patients. *Perceptual and Motor Skills,* 1969, **28**, 957–958.

Liederman, P. C., Green, R., & Liederman, V. R. Out-patient group therapy with geriatric patients. *Geriatrics,* 1967, **22**, 148–153.

Linden, M. E. Group psychotherapy with institutionalized senile women. *International Journal of Group Psychotherapy,* 1953, **3**, 150–170.

Linden, M. E. Significance of dual leadership in gerontologic group psychotherapy. *International Journal of Group Psychotherapy,* 1954, **4**, 262–273.

Lindsley, O. R. Geriatric behavioral prosthetics. In R. Kastenbaum (Ed.), *New thoughts on old age.* New York: Springer, 1964.

Lindzey, G., & Boring, E. G. (Eds.) *A history of psychology in autobiography.* Vol. 5. New York: Appleton-Century-Crofts, 1967.

Linton, H. B. Dependence on external influence: Correlates in perception, attitudes, and judgment. *Journal of Abnormal and Social Psychology,* 1955, **51**, 502–507.

Linton, R. *The cultural background of personality.* New York: Appleton-Century-Crofts, 1942.

Little, K. B. Epilogue: Academic marketplace 1984. *American Psychologist,* 1972, **27**, 504–506.

Liu, W. T. Family interactions among local and refugee Chinese families in Hong Kong. *Journal of Marriage and the Family,* 1966, **28**, 314–323.

Livson, N. Person cluster analysis of case-record *Q* sorts. Institute of Human Development Report, University of California at Berkeley, 1962.

Livson, N. Developmental dimensions of personality: A longitudinal analysis. In R. C. Tryon (Chm.), Personality dimensions and typologies revealed by modern cluster analysis. Symposium presented at the meeting of the Western Psychological Association, Honolulu, June, 1965.

Livson, N., & Peskin, H. Prediction of adult psychological health in a longitudinal study. *Journal of Abnormal Psychology*, 1967, **72**, 509–518.

Lloyd, B. B., & Light, R. A. Cognitive stages in dream concept development in English children. *Journal of Social Psychology*, 1970, **82**, 271–272.

Loevinger, J. The meaning and measurement of ego development. *American Psychologist*, 1966, **214, 195**–206.

Loevinger, J. Theories of ego development. In L. Breger (Ed.), *Clinical-cognitive psychology: Models and integrations*. Englewood Cliffs: Prentice-Hall, 1969.

Loevinger, J., & Wessler, R. *Measuring ego development: Construction and use of a sentence completion test*. Vol. 1. San Francisco: Jossey-Bass, 1970.

Loevinger, J., Wessler, R., & Redmore, C. *Measuring ego development: Scoring manual for women and girls*. Vol. 2. San Francisco: Jossey-Bass, 1970.

Lohnes, P. R. Research frontier: Markov models for human development research. *Journal of Counseling Psychology*, 1965, **12**, 322–327.

Looft, W. R. Children's judgments of age. *Child Development*, 1971, **42**, 1282–1284. (a)

Looft, W. R. The psychology of more. *American Psychologist*, 1971, **26**, 561–565. (b)

Looft, W. R. Egocentrism and social interaction across the life span. *Psychological Bulletin*, 1972, **78**, 73–92.

Looft, W. R. Reflections on intervention in old age: Motives, goals and assumptions. In P. B. Baltes (Ed.), Strategies for psychological intervention in old age. *Gerontologist*, 1973, **13**, 6–10.

Looft, W. R., & Bartz, W. H. Animism revived. *Psychological Bulletin*, 1969, **71**, 1–19.

Looft, W. R., & Charles, D. C. Egocentrism and social interaction in young and old adults. *Aging and Human Development*, 1971, **2**, 21–28.

Looft, W. R., Rayman, J. R., & Rayman, B. B. Children's judgments of age in Sarawak. *Journal of Social Psychology*, 1972, **86**, 181–185.

Lorge, I. Capacities of older adults. In W. T. Donahue (Ed.), *Education for later maturity: A handbook*. New York: Whiteside & Morrow, 1955.

Lowy, L. The group in social work with the aged. *Social Work*, 1962, **7**, 43–50.

Lusk, D., & Lewis, M. Mother-infant interaction and infant development among the Wolof of Senegal. *Human Development*, 1972, **15**, 58–69.

Lynn, D. B. *Parental and sex role identification: A theoretical formulation*. Berkeley: McCutchan, 1969.

Maas, H. Long term effects of early childhood separation and group care. *Vita Humana*, 1963, **6**, 34–56.

Maccoby, E. E. Role-taking in childhood and its consequences for social learning. *Child Development*, 1959, **30**, 239–252.

Maccoby, E. E. Sex differences in intellectual functioning. In E. E. Maccoby (Ed.), *The development of sex differences*. Stanford: Stanford University Press, 1966.

Maccoby, E. E. The development of moral values and behavior in childhood. In J. A. Clausen (Ed.), *Socialization and society*. Boston: Little, Brown & Co., 1968.

Maccoby, E. E., Dowley, E. M., Hagen, J. W., & Degerman, R. Activity level and intellectual functioning in normal preschool children. *Child Development*, 1965, **36**, 761–770.

Maccoby, E. E., & Feldman, S. Mother-attachment and stranger-reactions in the third year of life. *Monographs of the Society for Research in Child Development*, 1972, **37**, No. 146.

Maccoby, E. E., & Masters, J. C. Attachment and dependency. In P. H. Mussen (Ed.), *Carmichael's manual of child psychology*. Vol. 2. New York: Wiley, 1970.

MacKinnon, D. W. The structure of personality. In J. McV. Hunt (Ed.), *Personality and the behavior disorders*. Vol. 1. New York: Ronald Press, 1944.

MacKinnon, D. W. The personality correlates of creativity: A study of American architects.

In G. S. Nielsen (Ed.), *Proceedings of the XIV International Congress of Applied Psychology*. Vol. II. Copenhagen: Munksgaard, 1962.

Maddox, G. L. Disengagement theory: A critical evaluation. *Gerontologist,* 1964, **4**, 80–82.

Maddox, G. L. Persistence of life style among the elderly: A longitudinal study of social activity in relation to life satisfaction. In B. L. Neugarten (Ed.), *Middle age and aging*. Chicago: University of Chicago Press, 1968.

Magrabi, F. M., & Marshall, W. H. Family developmental tasks: A research model. *Journal of Marriage and the Family,* 1965, **27**, 454–461.

Mahrer, A. R. *New approaches to personality classification*. New York: Columbia University Press, 1970.

Maltzman, I. On the training of originality. *Psychological Review,* 1960, **67**, 229–242.

Mannheim, K. *Essays on the sociology of knowledge*. London: Routledge & Kegan Paul, 1952. (a)

Mannheim, K. The problem of generations. In K. Mannheim (Ed.), *Essays on the sociology of knowledge*. New York: Oxford University Press, 1952. (b)

Marcia, J. E. Development and validation of ego-identity status. *Journal of Personality and Social Psychology,* 1966, **3**, 551–558.

Marias, J. Generations: The concept. *International encyclopedia of the social sciences*. Vol. 6. New York: Free Press, 1968.

Marshall, M. Living a lifetime—A proposed television series for older adults. Unpublished master's thesis, California State College at Los Angeles, 1970.

Martin, W. C., Bengtson, V. L., & Acock, A. A. Alienation and age: A cohort-specific approach. Unpublished manuscript, University of Southern California, 1972.

McArthur, A. Developmental tasks and parent-adolescent conflict. *Journal of Marriage and the Family,* 1962, **24**, 189–191.

McCall, G., & Simmons, J. L. *Identities and interaction*. New York: New York Free Press, 1966.

McCandless, B. R., & Evans, E. E. *Human Development and society: A psychological view*. Hinsdale, Illinois: Dryden, 1973.

McClearn, G. E. Genes, generality, and behavioral research. In J. Hirsch (Ed.), *Behavior-genetic analysis*. New York: McGraw-Hill, 1967.

McClelland, D. C., Atkinson, J. W., Clark, R. A., & Lowell, E. L. *The achievement motive*. New York: Appleton-Century-Crofts, 1953.

McClusky, H. Y. *Education: Background*. Washington, D.C.: White House Conference on Aging, 1971.

McFarland, R. A. The sensory and perceptual processes in aging. In K. W. Schaie (Ed.), *Theory and methods of research on aging*. Morgantown, West Virginia: West Virginia University Library, 1968.

McTavish, D. G. Perceptions of old people: A review of research methodologies and findings. *Gerontologist,* 1971, **11**, 90–101.

Mead, M. *Culture and commitment: A study of the generation gap*. New York: Doubleday, 1970.

Mead, M. Youth revolt: The future is now. *Saturday Review,* 1970, **53**, 23–25, 113.

Mednick, S. A. The associative bases of the creative process. *Psychological Review,* 1962, **69**, 220–232.

Meehl, P. E. Theory-testing in psychology and physics: A methodological paradox. *Philosophy of Science,* 1967, **34**, 103–115.

Meili, G., & Meili, R. *Grundlagen individueller Persoenlichkeitsunterschiede* (Foundations of Individual Differences in Psychology). Bern: Hans Huber, 1972.

Melton, A. W. Individual differences and theoretical process variables. In R. M. Gagne (Ed.), *Learning and individual differences*. Columbus, Ohio: Merrill, 1967.

Mendelsohn, G. A., & Griswold, B. B. Differential use of incidental stimuli in problem solving as a function of creativity. *Journal of Abnormal and Social Psychology,* 1964, **68**, 431–436.

Mendelsohn, G. A., & Griswold, B. B. Assessed creative potential, vocabulary level, and sex as predictors of the use of incidental cues in verbal problem solving. *Journal of Personality and Social Psychology,* 1966, **4**, 423–431.

Mentre, F. *Les générations sociales.* Paris: Bossard, 1920.

Meredith, W. Rotation to achieve factorial invariance. *Psychometrika,* 1964, **29**, 187–206.

Messick, S., & Damarin, F. Cognitive styles and memory for faces. *Journal of Abnormal and Social Psychology,* 1964, **69**, 313–318.

Messick, S., & Kogan, N. Differentiation and compartmentalization in object-sorting measures of categorizing style. *Perceptual and Motor Skills,* 1963, **16**, 47–51.

Metz, A. S. A comparison of husbands and wives' dissatisfactions with marriage partner based on a factor analytic study of marital interpersonal behavior. Unpublished doctoral dissertation, University of Pennsylvania, 1962.

Meyer, J. W., & Sobieszek, B. I. Effect of a child's sex on adult interpretations of its behaviors. *Developmental Psychology,* 1972, **6**, 42–48.

Meyerowitz, J. H. Satisfaction during pregnancy. *Journal of Marriage and the Family,* 1970, **32**, 38–42.

Michaux, W. W., Gansereit, K. W., McCabe, O. L., & Kurland, A. A. The psychopathology and measurement of environmental stress. *Community Mental Health Journal,* 1967, **3**, 358–372.

Mikesell, R. M., & Tesser, A. Life history antecedents of authoritarianism: A quasi-longitudinal approach. Proceedings of the 79th Annual Convention of the American Psychological Association, 1971, 369–370.

Miller, N. E., & Dollard, J. *Social learning and imitation.* New Haven: Yale University Press, 1941.

Mischel, W. A social-learning view of sex differences in behavior. In E. E. Maccoby (Ed.), *The development of sex differences.* Stanford: Stanford University Press, 1966.

Mischel, W. *Personality and assessment.* New York: Wiley, 1968.

Mischel, W. Continuity and change in personality. *American Psychologist,* 1969, **24**, 1012–1018.

Mischel, W. Sex-typing and socialization. In P. H. Mussen (Ed.), *Carmichael's handbook of child psychology.* Vol. 2. New York: Wiley, 1970.

Mishara, B. L. Comparison of two types of milieu programs for rehabilitation of chronic geriatric patients. Paper presented at the 24th Annual Meeting of the Gerontological Society, Houston, 1971.

Mönks, F. J., Hartup, W. W., & DeWitt, J. (Eds.). *Determinants of behavioral development.* New York: Academic Press, 1972.

Morris, C. Theory of signs. In O. Neurath, R. Carnap, & C. Morris (Eds.), *International encyclopedia of a unified science.* Chicago: University of Chicago Press, 1955.

Moss, H. A. Sex, age, and state as determinants of mother-infant interaction. *Merrill-Palmer Quarterly,* 1967, **13**, 19–36.

Moss, H. A., & Robson, K. S. Maternal influences in early social behavior. *American Journal of Orthopsychiatry,* 1967, **37**, 394–395.

Moss, H. A., & Robson, K. S. Maternal influences in early social visual behavior. *Child Development,* 1968, **39**, 401–408. (a)

Moss, H. A., & Robson, K. S. The role of protest behavior in the development of mother-infant attachment. Paper presented at the meeting of the American Psychological Association, San Francisco, 1968. (b)

Muller, P. *The tasks of childhood.* New York: McGraw-Hill, 1969.

Murphy, G. Shall we ever really understand personality? *Journal of Projective Techniques and Personality Assessment,* 1964, **28**, 140–143.

Murphy, G., Murphy, L. B., & Newcomb, T. M. *Experimental social psychology.* New York: Harper, 1937.

Musgrove, F. Inter-generation attitudes. In F. Musgrove (Ed.), *Youth and the social order*. Bloomington: Indiana Press, 1964.

Mussen, P. H. Early sex-role development. In D. A. Goslin (Ed.), *Handbook of socialization theory and research*. Chicago: Rand McNally, 1969.

Nagel, E. Determinism and development. In D. B. Harris (Ed.), *The concept of development*. Minneapolis: University of Minnesota Press, 1957.

Nardi, A. H. Autoperception and heteroperception of personality traits in adolescents, adults, and the aged. Unpublished doctoral dissertation, West Virginia University, 1971.

National Center for Educational Statistics. *Adult basic education program statistics—students and staff data*. Washington, D.C.: U.S. Office of Education, 1970.

Navran, L. Communication and adjustment in marriage. *Family Process,* 1967, **6**, 173–184.

Nesselroade, J. R., & Reese, H. W. (Eds.). *Life-span developmental psychology: Methodological issues*. New York: Academic Press, 1973.

Nesselroade, J. R., Schaie, K. W., & Baltes, P. B. Ontogenetic and generational components of structural and quantitative change in adult cognitive behavior. *Journal of Gerontology,* 1972, **27**, 222–228.

Neugarten, B. L. *Personality in middle and late life*. New York: Atherton Press, 1964.

Neugarten, B. L. Adult personality: A developmental view. *Human Development,* 1966, **9**, 61–73.

Neugarten, B. L. *Middle age and aging: A reader in social psychology*. Chicago: University of Chicago Press, 1968. (a)

Neugarten, B. L. Toward a psychology of the life cycle. In B. L. Neugarten (Ed.), *Middle age and aging: A reader in social psychology*. Chicago: University of Chicago Press, 1968. (b)

Neugarten, B. L. Continuities and discontinuities of psychological issues into adult life. *Human Development,* 1969, **12**, 121–130.

Neugarten, B. L., & Gutmann, D. L. Age-sex roles and personality in middle age: A thematic apperception study. *Psychological Monographs,* 1958, **72**, No. 470.

Neugarten, B. L., & Gutmann, D. L. Age-sex roles and personality in middle age: A thematic apperception study. In B. L. Neugarten (Ed.), *Middle age and aging: A reader in social psychology*. Chicago: University of Chicago Press, 1968.

Neugarten, B. L., & Moore, J. W. The changing age-status system. In B. L. Neugarten (Ed.), *Middle age and aging: A reader in social psychology*. Chicago: University of Chicago Press, 1968.

Neugarten, B. L., Moore, J. W., & Lowe, J. C. Age norms, age constraints, and adult socialization. *American Journal of Sociology,* 1965, **70**, 710–717.

Neugarten, B. L., & Paterson, W. A. A study of the American age-grade system. In *Proceedings of the Fourth Congress of the International Association of Gerontology,* Vol. 3, 1957.

Newcomb, T. *The acquaintance process*. New York: Holt, Rinehart & Winston, 1961.

Nicholls, J. G. Some effects of testing procedure on divergent thinking. *Child Development,* 1971, **42**, 1647–1651.

Nielsen, A. C., Company. *Nielsen TV 1970*. Chicago: Media Research Division, 1970.

Nisbet, R. A. *Social change and history: Aspects of the western theory of development*. New York: Oxford University Press, 1969.

Nunnally, J. *Psychometric theory*. New York: McGraw-Hill, 1967.

Odum, E. P. *Ecology*. New York: Holt, Rinehart & Winston, 1963.

Ogburn, W. F. *Social change with respect to culture and original nature*. New York: Viking Press, 1950.

Opler, M. K. Social identity and self-control. In S. Z. Klausner (Ed.), *The quest for self-control*. New York: Free Press, 1965.

O'Rourke, J. Field and laboratory. The decision making behaviors of family groups in two experimental conditions. *Sociometry,* 1963, **26**, 422–435.

Osmond, H. Function as the basis of psychiatric ward design. *Mental Hospitals,* 1957, **8**, 23–30.

Osofsky, J. D. The shaping of mothers' behavior by children. *Journal of Marriage and the Family*, 1970, **32**, 400–405.

Osofsky, J. D. Children's influence upon parental behavior: An attempt to define the relationship with the use of a laboratorium task. *Generic Psychology Monographs*, 1971, **83**, 147–169.

Overton, W. F., & Reese, H. W. Models of development: Methodological implications. In J. R. Nesselroade & H. W. Reese (Eds.), *Life-span developmental psychology: Methodological issues*. New York: Academic Press, 1973.

Owens, W. A. Age and mental abilities: A longitudinal study. *Genetic Psychology Monographs*, 1953, **48**, 3–54.

Owens, W. A. Age and mental abilities: A second follow-up. *Journal of Educational Psychology*, 1966, **51**, 311–325.

Owens, W. A. Toward one discipline of scientific psychology. *American Psychologist*, 1968, **23**, 782–785.

Owens, W. A. A quasi-actuarial basis for individual assessment. *American Psychologist*, 1971, **26**, 992–999.

Palmore, E., & Whittington, F. Trends in the relative status of the aged. *Social Forces*, 1971, **50**, 84–91.

Pankove, E., & Kogan, N. Creative ability and risk taking in elementary school children. *Journal of Personality*, 1968, **36**, 420–439.

Papalia, D. E. The status of several conservation abilities across the life-span. *Human Development*, 1972, **15**, 229–243.

Parsons, T. Age and sex in the social structure of the United States. *American Sociological Review*, 1942, **7**, 604–616.

Parsons, T. *The structure of social action*. Glencoe, Illinois: Free Press, 1949.

Parsons, T. *Social structure and personality*. New York: Free Press, 1967.

Parsons, T., & Bales, R. F. *Family, socialization, and interaction process*. Glencoe, Illinois: Free Press, 1955.

Parsons, T., & Shils, E. A. (Eds.) *Toward a general theory of action*. Cambridge: Harvard University Press, 1951. (a)

Parsons, T., & Shils, E. A. The social system. In T. Parsons & E. A. Shils (Eds.), *Toward a general theory of action*. Cambridge: Harvard University Press, 1951. (b)

Patterson, G. R. Social learning: An additional base for developing behavior modification techniques. In D. Frank (Ed.), *Assessment and status of the behavior therapies and associated development*. New York: McGraw-Hill, 1967.

Patterson, G. R. *Families: Applications of social learning to family life*. Champaigne, Illinois: Research, 1971.

Patterson, G. R., & Cobb, J. A. A diagnostic analysis of "aggressive" behavior: An additional step toward a theory of aggression. In J. P. Hill (Ed.), *Minnesota symposia on child psychology*. Minneapolis: University of Minnesota Press, 1971.

Patterson, G. R., & Reid, J. B. Reciprocity and coercion: Two facets of social systems. Unpublished manuscript, Oregon Research Institute, University of Oregon, 1969.

Patterson, G. R., & Hops, H. Coercion, a game for two: Intervention techniques for marital conflict. Unpublished report (Technical Report 6), University of Oregon, June, 1971.

Pattishall, E. Programs for health maintenance and primary health care. In H. B. Urban & W. R. Looft (Eds.), *Human development intervention*, in preparation.

Payne, T. R. *S. L. Rubinstein and the philosophical foundations of Soviet psychology*. New York: Humanities Press, 1968.

Peskin, H. Multiple prediction of adult psychological health and preadolescent and adolescent behavior. *Journal of Consulting and Clinical Psychology*, 1972, **38**, 155–160.

Peterson, W. A. Research priorities on perceptions and orientations toward aging and toward older people. *Gerontologist*, 1971, **11**, 60–63.

Peterson, W. A., & Peters, G. R. (Eds.). Perceptions of aging. *Gerontologist*, 1971, **11**, 59–108.

Pettigrew, T. F. The measurement and correlates of category width as a cognitive variable. *Journal of Personality,* 1958, **26**, 532–544.

Piaget, J. Children's philosophies. In C. Murchison (Ed.), *A handbook of child psychology.* Worcester: Clark University Press, 1933.

Piaget, J. *Play, dreams, and imitation in childhood.* New York: Norton, 1951.

Piaget, J. The general problem of the psychobiological development of the child. In J. M. Tanner & B. Inhelder (Eds.), *Discussions on child development.* Vol. 4. New York: International University Press, 1960. (a)

Piaget, J. *The moral judgment of the child.* Translated by M. Gabain. New York: Free Press, 1960. (b)

Piaget, J. *Genetic epistemology.* New York: Columbia University Press, 1970. (a)

Piaget, J. *Structuralism.* New York: Basic Books, 1970. (b)

Piaget, J. Intellectual evolution from adolescence to adulthood. *Human Development,* 1972, **15**, 1–12.

Piers, E. V., Daniels, J. M., & Quackenbush, J. I. The identification of creativity in adolescents. *Journal of Educational Psychology,* 1960, **51**, 346–351.

Pikunas, J. *Human development: A science of growth.* New York: McGraw-Hill, 1961, 1969.

Podd, M. H. Ego identity status and morality: An empirical investigation of two developmental concepts. Unpublished doctoral dissertation, University of Chicago, 1969.

Pomeroy, E. L. Group approaches to treatment of the aged. Paper presented at the 80th Annual Meeting of the American Psychological Association, Honolulu, September, 1972.

Precker, J. A. Similarity in valuings as a factor in the selection of peers and a near authority figure. *Journal of Abnormal and Social Psychology,* 1952, **47**, 406–414.

Pressey, S. L. Major problems—and the major problem—motivation, learning and education in the later years. In J. E. Anderson (Ed.), *Psychological aspects of aging.* Washington, D.C.: American Psychological Association, 1956.

Pressey, S. L., & Kuhlen, R. G. *Psychological development through the life-span.* New York: Harper & Row, 1939, 1957.

Provence, S., & Lipton, R. G. *Infants in institutions.* New York: International University Press, 1962.

Rachlis, D. Suicide and loss adjustment in the aging. Bulletin of Suicidology, No. 7, 1970, National Institute of Mental Health, Bethesda, Maryland.

Rahe, R., McKean, J. D., Jr., & Arthur, R. J. A longitudinal study of life change and illness patterns. *Journal of Psychosomatic Research,* 1967, **10**, 355–366.

Rapaport, A., & Chammah, A. M. *Prisoner's dilemma: A study in conflict and cooperation.* Ann Arbor: University of Michigan Press, 1965.

Rapaport, D., Gill, M., & Schafer, R. *Diagnostic psychological testing.* Vol. 1. Chicago: Year Book Publishers, 1945.

Raush, H. L., Dittman, A. L., & Taylor, T. J. The interpersonal behavior of children in residential treatment. *Journal of Abnormal and Social Psychology,* 1959, **58**, 9–26.

Raush, H. L., Farbman, I., & Llewellyn, L. G. Person, setting, and change in social interaction: Vol. 2. A normal-control study. *Human Relations,* 1960, **13**, 305–331.

Reese, H. W., & Overton, W. F. Models of development and theories of development. In L. R. Goulet & P. B. Baltes (Eds.), *Life-span developmental psychology: Research and theory.* New York: Academic Press, 1970.

Reich, C. *The greening of America.* New York: Random House, 1970.

Reichard, S., Livson, F., & Peterson, P. *Aging and personality.* New York: Wiley, 1962.

Reichenbach, M., & Mathers, R. A. The place of time and aging in the natural sciences and scientific philosophy. In J. E. Birren (Ed.), *Handbook of aging and the individual: Psychological and biological aspects.* Chicago: University of Chicago Press, 1959.

Rest, J. The hierarchical nature of moral judgment: Patterns of comprehension and preference of moral stages. In L. Kohlberg & E. Turiel (Eds.), *Recent research in moral development.* New York: Holt, Rinehart & Winston, 1973, in press.

Rheingold, H. L. The social and socializing infant. In D. A. Goslin (Ed.), *Handbook of socialization theory and research.* Chicago: Rand McNally, 1969.

Rheingold, H. L., & Eckerman, L. O. The infant's free entry into a new environment. *Journal of Experimental Child Psychology,* 1969, **8**, 271–283.

Richer, S. The economics of child-rearing. *Journal of Marriage and the Family,* 1968, **30**, 462–466.

Richman, F. The disenfranchised majority. *Center Occasional Paper,* 1968, **1**, 4–14.

Riegel, K. Personality theory and aging. In J. E. Birren (Ed.), *Handbook of aging and the individual.* Chicago: University of Chicago Press, 1959.

Riegel, K. F. Development of language: Suggestions for a verbal fallout model. *Human Development,* 1966, **9**, 97–120.

Riegel, K. F. History as a nomothetic science. Some generalizations from theories and research in developmental psychology. *Journal of Social Issues,* 1969, **25**, 99–127.

Riegel, K. F. The influence of economic and political ideology upon the development of developmental psychology. *Psychological Bulletin,* 1972, **78**, 129–141. (a)

Riegel, K. F. On the dialectics of cognitive changes during the life span. Paper presented at the Ninth International Congress of Gerontology, Kiev, U.S.S.R., July, 1972. (b)

Riegel, K. F. Time and change in the development of the individual and society. In H. W. Reese (Ed.), *Advances in child development and behavior.* Vol. 7. New York: Academic Press, 1972. (c)

Riegel, K. F. Developmental psychology and society: Some historical and ethical considerations. In J. R. Nesselroade & H. W. Reese (Eds.), *Life-span developmental psychology: Methodological issues.* New York: Academic Press, 1973.

Riegel, K. F., & Riegel, R. M. Development, drop, and death. *Developmental Psychology,* 1972, **6**, 306–319.

Riley, M. W. Social gerontology and the age stratification of society. *Gerontologist,* 1971, **11**, 79–87.

Riley, M. W., & Foner, A. *Aging and society.* Vol. 1. *An inventory of research findings.* New York: Russell Sage, 1968.

Riley, M. W., Foner, A., Hess, B., & Toby, M. L. Socialization for the middle and later years. In D. A. Goslin (Ed.), *Handbook of socialization theory and research.* Chicago: Rand McNally, 1969.

Riley, M. W., Johnson, M. E., & Foner, A. (Eds.). *Aging and society: A sociology of age stratification.* Vol. 3. New York: Russell Sage, 1972.

Roberton, M. A. Uni-directionality in life-span development: A necessary or unnecessary corollary of organismic theory? Unpublished manuscript, University of Wisconsin, 1972.

Robson, K. S. The role of eye-to-eye contact in maternal-infant attachment. *Journal of Child Psychology and Psychiatry and Allied Disciplines,* 1967, **8**, 13–25.

Robson, K. S., & Moss, H. A. Subjective aspects of maternal attachment in man. Unpublished manuscript, National Institute of Mental Health, Bethesda, Md., 1969.

Robson, K. S., Pedersen, F. A., & Moss, H. A. Developmental observations of dyadic gazing in relation to the fear of strangers and social approach behavior. *Child Development,* 1969, **40**, 619–627.

Roe, A. *The making of a scientist.* New York: Dodd & Mead, 1953.

Roff, M. (Ed.). *Life history research in psychopathology.* Minneapolis: University of Minnesota Press, 1970, 1972. 2 vols.

Rogers, C. Autobiography. In E. G. Boring & G. Lindzey (Eds.), *History of psychology in autobiography.* Vol. 5. New York: Appleton-Century-Crofts, 1967.

Rohwer, W. D. Implications of cognitive development for education. In P. H. Mussen (Ed.), *Carmichael's manual of child psychology.* Vol. 1. New York: Wiley, 1970.

Rohwer, W. D. Prime time for education: Early childhood or adolescence? *Harvard Educational Review,* 1971, **41**, 316–341.

Roosevelt, E. *The autobiography of Eleanor Roosevelt.* New York: Harper & Row, 1961.

Roper, B. W. *An extended view of public attitudes toward television and other mass media, 1959–71.* New York: Roper, 1971.

Rose, A. M. A current theoretical issue in social gerontology. *Gerontologist,* 1964, **4**, 46–50.

Rosencranz, H., & McNevin, T. A factor analysis of attitudes toward the aged. *Gerontologist,* 1969, **9**, 55–59.

Rossi, A. S. Transition to parenthood. *Journal of Marriage and the Family,* 1968, **30**, 26–29.

Rozak, T. *The making of a counter culture.* Garden City, New Jersey: Doubleday, 1969.

Rozelle, R. M., & Campbell, D. T. More plausible rival hypotheses in the cross-lagged panel correlational technique. *Psychological Bulletin,* 1969, **71**, 74–80.

Ryan, W. *Distress in the city.* Cleveland: Case Western Reserve University, 1969.

Ryder, N. The cohort as a concept in the study of social change. *American Sociological Review,* 1965, **30**, 843–861.

Ryder, N. Notes on the concept of a population. In M. W. Riley, *et al.* (Eds.), *Aging and society: A sociology of age stratification.* Vol. 3. New York: Russell Sage, 1972.

Safilios-Rothschild, C. Family sociology or wives' family sociology? A cross-cultural examination of decision making. *Journal of Marriage and the Family,* 1969, **31**, 290–301.

Safilios-Rothschild, C. The study of family power structure. *Journal of Marriage and the Family,* 1970, **32**, 539–552.

Sanders, S., Laurendeau, M. & Bergeron, J. Aging and the concept of space: The conservation of surfaces. *Journal of Gerontology,* 1966, **21**, 281–285.

Sanford, N. Personality: I. The field. *International encyclopedia of the social sciences.* Vol. 12. New York: MacMillan & Free Press, 1968.

Santayana, G. *Life of reason.* New York: Scribner, 1954.

Santostefano, S. G., & Paley, E. Development of cognitive controls in children. *Child Development,* 1964, **35**, 939–949.

Sapolsky, A. Effect of interpersonal relationships on verbal conditioning. *Journal of Abnormal and Social Psychology,* 1960, **60**, 241–246.

Schachter, S. The interaction of cognitive and physiological determinants of emotional state. In L. Berkowitz (Ed.), *Advances in experimental social psychology.* Vol. 1. New York: Academic Press, 1964.

Schaefer, E. F. A circumplex model for maternal behavior. *Journal of Abnormal Social Psychology,* 1959, **59**, 226–235.

Schaefer, M. Politics and public health. Unpublished doctoral dissertation in Public Administration, Syracuse University, 1962.

Schaffer, H. R., & Emerson, P. E. The development of social attachments in infancy. *Monographs of the Society for Research in Child Development,* 1964, **29**, Whole No. 3.

Schaie, K. W. A general model for the study of developmental problems. *Psychological Bulletin,* 1965, **64**, 92–107.

Schaie, K. W. Age changes and age differences. In B. L. Neugarten (Ed.), *Middle age and aging: A reader in social psychology.* Chicago: University of Chicago Press, 1968.

Schaie, K. W. A reinterpretation of age related changes in cognitive structure and functioning. In L. R. Goulet, & P. B. Baltes (Eds.), *Life-span developmental psychology: Research and theory.* New York: Academic Press, 1970.

Schaie, K. W. Reflections on papers by Looft, Peterson, and Sparks: Intervention towards an ageless society? In P. B. Baltes (Ed.), Strategies for psychological intervention in old age. *Gerontologist*, 1973, **13**, 31–36. (a)

Schaie, K. W. Methodological problems in descriptive developmental research on adulthood and aging. In J. R. Nesselroade & H. W. Reese (Eds.), *Life-span developmental psychology: Methodological issues*. New York: Academic Press, 1973. (b)

Schaie, K. W., Labouvie, G. V., & Buech, B. Ontogenetic versus generational components of adult intellectual development: A second follow-up. Unpublished manuscript, Department of Psychology, West Virginia University, 1973.

Schaie, K. W., & Marquette, B. Personality in maturity and old age. In R. M. Dreger (Ed.), *Multivariate personality research: Contributions to the understanding of personality in honor of Raymond B. Cattell*. Baton Rouge: Claitor's Publishing, 1972.

Schaie, K. W., & Strother, C. W. The cross-sequential study of age changes in cognitive behavior. *Psychological Bulletin*, 1968, **70**, 671–680.

Schalinsie, T. F. The role of television in the life of the aged person. Unpublished doctoral dissertation, Ohio State University, 1968.

Schmidt, L. R. Testing the limits im Leistungsverhalten: Möglichkeiten und Grenzen. In E. Duhm (Ed.), *Praxis der Klinischen Psychologie*. Vol. 2. Göttingen: Hogrefe, 1970.

Schoenfeldt, L. F. Life history subgroups as moderators in the prediction of intellectual change. Unpublished manuscript, Department of Psychology, University of Georgia, 1972.

Schooler, C. Childhood family structure and adult characteristics. *Sociometry*, 1971, **35**, 255–269.

Schramm, W. *Television in the lives of our children*. Palo Alto: Stanford Univ. Press, 1961.

Schramm, W. Aging and mass communication. In M. W. Riley, J. W. Riley, Jr., M. E. Johnson, A. Foner, & B. Hess (Eds.), *Aging and society: Aging and the professions*. Vol. 2. New York: Russell Sage, 1969.

Schwartz, D. W., & Karp, S. A. Field dependence in a geriatric population. *Perception and Motor Skills*, 1967, **24**, 495–504.

Sears, R. R. A theoretical framework for personality and social behavior. *American Psychologist*, 1951, **6**, 476–483.

Sears, R. R., Maccoby, E. E., & Levin, H. *Patterns of child rearing*. Evanston, Illinois: Row & Peterson, 1957.

Sears, R. R., Rau, L., & Alpert, R. *Identification and child rearing*. Stanford: Stanford University Press, 1965.

Secord, P., & Backman, C. Interpersonal congruency, perceived similarity and friendship. *Sociometry*, 1964, **27**, 115–127.

Selye, H. *The stress of life*. New York: McGraw-Hill, 1956.

Selznick, P. *TVA and the grass roots*. Berkeley: Univ. of California Press, 1949.

Seward, G. H., & Williamson, R. C. (Eds.) *Sex roles in changing society*. New York: Random House, 1970.

Shanas, E., Townsend, P., Wedderburn, D., Frus, H., Mehhaj, P., & Stehouwer, I. *Older people in three industrial societies*. New York: Atherton Press, 1968.

Sheldon, H. *Varieties of temperament*. New York: Harper & Row, 1942.

Shibutani, T. Reference groups and social control. In A. M. Rose (Ed.), *Human behavior and social processes*. Boston: Houghton Mifflin, 1962.

Shipman, V. C., Barone, J., Beaton, A., Emmerich, W., & Ward, W. Disadvantaged children and their first school experiences: Structure and development of cognitive competencies and styles prior to school entry. Report No. 71-19, Educational Testing Service, December, 1971.

Shneidman, E. S., & Fareberow, N. L. (Eds.) *Clues to suicide*. New York: McGraw-Hill, 1957.

Shrauger, S., & Altrocchi, J. The personality of the perceiver as a factor in person perception. *Psychological Bulletin*, 1964, **62**, 289–308.

Sigel, I. E. Developmental theory: Its place and relevance in early intervention programs. Paper presented at the Biennial Meeting of the Society for Research in Child Development, Minneapolis, Minnesota, April, 1971.

Simmons, L. (Ed.) *Sun chief: The autobiography of a Hopi Indian.* New Haven: Yale Univ. Press, 1942.

Simon, B., & Lawton, M. P. Proximity and other determinants of friendship formation among the elderly. Paper presented at the Annual Meeting of the Eastern Psychological Association, Boston, April, 1967.

Simon, W., & Gagnon, J. H. On psychosexual development. In D. A. Goslin (Ed.), *Handbook of socialization theory and research.* Chicago: Rand McNally, 1969.

Skinner, B. F. *The behavior of organisms.* New York: Appleton-Century-Crofts, 1938.

Skinner, B. F. *Science and human behavior.* New York: Appleton-Century-Crofts, 1953.

Slater, P. E. *The pursuit of loneliness: American culture at the breaking point.* Boston: Beacon, 1970.

Smelser, W. T., & Stewart, L. H. Where are the siblings? A re-evaluation of the relationship between birth order and college attendance. *Sociometry,* 1968, **31,** 294–303.

Smith, H. T. A comparison of interview and observation measures of mother behavior. *The Journal of Abnormal and Social Psychology,* 1958, **57,** 278–282.

Smoller, A. J. Shifts in psychological concerns from adolescence to later maturity. Unpublished doctoral dissertation, University of Southern California, 1971.

Snow, C. P. *The two cultures and the scientific revolution.* London and New York: Cambridge Univ. Press, 1959.

Sommer, R. The ecology of privacy. *The Library Quarterly,* 1966, **36,** 234–248.

Spence, J. T. Learning theory and personality. In J. M. Wepman & R. W. Heine (Eds.), *Concepts of personality.* Chicago: Aldine, 1963.

Spence, D. L., & Lonner, T. D. Divorce and the life-course of middle-aged women. Paper presented at the Annual Meeting of the American Sociological Association, Denver, August, 1971.

Spiker, C. C. The concept of development: Relevant and irrelevant issues. *Monographs of the Society for Research in Child Development,* 1966, **31,** 40–54.

Stanton, A. H., & Schwartz, M. S. *The mental hospital.* New York: Basic Books, 1954.

Stea, D., & Downs, R. M. From the outside looking in at the inside looking out. *Environment and Behavior,* 1970, **2,** 3–12.

Stein, A. H. The effects of sex-role standards for achievement and sex-role preference on three determinants of achievement motivation. *Developmental Psychology,* 1971, **4,** 219–231.

Stein, A. H., & Smithells, J. Age and sex differences in children's sex-role standards about achievement. *Developmental Psychology,* 1969, **1,** 252–259.

Stendler, C. B. Critical periods in socialization and overdependency. *Child Development,* 1952, **23,** 3–12.

Stevenson, H. W. Children's learning: Crossword of developmental and educational psychology. Paper presented at the Annual Meeting of the American Psychological Association, San Francisco, September, 1968.

Stolz, L. M. *Influences on parent behavior.* Stanford: Stanford Univ. Press, 1967.

Stone, A. A., & Onque, G. C. *Longitudinal studies of child personality.* Cambridge, Massachusetts: Harvard Univ. Press, 1959.

Storck, P. A., Looft, W. R., & Hooper, F. H. Interrelationships among Piagetian tasks and traditional measures of cognitive abilities in mature and aged adults. *Journal of Gerontology,* 1972, **27,** 461–465.

Straus, M. A. Power and support structure of the family in relation to socialization. *Journal of Marriage and the Family,* 1964, **26,** 318–326.

Strauss, A. *Mirrors and masks: The search for identity.* San Francisco: Sociology Press, 1969.

Streib, G. F. Intergenerational relations: Perspectives of the two generations on the older parent. *Journal of Marriage and the Family,* 1965, **27**, 469–476.

Strodtbeck, F. L. Husband–wife interaction over revealed differences. *American Sociological Review,* 1951, **16**, 468–473.

Strodtbeck, F. L. Family interaction, values and achievement. In D. McClelland (Ed.), *Talent and society.* Princeton, New Jersey: Van Nostrand, 1958.

Stroop, J. R. Studies in interference in serial verbal reactions. *Journal of Experimental Psychology,* 1935, **18**, 643–662.

Sutton-Smith, B. Developmental laws and the experimentalists' ontology. *Merrill-Palmer Quarterly,* 1970, **16**, 253–259.

Sutton-Smith, B., & Rosenberg, B. *The sibling.* New York: Holt, Rinehart & Winston, 1970.

Svoboda, C. P. The mind–body problem: Stalemate or paradox? Unpublished manuscript, Department of Educational Psychology, University of Wisconsin, 1972.

Swain, M. A. Husband–wife patterns of interaction at three stages of marriage. *Dissertation Abstract International,* 1970, **31**, 904–905.

Tagiuri, R. Person perception. In G. Lindzey & E. Aronson (Eds.), *Handbook of social psychology,* Vol. 3. Reading, Massachusetts: Addison-Wesley, 1969.

Tagiuri, R., & Petrullo, L. (Eds.) *Person perception and interpersonal behavior.* Stanford: Stanford Univ. Press, 1958.

Tajfel, H. Social and cultural factors in perception. In G. Lindzey & E. Aronson (Eds.), *Handbook of Social Psychology,* Vol. 5. Reading, Massachusetts: Addison-Wesley, 1969.

Terman, L. M., & Miles, C. C. *Sex and personality: Studies in masculinity and femininity.* New York: Russell & Russell, 1936.

Terman, L. M., & Oden, M. *The gifted child grows up.* Stanford: Stanford Univ. Press, 1947.

Thaler, M. Relationships among Wechsler, Weigl, Rorschach, EEG findings, and abstract-concrete behavior in a group of normal aged subjects. *Journal of Gerontology,* 1956, **11**, 404–409.

Tharp, R. G. Psychological patterning in marriage. *Psychological Bulletin,* 1963, **60**, 97–117.

Thibaut, J., & Kelly, H. *The social psychology of groups.* New York: Wiley, 1967.

Thibaut, J., & Strickland, L. Psychological set and social conformity. *Journal of Personality,* 1956, **25**, 115–129.

Thomae, H. Theory of aging and cognitive theory of personality. *Human Development,* 1970, **13**, 1–16.

Thomae, H., & Lehr, U. (Eds.) *Altern: Probleme und Tatsachen.* Frankfurt: Akademische Verlagsgesellschaft, 1968.

Thomas, E. L. Family correlates of student political activism. *Developmental Psychology,* 1971, **4**, 206–214. (a)

Thomas, E. L. Studying the generation gap: The case of the blind man and the elephant? Paper presented for discussion at the National Council on Family Relations, Estes Park, Colorado, August, 1971. (b)

Thompson, N. L., & McCandless, B. IT score variations by instructional style. *Child Development,* 1970, **41**, 425–436.

Thompson, W. R. Development and biophysical bases of personality. In E. F. Borgatta & W. W. Lambert (Eds.) *Handbook of personality theory and research.* Chicago: Rand McNally, 1968.

Thorndike, E. L. Autobiography. In C. D. Murchison (Ed.), *A history of psychology in autobiography.* Vol. 3. Worcester, Massachusetts: Clark Univ. Press, 1936.

Thorndike, E. L. Objections to the theory of recapitulation. In R. Grinder (Ed.), *A history of genetic psychology.* New York: Wiley, 1967.

Thorndike, R. L. Some methodological issues in the study of creativity. In *Proceedings of the 1962 invitational conference on testing problems*. Princeton, New Jersey: Educational Testing Service, 1963.

Toffler, A. *Future shock,* New York: Random House, 1970.

Tomlinson-Keasey, C. Formal operations in females from eleven to fifty-four years of age. *Developmental Psychology,* 1972, **6**, 364.

Toulmin, S. The concept of "stages" in psychological development. In T. Mischel (Ed.), *Cognitive development and epistemology*. New York: Academic Press, 1971.

Toynbee, A. *The study of history*. Vol. 1. Abridgement by D. C. Sommervell, New York: Oxford Univ. Press, 1947.

Triandis, L. M., & Lambert, W. W. Pancultural factor analysis of reported socialization practices. *Journal of Abnormal and Social Psychology,* 1961, **62**, 631–639.

Troeltsch, E. *The social teaching of the Christian churches*. Translated by O. Wyon. New York: Harper & Row, 1960.

Troll, L. E. Issues in the study of generations. *Aging and Human Development,* 1970, **1**, 199–218.

Troll, L. E. The family of later life: A decade review. *Journal of Marriage and the Family,* 1971, **33**, 263–290.

Troll, L. E., Neugarten, B. L., & Kraines, R. Similarities in values and other personality characteristics in college students and their parents. *Merrill-Palmer Quarterly,* 1969, **15**, 323–326.

Troll, L. E., & Schlossberg, N. A preliminary investigation of "Age Bias" in helping professions. *Gerontologist,* 1970, **10**, Part 2. (Abstract).

Tryon, C. Fostering mental health in our schools. In C. Tryon & J. W. Lilienthal (Eds.), *Developmental tasks. Yearbook of the national association for supervision and curriculum development*. Washington, D.C.: U.S. Government Printing Office, 1950. 2 vols.

Tryon, R. C. *Cluster analysis*. Ann Arbor: Edwards Brothers, 1939.

Tryon, R. C., & Bailey, D. E. The BC TRY computer system of cluster and factor analysis. *Multivariate Behavioral Research,* 1966, **1**, 95–111.

Tryon, R. C., & Bailey, D. E. *Cluster analysis*. New York: McGraw-Hill, 1970.

Tuckman, J., & Lorge, I. The attitudes of the aged toward the older worker for institutionalized and noninstitutionalized adults. *Journal of Gerontology,* 1952, **7**, 559–564. (a)

Tuckman, J., & Lorge, I. The effect of institutionalization on attitudes toward old people. *Journal of Abnormal and Social Psychology,* 1952, **47**, 337–344. (b)

Tuckman, J., & Lorge, I. Attitudes toward old workers. *Journal of Applied Psychology,* 1952, **36**, 149–153. (c)

Tuckman, J., & Lorge, I. Attitudes toward old people. *Journal of Social Psychology,* 1953, **37**, 249–260.

Tuckman, J., & Lorge, I. Attitudes toward aging of individuals with experiences with the aged. *Journal of Genetic Psychology,* 1958, **92**, 199–215. (a)

Tuckman, J., & Lorge, I. The projection of personal symptoms into stereotypes about aging. *Journal of Gerontology,* 1958, **13**, 70–73. (b)

Tuckman, J., Lorge, I., & Spooner, G. A. The effect of family environment on attitudes toward old people and the old worker. *Journal of Social Psychology,* 1953, **38**, 207–218.

Turiel, E. Developmental processes in the child's moral thinking. In P. H. Mussen, J. Langer, & M. Covington (Eds.), *Trends and issues in developmental psychology*. New York: Holt, Rinehart & Winston, 1969.

Turiel, E. The effects of cognitive conflict on moral judgment development. In L. Kohlberg & E. Turiel (Eds.), *Recent research in moral development*. New York: Holt, Rinehart & Winston, 1973, in press. (a)

Turiel, E. An experimental test of the sequentiality of developmental stages in the child's moral development. In L. Kohlberg & E. Turiel (Eds.), *Recent research in moral development.* New York: Holt, Rinehart & Winston, 1973, in press. (b)

Turner, H., & Goldfarb, A. Psychotherapy of aged persons: Utilization and effectiveness of brief therapy. *American Journal of Psychiatry,* 1953, **109**, 916–921.

Uhr, L. M. Personality changes during marriage. Unpublished doctoral dissertation, University of Michigan, 1957.

Urban, H. B., & Looft, W. R. Issues in human development intervention. In H. B. Urban & W. R. Looft (Eds.), *Human development intervention,* in preparation.

U.S. Bureau of the Census. *Census of population.* Vol. 1. Part 1. Washington, D.C.: U.S. Government Printing Office, 1960.

U.S. Bureau of the Census. *Current population reports.* Washington, D.C.: U.S. Government Printing Office, 1965.

U.S. Bureau of the Census. *Current population reports.* Washington, D.C.: U.S. Government Printing Office, 1968.

U.S. Bureau of the Census. *Current population reports.* Washington, D.C.: U.S. Government Printing Office, 1970.

U.S. Bureau of the Census. *Current population reports.* Washington, D.C.: U.S. Government Printing Office, 1971.

U.S.D.H.E.W., National Institute of Child Health and Human Development. *Final report: A survey of the training needs and mechanisms in gerontology.* St. Louis, Mo.: Gerontological Society, 1968.

U.S.D.H.E.W. Office of Education. *Educational research and development in the United States.* Washington, D.C.: U.S. Government Printing Office, 1969.

U.S. White House Conference on Aging: 1971. *A report to the delegates from the conference sections and special concerns sessions.* Report No. 0–448–917. Washington, D.C.: U.S. Government Printing Office, 1971.

Uzgiris, I. C. Patterns of vocal and gestural imitation. In F. J. Monks, W. W. Hartup, & J. DeWit (Eds.), *Determinants of behavioral development.* New York: Academic Press, 1972.

Vale, J. R., & Vale, C. A. Individual differences and general laws in psychology. *American Psychologist,* 1969, **24**, 1093–1108.

Van den Daele, L. D. Qualitative models in developmental analysis. *Developmental Psychology,* 1969, **1**, 303–310.

Van Gennep, A. *The rites of passage.* Chicago: Univ. of Chicago Press, 1960.

Vernon, P. E. Effects of administration and scoring on divergent thinking tests. *British Journal of Educational Psychology,* 1971, **41**, 245–257.

Vroegh, K. Masculinity and femininity in the preschool years. *Child Development,* 1968, **39**, 1253–1257.

Vroegh, K. Masculinity and femininity in the elementary and junior high school years. *Developmental Psychology,* 1971, **4**, 254–261.

Vygotsky, L. *Thought and language.* Cambridge, Massachusetts: MIT Press, 1962.

Wachtel, P. L. Style and capacity in analytic functioning. *Journal of Personality,* 1968, **36**, 202–212.

Wallach, M. A. Creativity. In P. H. Mussen (Ed.), *Carmichael's manual of child psychology,* Vol. 1. New York: Wiley, 1970.

Wallach, M. A. *The intelligence/creativity distinction.* New York: General Learning Press, 1971.

Wallach, M. A., & Kogan, N. *Modes of thinking in young children.* New York: Holt, Rinehart & Winston, 1965.

Wallach, M. A., Kogan, N., & Burt, R. B. Group risk taking and field dependence-independence of group members. *Sociometry,* 1967, **30**, 323–338.

Wallach, M. A., & Wing, C. W., Jr. *The talented student: A validation of the creativity-intelligence distinction.* New York: Holt, Rinehart & Winston, 1969.

Waller, W. *The family: A dynamic interpretation.* New York: Dryden, 1938.

Ward, W. C. Creativity in young children. *Child Development,* 1968, **38,** 737–754.

Ward, W. C. Rate and uniqueness in children's creative responding. *Child Development,* 1969, **40,** 869–878.

Ward, W. C., Kogan, N., & Pankove, E. Incentive effects in children's creativity. *Child Development,* 1972, **43,** 669–676.

Warner, W. L. *A black civilization.* New York: Harper & Row, 1958.

Warr, P. B., & Knapper, C. *The perception of people and events.* New York: Wiley, 1968.

Washburn, R. V. A study of the smiling and laughing of infants in the first year of life. *Genetic Psychology Monographs,* 1929, **6,** 396–535 (Nos. 5 & 6).

Waterman, A. S., & Waterman, C. K. A longitudinal study of changes in ego identity status during the freshman year at college. *Developmental Psychology,* 1971, **5,** 167–173.

Watson, R. I. Psychology: A prescriptive science. *American Psychologist,* 1967, **22,** 435–443.

Watson, R. I. Prescriptions as operative in the history of psychology. *Journal of the History of the Behavioral Sciences,* 1971, **7,** 311–322.

Waxler, N. E., & Mishler, E. G. Experimental studies of families. In L. Berkowitz (Ed.), *Advances in experimental social psychology.* Vol. 5. New York: Academic Press, 1970.

Webber, E. L. The educable aged. In J. C. D. Dixon (Ed.), *Continuing education in the later years.* Gainesville: Univ. of Florida Press, 1963.

Weber, M. *The theory of social and economic organization.* Translated by A. M. Henderson and T. Parsons. New York: Free Press, 1947.

Weber, M. In E. A. Shils & H. A. Finch (Eds. and Trans.), *The methodology of the social sciences.* New York: Free Press, 1949.

Weber, M. *The sociology of religion.* Translated by E. Fischoff. Boston: Beacon Press, 1964.

Welford, A. T. *Aging and human skill.* London: Oxford University Press, 1958.

Werner, H. *Comparative psychology of mental development.* New York: International Universities Press, 1948.

Werner, H. The concept of development from a comparative and organismic point of view. In D. B. Harris (Ed.), *The concept of development.* Minneapolis: University of Minnesota Press, 1957.

Westby, D., & Braungart, R. Activists and the history of the future. In J. Foster & D. Long (Eds.), *Protest!: Student activism in America.* New York: William Morrow, 1968.

White, R. W. *Lives in progress.* New York: Holt, 1952.

Whiting, B. B. (Ed.) *Six cultures: Studies of child rearing.* New York: Wiley, 1963.

Wild, C. Creativity and adaptive regression. *Journal of Personality and Social Psychology,* 1965, **2,** 161–169.

Willems, E. P. Behavioral ecology and experimental analysis: Courtship is not enough. In J. R. Nesselroade & H. W. Reese (Eds.), *Life-span developmental psychology: Methodological issues.* New York: Academic Press, 1973.

Williams, R. Changing status, roles, and relationships. In C. Tibbits (Ed.), *Handbook of social gerontology.* Chicago: Univ. of Chicago Press, 1960.

Williams, T. M., & Fleming, J. W. Methodological study of the relationship between associative fluency and intelligence. *Developmental Psychology,* 1969, **1,** 155–162.

Witkin, H. A. Social influences in the development of cognitive style. In D. A. Goslin (Ed.), *Handbook of socialization theory and research.* Chicago: Rand McNally, 1969.

Witkin, H. A., Dyk, R. B., Faterson, H. F., Goodenough, D. R., & Karp, S. A. *Psychological differentiation.* New York: Wiley, 1962.

Witkin, H. A., Dyk, R. B., Faterson, H. F., Goodenough, D. R., & Birnbaum, J. Cognitive patterning in mildly retarded boys. *Child Development,* 1966, **37,** 301–316.

Witkin, H., Goodenough, D. R., & Karp, S. Stability of cognitive style from childhood to young adulthood. *Journal of Personality and Social Psychology*, 1967, **7**, 291–300.

Witkin, H. A., Lewis, H. B., Hertzman, M., Machover, K., Meissner, P. B., & Wapner, S. *Personality through perception*. New York: Harper & Row, 1954.

Witkin, H. A., Lewis, H. B., & Weil, E. Affective reactions and patient-therapist interactions among more differentiated and less differentiated patients early in therapy. *Journal of Nervous and Mental Disease*, 1968, **146**, 193–208.

Witty, P. A. Studies of the mass media, 1949–1965. *Science Education*, 1966, **50**, 119–126.

Witty, P. A. Some research on TV. In *Children and TV: Television's impact on the child*. Washington, D.C.: Bulletin 2PA, 1967, Association for Childhood Education International.

Wohlwill, J. F. The age variable in psychological research. *Psychological Review*, 1970, **77**, 49–64. (a)

Wohlwill, J. F. Methodology and research strategy in the study of developmental change. In L. R. Goulet & P. B. Baltes (Eds.), *Life-span developmental psychology: Research and theory*. New York: Academic Press, 1970. (b)

Wohlwill, J. F. The emerging discipline of environmental psychology. *American Psychologist*, 1970, **15**, 303–312. (c)

Wolff, K. Group psychotherapy with geriatric patients in a mental hospital. *Journal of the American Geriatrics Society*, 1957, **5**, 13–19.

Wolfle, D., & Kidd, C. V. The future market for Ph.D.'s. *Science*, 1971, **173**, 784–793.

Wood, J. L. Student political activism at Berkeley: A test of three theories. Unpublished manuscript, Department of Sociology, University of California, Berkeley, 1972.

Woodruff, D. S. Biofeedback—implications for gerontology. Paper presented at the 24th Annual Meeting of the Gerontological Society, Houston, October, 1971.

Woodruff, D. S. Biofeedback control of the EEG alpha rhythm and its effect on reaction time in the young and old. Unpublished doctoral dissertation, University of Southern California, 1972.

Woodruff, D. S. The usefulness of the life-span approach for the psychophysiology of aging. In P. B. Baltes (Ed.), Life-span models of psychological aging: A symposium, *Gerontologist*, 1973, in press.

Woodruff, D. S., & Birren, J. E. Age changes and cohort differences in personality. *Developmental Psychology*, 1972, **6**, 252–259.

Woodruff, D. S., & Birren, J. E. Training for professionals in the field of aging: Needs, goals, models, and means. In I. N. Mensh & A. N. Schwartz (Eds.), *New professional approaches to the old*. New York: Thomas, 1973.

Yarrow, L. J., & Yarrow, M. R. Personality continuity and change in the family context. In P. Worchel & D. Byrne (Eds.), *Personality change*. New York: Wiley, 1964.

Yarrow, M. R., Waxler, C. Z., & Scott, P. M. Child effects on adult behavior. *Developmental Psychology*, 1971, **5**, 300–311.

Zelditch, M., Jr. Role differentiation in the nuclear family: A comparative study. In T. Parsons & R. F. Bales (Eds.), *Family, socialization and interaction process*. New York: Free Press, 1955.

Zigler, E. Review of research on social class and the socialization process. *Review of Educational Research*, 1970, **40**, 87–110.

Zinberg, N. E. The relationship of regressive phenomena to the aging process. In N. E. Zinberg & I. J. Kaufman (Eds.), *Normal psychology of the aging process*. New York: International Universities Press, 1963.

Author Index

Numbers in italics refer to the pages on which the complete references are listed.

433

Subject Index

A

Adolescent development, 5
Adult affectional system, 237
Adult development, 5
  interest in, 12–13
  research and theory, 13–19
  role of experience, 256
  social learning theory, 254–257
  sociological perspective, 253–254
Adulthood
  cognitive stage development, 183–186
  concepts of stage, 180–183
Adult personality
  Chicago approach, 44–46
Age
  as dependent variable, 44
  as independent and dependent variable, 35,
    36
  as index versus causal variable, 87–88
  phenomenological perceptions, 35
  as a physical object of orientation, 87–89
  relation to development, 37, 43, 47
  simulation, 35, 300–301
Age cohort, 63–64
  and age-grading, 215
  cohort differences, 215
  differential mobility, 215–216
  and intergenerational relations, 214–216
  and social change, 216
Age differences
  perceived versus actual, 285–286, 295–298,
    326

rate of behavior change, 283
in stimulus–response functional relationships,
  256–257
Age expectations
  regularities among adults, 60–61
Age function, 83
Age-functional behavior
  perceptions of, 293–298
  perceptual determinants, 299
Age-grading, 45, 57, 59
Age norms, 60–61
  conformity and deviation, 61–62
  internalization of, 61–62
  perceptions of, 294
Age psychology versus developmental psychology, 36
Age-specific theories of development, 5
Age-specific versus life-span theories, 394
Age status, 59–60
Age stratification, 62–64, 293–294
  and intergenerational relations, 214–216
Age variable
  status of, 34–37
Aging
  intellectual decline, 320
  and personality structure, 11
  psychosexual, 19
Attachment, *see also* Family attachment
  dyadic conceptions, 238–242
  experimental analysis, 251
  group profile, 243–244
  individual differences, 237–238
  interactional conceptions, 242–250

444